Models for Writers

Short Essays for Composition

Models for Writers

Short Essays for Composition

TWELFTH EDITION

Alfred Rosa
Paul Eschholz

University of Vermont

BEDFORD/ST. MARTIN'S
Boston ◆ New York

For Bedford/St. Martin's

Vice President, Editorial, Macmillan Higher Education Humanities: Edwin Hill
Editorial Director for English and Music: Karen S. Henry
Publisher for Composition, Business and Technical Writing and Developmental Writing: Leasa Burton
Executive Editor: John Sullivan
Developmental Editors: Karrin M. Varucene; Jonathan Douglas
Senior Production Editor: Harold Chester
Senior Production Supervisor: Jennifer Wetzel
Senior Marketing Manager: Jane Helms
Copy Editor: Jamie Nan Thaman
Director of Rights and Permissions: Hilary Newman
Senior Art Director: Anna Palchik
Cover Design: William Boardman
Cover Photo: Origami cranes. © Michelle McMahon/Getty Images
Chapter Openers: Julia Ra/Shutterstock
Composition: Cenveo Publisher Services
Printing and Binding: RR Donnelley and Sons-Crawfordsville

1 2 3 4 5 6 18 17 16 15 14

For information, write: Bedford/St. Martin's, 75 Arlington Street, Boston, MA 02116 (617-399-4000)

ISBN 978-1-4576-6784-8 (paperback)
ISBN 978-1-4576-8155-4 (High School Edition)

Acknowledgments
Text acknowledgments and copyrights appear at the back of the book on pages 665–68, which constitute an extension of the copyright page. Art acknowledgments and copyrights appear on the same page as the art selections they cover. It is a violation of the law to reproduce these selections by any means whatsoever without the written permission of the copyright holder.

Preface

Models for Writers continues to offer students and instructors brief, accessible, high-interest models of rhetorical elements, principles, and patterns. As important as it is for students to read while they are learning to write college-level essays, *Models for Writers* offers more than a collection of essays. Through the abundant study materials that accompany each selection, students master the writing skills they will need for all their college classes. Writing activities and assignments give students the chance to stitch together the various rhetorical elements into coherent, forceful essays of their own. This approach, which has helped several million students become better writers, remains at the heart of the book.

In this edition, we continue to emphasize the classic features of *Models for Writers* that have won praise from teachers and students alike. In addition, we have strengthened the book by introducing new selections and new voices as well as new instruction for some of the more challenging writing concepts.

FAVORITE FEATURES OF *MODELS FOR WRITERS*

• **Brief, lively readings that provide outstanding models.** Most of the seventy-two professional selections and all six of the sample student essays in *Models for Writers* are comparable in length (two to three pages) to the essays students will write themselves, and each clearly illustrates a basic rhetorical element, principle, or pattern. Just as important, the essays deal with subjects that we know from our own teaching experience will spark the interest of most college students. In addition, the range of voices, cultural perspectives, and styles represented in the essays will resonate with today's students. They will both enjoy and benefit from reading and writing about selections by many well-known authors, including Judith Ortiz Cofer, Stephen King, Anne Lamott, Amy Tan, Maya Angelou, David Sedaris, Martin Luther King Jr., and Steven Pinker.

• **Introductory chapters on reading and writing.** Throughout the chapters in Part One, students review the writing process from fresh angles and use the essays they read to improve their own writing. Chapter 1, The Writing Process, details the steps in the writing process and illustrates them with a student essay in progress. Chapter 2, From Reading to Writing, shows students how to use the apparatus in the text, provides them with guidelines for critical reading, and demonstrates with three student essays (narrative, responsive, and argumentative) how they can generate their own writing from reading.

• **An easy-to-follow rhetorical organization.** Each of the twenty rhetorically based chapters in *Models for Writers* is devoted to a particular element or pattern important to college writing. Chapters 3 through 10 focus on the concepts of thesis, unity, organization, beginnings and endings, paragraphs, transitions, effective sentences, and writing with sources. Chapter 11 illustrates the importance of controlling diction and tone, and Chapter 12, the uses of figurative language. Chapters 13 through 21 explore the types of writing most often required of college students: illustration, narration, description, process analysis, definition, division and classification, comparison and contrast, cause and effect, and argument. The final chapter is a brief guide to writing a research paper, which now includes both MLA and APA documentation guidelines.

• **Abundant study materials.** To help students use the readings to improve their writing, every essay is accompanied by ample study materials.

Reflecting on What You Know activities precede each reading and prompt students to explore their own ideas and experiences regarding the issues presented in the reading.

A *Thinking Critically about This Reading* question follows each essay. It encourages students to consider the writer's assumptions, make connections not readily apparent, or explore the broader implications of the selection.

Questions for Study and Discussion focus on the selection's content and on the author's purpose and the particular strategy used to achieve that purpose. To remind students that good writing is never one-dimensional, at least one question in each series focuses on a writing concern other than the one highlighted in the chapter.

Classroom Activities provide brief exercises that enable students to work (often in groups) on rhetorical elements, techniques, or patterns. These activities range from developing thesis statements to using strong action verbs and building argumentative evidence, and they encourage students to apply concepts modeled in the readings to their own writing. Additionally, several new activities throughout the book provide students with examples of career-related writing to demonstrate that critical reading, writing, and thinking skills are crucial beyond the college classroom.

Suggested Writing Assignments provide at least two writing assignments for each essay, with one encouraging students to use the reading selection as a direct model and another asking them to respond to the content of the reading.

• **Concise and interesting chapter introductions.** Writing instructors who use *Models for Writers* have continued to be generous in their praise for the brief, clear, practical, and student-friendly chapter introductions, which explain the various elements and patterns. In each introduction, students will find illuminating examples—many written by students—of the feature or principle under discussion.

• **Practical instruction on working with sources.** One of the biggest challenges student writers face is incorporating supporting evidence from other writers into their essays. In Chapter 1, The Writing Process, students find clear advice on developing strong thesis statements and marshaling evidence and support. Chapter 10 models strategies for taking effective notes from sources; using signal phrases to integrate quotations, summaries, and paraphrases smoothly; synthesizing sources; and avoiding plagiarism. Further reviewing the steps and skills involved in research and synthesis, Chapter 22, A Brief Guide to Writing a Research Paper, provides one full-length MLA-style model student research paper and the cover sheet, first page, and list of references for one APA-style model student research paper (the entire paper is offered online in LaunchPad Solo). Thus, students become more confident in joining academic conversations and in writing the kinds of essays that they will be called on to write in their college courses.

• **Targeted instruction on sentence grammar.** Chapter 1, The Writing Process, addresses editing concerns that instructors across the country have identified as the most problematic for their students, such as run-on sentences, verb tense shifts, comma splices, sentence fragments, and dangling and misplaced modifiers. Brief explanations and hand-edited examples show students how to find and correct these common errors in their own writing. Also available in this new edition are a host of online tutorials and self-paced, adaptive activities for further practice with grammatical and mechanical concepts.

• **Flexible arrangement.** Each chapter is self-contained so that instructors can easily follow their own teaching sequences, omitting or emphasizing certain chapters according to the needs of their students or the requirements of the course.

• **Alternate table of contents showing thematic clusters.** The alternate table of contents (pp. xxvii–xxxii) groups readings into twenty-four clusters, each with three to eight essays sharing a common theme. Students and instructors attracted to the theme of one essay in *Models for Writers* can consult this alternate table of contents to find other essays in the book that address the same theme.

• **Glossary of Useful Terms.** Cross-referenced in many of the questions and writing assignments throughout the book, this list of key terms defines rhetorical and literary terms that student writers need to know. Terms that are explained in the Glossary (pp. 651–63) are shown in boldface the first time they appear in a chapter.

■ NEW TO THE TWELFTH EDITION OF *MODELS FOR WRITERS*

• **Engaging, informative, and diverse new readings.** Twenty-nine of the book's seventy-two readings are new to this edition of *Models for Writers*—ideal models by both new and established writers. We selected these essays for their brevity and clarity, for their effectiveness as models, and for their potential to develop critical thinking and writing. Among the new readings are Robert G. Lake-Thom's "An Indian Father's Plea," Judith Ortiz Cofer's "My Rosetta," Michael Dirda's "Listening to My Father," Susan Orlean's "The American Man: Age Ten," and Marion Winik's "Guacamole Is a Cruel Mistress."

• **Carefully curated multimodal readings.** Fifteen multimodal e-readings go beyond the print page, with support for analyzing a variety of texts, such as video, images, and audio. Clear cross-references at the end of chapter introductions direct students to the e-readings for that strategy or topic. You and your students can access the e-readings at **macmillanhighered.com/mfw12e**. See the LaunchPad Solo description on pages ix–x of this preface to learn more about the online resources available to you and your students.

• **Compelling new examples of argument.** The argument chapter now features a revised cluster on crime and punishment (Crime: Finding an Effective Punishment) and two brand-new clusters: one that debates the effectiveness of activism through social media (Slacktivism: Social Media Meets Activism) and an entirely online multimodal cluster that examines the effects of media and society on self-image (Body Image: How We See Ourselves). These three argument clusters are designed to spark lively debate, both in class discussions and in students' writing. Additionally, the argument chapter now includes expanded explanations and examples of each of the most common logical fallacies to help students better understand these kinds of errors, advice on anticipating and fixing logical fallacies, and a new activity on identifying and correcting fallacies.

- **New and enhanced research coverage.** In Chapter 22, new material on detecting bias and understanding the differences between fact and opinion helps students better evaluate and analyze sources in their research writing. A new section in Chapter 22 includes APA documentation guidelines and an accompanying annotated model student paper.

- **New strategies for developing a strong thesis statement.** A new section in Chapter 1, Develop Your Thesis, includes a clear five-step process to help students through the challenge of arriving at an effective thesis statement from a broad topic.

GET THE MOST OUT OF YOUR COURSE WITH *MODELS FOR WRITERS*

Bedford/St. Martin's offers resources and format choices that help you and your students get even more out of your book and course. To learn more about or to order any of the following products, contact your Macmillan sales representative, e-mail sales support (sales_support@bfwpub.com), or visit the website at **macmillanhighered.com/mfw/catalog.**

LaunchPad Solo for Models for Writers: Where Students Learn

LaunchPad Solo provides engaging content and new ways to get the most out of your course.

- **Multimedia selections** include an online multimodal argument cluster on body image, and a multimodal reading and activity for each of the nine rhetorical patterns.
- **Prebuilt units**—including readings, videos, quizzes, and discussion groups—are **easy to adapt and assign** by adding your

own materials and mixing them with our high-quality multimedia content and ready-made assessment options, such as **LearningCurve** adaptive quizzing.

- LaunchPad Solo also provides access to a **gradebook** that provides a clear window on student performance—as a class, by individual student, and even by assignment.

- A **streamlined interface** helps students focus on what's due, and social commenting tools let them engage, make connections, and learn from one another. Use LaunchPad Solo on its own, or integrate it with your school's learning management system so that your class is always on the same page.

To get the most out of your course, order LaunchPad Solo for *Models for Writers* packaged with the print book at no additional charge. (**LaunchPad Solo for** *Models for Writers* **can also be purchased on its own.**) An activation code is required. To order LaunchPad Solo for *Models for Writers* with the print book, use ISBN: 978-1-319-01381-3.

Select Value Packages

Add value to your text by packaging one of the following resources with *Models for Writers*. To learn more about package options for any of the following products, contact your Beford/St. Martin's sales representative or visit **macmillanhighered.com/mfw/catalog.**

LearningCurve for Readers and Writers, Bedford/St. Martin's adaptive quizzing program, quickly learns what students already know and helps them practice what they don't yet understand. Game-like quizzing motivates students to engage with their course, and reporting tools help teachers discern their students' needs. *LearningCurve for Readers and Writers* can be packaged with *Models for Writers* at a significant discount. An activation code is required. To order LearningCurve packaged with the print book, use ISBN: 978-1-319-01517-6. For details, visit **macmillanhighered.com/englishlearningcurve.**

***EasyWriter*, Fifth Edition, by Andrea Lunsford** provides essential information students need to understand the conventions of formal written English. Whether you're looking for an affordable way to focus your writing classroom on rhetorical choices, or just a pocket-sized quick reference that your students can use on the go, you'll find what you need in *EasyWriter*. To order *EasyWriter* packaged with the print book, use ISBN: 978-1-319-01515-2.

***A Pocket Style Manual*, Seventh Edition, by Diana Hacker and Nancy Sommers** provides students with clear, complete answers to their questions about research, writing, and grammar. With 325 documentation models in four styles and coverage of drafting thesis statements, writing correctly and effectively, finding and evaluating sources, and writing research papers, *A Pocket Style Manual* supports writers across the disciplines. To order *A Pocket Style Manual* packaged with the print book, use ISBN: 978-1-319-01516-9.

Make Learning Fun with *Re:Writing 3*

New open online resources with videos and interactive elements engage students in new ways of writing. You'll find tutorials about using common digital writing tools, an interactive peer review game, Extreme Paragraph Makeover, and more—all for free and for fun. Visit **bedfordstmartins.com/rewriting.**

Instructor Resources

You have a lot to do in your course. Bedford/St. Martin's wants to make it easy for you to find the support you need—and to find it quickly.

• **The *Instructor's Manual for Models for Writers***, Twelfth Edition, contains suggested answers for each selection's critical reading and study questions. The Instructor's Manual also includes essay analysis and discussion, as well as tips to help students think critically about what they have read. Also included in the manual are two sample course plans for first-year composition courses—one fifteen weeks, the other, ten weeks—and a complete sample syllabus for a fifteen-week developmental English course. This manual may be found in the Instructor's Edition of *Models for Writers*, Twelfth Edition, and is also available as a separate booklet or as a downloadable PDF from **macmillanhighered.com/mfw/catalog.**

• ***Teaching Central*** (**macmillanhighered.com/teachingcentral**) offers the entire list of Bedford/St. Martin's print and online professional resources in one place. You will find landmark reference works, sourcebooks on pedagogical issues, award-winning collections, and practical advice for the classroom—all free for instructors.

• *Bits* (**bedfordbits.com**) collects creative ideas for teaching a range of composition topics in an easily searchable blog. A community of teachers—leading scholars, authors, and editors—discusses revision, research, grammar and style, technology, peer review, and much more. Take, use, adapt, and pass the ideas around; then, come back to the site to comment or share your own suggestions.

ACKNOWLEDGMENTS

In response to the many thoughtful reviews from instructors who use this book, we have maintained the solid foundation of the previous edition of *Models for Writers* while adding fresh readings and writing topics to stimulate today's student writers.

We are indebted to many people for their advice as we prepared this twelfth edition. We are especially grateful to Nancy Beasley, Georgia College & State University; Mara Beckett, Glendale Community College/Los Angeles City College; Brody Bluemel, The Pennsylvania State University; Stefanie Book, Vines High School; Susan Browning, Central Piedmont Community College; Connie Bubash, The Pennsylvania State University; Adam Burningham, Snow College; Shawn Durso, Milford High School; Taylor Emery, Austin Peay State University; Sherry Faithful, Carteret Community College; Kathleen Flynn, Glendale Community College; Lynee Gaillet, Georgia State University; Cynthia Galvan, Milwaukee Area Technical College; Elizabeth Genovise, Roane State Community College; Rose Gubele, University of Central Missouri; Nile Hartline, Des Moines Area Community College; Amy Havel, Southern Maine Community College; Robin Havenick, Linn-Benton Community College; Waddle Joette, Roane State Community College; Justine Keltz, South Hagerstown High School; Michael Kuelker, St. Charles Community College; Laurie Lyda, Georgia College & State University; Charla Major, Austin Peay State University; Cheryl Presswood-Hunter, Middle Georgia Technical College; Doug Rigby, Lehigh Carbon Community College; Heather Rodgers, Saint Charles Community College; Robin Runyan, Linn-Benton Community College; Joshua Taft, University of Central Missouri; Jon Tuttle, Francis Marion University; Vita Watkins, Glendale Community College; Maggie Whitehead, Lakeland High School; Melissa Williams, Central Georgia Technical College; and Katherine Woodbury, Southern Maine Community College.

It has been our good fortune to have the editorial guidance and good cheer of Karrin Varucene and Jonathan Douglas, our developmental editors on this book. We have also benefited from the great contributions to this edition by Stefanie Wortman as well as the careful eye of Harold Chester, our production editor, and the rest of the excellent team at Bedford/St. Martin's—Edwin Hill, Karen Henry, John Sullivan, Steve Scipione, and Jane Helms—as we planned, developed, and wrote this new edition. Our special thanks go to the late Tom Broadbent—our mentor and original editor at St. Martin's Press—who helped us breathe life and soul into *Models for Writers* in its earliest editions. The lessons that he shared with us during our fifteen-year partnership have stayed with us throughout our careers.

Thanks also to Sarah Federman, who authored the new material for the *Instructor's Manual*, and to Brian Kent, Cara Simone Bader, Tom Juvan, and Betsy Eschholz, who have shared their experiences using *Models for Writers* in the classroom. Our greatest debt is, as always, to our students—especially James Duffy, Trena Isley, Jake Jamieson, Zoe Ockenga, and Jeffrey Olesky, whose papers appear in this text—for all they have taught us over the years. Finally, we thank each other, partners in this writing and teaching venture for over four decades.

Alfred Rosa
Paul Eschholz

Contents

e For online videos, readings, and LearningCurve activities, go to **macmillanhighered.com/mfw12e.**

part four **Types of Essays**

22 A Brief Guide to Writing a Research Paper 611

Thematic Clusters

The thematic clusters that follow focus on themes that students can pursue in their own compositions. The essays themselves provide ideas and information that will stimulate their thinking as well as provide source material for their writing. The clusters—the themes and the essays associated with them—are meant to be suggestive rather than comprehensive and fairly narrow in scope rather than far ranging. Instructors and students are, of course, free to develop their own thematic groupings on which to base written work and are not limited by our groupings.

The American Dream

Discoveries/Epiphanies

Family and Friends

Heroes/Role Models

The Immigrant Experience

Life's Decisions

Medical Dilemmas

Moral Values

The Natural World

Parenting

Peer Pressure

People and Personalities

Personal Dilemmas

Power of Language

Punishment and Crime

Race in America

Sense of Place

Sense of Self

Sensual World

Social Activism

Teachers and Students

Technology

What's in a Name?

Writing about Writing

Models for Writers

Short Essays for Composition

Introduction for Students

Models for Writers is designed to help you learn to write by providing you with a collection of model essays — that is, essays that are examples of good writing. Good writing is direct and purposeful and communicates its message without confusing the reader. It doesn't wander from the topic, and it answers the reader's questions. Although good writing is well developed and detailed, it also accomplishes its task with the fewest possible words and with the simplest language appropriate to the writer's topic and thesis.

We know that one of the best ways to learn to write and to improve our writing is to read. By reading, we can see how other writers have communicated their experiences, ideas, thoughts, and feelings. We can study how they have used the various elements of the essay (words, sentences, paragraphs, organizational patterns, transitions, examples, evidence, and so forth) and thus learn how we might effectively do the same. When we see how a writer like James Lincoln Collier develops his essay "Anxiety: Challenge by Another Name" from a strong thesis statement, for example, we can better appreciate the importance of having a clear thesis statement in our own writing. When we see the way Russell Baker uses transitions in "Becoming a Writer" to link key phrases and important ideas so that readers can recognize how the parts of his essay fit together, we have a better idea of how to write coherently.

But we do not learn only by reading. We also learn by doing — that is, by writing — and in the best of all situations, we engage in reading and writing in conjunction with each other. *Models for Writers* therefore encourages you to practice what you are learning and to move from reading to writing.

Part One of *Models for Writers* provides you with strategies to do just that. Chapter 1, The Writing Process, introduces you to the important steps of the writing process, gives you guidelines for writing, and illustrates the writing process with a student essay. It also includes online tutorials on important digital writing skills as well as online LearningCurve activities on important grammar topics that will help you better edit your own writing. Chapter 2, From Reading to Writing, shows you how to use the apparatus that accompanies each selection in this text, provides you with guidelines for critical reading, and demonstrates with three annotated student essays how you can generate your own writing from reading. Also included in Chapter 2 are online tutorials on active reading strategies and reading visuals, as well as an online LearningCurve activity for practicing critical reading. (Icons and instructions at the bottom of the page will direct you to these online activities.) You will soon see that an effective essay has a clear purpose, often provides useful information, has an effect on the reader's thoughts and feelings, and is usually a pleasure to read. The essays that you will read in *Models for Writers* were chosen because they are effective.

All well-written essays share a number of structural and stylistic features that are illustrated by the various essays in *Models for Writers*. One good way to learn what these features are and how you can incorporate them into your own writing is to look at each of them in isolation. For this reason, we have divided the readings in *Models for Writers* into three major parts and, within these parts, into twenty chapters, each with its own particular focus and emphasis.

Part Two, The Elements of the Essay, includes eight chapters on the elements that are essential to a well-written essay, but because the concepts of thesis, unity, and organization underlie all the others, they come first in our sequence. Chapter 3, Thesis, shows how authors put forth, or state, the main ideas of their essays and how they use such statements to develop and control content. Chapter 4, Unity, shows how authors achieve a sense of wholeness in their essays, and Chapter 5, Organization, illustrates some important patterns that authors use to organize their thinking and writing. Chapter 6, Beginnings and Endings, offers advice on and models of ways to begin and conclude essays, while Chapter 7, Paragraphs, concentrates on the importance of well-developed paragraphs and what is necessary to achieve them. Chapter 8, Transitions, concerns various devices writers use to move from one idea or section of an essay to the next, and Chapter 9, Effective Sentences, focuses on techniques to make sentences powerful and to create stylistic variety. Finally, Chapter 10, Writing with Sources, provides proven strategies for taking effective notes from sources; for using signal phrases to integrate quotations, summaries, and paraphrases smoothly into the text of an essay; and for avoiding plagiarism.

Part Three, The Language of the Essay, starts with Chapter 11, Diction and Tone, which shows how writers carefully choose words either to convey exact meaning or to be purposely suggestive. In addition, this chapter shows how the words a writer uses can create a particular tone or relationship between writer and reader—one of irony, humor, or seriousness, for example. This part also includes Chapter 12, Figurative Language, which concentrates on the usefulness of the special devices of language—such as simile, metaphor, and personification—that add richness and depth to writing.

Part Four of *Models for Writers*, Types of Essays, is made up of Chapters 13 to 22, which focus on the types of writing that are most often required of college writing students—illustration (how to use examples to illustrate a point or an idea), narration (how to tell a story or give an account of an event), description (how to present a verbal picture), process analysis (how to explain how something is done or happens), definition (how to explain what something is), division and classification (how to divide a subject into its parts and place items into appropriate categories), comparison and contrast (how to explain the similarities and differences between two or more items), cause and effect (how to explain the causes of an event or the effects of an action), argument (how to use reason and logic to persuade someone to your way of thinking), and the research paper. These types of writing are referred to as *organizational patterns* or *rhetorical modes*.

Studying and practicing the organizational patterns are important in any effort to broaden your writing skills. In *Models for Writers*, we look at each pattern separately because we believe that this is the simplest and most effective way to introduce them. However, it does not mean that the writer of a well-written essay necessarily chooses a single pattern and sticks to it exclusively and rigidly. Confining yourself to cause-and-effect analysis or definition throughout an entire essay, for example, might prove impractical and may yield an awkward or unnatural piece of writing. In fact, it is often best to use a single pattern to organize your essay and then to use other patterns as your material dictates. As you read the model essays in this text, you will find that a good many of them use one dominant pattern in combination with other patterns.

Combining organizational patterns is not something that you usually think about when you first tackle a writing assignment. Rather, such combinations of patterns develop naturally as you organize, draft, and revise your materials. Combinations of patterns also make your writing more interesting and effective. See Chapter 1 (pp. 20–22) for a discussion of combining patterns.

Chapters 3 to 21 are organized in the same way. Each opens with an explanation of the element or principle under discussion. These introductions are brief, clear, and practical and usually provide one or more short examples of the feature or principle being studied, including examples from students such as yourself. Following the chapter introduction, we present three or four model essays (Chapter 21, with ten essays, is an exception). Each essay has a brief introduction of its own, providing information about the author and directing your attention to the way the essay demonstrates the featured technique. A Reflecting on What You Know prompt precedes each reading and invites you to explore your own ideas and experiences regarding some issue presented in the reading. Each essay is followed by four kinds of study materials—Thinking Critically about This Reading, Questions for Study and Discussion, Classroom Activity, and Suggested Writing Assignments. Read Chapter 2, From Reading to Writing, for help on improving your writing by using the materials that accompany the readings.

In addition to the model essays you'll find in Chapters 13–21, we have carefully chosen one multimodal reading (a video, an infographic, a speech, an audio clip) to illustrate each of the rhetorical modes. Look for this icon e and directions for accessing these multimodal readings at the end of the introductions for Chapters 13–20. Chapter 21, Argument, has an entirely multimodal argument cluster — Body Image: How We See Ourselves — offered online. You will find an introduction to this argument cluster on pages 609–10, along with directions for accessing the online cluster.

Chapter 22, A Brief Guide to Writing a Research Paper, offers an annotated MLA-style student research paper, "An Argument for Corporate Responsibility," and an annotated APA-style student research paper, "The Role of Spirituality and Religion in Mental Health" (available online). This chapter provides clear guidance on establishing a realistic schedule for a research project, conducting research on the Internet using directory and keyword searches, evaluating sources, analyzing sources, developing a working bibliography, taking useful notes, and using MLA and APA citation styles to document your paper. This chapter, in combination with Chapter 10, Writing with Sources, helps you build confidence in your academic writing skills.

Models for Writers provides information, instruction, and practice in writing effective essays. By reading thoughtfully and critically and by applying the writing strategies and techniques you observe other writers using, you will learn to write more expressively and effectively.

part ■ one

On Reading and Writing Well

CHAPTER 1

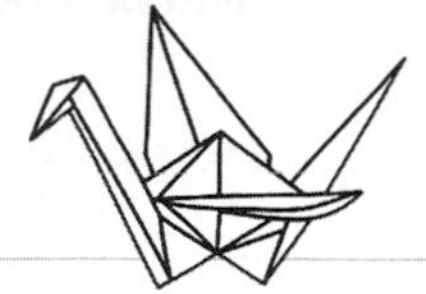

The Writing Process

The essays in this book will help you understand the elements of good writing and provide ample opportunity for you to practice writing in response to the model essays. As you write your essays, pay attention to your writing process. This chapter focuses on the stages of the writing process—prewriting, writing the first draft, revising, editing, and proofreading. It concludes with a sample of one student's writing process that you can model your own writing after. The strategies suggested in this chapter for each stage of the writing process will help you overcome many of the challenges you may face while writing essays.

PREWRITING

Writers rarely rely on inspiration alone to produce an effective piece of writing. Good writers prewrite or plan, write the first draft, revise, edit, and proofread. It is worth remembering, however, that often the process is recursive, moving back and forth among the five stages. Moreover, writing is personal; no two people go about it exactly the same way. Still, it is possible to learn the steps in the process and thereby have a reliable method for undertaking a writing task.

Reading can give you ideas and information, of course. But reading also helps expand your knowledge of the organizational patterns available to you; consequently, it can help direct all your prewriting activities. During *prewriting*, you select your subject and topic, gather ideas and information, and determine the thesis and organizational pattern or patterns you will use. Once you have worked through the prewriting process, you will be ready to start on your first draft. Let's explore how this works.

Understand Your Assignment

When you first receive an assignment, read it over several times to make sure you understand what you are being asked to do. Try restating the assignment in your own words to make sure you understand it. For example, consider the following assignments:

1. Narrate an experience that taught you that every situation has at least two sides.
2. Explain what is meant by *theoretical modeling* in the social sciences.
3. Write a persuasive essay in which you support or refute the following proposition: "Violence in the media is in large part responsible for an increase in violence in American society today."

Each of these assignments asks you to write in different ways. The first assignment asks you to tell the story of an event that showed you that every situation has more than one perspective. To complete the assignment, you might choose simply to narrate the event, or you might choose to analyze it in depth. In either case, you will need to explain to your reader how you came to this new understanding of multiple perspectives and why it was important to you. The second assignment asks you to explain what theoretical modeling is and why it is used. To accomplish this assignment, you will first need to read about the concept to gain a thorough understanding of it, and then you'll need to define it in your own words and explain its purpose and usefulness to your readers. You will also want to demonstrate the abstract concept with concrete examples to help your readers understand it. Finally, the third assignment asks you to take a position on a controversial issue for which there are many studies on both sides of the question. You will need to research the studies, consider the evidence they present, and then take a stand of your own. Your argument will necessarily have to draw on the sources and evidence you have researched, and you will need to refute the arguments and evidence presented by those experts who take an opposing position.

If, after reading the assignment several times, you are still unsure about what is being asked of you or about any additional requirements of the assignment, such as length or format, be sure to consult with your instructor.

Choose a Subject Area, and Focus on a Topic

Although you will usually be given specific assignments in your writing course, you may sometimes have the freedom to write on any subject that interests you. In such a case, you may already have a specific idea in mind. For example, if you are interested in sports, you might argue against the use of performance-enhancing drugs by athletes. What happens, however, when you are free to choose your own subject and cannot think of anything to write about? If you find yourself in this situation, begin by determining a broad subject that you might enjoy writing about—a general subject like medical ethics, amateur sports, or foreign travel. Also consider what you've recently read—essays in *Models for Writers*, for example—or your career ambitions when choosing a subject. Select several likely subjects, and let your mind explore their potential for interesting topics. Your goal is to arrive at an appropriately narrowed *topic*.

A topic is the specific part of a subject on which a writer focuses. Subjects such as the environment, literature, and sports are too broad to be dealt with adequately in a single essay. Entire books are written about these and other subjects. Start with your broad subject, and make it more specific.

Suppose, for example, you select farming and advertising as possible subject areas. The examples on the following page illustrate how to narrow these broad subjects into manageable topics. Notice how each successive topic is more narrowed than the one before it. Moving from the general to the specific, the topics become appropriate for essay-length writing.

In moving from a broad subject to a particular topic, you should take into account any assigned constraints on length or format. You will also want to consider the amount of time you have to write. These practical considerations will affect the scope of your topic.

macmillanhighered.com/mfw12e
LearningCurve > Topics and Main Ideas

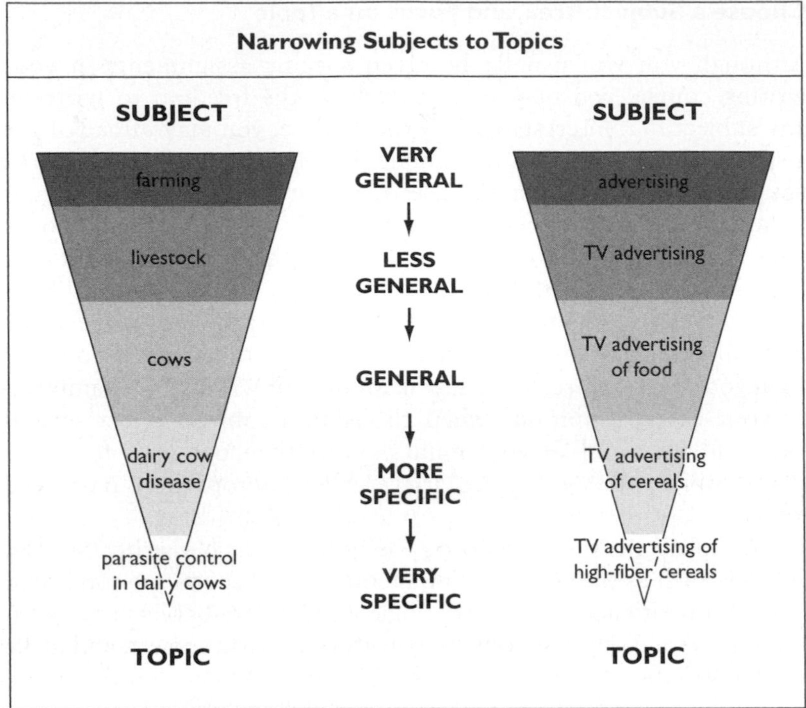

Get Ideas and Collect Information

Once you have found your topic, you will need to determine what you want to say about it. The best way to do this is to gather information. Your ideas about a topic must be supported by information, such as facts and examples. The information you gather about a topic will influence your ideas about the topic and what you want to say. Here are some of the ways you can gather information:

1. *Brainstorm.* Jot down the things you know about a topic, freely associating ideas and information as a way to explore the topic and its possibilities. (See p. 38 for an example.) Don't censor or edit your notes, and don't worry about spelling or punctuation. Don't write your notes in list form because such an organization will imply a hierarchy of ideas, which may hamper your creativity and

the free flow of your thoughts. The objective of *brainstorming* is to free up your thinking before you start to write. You may want to set aside your notes and return to them over several days. Once you generate a substantial amount of brainstormed material, you will want to study the items, attempt to see relationships among them, or sort and group the entries by using different colored highlighters.

2. *Cluster.* Another strategy for stimulating your thinking about a topic is *clustering*. Place your topic in a circle, and draw lines from that circle to other circles in which you write related key words or phrases. Around each of these key words, generate more circles representing the various aspects of the key word that come to mind. (See p. 39 for an example.) The value of clustering over brainstorming is that you are generating ideas and organizing them at the same time. Both techniques work very well, but you may prefer one over the other or find that one works better with one topic than another.
3. *Research.* You may want to add to what you already know about your topic with research. Research can take many forms beyond formal research carried out in your library. For example, firsthand observations and interviews with people knowledgeable about your topic can provide up-to-date information. Whatever your form of research, take careful notes so you can accurately paraphrase an author or quote an interviewee. Chapters 10 and 22 (see pp. 240–57 and 611–22) will help with all aspects of researching a topic.

Understand What a Thesis Is

Once you have generated ideas and information about your topic, you are ready to begin the important task of establishing a controlling idea, or *thesis* for your essay. The thesis of an essay is its main idea, the point you are trying to make. It is important because everything in your essay, all the ideas and information you have gathered, should be connected to the thesis. It is the glue that holds your writing together.

In his essay "The Ways of Meeting Oppression" (pp. 467–70), Martin Luther King Jr. offers the following thesis statement: "Oppressed people deal with their oppression in three characteristic ways." King supports his thesis by describing the three ways that oppressed people have traditionally dealt with oppression and explaining why two of those responses—acquiescing to their oppressors or violently resisting them—have not traditionally worked and are not responses he would recommend. He then works his way to the conclusion of his essay, recommending the path of nonviolent resistance as the best way to achieve social justice. His thesis statement carries with it the answer to several implied or built-in questions: What are the characteristic ways of meeting oppression, and which one is to be recommended? The structure of his essay, then, is also built into his thesis statement.

Remember that a weak thesis cannot produce a successful essay no matter how much effort you put into your writing. A strong thesis, on the other hand, will succeed, but only if it is properly supported.

Develop Your Thesis

You might think that creating a thesis requires some kind of clever thinking or special skills on your part when, in fact, it's a fairly straightforward task. Rather than staring at a blank screen or sheet of paper hoping for a thesis to magically appear, you need to look at the ideas and information you have generated about your topic and ask questions about them in order to understand the topic completely.

Step 1: Question

Let's say that you chose or were assigned the topic of internships, the practice of employing relatively inexperienced people, often students, so that they become familiar with particular work environments and business practices. Through your reading you have learned that internships are often mutually beneficial. Interns can gain useful work-related experience and businesses get inexpensive temporary help (which sometimes leads to permanent positions).

Now you need to more deeply inform yourself about internships by asking questions about the information and ideas you have gathered. For example, Why did internships develop as an educational and business practice? Where and when are they now used? Are there internship programs at your school? If so, what informational materials are available to you? Who can help you find an internship? Can you get an internship on your own? Do any businesses in your area offer internships? What are the negative aspects of an internship for both parties? Do you have family or friends who have employed interns? Do you have family or friends who have had internships? What information have you been able to gain from those on both sides of the relationship? Are interns usually paid? How are internships funded?

Once the questioning starts, one question will lead to another, and the answers to these questions—often found through more reading, interviews, and discussions—will inform you about the depth and breadth of your topic. If all this is done well, you will soon begin to think like an expert on your topic.

At this point, the likelihood of developing a thesis, or a number of them, will greatly increase. In fact, trying to develop not just one thesis but several of them can be a very helpful strategy in refining your ideas and coming up with the best possible thesis. Also, keep in mind that a thesis can be considered a *working thesis* until you are sure it conveys exactly what you want to say, or until you revise it into its final form. It is out of the facts and ideas that you have collected and the questions you ask of that material that a thesis will come to mind.

Step 2: List Several Possible Thesis Statements

Once you have asked all the questions you think necessary and have supplied answers to those questions, you are ready to list possible thesis statements. Here are some theses that might be developed as a result of a deeper investigation into the topic of internships:

- All effective internship programs have five key elements.
- Research is necessary before applying to an internship program.
- Employers must have a clearly defined set of expectations for internship programs.
- Record keeping and reporting are the keys to an effective internship program.
- There are no standard practices for funding internships.
- We need a federally funded internship program.

Step 3: Choose the Direction in Which You Would Like to Go

The potential theses listed in Step 2 reflect different approaches to and aspects of the topic of internships. Let's take a closer look at how each one may have been arrived at and where each might lead the writer:

All effective internship programs have five key elements.
This thesis is most likely the product of an examination of successful internship programs to learn their key elements. The supporting information might also serve to explain the establishment of an internship program or how to improve an existing one.

Research is necessary before applying to an internship program.
This thesis might be the product of learning what can go right and wrong with an internship and might even suggest what individuals need to know about a program before entering it.

Employers must have a clearly defined set of expectations for internship programs.
This thesis suggests that successful internships are the result of clear expectations for the intern and well-defined pathways for achieving success.

Record keeping and reporting are the keys to an effective internship program.
This thesis suggests that communication is important in any internship relationship. It implies that all parties should document projects, goals, and steps toward achieving those goals, as well as efforts in accomplishing them.

There are no standard practices for funding internships.
This thesis suggests that the way internships are financed is not standardized and that because each internship must be arranged for individually, arrangements vary greatly.

We need a federally funded internship program.
This thesis suggests that internships are so worthwhile that they need to be made available nationally and be federally funded.

Step 4: Write Your Thesis Statement

A thesis statement should be

- the most important point you make about your topic,
- more general than the ideas and facts you use to support it, and
- focused enough to be covered in the space allotted for the essay.

A thesis statement is not a question, although it might be prompted by one or many, as we have seen with the topic of internships.

An effective method for developing a thesis statement is to begin by writing, "What I want to say is that . . ."

> What I want to say is that unless language barriers between patients and healthcare providers are overcome, the lives of many patients in our more culturally diverse cities will be endangered.

Later, when you delete the formulaic opening and streamline the text, you will be left with a thesis statement:

> Unless language barriers between patients and healthcare providers are overcome, many patients' lives in our more culturally diverse cities will be endangered.

A good way to determine whether your thesis is too general or too specific is to consider how easy it will be to present information and examples to support it. If you stray too far in either direction, your task will become much more difficult. A thesis statement that is too general will leave you overwhelmed by the number of issues you must address. For example, the statement "Malls have ruined the fabric of American life" would lead to the question "How?" To answer it, you would probably have to include information about traffic patterns, urban decay, environmental damage, economic studies, and so on. You would obviously have to take shortcuts, and your essay would be ineffective. On the other hand, too specific a thesis statement will leave you with too little information to present. "The Big City Mall should not have been built because it reduced retail sales at the existing Big City stores by 21.4 percent" does not leave you with many options to develop an argument.

The thesis statement is usually set forth near the beginning of the essay, although writers sometimes begin with a few sentences that establish a context for the piece. One common strategy is to position the thesis as the final sentence of the first paragraph. In the opening paragraph of an essay on the harmful effects of quick weight-loss diets, student Marcie Turple builds a context for her thesis statement, which she presents in her last sentence:

> Americans are obsessed with thinness—even at the risk of dying. In the 1930s, people took dinitrophenol, an industrial poison, to lose weight. It boosted metabolism but caused blindness and some deaths. Since then dieters have used hormone injections, amphetamines, liquid protein diets, and, more recently, the controversial fen-phen. What most dieters need to realize is that there is no magic way to lose weight—no pill, no crash diet plan. *The only way to permanent weight loss is through sensible eating and exercise.*
>
> –Marcie Turple, student

Step 5: Revise Your Thesis Statement If Necessary

Remember that you are not unalterably committed to the wording of your original thesis, what writers call a *working thesis*. Just as you provide evidence to support the thesis statement, you are free to revise the statement to fit the evidence. For example, let's suppose you decide to use the following thesis statement for an essay on internships:

> We need a federally funded internship program.

You discover as you draft your essay that your evidence is largely financial. You learn that schools and businesses, especially in poorer parts of the country, refrain from establishing internships because there is little money for such efforts. You reason that if there were a federally funded program, students and businesses from any part of the country, regardless of local resources, would have an equal opportunity to participate. You then revise your working thesis to reflect this additional, more pertinent evidence:

> We need a nationwide federally funded internship program that will provide equal opportunity for all students and businesses, regardless of their regional economic differences.

Models for Writers abounds in essays with excellent thesis statements, and we often ask you to identify them. Reading essays with strong thesis statements and locating the controlling idea in each is a great way to learn how to write your own strong thesis statements. Here are some more examples of thesis statements drawn from the essays in *Models for Writers*:

James Lincoln Collier states his thesis in paragraph 20 of "Anxiety: Challenge by Another Name" (p. 96):

> The point is that the new, the different, is almost by definition scary. But each time you try something, you learn, and as the learning piles up, the world opens to you.

Collier's thesis appears near the end of his essay and consists of two sentences instead of a single statement.

William Lutz presents his thesis at the beginning of paragraph 2 in "Doubts about Doublespeak" (p. 473):

> Doublespeak is language which pretends to communicate but doesn't.

Writers occasionally reiterate their thesis statements in different language so as to elaborate on them and give them more emphasis. Lutz does this in paragraph 9:

> Doublespeak is not the product of careless language or sloppy thinking. Quite the opposite. Doublespeak is language carefully designed and constructed to appear to communicate when in fact it doesn't. It is language designed not to lead but mislead.

Finally, in an essay about finding appropriate punishment for minor crimes, Dan M. Kahan in "Shame Is Worth a Try" (pp. 581–83) offers the following thesis statement in paragraph 3:

> [W]hat the shame proponents seem to be getting, and the critics ignoring, is the potential of shame as an effective, cheap, and humane alternative to imprisonment.

With this thesis, Kahan expresses his argument and provides the reader with an outline of the three main points he'll expand on in his essay to support that argument.

As you read through the essays in this book, be on the lookout for thesis statements that you find especially effective: Note their placement within the essay and think about why they've caught your eye. These can serve, then, as models for you when you write your thesis statement. For more on the various ways of developing an effective thesis, see Chapter 3, Thesis (pp. 79–81).

Know Your Audience

Although it is not always possible to know who your readers are, you nevertheless need to consider your intended audience. Your attitude toward your topic, your tone, your sentence structure, and your choice of words are just some of the important considerations that rely on your awareness of audience. For a list of questions to help you determine your audience, see the box below.

Audience Questions

1. Who are my readers?
2. Is my audience specialized (for example, those in my geology lab) or more general (college students)?
3. What do I know about my audience's age, gender, education, religious affiliation, socioeconomic status, and political attitudes?
4. What do my readers need to know that I can tell them?
5. Will my audience be interested, open-minded, resistant, objective, or hostile to what I am saying?
6. Is there any specialized language that my audience must have to understand my subject or that I should avoid?
7. What do I want my audience to do as a result of reading my essay?

Determine Your Method of Development

Part Four of *Models for Writers* includes chapters on the various types of writing most often required of college students. Often these types of writing are referred to as *methods of development, rhetorical patterns*, or *organizational patterns*.

Studying these organizational patterns and practicing the use of them are important in any effort to broaden your writing skills. In *Models for Writers*, we look at each pattern separately because we believe this is the most effective way to introduce them, but it does not necessarily mean that a well-written essay adheres exclusively and rigidly to a single pattern of development. Confining yourself exclusively to comparison and contrast throughout an entire essay, for instance, might prove impractical and result in a formulaic or stilted essay. As you read the model essays in this text, you will find that many of them use a combination of patterns to support the dominant pattern. For a description of what each organizational pattern involves, see the box below.

Organizational Patterns	
Illustration	Using examples to illustrate a point or an idea
Narration	Telling a story or giving an account of an event
Description	Presenting a picture with words
Process Analysis	Explaining how something is done or happens
Definition	Explaining what something is
Division and Classification	Dividing a subject into its parts and placing them in appropriate categories
Comparison and Contrast	Demonstrating likenesses and differences
Cause and Effect	Explaining the causes of an event or the effects of an action
Argument	Using reason and logic to persuade someone to your way of thinking

Combining organizational patterns is probably not something you want to plan or even think about when you first tackle a writing assignment. Instead, let these patterns develop naturally as you organize, draft, and revise your materials.

If you're still undecided or concerned about combining patterns, try the following steps:

1. Summarize the point you want to make in a single phrase or sentence.
2. Restate the point as a question (in effect, the question your essay will answer).
3. Look closely at both the summary and the question for key words or concepts that suggest a particular pattern.
4. Consider other strategies that could support your primary pattern.

Here are some examples:

SUMMARY: Venus and Serena Williams are among the best female tennis players in the history of the game.

QUESTION: How do Venus and Serena Williams compare with other tennis players?

PATTERN: Comparison and contrast. The writer must compare the Williams sisters with other female players and provide evidence to support the claim that they are "among the best."

SUPPORTING PATTERNS: Illustration and description. Good evidence includes examples of the Williams sisters' superior ability and accomplishments as well as descriptions of their athletic feats.

SUMMARY: How to build a personal website.

QUESTION: How do you build a personal website?

PATTERN: Process analysis. The word *how,* especially in the phrase *how to,* implies a procedure that can be explained in steps or stages.

SUPPORTING PATTERNS: Description. It will be necessary to describe the website, especially the look and design of the site, at various points in the process.

SUMMARY: Petroleum and natural gas prices should be federally controlled.

QUESTION: What should be done about petroleum and natural gas prices?

PATTERN: Argument. The word *should* signals an argument, calling for evidence and reasoning in support of the conclusion.

SUPPORTING PATTERNS: Comparison and contrast and cause and effect. The writer should present evidence from a comparison of federally controlled pricing with deregulated pricing as well as from a discussion of the effects of deregulation.

These are just a few examples showing how to decide on a pattern of development and supporting patterns that are suitable for your topic and what you want to say about it.

Map Your Organization

Once you decide what you want to write about and come up with some ideas about what you might like to say, your next task is to organize the main ideas for your essay in a way that seems both natural and logical to you. In other words, make an outline. In constructing this outline, if you discover that a particular organizational pattern will help you in generating ideas, you might consider using that as your overall organizing principle.

Whether you write a formal outline, simply set down a rough sequence of the major points of your thesis, or take a middle ground between those two strategies, you need to think about the overall organization of your paper. Some writers make a detailed outline and fill it out point by point, whereas others follow a general plan and let the writing take them where it will, making any necessary adjustments to the plan when they revise.

Here are some major patterns of organization you may want to use for your outline:

- Chronological (oldest to newest, or the reverse)
- Spatial (top to bottom, left to right, inside to outside, and so forth)
- Least familiar to most familiar
- Easiest to most difficult to comprehend
- Easiest to most difficult to accept
- According to similarities or differences

Notice that some of these organizational patterns correspond to the rhetorical patterns in Part Four of this book. For example, a narrative essay generally follows a chronological organization. If you are having trouble developing or mapping an effective organization, refer to the introduction and readings in Chapter 5, Organization. Once you have settled on an organizational pattern, you are ready to write a first draft.

WRITING THE FIRST DRAFT

Your goal in writing a first draft is to get your ideas down on paper. Write quickly, and let the writing follow your thinking. Do not be overly concerned about spelling, word choice, or grammar because such concerns will break the flow of your ideas. After you have completed your first draft, you will go over your essay to revise and edit it.

As you write your draft, pay attention to your outline, but do not be a slave to it. It is there to help you, not restrict you. Often, when writing, you discover something new about your subject; if so, follow that idea freely. Wherever you deviate from your plan, place an X in the margin to remind yourself of the change. When you revise, you can return to that part of your writing and reconsider the change you made, either developing it further or abandoning it.

It may happen that while writing your first draft, you run into difficulty that prevents you from moving forward. For example, suppose you want to tell the story of something that happened to you, but you aren't certain whether you should be using the pronoun *I* so often. Turn to the essays in Chapters 11 and 14 to see how the authors use diction and tone and how other narrative essays handle this problem. You will find that the frequent use of *I* isn't necessarily a problem at all. For an account of a personal experience, it's perfectly acceptable to use *I* as often as you need to. Or suppose that after writing several pages describing someone who you think is quite a character, you find that your draft seems flat and doesn't express how lively and funny the person really is. If you read the introduction to Chapter 15, you will learn that descriptions need lots of factual, concrete detail; the selections in that chapter give further proof of this. You can use those guidelines to add details that are missing from your draft.

If you run into difficulties writing your first draft, don't be discouraged. Even experienced writers run into problems at the beginning. Just try to keep going, and take the pressure off yourself. Think about your topic, and consider your details and what you want to say. You may even want to go back and look over the ideas and information you've gathered.

Create a Title

What makes a good title? There are no hard-and-fast rules, but most writers would agree that an effective title hooks the reader into reading the essay, either because the title is unusual and intrigues the reader or because it asks a question and the reader is curious to know the answer. A good title announces your subject and prepares your reader for the approach you take. You can create a title while writing your first draft or after you have seen how your ideas develop. Either way, the important thing is to brainstorm for titles and not simply use the first one that comes to mind. With at least a half dozen to choose from, preferably more, you will have a much better sense of how to pick an effective title—one that does important work explaining your subject to the reader and that is lively and inviting. Spend several minutes reviewing the titles of the essays in *Models for Writers* (see the table of contents, pp. xvi–xxv). You'll like some better than others, but reflecting on the effectiveness of each one will help you strengthen your own titles.

Focus on Beginnings and Endings

The beginning of your essay is vitally important to its success. Indeed, if your opening doesn't attract and hold your readers' attention, readers may be less than enthusiastic about proceeding.

Notes on Beginnings and Endings

Beginnings and endings are important to the effectiveness of essays, but they can be difficult to write. Inexperienced writers often think that they must write their essays sequentially when, in fact, it is better to write both the beginning and the ending after most of the rest of an essay is completed. Pay particular attention to both parts during revision. Ask yourself the following questions:

1. Does my introduction grab the reader's attention?
2. Is my introduction confusing in any way? How well does it relate to the rest of the essay?
3. If I state my thesis in the introduction, how effectively is it presented?
4. Does my essay come to a logical conclusion, or does it just stop short?
5. How well does the conclusion relate to the rest of the essay? Am I careful not to introduce new topics or issues that I did not address in the body of the essay?
6. Does the conclusion help underscore or illuminate important aspects of the body of the essay, or is it just another version of what I wrote earlier?

Your ending is almost always as important as your beginning. An effective conclusion does more than end your essay. It wraps up your thoughts and leaves readers satisfied with the presentation of your ideas and information. Your ending should be a natural outgrowth of the development of your ideas. Avoid trick endings, mechanical summaries, and cutesy comments, and never introduce new concepts or information in the ending. Just as with the writing of titles, the writing of beginnings and endings is perhaps best done by generating several alternatives and then selecting from among them. Review the box on page 24 and see Chapter 6 for more help developing your beginnings and endings.

REVISING

Once you have completed a first draft, set it aside for a few hours or even until the next day. Removed from the process of drafting, you can approach the revision of your draft with a clear mind. When you revise, consider the most important elements of your draft first. You should focus on your thesis, purpose, content, organization, and paragraph structure. You will have a chance to look at grammar, punctuation, and mechanics after you revise. This way you will make sure that your essay is fundamentally solid and says what you want it to say before dealing with the task of editing.

Questions for Revising

1. Have I focused on my topic?
2. Does my thesis make a clear statement about my topic?
3. Is the organizational pattern I have used the best one, given my purpose?
4. Does the topic sentence of each paragraph relate to my thesis? Does each paragraph support its topic sentence?
5. Do I have enough supporting details, and are my examples the best ones that I can develop?
6. How effective are my beginning and my ending? Can I improve them?
7. Do I have a good title? Does it indicate what my subject is and hint at my thesis?

macmillanhighered.com/mfw12e
LearningCurve > Topic Sentences and Supporting Details

It is helpful to have someone—a friend or a member of your writing class—listen to your essay as you read it aloud. The process of reading aloud allows you to determine if your writing sounds clear and natural. If you have to alter your voice to provide emphasis, try rephrasing the idea to make it clearer. Whether you revise your work on your own or have someone assist you, the questions in the box on page 25 will help you focus on the largest, most important elements of your essay early in the revision process.

EDITING

Once you are sure that the large elements of your essay are in place and that you have said what you intended, you are ready to begin editing your essay. At this stage, correct any mistakes in grammar, punctuation, mechanics, and spelling because a series of small errors can distract readers. Such errors can also cause readers to doubt the important points you are trying to make.

In this section we provide sound advice and solutions for the editing problems that trouble students most. For more guidance with these or other editing or grammar concerns, refer to your grammar handbook, make an appointment with a writing center tutor, or ask your instructor for help.

Run-ons: Fused Sentences and Comma Splices

Writers can become so absorbed in getting their ideas down on paper that they often combine two independent clauses (complete sentences that can stand alone when punctuated with a period) incorrectly, creating a *run-on sentence*. A run-on sentence fails to show where one thought ends and where another begins and can confuse readers. There are two types of run-on sentences: the fused sentence and the comma splice.

A *fused sentence* occurs when a writer combines two independent clauses with no punctuation at all. To correct a fused sentence, divide the independent clauses into separate sentences, or join them by adding words, punctuation, or both.

macmillanhighered.com/mfw12e
LearningCurve > Run-ons and Comma Splices; Commas

INCORRECT	Jen loves Harry Potter she was the first in line to buy the latest book.
EDITED	Jen loves Harry Potter ^. She^ she was the first in line to buy the latest book.
EDITED	Jen loves Harry Potter ^; in fact,^ she was the first in line to buy the latest book.

A *comma splice* occurs when writers use only a comma to combine two independent clauses. To correct a comma splice, divide the independent clauses into separate sentences or join them by adding words, punctuation, or both.

INCORRECT	The e-mail looked like spam, Marty deleted it.
EDITED	The e-mail looked like spam ^;^ Marty deleted it.
EDITED	The e-mail looked like spam, ^so^ Marty deleted it.

Sentence Fragments

A *sentence fragment* is a word group that cannot stand alone as a complete sentence. Even if a word group begins with a capital letter and ends with punctuation, it is not a sentence unless it has a subject (the person, place, or thing the sentence is about) and a verb (a word that tells what the subject does) and expresses a complete thought. Word groups that do not express complete thoughts often begin with a subordinating conjunction such as *although, because, since,* or *unless.* To correct a fragment, add a subject or a verb, or integrate the fragment into a nearby sentence to complete the thought.

INCORRECT	Divided my time between work and school last semester.

macmillanhighered.com/mfw12e
LearningCurve > Fragments

EDITED *I divided* ~~Divided~~ my time between work and school last semester.

INCORRECT Terry's essay was really interesting. Because it brought up good points about energy conservation.

EDITED Terry's essay was really interesting/ *because* ~~Because~~ it brought up good points about energy conservation.

Creative use of intentional sentence fragments is occasionally acceptable—in narration essays, for example—when writers are trying to establish a particular mood or tone.

> I asked him about his recent trip. He asked me about work. Short questions. One-word answers. Then an awkward pause.
>
> –David P. Bardeen, "LIVES; Not Close Enough for Comfort"

Subject-Verb Agreement

Subjects and verbs must agree in number—that is, a singular subject (one person, place, or thing) must take a singular verb, and a plural subject (more than one person, place, or thing) must take a plural verb. Most native speakers of English use proper subject-verb agreement in their writing without conscious awareness. Even so, some sentence constructions can be troublesome.

When a prepositional phrase (a phrase that includes a preposition such as *on, of, in, at,* or *between*) falls between a subject and a verb, it can obscure their relationship. To make sure the subject agrees with its verb in a sentence with an intervening prepositional phrase, mentally cross out the phrase (*of basic training* in the following example) to isolate the subject and verb and determine if they agree.

INCORRECT The first three weeks of basic training is the worst.

EDITED The first three weeks of basic training *are* ~~is~~ the worst.

macmillanhighered.com/mfw12e
LearningCurve > Subject-Verb Agreement

Writers often have difficulty with subject-verb agreement in sentences with compound subjects (two or more subjects joined together with the word *and*). As a general rule, compound subjects take plural verbs.

INCORRECT	My mother, sister, and cousin is visiting me next month.
EDITED	My mother, sister, and cousin ~~is~~ ^are^ visiting me next month.

However, in sentences with subjects joined by *either . . . or, neither . . . nor,* or *not only . . . but also,* the verb must agree with the subject closest to it.

INCORRECT	Neither the mechanics nor the salesperson know what's wrong with my car.
EDITED	Neither the mechanics nor the salesperson ~~know~~ ^knows^ what's wrong with my car.

While editing your essay, be sure to identify the subjects and verbs in your sentences and to check their agreement.

Pronoun-Antecedent Agreement

A *pronoun* is a word that takes the place of a noun in a sentence. To avoid repeating nouns in our speech and writing, we use pronouns as noun substitutes. The noun to which a pronoun refers is called its *antecedent*. A pronoun and its antecedent are said to *agree* when the relationship between them is clear. Pronouns must agree with their antecedents in both *person* and *number.*

There are three types of pronouns: first person (*I* and *we*), second person (*you*), and third person (*he, she, they,* and *it*). First-person pronouns refer to first-person antecedents, second-person pronouns refer to second-person antecedents, and third-person pronouns refer to third-person antecedents.

INCORRECT House hunters should review their finances carefully before you make an offer.

EDITED House hunters should review their finances carefully before ~~you~~ *they* make an offer.

A pronoun must agree in number with its antecedent; that is, a singular pronoun must refer to a singular antecedent, and a plural pronoun must refer to a plural antecedent. When two or more antecedents are joined by the word *and*, the pronoun must be plural.

INCORRECT Gina, Kim, and Katie took her vacations in August.

EDITED Gina, Kim, and Katie took ~~her~~ *their* vacations in August.

When the subject of a sentence is an indefinite pronoun such as *everyone, each, everybody, anyone, anybody, everything, either, one, neither, someone,* or *something,* use a singular pronoun to refer to it or recast the sentence to eliminate the agreement problem.

INCORRECT Each of the women submitted their résumé.

EDITED Each of the women submitted ~~their~~ *her* résumé.

EDITED ~~Each~~ *Both* of the women submitted their ~~resume~~ *résumés*.

Verb Tense Shifts

A verb's tense indicates when an action takes place—sometime in the past, right now, or in the future. Using verb tense consistently helps your readers understand time changes in your writing. Inconsistent verb tenses, or *shifts,* within a sentence confuse readers and are especially noticeable in narration and process analysis writing, which are sequence and time oriented. Generally, you should write in the past or present tense and maintain that tense throughout your sentence.

INCORRECT The painter studied the scene and pulls a fan brush decisively from her cup.

EDITED — The painter studied the scene and ~~pulls~~ *pulled* a fan brush decisively from her cup.

Misplaced and Dangling Modifiers

A *modifier* is a word or words that describe or give additional information about other words in a sentence. Always place modifiers as close as possible to the words they modify. An error in modifier placement could be unintentionally confusing (or amusing) to your readers. Two common problems arise with modifiers: the misplaced modifier and the dangling modifier.

A *misplaced modifier* unintentionally modifies the wrong word in a sentence because it is placed incorrectly.

INCORRECT — The waiter brought a steak to the man covered with onions.

EDITED — The waiter brought a steak *covered with onions* to the man. ~~covered with onions.~~

A *dangling modifier* appears at the beginning or end of a sentence and modifies a word that does not appear in the sentence—often an unstated subject.

INCORRECT — Staring into the distance, large rain clouds form.

EDITED — Staring into the distance, *Jon saw* large rain clouds form.

While editing your essay, make sure you have positioned your modifiers as close as possible to the words they modify, and make sure each sentence has a clear subject that is modified correctly.

Faulty Parallelism

Parallelism means using similar grammatical forms to show that ideas in a sentence are of equal importance. Faulty parallelism can interrupt the flow of your writing and confuse your readers. Writers have trouble with parallelism in three kinds of sentence constructions.

In sentences that include items in a pair or series, make sure the elements of the pair or series are parallel in form. Delete any unnecessary or repeated words.

INCORRECT Nina likes snowboarding, roller skating, and to hike.

EDITED Nina likes snowboarding, roller skating, and ~~to hike.~~ ^*hiking.*

In sentences that include connecting words such as *both . . . and, either . . . or, neither . . . nor, rather . . . than,* and *not only . . . but also,* make sure the elements being connected are parallel in form. Delete any unnecessary or repeated words.

INCORRECT The lecture was both enjoyable and it was a form of education.

EDITED The lecture was both enjoyable and ~~it was a form of education.~~ ^*educational.*

In sentences that include the comparison word *as* or *than,* make sure the elements of the comparison are parallel in form. Delete any unnecessary or repeated words.

INCORRECT It would be better to study now than waiting until the night before the exam.

EDITED It would be better to study now than ~~waiting~~ ^*to wait* until the night before the exam.

Weak Nouns and Verbs

Inexperienced writers often believe that adjectives and adverbs are the stuff of effective writing. They're right in one sense but not wholly so. Although strong adjectives and adverbs are crucial, good writing depends on strong, well-chosen nouns and verbs. The noun *vehicle* is not nearly as descriptive as *Jeep, snowmobile, pickup truck,* or *SUV,* for example. Why use the weak verb *look* when your meaning would be conveyed more precisely with *glance, stare, spy, gaze, peek, examine,* or *witness*? Instead of the weak verb *run,* use *fly, gallop, hustle, jog, race, rush, scamper, scoot, scramble,* or *trot.*

While editing your essay, look for instances of weak nouns and verbs. If you can't form a clear picture in your mind of what a noun looks like or what a verb's action is, your nouns and verbs are likely weak. The more specific and strong you make your nouns and verbs, the more lively and descriptive your writing will be.

WEAK The flowers moved toward the bright light of the sun.

EDITED The ~~flowers moved~~ *tulips stretched* toward the bright light of the sun.

When you have difficulty thinking of strong, specific nouns and verbs, reach for a thesaurus—but only if you are sure you can identify the best word for your purpose. Thesauruses are available free online and in inexpensive paperback editions; most word processing programs include a thesaurus as well. A thesaurus will help you avoid redundancy in your writing and find specific words with just the right meaning.

Academic Diction and Tone

The language that you use in your college courses, known as *American Standard English,* is formal in diction and objective in tone. American Standard English is the language used by educators, civic leaders, the media, and professionals in all fields. Although the standard is fairly narrow in scope, it allows for individual differences in expression and voice so that your writing can retain its personality and appeal.

Tone is the distance that you establish between yourself and your audience and is created by your *diction* (the particular words you choose) and the complexity of your sentences. Formal writing creates a distance between yourself and your audience through the use of third-person pronouns (*he*, *she*, *it*, *they*) and provides the impression of objectivity. Formal writing values logic, evidence, and reason over opinion and bias. Informal writing, on the other hand, uses first-person pronouns (*I*, *we*); is usually found in narratives; and respects feelings, individual tastes, and personal preferences. Similarly, the second-person pronoun (*you*) is used to bring your reader close to you, as is

macmillanhighered.com/mfw12e
LearningCurve > Appropriate Language

done in this text, but it is too familiar for most academic writing and is best avoided if there is any question about its appropriateness.

INFORMAL	The experiment looked like it was going to be a bust.
FORMAL	After detecting a number of design flaws in the experiment, we concluded that it was going to be a failure.
SUBJECTIVE	The governor said that the shortfall in tax revenues was quite a bit bigger than anyone expected.
OBJECTIVE	The governor reported that tax revenues fell by 9 percent over last year.

When writing in a particular discipline, use discipline-specific language and conventions that reflect your understanding of the discipline. Key resources are your readings and the language you use with your instructors and classmates in each discipline. As you read, note how the writer uses technical language (for example, *point of view* and *denouement* in literature; *mean distribution* in statistics; *derivatives* in financial analysis; *pan, tilt,* and *track* in film study; *exogamy* and *endogamy* in anthropology; and *polyphony* and *atonality* in music) to communicate difficult concepts, recognized phenomena in the discipline, and characteristic nuances of the discipline.

Discipline-Specific Prose (Psychology)

How does information get "into" long-term memory? One very important function that takes place in short-term memory is *encoding*, or transforming the new information into a form that can be retrieved later. As a student, you may have tried to memorize dates, facts, or definitions by simply repeating them to yourself over and over. This strategy reflects an attempt to use maintenance rehearsal to encode material into long-term memory. However, maintenance rehearsal is *not* a very effective strategy for encoding information into long-term memory.

A much more effective encoding strategy is *elaborative rehearsal*, which involves focusing on the *meaning* of information to help encode and transfer it to long-term memory. With elaborative rehearsal, you relate the information to other information you already know. That is, rather than simply repeating the information, you *elaborate* on the new information in some meaningful way.

–"Encoding Long-Term Memories," Don H. Hockenbury and Sandra E. Hockenbury, from *Psychology*, Sixth Edition

If you listen carefully and read closely, you will be able to discern the discipline-specific language cues that make a writer sound more like, say, a historian or an anthropologist than a psychologist. In turn, you will be able to use the language of your own discipline with greater ease and accuracy and achieve the subtleties of language that will allow you to carry out your research, draw sound conclusions, and write effectively and with authority.

ESL Concerns (Articles and Nouns)

Two areas of English grammar that can be especially problematic for nonnative speakers of English are articles and nouns. In English, correct use of articles and nouns is necessary for sentences to make sense.

There are two kinds of articles in English: *indefinite* (*a* and *an*) and *definite* (*the*). Use *a* before words beginning with a consonant sound and *an* before words beginning with a vowel sound. Note, too, that *a* is used before an *h* with a consonant sound (*happy*) and *an* is used before a silent *h* (*hour*).

There are two kinds of nouns in English: count and noncount. *Count nouns* name individual things or units that can be counted or separated out from a whole, such as *students* and *pencils*. *Noncount nouns* name things that cannot be counted because they are considered wholes in themselves and cannot be divided, such as *work* and *furniture*.

Use the indefinite article (*a* or *an*) before a singular count noun when you do not specify which one.

I would like to borrow *a* colored pencil.

Plural count nouns take *the*.

I would like to borrow *the* colored pencils.

If a plural count noun is used in a general sense, it does not take an article at all.

I brought colored pencils to class today.

Noncount nouns are always singular and never take an indefinite article.

> We need new living room furniture.

The is sometimes used with noncount nouns to refer to a specific idea or thing.

> *The* furniture will be delivered tomorrow.

When editing your essay, be sure you have used articles and nouns correctly.

INCORRECT I love an aroma of freshly baked cookies.

EDITED I love ~~an~~ *the* aroma of freshly baked cookies.

INCORRECT I have never had the chicken pox.

EDITED I have never had ~~the~~ chicken pox.

Questions for Editing Sentences

1. Do I include any fused sentences or comma splices?
2. Do I include any unintentional sentence fragments?
3. Do my verbs agree with their subjects?
4. Do my pronouns agree with their antecedents?
5. Do I make any unnecessary shifts in verb tense?
6. Do I have any misplaced or dangling modifiers?
7. Are my sentences parallel?
8. Do I use strong nouns and verbs?
9. Do I pair articles and nouns correctly?

PROOFREADING

Do not assume that because you made edits and corrections to your essay electronically in your word processor that all your changes were saved or that your essay will print out correctly. Also do not assume that because you used your word processor's spell-check or grammar-check

Questions for Proofreading Essays

1. Have I printed a hard copy of my essay for proofreading?
2. Have I misspelled or incorrectly typed any words? Has my spell-checker inadvertently approved commonly confused words like *its* and *it's,* or *their, there,* and *they're*?
3. Have I checked my essay for errors I make often?
4. Do all my edits and corrections appear in my hard copy?
5. Have I formatted my essay according to my instructor's directions?
6. Have I given the hard copy of my final draft a thorough review before turning it in?

function you've found and corrected every spelling and grammatical error. In fact, such checkers often allow incorrect or misspelled words to pass while flagging correct grammatical constructions as incorrect. Although your word processor's spell-checker and grammar-checker are a good first line of defense against certain types of errors, there is no replacement for a human proofreader—you.

Print out your essay and carefully proofread it manually. Check to make sure you do not use *your* where you intend *you're, its* where you mean *it's,* or *to* where you want *too*. Spell-checkers *never* catch these types of errors. If you know you are prone to certain mistakes, go through your essay looking for those particular errors.

Make sure that all your electronic changes appear on the hard copy and that you have caught and corrected any grammatical problems. (Be sure to refer to the Questions for Editing Sentences box on page 36 and to the Questions for Proofreading Essays box above.) Check to be certain you have followed your instructor's formatting guidelines. Above all, give your hard-copy essay one final read-through before submitting it to your instructor.

WRITING AN EXPOSITORY ESSAY: A STUDENT ESSAY IN PROGRESS

While he was a student in a writing class at the University of Vermont, Jeffrey Olesky was asked to write an essay on any topic using a suitable method of development. After making a brief list of the subjects that interested him, he chose to write about golf. Golf had been a part of Olesky's life since he was a youngster, so he figured he would have enough material for an essay.

First, he needed to focus on a specific topic within the broad subject area of golf. Having considered a number of aspects of the game—how it's played, its rise in popularity, the controversies over the exclusion of women and minorities from private clubs—he kept coming back to how much golf meant to him. Focusing on his love of golf, he then established his tentative thesis: Golf has taught me a lot.

Olesky needed to develop a number of examples to support his thesis, so he brainstormed for ideas, examples, and anecdotes—anything that came to mind to help him develop his essay. These are his notes:

Brainstorming Notes

Golf is my life — I can't imagine being who I am without it.

I love to be out on the course early in the morning.

It's been embarrassing and stressful sometimes.

There's so much to know and remember about the game, even before you try to hit the ball.

The story about what my father taught me — felt badly and needed to apologize.

"You know better than that, Jeffrey."

I have pictures of me on the greens with a cut-down golf putter.

All kinds of character building goes on.

It's all about rules and playing fairly.

Wanted to be like my father.

The frustration is awesome, but you can learn to deal with it.

Golf is methodical.

I use golf to clear my head.

Golf teaches life's lessons.

Golf teaches you manners, to be respectful of others.

Golf teaches you to abide by the rules.

Golf is an internal tool.

When he thought that he had gathered enough information, he began to consider an organizational plan, a way to present his information in a logical manner. He realized that the character-building

Clustering Diagram

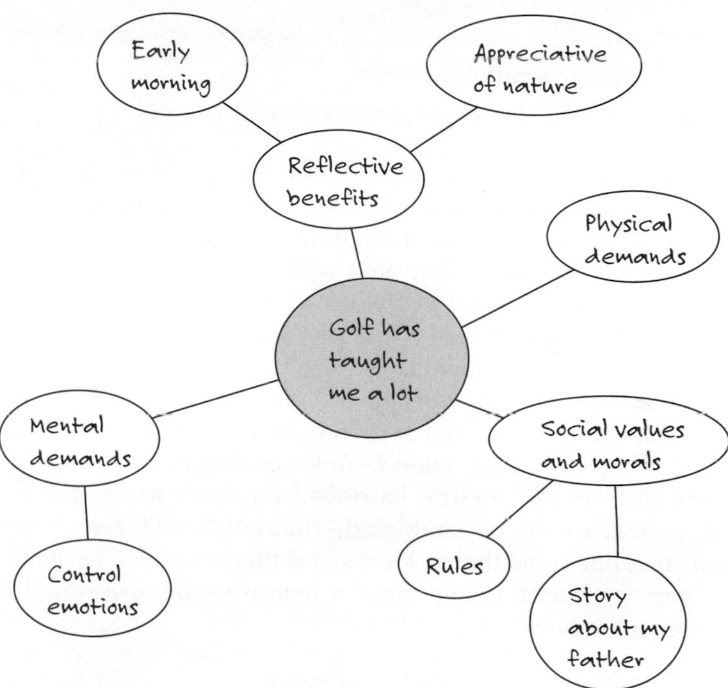

benefits of golf that he included in his brainstorming notes clustered around some key subtopics. He decided to do some clustering and drew circles that included his ideas about golf: the physical and mental demands of the game, the social values and morals it teaches, and the reflective benefits of golf. He then sorted out his related ideas and examples and added them, mapping their relationship in this diagram.

Before beginning to write the first draft of his essay, Olesky thought it would be a good idea to list in an informal outline the major points he wanted to make. Here is his informal outline:

Informal Outline

1. *Brief introductory paragraph announcing the topic*
2. *An expansion of the introductory paragraph and the thesis statement: Golf has taught me a lot*
3. *A discussion of how, above all, golf teaches one to control one's emotions*

4. *A discussion of how much one needs to know and remember to play golf well*
5. *The social values that golf teaches*
6. *A multiparagraph example illustrating a valuable lesson taught through golf*
7. *Golf provides an opportunity to reflect*
8. *Reflection, in turn, leads to a deeper appreciation of nature*

With his outline before him, Olesky felt ready to try a rough draft of his essay. He wrote quickly, keeping his organizational plan in mind but striving to keep the writing going and get his thoughts down on paper. He knew that once he had a draft, he could determine how to improve it. Olesky wrote some fairly solid paragraphs, but he sensed that they were on different aspects of his topic and that the logical order of the points he was making was not quite right. He needed a stronger organizational plan, some way to present his information that was not random but rather showed a logical progression.

Reviewing his outline, Olesky could see that there was a natural progression from the physical lessons of the sport to the social and moral lessons to the psychological, emotional, and even spiritual benefits that one could derive. He decided therefore to move item 3 in his original organization and make it item 6 in the revision. Here is his reordered outline:

Reordered Outline

1. *Brief introductory paragraph announcing the topic*
2. *An expansion of the introductory paragraph and the thesis statement: Golf has taught me a lot*
3. *A discussion of how much one needs to know and remember to play golf well*
4. *The social values that golf teaches*
5. *A multiparagraph example illustrating a valuable lesson taught through golf*
6. *A discussion of how, above all, golf teaches one to control one's emotions*
7. *Golf provides an opportunity to reflect*
8. *Reflection, in turn, leads to a deeper appreciation of nature*

Olesky was satisfied that his essay now had a natural and logical organization: it moved from matters of lesser to greater importance to him personally. However, he now needed to revise his thesis to suit the argument he had established. He wanted his revised thesis to be focused and specific and to include the idea that the lessons and values golf has taught him could not have been learned as easily in other ways. Here is his revised thesis statement:

Revised Thesis Statement

In its simplicity, golf has taught me many lessons and values that other people have trouble learning elsewhere.

After revising the organization, he was now ready to edit his essay and to correct those smaller but equally important errors in word choice, wordiness, punctuation, and mechanics. He had put aside these errors to make sure his essay had the appropriate content. Now he needed to make sure it was grammatically correct. Here are several sample paragraphs showing the editing Olesky did on his essay:

Edited Paragraphs

Addition for clarity

Elimination of unessential information

Change of period to colon to eliminate sentence fragment and introduce appositive phrase

Correction of it's to its

Ever since I was a little boy, no older than two or three, I have had a golf club in my hand. My mother has pictures of me *as a toddler* with my father on the putting green of the local golf course. ~~that my father belonged to.~~ With a cut-down putter, the shaft ~~had been~~ reduced in length so that it would fit me, I would spend hours trying to place the small white ball into the little round hole. I'm sure at first that I took to the game to be like my father: ~~T~~to act like him, play like him, and hit the ball like him. However, it is not what I have learned about the mechanics of the golf swing or *about* ~~all~~ the facts ~~and figures~~ of the game that have caused golf to mean so much to me but rather the things golf has taught me about everyday life *in general*. In it~~'~~s simplicity, golf has taught me many lessons and values other people have trouble learning elsewhere.

Elimination of wordiness

Golf is a good teacher because ~~Along the same lines,~~ there are many variables and aspects to the game. ~~of golf.~~ You ~~are~~ constantly hav~~ing~~*e* to think, analyze, and evaluate *your position and strategy.* ~~That is the difficulty of the game of golf.~~ Unlike many sports *that rely on* ~~once you~~ committ*ing* ~~ed the~~ the action*s* to muscle memory, *golf requires* ~~there is no guarantee you will still perform well. There is~~ a phenomenal amount of information to think about and keys to remember. Legs shoulder-width apart, knees flexed, fingers interlocked, body loose . . . and you haven't even tried to hit the ball yet. But having to go about things so methodically *in golf* has enabled me to apply *the skills of patience and analysis* ~~the methods of golf~~ to many other parts of my life. I don't believe I would have nearly the same personality if golf had not played such an *integral* ~~intricate~~ role in my development.

Addition of specific information for clarity

Improved dicton

In addition to editing his revised paper, Olesky reexamined his title, "Character Builder." He considered a half dozen alternatives and finally settled on the use of "Golf" as a main title because it was such a key word for his topic and thesis; he used "A Character Builder" as his subtitle. He also thought about his conclusion, wondering whether it was forceful enough. After giving it considerable thought and seeking the advice of his classmates, Olesky decided to end with the low-key but meaningful final paragraphs he generated in his original draft. Here is the final version of his essay:

Final Essay

Title: suggests what the essay will be about

Golf: A Character Builder

Jeffrey Olesky

Beginning: effective opening paragraph sets the context for the essay

Golf is what I love. It is what I do, and it is who I am. In many respects, it has defined and shaped my character and personality. I couldn't possibly imagine my life without golf and what it has meant for me.

Ever since I was a little boy, no older than two or three, I have had a golf club in my hand. My mother has pictures of me as a toddler with my father on the putting green of the local golf course.

With a cut-down putter, the shaft reduced in length so that it would fit me, I would spend hours trying to place the small white ball into the little round hole. I'm sure at first that I took to the game to be like my father: to act like him, play like him, and hit the ball like him. However, it is not what I have learned about the mechanics of the golf swing or about the facts of the game that have caused golf to mean so much to me but rather the things golf has taught me about everyday life in general. In its simplicity, golf has taught me many lessons and values other people have trouble learning elsewhere.

Thesis statement: sets clear expectation in the reader's mind

Transition: discussion moves to how the game influences personality

Golf requires lots of information, both physical and mental

Golf is a good teacher because there are many variables and aspects to the game. You constantly have to think, analyze, and evaluate your position and strategy. Unlike many sports that rely on committing actions to muscle memory, golf requires a phenomenal amount of information to think about and keys to remember. Legs shoulder-width apart, knees flexed, fingers interlocked, body loose . . . and you haven't even tried to hit the ball yet. But having to go about things so methodically in golf has enabled me to apply the skills of patience and analysis to many other parts of my life. I don't believe I would have nearly the same personality if golf had not played such an integral role in my development.

Golf teaches life lessons

Golf has also changed and shaped my personality by repeatedly reinforcing many of the lessons of life. You know the ones I'm referring to, the rules you learn in kindergarten: treat others as you would like to be treated; respect other people and their property . . . the list goes on. Golf may not blare them out as obviously as my kindergarten teacher did, but in its own subtle, respectful tone, golf has imbued me with many of the values and morals I have today. Simply by learning the rules of such a prestigious, honest, and respected game, you gradually learn the reasoning behind them and the ways that they relate to life.

Illustration: extended example in narrative of some lessons that golf teaches

A good example of such a life lesson comes from the first time my father ever took me out on an actual golf course. I had been waiting for this day for quite some time and was so excited when he finally gave me the chance. He had gone out to play with a few of his friends early one Saturday morning in one of the larger tournaments. I was caddying for my father. Although I was too young to actually carry his bag, I would clean his golf ball, rake the bunkers for him, and do the other minor tasks that caddies do. But the fact that I was actually out "with the big boys," watching them play golf, was enough to make me happy. Besides, none of the other gentlemen my father was playing with seemed to mind that I was along for the ride.

Narrative example continues

The lesson I learned that day appears rather simple now. It came on the putting green of the second hole. My father had finished putting out, and I was holding the flagstick off to the side of the green while the other players finished. Generally, my father would come stand next to me and give me a hand, but due to circumstances we ended up on opposite sides of the green. During the next player's putt, my father lowered his eyebrows at me and nodded his head to one side a few times. Curious as to what he wanted me to do, I almost let the question slip out of my mouth. But I knew better. I had already learned the rules of not talking or moving while other golfers were hitting. I quietly stood my ground until everyone was finished and then placed the flagstick back in the hole. While walking toward the next tee box, I neared my father. Regardless of what he had wanted me to do, I thought he would commend me for not talking or moving during the ordeal.

Dialogue: shows rather than tells, and puts the reader in the scene

"You know better than that, Jeffrey," he said.

"What?" I asked curiously, disappointed that he had not praised me on a job well done.

"You never stand so that your shadow is in someone's line."

How could I be so stupid? He had reminded me a thousand times before. You never allow your shadow to fall in the line of someone's putt because it is distracting to the person putting.

I rationalized to my father that maybe the man hadn't noticed or that it didn't bother him. Unfortunately, my father wasn't going to take that as an excuse. After explaining to me what I had done wrong, he suggested that I go over and apologize to the gentleman. I was still a young boy, and the figure of the older man was somewhat intimidating. This task was no easy chore because I was obviously very scared, and this is perhaps what made the lesson sink in a little deeper. I remember slowly approaching my father's friend and sheepishly looking back to my father for help. Once I realized I was on my own, I bashfully gave him my apologies and assured him that it wouldn't happen again. As you can probably guess, the repercussions were not as dramatic as I had envisioned them to be. Once my father had pointed out my mistake, I begged him to reconcile with the gentleman for me. However, in apologizing for myself, I learned a valuable lesson. Golf is important because it has taught me many social values such as this, but it can also be a personal, internal tool.

Transition: golf can also be a personal, internal tool

Golf has taught me how to deal with frustration and to control myself mentally in difficult and strenuous situations. Golf is about mastering your emotions in stressful times and prevailing with a methodical, calm mind. I have dealt with the disappointment of missing a two-foot putt on the last hole to break eighty and the embarrassment of shanking my drive off the first hole in front of dozens of people. In dealing with these circumstances and continuing with my game, I have learned how to control my emotions. Granted, golf is not the most physically strenuous sport, but it is the mental challenge of complete and utter concentration that makes it difficult. People who are not able to control their temper or to take command of their emotions generally do not end up playing this game for very long.

Organization continues to move from concrete practical concerns to those that are more abstract

Golf gives me the opportunity to be reflective — time to myself when I can debate and organize the thoughts in my head. There are few places where you can find the peace and tranquility

Organization: Olesky moves to more philosophic influences

like that of a golf course in the early morning or late afternoon. When I am playing by myself, which I make an effort to do when I need to get away, I am able to reflect and work out some of the difficulties I am facing. I can think in complete quietness, but at the same time I have something to do while I am thinking. There are few places in the world offering this type of sanctuary that are easily accessible.

Organization: Olesky discusses golf's ability to bring him close to nature

It is in these morning reflections that I also gain an appreciation of my surroundings. I often like to get up early on a Saturday or Sunday and be the first one on the course. There are many things I love about the scenery of a golf course during the morning hours. I love the smell of the freshly cut grass as the groundskeepers crisscross their patterns onto the fairways and greens. I love looking back on my progress toward the tee box on the first hole to witness my solitary foot tracks in the morning dew. I love the chirp of the yellow finches as they signal the break of dawn. All these conditions help to create the feeling of contentment as I walk down the first fairway. Thinking back to those days on the putting green with my father, I realize how dear golf is to me. Golf has created my values, taught me my lessons, and been my outlet. I love the game for all these reasons.

Ending: a quiet but appropriate conclusion

macmillanhighered.com/mfw12e
Tutorials > Digital Writing > Photo Editing Basics with GIMP; Audio Editing with Audacity; Presentations; Word Processing; Job Search/Personal Branding

CHAPTER **2**

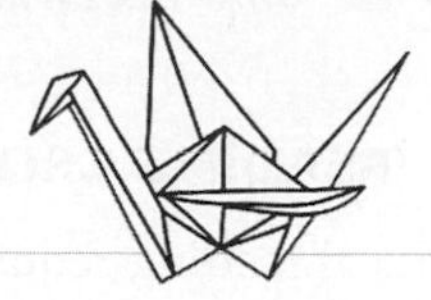

From Reading to Writing

To move from reading to writing, you need to read actively and critically, with an alert, inquiring mind. Reading critically means learning how to analyze and respond to what you read. You must be able to discover what is going on in an essay, to figure out the writer's reasons for shaping the essay in a particular way, to decide whether the result works well or poorly—and why. At first, such digging may seem odd, and for good reason. After all, we all know how to read. But do we know how to read *critically*?

Critical reading is a skill that takes time to acquire. By becoming more familiar with different types of writing, you will sharpen your critical thinking skills and learn how good writers make decisions in their writing. After reading an essay, most people feel more confident talking about the content of the piece than about the writer's style because content is more tangible. In large part, this discrepancy results from our schooling. Most of us have been taught to read for ideas. Not many of us, however, have been trained to read critically, to engage a writer and his or her writing, to ask why we like one piece of writing and not another. Similarly, most of us do not ask ourselves why one piece of writing is more convincing than another. When you learn to read and think critically, you begin to answer these important questions and come to appreciate the craftsmanship involved in writing. Critical reading, then, is a skill you need if you are truly to engage and understand the content of a piece of writing as well as the craft that shapes the writer's ideas into a presentable form. Critical reading will repay your efforts by helping you read more effectively, think more critically, and grow as a writer.

e **macmillanhighered.com/mfw12e**
Tutorials > Critical Reading > Active Reading Strategies
Learning Curve > Critical Reading

READING CRITICALLY

Critical reading requires, first of all, that you commit time and effort. Second, try to take a positive interest in what you are reading, even if the subject matter is not immediately appealing. Remember that you are reading not for content alone but also to understand a writer's methods—to see firsthand the kinds of choices writers make while they write.

To get the most out of your reading, follow the five steps of the reading process.

1. Prepare yourself to read the selection.
2. Read the selection.
3. Reread the selection.
4. Annotate the text with marginal notes.
5. Analyze and evaluate the text with questions.

Step 1: Prepare Yourself to Read the Selection

Before diving into any given selection, it's helpful to get a context for the reading: What's the essay about? What do you know about the writer's background and reputation? Where was the essay first published? Who was the intended audience for the essay? How much do you already know about the subject of the reading selection? We encourage you, therefore, to review the materials that precede each selection in this book.

Each selection begins with a title, a portrait of the writer, a headnote, and a writing prompt. From the *title,* you often discover the writer's position on an issue or attitude toward the topic. On occasion, the title provides clues about the intended audience and the writer's purpose in writing the piece. The *headnote* contains three essential elements: a biographical note about the author, publication information, and rhetorical highlights of the selection. In addition to information on the person's life and work, the *biographical note* will tell you something about his or her reputation and authority to write on the subject of the piece. The *publication information* tells you when the selection was published and in what book or magazine it appeared. This information gives you insights about the intended audience and the historical context. The *rhetorical highlights* direct your attention to one or more of the model features of the selection.

Finally, the *writing prompt*, called Reflecting on What You Know, encourages you to collect your own thoughts and opinions about the topic or related subjects before you commence reading. This prompt makes it easy for you to keep a record of your own knowledge or thinking about a topic before you see what the writer has to offer in the essay.

To demonstrate how these context-building materials can work for you, carefully review the following materials that accompany Isaac Asimov's "Intelligence." The essay itself appears later in this chapter (pp. 53–55).

Intelligence

Title

Isaac Asimov

Headnote

1. Biographical note

Frank Capri/Hulton Archive/Getty Images

Born in Russia, Isaac Asimov immigrated to the United States in 1923. His death in 1992 ended a long, prolific career as a science-fiction and nonfiction writer. Asimov was uniquely talented at making a diverse range of topics—from Shakespeare to atomic physics—comprehensible and entertaining to the general reader. Asimov earned three degrees at Columbia University and later taught biochemistry at Boston University. At the time of his death, he had published more than five hundred books. It's Been a Good Life, *published in 2002, was compiled from selections made from Asimov's three previous autobiographical volumes:* In Memory Yet Green *(1979),* In Joy Still Felt *(1980), and* I. Asimov: A Memoir *(1994). Edited by Janet Jeppson Asimov, the book also features "A Way of Thinking," Asimov's four hundredth essay for the* Magazine of Fantasy and Science Fiction.

In the following essay, which first appeared in Please Explain: The Myriad Mysteries of the Universe Revealed *(1973), Asimov, an intellectually gifted man, ponders the nature of intelligence. His academic brilliance, he concedes, would mean little or nothing if like-minded intellectuals had not established the standards for intelligence in our society. Notice how he uses personal experience and the example of his auto mechanic to develop his definition of intelligence.*

2. Publication information

3. Rhetorical highlights

Reflecting on What You Know

Writing prompt

Our society defines the academically gifted as intelligent, but perhaps *book smart* would be a better term. IQ tests don't take into account common sense or experience, attributes that the academically gifted sometimes lack outside of a scholarly setting. Who's the smartest person you know? Is he or she academically gifted or smart in some way that would not be readily recognized as a form of intelligence?

From these preliminary materials, what expectations do you have for the selection itself? And how does this knowledge equip you to engage the selection before you read it? Asimov's title suggests the question, What is intelligence? You can reasonably infer that Asimov will discuss the nature of intelligence. His purpose clearly seems to be to explore the subject with his readers. The short biographical note reveals that Asimov—a scientist, teacher, and prolific author—is no longer living, that he enjoyed a reputation as a renaissance man, and that he wrote with an ease and understanding that make difficult subjects readily accessible to the general public. This background material suggests that in the essay you'll get a thoughtful, balanced, and easy-to-comprehend discussion of intelligence. The publication information indicates that this essay first appeared in a 1973 book in which Asimov explains popular "mysteries of the universe." The rhetorical highlights advise you to pay particular attention to how Asimov uses the examples of himself and his auto mechanic to think about the meaning of intelligence. Finally, the writing prompt asks you to consider how society defines the term *intelligence,* first by identifying the smartest person in your life and then by thinking about whether that person is more academically gifted (book smart) or experientially gifted (street smart). After reading the essay, you can compare your thoughts about the nature of intelligence with Asimov's.

Step 2: Read the Selection

Always read the selection at least twice, no matter how long it is. The first reading gives you a chance to get acquainted with the essay and to form your first impressions of it. With the first reading, you want to get an overall sense of what the writer is saying, keeping in mind the essay's title and the facts that you know about the writer from the essay's headnote. The essay will offer you information, ideas, and arguments—some you may have expected, some you may not have expected. As you read, you may find yourself modifying your sense of the writer's message and purpose. Does the writer reveal a bias? Any unsupported opinions? If there are any words that you do not recognize, circle them so that you can look them up later in a dictionary. Put question marks alongside any passages that are not immediately clear. You may, in fact, want to delay most of your annotating until a second reading so that your first reading can be fast and free.

Step 3: Reread the Selection

Your second reading should be quite different from the first. You will know what the essay is about, where it is going, and how it gets there. Now you can relate the parts of the essay more accurately to the whole. Use your second reading to test your first impressions against the words on the page, developing and deepening your sense of how the essay is written and how well. Because you now have a general understanding of the essay, you can pay special attention to the author's purpose and means of achieving that purpose. You can also determine whether the writer reveals a bias and whether the writer adequately supports his or her opinions. (For more information about detecting a writer's bias and determining how well the writer supports his or her opinions, see pp. 618–19.) Finally, you can look for features of organization and style that you can learn from and adapt to your own work.

Step 4: Annotate the Text with Marginal Notes

When you annotate a text, you should do more than simply underline or highlight important points to remember. It is easy to highlight so much that the efforts of your highlighting can become almost meaningless because you forget why you highlighted the passages in the first place. Instead, as you read, write down your thoughts in the margins or on a separate piece of paper. (See pp. 53–55 for Asimov's "Intelligence" with student annotations.) Mark the selection's main point when you find it stated directly. Look for the pattern or patterns of development the author uses to explore and support that point, and jot the information down. If you disagree with a statement or conclusion, object in the margin: "No!" If you feel skeptical, indicate that response: "Why?" or "Explain." If you are impressed by an argument or turn of phrase, compliment the writer: "Good point!" Place vertical lines or stars in the margin to indicate important points.

Jot down whatever marginal notes come to mind. Most readers combine brief responses written in the margins with underlining, circling, highlighting, stars, or question marks. Here are some suggestions of elements you may want to mark to help you record your responses as you read:

What to Annotate in a Text

- Memorable statements of important points
- Key terms or concepts
- Central issues or themes
- Examples that support a main point
- Unfamiliar words
- Questions you have about a point or passage
- Your response to a specific point or passage

Remember that there are no hard-and-fast rules for which elements you should annotate. Choose a method of annotation that works best for you and that will make sense when you go back to recollect your thoughts and responses to the essay. When annotating a text, don't be timid. Mark up your book as much as you like, or jot down as many responses in your notebook as you think will be helpful. Don't let annotating become burdensome. A word or phrase is usually as good as a sentence. One helpful way to focus your annotations is to ask yourself questions as you read the selection a second time.

Step 5: Analyze and Evaluate the Text with Questions

As you read the essay a second time, probe for a deeper understanding of and appreciation for what the writer has done. Focus your attention by asking yourself some basic questions about its content and form. Here are some questions you may find useful:

Questions to Ask Yourself as You Read

1. What does the writer want to say? What is the writer's main point or thesis?
2. Why does the writer want to make this point? What is the writer's purpose?
3. Does the writer take a position on the subject and adequately support it?
4. What pattern or patterns of development does the writer use?
5. How does the writer's pattern of development suit his or her subject and purpose?
6. What, if anything, is noteworthy about the writer's use of this pattern?
7. How effective is the essay? Does the writer make his or her points clearly?

Each essay in *Models for Writers* is followed by study questions that are similar to the ones suggested here but specific to the essay. These questions help you analyze both the content of the essay and the writer's craft. As you read the essay a second time, look for details that will support your answers to these questions, and then answer the questions as fully as you can.

An Example: Annotating Isaac Asimov's "Intelligence"

Notice how one of our students, guided by the seven preceding questions, recorded her responses to Asimov's text with marginal notes.

Asks question central to the essay and relates army experience

What is intelligence, anyway? When I was in the army I received a kind of aptitude test that soldiers took and, against a norm of 100, scored 160. No one at the base had ever seen a figure like that, and for two hours they made a big fuss over me. (It didn't mean anything. The next day I was still a buck private with KP as my highest duty.)

All my life I've been registering scores like that, so that I have the complacent feeling that I'm highly intelligent, and I expect other people to think so, too. Actually, though, don't such scores simply mean that I am very good at answering the type of academic questions that are considered worthy of answers by the people who make up the intelligence tests—people with intellectual bents similar to mine?

Questions the meaning of high test scores. What do I think they mean?

Auto repair example. Any relationship between test scores and ability to fix cars?

For instance, I had an auto-repair man once, who, on these intelligence tests, could not possibly have scored more than 80, by my estimate. I always took it for granted that I was far more intelligent than he was. Yet, when anything went wrong with my car I hastened to him with it, watched him anxiously as he explored its vitals, and listened to his pronouncements as though they were divine oracles—and he always fixed my car.

Well, then, suppose my auto-repair man devised questions for an intelligence test. Or suppose a carpenter did, or a farmer, or, indeed, almost anyone but an academician. By every one of those tests, I'd prove myself a moron. And I'd *be* a moron, too. In a world where I could not use my academic training and my verbal talents but had to do something intricate or hard, working with my hands, I would do poorly. My intelligence, then, is not absolute but is a function of the society I live in and of the fact that a small subsection of that society has managed to foist itself on the rest as an arbiter of such matters.

Sees intelligence as function of roles in society. Good point!

Mechanic's joke about "deaf-and-dumb carpenter."

Consider my auto-repair man, again. He had a habit of telling me jokes whenever he saw me. One time he raised his head from under the automobile hood to say, "Doc, a deaf-and-dumb guy went into a hardware store to ask for some nails. He put two fingers together on the counter and made hammering motions with the other hand. The clerk brought him a hammer. He shook his head and pointed to the two fingers he was hammering. The clerk brought him nails. He picked out the sizes he wanted, and left. Well doc, the next guy who came in was a blind man. He wanted scissors. How do you suppose he asked for them?"

Traps Asimov with question about blind customer.

Indulgently, I lifted my right hand and made scissoring motions with my first two fingers. Whereupon my auto-repair man laughed raucously and said, "Why you dumb jerk, he used his *voice* and asked for them." Then he said, smugly, "I've been trying that on all my customers today." "Did you catch many?" I asked. "Quite a few," he said, "but I knew for sure I'd catch *you*." "Why is that?" I asked. "Because you're so goddamned educated, doc, I *knew* you couldn't be very smart."

What point did mechanic have?

Brings up question, Are all educated people smart? Not in my experience!

And I have an uneasy feeling he had something there.

Practice: Reading and Annotating Rachel Carson's "Fable for Tomorrow"

Before you read the following essay, think about its title, the biographical and rhetorical information in the headnote, and the writing prompt. Make some marginal notes of your expectations for the essay, and write out a response to the prompt. Then, as you read the essay itself for the first time, try not to stop; take it all in as if in one breath. The second time, however, pause to annotate key points in the text, using the marginal fill-in lines provided alongside each paragraph. As you read, remember the seven basic questions mentioned earlier:

1. What does Carson want to say? What is her main point, or thesis?
2. Why does she want to make this point? What is her purpose?
3. Does Carson take a position on her subject and adequately support it?
4. What pattern or patterns of development does Carson use?
5. How does Carson's pattern of development suit her subject and purpose?
6. What, if anything, is noteworthy about Carson's use of this pattern?
7. How effective is Carson's essay? Does she make her points clearly?

Fable for Tomorrow

Rachel Carson

© Underwood & Underwood/Corbis

Naturalist Rachel Carson (1907–1964) majored in biology at the Pennsylvania College for Women (which later became Chatham College) in the mid-1920s and earned a master's degree in marine zoology from Johns Hopkins University. Later she worked as an aquatic biologist for the U.S. Bureau of Fisheries in Washington, D.C. She wrote Under the Sea Wind *(1941),* The Sea around Us *(1951), and* The Edge of the Sea *(1955)—all sensitive investigations of marine life. But it was* Silent Spring *(1962), her study of herbicides and insecticides, that made Carson a controversial figure. Once denounced as an alarmist, she is now regarded as an early prophet of the ecology movement.*

In the following fable (a short tale teaching a moral) taken from Silent Spring, *Carson uses contrast to show her readers the devastating effects of the indiscriminate use of pesticides.*

Title:

____

____

Headnote:

1. Biographical note:

____

____

____

____

____

2. Publication information:

____

____

3. Rhetorical highlights:

____

____

Reflecting on What You Know

Hardly a week goes by that we don't hear a news story about the poisoning of the environment. Popular magazines have run cover stories about Americans' growing interest in organic foods. Where do you stand on the issue of using chemical fertilizers, herbicides, and pesticides to grow our nation's food? Do you seek out organic products when you shop? Why or why not?

Writing prompt:

____

____

____

Annotations:

1 There was once a town in the heart of America where all life seemed to live in harmony with its surroundings. The town lay in the midst of a checkerboard of prosperous farms, with fields of grain and hillsides of orchards where, in spring, white clouds of bloom drifted above the green fields. In autumn, oak and maple and birch set up a blaze of color that flamed and flickered across a backdrop of pines. Then foxes barked in the hills and deer silently crossed the fields, half hidden in the mists of the fall mornings.

2 Along the roads, laurels, viburnum and alder, great ferns and wildflowers delighted the traveler's eye through much of the year. Even in winter the roadsides were places of beauty, where countless birds came to feed on the berries and on the seed heads of the dried weeds rising above the snow. The countryside was, in fact, famous for the abundance and variety of its bird life, and when the flood of migrants was pouring through in spring and fall people traveled from great distances to observe them. Others came to fish the streams, which flowed clear and cold out of the hills and contained shady pools where trout lay. So it had been from the days many years ago when the first settlers raised their houses, sank their wells, and built their barns.

3 Then a strange blight crept over the area and everything began to change. Some evil spell had settled on the community: mysterious maladies swept the flocks of chickens; the cattle and sheep sickened and died. Everywhere was a shadow of death. The farmers spoke of much illness among their families. In the town the doctors had become more and more puzzled by new kinds of sickness appearing among their patients. There had been several sudden and unexplained deaths, not only among adults but even among children, who would be stricken suddenly while at play and die within a few hours.

4 There was a strange stillness. The birds, for example—where had they gone? Many people spoke of them, puzzled and disturbed. The feeding stations

in the backyards were deserted. The few birds seen anywhere were moribund; they trembled violently and could not fly. It was a spring without voices. On the mornings that had once throbbed with the dawn chorus of robins, catbirds, doves, jays, wrens, and scores of other bird voices there was now no sound; only silence lay over the fields and woods and marsh.

5 On the farms the hens brooded, but no chicks hatched. The farmers complained that they were unable to raise any pigs—the litters were small and the young survived only a few days. The apple trees were coming into bloom but no bees droned among the blossoms, so there was no pollination and there would be no fruit.

6 The roadsides, once so attractive, were now lined with browned and withered vegetation as though swept by fire. These, too, were silent, deserted by all living things. Even the streams were now lifeless. Anglers no longer visited them, for all the fish had died.

7 In the gutters under the eaves and between the shingles of the roofs, a white granular powder still showed a few patches; some weeks before it had fallen like snow upon the roofs and the lawns, the fields and streams.

8 No witchcraft, no enemy action had silenced the rebirth of new life in this stricken world. The people had done it themselves.

9 This town does not actually exist, but it might easily have a thousand counterparts in America or elsewhere in the world. I know of no community that has experienced all the misfortunes I describe. Yet every one of these disasters has actually happened somewhere, and many real communities have already suffered a substantial number of them. A grim specter has crept upon us almost unnoticed, and this imagined tragedy may easily become a stark reality we all shall know.

Once you have read and reread Carson's essay and annotated the text, write your own answers to the seven basic questions listed on page 55. Then compare your answers with the set of answers that follows.

1. *What does Carson want to say? What is her main point, or thesis?* Carson wants to tell her readers a fable, a short narrative that makes an edifying or cautionary point. Carson draws the "moral" of her fable in the final paragraph. She believes that we have in our power the ability to upset the balance of nature, to turn what is an idyllic countryside into a wasteland. As she states in paragraph 8, "The people had done it [silenced the landscape] themselves." Human beings need to take heed and understand their role in environmental stewardship.
2. *Why does she want to make this point? What is her purpose?* Carson's purpose is to alert us to the clear danger of pesticides (the "white granular powder," paragraph 7) to the environment. Even though the composite environmental disaster she describes has not occurred yet, she feels compelled to inform her readers that each of the individual disasters has happened somewhere in a real community. Although Carson does not make specific recommendations for what each of us can do, her message is clear: to do nothing about pesticides is to invite environmental destruction.
3. *Does Carson take a position on her subject and adequately support it?* Carson takes the position that Americans should be more careful in their use of pesticides. She believes that when farmers use pesticides indiscriminately, the environment suffers unintended consequences. As her fable develops, Carson shows the widespread effects of pesticides and herbicides on the landscape. Her evidence—though controversial in 1962—adequately supports her position. Carson tells us that every one of these disasters has actually happened somewhere in America.
4. *What pattern or patterns of development does Carson use?* Carson's dominant pattern of development is comparison and contrast. In paragraphs 1 and 2, she describes the mythical town before the blight ("all life seemed to live in harmony with its surroundings"); in paragraphs 3–7, she portrays the same town after the blight ("some evil spell had settled on the community"). Carson seems less interested in making specific contrasts than in drawing a total picture of the town before and after the blight. In

this way, she makes the change dramatic and powerful. Carson enhances her contrast by using vivid descriptive details that appeal to our senses to paint her pictures of the town before and after the "strange blight." The countryside before the blight is full of life; the countryside after, barren and silent.

5. *How does Carson's pattern of development suit her subject and purpose?* Carson selects comparison and contrast as her method of development because she wants to shock her readers into seeing what happens when humans use pesticides indiscriminately. By contrasting a mythical American town before the blight with the same town after the blight, Carson is able to *show* us the differences, not merely tell us about them. The descriptive details enhance this contrast: for example, "checkerboard of prosperous farms," "white clouds of bloom," "foxes barked," "seed heads of the dried weeds," "cattle and sheep sickened," "they trembled violently," "no bees droned," and "browned and withered vegetation." Perhaps the most striking detail is the "white granular powder" that "had fallen like snow upon the roofs and the lawns, the fields and streams" (7). The powder is the residue of the pervasive use of insecticides and herbicides in farming. Carson waits to introduce the powder for dramatic impact. Readers absorb the horror of the changing scene, wonder at its cause, and then suddenly realize it is not an unseen, uncontrollable force but human beings who have caused the devastation.
6. *What, if anything, is noteworthy about Carson's use of this pattern?* In her final paragraph, Carson writes, "A grim specter has crept upon us almost unnoticed." And this is exactly what happens in her essay. By starting with a two-paragraph description of "a town in the heart of America where all life seemed to live in harmony with its surroundings," Carson lulls her readers into thinking that all is well. But then at the beginning of paragraph 3, she introduces the change: "a strange blight crept over the area." By opting to describe the preblight town in its entirety first and then contrast it with the blighted town, she makes the change more dramatic and thus enhances its impact on readers.
7. *How effective is Carson's essay? Does she make her points clearly?* Instead of writing a strident argument against the indiscriminate

macmillanhighered.com/mfw12e
Tutorials > Critical Reading > Reading Visuals: Purpose; Reading Visuals: Audience

use of pesticides, Carson chooses to engage her readers in a fable with an educational message. In reading her story of this American town, we witness what happens when farmers blanket the landscape with pesticides. When we learn in the last paragraph that "this town does not actually exist," we are given cause for hope. Even though "every one of these disasters has actually happened somewhere," we are led to believe that there is still time to act before "this imagined tragedy" becomes "a stark reality we all shall know." When she wrote *Silent Spring* in 1962, Carson was considered an outspoken alarmist, and now almost daily we read reports of water pollution, oil spills, hazardous waste removal, toxic waste dumps, and climate change. Her warning is as appropriate today as it was when she first wrote it.

USING YOUR READING IN THE WRITING PROCESS

Reading and writing are two sides of the same coin. Many people view writing as the making of reading, but the connection does not end there. We know that one of the best ways to learn to write and to improve our writing is to read. By reading, we can begin to see how other writers have communicated their experiences, ideas, thoughts, and feelings in their writing. We can study how they have effectively used the various elements of the essay—thesis, unity, organization, beginnings and endings, paragraphs, transitions, effective sentences, diction and tone, and figurative language—to say what they wanted to say. By studying the style, technique, and rhetorical strategies of other writers, we learn how we might effectively do the same. The more we read and write, the more we begin to read as writers and, in turn, to write knowing what readers expect.

Reading as a Writer

What does it mean to read as a writer? As mentioned earlier, most of us have not been taught to read with a writer's eye, to ask why we like one piece of writing and not another. Similarly, most of us do not ask ourselves why one piece of writing is more convincing than another. When you learn to read with a writer's eye, you begin to answer these important questions. You read beyond the content to see how certain aspects of the writing itself affect you. You come to appreciate what is involved in selecting and focusing a subject as well as the craftsmanship involved in writing: how a writer selects descriptive details, uses an unobtrusive organizational pattern, opts for fresh and lively language, chooses representative and persuasive examples, and emphasizes important points with sentence variety. You come to see writing as a series of decisions the writer makes.

On one level, reading stimulates your thinking by providing you with subjects to write about. For example, after reading Helen Keller's "The Most Important Day," you might take up your pen to write about a turning point in your life. Or by reading Russell Baker's "Becoming a Writer," Carl T. Rowan's "Unforgettable Miss Bessie," Thomas L. Friedman's "My Favorite Teacher," and Michael Dirda's "Listening to My Father," you might see how each of these writers creates a dominant impression of an influential person in his or her life and write about an influential person in your own life.

On a second level, reading provides you with information, ideas, and perspectives for developing your own essay. In this way, you respond to what you read, using material from what you've read in your essay. For example, after reading June Tangney's essay "Condemn the Crime, Not the Person," you might want to elaborate on what she has written and either agree with her examples or generate ones of your own. You could also qualify her argument or take issue with it. Similarly, if you want to write about the effects of new technologies and engineering on our health and well-being, you will find Julie Zhou's "Where Anonymity Breeds Contempt" and Christina Baker Kline's "Taking My Son to College, Where Technology Has Replaced Serendipity" invaluable resources.

On a third level, critical reading can increase your awareness of how others' writing affects you, thus making you more sensitive to how your own writing will affect your readers. For example, if you have ever been impressed by an author who uses convincing evidence to support each of his or her claims, you might be more likely to back up your own claims carefully. If you have been impressed by an apt turn of phrase or absorbed by a writer's new idea, you may be less inclined to feed your readers dull, worn-out, and trite phrases.

More to the point, however, the critical reading that you are encouraged to do in *Models for Writers* will help you recognize and analyze the essential elements of the essay. When you see, for example, how a writer like Stanley McChrystal uses a strong thesis statement to control the parts of his essay calling for civic service for young

Americans, you can better appreciate what a clear thesis statement is and see the importance of having one in your essay. When you see the way Nancy Gibbs uses transitions to link key phrases and important ideas so that readers can clearly recognize how the parts of her essay are meant to flow together, you have a better idea of how to achieve such coherence in your own writing. And when you see how Martin Luther King Jr. divides the ways in which people characteristically respond to oppression into three distinct categories, you witness a powerful way in which you, too, can organize an essay using division and classification.

Another important reason, then, to master the skills of critical reading is that for everything you write, you will be your own first reader and critic. How well you are able to scrutinize your own drafts will powerfully affect how well you revise them, and revising well is crucial to writing well. So reading others' writing with a critical eye is a useful and important practice; the more you read, the more skilled you will become at seeing the rhetorical options available to you and making conscious choices in your own writing.

WRITING FROM READING: THREE SAMPLE STUDENT ESSAYS

A Narrative Essay

Reading often triggers memories of pesonal experiences. After reading several narratives about growing up—Maya Angelou's "Momma, the Dentist, and Me" (p. 381) and Dick Gregory's "Shame" (p. 163), in particular—and discussing with her classmates how memorable events often signal significant changes in life, student Trena Isley decided to write a narrative about such a turning point in her own life. Isley focused on the day she told her father that she no longer wished to participate in sports. Recalling that event led her to reconsider her childhood experiences of running track. Isley welcomed the opportunity to write about this difficult period in her life. As she tried to make her dilemma clear to her classmates, she found that she clarified it for herself. She came to a deeper understanding of her own fears and feelings about striking out on her own and ultimately to a better appreciation of her difficult relationship with her father. What follows is the final draft of Isley's essay.

On the Sidelines

Trena Isley

Point of view: first-person narrative

It was a Monday afternoon, and I was finally home from track practice. The coach had just told me that I had a negative attitude and should contemplate why I was on the team. My father greeted me in the living room.

"Hi, honey. How was practice?"

"Not good. Dad. Listen. I don't want to do this anymore. I hate the track team."

Opening: critical dialogue between writer and her father highlights conflict

"What do you mean *hate*?"

"This constant pressure is making me crazy."

"How so?"

"It's just not fun anymore."

"Well, I'll have to talk to Coach — "

"No! You're supposed to be my father, not my coach."

"I am your father, but I'm sure . . . "

"Just let me do what I want. You've had your turn."

He just let out a sigh and left the room. Later he told me that I was wasting my "God-given abilities." The funny part was that none of my father's anger hit me at first. All I knew was that I was free.

Flashback: writer returns to beginning of story and sets context

My troubles began the summer I was five years old. It was late June, and the sticky weather had already settled into the Champlain Valley. My father was yanking my hair into a ponytail in preparation for the first day of the summer track and field season.

As our truck pulled into the upper parking lot I could look down on the scene below. The other kids resembled ants against the massive black track, all of them parading around with no obvious purpose. I stepped out of the truck, never taking my eyes off the colony beneath me, and fell. As I stood there, both knees skinned and bleeding, the last thing I wanted to do was join the other kids. My father quickly hushed my sobs and escorted me down into the throng of children. Around the track we ran, each step stinging my knees as the tears in my eyes continued to rise. Through blurred

Echo of title

vision I could see my father on the sidelines, holding his stopwatch in one hand and wearing a grin from ear to ear.

Organization: chronological sequence of events

Writer provides details of her track "career" and relationship with her father

For most of my childhood I was content to let my father make me a track star. As my collection of blue ribbons grew, I was perfect in my father's eyes. By the time I was ten, college coaches were joking with me about scholarships. So I continued to run. It was fun in the beginning, and Dad always had nice things to say about me. I can remember him talking to my grandmother over the holidays: "Trena's got a real shot at winning the 200 meters at the state meet this year, but she's got to train hard."

I began to alter my opinion of competition as I entered my teenage years. At this point I wasn't having fun anymore. My father took me to the gym for "training" sessions four days a week before school. I knew my friends weren't getting up at 5:00 A.M., so I didn't understand why I had to. At thirteen years old all I wanted was to be considered normal. I wanted to fit in with the other kids and do regular teenage stuff.

My father didn't understand my waning interest in track. He still looked forward to my competitions and practice every morning. When my alarm would go off, I would not jump out of bed, often claiming that I didn't feel well or pretending to oversleep. When I began not winning all or even most of my races, my father pushed me to work harder. He would talk incessantly about other competitors and how often they practiced. He never stopped trying to coax me into practicing by buying me breakfast or taking me out to lunch. He tried endlessly, but I just didn't care about track. I resented him more and more with each attempt. I needed to do something that I was truly interested in. And I needed to do it alone.

Dialogue: shows the disconnect between writer and her father

"Hey, Dad, what do you think about me trying out for the school play this term? I was told I have a good shot at a part."

"I don't think you'd have time. Track practice is every day, isn't it? I've been talking with the coach, and he says the team is looking strong this year. He tells me the state meet should be tough, though. Do you need new spikes?"

"No, Dad. The ones I have are fine, but I just thought . . ."

"Great, 'cause you'll need good spikes when you run on some of those dirt tracks."

So that was that. It got so bad that my father didn't hear me unless "track" was in the sentence. I was starving for my own identity. The mold "Trena the track star" that my father had created for me was crumbling rapidly. Sadly, he wasn't noticing; however, I knew I wanted to quit the track team, but I was afraid that if I gave up sports there would be nothing left for me to be good at. The worst thing someone could be in my family was average.

Writer returns to confrontation with father in opening scene

When I finally did it — told my father the pressure was making me crazy and that I was quitting — I felt three times lighter. I came to find out, though, that this freedom did have its price. I got to sleep late, but Dad didn't ask me how my day was anymore. He didn't ask me much of anything except when I'd be home at night and with whom I was going out. He wasn't my coach anymore — he was my warden.

Every night I was grilled for details. He needed to know everyone I was with and what we were doing. When I'd tell him, he never seemed to believe me. My dreams of living on a farm and building my own house were laughed at. In the same conversation my younger sister could tell my parents that she was hoping to work for the United Nations, and she would be applauded. The shift had been made. I gained my personal and creative independence but lost a parent.

Organization: time reference "five years"

It has been five years since I retired from athletics and slipped out of my father's graces. Presently my father and I do speak, but it's all on the surface. I now realize that I didn't need the extra morning practices to be good at something. This transition was normal and healthy. It happened quickly, so quickly that I left my father holding the remains of our relationship. The problem was that neither of us bothered to reinvent one for our future as adults. It's not hard for me to understand why we still have a difficult time relating to each other. We really don't know each other very well.

Ending: writer reflects on relationship with her father

Eventually we'll be able to talk about my quitting track as just that, a small incident that marked the turn of a page in both our lives. We both have unresolved feelings that are standing in the way of our friendship. I need to stop blaming him for my blemished self-image, and he needs to realize that I can succeed without his coaching. In the end we both have to forgive each other.

A Response Essay

For an assignment following James Lincoln Collier's essay "Anxiety: Challenge by Another Name" (pp. 93–96), Zoe Ockenga tackled the topic of anxiety. In her first draft, she explored how anxious she felt the night before her first speech in a public speaking class and how in confronting that anxiety she benefited from the course. Ockenga read her essay aloud in class, and other students had an opportunity to ask her questions and to offer constructive criticism. Several students suggested that she might want to relate her experiences to those that Collier recounts in his essay. Another asked if she could include other examples to bolster the point she wanted to make. At this point in the discussion, Ockenga recalled a phone conversation she had had with her mother regarding her mother's indecision about accepting a new job. The thought of working outside the home for the first time in more than twenty years brought out her mother's worst fears and threatened to keep her from accepting the challenge. Armed with these valuable suggestions and ideas, Ockenga began revising. In subsequent drafts, she worked on the Collier connection, actually citing his essay on several occasions, and developed the example of the anxiety surrounding her mother's decision. What follows is the final draft of her essay, which incorporates the changes she made based on the peer evaluation of her first draft.

Title: indicates main idea of the essay

The Excuse "Not To"

Zoe Ockenga

I cannot imagine anything worse than the nervous, anxious feeling I got the night before my first speech in public speaking class last spring semester. The knots in my stomach were so fierce that I racked my brain for an excuse to give the teacher so that I would not have to go through with the dreaded assignment. Once in bed, I lay awake thinking of all the mistakes that I might make while standing

Beginning: captures readers' attention with personal experience most college students can relate to

alone in front of my classmates. I spent the rest of the night tossing and turning, frustrated that now, on top of my panic, I would have to give my speech with huge bags under my eyes.

Thesis

Anxiety is an intense emotion that can strike at any time or place, before a simple daily activity or a life-changing decision. For some people, anxiety is only a minor interference in the process of achieving a goal. For others, it can be a force that is impossible to overcome. In these instances, anxiety can prevent the accomplishment of lifelong hopes and dreams. Avoiding the causes of stress or fear can make us feel secure and safe. Avoiding anxiety, however, may mean forfeiting a once-in-a-lifetime opportunity. Confronting anxiety can make for a richer, more fulfilling existence.

First example: continues story introduced in opening paragraph to support thesis

The next day I trudged to class and sat on the edge of my seat until I could not stand the tension any longer. At this point, I forced myself to raise my hand to volunteer to go next simply to end my suffering. As I walked to the front of the room and assumed my position at the podium, the faces of the twenty-five classmates I had been sitting beside a minute ago suddenly seemed like fifty. I probably fumbled over a word or two as I discussed the harmful aspects of animal testing, but my mistakes were not nearly as severe as I had imagined the night before. Less than five minutes later the whole nightmare was over, and it had been much less painful than I had anticipated. As I sat down with a huge sigh of relief to listen to the next victim stumble repeatedly over how to milk dairy cows, I realized that I had not been half bad.

Although I still dreaded giving the next series of speeches, I eventually became more accustomed to speaking in front of my peers. I would still have to force myself to volunteer, secretly hoping the teacher would forget about me, but the audience that once seemed large and forbidding eventually became much more human. A speech class is something that I would never have taken if it had not been a requirement, but I can honestly say that I am better off because of it. I was forced to grapple with my anxiety and in the process became a stronger, more self-confident individual. Before this class I had been able to hide out in large lectures, never offering any comments or insights. For the first time at college I was forced to participate, and I realized that I could speak effectively in front of strangers and, more important, that I had something to say.

Second example: cites essay from Models for Writers *to support thesis*

The insomnia-inducing anticipation of giving a speech was a type of anxiety that I had to overcome to meet my distribution requirements for graduation. In the essay "Anxiety: Challenge by Another Name" by James Lincoln Collier, the author tells of his own struggles with anxiety. He tells of one particular event that happened between his sophomore and junior years in college when he was asked to spend a summer in Argentina with a good friend. He writes about how he felt after he made his decision not to go:

Block quote in MLA style

> I had turned down something I wanted to do because I was scared, and had ended up feeling depressed. I stayed that way for a long time. And it didn't help when I went back to college in the fall to discover that Ted and his friend had had a terrific time. (94)

The proposition of going to Argentina was an extremely difficult choice for Collier, as it meant abandoning the comfortable routine of the past and venturing completely out of his element. Although the idea of the trip was exciting, the author could not bring himself to choose the summer in Argentina because of his uncertainties.

The summer abroad that Collier denied himself in his early twenties left him with such a feeling of regret that he vowed to change his approach to life. From then on, he faced challenges that made him uncomfortable and was able to accomplish feats he would never have dreamed possible — interviewing celebrities, traveling extensively throughout Europe, parachuting, and even learning to ski at age forty. Collier emphasizes that he was able to make his life fulfilling and exciting by adhering to his belief that anxiety cannot be stifled by avoidance; it can be stifled only by confrontation (95–96).

Third example: introduces mother's dilemma

Anxiety prevents many individuals from accepting life's challenges and changes. My own mother is currently struggling with such a dilemma. At age fifty-three, having never had a career outside the home, my mother has been recommended to manage a new art gallery. The River Gallery, as it will be called, will be opening in our town of Ipswich, Massachusetts, this spring. An avid collector and art lover as well as a budding potter, my mother would, I believe, be exceptional at this job.

Anticipating this new opportunity and responsibility has caused my mother great anxiety. Reentering the workforce after over twenty years is as frightening for my mother as the trip to Argentina was for Collier. When I recently discussed the job prospect with my mother, she was negative and full of doubt. "There's no way I could ever handle such a responsibility," she commented. "I have no business experience. I would look like a fool if I actually tried to pull something like this off. Besides, I'm sure the artists would never take me seriously." Just as my mother focused on all the possible negative aspects of the opportunity in front of her, Collier questioned the value of his opportunity to spend a summer abroad. He describes having second thoughts about just how exciting the trip would be:

Quotation: quotes Collier to help explain mother's indecision

> I had never been very far from New England, and I had been homesick my first few weeks at college. What would it be like in a strange country? What about the language? And besides, I had promised to teach my younger brother to sail that summer. (94)

Focusing on all the possible problems accompanying a new opportunity can arouse such a sense of fear that it can overpower the ability to take a risk. Both my mother and Collier found out that dwelling on possible negative outcomes allowed them to ignore the benefits of a new experience and thus maintain their safe current situations.

Currently my mother is using anxiety as an excuse "not to" act. To confront her anxiety and take an opportunity in which there is a possibility of failure as well as success is a true risk. Regardless of the outcome, to even contemplate a new challenge has changed her life. The summer forgone by Collier roused him to never again pass up an exciting opportunity and thus to live his life to the fullest. Just the thought of taking the gallery position has prompted my mother to contemplate taking evening classes so that if she refuses the offer she may be better prepared for a similar challenge in the future. Although her decision is unresolved, her anxiety has made her realize the possibilities that may be opening for her, whether or not she chooses to take them. If in the end her answer is no, I believe that a lingering "What if?" feeling will cause her to reevaluate her expectations and goals for the future.

Conclusion: includes strong statement about anxiety that echoes optimism of thesis

Anxiety can create confidence and optimism or depression, low self-esteem, and regret. The outcome of anxiety is entirely dependent on whether the individual runs from it or embraces it. Some forms of anxiety can be conquered merely by repeating the activity that causes them, such as giving speeches in a public speaking class. Anxiety brought on by unique opportunities or life-changing decisions, such as a summer in a foreign country or a new career, must be harnessed. Opportunities forgone due to anxiety and fear could be the chances of a lifetime. Although the unpleasant feelings that may accompany anxiety may make it initially easier to do nothing, the road not taken will never be forgotten. Anxiety is essentially a blessing in disguise. It is a physical and emotional trigger that tells us when and where there is an opportunity for us to grow and become stronger human beings.

MLA-style works cited list

Works Cited

Collier, James Lincoln. "Anxiety: Challenge by Another Name." *Models for Writers*. Ed. Alfred Rosa and Paul Eschholz. 12th ed. Boston: Bedford, 2015. 93–96. Print.

An Argumentative Essay

James Duffy's assignment was to write a thesis-driven argument, and he was free to choose his own topic. He knew from past experience that to write a good essay he would have to write on a topic he cared about. He also knew that he should allow himself a reasonable amount of time to find a topic and to gather his ideas. A premedical student, James found himself reading the essays in *Models for Writers* that had a scientific bent. He was particularly struck by Barbara Huttmann's essay, "A Crime of Compassion" (pp. 342–45), because it dealt with the issues of the right to die and treating pain in terminally ill patients, issues that he would be confronting as a medical doctor.

James wrote this particular essay on a patient's right to choose death during the second half of the semester, after he had read a number of model arguments and had learned the importance of incorporating such elements as good paragraphing, unity, and transitions in his earlier essays. He began by brainstorming about his topic: he made lists of all the ideas, facts, issues, arguments, opposing arguments, and refutations that came to mind as a result of his own firsthand experiences with dying patients while on an internship. Once he was confident that he had amassed enough information to begin writing, he made a rough outline of an organizational plan and then wrote a first draft of his essay. After conferencing with several peers as well as his instructor, James revised what he had written.

The final draft of James's essay illustrates that he had learned how the parts of a well-written essay fit together and how to make revisions that emulate some of the qualities in the model essays he had read and studied. The following is the final draft of James's essay.

One Dying Wish

James Duffy

Opening: context-setting story focuses attention on the central issue

It was an interesting summer. I spent most of my internship assisting postdoctoral students doing research in Cincinnati. One day I came across a file I will never forget. Within the thick file was the story of a fifty-something cancer patient. The man's cancer had metastasized and was now spread throughout his entire body. Over a period of two months he went under the knife seven times to repair and remove parts of his battle-weary body. He endured immeasurable pain. The final surgery on record was done in an effort to stop the pain — doctors intentionally severed the man's spinal cord.

Thesis: writer presents clear statement of position

Terminally ill patients experience intractable pain, and many lose the ability to live a life that has any real meaning to them. To force these people to stay alive when they are in pain and there is no hope for recovery is wrong. They should have the choice to let nature take its course. Forcing people to live in pain when only machines are keeping them alive is unjust.

Presentation of opposing argument: troublesome hospital policy

The hospital I was doing my internship in that summer had a policy that as long as someone was alive, they would do anything to keep him or her alive. The terminal cancer patient whose file I stumbled across fit into this category. He was on narcotics prescribed to alleviate his pain. The problem was that the doctors could not prescribe above a certain life-threatening dosage, a level far below what was necessary to manage the patient's pain. In such a situation, the doctors can't raise a dose because they risk sedating the patient to the point of heart failure.

Discussion of what writer believes is wrong with hospital policy

The hospital I was working at had fallen on hard times; the last thing they needed was to lose a large malpractice suit. If a doctor prescribes above the highest recommended dosage, his or her hospital is at risk if the patient dies. Keeping patients on life support at low dosages, however, is cruel. The doctors at many hospitals have their hands tied. They simply can't give dosages high enough to treat the pain without putting the hospital at risk, and the other option, stopping life support, is forbidden by many hospitals.

Evidence: writer uses example of his Aunt Eileen to show how patient choice and compassionate care should work

When I was fifteen, my Aunt Eileen, who was thirty-four, was diagnosed with a malignant skin cancer. The disease was caught late, and the cancer had metastasized throughout her body. At the time, Eileen had been married for eight years and had a four-year-old daughter and a six-year-old son. They were and are adorable children. When Eileen learned of the disease, she was devastated. She loved her husband and children very much and could not bear the thought of not being with them. Eileen fought the disease fiercely. She tried all the conventional treatments available. Her father and brother were both doctors, so she had access to the best possible care, but the disease did not succumb to the treatment. She tried unconventional and experimental treatments as well, but it was all for naught. The disease had an unshakable grip on her. She had wasted away to well below one hundred pounds; a tumor had grown to the size of a grapefruit on her stomach. It was the end, and everyone knew it. Luckily Eileen was able to get into a hospice center. While she was there, she was able to make peace with herself, her family, and God and die calmly without pain.

If Eileen had been forced to keep living, her pain undertreated and her body resuscitated again and again, the damage to her and her family would have been enormous. It would have been almost impossible to make peace with herself and God if she had been in pain so intense she couldn't think. The hospice personnel managed the pain and helped Eileen and her family avoid the anguish of a prolonged and painful death.

Evidence: writer introduces outside source to support his argument for patient choice

Writer summarizes Huttmann's story about her patient Mac, taking care to put any directly quoted material in quotation marks followed by an in-text citation

In "A Crime of Compassion," Barbara Huttmann, a registered nurse, recounts her hospital's disregard for a patient named Mac. Mac's story is one of a prolonged and painful death, without options. Mac came into the hospital with a persistent cough and walked out with a diagnosis of lung cancer. He battled the disease but lost ground fast. Over the course of six months, Mac lost "his youth, . . . his hair, his bowel and bladder control, . . . and his ability to do the slightest thing for himself" (343). Mac wasted away to a mere sixty pounds. He was in constant pain, which the hospital was unable to manage. His young wife now looked "haggard" and "beaten" (343). Mac went into arrest three times some days. Every time his wife broke down into tears. The nurses ordered "code blue" every time it happened, and the hospital staff resuscitated Mac. This situation repeated itself for over a month. During one month, Mac was resuscitated fifty-two times. Mac had long ago realized the battle was over. He pleaded with his doctors and nurses to let him die. The problem was that the hospital did not issue no-code orders. A no-code order meant that if Mac went into arrest again they would let him die. Days passed as Barbara Huttmann, his nurse, pleaded for a no-code order. Each time he went into arrest his wife, Maura, took another step toward becoming psychologically crippled. As Barbara worked to resuscitate Mac, she'd look into his eyes as he pleaded for her to stop. Finally, Barbara decided enough was enough. Mac went into arrest and she did not call the code blue until she was certain he could not be resuscitated. For granting Mac his dying wish, Barbara was charged with murder (342–45).

Writer uses anti–capital punishment argument to bolster his call for more humane treatment of the terminally ill

The situation of Mac illustrates the death many people are forced to endure. These situations constitute an irony in today's society. Many complain that executions are inhumane or cruel and unusual. A principal argument of these anti–capital punishment people is that the death is not pain-free. People also think that regardless of the situation a patient should be allowed to die and should not be medicated to the point of death. Mac was forced to live on the brink of death for over a month, watching as his wife was also destroyed by his ordeal. The treatment Mac received can only be described as inhumane. To force a man to live in pain when there is no reasonable hope he will ever get better is truly cruel and unusual. Had Mac had the option of a peaceful and pain-free death, it would have saved himself and his wife the pain of being forced to live on the edge of death for such an extended period of time. Maura must have looked into Mac's tortured eyes and wondered why he had no choices concerning his life or death. Almost any choice would have been better than the treatment he received.

American society needs to follow the lead of countries like the Netherlands and Belgium or a state like Oregon with its Death with Dignity Act and reevaluate the right of the terminally ill to die. Keeping people in agonizing pain for a long period is uncivilized. Everyone would agree with that. Many people do not

Conclusion: Writer calls for action on the rights of the terminally ill

understand, however, that prolonging the life of a terminally ill patient with unmanageable pain is the same thing. Laws need to be passed to protect doctors who accidently overmedicate a terminally ill patient in the interest of pain management. Patients also deserve the right to determine if they want to go off life support, no matter what hospital they are in. Until people demand that action be taken to resolve this issue, the terminally ill will continue to suffer.

Works Cited

Huttmann, Barbara. "A Crime of Compassion." *Models for Writers*. Ed. Alfred Rosa and Paul Eschholz. 12th ed. Boston: Bedford, 2015. 342–45. Print.

part ■ two

The Elements of the Essay

CHAPTER **3**

Thesis

The **thesis** of an essay is its main or controlling idea, the point the writer is trying to make. The thesis is often expressed in a one- or two-sentence statement, although sometimes it is implied or suggested rather than stated directly. The thesis statement determines the content of the essay: everything the writer says must be logically related to the thesis statement.

Because everything you say in your composition must be logically related to your thesis, the thesis statement controls and directs the choices you make about the content of your essay. This does not mean that your thesis statement is a straitjacket. As your essay develops, you may want to modify your thesis statement to accommodate your new thinking. This urge is not only acceptable but also normal.

One way to develop a working thesis is to determine what question you are trying to answer in your essay. A one- or two-sentence answer to this question often produces a tentative thesis statement. For example, a student wanted to answer the following question in her essay:

Do men and women have different conversational speaking styles?

Her preliminary answer to this question was this:

Men and women appear to have different objectives when they converse.

After writing two drafts, she modified her thesis to better fit the examples she had gathered:

Very often, conversations between men and women become situations in which the man gives a mini-lecture and the woman unwittingly turns into a captive audience.

A thesis statement should be

- the most important point you make about your topic,
- more general than the ideas and facts used to support it, and
- appropriately focused for the length of your paper.

A thesis statement is not a question but an assertion—a claim made about a debatable issue that can be supported with evidence.

Another effective strategy for developing a thesis statement is to begin by writing "What I want to say is that . . ."

> *What I want to say is that unless the university administration enforces its strong anti-hazing policy, the well-being of many of its student-athletes will be endangered.*

Later, when you delete the formulaic opening, you will be left with a thesis statement:

> *Unless the university administration enforces its strong anti-hazing policy, the well-being of many of its student-athletes will be endangered.*

Usually the thesis is presented early in the essay, sometimes in the first sentence. Here are some examples of strong thesis statements:

> Mutual respect is the most important ingredient in a healthy marriage.
>
> Mark Twain's great contribution to American literature is his use of vernacular English, and this is no more pronounced than in his novel *The Adventures of Huckleberry Finn.*
>
> Professional sports organizations need to address the long-term effects of player concussions with rule changes and more technologically advanced equipment.
>
> Many people believe that the American legal system is flooded with frivolous lawsuits, but there is little agreement on what is meant by "frivolous."

Each of these sentences does what a good thesis statement should do: it identifies the topic and makes an assertion about it.

Often writers prepare readers for the thesis statement with one or several sentences that establish a context. Notice in the following example how the author eases the reader into his thesis about the stages of life instead of presenting it abruptly in the first sentence:

> There used to be four common life phases: childhood, adolescence, adulthood and old age. Now, there are at least six: childhood, adolescence, odyssey, adulthood, active retirement and old age. Of the new ones, the least understood is odyssey, the decade of wandering that frequently occurs between adolescence and adulthood.
>
> –David Brooks, "The Odyssey Years"

On occasion a writer may even purposely delay the presentation of a thesis until the middle or the end of an essay. If the thesis is controversial or needs extended discussion and illustration, the writer might present it later to make it easier for the reader to understand and accept it. Appearing near or at the end of an essay, a thesis also gains prominence. For example, after an involved discussion about why various groups put pressure on school libraries to ban books, a student ended an essay with her thesis:

> The effort to censor what our children are reading can turn into a potentially explosive situation and cause misunderstanding and hurt feelings within our schools and communities. If we can gain an understanding of why people have sought to censor children's books, we will be better prepared to respond in a sensitive and reasonable manner. More importantly, we will be able to provide the best educational opportunity for our children through a sensible approach, one that neither overly restricts the range of their reading nor allows them to read all books, no matter how inappropriate. *Thesis*
>
> –Tara Ketch, student

Some kinds of writing do not need thesis statements. These include descriptions, narratives, and personal writing such as letters and diaries. But any essay that seeks to explain or prove a point has a thesis that is usually set forth in a formal thesis statement.

For more information on thesis statements, see Chapter 1, pages 13–19.

The Most Important Day

■ Helen Keller

© Bettmann/CORBIS

Helen Keller (1880–1968) was afflicted by a disease that left her blind and deaf at the age of eighteen months. With the aid of her teacher, Anne Mansfield Sullivan, she was able to overcome her severe handicaps, to graduate from Radcliffe College, and to lead a productive and challenging adult life. In the following selection from her autobiography, The Story of My Life *(1902), Keller tells of the day she first met Anne Sullivan, a day she regarded as the most important in her life.*

As you read, note that Keller states her thesis in the first paragraph and that the remaining paragraphs maintain unity by emphasizing the importance of the day her teacher arrived, even though they deal with the days and weeks following.

Reflecting on What You Know

Reflect on the events of what you consider "the most important day" of your life. Briefly describe what happened. Why was that particular day so significant?

The most important day I remember in all my life is the one on which my teacher, Anne Mansfield Sullivan, came to me. I am filled with wonder when I consider the immeasurable contrast between the two lives which it connects. It was the third of March, 1887, three months before I was seven years old. 1

On the afternoon of that eventful day, I stood on the porch, dumb,[1] expectant. I guessed vaguely from my mother's signs and from the hurrying to and fro in the house that something unusual was about to happen, so I went to the door and waited on the steps. The afternoon sun penetrated the mass of honeysuckle that covered the porch and fell on my upturned face. My fingers lingered almost unconsciously on the familiar leaves and blossoms which had just come forth to greet the 2

[1]*dumb*: unable to speak; mute.

sweet southern spring. I did not know what the future held of marvel or surprise for me. Anger and bitterness had preyed upon me continually for weeks and a deep languor[2] had succeeded this passionate struggle.

Have you ever been at sea in a dense fog, when it seemed as if a 3
tangible white darkness shut you in, and the great ship, tense and anxious, groped her way toward the shore with plummet and sounding-line,[3] and you waited with beating heart for something to happen? I was like that ship before my education began, only I was without compass or sounding-line, and had no way of knowing how near the harbor was. "Light! Give me light!" was the wordless cry of my soul, and the light of love shone on me in that very hour.

I felt approaching footsteps. I stretched out my hand as I supposed 4
to my mother. Someone took it, and I was caught up and held close in the arms of her who had come to reveal all things to me, and, more than all things else, to love me.

The morning after my teacher came she led me into her room and 5
gave me a doll. The little blind children at the Perkins Institution[4] had sent it and Laura Bridgman[5] had dressed it; but I did not know this until afterward. When I had played with it a little while, Miss Sullivan slowly spelled into my hand the word "d-o-l-l." I was at once interested in this finger play and tried to imitate it. When I finally succeeded in making the letters correctly I was flushed with childish pleasure and pride. Running downstairs to my mother I held up my hand and made the letters for doll. I did not know that I was spelling a word or even that words existed; I was simply making my fingers go in monkeylike imitation. In the days that followed I learned to spell in this uncomprehending way a great many words, among them *pin, hat, cup* and a few verbs like *sit, stand,* and *walk*. But my teacher had been with me several weeks before I understood that everything has a name.

One day, while I was playing with my new doll, Miss Sullivan put 6
my big rag doll into my lap also, spelled "d-o-l-l" and tried to make me understand that "d-o-l-l" applied to both. Earlier in the day we had had a tussle over the words "m-u-g" and "w-a-t-e-r." Miss Sullivan had tried to impress it upon me that "m-u-g" is *mug* and that

[2]*languor:* sluggishness.

[3]*plummet . . . line:* a weight tied to a line that is used to measure the depth of the ocean.

[4]*Perkins Institution:* the first school for blind children in the United States, opened in 1832 and located in South Boston during her time there. The school moved to Watertown, Massachusetts, in 1912.

[5]*Laura Bridgman* (1829–1889): a deaf-blind girl who was educated at the Perkins Institution in the 1840s.

"w-a-t-e-r" is *water*, but I persisted in confounding the two. In despair she had dropped the subject for the time, only to renew it at the first opportunity. I became impatient at her repeated attempts and, seizing the new doll, I dashed it upon the floor. I was keenly delighted when I felt the fragments of the broken doll at my feet. Neither sorrow nor regret followed my passionate outburst. I had not loved the doll. In the still, dark world in which I lived there was no strong sentiment or tenderness. I felt my teacher sweep the fragments to one side of the hearth, and I had a sense of satisfaction that the cause of my discomfort was removed. She brought me my hat, and I knew I was going out into the warm sunshine. This thought, if a wordless sensation may be called a thought, made me hop and skip with pleasure.

We walked down the path to the well-house, attracted by the fra- 7
grance of the honeysuckle with which it was covered. Someone was drawing water and my teacher placed my hand under the spout. As the cool stream gushed over one hand she spelled into the other the word *water*, first slowly, then rapidly. I stood still, my whole attention fixed upon the motions of her fingers. Suddenly I felt a misty consciousness as of something forgotten—a thrill of returning thought; and somehow the mystery of language was revealed to me. I knew then that "w-a-t-e-r" meant the wonderful cool something that was flowing over my hand. The living word awakened my soul, gave it light, hope, joy, set it free! There were barriers still, it is true, but barriers that could in time be swept away.

I left the well-house eager to learn. Everything had a name, and 8
each name gave birth to a new thought. As we returned to the house every object which I touched seemed to quiver with life. That was because I saw everything with the strange, new sight that had come to me. On entering the door I remembered the doll I had broken. I felt my way to the hearth and picked up the pieces. I tried vainly to put them together. Then my eyes filled with tears; for I realized what I had done, and for the first time I felt repentance and sorrow.

I learned a great many new words that day. I do not remember 9
what they all were; but I do know that *mother, father, sister, teacher* were among them—words that were to make the world blossom for me, "like Aaron's rod,[6] with flowers." It would have been difficult to find a happier child than I was as I lay in my crib at the close of that

[6]*Aaron's rod:* in Jewish and Christian traditions, a rod similar to Moses's staff that, in the high priest Aaron's hands, had miraculous power.

eventful day and lived over the joys it had brought me, and for the first time longed for a new day to come.

Thinking Critically about This Reading

Keller writes that "'Light! Give me light!' was the wordless cry of [her] soul" (paragraph 3). What was the "light" Keller longed for, and how did receiving it change her life?

Questions for Study and Discussion

1. What is Keller's thesis? What question do you think Keller is trying to answer? Does her thesis answer her question?
2. What is Keller's purpose? (Glossary: *Purpose*)
3. What was Keller's state of mind before Anne Sullivan arrived to help her? To what does she compare herself? (Glossary: *Analogy*) How effective is this comparison? Explain.
4. Why was the realization that everything has a name important to Keller?
5. How was the "mystery of language" (7) revealed to Keller? What were the consequences for her of this new understanding of the nature of language?
6. Keller narrates the events of the day Sullivan arrived (2–4), the morning after she arrived (5), and one day several weeks after her arrival (6–9). (Glossary: *Narration*) Describe what happens on each day, and explain how these separate incidents support Keller's thesis.

Classroom Activity Using Thesis

One effective way of focusing on your subject is to develop a list of specific questions about it at the start. This strategy has a number of advantages. Each question narrows the general subject area, suggesting a more manageable essay. Also, simply phrasing your topic as a question gives you a starting point; your work has focus and direction from the outset. Finally, a one- or two-sentence answer to your question often provides you with a preliminary thesis statement.

To test this strategy, develop a list of five questions about the subject "recycling paper waste on campus." To get you started, here is one possible question: should students be required to recycle paper waste?

1. ______________________________
2. ______________________________
3. ______________________________
4. ______________________________
5. ______________________________

Now develop a preliminary thesis statement by answering one of your questions.

Suggested Writing Assignments

1. Think about an important day in your own life. Using the thesis statement "The most important day of my life was ________," write an essay in which you show the significance of that day by recounting and explaining the events that took place, as Keller does in her essay. Before you write, you might find it helpful to reflect on your response to the prompt on page 82 for this reading.
2. For many people around the world, the life of Helen Keller symbolizes what a person can achieve despite seemingly insurmountable obstacles. Her achievements have inspired people with and without disabilities, leading them to believe they can accomplish more than they ever thought possible. Consider the role of people with disabilities in our society, develop an appropriate thesis, and write an essay on the topic.
3. Keller was visually and hearing impaired from the age of eighteen months, which meant she could neither read nor hear people speak. She was eventually able to read and write using braille, a system of "touchable symbols" invented by Louis Braille. Write an essay in which you put forth the thesis that the invention of braille has liberated countless numbers of people who have shared Keller's visual impairment.

Where Anonymity Breeds Contempt

■ **Julie Zhuo**

AP Photo/Jeff Chiu

Julie Zhuo began working at Facebook in 2006 and is currently the director of product design. She also writes a weekly series called "The Year of the Looking Glass" on Medium.com, featuring her thoughts on creative pursuits, management problems, and the business of social media. She attended Stanford University, where she completed both a bachelor's and a master's degree in computer science.

In the following essay, which appeared in the Opinion Pages of the New York Times *in November 2010, Zhuo gives readers a definition of the term* trolling *and offers examples to show why it is problematic. As you read, pay attention to how Zhuo's thesis answers a question that arises from this discussion of trolling: what can we do to combat the problem?*

Reflecting on What You Know

Do you think people interact differently online than they do face-to-face? Why or why not? Think of an example that supports your answer.

There you are, peacefully reading an article or watching a video on the Internet. You finish, find it thought-provoking, and scroll down to the comments section to see what other people thought. And there, lurking among dozens of well-intentioned opinions, is a troll. 1

"How much longer is the media going to milk this beyond tired story?" "These guys are frauds." "Your idiocy is disturbing." "We're just trying to make the world a better place one brainwashed, ignorant idiot at a time." These are the trollish comments, all from anonymous sources, that you could have found after reading a CNN article on the rescue of the Chilean miners. 2

Trolling, defined as the act of posting inflammatory, derogatory 3
or provocative messages in public forums, is a problem as old as the Internet itself, although its roots go much farther back. Even in the fourth century B.C., Plato touched upon the subject of anonymity and morality in his parable of the ring of Gyges.

That mythical ring gave its owner the power of invisibility, and 4
Plato observed that even a habitually just man who possessed such a ring would become a thief, knowing that he couldn't be caught. Morality, Plato argues, comes from full disclosure; without accountability for our actions we would all behave unjustly.

This certainly seems to be true for the anonymous trolls today. 5
After Alexis Pilkington, a 17-year-old Long Island girl, committed suicide earlier this year, trolls descended on her online tribute page to post pictures of nooses, references to hangings and other hateful comments. A better-known example involves Nicole Catsouras, an 18-year-old who died in a car crash in California in 2006. Photographs of her badly disfigured body were posted on the Internet, where anonymous trolls set up fake tribute pages and in some cases e-mailed the photos to her parents with subject lines like "Hey, Daddy, I'm still alive."

Psychological research has proven again and again that ano- 6
nymity increases unethical behavior. Road rage bubbles up in the relative anonymity of one's car. And in the online world, which can offer total anonymity, the effect is even more pronounced. People—even ordinary, good people—often change their behavior in radical ways. There's even a term for it: the online disinhibition effect.

Many forums and online communities are looking for ways to 7
strike back. Back in February, Engadget, a popular technology review blog, shut down its commenting system for a few days after it received a barrage of trollish comments on its iPad coverage.

Many victims are turning to legislation. All 50 states now have 8
stalking, bullying or harassment laws that explicitly include electronic forms of communication. Last year, Liskula Cohen, a former model, persuaded a New York judge to require Google to reveal the identity of an anonymous blogger who she felt had defamed her, and she has now filed a suit against the blogger. Last month, another former model, Carla Franklin, persuaded a judge to force YouTube to reveal the identity of a troll who made a disparaging comment about her on the video-sharing site.

But the law by itself cannot do enough to disarm the Internet's 9
trolls. Content providers, social networking platforms and community sites must also do their part by rethinking the systems they have in place for user commentary so as to discourage—or disallow—anonymity. Reuters, for example, announced that it would start to block anonymous comments and require users to register with their names and e-mail addresses in an effort to curb "uncivil behavior."

Some may argue that denying Internet users the ability to post 10
anonymously is a breach of their privacy and freedom of expression. But until the age of the Internet, anonymity was a rare thing. When someone spoke in public, his audience would naturally be able to see who was talking.

Others point out that there's no way to truly rid the Internet of 11
anonymity. After all, names and e-mail addresses can be faked. And in any case many commenters write things that are rude or inflammatory under their real names.

But raising barriers to posting bad comments is still a smart first 12
step. Well-designed commenting systems should also aim to highlight thoughtful and valuable opinions while letting trollish ones sink into oblivion.

The technology blog Gizmodo is trying an audition system for 13
new commenters, under which their first few comments would be approved by a moderator or a trusted commenter to ensure quality before anybody else could see them. After a successful audition, commenters can freely post. If over time they impress other trusted commenters with their contributions, they'd be promoted to trusted commenters, too, and their comments would henceforth be featured.

Disqus, a comments platform for bloggers, has experimented with 14
allowing users to rate one another's comments and feed those ratings into a global reputation system called Clout. Moderators can use a commenter's Clout score to "help separate top commenters from trolls."

At Facebook, where I've worked on the design of the public com- 15
menting widget, the approach is to try to replicate real-world social norms by emphasizing the human qualities of conversation. People's faces, real names and brief biographies ("John Doe from Lexington") are placed next to their public comments, to establish a baseline of responsibility.

Facebook also encourages you to share your comments with your 16
friends. Though you're free to opt out, the knowledge that what you

say may be seen by the people you know is a big deterrent to trollish behavior.

This kind of social pressure works because, at the end of the day, most trolls wouldn't have the gall to say to another person's face half the things they anonymously post on the Internet. 17

Instead of waiting around for human nature to change, let's start to rein in bad behavior by promoting accountability. Content providers, stop allowing anonymous comments. Moderate your comments and forums. Look into using comment services to improve the quality of engagement on your site. Ask your users to report trolls and call them out for polluting the conversation. 18

In slowly lifting the veil of anonymity, perhaps we can see the troll not as the frightening monster of lore, but as what we all really are: human. 19

Thinking Critically about This Reading

Zhuo points out several legal efforts to curb "trolling" but argues that "the law by itself cannot do enough" to stop abusive comments (paragraph 9). Where does she think the responsibility lies? Do you agree? Why or why not?

Questions for Study and Discussion

1. What is Zhuo's thesis, and where does she state it?
2. What problem does Zhuo address in this essay? How does her thesis offer an approach to this problem?
3. Why does Zhuo think Plato's story about the ring of Gyges (4) is relevant to Internet users?
4. How does Zhuo define the "online disinhibition effect" (6)? Which of Zhuo's examples of this effect do you find most powerful? (Glossary: *Definition*)
5. Zhuo identifies anonymity as a source of the problem. How does she think Internet culture allows, or even encourages, users to remain anonymous?
6. At the beginning of her essay, Zhuo says a troll can lurk "among dozens of well-intentioned opinions" (1). What does this say about the balance of thoughtful responses and inflammatory

comments online? How much of the latter do you think it takes to derail a discussion?

Classroom Activity Using Thesis

A strong thesis makes a claim rather than stating something obvious about the topic. One way to check whether your thesis makes a claim is to try stating its opposite as an alternative. If this new thesis seems absurd or wrong, your original thesis might benefit from greater specificity.

Imagine that you were going to write a response to Zhuo's argument about online trolling. Which of the following could be a thesis statement for a substantial counterargument? If you're not sure, test each one by stating its opposite. Note: often a good thesis cannot be easily reversed because it does not frame the issues in black and white.

1. Something should be done to decrease irresponsible commenting online.
2. Trolling can best be addressed through stronger laws.
3. Online forums often become a platform for inflammatory comments.
4. Web developers are inventing new systems to discourage trolling.
5. Though it is important to combat trolling, websites should preserve open commenting policies.
6. Zhuo overstates the problem of trolling on the Internet.

Now that you've eliminated some, how many potential theses are left? When writers like Zhuo address complex issues, thoughtful readers can respond with an array of ideas, concerns, or questions. Look at the remaining thesis statements, and discuss how each one takes a different approach to the problem.

Suggested Writing Assignments

1. Find a newspaper article posted in the past weeks and survey the comments section. Do your findings support Zhuo's assertions about trolling? Write an essay that summarizes what you observe. Your thesis should state what these comments reveal about online commenting behavior.

2. Though Zhuo is optimistic in offering her solution to the problem, her thesis about how to curb trolling depends on a skeptical view about when humans behave morally. Do you agree with her that we are far more likely to be moral when we're being watched? Is there a better way to assure moral behavior? Write an essay supporting Zhuo's call for "full disclosure" or arguing for an alternative way to encourage more responsible interactions.
3. Zhuo asks developers of online content to find new ways to inhibit the posting of destructive comments. In an essay, compare the different approaches she mentions, such as those by Engadget and Gizmodo. Your thesis should clearly state which approach you think would be most acceptable to users and which would be most effective at blocking trolls.

Anxiety: Challenge by Another Name

■ **James Lincoln Collier**

Photo © Miriam Berkley

James Lincoln Collier is a freelance writer with more than six hundred articles to his credit. He was born in New York in 1928 and graduated from Hamilton College in 1950. An accomplished jazz musician, Collier has often focused his nonfiction writing on American music. His best-known book is The Making of Jazz: A Comprehensive History *(1978). With his brother Christopher he has written a number of history books, including* A Century of Immigration: 1820–1924 *(2000),* The Civil War *(2000),* The Changing Face of American Society: 1945–2000 *(2001), and a series of biographies for young readers covering major figures in American history. Collier has also written a number of children's books, one of which,* My Brother Sam Is Dead *(1974), was awarded a Newbery Honor and named a Notable Children's Book.*

As you read the following essay, which first appeared in Reader's Digest *in 1986, pay attention to where Collier places his thesis. Note also how his thesis statement identifies the topic (anxiety) and makes an assertion about it (that it can have a positive effect on our lives).*

Reflecting on What You Know

Many people associate anxiety with stress and think of it as a negative thing. Are there good kinds of anxiety, too? Provide an example of anxiety that has been beneficial to you or to someone you know.

Between my sophomore and junior years at college, a chance came up for me to spend the summer vacation working on a ranch in Argentina. My roommate's father was in the cattle business, and he wanted Ted to see something of it. Ted said he would go if he could take a friend, and he chose me. 1

The idea of spending two months on the fabled Argentine Pampas[1] was exciting. Then I began having second thoughts. I had never been very far from New England, and I had been homesick my first few weeks at college. What would it be like in a strange country? What about the language? And besides, I had promised to teach my younger brother to sail that summer. The more I thought about it, the more the prospect daunted[2] me. I began waking up nights in a sweat. 2

In the end I turned down the proposition. As soon as Ted asked somebody else to go, I began kicking myself. A couple of weeks later I went home to my old summer job, unpacking cartons at the local supermarket, feeling very low. I had turned down something I wanted to do because I was scared, and had ended up feeling depressed. I stayed that way for a long time. And it didn't help when I went back to college in the fall to discover that Ted and his friend had had a terrific time. 3

In the long run that unhappy summer taught me a valuable lesson out of which I developed a rule for myself: *do what makes you anxious; don't do what makes you depressed.* 4

I am not, of course, talking about severe states of anxiety or depression, which require medical attention. What I mean is that kind of anxiety we call stage fright, butterflies in the stomach, a case of nerves—the feelings we have at a job interview, when we're giving a big party, when we have to make an important presentation at the office. And the kind of depression I am referring to is that downhearted feeling of the blues, when we don't seem to be interested in anything, when we can't get going and seem to have no energy. 5

I was confronted by this sort of situation toward the end of my senior year. As graduation approached, I began to think about taking a crack at making my living as a writer. But one of my professors was urging me to apply to graduate school and aim at a teaching career. 6

I wavered. The idea of trying to live by writing was scary—a lot more scary than spending a summer on the Pampas, I thought. Back and forth I went, making my decision, unmaking it. Suddenly, I realized that every time I gave up the idea of writing, that sinking feeling went through me; it gave me the blues. 7

The thought of graduate school wasn't what depressed me. It was giving up on what deep in my gut I really wanted to do. Right then I learned another lesson. To avoid that kind of depression meant, inevitably, having to endure a certain amount of worry and concern. 8

[1]*Pampas:* a vast plain in central Argentina.
[2]*daunted:* discouraged.

The great Danish philosopher Søren Kierkegaard believed that anxiety always arises when we confront the possibility of our own development. It seems to be a rule of life that you can't advance without getting that old, familiar, jittery feeling. 9

Even as children we discover this when we try to expand ourselves by, say, learning to ride a bike or going out for the school play. Later in life we get butterflies when we think about having that first child, or uprooting the family from the old hometown to find a better opportunity halfway across the country. Any time, it seems, that we set out aggressively to get something we want, we meet up with anxiety. And it's going to be our traveling companion, at least part of the way, into any new venture. 10

When I first began writing magazine articles, I was frequently required to interview big names—people like Richard Burton,[3] Joan Rivers,[4] sex authority William Masters, baseball-great Dizzy Dean. Before each interview I would get butterflies and my hands would shake. 11

At the time, I was doing some writing about music. And one person I particularly admired was the great composer Duke Ellington. Onstage and on television, he seemed the very model of the confident, sophisticated man of the world. Then I learned that Ellington still got stage fright. If the highly honored Duke Ellington, who had appeared on the bandstand some 10,000 times over thirty years, had anxiety attacks, who was I to think I could avoid them? 12

I went on doing those frightening interviews, and one day, as I was getting onto a plane for Washington to interview columnist Joseph Alsop, I suddenly realized to my astonishment that I was looking forward to the meeting. What had happened to those butterflies? 13

Well, in truth, they were still there, but there were fewer of them. I had benefited, I discovered, from a process psychologists call "extinction." If you put an individual in an anxiety-provoking situation often enough, he will eventually learn that there isn't anything to be worried about. 14

Which brings us to a corollary[5] to my basic rule: *you'll never eliminate anxiety by avoiding the things that caused it.* I remember how my son Jeff was when I first began to teach him to swim at the lake cottage where we spent our summer vacations. He resisted, and when I got him into the water he sank and sputtered and wanted to 15

---

[3]*Richard Burton* (1925–1984): a well-known British stage and Hollywood movie actor.
[4]*Joan Rivers* (1933–2014): a stand-up comedian and talk-show host.
[5]*corollary:* a proposition that follows with little or no proof required.

quit. But I was insistent. And by summer's end he was splashing around like a puppy. He had "extinguished" his anxiety the only way he could—by confronting it.

The problem, of course, is that it is one thing to urge somebody else to take on those anxiety-producing challenges; it is quite another to get ourselves to do it. 16

Some years ago I was offered a writing assignment that would require three months of travel through Europe. I had been abroad a couple of times on the usual "If it's Tuesday this must be Belgium" trips, but I hardly could claim to know my way around the continent. Moreover, my knowledge of foreign languages was limited to a little college French. 17

I hesitated. How would I, unable to speak the language, totally unfamiliar with local geography or transportation systems, set up interviews and do research? It seemed impossible, and with considerable regret I sat down to write a letter begging off. Halfway through, a thought—which I subsequently made into another corollary to my basic rule—ran through my mind: *you can't learn if you don't try.* So I accepted the assignment. 18

There were some bad moments. But by the time I had finished the trip I was an experienced traveler. And ever since, I have never hesitated to head for even the most exotic of places, without guides or even advanced bookings, confident that somehow I will manage. 19

The point is that the new, the different, is almost by definition scary. But each time you try something, you learn, and as the learning piles up, the world opens to you. 20

I've made parachute jumps, learned to ski at forty, flown up the Rhine[6] in a balloon. And I know I'm going to go on doing such things. It's not because I'm braver or more daring than others. I'm not. But I don't let the butterflies stop me from doing what I want. Accept anxiety as another name for challenge and you can accomplish wonders. 21

Thinking Critically about This Reading

Collier writes that "Kierkegaard believed that anxiety always arises when we confront the possibility of our own development" (paragraph 9). How do Collier's own experiences and growth substantiate Kierkegaard's belief in the value of anxiety?

[6]*Rhine:* a major river and waterway of western Europe.

Questions for Study and Discussion

1. What is Collier's thesis? Based on your own experiences, do you think Collier's thesis is valid? Explain.
2. What is the process known to psychologists as "extinction"?
3. What causes Collier to come up with his basic rule for himself: "Do what makes you anxious; don't do what makes you depressed" (4)? (Glossary: *Cause and Effect*) How does he develop the two corollaries to his basic rule? How do the basic rule and the two corollaries prepare you for his thesis?
4. What is Collier's purpose? (Glossary: *Purpose*)
5. What function do paragraphs 17–19 serve in Collier's essay?

Classroom Activity Using Thesis

A good thesis statement identifies the topic and makes an assertion about it. Evaluate each of the following sentences, and explain why each one either works or doesn't work as a thesis statement.

1. Americans are suffering from overwork.
2. Life is indeed precious, and I believe the death penalty helps to affirm this fact.
3. Birthday parties are loads of fun.
4. New York is a city of sounds: muted sounds and shrill sounds, shattering sounds and soothing sounds, urgent sounds and aimless sounds.
5. Everyone is talking about the level of violence in American society.

Suggested Writing Assignments

1. Building on your own experiences and the reading you have done, write an essay in which you use as your thesis either Collier's basic rule or one of his corollaries to that basic rule.
2. Write an essay using any one of the following as your thesis:

   Good manners are a thing of the past.

   We need rituals in our lives.

   To tell a joke well is an art.

   We are a drug-dependent society.

   Regular exercise offers many benefits.

CHAPTER **4**

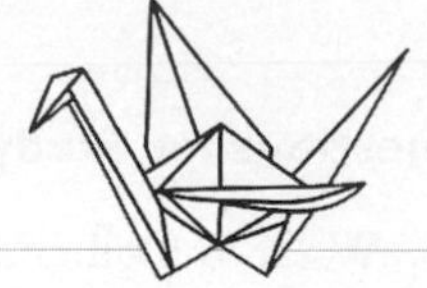

Unity

Unity is an essential quality in a well-written essay. The principle of unity requires that every element in a piece of writing—whether a paragraph or an essay—be related to the main idea. Sentences that stray from the main idea, even though they might be related to it or provide additional information, can weaken an otherwise strong piece of writing. Notice how the italicized segments in the following paragraph undermine its unity and divert our attention from its main idea:

> When I was growing up, one of the places I enjoyed most was the cherry tree in the backyard. *Behind the yard was an alley and then more houses.* Every summer when the cherries began to ripen, I used to spend hours high up in the tree, picking and eating the sweet, sun-warmed cherries. *My mother always worried about my falling out of the tree, but I never did.* But I had some competition for the cherries—flocks of birds that enjoyed them as much as I did would perch all over the tree, devouring the fruit whenever I wasn't there. I used to wonder why the grown-ups never ate any of the cherries—*my father loved all kinds of fruit*—but actually, when the birds and I had finished, there weren't many left.
>
> –Betty Burns, student

When the italicized sentences are eliminated, the paragraph is unified and reads smoothly.

Now consider another paragraph, this one from an essay about family photographs and how they allow the author to learn about her past and to stay connected with her family in the present:

> Photographs have taken me to places I have never been and have shown me people alive before I was born. I can visit my grandmother's childhood home in Vienna, Austria, and walk down the high-ceilinged, iron staircase by looking through the small,

white album my grandma treasures. I also know of the tomboy she once was, wearing lederhosen instead of the dirndls worn by her friends. And I have seen her as a beautiful young woman who traveled with the Red Cross during the war, uncertain of her future. The photograph that rests in a red leather frame on my grandma's nightstand has allowed me to meet the man she would later marry. He died before I was born. I have been told that I would have loved his calm manner, and I can see for myself his gentle smile and tranquil expression.

–Carrie White, student

Did you notice that the first sentence gives focus and direction to the paragraph and that all of the subsequent sentences are directly related to it?

A well-written essay should be unified both within and between paragraphs; that is, everything in it should be related to its **thesis**, the main idea of the essay. The first requirement for unity is that the thesis itself be clear, either through a direct statement, called the *thesis statement,* or by implication. (See Chapter 3 for more on thesis.) The second requirement is that there be no digressions—no discussion or information that is not shown to be logically related to the thesis. A unified essay stays within the limits of its thesis.

Here, for example, is a short essay by Stuart Chase about the dangers of making generalizations. As you read, notice how carefully Chase sticks to his point.

Overgeneralizing

One swallow does not make a summer, nor can two or three cases often support a dependable generalization. Yet all of us, including the most polished eggheads, are constantly falling into this mental peopletrap. It is the most common, probably the most seductive, and potentially the most dangerous, of all the fallacies. 1

You drive through a town and see a drunken man on the sidewalk. A few blocks further on you see another. You turn to your companion: "Nothing but drunks in this town!" Soon you are out in the country, bowling along at fifty. A car passes you as if you were parked. On a curve a second whizzes by. Your companion turns to you: "All the drivers in this state are crazy!" Two thumping 2 generalizations, each built on two cases. If we stop to think, we usually recognize the exaggeration and the unfairness of such generalizations. Trouble comes when we do not stop to think—or when we build them on a prejudice.

This kind of reasoning has been around for a long time. 3
Aristotle was aware of its dangers and called it "reasoning by example," meaning too few examples. What it boils down to is failing to count your swallows before announcing that summer is here. Driving from my home to New Haven the other day, a distance of about forty miles, I caught myself saying: "Every time I look around I see a new ranch-type house going up." So on the return trip I counted them; there were exactly five under construction. And how many times had I "looked around"? I suppose I had glanced to right and left—as one must at side roads and so forth in driving—several hundred times.

In this fallacy, we do not make the error of neglecting facts 4
altogether and rushing immediately to the level of opinion. We start at the fact level properly enough, but *we do not stay there*. A case or two and up we go to a rousing oversimplification about drunks, speeders, ranch-style houses—or, more seriously, about foreigners, African Americans, labor leaders, teenagers.

Why do we overgeneralize so often and sometimes so disas- 5
trously? One reason is that the human mind is a generalizing machine. We would not be people without this power. The old academic crack: "All generalizations are false, including this one," is only a play on words. We *must* generalize to communicate and to live. But we should beware of beating the gun; of not waiting until enough facts are in to say something useful. Meanwhile it is a plain waste of time to listen to arguments based on a few handpicked examples.

–Stuart Chase, *Guides to Straight Thinking*

Everything in the essay relates to Chase's thesis statement, which is included in the essay's first sentence: "nor can two or three cases often support a dependable generalization." Paragraphs 2 and 3 document the thesis with examples; paragraph 4 explains how overgeneralizing occurs; paragraph 5 analyzes why people overgeneralize; and, for a conclusion, Chase restates his thesis in different words. An essay may be longer, more complex, and more wide-ranging than this one, but to be effective it must also avoid digressions and remain close to the author's main idea.

A good way to check that your essay is indeed unified is to underline your thesis and then explain to yourself how each paragraph in your essay is related to the thesis. If you find a paragraph that does not appear to be logically connected, you can revise it so that the relationship is clear. Similarly, it is useful to make sure that each sentence in a paragraph is related to the topic sentence. (See pp. 169–72 for a discussion of topic sentences.)

My Favorite Teacher

■ Thomas L. Friedman

Nancy Ostertag/Getty Images for AFI

New York Times *foreign affairs columnist Thomas L. Friedman was born in Minneapolis, Minnesota, in 1953. He graduated from Brandeis University in 1975 and received a Marshall Scholarship to study modern Middle East studies at St. Antony's College, Oxford University, where he earned a master's degree. He has worked for the* New York Times *since 1981, first in Lebanon, then in Israel, and since 1989 in Washington, D.C. He has won three Pulitzer Prizes. His 1989 best seller,* From Beirut to Jerusalem, *received the National Book Award for nonfiction. Friedman's most recent books include* The World Is Flat: A Brief History of the Twenty-First Century *(2005);* Hot, Flat, and Crowded: Why We Need a Green Revolution—and How It Can Renew America *(2008); and* That Used to Be Us: How America Fell Behind in the World It Invented and How We Can Come Back *(2011), co-written with Michael Mandelbaum.*

In the following essay, which first appeared in the New York Times *on January 9, 2001, Friedman pays tribute to his tenth-grade journalism teacher. As you read Friedman's profile of Hattie M. Steinberg, note the descriptive detail he selects to create a unified, dominant impression of "a woman of clarity in an age of uncertainty."*

Reflecting on What You Know

If you had to name your three favorite teachers to date, who would be on your list? Why do you consider each of the teachers a favorite? Which one, if any, are you likely to remember twenty-five years from now? Why?

Last Sunday's *New York Times Magazine* published its annual review of people who died last year who left a particular mark on the world. I am sure all readers have their own such list. I certainly do. 1

Indeed, someone who made the most important difference in my life died last year—my high school journalism teacher, Hattie M. Steinberg.

I grew up in a small suburb of Minneapolis, and Hattie was the legendary journalism teacher at St. Louis Park High School, Room 313. I took her intro to journalism course in 10th grade, back in 1969, and have never needed, or taken, another course in journalism since. She was that good. 2

Hattie was a woman who believed that the secret for success in life was getting the fundamentals right. And boy, she pounded the fundamentals of journalism into her students—not simply how to write a lead or accurately transcribe a quote, but, more important, how to comport yourself in a professional way and to always do quality work. To this day, when I forget to wear a tie on assignment, I think of Hattie scolding me. I once interviewed an ad exec for our high school paper who used a four-letter word. We debated whether to run it. Hattie ruled yes. That ad man almost lost his job when it appeared. She wanted to teach us about consequences. 3

Hattie was the toughest teacher I ever had. After you took her journalism course in 10th grade, you tried out for the paper, *The Echo,* which she supervised. Competition was fierce. In 11th grade, I didn't quite come up to her writing standards, so she made me business manager, selling ads to the local pizza parlors. That year, though, she let me write one story. It was about an Israeli general who had been a hero in the Six-Day War,[1] who was giving a lecture at the University of Minnesota. I covered his lecture and interviewed him briefly. His name was Ariel Sharon.[2] First story I ever got published. 4

Those of us on the paper, and the yearbook that she also supervised, lived in Hattie's classroom. We hung out there before and after school. Now, you have to understand, Hattie was a single woman, nearing 60 at the time, and this was the 1960s. She was the polar opposite of "cool," but we hung around her classroom like it was a malt shop and she was Wolfman Jack.[3] None of us could have articulated it then, but it was because we enjoyed being harangued[4] by her, 5

[1]*Six-Day War:* the short but pivotal war in June 1967 between Israel and the allied countries of Egypt, Syria, and Jordan.

[2]*Ariel Sharon* (1928–2014): Israeli general and politician, elected prime minister of Israel in 2001.

[3]*Wolfman Jack:* pseudonym of Robert Weston Smith (1938–1995), a famous American rock-and-roll radio disc jockey.

[4]*harangued:* given a long, scolding lecture.

disciplined by her, and taught by her. She was a woman of clarity in an age of uncertainty.

We remained friends for 30 years, and she followed, bragged about, and critiqued every twist in my career. After she died, her friends sent me a pile of my stories that she had saved over the years. Indeed, her students were her family—only closer. Judy Harrington, one of Hattie's former students, remarked about other friends who were on Hattie's newspapers and yearbooks: "We all graduated 41 years ago; and yet nearly each day in our lives something comes up—some mental image, some admonition[5] that makes us think of Hattie." 6

Judy also told the story of one of Hattie's last birthday parties, when one man said he had to leave early to take his daughter somewhere. "Sit down," said Hattie. "You're not leaving yet. She can just be a little late." 7

That was my teacher! I sit up straight just thinkin' about her. 8

Among the fundamentals Hattie introduced me to was *The New York Times*. Every morning it was delivered to Room 313. I had never seen it before then. Real journalists, she taught us, start their day by reading the *Times* and columnists like Anthony Lewis and James Reston. 9

I have been thinking about Hattie a lot this year, not just because she died on July 31, but because the lessons she imparted seem so relevant now. We've just gone through this huge dot-com-Internet-globalization bubble—during which a lot of smart people got carried away and forgot the fundamentals of how you build a profitable company, a lasting portfolio, a nation state, or a thriving student. It turns out that the real secret of success in the information age is what it always was: fundamentals—reading, writing, and arithmetic; church, synagogue, and mosque; the rule of law; and good governance. 10

The Internet can make you smarter, but it can't make you smart. It can extend your reach, but it will never tell you what to say at a P.T.A. meeting. These fundamentals cannot be downloaded. You can only upload them, the old-fashioned way, one by one, in places like Room 313 at St. Louis Park High. I only regret that I didn't write this column when the woman who taught me all that was still alive. 11

Thinking Critically about This Reading

What do you think Friedman means when he states, "The Internet can make you smarter, but it can't make you smart" (paragraph 11)?

---

[5]*admonition:* a cautionary advice or warning.

Questions for Study and Discussion

1. Friedman claims that his high school journalism teacher, Hattie M. Steinberg, was "someone who made the most important difference in my life" (1). What descriptive details does Friedman use to support this thesis? (Glossary: *Thesis*)
2. Hattie M. Steinberg taught her students the fundamentals of journalism—"not simply how to write a lead or accurately transcribe a quote, but, more important, how to comport yourself in a professional way and to always do quality work" (3). According to Friedman, what other fundamentals did she introduce to her students? Why do you think he values these fundamentals so much?
3. Friedman punctuates his description of Steinberg's teaching with short, pithy sentences. For example, he ends paragraph 2 with the sentence "She was that good" and paragraph 3 with "She wanted to teach us about consequences." Identify several other short sentences Friedman uses. What do these sentences have in common? How do short sentences like these affect you as a reader? Explain.
4. Why do you think Friedman tells us three times that Steinberg's classroom was number 313 at St. Louis Park High School?
5. What details in Friedman's portrait of his teacher stand out for you? Why do you suppose Friedman chose the details that he did? What dominant impression of Hattie M. Steinberg do they collectively create? (Glossary: *Dominant Impression*)
6. According to Friedman, what went wrong when the "huge dot-com-Internet-globalization bubble" (10) of the late 1990s burst? Do you agree?

Classroom Activity Using Unity

Mark Wanner, a student, wrote the following essay using this thesis statement:

> In order to provide a good learning environment in school, the teachers and administrators need to be strong leaders.

Unfortunately, some of the sentences disrupt the unity of the essay. Find these sentences, eliminate them, and reread the essay.

Strong School Leaders

School administrators and teachers must do more than simply supply students with information and a school building. They must also provide students with an atmosphere that allows them to focus on learning within the walls of the school. Whether the walls are brick, steel, or cement, they are only walls, and they do not help to create an appropriate atmosphere. Strong leadership both inside and outside the classroom yields a school in which students are able to excel in their studies because they know how to conduct themselves in their relationships with their teachers and fellow students. 1

A recent change in the administration of Eastside High School demonstrated how important strong leadership is to learning. Under the previous administration, parents and students complained that not enough emphasis was placed on studies. Most of the students lived in an impoverished neighborhood that had only one park for several thousand residents. Students were allowed to leave school at any time of the day, and little was done to curb the growing substance abuse problem. "What's the point of trying to teach algebra to students who are just going to get jobs as part-time sales clerks, anyway?" Vice Principal Iggy Norant said when questioned about his school's poor academic standards. Mr. Norant was known to students as Twiggy Iggy because of his tall, thin frame. Standardized test scores at the school lagged well behind the state average, and only 16 percent of the graduates attended college within two years. 2

Five years ago, the school board hired Mary Peña, former chair of the state educational standards committee, as principal. A cheerleader in college, Ms. Peña got her BA in recreation science before getting her master's in education. She immediately emphasized the importance of learning, replacing any faculty members who did not share her high expectations of the students. Among those she fired was Mr. Norant; she also replaced two social studies teachers, one math teacher, four English teachers, and a lab instructor who let students play Gameboy in lab. She also established a code of conduct, which clearly stated the rules all students had to follow. Students were allowed second chances, but those who continued to conduct themselves in a way that interfered with the other students' ability to learn were dealt with quickly and severely. "The attitude at Eastside has changed so much since Mary Peña arrived," said math teacher Jeremy Rifkin after Peña's second year. "Students come to class much more relaxed and ready to learn. I feel like 3

I can teach again." Test scores at Eastside are now well above state averages, and 68% of the most recent graduating class went straight to college.

–Mark Wanner, student

Suggested Writing Assignments

1. Friedman believes that "the real secret of success in the information age is what it always was: fundamentals—reading, writing, and arithmetic; church, synagogue, and mosque; the rule of law; and good governance" (10). Do you agree? What are the fundamentals that you value most? Write a unified essay in which you discuss what you believe to be the secret of success today.
2. Who are your favorite teachers? What important differences did these people make in your life? What characteristics do these teachers share with Hattie M. Steinberg in this essay, Miss Bessie in Carl T. Rowan's "Unforgettable Miss Bessie" (pp. 410–14), or Anne Mansfield Sullivan in Helen Keller's "The Most Important Day" (pp. 82–85)? Using examples from your own school experience as well as from one or more of the essays noted above, write an essay in which you explore what makes a great teacher. Be sure to choose examples that clearly illustrate each of your points.

Our Vanishing Night

■ Verlyn Klinkenborg

Fred Conrad/The New York Times/Redux

Born in 1952 in Meeker, Colorado, Verlyn Klinkenborg grew up on farms in Iowa and Minnesota, where he developed his keen observation skills and love for life in rural America. After graduating from Pomona College and receiving a PhD from Princeton University, he embarked on a career as a writer and farmer. His first book, Making Hay *(1986), reflects Klinkenborg's fascination with small family farms.* The Last Fine Time *(1991) is a history of immigrant life in Buffalo, New York, where his father-in-law owned a neighborhood bar. From 1997 to 2013, his column "The Rural Life" appeared regularly on the editorial pages of the* New York Times, *and in 2003 those essays were published in the collection* The Rural Life. *His most recent book is* Several Short Sentences about Writing *(2013). Klinkenborg's essays have also appeared in* Harper's, Smithsonian, Audubon, National Geographic, *and the* New Yorker. *He has taught literature and creative writing at Fordham University, St. Olaf College, Bennington College, and Harvard University.*

The following essay first appeared in the November 2008 issue of National Geographic. *Notice how Klinkenborg unifies his essay with striking examples of the negative effects of light pollution, all of which relate to his main idea and support his thesis.*

Reflecting on What You Know

As a child, did you ever go outside on a clear night to look at the stars? Do you remember the names of some of the constellations and planets—like Orion, the Big Dipper, or Venus—that you were able to identify? When you find yourself outside walking now, do you look up at the evening sky? Are the heavens still as you remember them as a child? If not, what's changed?

If humans were truly at home under the light of the moon and stars, we would go in darkness happily, the midnight world as visible to us as it is to the vast number of nocturnal species on this planet. Instead, we are diurnal creatures, with eyes adapted to living in the sun's light. This is a basic evolutionary fact, even though most of us don't think of ourselves as diurnal beings any more than we think of ourselves as primates or mammals or Earthlings. Yet it's the only way to explain what we've done to the night: We've engineered it to receive us by filling it with light. 1

This kind of engineering is no different than damming a river. Its benefits come with consequences—called light pollution—whose effects scientists are only now beginning to study. Light pollution is largely the result of bad lighting design, which allows artificial light to shine outward and upward into the sky, where it's not wanted, instead of focusing it downward, where it is. Ill-designed lighting washes out the darkness of night and radically alters the light levels—and light rhythms—to which many forms of life, including ourselves, have adapted. Wherever human light spills into the natural world, some aspect of life—migration, reproduction, feeding—is affected. 2

For most of human history, the phrase "light pollution" would have made no sense. Imagine walking toward London on a moonlit night around 1800, when it was Earth's most populous city. Nearly a million people lived there, making do, as they always had, with candles and rushlights and torches and lanterns. Only a few houses were lit by gas, and there would be no public gaslights in the streets or squares for another seven years. From a few miles away, you would have been as likely to *smell* London as to see its dim collective glow. 3

Now most of humanity lives under intersecting domes of reflected, refracted light, of scattering rays from overlit cities and suburbs, from light-flooded highways and factories. Nearly all of nighttime Europe is a nebula of light, as is most of the United States and all of Japan. In the south Atlantic the glow from a single fishing fleet—squid fishermen luring their prey with metal halide lamps—can be seen from space, burning brighter, in fact, than Buenos Aires or Rio de Janeiro. 4

In most cities the sky looks as though it has been emptied of stars, leaving behind a vacant haze that mirrors our fear of the dark and resembles the urban glow of dystopian science fiction. We've 5 grown so used to this pervasive orange haze that the original glory of an unlit night—dark enough for the planet Venus to throw shadows on Earth—is wholly beyond our experience, beyond memory almost. And yet above the city's pale ceiling lies the rest of the universe, utterly undiminished by the light we waste—a bright shoal of stars and planets and galaxies, shining in seemingly infinite darkness.

We've lit up the night as if it were an unoccupied country, when 6
nothing could be further from the truth. Among mammals alone, the number of nocturnal species is astonishing. Light is a powerful biological force, and on many species it acts as a magnet, a process being studied by researchers such as Travis Longeore and Catherine Rich, co-founders of the Los Angeles–based Urban Wildlands Group. The effect is so powerful that scientists speak of songbirds and seabirds being "captured" by searchlights on land or by the light from gas flares on marine oil platforms, circling and circling in the thousands until they drop. Migrating at night, birds are apt to collide with brightly lit tall buildings; immature birds on their first journey suffer disproportionately.

Insects, of course, cluster around streetlights, and feeding at 7
those insect clusters is now ingrained in the lives of many bat species. In some Swiss valleys the European lesser horseshoe bat began to vanish after streetlights were installed, perhaps because those valleys were suddenly filled with light-feeding pipistrelle bats. Other nocturnal mammals—including desert rodents, fruit bats, opossums, and badgers—forage more cautiously under the permanent full moon of light pollution because they've become easier targets for predators.

Some birds—blackbirds and nightingales, among others—sing at 8
unnatural hours in the presence of artificial light. Scientists have determined that long artificial days—and artificially short nights—induce early breeding in a wide range of birds. And because a longer day allows for longer feeding, it can also affect migration schedules. One population of Bewick's swans wintering in England put on fat more rapidly than usual, priming them to begin their Siberian migration early. The problem, of course, is that migration, like most other aspects of bird behavior, is a precisely timed biological behavior. Leaving early may mean arriving too soon for nesting conditions to be right.

Nesting sea turtles, which show a natural predisposition for dark 9
beaches, find fewer and fewer of them to nest on. Their hatchlings, which gravitate toward the brighter, more reflective sea horizon, find themselves confused by artificial lighting behind the beach. In Florida

alone, hatchling losses number in the hundreds of thousands every year. Frogs and toads living near brightly lit highways suffer nocturnal light levels that are as much as a million times brighter than normal, throwing nearly every aspect of their behavior out of joint, including their nighttime breeding choruses.

Of all the pollutions we face, light pollution is perhaps the most easily remedied. Simple changes in lighting design and installation yield immediate changes in the amount of light spilled into the atmosphere and, often, immediate energy savings. 10

It was once thought that light pollution only affected astronomers, who need to see the night sky in all its glorious clarity. And, in fact, some of the earliest civic efforts to control light pollution—in Flagstaff, Arizona, half a century ago—were made to protect the view from Lowell Observatory, which sits high above that city. Flagstaff has tightened its regulations since then, and in 2001 it was declared the first International Dark Sky City. By now the effort to control light pollution has spread around the globe. More and more cities and even entire countries, such as the Czech Republic, have committed themselves to reducing unwanted glare. 11

Unlike astronomers, most of us may not need an undiminished view of the night sky for our work, but like most other creatures we do need darkness. Darkness is as essential to our biological welfare, to our internal clockwork, as light itself. The regular oscillation of waking and sleep in our lives—one of our circadian rhythms—is nothing less than a biological expression of the regular oscillation of light on Earth. So fundamental are these rhythms to our being that altering them is like altering gravity. 12

For the past century or so, we've been performing an open-ended experiment on ourselves, extending the day, shortening the night, and short-circuiting the human body's sensitive response to light. The consequences of our bright new world are more readily perceptible in less adaptable creatures living in the peripheral glow of our prosperity. But for humans, too, light pollution may take a biological toll. At least one new study has suggested a direct correlation between higher rates of breast cancer in women and the nighttime brightness of their neighborhoods. 13

In the end, humans are no less trapped by light pollution than the frogs in a pond near a brightly lit highway. Living in a glare of our own making, we have cut ourselves off from our evolutionary and cultural patrimony—the light of the stars and the rhythms of 14 day and night. In a very real sense, light pollution causes us to lose sight of our true place in the universe, to forget the scale of our being, which is best measured against the dimensions of a deep night with the Milky Way—the edge of our galaxy—arching overhead.

Thinking Critically about This Reading

According to Klinkenborg, are there any benefits to lighting up the night? What are the consequences? (Glossary: *Cause and Effect*) For you, do the benefits outweigh the consequences? Explain.

Questions for Study and Discussion

1. What is Klinkenborg's thesis, and where does he present it? (Glossary: *Thesis*)
2. Are there any digressions, discussions, or information in this essay that do not logically connect to Klinkenborg's thesis? (Glossary: *Thesis*) Explain how each paragraph in the essay relates to his thesis.
3. What does Klinkenborg mean when he says that "we are diurnal creatures" (paragraph 1)?
4. In what ways is light "a powerful biological force" (6)?
5. What can be done to remedy the problem of light pollution?
6. Klinkenborg claims that "light pollution causes us to lose sight of our true place in the universe" (14). What do you think he means? Do you agree or disagree with his conclusion? Why?

Classroom Activity Using Unity

Carefully read the following progress report from an elementary school teacher, paying special attention to how well the opening paragraph establishes a unified set of themes that are addressed in the body of the report. Identify places in the body paragraphs that touch on those themes. What opportunities do you see for improving the unity of this report?

PROGRESS REPORT

Student: Jared Greene
Teacher: Melissa Holman
Report: December 2014

It has been a pleasure to welcome Jared to second grade. A responsible member of our classroom community, his behavior at school is respectful and appropriate, and he is a student who can be counted on to do the right thing. At all times, he works hard, takes pride in his work, and is eager to share what he has accomplished with teachers, family members, and classmates.

Reading: The reading curriculum is taught through the structure of Reading Workshop. This includes reading independently, reading with a teacher, reading with other students in a weekly reading group, and taking lessons on reading strategies and phonics. . . . Jared is an enthusiastic participant during group meetings. He likes to discuss literature, and he frequently makes text connections and predictions during group mini-lessons.

Writing and Spelling: During Writers' Workshop, instruction has focused on generating story ideas; developing one idea into a story with a beginning, a middle, and an end; "reading like a writer" to notice choices authors make in the structure and language of their published works; and expanding "small moments" into detailed stories. Jared is working on a research piece about the Wampanoag (Native American) language. Jared has a strong sense of story structure (beginning, middle, end) as well as many of the conventions of nonfiction (table of contents, index, glossary).

Mathematics: We have completed three units in our *Everyday Math* curriculum, incorporating lessons in money, telling time, addition and subtraction, place value, and "number stories" (word problems). Mathematical thinking is an area of true strength for Jared. He understands concepts of operation (addition, subtraction, etc.) and demonstrates comfort with basic and more complex math facts. He is growing increasingly limber with his use of numbers and is able to see that there are many strategies for solving any given problem.

Social Studies and Science: We are wrapping up the work of our first three Charles River research units, which focused on river geology and erosion, mapping, and the water cycle. Jared has been an active participant in our Charles River research. He is naturally inquisitive, enthusiastic about the material, and careful in his hypotheses and observations. He is able to record detailed notes and enjoys predicting the outcome of experiments and projects.

It has been wonderful to have Jared in my classroom since September. I look forward to fostering his intellectual and social development throughout the remainder of the school year.

Suggested Writing Assignments

1. What examples of light pollution can you identify on campus or in town? Some things you might look for include overilluminated parking lots, walkways, and streets; lights not properly shielded; and lighting left on in buildings after closing. How might the light pollution you identify be corrected? Write a letter to the building and grounds administrator at your school or to your town manager in which you argue to have the light pollution reduced or eliminated. Be sure that all of your reasons support your thesis.
2. Klinkenborg claims, "Wherever human light spills into the natural world, some aspect of life—migration, reproduction, feeding—is affected" (2). Do some research in your library or on the Internet about how human light affects the migration and feeding patterns of certain migratory birds or the reproduction of certain animals, such as sea turtles. Write a unified essay in which you report your findings.

The Meanings of a Word

■ **Gloria Naylor**

AP Photo/Tom Keller

American novelist, essayist, and screenwriter Gloria Naylor was born in 1950 in New York City, where she lives today. She worked first as a missionary for the Jehovah's Witnesses from 1967 to 1975 and then as a telephone operator until 1981. That year she graduated from Brooklyn College of the City University of New York. She also holds a graduate degree in African American studies from Yale University. Naylor has taught writing and literature at George Washington University, New York University, and Cornell University, in addition to publishing several novels: The Women of Brewster Place *(1982),* Linden Hills *(1985),* Mama Day *(1988),* Bailey's Cafe *(1992), and* The Men of Brewster Place *(1998). Naylor's most recent novel is 1996 (2005), a book that has been described as a "fictionalized memoir."*

The following essay first appeared in the New York Times *in 1986. In it Naylor examines the ways in which words can take on meaning, depending on who uses them and for what purpose. Notice how the paragraphs describing her experiences with the word* nigger *relate back to a clearly stated thesis at the end of paragraph 2.*

Reflecting on What You Know

Have you ever been called a derogatory name? What was the name, and how did you feel about it?

Language is the subject. It is the written form with which I've managed to keep the wolf away from the door and, in diaries, to keep my sanity. In spite of this, I consider the written word inferior to the spoken, and much of the frustration experienced by novelists is the awareness that whatever we manage to capture in even the most transcendent[1] passages falls far short of the richness of life. Dialogue 1

[1]*transcendent:* preeminent; above all others.

achieves its power in the dynamics of a fleeting moment of sight, sound, smell, and touch.

I'm not going to enter the debate here about whether it is language that shapes reality or vice versa. That battle is doomed to be waged whenever we seek intermittent reprieve from the chicken and egg dispute. I will simply take the position that the spoken word, like the written word, amounts to a nonsensical arrangement of sounds or letters without a consensus that assigns "meaning." And building from the meanings of what we hear, we order reality. Words themselves are innocuous;[2] it is the consensus that gives them true power. 2

I remember the first time I heard the word *nigger*.[3] In my third-grade class, our math tests were being passed down the rows, and as I handed the papers to a little boy in back of me, I remarked that once again he had received a much lower mark than I did. He snatched his test from me and spit out that word. Had he called me a nymphomaniac or a necrophiliac, I couldn't have been more puzzled. I didn't know what a nigger was, but I knew that whatever it meant, it was something he shouldn't have called me. This was verified when I raised my hand, and in a loud voice repeated what he had said and watched the teacher scold him for using a "bad" word. I was later to go home and ask the inevitable question that every black parent must face—"Mommy, what does *nigger* mean?" 3

And what exactly did it mean? Thinking back, I realize that this could not have been the first time the word was used in my presence. I was part of a large extended family that had migrated from the rural South after World War II and formed a close-knit network that gravitated around my maternal grandparents. Their ground-floor apartment in one of the buildings they owned in Harlem[4] was a weekend mecca for my immediate family, along with countless aunts, uncles, and cousins who brought along assorted friends. It was a bustling and open house with assorted neighbors and tenants popping in and out to exchange bits of gossip, pick up an old quarrel, or referee the ongoing checkers game in which my grandmother cheated shamelessly. They were all there to let down their hair and put up their feet after a week of labor in the factories, laundries, and shipyards of New York. 4

---

[2]*innocuous:* harmless; lacking significance or effect.

[3]"The use of the word 'nigger' is reprehensible in today's society. This essay speaks to a specific time and place when that word was utilized to empower African-Americans; today it is used to degrade them even if spoken from their own mouths."–Gloria Naylor

[4]*Harlem:* a predominantly African American neighborhood located in New York City.

Amid the clamor, which could reach deafening proportions— 5
two or three conversations going on simultaneously, punctuated by the sound of a baby's crying somewhere in the back rooms or out on the street—there was still a rigid set of rules about what was said and how. Older children were sent out of the living room when it was time to get into the juicy details about "you-know-who" up on the third floor who had gone and gotten herself "p-r-e-g-n-a-n-t!" But my parents, knowing that I could spell well beyond my years, always demanded that I follow the others out to play. Beyond sexual misconduct and death, everything else was considered harmless for our young ears. And so among the anecdotes[5] of the triumphs and disappointments in the various workings of their lives, the word *nigger* was used in my presence, but it was set within contexts and inflections[6] that caused it to register in my mind as something else.

In the singular, the word was always applied to a man who had 6
distinguished himself in some situation that brought their approval for his strength, intelligence, or drive:

"Did Johnny *really* do that?" 7

"I'm telling you, that nigger pulled in $6,000 of overtime last 8
year. Said he got enough for a down payment on a house."

When used with a possessive adjective by a woman—"my nig- 9
ger"—it became a term of endearment for her husband or boyfriend. But it could be more than just a term applied to a man. In their mouths it became the pure essence of manhood—a disembodied force that channeled their past history of struggle and present survival against the odds into a victorious statement of being: "Yeah, that old foreman found out quick enough—you don't mess with a nigger."

In the plural, it became a description of some group within the 10
community that had overstepped the bounds of decency as my family defined it. Parents who neglected their children, a drunken couple who fought in public, people who simply refused to look for work, those with excessively dirty mouths or unkempt households were all "trifling niggers." This particular circle could forgive hard times, unemployment, the occasional bout of depression—they had gone through all of that themselves—but the unforgivable sin was a lack of self-respect.

[5]*anecdotes:* short accounts or stories of life experiences.
[6]*inflections:* alterations in pitch or tone of voice.

A woman could never be a "nigger" in the singular, with its connotation of confirming worth. The noun *girl* was its closest equivalent in that sense, but only when used in direct address and regardless of the gender doing the addressing. *Girl* was a token of respect for a woman. The one-syllable word was drawn out to sound like three in recognition of the extra ounce of wit, nerve, or daring that the woman had shown in the situation under discussion. 11

"G-i-r-l, stop. You mean you said that to his face?" 12

But if the word was used in a third-person reference or shortened so that it almost snapped out of the mouth, it always involved some element of communal disapproval. And age became an important factor in these exchanges. It was only between individuals of the same generation, or from any older person to a younger (but never the other way around), that *girl* would be considered a compliment. 13

I don't agree with the argument that use of the word *nigger* at this social stratum of the black community was an internalization of racism. The dynamics were the exact opposite: the people in my grandmother's living room took a word that whites used to signify worthlessness or degradation and rendered it impotent.[7] Gathering there together, they transformed *nigger* to signify the varied and complex human beings they knew themselves to be. If the word was to disappear totally from the mouths of even the most liberal of white society, no one in that room was naive enough to believe it would disappear from white minds. Meeting the word head-on, they proved it had absolutely nothing to do with the way they were determined to live their lives. 14

So there must have been dozens of times that *nigger* was spoken in front of me before I reached the third grade. But I didn't "hear" it until it was said by a small pair of lips that had already learned it could be a way to humiliate me. That was the word I went home and asked my mother about. And since she knew that I had to grow up in America, she took me in her lap and explained. 15

Thinking Critically about This Reading

What does Naylor mean when she states that "words themselves are innocuous; it is the consensus that gives them true power" (paragraph 2)? How does she use the two meanings of the word *nigger* to illustrate her point?

[7] *impotent:* weak; powerless.

Questions for Study and Discussion

1. Naylor states her thesis in the last sentence of paragraph 2. (Glossary: *Thesis*) How does what she says in the first two paragraphs build unity by connecting to her thesis statement?
2. What are the two meanings of the word *nigger* as Naylor uses it in her essay? Where is the clearest definition of each use of the word presented? (Glossary: *Definition*)
3. Naylor says she must have heard the word *nigger* many times while she was growing up, yet she "heard" it for the first time when she was in the third grade. How does she explain this seeming contradiction?
4. Naylor gives a detailed narration of her family and its lifestyle in paragraphs 4 and 5. (Glossary: *Narration*) What kinds of details does she include in her brief story? (Glossary: *Details*) How does this narration contribute to your understanding of the word *nigger* as used by her family? Why do you suppose she offers so little in the way of a definition of the other use of the word *nigger*? (Glossary: *Definition*) Explain.
5. Would you characterize Naylor's tone as angry, objective, cynical, or something else? (Glossary: *Tone*) Cite examples of her diction to support your answer. (Glossary: *Diction*)
6. What is the meaning of Naylor's last sentence? How well does it work as an ending for her essay? (Glossary: *Beginnings and Endings*)

Classroom Activity Using Unity

Write a unified paragraph that makes a clear statement about the following list of items. Then compare your paragraph with another student's work. How did each of you establish relationships among the items on the list? How does your writing help your reader make these connections?

A college library

A student's book bag

A laptop computer

A paper notebook

A professor

Suggested Writing Assignments

1. Naylor disagrees with the notion that use of the word *nigger* in the African American community can be taken as an "internalization of racism" (14). Reexamine her essay, and discuss in what ways her definition of the word *nigger* affirms or denies her position. (Glossary: *Definition*) Draw on your own experiences, observations, and reading to support your answer.
2. Write a short essay in which you define a word—for example, *wife, macho, liberal, success,* or *marriage*—that has more than one meaning depending on one's point of view.

CHAPTER **5**

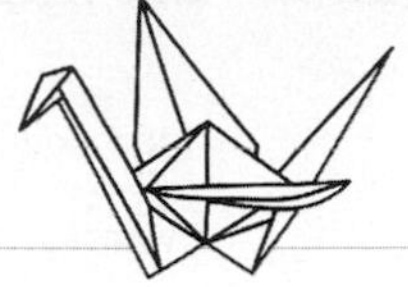

Organization

In an essay, ideas and information cannot be presented all at once; they have to be arranged in some order. That order is the essay's **organization.**

The pattern of organization in an essay should be suited to the writer's subject and **purpose.** For example, if you are writing about your experience working in a fast-food restaurant and your purpose is to tell about the activities of a typical day, you might present those activities in chronological order. If, on the other hand, you wish to argue that working in a bank is an ideal summer job, you might proceed from the least rewarding to the most rewarding aspect of this job; this is called *climactic order.*

Some common patterns of organization are time order, space order, and logical order. Time order, or chronological order, is used to present a sequence of events as they occurred. A personal narrative, a report of a campus incident, or an account of a historical event can be most naturally and easily related in chronological order. In the following paragraphs, student writer Jeffrey Olesky uses chronological order to recount an important lesson he learned. You can read Olesky's entire essay on pages 42–46 of this book.

> The lesson I learned that day appears rather simple now. It came on the putting green of the second hole. My father had finished putting out, and I was holding the flagstick off to the side of the green while the other players finished. Generally, my father would come stand next to me and give me a hand, but due to circumstances we ended up on opposite sides of the green. During the next player's putt, my father lowered his eyebrows at me

and nodded his head to one side a few times. Curious as to what he wanted me to do, I almost let the question slip out of my mouth. But I knew better. I had already learned the rules of not talking or moving while other golfers were hitting. I quietly stood my ground until everyone was finished and then placed the flagstick back in the hole. While walking toward the next tee box, I neared my father. Regardless of what he had wanted me to do, I thought he would commend me for not talking or moving during the ordeal.

"You know better than that, Jeffrey," he said.

"What?" I asked curiously, disappointed that he had not praised me on a job well done.

"You never stand so that your shadow is in someone's line."

How could I be so stupid? He had reminded me a thousand times before. You never allow your shadow to fall in the line of someone's putt because it is distracting to the person putting. I rationalized to my father that maybe the man hadn't noticed or that it didn't bother him. Unfortunately, my father wasn't going to take that as an excuse. After explaining to me what I had done wrong, he suggested that I go over and apologize to the gentleman. I was still a young boy, and the figure of the older man was somewhat intimidating. This task was no easy chore because I was obviously very scared, and this is perhaps what made the lesson sink in a little deeper. I remember slowly approaching my father's friend and sheepishly looking back to my father for help. Once I realized I was on my own, I bashfully gave him my apologies and assured him that it wouldn't happen again. As you can probably guess, the repercussions were not as dramatic as I had

> envisioned them to be. Once my father had pointed out my mistake, I begged him to reconcile with the gentleman for me. However, in apologizing for myself, I learned a valuable lesson. Golf is important because it has taught me many social values such as this, but it can also be a personal, internal tool.

Of course, the order of events can sometimes be rearranged for special effect. For example, an account of an auto accident may begin with the collision itself and then flash back in time to the events leading up to it. The description of a process—such as framing a poster or serving a tennis ball—almost always calls for a chronological organization.

When analyzing a causally related series of events, writers often use a chronological organization to clarify for readers the exact sequence of events. In the following example, the writer examines sequentially the series of malfunctions that led to the near disaster at the Three Mile Island nuclear facility in Harrisburg, Pennsylvania, showing clearly how each one led to the next:

> On March 28, 1979, at 3:53 A.M., a pump at the Harrisburg plant failed. Because the pump failed, the reactor's heat was not drawn off in the heat exchanger and the very hot water in the primary loop overheated. The pressure in the loop increased, opening a release valve that was supposed to counteract such an event. But the valve stuck open and the primary loop system lost so much water (which ended up as a highly radioactive pool, six feet deep, on the floor of the reactor building) that it was unable to carry off all the heat generated within the reactor core. Under these circumstances, the intense heat held within the reactor could, in theory, melt its fuel rods, and the resulting "meltdown" could then carry a hugely radioactive mass through the floor of the reactor. The reactor's emergency cooling system, which is designed to prevent this disaster, was then automatically activated, but when it was, apparently, turned off too soon, some of the fuel rods overheated. This produced a bubble of hydrogen gas at the top of the reactor. (The hydrogen is dissolved in the water in order to react with oxygen that is produced when the intense reactor radiation splits water molecules into their atomic constituents. When heated, the dissolved hydrogen bubbles out of the solution.) This bubble blocked the flow of cooling water so that despite the action of the emergency cooling system the reactor core was again in danger of melting down. Another danger was that the

gas might contain enough oxygen to cause an explosion that could rupture the huge containers that surround the reactor and release a deadly cloud of radioactive material into the surrounding country-side. Working desperately, technicians were able to gradually reduce the size of the gas bubble using a special apparatus brought in from the atomic laboratory at Oak Ridge, Tennessee, and the danger of a catastrophic release of radioactive materials subsided. But the sealed-off plant was now so radioactive that no one could enter it for many months—or, according to some observers, for years—without being exposed to a lethal dose of radiation.

–Barry Commoner, *The Politics of Energy*

Space order is used when describing a person, place, or thing. This organizational pattern begins at a particular point and moves in some direction, such as left to right, top to bottom, east to west, outside to inside, front to back, near to far, around, or over. In describing a house, for example, a writer could move from top to bottom, from outside to inside, or in a circle around the outside.

In the following paragraph, the subject is a baseball, and the writer describes it from the inside out, moving from its "composition-cork nucleus" to the print on its stitched cowhide cover:

It weighs just over five ounces and measures between 2.86 and 2.94 inches in diameter. It is made of a composition-cork nucleus encased in two thin layers of rubber, one black and one red, surrounded by 121 yards of tightly wrapped blue-gray wool yarn, 45 yards of white wool yarn, 54 more yards of blue-gray wool yarn, 150 yards of fine cotton yarn, a coat of rubber cement, and a cowhide (formerly horsehide) exterior, which is held together with 216 slightly raised red cotton stitches. Printed certifications, endorsements, and outdoor advertising spherically attest to its authenticity.

–Roger Angell, *Five Seasons: A Baseball Companion*

Logical order can take many forms, depending on the writer's purpose. Often-used patterns include general to specific, most familiar to least familiar, and smallest to biggest. Perhaps the most common type of logical order is order of importance. Notice how the writer uses this order in the following paragraph:

The Egyptians have taught us many things. They were excellent farmers. They knew all about irrigation. They built temples which were afterwards copied by the Greeks and which served as the earliest models for the churches in which we worship nowadays. They invented a calendar which proved such a useful instrument for the purpose of measuring time that it has survived with few changes until today. But most important of all, the Egyptians learned how to preserve speech for the benefit of future generations. They invented the art of writing.

–Hendrick Willem Van Loon, *The Story of Mankind*

By organizing the material according to the order of increasing importance, the writer places special emphasis on the final sentence.

A student essay on outdoor education provides another example of logical order. In the paragraph that follows, the writer describes some of the special problems students have during the traditionally difficult high school years. She then explains the benefits of involving such students in an outdoor education curriculum as a possible remedy, offers a quotation from a noteworthy text on outdoor education to support her views, and presents her thesis statement in the final sentence of the paragraph—all logical steps in her writing.

For many students, the normally difficult time of high school is especially troublesome. These students may have learning disabilities, emotional-behavioral disorders, or low self-esteem, or they may be labeled "at-risk" because of socioeconomic background, delinquency, or drug and alcohol abuse. Any combination of these factors contributes negatively to students' success in school. Often the traditional public or private high school may not be the ideal environment in which these students can thrive and live up to their highest potential. Outdoor education can benefit these high schoolers and provide them with the means necessary to overcome their personal issues and develop skills, knowledge, and self-esteem that will enable them to become successful, self-aware, emotionally stable, and functional adults. In their book *Outdoor Education*, authors Smith, Carlson, Donaldson, and Masters state poignantly that outdoor education "can be one of the most effective forces in the community to prevent human erosion as well as land erosion; it can be one of

Statement of the problem

A possible remedy is offered and explained

Authorities are quoted to support the suggested solution

The thesis is given after a preliminary discussion to increase its acceptability

the means of saving youngsters from the education scrap heap" (49). Outdoor education builds a relationship between students and the natural environment that might not be formed otherwise and gives students a respect for the world in which they live. Aspects of outdoor education should be implemented in the curriculums of high schools in order to achieve these results in all students.

–Jinsie Ward, student

Although logical order can take many forms, the exact rationale always depends on the topic of the writing. For example, in writing a descriptive essay about a place you visited, you can move from the least striking to the most striking detail to keep your readers interested and involved in the description. In an essay explaining how to pick individual stocks for investment, you can start with the point that readers will find the least difficult to understand and move on to the most difficult point. (That's how many teachers organize their courses.) Or in writing an essay arguing for more internships and service learning courses, you can move from your least controversial to your most controversial point, preparing your reader gradually to accept your argument.

A simple way to check the organization of an essay is to outline it once you have a draft. Does the outline represent the organizational pattern—chronological, spatial, or logical—that you set out to use? Problems in outlining will naturally indicate sections that you need to revise.

A View from the Bridge

■ Cherokee Paul McDonald

Courtesy of Cherokee Paul McDonald

A fiction writer, memoirist, and journalist, Cherokee Paul McDonald was raised and schooled in Fort Lauderdale, Florida. In 1970, he returned home from a tour of duty in Vietnam and joined the Fort Lauderdale Police Department, where he rose to the rank of sergeant. In 1980, after receiving a degree in criminal science from Broward Community College, McDonald left the police department to become a writer. He worked a number of odd jobs before publishing his first book, The Patch, *in 1986. In 1991, he published* Blue Truth, *a memoir. His novel* Summer's Reason *was released in 1994, and his most recent book, a memoir of the Vietnam War titled* Into the Green: A Reconnaissance by Fire, *was published in 2001.*

"A View from the Bridge" was originally published in Sunshine *magazine in 1990. As you read, notice how McDonald organizes his narrative. He tells us what the narrator and the boy are doing, but he also relies heavily on their dialogue to structure his story, which unfolds as the two talk. McDonald makes the story come alive by showing us, rather than by simply telling us, what happens.*

Reflecting on What You Know

Make a list of your interests, focusing on those to which you devote a significant amount of time. Do you share any of these interests with people you know? What does a shared interest do for a relationship between two people?

I was coming up on the little bridge in the Rio Vista neighborhood of Fort Lauderdale, deepening my stride and my breathing to negotiate the slight incline without altering my pace. And then, as I neared the crest, I saw the kid. 1

He was a lumpy little guy with baggy shorts, a faded T-shirt and heavy sweat socks falling down over old sneakers. 2

3 Partially covering his shaggy blond hair was one of those blue baseball caps with gold braid on the bill and a sailfish patch sewn onto the peak. Covering his eyes and part of his face was a pair of those stupid-looking '50s-style wrap-around sunglasses.

4 He was fumbling with a beat-up rod and reel, and he had a little bait bucket by his feet. I puffed on by, glancing down into the empty bucket as I passed.

5 "Hey, mister! Would you help me, please?"

6 The shrill voice penetrated my jogger's concentration, and I was determined to ignore it. But for some reason, I stopped.

7 With my hands on my hips and the sweat dripping from my nose I asked, "What do you want, kid?"

8 "Would you please help me find my shrimp? It's my last one and I've been getting bites and I know I can catch a fish if I can just find that shrimp. He jumped outta my hand as I was getting him from the bucket."

9 Exasperated, I walked slowly back to the kid, and pointed.

10 "There's the damn shrimp by your left foot. You stopped me for *that*?"

11 As I said it, the kid reached down and trapped the shrimp.

12 "Thanks a lot, mister," he said.

13 I watched as the kid dropped the baited hook down into the canal. Then I turned to start back down the bridge.

14 That's when the kid let out a "Hey! Hey!" and the prettiest tarpon[1] I'd ever seen came almost six feet out of the water, twisting and turning as he fell through the air.

15 "I got one!" the kid yelled as the fish hit the water with a loud splash and took off down the canal.

16 I watched the line being burned off the reel at an alarming rate. The kid's left hand held the crank while the extended fingers felt for the drag setting.

17 "No, kid!" I shouted. "Leave the drag alone . . . just keep that damn rod tip up!"

18 Then I glanced at the reel and saw there were just a few loops of line left on the spool.

19 "Why don't you get yourself some decent equipment?" I said, but before the kid could answer I saw the line go slack.

20 "Ohhh, I lost him," the kid said. I saw the flash of silver as the fish turned.

---

[1]*tarpon:* a large, silvery fish.

"Crank, kid, crank! You didn't lose him. He's coming back toward you. Bring in the slack!" 21

The kid cranked like mad, and a beautiful grin spread across his face. 22

"He's heading in for the pilings,"[2] I said. "Keep him out of those pilings!" 23

The kid played it perfectly. When the fish made its play for the pilings, he kept just enough pressure on to force the fish out. When the water exploded and the silver missile hurled into the air, the kid kept the rod tip up and the line tight. 24

As the fish came to the surface and began a slow circle in the middle of the canal, I said, "Whooee, is that a nice fish or what?" 25

The kid didn't say anything, so I said, "Okay, move to the edge of the bridge and I'll climb down to the seawall and pull him out." 26

When I reached the seawall I pulled in the leader, leaving the fish lying on its side in the water. 27

"How's that?" I said. 28

"Hey, mister, tell me what it looks like." 29

"Look down here and check him out," I said. "He's beautiful." 30

But then I looked up into those stupid-looking sunglasses and it hit me. The kid was blind. 31

"Could you tell me what he looks like, mister?" he said again. 32

"Well, he's just under three, uh, he's about as long as one of your arms," I said. "I'd guess he goes about 15, 20 pounds. He's mostly silver, but the silver is somehow made up of *all* the colors, if you know what I mean." I stopped. "Do you know what I mean by colors?" 33

The kid nodded. 34

"Okay. He has all these big scales, like armor all over his body. They're silver too, and when he moves they sparkle. He has a strong body and a large powerful tail. He has big round eyes, bigger than a quarter, and a lower jaw that sticks out past the upper one and is very tough. His belly is almost white and his back is a gunmetal gray. When he jumped he came out of the water about six feet, and his scales caught the sun and flashed it all over the place." 35

By now the fish had righted itself, and I could see the bright-red gills as the gill plates opened and closed. I explained this to the kid, and then said, more to myself, "He's a beauty." 36

---

[2]*pilings:* support columns driven vertically into the ground or ocean floor.

"Can you get him off the hook?" the kid asked. "I don't want to 37
kill him."

I watched as the tarpon began to slowly swim away, tired but still 38
alive.

By the time I got back up to the top of the bridge the kid had his 39
line secured and his bait bucket in one hand.

He grinned and said, "Just in time. My mom drops me off here, 40
and she'll be back to pick me up any minute."

He used the back of one hand to wipe his nose. 41

"Thanks for helping me catch that tarpon," he said, "and for 42
helping me to see it."

I looked at him, shook my head, and said, "No, my friend, thank 43
you for letting *me* see that fish."

I took off, but before I got far the kid yelled again. 44

"Hey, mister!" 45

I stopped. 46

"Someday I'm gonna catch a sailfish and a blue marlin and a 47
giant tuna and *all* those big sportfish!"

As I looked into those sunglasses I knew he probably would. I 48
wished I could be there when it happened.

Thinking Critically about This Reading

Near the end of the story, why does the narrator say to the boy, "No, my friend, thank you for letting *me* see that fish" (paragraph 43)? What happens to the narrator's attitude as a result of his encounter with the boy? What lesson do you think the narrator learns?

Questions for Study and Discussion

1. How does McDonald organize his essay? What period of time would you estimate is covered in this essay?
2. What clues lead up to the revelation that the boy is blind? Why does it take McDonald so long to realize it?
3. Notice the way McDonald chooses and adjusts some of the words he uses to describe the fish to the boy in paragraphs 33–36. Why does he do this? How does he organize his description of the fish so that the boy can visualize it better?

4. By the end of the essay, we know much more about the boy beyond that he is blind, but after the initial description, McDonald characterizes him only indirectly. As the essay unfolds, what do we learn about the boy, and how does the author convey this knowledge?
5. McDonald tells much of his experience through dialogue. (Glossary: *Dialogue*) What does this dialogue add to the narration? (Glossary: *Narration*) What would have been lost had McDonald not used dialogue?
6. What is the connotation of the word *view* in the title? (Glossary: *Connotation/Denotation*) Of the word *bridge*?

Classroom Activity Using Organization

Consider the ways in which you might organize a discussion of the seven states listed below. For each state, we have provided some basic information: the date it entered the Union, population (2010 census), land area, and number of electoral votes in a presidential election.

ALASKA
January 3, 1959
710,231 people
570,374 square miles
3 electoral votes

ARIZONA
February 14, 1912
6,392,017 people
113,642 square miles
11 electoral votes

FLORIDA
March 3, 1845
18,801,310 people
53,937 square miles
29 electoral votes

MAINE
March 15, 1820
1,328,361 people
30,865 square miles
4 electoral votes

MISSOURI
August 10, 1821
5,988,927 people
69,709 square miles
10 electoral votes

MONTANA
November 8, 1889
989,415 people
145,556 square miles
3 electoral votes

OREGON
February 14, 1859
3,831,074 people
98,386 square miles
7 electoral votes

Suggested Writing Assignments

1. In groups of two or three, take turns describing a specific beautiful or remarkable thing to the others as if they were blind. You may want to bring in an actual object to observe while your classmates cover their eyes. Help each other find the best words to create a vivid verbal picture. Using paragraphs 33–36 of McDonald's story as a model, write a brief description of your object, retaining the informal style of your speaking voice.
2. Recall a time when you and one other person held a conversation that helped you see something more clearly—visually, in terms of understanding, or both. Using McDonald's narrative as an organizational model, tell the story of that moment, re-creating the dialogue exactly as you remember it.
3. McDonald's "A View from the Bridge" is just one "fish story" in the long and rich tradition of that genre. In its own way, the story plays on the ironic notion that fishing is a quiet sport but one in which participants come to expect the unexpected. (Glossary: *Irony*) For the narrator in the story, there is a lesson in not merely looking but truly seeing, in describing the fish so that the blind boy can "see" it. It is interesting that a sport in which "nothing happens" can be the source of so much storytelling. Write an essay in which you tell a "fish story" of your own, one that reveals a larger, significant truth or life lesson. Pay particular attention to the pattern of organization you choose, and be sure to revise your essay to tighten up your use of that pattern. If possible, incorporate some elements of surprise as well.

The American Man: Age Ten

Susan Orlean

Gasper Tringale

Susan Orlean grew up in Cleveland, Ohio, and studied literature and history at the University of Michigan. She began her writing career in Portland, Oregon, writing first for a small monthly magazine and then eventually for Rolling Stone *and the* Village Voice. *Orlean is currently a staff writer for the* New Yorker *and has published articles in the* New York Times Magazine, Spy, Esquire, *and* Outside. *She is the author of six nonfiction books, including* The Bullfighter Checks Her Makeup *(2001) and* My Kind of Place *(2004). Her book* The Orchid Thief *(1998) was the basis for the 2002 movie* Adaptation, *directed by Charlie Kaufman and starring Nicolas Cage and Meryl Streep. Her most recent book,* Rin Tin Tin: The Life and the Legend *(2011), tells the story of a real dog—rescued from a shelled building in France during World War I—that became an international celebrity.*

In this excerpt from "The American Man: Age Ten," which originally appeared in Esquire *in 1992, Orlean gives readers a glimpse into the life of ten-year-old Colin Duffy. As she catalogs his particular interests, habits, and ways of thinking, she paints a portrait of American boyhood more generally. As you read, take note of how she organizes her observations about Colin, beginning with his exterior appearance and moving to his internal feelings and desires.*

Reflecting on What You Know

What do you remember about yourself at age ten? What do you think it would be like if your adult self could observe that ten-year-old?

Here are the particulars about Colin Duffy: He is ten years old, on the nose. He is four feet eight inches high, weighs seventy-five pounds, and appears to be mostly leg and shoulder blade. He is a 1 handsome kid. He has a broad forehead, dark eyes with dense lashes, and a sharp, dimply smile. I have rarely seen him without a baseball cap. He owns several, but favors a University of Michigan Wolverines model, on account of its pleasing colors. The hat styles his hair into wild disarray. If you ever managed to get the hat off his head, you would see a boy with a nimbus of golden-brown hair, dented in the back, where the hat hits him.

Colin lives with his mother, Elaine; his father, Jim; his older sister, 2
Megan; and his little brother, Chris, in a pretty pale blue Victorian house on a bosky street in Glen Ridge, New Jersey. Glen Ridge is a serene and civilized old town twenty miles west of New York City. It does not have much of a commercial district, but it is a town of amazing lawns. Most of the houses were built around the turn of the century and are set back a gracious, green distance from the street. The rest of the town seems to consist of parks and playing fields and sidewalks and backyards—in other words, it is a far cry from South-Central Los Angeles and from Bedford-Stuyvesant and other, grimmer parts of the country where a very different ten-year-old American man is growing up today.

There is a fine school system in Glen Ridge, but Elaine and Jim, 3
who are both schoolteachers, choose to send their children to a parents' cooperative elementary school in Montclair, a neighboring suburb. Currently, Colin is in fifth grade. He is a good student. He plans to go to college, to a place he says is called Oklahoma City State College University. OCSCU satisfies his desire to live out west, to attend a small college, and to study law enforcement, which OCSCU apparently offers as a major. After four years at Oklahoma City State College University, he plans to work for the FBI. He says that getting to be a police officer involves tons of hard work, but working for the FBI will be a cinch, because all you have to do is fill out one form, which he has already gotten from the head FBI office. Colin is quiet in class but loud on the playground. He has a great throwing arm, significant foot speed, and a lot of physical confidence. He is also brave. Huge wild cats with rabies and gross stuff dripping from their teeth, which he says run rampant throughout his neighborhood, do not scare him. Otherwise, he is slightly bashful. This combination of athletic grace and valor and personal reserve accounts for considerable popularity. He has a fluid relationship to many social groups, including the superbright nerds, the ultra-jocks, the flashy kids who will someday become extremely popular and socially successful

juvenile delinquents, and the kids who will be elected president of the student body. In his opinion, the most popular boy in his class is Christian, who happens to be black, and Colin's favorite television character is Steve Urkel on *Family Matters*, who is black, too, but otherwise he seems uninterested in or oblivious to race. Until this year, he was a Boy Scout. Now he is planning to begin karate lessons. His favorite schoolyard game is football, followed closely by prison dodgeball, blob tag, and bombardo. He's crazy about athletes, although sometimes it isn't clear if he is absolutely sure of the difference between human athletes and Marvel Comics action figures. His current athletic hero is Dave Meggett. His current best friend is named Japeth. He used to have another best friend named Ozzie. According to Colin, Ozzie was found on a doorstep, then changed his name to Michael and moved to Massachusetts, and then Colin never saw him or heard from him again.

He has had other losses in his life. He is old enough to know 4
people who have died and to know things about the world that are worrisome. When he dreams, he dreams about moving to Wyoming, which he has visited with his family. His plan is to buy land there and have some sort of ranch that would definitely include horses. Sometimes when he talks about this, it sounds as ordinary and hard-boiled as a real estate appraisal; other times it can sound fantastical and wifty and achingly naive, informed by the last inklings of childhood—the musings of a balmy real estate appraiser assaying a wonderful and magical landscape that erodes from memory a little bit every day. The collision in his mind of what he understands, what he hears, what he figures out, what popular culture pours into him, what he knows, what he pretends to know, and what he imagines makes an interesting mess. The mess often has the form of what he will probably think like when he is a grown man, but the content of what he is like as a little boy.

He is old enough to begin imagining that he will someday get 5
married, but at ten he is still convinced that the best thing about being married will be that he will be allowed to sleep in his clothes. His father once observed that living with Colin was like living with a Martian who had done some reading on American culture. As it happens, Colin is not especially sad or worried about the prospect of growing up, although he sometimes frets over whether he should be called a kid or a grown-up; he has settled on the word *kid-up*. Once, I asked him what the biggest advantage to adulthood will be, and he

said, "The best thing is that grown-ups can go wherever they want." I asked him what he meant, exactly, and he said, "Well, if you're grown up, you'd have a car, and whenever you felt like it, you could get into your car and drive somewhere and get candy."

Thinking Critically about This Reading

Orlean calls Colin's mind an "interesting mess" (paragraph 4). What accounts for its messiness? Why does she find it interesting?

Questions for Study and Discussion

1. What features does Orlean focus on in her description of Colin? What does she tell us about his appearance, his tastes, and the way he thinks?
2. How is Colin a product of the town where he is growing up? What does Orlean tell readers about the town?
3. How does Orlean convey Colin's way of talking to the reader? As a reader, do you find this technique effective for describing Colin?
4. How and why does Colin invent the term *kid-up* (5)? Do you think it's a good term to represent how Orlean sees him? Why?
5. Orlean's observations about Colin are often funny even when, or especially when, she is recounting moments when he doesn't know he's being funny. Why do you think this is the case? What is funny about the things Colin says? (Glossary: *Irony*)
6. What claims is Orlean making about American men? How does she think Colin is representative of the American man?

Classroom Activity Using Organization

Like Orlean, Thomas L. Friedman faces the task of organizing his observations about an interesting, complex person. Go back to "My Favorite Teacher" (pp. 102–4), and jot down next to each paragraph a few words about what kind of information it conveys about Hattie M. Steinberg. Then discuss how Friedman's strategies for organizing his description differ from those Orlean uses to describe Colin.

Suggested Writing Assignments

1. Orlean points out that Colin's life is a "far cry" (2) from the experience of other ten-year-olds. Is his life similar to that of kids growing up in your childhood neighborhood? Or the place where you live now? Write an essay about childhood as you see it, paying particular attention to how you organize the ideas to make your point.
2. Taking Orlean's method as a model, conduct an interview with a young person. Write an essay that both conveys your interaction with the child to a reader and makes an argument for what is interesting or representative about his or her experiences and ideas. Make sure to organize your essay so that it will be easy for readers to discern when you are summarizing your conversation and when you are interpreting what you heard.

Revolution on Eight Wheels

Diane "Lady Hulk" Williams

Janine Norton

Diane Williams was born in San Mateo, California. She earned a bachelor's degree from Williams College and master's degrees from the University of Massachusetts–Amherst and Smith College. She is currently working toward a PhD in American studies with a focus on sport studies at the University of Iowa, where she is a Presidential Research Graduate Fellow. She was an associate producer for the documentary Not Just a Game: Power, Politics and American Sports *(2010). She has been playing roller derby since 2009, now with the Old Capitol City Roller Girls.*

In "Revolution on Eight Wheels," originally published in the Nation, *Williams uses her first encounter with roller derby as an entry point and considers what makes the sport so popular. She says that in the essay, which is distilled from a longer project, she "wanted to convey the feel of a bout, the energy and excitement, along with some history and critical discussion of the sport/culture." As you read, think about how she organizes these elements in her writing.*

Reflecting on What You Know

Think about the differences between men's and women's sports. How do you think audiences perceive female athletes in comparison to male athletes? What would you expect from a sport primarily played by women?

I had no idea what to expect when I arrived at my first roller derby bout in Tucson, in 2005. As a former college athlete and coach, an amateur women's sports historian and a gender studies nerd, I had heard buzz about derby and wanted to check it out. That night, the Furious Truckstop Waitresses, clad in pink waitress dresses, were playing the police-themed Vice Squad. As women of all shapes and sizes whizzed by me in warm-ups, I noticed names like Barbicide, Whiskey 1

Mick and Sloppy Flo emblazoned on their uniforms. Some wore fish-net tights, itty-bitty skirts and funky makeup. As excited as I was, I paused: Was this objectification disguised as empowerment? Were these women being exploited or were they totally awesome? I couldn't tell. I settled in near the track, intrigued.

At the first whistle, the spectacle transformed into an exhilarating celebration of women and sport, complete with referees and play-by-play announcers. I'd never seen this many paying fans support an amateur women's sport. After the game, I watched the skaters pack up the merchandise, sweep the floor and stack the chairs. Everyone did everything. This was a woman-focused, do-it-yourself sports culture, and I was hooked. 2

Roller derby has existed on and off since the 1930s, but this new wave originated in Austin, Texas, in 2001, the vision of a man known as "Devil Dan" and some feisty women. After he reportedly stole their money and skipped town, the burned-but-determined team captains carried on, reviving roller derby for the new millennium. Sassy, strong and aggressive, "derby girls" challenged traditional notions of acceptable female behavior through the male-dominated world of sports. 3

In 2005 the Women's Flat Track Derby Association (WFTDA) was formed, creating a standard set of rules and supporting the growing derby community. Women held leadership positions in the association; men were involved as referees, coaches and announcers, but not skaters. This was a deviation from the sport's co-ed history, but organizers insisted that the new derby have little connection to the promoter-owned derby their parents remembered. This roller derby was skater-owned, and WFTDA adopted the motto "Real. Strong. Athletic. Revolutionary." I wore my WFTDA shirt proudly and cheered when Tucson hosted twenty teams for the first-ever national competition, the Dust Devil Tournament, in 2006. 4

Two years later, as a burned-out graduate student in need of adventure, I found myself on a date at a roller rink in Hadley, Massachusetts. I spent the whole night imagining myself playing derby as I swerved around the rink. Soon afterward, I attended "Fresh Meat Night" with the local league, Pioneer Valley Roller Derby. PVRD had a women's team and the first men's team in the country. They practiced together, a unique and progressive approach that I loved, and I found that the toughest-looking skaters were incredibly supportive and encouraging. Personally, politically and athletically, I'd found my home. "Lady Hulk" was born. 5

Roller derby marries an underground vibe with the fun of athletic 6
competition in a blend of sport and spectacle that is as much fun to play as it is to watch. Teams compete on a small flat or banked track. Each team has four blockers and one jammer. Everyone skates around the track in a series of two-minute "jams," trying to get their team's jammer through the opposing pack of blockers, while holding the other team's jammer back. Once through the pack, the jammers skate quickly around the track, earning points for each opposing player they lap. At the end of each jam, new skaters get on the track and a new jam begins. Games last for around sixty minutes, divided into two or three periods. Unlike in the old days of derby, today you usually earn a penalty for throwing elbows and get ejected for fighting.

Skaters come to derby from different backgrounds, and they all 7
bring unique stories and style. Some rock fishnets and booty shorts, some have tattoos and piercings, and some practice in gym shorts and T-shirts. Many started after attending a bout or learning that a friend joined a team; others were drawn in through media coverage, Facebook, the movie *Whip It* or the A&E show *Rollergirls*. Some are former Division I athletes, while others were kids who hated PE.

For those burned out on traditional sports, derby provides a chal- 8
lenging, refreshing alternative. It's a "love of the game" world where passion, community and the spirit of competition support leagues through the growing pains, budgetary challenges and inevitable derby drama. Even the refs and officials donate their time. One skater summed up the culture this way: "We don't care about your body type or sexual orientation or whether you were the popular kid in school. As long as you want to come out and strap on skates and pads, work your butt off, and offer support and respect for those around you, there is a place for you here."

According to Roller Derby WorldWide, there are 960 amateur 9
leagues around the globe. This includes banked-track teams, WFTDA-affiliated and unaffiliated flat-track women's teams, men's teams (many affiliated with the Men's Roller Derby Association), junior teams, recreational teams and teams that play by "old-school rules." Some leagues are nationally ranked and participate in official seasons and championships; others are just starting up, with little more than a few skaters, new knee pads and a dream. Teams are playing in increasingly large venues, and more and more fans are cheering them on. Players can read game recaps and articles on strategy in the derby community trade magazines *Five on Five* and *Blood and Thunder*, and bouts are often streamed on the hugely popular online Derby News Network.

As roller derby continues to grow and evolve, many questions are popping up. Will it become an Olympic sport? Join the X Games? Can it remain local? Might the development of girls' junior leagues lead to an increasingly competitive derby market? Will roller derby be on TV again? Will men's derby push the community to be more inclusive? Everyone involved has an opinion and a hope for the future; but on the local level, we're also busy getting ready for our next bout. 10

Those of us who play roller derby are part of history, part of making the spectacle of sport more apparent and celebratory, and leaving limiting ideas about appropriate sports for women and men in our eight-wheeled wake. Check out your local team and support the roller derby revolution! 11

Thinking Critically about This Reading

Williams raises several questions about propriety in her essay: Which sports are appropriate for men and which for women? What is the appropriate body type or personal style for an athlete? What are the appropriate authorities or organizations to regulate a sport?

After reading her essay, how do you think watching, and then participating in, roller derby has helped Williams answer these questions? How do the "derby girls" determine what is appropriate?

Questions for Study and Discussion

1. How does Williams organize the information about roller derby in this essay? Where does she introduce research, and where does she convey personal experience? How do her organizational decisions affect the reader's experience?
2. What impresses Williams about the first roller derby match she watches? What are her hesitations about the sport?
3. What is unique about roller derby both as a sport and as a business? How is its culture different from that of other sports?
4. When Williams introduces her derby name, Lady Hulk, she does it in the third person, as if she were a separate character (paragraph 5). Why does she do this? Do you think it reveals anything about the appeal of roller derby? (Glossary: *Point of View*)
5. What does Williams think is important about the story of the origin of roller derby? What does it have to do with the way the sport is played now?

6. Near the end of her essay, Williams asks a series of questions about the future of roller derby (10). Why do you think she raises all these questions? What do they show readers about the state of the sport now?

Classroom Activity Using Organization

As in Williams's essay, the following application letter has to organize a lot of information for its reader. Read the letter, then discuss how its writer, Joshua S. Goodman, constructs the three paragraphs that summarize his skills and experience. How would you describe Goodman's goals in the letter? How does he organize highlights from his résumé to accomplish those goals?

222 Morewood Ave.
Pittsburgh, PA 15212
April 16, 2014

Ms. Judith Castro
Director, Human Resources
Natural History Museum
1201 S. Figueroa Street
Los Angeles, CA 90015

Dear Ms. Castro:

I have recently learned from Jodi Hammel, a graphic designer at Dyer/Khan, that you are recruiting for a graphic designer in your Marketing Department. Your position interests me greatly because it offers me an opportunity both to fulfill my career goals and to promote the work of an internationally respected institution. Having participated in substantial volunteer activities at a local public museum, I am aware of the importance of your work.

I bring strong up-to-date academic and practical skills in multimedia tools and graphic arts production, as indicated in my enclosed résumé. Further, I have recent project management experience at Dyer/Khan, where I was responsible for the development of client brochures, newsletters, and posters. As project manager, I coordinated the project time lines, budgets, and production with clients, staff, and vendors.

My experience and contacts in the Los Angeles area media and entertainment community should help me make use of state-of-the-art design expertise. As you will see on my résumé, I have worked with the leading motion picture, television, and music companies — that experience should help me develop exciting marketing tools Museum visitors and patrons will find attractive. For example, I helped design an upgrade of the CGI logo for Paramount Pictures and was formally commended by the Director of Marketing.

Could we schedule a meeting at your convenience to discuss this position further? Call me any weekday morning at 412-555-1212 (cell) or e-mail me at jgoodman@aol.com if you have questions or need additional information. Thank you for your consideration.

Sincerely,

Joshua S. Goodman

Joshua S. Goodman

Suggested Writing Assignments

1. In paragraph 6, Williams explains the basic rules of roller derby. Note that Williams organizes this paragraph chronologically, following the match from beginning to end. Using her paragraph as a model, write an explanation of your favorite sport or hobby to someone unfamiliar with it. Try to organize your explanation so that it will be as clear and comprehensive as possible. (Glossary: *Process Analysis*)
2. Williams begins "Revolution on Eight Wheels" by telling the story of her first encounter with roller derby. This approach lets the reader in on a personal connection to the subject and provides a clear viewpoint. Williams then broadens her view to write more generally about roller derby, including information about its rules and recent history. Write an essay that begins with your own anecdote about a first encounter with something new to you. Following Williams's lead, expand on your personal experience by folding some research into your essay. Make calculated decisions, as Williams does, on where to include the research and where to refer to personal experience to keep your reader engaged. (Glossary: *Anecdote*)

CHAPTER **6**

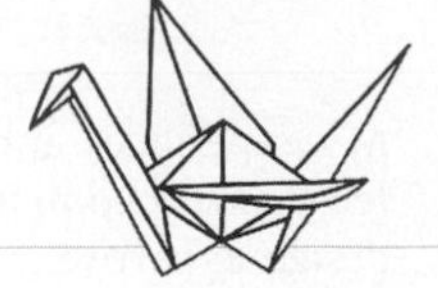

Beginnings and Endings

"Begin at the beginning and go on till you come to the end: then stop," advised the King of Hearts in *Alice in Wonderland.* "Good advice, but more easily said than done," you might be tempted to reply. Certainly, no part of writing essays can be more daunting than coming up with effective **beginnings and endings**. In fact, many writers believe that beginnings and endings are the most important parts of any piece of writing, regardless of its length. Even before coming to your introduction, your readers will usually know something about your intentions from your title. Titles such as "The Case against Euthanasia," "How to Buy a Used Car," and "What Is a Migraine Headache?" indicate both your subject and your approach and prepare your readers for what follows.

■ BEGINNINGS

What makes for an effective beginning? Not unlike a personal greeting, a good beginning should catch a reader's interest and then hold it. The experienced writer realizes that many readers would rather do almost anything than make a commitment to read, so the opening—or *lead,* as journalists refer to it—requires a lot of thought and much revising to make it right and to keep the reader's attention from straying. The inexperienced writer, on the other hand, knows that the beginning is important but tries to write it first and to perfect it before moving on to the rest of the essay. Although there are no "rules" for writing introductions, we can offer one bit of general advice: wait until the writing process is well under way or almost completed before focusing on your lead. Following this advice will keep you from spending too much time on an introduction that you will undoubtedly revise. More important, once you actually see how your essay develops, you will know better how to introduce it to your reader.

In addition to capturing your reader's attention, a good beginning usually introduces your thesis and either suggests or actually reveals the structure of the composition. Keep in mind that the best beginning is not necessarily the most catchy or the most shocking but the one most appropriate for the job you are trying to do.

There are many effective ways of beginning an essay. Consider using one of the following.

Anecdote

Introducing your essay with an **anecdote**—a brief narrative drawn from current news events, history, or your personal experience—can be an effective way to capture your reader's interest. In the following example, the writer introduces an essay on choosing her career path by recounting the moment she first encountered her most inspiring teacher.

> Picture this: it is my first day of AP European History, sophomore year of high school. I sit slumped over in my desk, listening to my teacher babbling on about some revolution or uprising somewhere in the world. I struggle to stay awake, wondering how I am ever going to get through this class today, let alone this year. All of a sudden a man enters our classroom, walks right up to my history teacher (who is sitting at a desk in the front of the classroom lecturing), whips out a hankie and a rubber band, and creates something like a keffiyeh (a traditional Middle Eastern head covering) on the head of my bald history teacher. My classmates and I wait in anxious anticipation for the outburst of angry words that are sure to follow. To our surprise and delight, Mr. C (our history teacher) cracks a smile, and we all burst into laughter. He introduces this strange man as our English teacher, Mr. R. This mysterious Mr. R then proceeds to walk to the far end of the classroom, hoist himself up onto a desk, and walk across each student's desk to the other side of the room. This accomplished, he waves a final farewell and exits the classroom. This would be the English teacher I would never forget. He would be the one to inspire me to pursue a career in education.
>
> –Karen Vaccaro, student

Analogy and Comparison

An **analogy**, or comparison, can be useful in getting readers to think about a topic they might otherwise reject as uninteresting or unfamiliar.

In the following multiparagraph example, William Zinsser introduces a subject few would consider engrossing—bloated, sloppy writing—with a comparison to disease. By pairing these two seemingly unrelated concepts, he both introduces and illustrates the idea he will develop in his essay: writing is a demanding craft, and to keep one's writing disease-free, one must edit with a watchful eye.

> Clutter is the disease of American writing. We are a society strangling in unnecessary words, circular constructions, pompous frills, and meaningless jargon.
>
> Who can understand the clotted language of everyday American commerce: the memo, the corporation report, the business letter, the notice from the bank explaining its latest "simplified" statement? What member of an insurance or medical plan can decipher the brochure explaining his costs and benefits? What father or mother can put together a child's toy from the instructions on the box? Our national tendency is to inflate and thereby sound important. The airline pilot who announces that he is presently anticipating experiencing considerable precipitation wouldn't think of saying it may rain. The sentence is too simple—there must be something wrong with it.
>
> But the secret of good writing is to strip every sentence to its cleanest components. Every word that serves no function, every long word that could be a short word, every adverb that carries the same meaning that's already in the verb, every passive construction that leaves the reader unsure of who is doing what—these are the thousand and one adulterants that weaken the strength of a sentence. And they usually occur in proportion to education and rank.
>
> –William Zinsser, "Simplicity," p. 174

Dialogue/Quotation

Although relying heavily on the ideas of others can weaken an effective introduction, opening your essay with a quotation or a brief **dialogue** can attract a reader's attention and succinctly illustrate a particular attitude or point you want to discuss. In the following example, the writer introduces an essay about the three main types of stress in our lives by recounting a brief dialogue with one of her roommates.

> My roommate, Megan, pushes open the front door, throws her keys on the counter, and flops down on the couch.
>
> "Hey, Megan, how are you?" I yell from the kitchen.

"I don't know what's wrong with me. I sleep all the time, but I'm still tired. No matter what I do, I just don't feel well."

"What did the doctor say?"

"She said it sounds like chronic fatigue syndrome."

"Do you think it might be caused by stress?" I ask.

"Nah, stress doesn't affect me very much. I like keeping busy and running around. This must be something else."

Like most Americans, Megan doesn't recognize the numerous factors in her life that cause her stress.

–Sarah Federman, student

Facts and Statistics

For the most part, you should use **facts** and statistics to support your argument rather than let them speak for you, but presenting brief and startling facts or statistics can be an effective way to engage readers in your essay.

One out of every five new recruits in the United States military is female.

The Marines gave the Combat Action Ribbon for service in the Persian Gulf to twenty-three women.

Two female soldiers were killed in the bombing of the USS *Cole*.

The Selective Service registers for the draft all male citizens between the ages of eighteen and twenty-five.

What's wrong with this picture?

–Anna Quindlen, "Uncle Sam and Aunt Samantha"

Irony or Humor

It is often effective to introduce an essay with irony or humor. Humor signals to the reader that your essay will be entertaining to read, and **irony** can indicate an unexpected approach to a topic. In his essay "The Principles of Poor Writing" (pp. 430–34), Paul W. Merrill begins his ironic instructional essay on how to write poorly by establishing a wry tone, even poking fun at himself, stating that "the author . . . can write poorly without half trying."

Books and articles on good writing are numerous, but where can you find sound, practical advice on how to write poorly? Poor writing is so common that every educated person ought to know something about it. Many scientists actually do write poorly, but they probably perform by ear without perceiving clearly how their results are achieved. An article on the principles of poor writing might help. The author considers himself well qualified to prepare such an article; he can write poorly without half trying.

The average student finds it surprisingly easy to acquire the usual tricks of poor writing. To do a consistently poor job, however, one must grasp a few essential principles:

1. Ignore the reader.
2. Be verbose, vague, and pompous.
3. Do not revise.

–Paul W. Merrill, "The Principles of Poor Writing," pp. 430–31

There are several other good ways to begin an essay; the following opening paragraphs illustrate each approach.

Short Generalization

Washington is a wonderful city. The scale seems right, more humane than other places. I like all the white marble and green trees, the ideals celebrated by the great monuments and memorials. I like the climate, the slow shift of the seasons here. Spring, so southern in feeling, comes early, and the long, sweet autumns can last into December. Summers are murder, equatorial—no question; the compensation is that Congress adjourns, the city empties out, eases off. Winter evenings in Georgetown with the snow falling and the lights just coming on are as beautiful as any I've known.

–David McCullough, *Brave Campanions*

Startling Claim

I've finally figured out the difference between neat and sloppy people. The distinction is, as always, moral. Neat people are lazier and meaner than sloppy people.

–Suzanne Britt, "Neat People vs. Sloppy People"

Strong Proposition

For the ambulatory individual, access for the mobility impaired on the University of Texas at Austin (UT) campus is easy to overlook. Automatic door entrances and bathrooms with the universal handicapped symbol make the campus seem sufficiently accessible. But for many students and faculty at UT, including me, maneuvering the UT campus in a wheelchair is a daily experience of stress and frustration. Although the university has made a concerted and continuing effort to improve access, students and faculty with physical disabilities still suffer from discriminatory hardship, unequal opportunity to succeed, and lack of independence.

The university must make campus accessibility a higher priority and take more seriously the hardship that the campus at present imposes on people with mobility impairments. Better accessibility would also benefit the numerous students and faculty with temporary disabilities and help the university recruit a more diverse body of students and faculty.

–Manasi Deshpande, student

Rhetorical Questions

Where does the universe begin? Where does it end? The universe is so immense that it is difficult to wrap our minds around the sheer magnitude of it. Yet, despite the immensity of our universe, there is only one known planet that can support life as we know it. That planet, of course, is Earth—a unique and precious sphere teeming with life, beauty, mysteries, and wonder. Unfortunately, we tend to take our valuable home for granted, for it is easy to forget just how much our actions impact the environment. Why do we ignore those who point out the negative effects of our behaviors and ask us to change our ways, especially when it comes to the issue of global warming? Evidence shows that humans are largely responsible for causing this phenomenon, yet we continue to engage in old habits that only make it worse. Global warming is a serious issue affecting everyone, and so it is up to all of us to be more aware of our actions and change our harmful behaviors in order to protect our one and only home—and us.

–Kristen Sadowski, student

On page 150 are some examples of how *not* to begin an essay. You should always *avoid* using beginnings such as these in your writing.

Beginnings to Avoid

Apology
I am a college student and do not consider myself an expert on intellectual property, but I think file sharing and movie downloads should be legal.

Complaint
I'd rather write about a topic of my own choice than the one that is assigned, but here goes.

Webster's Dictionary
Webster's New Collegiate Dictionary defines the verb *to snore* as follows: "to breathe during sleep with a rough hoarse noise due to vibration of the soft palate."

Platitude/Cliché
America is the land of opportunity, and no one knows that better than Martha Stewart.

Reference to Title
As you can see from my title, this essay is about why we should continue to experiment with embryonic stem cells.

ENDINGS

An effective ending does more than simply indicate where the writer stopped writing. A conclusion may summarize; may inspire the reader to further thought or even action; may return to the beginning by repeating key words, phrases, or ideas; or may surprise the reader by providing a particularly convincing example to support a thesis. Indeed, there are many ways to write a conclusion, but the effectiveness of any choice must be measured by how appropriately it fits what comes before it. You might consider concluding with a restatement of your thesis, with a prediction, or with a recommendation.

In an essay contrasting the traditional Hispanic understanding of the word *macho* with the meaning it has developed in mainstream American culture, Rose Del Castillo Guilbault begins her essay with a succinct, two-sentence paragraph offering her thesis:

What is *macho*? That depends which side of the border you come from.

She concludes her essay by restating her thesis, but in a manner that reflects the detailed examination she has given the concept of macho in her essay:

The impact of language in our society is undeniable. And the misuse of *macho* hints at a deeper cultural misunderstanding that extends beyond mere word definitions.

–Rose Del Castillo Guilbault, "Americanization Is Tough on 'Macho' "

In the following conclusion to her essay on global warming (you can read her introduction on p. 149), Kristen Sadowski summarizes the points she has made in her essay, ending with a clever use of figurative language to drive home her point. (See the introduction to Chapter 12, pp. 320–21, for a detailed discussion of figurative language.)

Clearly, there are numerous ways for us to reduce our greenhouse gas emissions and prevent global warming from worsening. In fact, there are so many ways that it can be overwhelming. But we do not have to change our lifestyles entirely or implement every single solution. Instead, we can be more aware of our actions and make small changes here and there until we are comfortable with our newly formed habits. Often, changing our behaviors can be the hardest thing for us to do, especially if we are content with our current way of life. By making conscious efforts to become more environmentally responsible, however, we can all be successful in our attempts to make the world a better place. One person acting alone cannot impact global warming, but individuals acting together can make a huge difference. The Earth has a fever, and we have the medicine of our actions to keep that fever at bay.

–Kristen Sadowski, student

In the following conclusion to her essay "Title IX Just Makes Sense," Jen Jarjosa offers an overview of her argument and concludes by predicting the outcome of the solution she advocates:

There have undeniably been major improvements in the treatment of female college athletes since the enactment of Title IX. But most colleges and universities still don't measure up to the actual

> regulation standards, and many have quite a ways to go. The Title IX fight for equality is not a radical feminist movement, nor is it intended to take away the privileges of male athletes. It is, rather, a demand for fairness, for women to receive the same opportunities that men have always had. When colleges and universities stop viewing Title IX budget requirements as an inconvenience and start complying with the spirit and not merely the letter of the law, collegiate female athletes will finally reach the parity they deserve.
>
> –Jen Jarjosa, student

If you are having trouble with your conclusion—which is not an uncommon occurrence—it may be because of problems with your essay itself. Frequently, writers do not know when to end because they are not sure about their overall purpose. For example, if you are taking a trip and your purpose is to go to Chicago, you will know when you get there and will stop. But if you don't really know where you are going, it's very difficult to know when to stop.

It's usually a good idea in your conclusion to avoid such overworked expressions as "In conclusion," "In summary," "I hope I have shown," or "Finally." Your conclusion should also do more than simply repeat what you've said in your opening paragraph. The most satisfying essays are those in which the conclusion provides an interesting way of wrapping up ideas introduced in the beginning and developed throughout, so that your reader has the feeling of coming full circle.

You might find it revealing as your course progresses to read with special attention the beginnings and endings of the essays throughout *Models for Writers*. Take special note of the varieties of beginnings and endings, the possible relationship between a beginning and an ending, and the general appropriateness of these elements to the writer's subject and purpose.

White Lies

■ Erin Murphy

Erin Murphy was born in New Britain, Connecticut, in 1968 and grew up in Richmond, Virginia. She earned a BA in English from Washington College in 1990 and an MFA in English and poetry from the University of Massachusetts in 1993. Murphy is author of six collections of poetry: Science of Desire *(2004);* Dislocation and Other Theories *(2008);* Too Much of This World *(2008), winner of the Anthony Piccione Poetry Prize;* Word Problems *(2011), winner of the Paterson Prize for Literary Excellence;* Distant Glitter *(2013); and* Ancilla *(2013). She is also coeditor of a poetry anthology,* Making Poems: Forty Poems with Commentary by the Poets *(2010). Other awards include a National Writers' Union Poetry Award judged by Donald Hall; a Dorothy Sargent Rosenberg Poetry Prize; a Foley Poetry Award; and fellowships from the Pennsylvania Council on the Arts, the Maryland State Arts Council, and the Virginia Center for the Creative Arts. Her poems have appeared in dozens of journals and several anthologies, including* 180 More: Extraordinary Poems for Every Day, *edited by Billy Collins. She is on the faculty at Pennsylvania State University's Altoona College, where she teaches English and creative writing.*

First published in 2010 in Brevity, *the following essay has been nominated for a Pushcart Prize. Murphy comments on her writing of the narrative and how she feels about it now: "This is a story that I carried with me for thirty years before I wrote about it. Now that I am a mother, I have a heightened awareness of the kind of bullying that is all too common in schools. When my own children came home with stories about classmates being ostracized, I thought of Connie and her candy. For decades, I've felt sympathy for Connie; from my current perspective, I also feel tremendous sympathy for her mother." Notice how Murphy captures the reader's attention in the opening paragraph.*

Reflecting on What You Know

At what point do repeated mocking comments directed at our classmates and school friends cross the line into bullying? Have you engaged in such mocking comments? Have you been bullied? Have you come to anyone's rescue who was being bullied? Explain.

Arpi, a Lebanese girl who pronounced *ask* as *ax* no matter how many times the teacher corrected her, must have been delighted by the arrival of Connie, the new girl in our fifth grade class. Connie was albino, exceptionally white even by the ultra-Caucasian standards of our southern suburb. Only her eyelids had color: mouse-nose pink, framed by moth-white lashes and brows. 1

We had been taught that there was no comparative or superlative for *different*. Things were either different or the same, the teacher said. Likewise for *perfect*—something was either perfect or not. But surely Arpi thought of Connie as *more different* than herself. Arpi may have had a name that sounded all too close to Alpo, a brand of dog food, but at least she had a family whose skin and hair and eyes looked like hers. Connie, by comparison, was alone in her difference. She was, perhaps, *most different. Differentest.* 2

This was confirmed by the ridicule, which was immediate and unrelenting: *Casper, Chalk Face, Q-Tip.* Connie, whose shoulders hunched in a permanent parenthesis, pretended not to hear the names or the taunting questions: *What'd ya do, take a bath in bleach? Who's your boyfriend—Frosty the Snowman?* She sat in the front of the classroom, and if she felt the boys plucking white hairs from her scalp, she didn't react. The teacher, who was serving the last nine months of a thirty-year sentence in the public school system, spent the bulk of each day perusing magazines and L.L. Bean catalogs in the back of the room. As far as I know, she never intervened. 3

All of this changed in mid-October when Connie's father got a job at a candy factory, news Connie announced tentatively one rainy day during indoor recess. 4

Can he get us candy? 5

Yes. 6

Any kind? As much as we want? For free? 7

Yes, yes, yes. 8

And so the daily ritual began. Kids placed orders for Reese's 9
Cups, Baby Ruth bars, Hubba-Bubba bubble gum. Connie kept a log of the requests in a pocket-sized notebook. The next day, she would tote a box full of candy into the classroom and distribute the promised sweets to eager hands. Overnight, Connie became the center of attention. Girls—even Marcia Miller, the first in our class to wear mascara—would beg to sit by Connie at lunch so they could update their orders.

And what about me? What was my role? Did I request my 10
favorites—Three Musketeers and coconut-centered Mounds bars? Or did I, as I have told myself and others in the years since, refuse to contribute to such cruelty? Or, in a more likely scenario, did I dump out my loot triumphantly at home one afternoon, only to be scolded by my mother? I don't remember, my memory obscured, I'm sure, by the wishful image of myself as a precocious champion of social justice. And I don't remember if I actually witnessed—or just imagined—Connie and her mother at the 7-Eleven one day after school. They were in the candy aisle. Her mother was filling a cardboard box. And Connie, bathed in unflinching fluorescence, was curved over her notebook making small, careful check marks.

Thinking Critically about This Reading

In her essay, Murphy introduces an interesting technique for an essay writer. Murphy explains:

> This essay hinges on the use of what the writer Lisa Knopp calls "perhapsing." Sometimes when we're writing, we can't recall the exact details of our experiences. In this case, we can "perhaps" or speculate about what actually happened. In the final paragraph of "White Lies," I speculate about whether I saw or dreamt about Connie and her mother in the convenience store. The result of this rhetorical strategy is two-fold: it establishes me as a reliable narrator and allows me to question my own motives in "re-membering" (as in the opposite of "dismembering") the past.

How well does this strategy work for Murphy in her final paragraph? Explain.

Questions for Study and Discussion

1. Murphy's story is brief, but how well does she satisfy the five essential features of good narration—a clear context; well-chosen details; a logical, often chronological organization; an appropriate and consistent point of view; and a meaningful point or purpose? Explain.
2. What point does Murphy make about the lack of comparative and superlative forms for some adjectives? Does reality support the grammatical rule? Explain.
3. Explain Murphy's ending. Do you think you know what Murphy's "role" was? On what evidence do you base your opinion?
4. What is Murphy's attitude toward Connie's classroom teacher? Why does she include information about her? (Glossary: *Attitude*)
5. What is the point of Murphy's story?
6. In the story, is Connie's mother a hero, or is she someone whose actions are ethically questionable, even wrong? Explain.
7. Assuming that the events in the convenience store actually took place, what motivates Connie's mother's actions? If you had been Connie's mother, what would you have done in her situation?

Classroom Activity Using Beginnings and Endings

Carefully read the following three possible beginnings for an essay on the world's most famous practical joker, Hugh Troy. What are the advantages and disadvantages of each? Which one would you select as an opening paragraph? Why?

> Whether questioning the values of American society or simply relieving the monotony of daily life, Hugh Troy always managed to put a little of himself into each of his stunts. One day he attached a plaster hand to his shirt sleeve and took a trip through the Holland Tunnel. As he approached the tollbooth, with his toll ticket between the fingers of the artificial hand, Troy left both ticket and hand in the grasp of the stunned tollbooth attendant and sped away.

> Nothing seemed unusual. In fact, it was a rather common occurrence in New York City. Five men dressed in overalls roped off a section of busy Fifth Avenue in front of the old Rockefeller residence, hung out MEN WORKING signs, and began ripping up the

pavement. By the time they stopped for lunch, they had dug quite a hole in the street. This crew was different, however, from all the others that had descended upon the streets of the city. It was led by Hugh Troy—the world's greatest practical joker.

Hugh Troy was born in Ithaca, New York, where his father was a professor at Cornell University. After graduating from Cornell, Troy left for New York City, where he became a successful illustrator of children's books. When World War II broke out, he went into the army and eventually became a captain in the 21st Bomber Command, 20th Air Force, under General Curtis LeMay. After the war he made his home in Garrison, New York, for a short while before finally settling in Washington, D.C., where he lived until his death.

Suggested Writing Assignments

1. Retell the story of "White Lies" from either Connie's or her mother's point of view, or tell of a similar situation drawn from your own experiences as a schoolchild. Where does your story begin? What information do you need to tell it? What information might you have to supply by using the "perhapsing" strategy Murphy employs at the end of her essay? Murphy's theme is one of prejudice and marginalization, so if you are telling a story from your childhood, you might want to base your narrative on a similar situation in which you felt isolated and powerless, or perhaps one in which you were responsible for making someone else feel like an outsider.
2. Write a brief essay in which you tell of a time one or both of your parents came to your rescue when you thought yourself to be in a tight spot. Did they intervene in answer to your request for help, or did they simply see that you were in need? Were you thankful for your parents' help, or did their involvement make the situation worse? How did the "rescue" work out? Consider how you will begin and end your essay. Look back at pages 144–52 to remind yourself of some of the possible ways you might choose to begin and end your essay.

The Case for Short Words

■ **Richard Lederer**

Courtesy of Richard Lederer

Born in 1938, Richard Lederer holds degrees from Haverford College, Harvard University, and the University of New Hampshire. He has been a prolific and popular writer about language and is the author of more than 40 books about language, history, and humor, including his best-selling Anguished English *series. He frequently appears on radio as a commentator on language, and his column, "Lederer on Language," appears in newspapers and magazines throughout the United States. Dr. Lederer has been named International Punster of the Year and Toastmasters International's Golden Gavel winner.*

In the following essay, taken from The Miracle of Language *(1999), pay attention to the strong proposition with which Lederer begins. He returns at the end to this proposition, which he expects might contradict what readers have assumed or have been taught about what makes good writing.*

Reflecting on What You Know

We all carry with us a vocabulary of short, simple-looking words that possess a special personal meaning. For example, to some the word *rose* represents not just a flower but a whole array of gardens, ceremonies, and romantic occasions. What little words have special meaning for you? What images do they bring to mind?

When you speak and write, there is no law that says you have to use big words. Short words are as good as long ones, and short, old words—like *sun* and *grass* and *home*—are best of all. A lot of small words, more than you might think, can meet your needs with a strength, grace, and charm that large words do not have. 1

Big words can make the way dark for those who read what you write and hear what you say. Small words cast their clear light on big things—night and day, love and hate, war and peace, and life and death. Big words at times seem strange to the eye and the ear and the mind and the heart. Small words are the ones we seem to have known from the time we were born, like the hearth fire that warms the home. 2

Short words are bright like sparks that glow in the night, prompt like the dawn that greets the day, sharp like the blade of a knife, hot like salt tears that scald the cheek, quick like moths that flit from flame to flame, and terse like the dart and sting of a bee. 3

Here is a sound rule: Use small, old words where you can. If a long word says just what you want to say, do not fear to use it. But know that our tongue is rich in crisp, brisk, swift, short words. Make them the spine and the heart of what you speak and write. Short words are like fast friends. They will not let you down. 4

The title of this [essay] and the four paragraphs that you have just read are wrought entirely of words of one syllable. In setting myself this task, I did not feel especially cabined, cribbed, or confined. In fact, the structure helped me to focus on the power of the message I was trying to put across. 5

One study shows that twenty words account for twenty-five percent of all spoken English words, and all twenty are monosyllabic. In order of frequency they are: *I, you, the, a, to, is, it, that, of, and, in, what, he, this, have, do, she, not, on,* and *they.* Other studies indicate that the fifty most common words in written English are each made of a single syllable. 6

For centuries our finest poets and orators have recognized and employed the power of small words to make a straight point between two minds. A great many of our proverbs punch home their points with pithy monosyllables: "Where there's a will, there's a way," "A stitch in time saves nine," "Spare the rod and spoil the child," "A bird in the hand is worth two in the bush." 7

Nobody used the short word more skillfully than William Shakespeare, whose dying King Lear laments: 8

> And my poor fool is hang'd! No, no, no life!
> Why should a dog, a horse, a rat have life,
> And thou no breath at all? . . .
> Do you see this? Look on her, look, her lips.
> Look there, look there!

Shakespeare's contemporaries made the King James Bible a centerpiece of short words—"And God said, Let there be light: and there was light. And God saw the light, that it was good." The descendants of such mighty lines live on in the twentieth century. When asked to explain his policy to Parliament, Winston Churchill[1] responded with these ringing monosyllables: "I will say: it is to wage war, by sea, land, and air, with all our might and with all the strength that God can give us." In his "Death of the Hired Man" Robert Frost[2] observes that "Home is the place where, when you have to go there, / They have to take you in." And William H. Johnson[3] uses ten two-letter words to explain his secret of success: "If it is to be, / It is up to me." 9

You don't have to be a great author, statesman, or philosopher to tap the energy and eloquence of small words. Each winter I ask my ninth graders at St. Paul's School to write a composition composed entirely of one-syllable words. My students greet my request with obligatory moans and groans, but, when they return to class with their essays, most feel that, with the pressure to produce high-sounding polysyllables relieved, they have created some of their most powerful and luminous prose. Here are submissions from two of my ninth graders: 10

> What can you say to a boy who has left home? You can say that he has done wrong, but he does not care. He has left home so that he will not have to deal with what you say. He wants to go as far as he can. He will do what he wants to do.
>
> This boy does not want to be forced to go to church, to comb his hair, or to be on time. A good time for this boy does not lie in your reach, for what you have he does not want. He dreams of ripped jeans, shorts with no starch, and old socks.
>
> So now this boy is on a bus to a place he dreams of, a place with no rules. This boy now walks a strange street, his long hair blown back by the wind. He wears no coat or tie, just jeans and an old shirt. He hates your world, and he has left it.
>
> –Charles Shaffer

> For a long time we cruised by the coast and at last came to a wide bay past the curve of a hill, at the end of which lay a small town. Our long boat ride at an end, we all stretched and stood up to watch as the boat nosed its way in.

---

[1] *Winston Churchill* (1874–1965): British orator, author, and statesman.
[2] *Robert Frost* (1874–1963): American poet.
[3] *William H. Johnson* (1771–1834): associate justice of the U.S. Supreme Court, 1804–1834.

> The town climbed up the hill that rose from the shore, a space in front of it left bare for the port. Each house was a clean white with sky blue or gray trim; in front of each one was a small yard, edged by a white stone wall strewn with green vines.
>
> As the town basked in the heat of noon, not a thing stirred in the streets or by the shore. The sun beat down on the sea, the land, and the back of our necks, so that, in spite of the breeze that made the vines sway, we all wished we could hide from the glare in a cool, white house. But, as there was no one to help dock the boat, we had to stand and wait.
>
> At last the head of the crew leaped from the side and strode to a large house on the right. He shoved the door wide, poked his head through the gloom, and roared with a fierce voice. Five or six men came out, and soon the port was loud with the clank of chains and creak of planks as the men caught ropes thrown by the crew, pulled them taut, and tied them to posts. Then they set up a rough plank so we could cross from the deck to the shore. We all made for the large house while the crew watched, glad to be rid of us.
>
> –Celia Wren

You too can tap into the vitality and vigor of compact expression. Take a suggestion from the highway department. At the boundaries of your speech and prose place a sign that reads "Caution: Small Words at Work." 11

Thinking Critically about This Reading

In his opening paragraph, Lederer states that "short, old words—like *sun* and *grass* and *home*—are best of all." What attributes make these words the "best"? Does this claim surprise you by running counter to what we've always heard about "big words" and a large vocabulary?

Questions for Study and Discussion

1. In this essay, written to encourage the use of short words, Lederer himself employs many polysyllabic words in paragraphs 5–11. What is his purpose in doing so? (Glossary: *Purpose*)
2. Lederer quotes a variety of passages to illustrate the effectiveness of short words. For example, he quotes from famous, universally familiar sources, such as Shakespeare and the King James Bible, as well as his own ninth-grade students. How does the variety of

his illustrations serve to inform his readers? How does each example gain impact from the inclusion of the others?

3. To make clear to the reader why short words are effective, Lederer relies heavily on metaphors and similes, especially in the first four paragraphs. (Glossary: *Figure of Speech*) Choose at least one metaphor and one simile from these paragraphs, and explain the comparison implicit in each.
4. In paragraph 10, Lederer refers to the relief his students feel when released from "the pressure to produce high-sounding polysyllables." Where does this pressure come from? How does it relate to the central purpose of this essay?
5. How does the final paragraph serve to close the essay effectively? (Glossary: *Beginnings and Endings*)
6. This essay abounds with examples of striking sentences and passages consisting entirely of one-syllable words. Choose four of the single-sentence examples or a section of several sentences from one of the longer examples, and rewrite them, using primarily words of two or more syllables. Notice how each revision differs from the original.

Classroom Activity Using Beginnings and Endings

Write the first four paragraphs of an essay that begins with an opposite proposition: "When you speak and write, there is no law that says you have to use small words." As you write, incorporate as many polysyllabic words as you can. Then compare your paragraphs with the opening of "The Case for Short Words." In what ways do they feel different? Do they prove Lederer's point?

Suggested Writing Assignments

1. Follow the assignment Lederer gives his own students, and write a composition composed entirely of one-syllable words. Make your piece approximately the length of his student examples or of his own four-paragraph opening.
2. Write a persuasive essay attempting to convince readers to give up a widely held belief. Using Lederer's essay as a model, state your argument directly in the first paragraph, and use the final paragraph to reiterate the value of your proposition.

Shame

Dick Gregory

Ethan Miller/Getty Images

Dick Gregory—activist, comedian, and nutrition expert—was born in St. Louis, Missouri, in 1932. While attending Southern Illinois University on an athletic scholarship, Gregory excelled in track, winning the university's Outstanding Athlete Award in 1953. In 1954, he was drafted into the army. After his discharge, he immediately became active in the civil rights movement led by Martin Luther King Jr. In the 1960s, Gregory was an outspoken critic of U.S. involvement in Vietnam, which in turn led to his run for the presidency in 1968 as a write-in candidate for the Freedom and Peace Party. Two of his books from this era are No More Lies: The Myth and Reality of American History *(1971) and* Dick Gregory's Political Primer *(1972). Throughout his life he has crusaded for economic reforms and minority rights, and spoken out on antidrug issues. In 2000, he published* Callus on My Soul, *the second volume of his autobiography. In recent years, Gregory has been active in the diet and health-food industry.*

In the following episode from Nigger *(1964), the first volume of his autobiography, Gregory narrates the story of a childhood experience that taught him the meaning of shame. Through his use of dialogue, he dramatically re-creates the experience for readers. Notice how he begins this essay in the shelter of home and ends with the feeling that his lesson in shame exposes him to the eyes of "the whole world."*

Reflecting on What You Know

We all learn many things in school beyond the lessons we study formally. Some of the extracurricular truths we learn stay with us for the rest of our lives. Write about something you learned in school—something that has made life easier or more understandable for you—that you still find useful.

I never learned hate at home, or shame. I had to go to school for that. I was about seven years old when I got my first big lesson. I was in love with a little girl named Helene Tucker, a light-complexioned little girl with pigtails and nice manners. She was always clean and she was smart in school. I think I went to school then mostly to look at her. I brushed my hair and even got me a little old handkerchief. It was a lady's handkerchief, but I didn't want Helene to see me wipe my nose on my hand. The pipes were frozen again, there was no water in the house, but I washed my socks and shirt every night. I'd get a pot, and go over to Mister Ben's grocery store, and stick my pot down into his soda machine. Scoop out some chopped ice. By evening the ice melted to water for washing. I got sick a lot that winter because the fire would go out at night before the clothes were dry. In the morning I'd put them on, wet or dry, because they were the only clothes I had. 1

Everybody's got a Helene Tucker, a symbol of everything you want. I loved her for her goodness, her cleanness, her popularity. She'd walk down my street and my brothers and sisters would yell, "Here comes Helene," and I'd rub my tennis sneakers on the back of my pants and wish my hair wasn't so nappy[1] and the white folks' shirt fit me better. I'd run out on the street. If I knew my place and didn't come too close, she'd wink at me and say hello. That was a good feeling. Sometimes I'd follow her all the way home, and shovel the snow off her walk and try to make friends with her Momma and her aunts. I'd drop money on her stoop late at night on my way back from shining shoes in the taverns. And she had a Daddy, and he had a good job. He was a paper hanger. 2

I guess I would have gotten over Helene by summertime, but something happened in that classroom that made her face hang in front of me for the next twenty-two years. When I played the drums in high school it was for Helene and when I broke track records in college it was for Helene and when I started standing behind microphones and heard applause I wished Helene could hear it, too. It wasn't until I was twenty-nine years old and married and making money that I finally got her out of my system. Helene was sitting in that classroom when I learned to be ashamed of myself. 3

It was on a Thursday. I was sitting in the back of the room, in a seat with a chalk circle drawn around it. The idiot's seat, the troublemaker's seat. 4

---

[1]*nappy:* shaggy or fuzzy.

The teacher thought I was stupid. Couldn't spell, couldn't read, 5
couldn't do arithmetic. Just stupid. Teachers were never interested in finding out that you couldn't concentrate because you were so hungry, because you hadn't had any breakfast. All you could think about was noontime, would it ever come? Maybe you could sneak into the cloakroom and steal a bite of some kid's lunch out of a coat pocket. A bite of something. Paste. You can't really make a meal of paste, or put it on bread for a sandwich, but sometimes I'd scoop a few spoonfuls out of the paste jar in the back of the room. Pregnant people get strange tastes. I was pregnant with poverty. Pregnant with dirt and pregnant with smells that made people turn away, pregnant with cold and pregnant with shoes that were never bought for me, pregnant with five other people in my bed and no Daddy in the next room, and pregnant with hunger. Paste doesn't taste too bad when you're hungry.

The teacher thought I was a troublemaker. All she saw from the 6
front of the room was a little black boy who squirmed in his idiot's seat and made noises and poked the kids around him. I guess she couldn't see a kid who made noises because he wanted someone to know he was there.

It was on a Thursday, the day before the Negro payday. The eagle 7
always flew on Friday. The teacher was asking each student how much his father would give to the Community Chest. On Friday night, each kid would get the money from his father, and on Monday he would bring it to the school. I decided I was going to buy me a Daddy right then. I had money in my pocket from shining shoes and selling papers, and whatever Helene Tucker pledged for her Daddy I was going to top it. And I'd hand the money right in. I wasn't going to wait until Monday to buy me a Daddy.

I was shaking, scared to death. The teacher opened her book and 8
started calling out names alphabetically.

"Helene Tucker?" 9

"My daddy said he'd give two dollars and fifty cents." 10

"That's very nice, Helene. Very, very nice indeed." 11

That made me feel pretty good. It wouldn't take too much to top 12
that. I had almost three dollars in dimes and quarters in my pocket. I stuck my hand in my pocket and held onto the money, waiting for her to call my name. But the teacher closed her book after she called everybody else in the class.

I stood up and raised my hand. 13

"What is it now?" 14

"You forgot me." 15

She turned toward the blackboard. "I don't have time to be play- 16
ing with you, Richard."

"My Daddy said he'd . . ." 17

"Sit down, Richard, you're disturbing the class." 18

"My Daddy said he'd give . . . fifteen dollars." 19

She turned around and looked mad. "We are collecting this 20
money for you and your kind, Richard Gregory. If your Daddy can give fifteen dollars you have no business being on relief."

"I got it right now, I got it right now, my Daddy gave it to me to 21
turn in today, my Daddy said . . ."

"And furthermore," she said, looking right at me, her nostrils get- 22
ting big and her lips getting thin and her eyes opening wide, "we know you don't have a Daddy."

Helene Tucker turned around, her eyes full of tears. She felt sorry 23
for me. Then I couldn't see her too well because I was crying, too.

"Sit down, Richard." 24

And I always thought the teacher kind of liked me. She always 25
picked me to wash the blackboard on Friday, after school. That was a big thrill, it made me feel important. If I didn't wash it, come Monday the school might not function right.

"Where are you going, Richard?" 26

I walked out of school that day, and for a long time I didn't go 27
back very often. There was shame there.

Now there was shame everywhere. It seemed like the whole world 28
had been inside that classroom, everyone had heard what the teacher had said, everyone had turned around and felt sorry for me. There was shame in going to the Worthy Boys Annual Christmas Dinner for you and your kind, because everybody knew what a worthy boy was. Why couldn't they just call it the Boys Annual Dinner; why'd they have to give it a name? There was shame in wearing the brown and orange and white plaid mackinaw[2] the welfare gave to three thousand boys. Why'd it have to be the same for everybody so when you walked down the street the people could see you were on relief? It was a nice warm mackinaw and it had a hood, and my Momma beat me and called me a little rat when she found out I stuffed it in the bottom of a pail full of garbage way over on Cottage Street. There was shame in running over to Mister Ben's at the end of the day and asking for his rotten peaches, there was

[2]*mackinaw:* a short, double-breasted wool coat.

shame in asking Mrs. Simmons for a spoonful of sugar, there was shame in running out to meet the relief truck. I hated that truck, full of food for you and your kind. I ran into the house and hid when it came. And then I started to sneak through alleys, to take the long way home so the people going into White's Eat Shop wouldn't see me. Yeah, the whole world heard the teacher that day, we all know you don't have a Daddy.

Thinking Critically about This Reading

In paragraph 28, Gregory states, "Now there was shame everywhere. It seemed like the whole world had been inside that classroom, everyone had heard what the teacher had said, everyone had turned around and felt sorry for me." What did Gregory's teacher say, and why did it hurt him so greatly?

Questions for Study and Discussion

1. How do the first three paragraphs of the essay help establish a context for the narrative that follows? (Glossary: *Narration*)
2. What does Gregory mean by "shame"? What precisely was he ashamed of, and what in particular did he learn from the incident? (Glossary: *Definition*)
3. In a word or phrase, how would you describe Gregory's tone? (Glossary: *Tone*) What specific words or phrases in his essay lead you to this conclusion?
4. What is the teacher's attitude toward Gregory? In arriving at your answer, consider her own words and actions as well as Gregory's opinion.
5. What role does money play in Gregory's experience? How does money relate to his sense of shame?
6. Specific details can enhance the reader's understanding and appreciation of a subject. (Glossary: *Details*) Gregory's description of Helene Tucker's manners or the plaid of his mackinaw, for example, makes his account vivid and interesting. Cite several other specific details he gives, and consider how the essay would be different without them.
7. Reread this essay's first and last paragraphs, and compare how much each one emphasizes shame. (Glossary: *Beginnings and Endings*) Which emotion other than shame does Gregory reveal

in the first paragraph, and does it play a role in the last one? Is the last paragraph an effective ending? Explain.

Classroom Activity Using Beginnings and Endings

Gregory begins his essay with a startling claim: that at school he learned about shame. Pick two from among the eight other methods for beginning essays discussed in the introduction to this chapter, and use them to write alternative openings for Gregory's essay. Share your beginnings with others in the class, and discuss their effectiveness.

Suggested Writing Assignments

1. Using Gregory's essay as a model, write an essay narrating an experience that made you feel especially afraid, angry, surprised, embarrassed, or proud. Include details that allow your readers to know exactly what happened. Pay attention to how you use your first and last paragraphs to present the emotion your essay focuses on.
2. Most of us grow up with some sense of the socioeconomic class that our family belongs to, and often we are aware of how we are, or believe we are, different from people of other classes. Write an essay in which you describe a possession or an activity that you thought revealed your socioeconomic standing and made you self-conscious about how you were different from others. Using Gregory's essay as a model, let your first and last paragraphs dramatize this realization by showing how your self-consciousness changed as you understood how others viewed you.

CHAPTER **7**

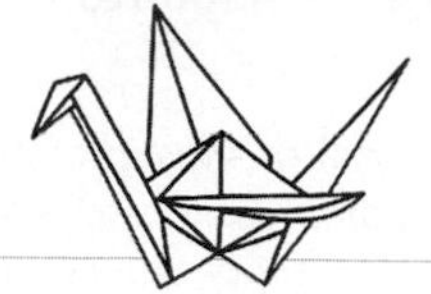

Paragraphs

Within an essay, the **paragraph** is the most important unit of thought. Like the essay, it has its own main idea, often stated directly in a topic sentence. Like a good essay, a good paragraph is unified: it avoids digressions and develops its main idea. Paragraphs use many of the rhetorical strategies that essays use—strategies like classification, comparison and contrast, and cause and effect. As you read the following three paragraphs, notice how each writer develops his or her topic sentence with explanations, concrete details and statistics, or vivid examples. The topic sentence in each paragraph is italicized.

> *Happiness is a slippery concept, a bundle of meanings with no precise, stable definition.* Lots of thinkers have taken a shot at it. "Happiness is when what you think, what you say, and what you do are in harmony," proposed Gandhi. Abraham Lincoln argued "most people are about as happy as they make up their minds to be." Snoopy, the beagle-philosopher in *Peanuts*, took what was to my mind the most precise stab at the underlying epistemological problem. "My life has no purpose, no direction, no aim, no meaning, and yet I'm happy. I can't figure it out. What am I doing right?"
>
> –Eduardo Porter, "What Happiness Is," p. 459

> The problem of substance abuse is far more complex and far more pervasive than any of us really knows or is willing to admit. *Most stories of illegal drugs overshadow Americans' struggles with alcohol, tobacco, food, and nonprescription drugs—our so-called legal addictions.* In 2000, for example, 17,000 deaths were attributed to cocaine and heroin. In that same year, 435,000 deaths were attributed to tobacco and 85,000 to alcohol. It's not surprising, then, that many sociologists believe we are a nation of substance abusers—drinkers, smokers, overeaters, and pill poppers. Although the statistics are alarming, they do not begin to suggest the heavy

toll of substance abuse on Americans and their families. Loved ones die, relationships are fractured, children are abandoned, job productivity falters, and the dreams of young people are extinguished.

–Alfred Rosa and Paul Eschholz

Photographs have let me know my parents before I was born, as the carefree college students they were, in love and awaiting the rest of their lives. I have seen the light blue Volkswagen van my dad used to take surfing down the coast of California and the silver dress my mom wore to her senior prom. Through pictures I was able to witness their wedding, which showed me that there is much in their relationship that goes beyond their children. I saw the look in their eyes as they held their first, newborn daughter, as well as the jealous expressions of my sister when I was born a few years later. There is something almost magical about viewing images of yourself and your family that you were too young to remember.

–Carrie White, student

Many writers find it helpful to think of the paragraph as a very small, compact essay. Here is a paragraph from Martin Luther King Jr.'s essay "The Ways of Meeting Oppression" (pp. 467–70).

Violence as a way of achieving racial justice is both impractical and immoral. It is impractical because it is a descending spiral ending in destruction for all. The old law of an eye for an eye leaves everybody blind. It is immoral because it seeks to humiliate the opponent rather than win his understanding; it seeks to annihilate rather than to convert. Violence is immoral because it thrives on hatred rather than love. It destroys community and makes brotherhood impossible. It leaves society in monologue rather than dialogue. Violence ends by defeating itself. It creates bitterness in the survivors and brutality in the destroyers. A voice echoes through time saying to every potential Peter, "Put up your sword." History is cluttered with the wreckage of nations that failed to follow this command.

This paragraph, like all well-written paragraphs, has several distinguishing characteristics: it is unified, coherent, and adequately developed. It is unified in that every sentence and every idea relates to the main idea, stated in the topic sentence, "Violence as a way of achieving racial justice is both impractical and immoral." It is coherent in that the sentences and ideas are arranged logically, and the relationships among them are made clear by the use of effective transitions. Finally, the paragraph is adequately developed in that it presents a short but persuasive argument supporting its main idea.

How much development is "adequate" development? The answer depends on many things—how complicated or controversial the main idea is, what readers already know and believe, how much space the writer is permitted. Nearly everyone agrees that the Earth circles around the sun; a single sentence would be enough to make that point. A writer arguing that affirmative action has outlived its usefulness, however, would need many sentences—indeed, many paragraphs—to develop that idea convincingly.

Here is another model of an effective paragraph. As you read this paragraph about the sport of roller derby, pay attention to its main idea, unity, development, and coherence.

> Roller derby marries an underground vibe with the fun of athletic competition in a blend of sport and spectacle that is as much fun to play as it is to watch. Teams compete on a small flat or banked track. Each team has four blockers and one jammer. Everyone skates around the track in a series of two-minute "jams," trying to get their team's jammer through the opposing pack of blockers, while holding the other team's jammer back. Once through the pack, the jammers skate quickly around the track, earning points for each opposing player they lap. At the end of each jam, new skaters get on the track and a new jam begins. Games last for around sixty minutes, divided into two or three periods. Unlike in the old days of derby, today you usually earn a penalty for throwing elbows and get ejected for fighting.
>
> –Diane "Lady Hulk" Williams, "Revolution on Eight Wheels," p. 140

The main idea is stated at the beginning in a topic sentence. Other sentences in the paragraph support this idea with examples. Because all the separate examples illustrate how the sport is played and offer a sense of how exciting it is to watch, the paragraph is unified. Because there are enough examples to convince the reader of the truth of the topic statement, the paragraph is adequately developed. Finally, the use of transitional words and phrases like *once, at the end,* and *unlike* lends the paragraph coherence.

How long should a paragraph be? In modern essays, most paragraphs range from 50 to 250 words, but some run a full printed page or more, and others may be only a few words long. The best answer is that a paragraph should be long enough to develop its main idea adequately. When some writers find a paragraph running very long, they break it into two or more paragraphs so that readers can pause and catch their breath. Other writers forge ahead, relying on the unity and coherence of their paragraph to keep their readers from getting lost.

Articles and essays that appear in magazines and newspapers (especially online versions) often have relatively short paragraphs, some of only one or two sentences. Short paragraphs are a convention in journalism because of the narrow columns, which make paragraphs of average length appear very long. But often you will find that these journalistic paragraphs could be joined together into a few longer paragraphs. Longer, adequately developed paragraphs are the kind you should use in all but journalistic writing.

Simplicity

■ William Zinsser

Courtesy of William Zinsser

William Zinsser was born in New York City in 1922. After graduating from Princeton University, he worked for the New York Herald Tribune, *first as a feature writer and later as its drama editor and film critic. During the 1970s, he taught writing at Yale University. A former executive editor of the Book-of-the-Month Club, Zinsser has also served on the Usage Panel of the* American Heritage Dictionary. *He has taught at the New School and Columbia University, and he continues to write and teach in New York. Zinsser's published works cover many aspects of contemporary American culture, but he is best known as the author of lucid and accessible books about writing, including* Writing to Learn *(1988);* Inventing the Truth: The Art and Craft of Memoir *(1998, with Russell Baker and Jill Ker Conway);* Writing about Your Life: A Journey into the Past *(2005);* On Writing Well, *a perennial favorite for college writing courses, published in a thirtieth anniversary edition in 2006; and* Writing Places: The Life Journey of a Writer and Teacher *(2009). His latest book,* The Writer Who Stayed *(2012), is a collection of essays adapted from his award-winning series for the* American Scholar, *"Zinsser on Friday."*

In the following piece from On Writing Well, *Zinsser reminds us, as did Henry David Thoreau before him, to "simplify, simplify." As you read each paragraph, notice the clarity with which Zinsser presents its main idea, and observe how he develops that idea with adequate and logically related supporting information. You should also notice that he follows his own advice about simplicity.*

Reflecting on What You Know

Sometimes we get so caught up in what's going on around us that we start to feel frantic, and we lose sight of what is really important or meaningful to us. At such times, it's a good idea to take stock of what we are doing and to simplify our lives by dropping activities that are no longer rewarding. Write about a time when you've felt the need to simplify your life.

Clutter is the disease of American writing. We are a society strangling in unnecessary words, circular constructions, pompous frills, and meaningless jargon. 1

Who can understand the clotted language of everyday American commerce: the memo, the corporation report, the business letter, the notice from the bank explaining its latest "simplified" statement? What member of an insurance or medical plan can decipher the brochure explaining his costs and benefits? What father or mother can put together a child's toy from the instructions on the box? Our national tendency is to inflate and thereby sound important. The airline pilot who announces that he is presently anticipating experiencing considerable precipitation wouldn't think of saying it may rain. The sentence is too simple—there must be something wrong with it. 2

But the secret of good writing is to strip every sentence to its cleanest components. Every word that serves no function, every long word that could be a short word, every adverb that carries the same meaning that's already in the verb, every passive construction that leaves the reader unsure of who is doing what—these are the thousand and one adulterants[1] that weaken the strength of a sentence. And they usually occur in proportion to education and rank. 3

During the 1960s the president of my university wrote a letter to mollify[2] the alumni after a spell of campus unrest. "You are probably aware," he began, "that we have been experiencing very considerable potentially explosive expressions of dissatisfaction on issues only partially related." He meant the students had been hassling them about different things. I was far more upset by the president's English than by the students' potentially explosive expressions of dissatisfaction. I would have preferred the presidential approach taken by Franklin D. Roosevelt when he tried to convert into English his own government's memos, such as this blackout order of 1942: 4

> Such preparations shall be made as will completely obscure all Federal buildings and non-Federal buildings occupied by the Federal government during an air raid for any period of time from visibility by reason of internal or external illumination.

[1]*adulterants:* unnecessary ingredients that taint the purity of something.
[2]*mollify:* to soothe in temper; appease.

"Tell them," Roosevelt said, "that in buildings where they have to keep the work going to put something across the windows." 5

Simplify, simplify. Thoreau[3] said it, as we are so often reminded, and no American writer more consistently practiced what he preached. Open *Walden* to any page and you will find a man saying in a plain and orderly way what is on his mind: 6

> I went to the woods because I wished to live deliberately, to front only the essential facts of life, and see if I could not learn what it had to teach, and not, when I came to die, discover that I had not lived.

How can the rest of us achieve such enviable freedom from clutter? The answer is to clear our heads of clutter. Clear thinking becomes clear writing; one can't exist without the other. It's impossible for a muddy thinker to write good English. He may get away with it for a paragraph or two, but soon the reader will be lost, and there's no sin so grave, for the reader will not easily be lured back. 7

Who is this elusive creature, the reader? The reader is someone with an attention span of about 30 seconds—a person assailed by many forces competing for attention. At one time those forces were relatively few: newspapers, magazines, radio, spouse, children, pets. Today they also include a galaxy of electronic devices for receiving entertainment and information—television, VCRs, DVDs, CDs, video games, the Internet, e-mail, cell phones, BlackBerries, iPods—as well as a fitness program, a pool, a lawn, and that most potent of competitors, sleep. The man or woman snoozing in a chair with a magazine or a book is a person who was being given too much unnecessary trouble by the writer. 8

It won't do to say that the reader is too dumb or too lazy to keep pace with the train of thought. If the reader is lost, it's usually because the writer hasn't been careful enough. The carelessness can take any number of forms. Perhaps a sentence is so excessively cluttered that the reader, hacking through the verbiage, simply doesn't know what it means. Perhaps a sentence has been so shoddily constructed that the reader could read it in several ways. Perhaps the writer has switched pronouns in midsentence, or has switched tenses, so the reader loses track of who is talking or when the action took place. Perhaps 9

[3]*Henry David Thoreau* (1817–1862): American essayist, poet, and philosopher activist. *Walden*, his masterwork, was published in 1854.

Sentence B is not a logical sequel to Sentence A; the writer, in whose head the connection is clear, hasn't bothered to provide the missing link. Perhaps the writer has used a word incorrectly by not taking the trouble to look it up.

Faced with such obstacles, readers are at first tenacious. They blame themselves—they obviously missed something, and they go back over the mystifying sentence, or over the whole paragraph, piecing it out like an ancient rune, making guesses and moving on. But they won't do that for long. The writer is making them work too hard, and they will look for one who is better at the craft. 10

Writers must therefore constantly ask: what am I trying to say? Surprisingly often they don't know. Then they must look at what they have written and ask: have I said it? Is it clear to someone encountering the subject for the first time? If it's not, some fuzz has worked its way into the machinery. The clear writer is someone clearheaded enough to see this stuff for what it is: fuzz. 11

I don't mean that some people are born clearheaded and are therefore natural writers, whereas others are naturally fuzzy and will never write well. Thinking clearly is a conscious act that writers must force on themselves, as if they were working on any other project that requires logic: making a shopping list or doing an algebra problem. Good writing doesn't come naturally, though most people seem to think it does. Professional writers are constantly bearded[4] by people who say they'd like to "try a little writing sometime"—meaning when they retire from their real profession, like insurance or real estate, which is hard. Or they say, "I could write a book about that." I doubt it. 12

Writing is hard work. A clear sentence is no accident. Very few sentences come out right the first time, or even the third time. Remember this in moments of despair. If you find that writing is hard, it's because it *is* hard. 13

Thinking Critically about This Reading

How does Zinsser support his claim that "we are a society strangling in unnecessary words, circular constructions, pompous frills, and meaningless jargon" (paragraph 1)? What are the implications of his claim for writers in general and for you in particular?

[4]*bearded:* confronted boldly.

Questions for Study and Discussion

1. What exactly does Zinsser mean by "clutter" (1)? How does he believe we can free ourselves of clutter?
2. Identify the main idea in each of the thirteen paragraphs. How is each paragraph related to Zinsser's topic and purpose?
3. In what ways do paragraphs 4–6 serve to illustrate the main idea of paragraph 3? (Glossary: *Illustration*)
4. In paragraph 11, Zinsser says that writers must constantly ask themselves some questions. What are these questions, and why are they important?
5. How do Zinsser's first and last paragraphs serve to introduce and conclude his essay? (Glossary: *Beginnings and Endings*)
6. What is the relationship between thinking and writing for Zinsser?

Classroom Activity Using Paragraphs

What follows is a passage from the final read-through manuscript of this chapter from the first edition of *On Writing Well.* Zinsser has included manuscript pages showing his editing for clutter in every edition of his book because he believes they are instructive. He says, "Although they look like a first draft, they had already been rewritten and retyped—like almost every other page—four or five times. With each rewrite I try to make what I have written tighter, stronger, and more precise, eliminating every element that's not doing useful work. Then I go over it once more, reading it aloud, and am always amazed at how much clutter can still be cut. (In later editions I eliminated the sexist pronoun 'he' denoting 'the writer' and 'the reader.')"

Carefully study these manuscript pages and Zinsser's editing, and be prepared to discuss how the changes enhance his paragraphs' unity, coherence, and logical development.

is too dumb or too lazy to keep pace with the ~~writer's~~ train of thought. My sympathies are ~~entirely~~ with him. ~~He's not so dumb.~~ If the reader is lost, it is generally because the writer ~~of the article~~ has not been careful enough to keep him on the ~~proper~~ path.

This carelessness can take any number of ~~different~~ forms. Perhaps a sentence is so excessively ~~long and~~ cluttered that the reader, hacking his way through ~~all~~ the verbiage, simply doesn't know what it ~~the writer~~ means. Perhaps a sentence has been so shoddily constructed that the reader could read it in any of several ~~two or three different~~ ways. ~~He thinks he knows what the writer is trying to say, but he's not sure.~~ Perhaps the writer has switched pronouns in midsentence, or ~~perhaps he~~ has switched tenses, so the reader loses track of who is talking ~~to whom~~ or ~~exactly~~ when the action took place. Perhaps Sentence B is not a logical sequel to Sentence A -- the writer, in whose head the connection is ~~perfectly~~ clear, has not bothered to provide ~~given enough thought to providing~~ the missing link. Perhaps the writer has used an important word incorrectly by not taking the trouble to look it up. ~~and make sure.~~ He may think that "sanguine" and "sanguinary" mean the same thing, but ~~I can assure you that~~ the difference is a bloody big one. ~~to the reader.~~ The reader ~~He~~ can only ~~try to~~ infer ~~xxx~~ (speaking of big differences) what the writer is trying to imply.

Faced with these ~~such a variety of~~ obstacles, the reader is at first a remarkably tenacious bird. He ~~tends to~~ blames himself. He obviously missed something, ~~he thinks,~~ and he goes back over the mystifying sentence, or over the whole paragraph, piecing it out like an ancient rune, making guesses and moving on. But he won't do this for long. ~~He will soon run out of patience.~~ The writer is making him work too hard, ~~-- harder than he should have to work --~~ and the reader will look for one ~~a writer~~ who is better at his craft.

The writer must therefore constantly ask himself: What am I trying to say? ~~in this sentence?~~

Surprisingly often, he doesn't know.

~~And~~ Then he must look at what he has ~~just~~ written and ask: Have I said it? Is it clear to someone encountering ~~who is coming upon~~ the subject for the first time? If it's not, ~~clear,~~ it is because some fuzz has worked its way into the machinery. The clear writer is a person ~~who is~~ clear-headed enough to see this stuff for what it is: fuzz.

I don't mean ~~to suggest~~ that some people are born clear-headed and are therefore natural writers, whereas others ~~other people~~ are naturally fuzzy and will ~~therefore~~ never write well. Thinking clearly is a ~~an entirely~~ conscious act that the writer must force ~~keep forcing~~ upon himself, just as if he were embarking ~~starting out~~ on any other ~~kind of~~ project that requires ~~calls for~~ logic: adding up a laundry list or doing an algebra problem. ~~or playing chess.~~ Good writing doesn't ~~just~~ come naturally, though most people obviously think it does. ~~it's as easy as walking.~~

Suggested Writing Assignments

1. If what Zinsser writes about clutter is an accurate assessment, we should easily be able to find numerous examples of clutter all around us. During the next few days, look for clutter in the written materials you come across. Choose one example that you find—an article, an essay, a form letter, or a section from a textbook, for example—and write an extended analysis explaining how it might have been written more simply. Develop your paragraphs well, make sure they are coherent, and try not to "clutter" your own writing.
2. Write a brief essay analyzing your need to simplify some aspect of your life. For example, are you involved in too many extracurricular activities, taking too many courses, working too many hours at a job, or not making sensible choices with regard to your social life? You may find it helpful to read what you wrote in response to the Reflecting on What You Know prompt at the beginning of this selection.

That Lean and Hungry Look

■ Suzanne Britt

Courtesy of Suzanne Britt

Born in Winston-Salem, North Carolina, Suzanne Britt now makes her home in Raleigh. She graduated from Salem College and Washington University, where she received her MA in English. A poet and essayist, Britt has been a columnist for the Raleigh News and Observer *and* Stars and Stripes, *European edition. Her work appears regularly in* North Carolina Gardens and Homes, *the* New York Times, Newsweek, *and the* Boston Globe. *Her essays have been collected in two books,* Skinny People Are Dull and Crunchy Like Carrots *(1982) and* Show and Tell *(1982). She is the author of* A Writer's Rhetoric *(1988)—a college writing textbook—and* Images: A Centennial Journey *(1991)—a history of Meredith College, a small, independent women's college in Raleigh, where she teaches English and continues to write.*

The following essay first appeared in Newsweek *and later became the basis for her book* Skinny People Are Dull and Crunchy Like Carrots, *titled after a line in this essay. In this selection, mingling humor with a touch of seriousness, Britt examines the differences between fat and thin people and gives us some insights about several important personality traits. Notice how she uses focused paragraphs to offer her insights about some relevant personality traits.*

Reflecting on What You Know

What are your thoughts about fat people and thin people? Into which category would you place yourself? How do you feel about being fat or thin? In talking about a person's body shape or size, what words other than *fat* and *thin* could you use? What difference, if any, would these words make? Explain.

Caesar was right. Thin people need watching. I've been watching them for most of my adult life, and I don't like what I see. When these narrow fellows spring at me, I quiver to my toes. Thin people come in all personalities, most of them menacing. You've got your "together" thin person, your mechanical thin person, your condescending thin person, your tsk-tsk thin person, your efficiency-expert thin person. All of them are dangerous. 1

In the first place, thin people aren't fun. They don't know how to goof off, at least in the best, fat sense of the word. They've always got to be adoing. Give them a coffee break, and they'll jog around the block. Supply them with a quiet evening at home, and they'll fix the screen door and lick S&H green stamps.[1] They say things like "there aren't enough hours in the day." Fat people never say that. Fat people think the day is too damn long already. 2

Thin people make me tired. They've got speedy little metabolisms that cause them to bustle briskly. They're forever rubbing their bony hands together and eyeing new problems to "tackle." I like to surround myself with sluggish, inert, easygoing fat people, the kind who believe that if you clean it up today, it'll just get dirty again tomorrow. 3

Some people say the business about the jolly fat person is a myth, that all of us chubbies are neurotic, sick, sad people. I disagree. Fat people may not be chortling all day long, but they're a hell of a lot *nicer* than the wizened and shriveled. Thin people turn surly, mean, and hard at a young age because they never learn the value of a hot-fudge sundae for easing tension. Thin people don't like gooey soft things because they themselves are neither gooey nor soft. They are crunchy and dull, like carrots. They go straight to the heart of the matter while fat people let things stay all blurry and hazy and vague, the way things actually are. Thin people want to face the truth. Fat people know there is no truth. One of my thin friends is always staring at complex, unsolvable problems and saying, "The key thing is . . ." Fat people never say that. They know there isn't any such thing as the key thing about anything. 4

Thin people believe in logic. Fat people see all sides. The sides fat people see are rounded blobs, usually gray, always nebulous and truly not worth worrying about. But the thin person persists. "If you 5

[1]*S&H green stamps:* popular trading stamps distributed to retail shoppers as part of a rewards program starting in the 1930s and running through the 1980s. Stamps could be redeemed for products.

consume more calories than you burn," says one of my thin friends, "you will gain weight. It's that simple." Fat people always grin when they hear statements like that. They know better.

Fat people realize that life is illogical and unfair. They know very 6
well that God is not in his heaven and all is not right with the world. If God was up there, fat people could have two doughnuts and a big orange drink anytime they wanted it.

Thin people have a long list of logical things they are always spout- 7
ing off to me. They hold up one finger at a time as they reel off these things, so I won't lose track. They speak slowly as if to a young child. The list is long and full of holes. It contains tidbits like "get a grip on yourself," "cigarettes kill," "cholesterol clogs," "fit as a fiddle," "ducks in a row," "organize," and "sound fiscal management." Phrases like that.

They think these 2,000-point plans lead to happiness. Fat people 8
know happiness is elusive at best and even if they could get the kind thin people talk about, they wouldn't want it. Wisely, fat people see that such programs are too dull, too hard, too off the mark. They are never better than a whole cheesecake.

Fat people know all about the mystery of life. They are the ones 9
acquainted with the night, with luck, with fate, with playing it by ear. One thin person I know once suggested that we arrange all the parts of a jigsaw puzzle into groups according to size, shape, and color. He figured this would cut the time needed to complete the puzzle by at least 50 percent. I said I wouldn't do it. One, I like to muddle through. Two, what good would it do to finish early? Three, the jigsaw puzzle isn't the important thing. The important thing is the fun of four people (one thin person included) sitting around a card table, working a jigsaw puzzle. My thin friend had no use for my list. Instead of joining us, he went outside and mulched the boxwoods. The three remaining fat people finished the puzzle and made chocolate, double-fudged brownies to celebrate.

The main problem with thin people is they oppress. Their good 10
intentions, bony torsos, tight ships, neat corners, cerebral machinations, and pat solutions loom like dark clouds over the loose, comfortable, spread-out, soft world of the fat. Long after fat people have removed their coats and shoes and put their feet up on the coffee table, thin people are still sitting on the edge of the sofa, looking neat as a pin, discussing rutabagas. Fat people are heavily into fits of laughter, slapping their thighs and whooping it up, while thin people are still politely waiting for the punch line.

Thin people are downers. They like math and morality and reasoned evaluation of the limitations of human beings. They have their skinny little acts together. They expound, prognose, probe, and prick. 11

Fat people are convivial. They will like you even if you're irregular and have acne. They will come up with a good reason why you never wrote the great American novel. They will cry in your beer with you. They will put your name in the pot. They will let you off the hook. Fat people will gab, giggle, guffaw, gallumph, gyrate, and gossip. They are generous, giving, and gallant. They are gluttonous and goodly and great. What you want when you're down is soft and jiggly, not muscled and stable. Fat people know this. Fat people have plenty of room. Fat people will take you in. 12

Thinking Critically about This Reading

What does Britt seem to have against thin people? Why does she consider thin people "dangerous" (paragraph 1)? What do you think Britt herself looks like? What in her essay led you to this conclusion?

Questions for Study and Discussion

1. How does Britt use topic sentences to establish the main idea of each paragraph? Choose a few sample paragraphs, and closely examine how the examples she uses develop that main idea.
2. How does Britt characterize thin people? Fat people?
3. What is Britt's purpose in this essay? (Glossary: *Purpose*) Is she serious, partially serious, mostly humorous? Are fat and thin people really her subject? Explain.
4. Britt makes effective use of the short sentence. Identify examples of sentences with three or fewer words, and explain what function each serves.
5. Britt uses many clichés in her essay. Identify at least a dozen examples. What do you suppose is her purpose in using them? (Glossary: *Cliché*)
6. It is somewhat unusual for an essayist to use alliteration (the repetition of initial consonant sounds), a technique more commonly found in poetry. Where has Britt used alliteration, and why do you suppose she has used this particular technique?

Classroom Activity Using Paragraphs

Write a unified, coherent, and well-developed paragraph using one of the following topic sentences. Be sure to select details that clearly demonstrate or support the general statement you choose. In a classroom discussion, students should compare and discuss the paragraphs developed from the same topic sentences as a way to understand the potential for variety in developing a topic sentence.

1. It was the noisiest place I had ever visited.
2. I was terribly frightened.
3. Signs of the sanitation strike were evident everywhere.
4. It was the best meal I've ever eaten.
5. Even though we lost, our team earned an A for effort.

Suggested Writing Assignments

1. Using Britt's argument against thin people as a model, write a counterargument in favor of thin people. Before beginning to write, make a list of the favorable points you would want to make about thin people. How would you counter Britt's points about fat people?
2. Reread paragraphs 3 through 6, paying careful attention to how these paragraphs are developed by contrasting the features of thin people and fat people. Now, select two specific examples from one of the following categories—people, products, events, institutions, places—and make a list of their contrasting features. For example, you could select Hillary Clinton and Sarah Palin, Beyoncé and Miley Cyrus, the Statue of Liberty and the Washington Monument, or the Grand Canyon and Yellowstone National Park. Finally, write an essay modeled after Britt's in which you use the contrasting features on your list.

The Home Place

■ Jimmy Carter

AP Photo/Richard Drew

James Earl Carter Jr. was the thirty-ninth president of the United States. Born in the small town of Plains, Georgia, he earned a BS from the U.S. Naval Academy and served for seven years as a naval officer. He completed two terms as Georgia's state senator and served as its governor before running for the presidency in 1976. During his term as president, he worked to combat energy shortages at home through conservation and other measures. He advocated for human rights abroad, helping to negotiate the Panama Canal Treaty and a peace agreement between Egypt and Israel. However, he faced continued economic problems at home and was defeated in his second run for the White House. After his presidency, Carter continued his service to the country, taking an active part in peace negotiations; in 2002, he was awarded the Nobel Peace Prize for his efforts at promoting peaceful conflict resolution around the world.

In this excerpt from his memoir, An Hour before Daylight *(2001), Carter describes the workings of his father's peanut farm. Each paragraph focuses on a different part of the farm, describing in loving detail the carpentry shop, the barn, and the unreliable water pump. In Carter's mind, these physical features of the farm, plus the men who work there, form "a fascinating system, like a huge clock."*

Reflecting on What You Know

What are your most vivid memories from childhood? What details do you recall when you think about your childhood home?

I still have vivid memories of the home place where I spent my boyhood. There was a dirt tennis court next to our house, unknown on any other farm in our area, which Daddy laid out as soon as we 1 moved there and kept clean and relatively smooth with a piece of angle iron nailed to a pine log that a mule could drag over it every week or so. Next was my father's commissary store, with the windmill in back, and then a large fenced-in garden. A two-rut wagon road ran from our back yard to the barn, which would become the center of my life as I matured and eagerly assumed increasing responsibilities for the work of a man.

Beyond the garden and alongside this small road was a combination blacksmith and carpenter shop surrounded by piles of all kinds of scrap metal, where everyone on the farm knew that rattlesnakes loved to breed. This is where we shod mules and horses, sharpened plow points, repaired machinery, made simple iron implements, and did woodwork, with Daddy providing the overall supervision. He was skilled with the forge and anvil, and did fairly advanced blacksmith work. This is one of the first places I was able to work alongside him. I could turn the hand crank on the forge blower fast enough to keep the charcoal fire ablaze, and to hold some of the red-hot pieces on the anvil with tongs while Daddy shaped them with a hammer and then plunged them, hissing, into water or oil for tempering. It required some skill to keep a plow point completely flat on the steel surface; otherwise a hammer blow would bring a violent and painful twisting, with the tongs and red-hot metal sometimes flying out of my hands. There was almost always something broken around the farm, and only rarely would anything be taken to town for welding. I learned a lot from Daddy, and also from Jack Clark, a middle-aged black man who was something of a supervisor on our farm and did most of the mule- and horse-shoeing. 2

In front of the shop was a large Sears, Roebuck grinding stone, and we would sit on a wooden seat and pedal to keep the thick disc spinning, with the bottom of the stone running in half an automobile tire filled with water. This was a busy place where we sharpened hoes, axes, scythes, knives, and scissors. Daddy didn't believe in paying for something we could do ourselves, so he also had an iron shoemaker's last in the shop that he used for replacing worn-out heels and soles for the family's shoes. As I got older, I helped with all the jobs in the shop, but was always most interested in working with wood, especially in shaping pieces with froe, plane, drawknife, and spokeshave. 3

The centerpiece of our farm life, and a place of constant exploration for me, was our large, perfectly symmetrical barn. It had been built by an itinerant Scottish carpenter named Mr. Valentine, whose 4 basic design was well known in our farming region. Daddy was very proud of its appearance and its practical arrangement, which minimized labor in handling the large quantities of feed needed for our livestock. There were special cribs, bins, and tanks for storing oats, ear corn, velvet beans, hay, fodder, and store-bought supplements, including molasses, a bran called "shorts," and cottonseed meal. The sheep, goats, and cattle were usually kept in stalls separate from each other and from the mules and horses, and animals requiring veterinary care could also be isolated while being treated. Hogs had their own pens, and were not permitted inside the barn.

Before I was big enough for real fieldwork, Daddy encouraged 5
me to spend time with Jack Clark, knowing that it was the best way for me to be educated about farm life, as Jack kept up a constant stream of comments about the world as he knew or envisioned it.

Jack was very black, of medium height, and strongly built. He 6
had surprisingly long arms, and invariably wore clean overalls, knee-high rubber boots, and a straw hat. Knowing (or at least claiming) that he spoke for my father, he issued orders or directions to the other hands in a somewhat gruff voice, always acting as the final arbiter over which field each hand would plow and which mule he would harness. He ignored the grumbled complaints. When all the other workers were off to their assigned duties, Jack was the sole occupant of the barn and the adjacent lots—except when I was following behind him like a puppy dog and bombarding him with questions. We became close friends, but there was always some restraint as to intimacy between us. For instance, although my daddy would pick me up on occasion to give me a hug or let me ride on his shoulders, this would have been inconceivable with Jack, except when he might lift me over a barbed-wire fence or onto the back of a mule or horse.

Radiating from the barn was a maze of fences and gates that let 7
us move livestock from one place to another with minimal risk of their escape. This was one of my earliest tasks, requiring only a modicum of skill and the ability to open and close the swinging gates. Within the first array of enclosures was a milking shed that would hold four cows at a time, adequate to accommodate our usual herd of eight to a dozen Jerseys and Guernseys that we milked in two shifts, twice a day. Later, we had a dozen A-frame hog-farrowing structures, which I helped my daddy build after bringing the innovative design home from my Future Farmer class in school. One shelter was assigned to each sow when birthing time approached, and the

design kept the animals dry, provided a convenient place for feed and water, and minimized the inadvertent crushing of the baby pigs by their heavy mamas. Except during extended dry seasons, the constantly used lots for hogs and milk cows were always ankle deep in mud and manure, which made bare feet much superior to brogans.

A little open shed near the barn enclosed a pump that lifted about 8
two cups of water from our shallow well with each stroke. It was driven by a small two-cycle gasoline engine that we cranked up and let run once or twice a day, just long enough to fill several watering troughs around the barn and sheds. This was the only motor-driven device on the farm, and was always viewed with a mixture of suspicion and trepidation. We were justifiably doubtful that it would crank when we needed it most, dreading the hour or two of hand pumping as the only alternative source of water for all the animals. Between the pump house and barn was a harness shed, an open-ended building where we stored a buggy, two wagons, and all the saddles, bridles, and other harness needed for an operating farm. Also near the barn was a concrete dipping-vat about four feet deep, filled with a pungent mixture containing creosote, through which we would drive our cattle, goats, and newly sheared sheep to protect them, at least temporarily, from flies and screwworms.

The farm operation always seemed to me a fascinating system, 9
like a huge clock, with each of its many parts depending on all the rest. Daddy was the one who designed, owned, and operated the complicated mechanism, and Jack Clark wound it daily and kept it on time. I had dreams that one day I would be master of this machine, with its wonderful intricacies.

The workers on our place, all black, lived in five small clapboard 10
houses, three right on the highway, one set farther back from the road, and another across the railroad tracks directly in front of our house. This was the community in which I grew up, all within a stone's throw of the barn.

Thinking Critically about This Reading

How does Carter show his role on the farm changing over time? As he describes the place, which features remind him of the times he took on more—and more difficult—work?

Questions for Study and Discussion

1. Carter uses the paragraphs of this essay to lead readers on a tour of the farm. Where does he start and end? Where does he stop along the way? How do his paragraphs help to focus our attention on different locations around the farm?
2. In this excerpt, Carter characterizes his father indirectly, not by telling us who he was but by showing us his habits and tendencies. Which details do you think tell readers the most about him?
3. Jack Clark is important to the running of the farm. Carter introduces him in paragraph 2, then offers a fuller portrait of him in paragraph 6. How does he develop this paragraph on Jack Clark's character? What information does he think is important for readers to know about him?
4. Carter discusses his increasing mastery of farm tasks and his role in the way the farm was run. What does he learn about the farm from his father? From Jack Clark? What does he contribute from his class at school?
5. The water pump, the only motorized device on the farm, was "viewed with a mixture of suspicion and trepidation" (paragraph 8). Using this quotation as a starting point, discuss the attitude of the family toward change and innovation.
6. Carter begins paragraph 9 with the metaphor of the farm as a well-kept machine. Why is this an apt way of thinking about it? How does the paragraph extend this metaphor? (Glossary: *Figure of Speech*)
7. The farm is the site of Carter's family business, but he also calls it a community. In what ways is this true?

Classroom Activity Using Paragraphs

In a business setting, writing usually has clear tasks to accomplish. The following paragraphs are from the opening of a proposal by a research consultant firm. Read the paragraphs, then write a brief description of each paragraph's purpose. What information does each paragraph provide for the clients? Discuss how the writers develop each paragraph to achieve its purpose.

PROPOSAL TO CONDUCT A MULTIYEAR EVALUATION OF PERMANENT SUPPORTIVE HOUSING IN LOWELL COUNTY

LS Group is pleased to partner with Barton Consulting, LLC, to provide the Supportive Housing Initiative (SHI) with a proposal to evaluate State-Financed Permanent Supportive Housing (PSH) in Lowell County. LS Group's national research and technical assistance experience in homelessness, housing, and community development, complemented by Barton's expertise in housing development, finance, and operations, provides an exceptional foundation on which to help SHI and its partners execute groundbreaking research on the long-term sustainability of PSH and its effectiveness over time for the tenants housed in various PSH settings. We are very excited about this study and believe the results have the opportunity to shape state policy, local practice, and national understanding of PSH and its ongoing impact and role.

LS Group and Barton offer SHI a *"full-service" research team*, with the breadth of staff and project skills necessary to complete *all three components* of the proposed study: program and cost effectiveness, community and neighborhood impact, and project stability and quality. This comprehensive approach allows us to achieve economies of scale across the three evaluation components, enabling us to propose richer analysis and more frequent interim reports than might otherwise be feasible. Most important, the technical approach is sufficiently rigorous to yield results that can guide important decision-making about the future of PSH in Lowell County.

Our proposal is organized as follows: In Section 1, we discuss the key elements of our technical approach and design considerations, including challenges that may be encountered and strategies to mitigate these challenges, and our plan for reporting and dissemination. Section 2 details the work plan and overall project time line. Section 3 describes our management plan and organizational and staff qualifications related to this study. Appendix A presents résumés for project staff, and Appendix B contains our references. Our budget and budget narrative and writing samples are included in separate documents.

Suggested Writing Assignments

1. Write a description of your campus or school. Following Carter's lead, make your virtual tour vivid for readers by focusing each of your paragraphs on one important feature of the place.
2. In the process of describing the "home place," Carter gives readers a clear picture of his father, though he does so indirectly. For example, rather than telling us his father was frugal and self-sufficient, he writes, "Daddy didn't believe in paying for something we could do ourselves," and describes how he repaired the family's shoes (3). Write an essay that paints a picture of a parent or another family member using that person's characteristic ways of speaking or acting to convey his or her personality. (Glossary: *Illustration*)

CHAPTER **8**

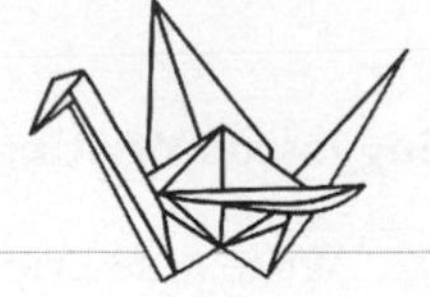

Transitions

A **transition** is a word or phrase used to signal the relationships among ideas in an essay and to join the various parts of an essay together. Writers use transitions to relate ideas within sentences, between sentences, and between paragraphs. Perhaps the most common type of transition is the transitional expression. Following is a list of transitional expressions categorized according to their functions.

Transitional Expressions
Addition and, again, too, also, in addition, further, furthermore, moreover, besides
Cause and Effect therefore, consequently, thus, accordingly, as a result, hence, then, so
Comparison similarly, likewise, by comparison
Concession to be sure, granted, of course, it is true, to tell the truth, certainly, with the exception of, although this may be true, even though, naturally
Contrast but, however, in contrast, on the contrary, on the other hand, yet, nevertheless, after all, in spite of
Example for example, for instance

Place
elsewhere, here, above, below, farther on, there, beyond, nearby, opposite to, around

Restatement
that is, as I have said, in other words, in simpler terms, to put it differently, simply stated

Sequence
first, second, third, next, finally

Summary
in conclusion, to conclude, to summarize, in brief, in short

Time
afterward, later, earlier, subsequently, at the same time, simultaneously, immediately, this time, until now, before, meanwhile, shortly, soon, currently, when, lately, in the meantime, formerly

Besides transitional expressions, there are two other important ways to make transitions: by repeating key words and ideas and by using pronoun references. This paragraph begins with the phrase "Besides transitional expressions," which contains the transitional word *besides* and also repeats wording from the last sentence of the previous paragraph. Thus, the reader knows that this discussion is moving toward a new but related idea. Repetition can also give a word or an idea emphasis: "Foreigners look to America as a land of freedom. Freedom, however, is not something all Americans enjoy."

Pronoun references avoid monotonous repetition of nouns and phrases. Without pronouns, these two sentences are wordy and tiring to read: "Jim went to the concert, where he heard Beethoven's Ninth Symphony. Afterward, Jim bought a recording of the Ninth Symphony." A more graceful and readable passage results if two pronouns are substituted in the second sentence: "Afterward, he bought a recording of it." The second version has another advantage in that it is now more tightly related to the first sentence. The transition between the two sentences is smoother.

In the following example, notice how Rachel Carson uses transitional expressions, repetition of words and ideas, and pronoun references:

> Under primitive agricultural conditions the farmer had few insect problems. *These* arose with the intensification of agriculture—the devotion of immense acreages to a single crop. *Such a system* set the stage for explosive increases in specific insect populations. Single-crop farming does not take advantage of the principles by which nature works; *it* is agriculture as an engineer might conceive it to be. Nature has introduced great variety into the landscape, but man has displayed a passion for simplifying *it*. *Thus he* undoes the built-in checks and balances by which nature holds the species within bounds. One important natural *check* is a limit on the amount of suitable habitat for each species. *Obviously then,* an insect that lives on wheat can build up its population to much higher levels on a farm devoted to wheat than on one in which wheat is intermingled with other crops to which the insect is not adapted.
>
> *The same thing* happens in other situations. A generation or more ago, the towns of large areas of the United States lined their streets with the noble elm tree. *Now* the beauty *they* hopefully created is threatened with complete destruction as disease sweeps through the elms, carried by a beetle that would have only limited chance to build up large populations and to spread from tree to tree if the elms were only occasional trees in a richly diversified planting.
>
> –Rachel Carson, *Silent Spring*

Pronoun reference (These)
Repeated key idea (Such a system)
Pronoun reference (it is agriculture)
Pronoun reference (simplifying it)
Transitional expression; pronoun reference (Thus he)
Repeated key word (check)
Transitional expression (Obviously then)
Repeated key idea (The same thing)
Transitional expression; pronoun reference (Now ... they)

Carson's transitions in this passage enhance its **coherence**—that quality of good writing that results when all sentences and paragraphs of an essay are effectively and naturally connected.

In the following four-paragraph sequence about a vegetarian's ordeal with her family at Thanksgiving each year, the writer uses transitions effectively to link one paragraph to another.

> The holiday that I dread the most is fast approaching. The relatives will gather to gossip and

bicker, the house will be filled with the smells of turkey, onions, giblets, and allspice, and I will be pursuing trivial conversations in the hope of avoiding any commentaries upon the state of my plate.

Reference to key idea in previous paragraph

Do not misunderstand me: I am not a scrooge. I enjoy the idea of Thanksgiving—the giving of thanks for blessings received in the past year and the opportunity to share an unhurried day with family and friends. The problem for me is that I am one of those freaky, misunderstood people who—as my family jokingly reminds me—eats "rabbit food." Because all traditional Western holidays revolve around food and more specifically around ham, turkey, lamb, or roast beef and their respective starchy accompaniments, it is no picnic for us vegetarians.

Repeated key word

The mention of the word *vegetarian* has, at various family get-togethers, caused my Great-Aunt Bertha to rant and rave for what seems like hours about those "liberal conspirators." Other relations cough or groan or simply stare, change the subject or reminisce about somebody they used to know who was "into that," and some proceed either to demand that I defend my position or try to talk me out of it. That is why I try to avoid the subject, but especially during the holidays.

Transitional time reference

Repeated key idea

In years past I have had about as many *successes as failures in steering comments about my food toward other topics.* Politics and religion are the easiest outs, guaranteed to immerse the family in a heated debate lasting until the loudest shouter has been abandoned amidst empty pie plates, wine corks, and rumpled linen napkins. I prefer, however, to use this tactic as a last resort. Holidays are supposed to be for relaxing.

–Mundy Wilson-Libby, student

An Indian Father's Plea

■ Robert G. Lake-Thom (Medicine Grizzly Bear)

Courtesy Robert Lake-Thom

Robert G. Lake-Thom, also known as Medicine Grizzly Bear, is a traditional Native American healer and spiritual teacher, following methods he learned from healers, ceremonial leaders, and religious leaders of several tribes. His ancestry is Karuk, Seneca, Cherokee, and Anglo. He was a professor of Native American studies for over twenty years, teaching at Gonzaga University, Humboldt State University, and Eastern Montana College (now Montana State University Billings). Lake-Thom is the author of three books on Native American shamanic life and ceremonies: Native Healer *(1991),* Spirits of the Earth *(1997), and* The Call of the Great Spirit *(2001).*

Lake-Thom wrote "An Indian Father's Plea" in response to the negative effects Western education practices were having on his children as well as Native American children across the nation. In this piece—which has been used for over two decades in both teacher training workshops and Indian education programs—Lake-Thom responds to a teacher who labeled his child a "slow learner," explaining the education his son has already received. Although he acknowledges that this education may seem foreign to the teacher, he explains that it has developed the boy's sensitivity to the world and honed skills important to his culture. As you read, notice how Lake-Thom uses transitions to lead the teacher through the stages of his son's education.

Reflecting on What You Know

Think about a time when your way of learning and understanding seemed out of sync with what you were being taught. What does it tell you about your education? Under what circumstances or with what methods do you learn best?

Wind-Wolf knows the names and migration patterns of more than 40 birds. He knows there are 13 tail feathers on a perfectly balanced eagle. What he needs is a teacher who knows his full measure. 1

Dear teacher, I would like to introduce you to my son, Wind-Wolf. He is probably what you would consider a typical Indian kid. He was born and raised on a reservation. He has black hair, dark brown eyes, olive complexion. And like so many Indian children his age, he is shy and quiet in the classroom. He is 5 years old, in kindergarten, and I can't understand why you have already labeled him a "slow learner." 2

At the age of 5, he has already been through quite an education compared with his peers in Western society. At his first introduction into this world, he was bonded to his mother and to the Mother Earth in a traditional native childbirth ceremony. And he has been continuously cared for by his mother, father, sisters, cousins, uncles, grandparents, and extended tribal family since this ceremony. 3

From his mother's warm and loving arms, Wind-Wolf was placed in a secure and specially designed Indian baby basket. His father and the medicine elders conducted another ceremony with him that served to bond him with the essence of his genetic father, the Great Spirit, the Grandfather Sun, and the Grandmother Moon. This was all done in order to introduce him properly into the new and natural world, not the world of artificiality, and to protect his sensitive and delicate soul. It is our people's way of showing the newborn respect, ensuring that he starts his life on the path of spirituality. 4

The traditional Indian baby basket became his "turtle's shell" and served as the first seat for his classroom. He was strapped in for safety, protected from injury by the willow roots and hazel wood construction. The basket was made by a tribal elder who had gathered her materials with prayer and in a ceremonial way. It is the same kind of basket that our people have used for thousands of years. It is specially designed to provide the child with the kind of knowledge and experience he will need in order to survive in his culture and environment. 5

Wind-Wolf was strapped in snuggly with a deliberate restriction upon his arms and legs. Although you in Western society may argue that such a method serves to hinder motor-skill development and abstract reasoning, we believe it forces the child to first develop his intuitive faculties, rational intellect, symbolic thinking, and five senses. Wind-Wolf was with his mother constantly, closely bonded physically, as she carried him on her back or held him in front while 6 breast-feeding. She carried him everywhere she went, and every night he slept with both parents. Because of this, Wind-Wolf's educational setting was not only a "secure" environment, but it was also very colorful, complicated, sensitive, and diverse. He has been with his mother at the ocean at daybreak when she made her prayers and gathered fresh seaweed from the rocks, he has sat with his uncles in a rowboat on the river while they fished with gill nets, and he has watched and listened to elders as they told creation stories and animal legends and sang songs around the campfires.

He has attended the sacred and ancient White Deerskin Dance of 7
his people and is well-acquainted with the cultures and languages of other tribes. He has been with his mother when she gathered herbs for healing and watched his tribal aunts and grandmothers gather and prepare traditional foods such as acorn, smoked salmon, eel, and deer meat. He has played with abalone shells, pine nuts, iris grass string, and leather while watching the women make beaded jewelry and traditional native regalia. He has had many opportunities to watch his father, uncles, and ceremonial leaders using different kinds of songs while preparing for the sacred dances and rituals.

As he grew older, Wind-Wolf began to crawl out of the baby bas- 8
ket, develop his motor skills, and explore the world around him. When frightened or sleepy, he could always return to the basket as a turtle withdraws into its shell. Such an inward journey allows one to reflect in privacy on what he has learned and to carry the new knowledge deeply into the unconscious and the soul. Shapes, sizes, colors, texture, sound, smell, feeling, taste, and the learning process are therefore functionally integrated—the physical and spiritual, matter and energy, conscious and unconscious, individual and social.

For example, Wind-Wolf was with his mother in South Dakota 9
while she danced for seven days straight in the hot sun, fasting, and piercing herself in the sacred Sun Dance Ceremony of a distant tribe. He has been doctored in a number of different healing ceremonies by medicine men and women from diverse places ranging from Alaska and Arizona to New York and California. He has been in more than 20 different sacred sweat-lodge rituals—used by native tribes to purify the mind, body, and soul—since he was 3 years old, and he has already been exposed to many different religions of his racial brothers: Protestant, Catholic, Asian Buddhist, and Tibetan Lamaist.

It takes a long time to absorb and reflect on these kinds of experi- 10
ences, so maybe that is why you think my Indian child is a slow learner. His aunts and grandmothers taught him to count and know

his numbers while they sorted out the complex materials used to make the abstract designs in the native baskets. He listened to his mother count each and every bead and sort out numerically according to color while she painstakingly made complex beaded belts and necklaces. He learned his basic numbers by helping his father count and sort the rocks to be used in the sweat-lodge—seven rocks for a medicine sweat, say, or 13 for the summer solstice ceremony. (The rocks are later heated and doused with water to create purifying steam.) And he was taught to learn mathematics by counting the sticks we use in our traditional native hand game. So I realize he may be slow in grasping the methods and tools that you are now using in your classroom, ones quite familiar to his white peers, but I hope you will be patient with him. It takes time to adjust to a new cultural system and learn new things.

He is not culturally "disadvantaged," but he is culturally "different." If you ask him how many months there are in a year, he will probably tell you 13. He will respond this way not because he doesn't know how to count properly, but because he has been taught by our traditional people that there are 13 full moons in a year according to the native tribal calender and that there are really 13 planets in our solar system and 13 tail feathers on a perfectly balanced eagle, the most powerful kind of bird to use in ceremonial healing. 11

But he also knows that some eagles may only have 12 tail feathers, or seven, that they do not all have the same number. He knows that the flicker has exactly 10 tail feathers; that they are red and black, representing the directions of east and west, life and death; and that this bird is considered a "fire" bird, a power used in native doctoring and healing. He can probably count more than 40 different kinds of birds, tell you and his peers what kind of bird each is and where it lives, the seasons in which it appears, and how it is used in a sacred ceremony. He may also have trouble writing his name on a piece of paper, but he knows how to say it and many other things in several different Indian languages. He is not fluent yet because he is only 5 years old and required by law to attend your educational system, learn your language, your values, your ways of thinking, and your methods of teaching and learning. 12

So you see, all of these influences together make him somewhat shy and quiet—and perhaps "slow" according to your standards. But if Wind-Wolf was not prepared for his first tentative foray into your world, neither were you appreciative of his culture. On the first day of class, you had difficulty with his name. You wanted to call him 13

Wind, insisting that Wolf must somehow be his middle name. The students in the class laughed at him, causing further embarrassment.

While you are trying to teach him your new methods, helping him learn new tools for self-discovery and adapt to his new learning environment, he may be looking out the window as if daydreaming. Why? Because he has been taught to watch and study the changes in nature. It is hard for him to make the appropriate psychic switch from the right to the left hemisphere of the brain when he sees the leaves turning bright colors, the geese heading south, and the squirrels scurrying around for nuts to get ready for a harsh winter. In his heart, in his young mind, and almost by instinct, he knows that this is the time of the year he is supposed to be with people gathering and preparing fish, deer meat, and native plants and herbs, and learning his assigned tasks in this role. He is caught between two worlds, torn by two distinct cultural systems. 14

Yesterday, for the third time in two weeks, he came home crying and said he wanted to have his hair cut. He said he doesn't have any friends at school because they make fun of his long hair. I tried to explain to him that in our culture, long hair is a sign of masculinity and balance and is a source of power. But he remained adamant in his position. 15

To make matters worse, he recently encountered his first harsh case of racism. Wind-Wolf had managed to adopt at least one good school friend. On the way home from school one day, he asked his new pal if he wanted to come home to play with him until supper. That was OK with Wind-Wolf's mother, who was walking with them. When they all got to the little friend's house, the two boys ran inside to ask permission while Wind-Wolf's mother waited. But the other boy's mother lashed out: "It is OK if you have to play with him at school, but we don't allow those kind of people in our house!" When my wife asked why not, the other boy's mother answered, "Because you are Indians, and we are white, and I don't want my kids growing up with your kind of people." 16

So now my young Indian child does not want to go to school anymore (even though we cut his hair). He feels that he does not belong. He is the only Indian child in your class, and he is well-aware of this fact. Instead of being proud of his race, heritage, and culture, he feels ashamed. When he watches television, he asks why the white people hate us so much and always kill our people in the movies and why they take everything away from us. He asks why the other kids in school are not taught about the power, beauty, and essence of 17 nature or provided with an opportunity to experience the world around them firsthand. He says he hates living in the city and that he misses his Indian cousins and friends. He asks why one young white girl at school who is his friend always tells him, "I like you, Wind-Wolf, because you are a good Indian."

Now he refuses to sing his native songs, play with his Indian artifacts, learn his language, or participate in his sacred ceremonies. When I ask him to go to an urban powwow or help me with a sacred sweat-lodge ritual, he says no because "that's weird" and he doesn't want his friends at school to think he doesn't believe in God. 18

So, dear teacher, I want to introduce you to my son, Wind-Wolf, who is not really a "typical" little Indian kid after all. He stems from a long line of hereditary chiefs, medicine men and women, and ceremonial leaders whose accomplishments and unique forms of knowledge are still being studied and recorded in contemporary books. He has seven different tribal systems flowing through his blood; he is even part white. I want my child to succeed in school and in life. I don't want him to be a dropout or juvenile delinquent or to end up on drugs and alcohol because he is made to feel inferior or because of discrimination. I want him to be proud of his rich heritage and culture, and I would like him to develop the necessary capabilities to adapt to, and succeed in, both cultures. But I need your help. 19

What you say and what you do in the classroom, what you teach and how you teach it, and what you don't say and don't teach will have a significant effect on the potential success or failure of my child. Please remember that this is the primary year of his education and development. All I ask is that you work with me, not against me, to help educate my child in the best way. If you don't have the knowledge, preparation, experience, or training to effectively deal with culturally different children, I am willing to help you with the few resources I have available or direct you to such resources. 20

Millions of dollars have been appropriated by Congress and are being spent each year for "Indian Education." All you have to do is take advantage of it and encourage your school to make an effort to use it in the name of "equal education." My Indian child has a constitutional right to learn, retain, and maintain his heritage and culture. By the same token, I strongly believe that non-Indian children also have a constitutional right to learn about our Native American heritage and culture, because Indians play a significant part in the history of Western society. Until this reality is equally understood and applied 21 in education as a whole, there will be a lot more schoolchildren in grades K-2 identified as "slow learners."

22 My son, Wind-Wolf, is not an empty glass coming into your class to be filled. He is a full basket coming into a different environment and society with something special to share. Please let him share his knowledge, heritage, and culture with you and his peers.

Thinking Critically about This Reading

The ritual introducing the child to his baby basket is a "way of showing the newborn respect" (paragraph 4). In what ways is Lake-Thom's essay more generally a call for showing respect? How would you expect the teacher to whom he is writing to respond?

Questions for Study and Discussion

1. Lake-Thom begins this essay with a few examples of what his son knows. Why do you think he starts in this way?
2. How do transitions help lead the reader through Wind-Wolf's development? Go back through the essay, identifying phrases that highlight the process of learning over time.
3. Lake-Thom describes the specially designed baby basket as a "turtle's shell" (5). Why does he use this metaphor? What similarities is he pointing out? (Glossary: *Figure of Speech*)
4. Discuss why Wind-Wolf would say there are thirteen months in a year. How does his father explain this "mistake" to the teacher?
5. What does Lake-Thom suggest are the advantages to the way his son has learned about the world? In what areas does he have greater knowledge than his classmates, who are not from Native American families?
6. What are the benefits of having Wind-Wolf attend school? What will this new form of education add to what he already knows?
7. Discuss Wind-Wolf's emotional reaction to his new school. What experiences have most affected him?
8. How does Lake-Thom think the teacher can make the school environment better for his child? Make note of where the essay transitions from describing Wind-Wolf's early education to making its "plea" to the teacher.

Classroom Activity Using Transitions

Instructions for constructing and hanging a tire swing appear here in scrambled order. First, read all nine sentences carefully. Next, arrange the sentences in what seems to you to be the logical sequence. Finally, identify places where transitional expressions, repetition of words and ideas, and pronoun references give coherence to the instructions.

1. Attach your tire to the rope with another tight square knot. (Make sure your tire is hanging with the holes on the bottom.)
2. After it's clean, drill a few holes, evenly spaced, along the bottom half of the tire to act as a drain for rainwater.
3. Then, using a ladder, loop your protected rope over the branch, and secure the rope to the branch with a tight square knot.
4. First pick a sturdy branch that is high enough to accommodate the length of your rope and strong enough to support your weight.
5. Once it's secured, spread some mulch around the base of your tire swing to absorb any falls.
6. Then find a tire that is large enough to comfortably fit one person.
7. Now test your swing and have some fun!
8. Next, clean the tire thoroughly before getting to work.
9. Once your tire is ready to be hung, get your rope and place rubber tubing over the section that will rest over the branch. (The tubing will help protect your rope from fraying.)

Suggested Writing Assignments

1. Write a history of your education, both inside and outside the classroom. When did you begin to learn? What have your greatest achievements and hardest challenges been? Make deliberate use of transitions to help your reader follow the time line and identify the key points in your development.
2. Though Lake-Thom is writing for a specific audience—the teacher—he published his letter so that the public could also learn from his experience with Wind-Wolf's first weeks of school. Think of a subject on which you have strong feelings, and write an open letter to persuade readers of your view. Using "An Indian Father's Plea" as a model, try to combine passionate expression with careful planning and structure. (Glossary: *Persuasion*)

Becoming a Writer

■ Russell Baker

Russell Baker has had a long and distinguished career as a newspaper reporter and columnist. He was born in Morrisonville, Virginia, in 1925 and graduated from Johns Hopkins University in 1947. He got his first newspaper job with the Baltimore Sun *and moved to the* New York Times *in 1954, where he wrote the "Observer" column from 1962 to 1998. His columns have been collected in numerous books over the years. In 1979, he was awarded the Pulitzer Prize, journalism's highest award, as well as the George Polk Award for commentary. Baker's memoir,* Growing Up *(1983), also received a Pulitzer. His autobiographical follow-up,* The Good Times, *appeared in 1989. His other works include* Russell Baker's Book of American Humor *(1993);* Inventing the Truth: The Art and Craft of Memoir *(1998, with William Zinsser and Jill Ker Conway); and* Looking Back *(2002), a collection of his essays for the* New York Review of Books. *From 1992 to 2004, he hosted the PBS television series* Exxon-Mobil Masterpiece Theater. *Baker now lives in Leesburg, Virginia.*

The following selection is from Growing Up. *As you read Baker's account of how he discovered his abilities as a writer, notice how effectively he uses repetition of key words and ideas to achieve coherence and to emphasize his emotional responses to the events he describes.*

Reflecting on What You Know

Life is full of moments that change us, for better or worse, in major and minor ways. We decide what hobbies we like and dislike, whom we want to date and perhaps eventually marry, what we want to study in school, what career we eventually pursue. Identify an event that changed your life or helped you make an important decision. How did it clarify your situation? How might your life be different if the event had never happened?

The notion of becoming a writer had flickered off and on in my head . . . but it wasn't until my third year in high school that the possibility took hold. Until then I'd been bored by everything associated with English courses. I found English grammar dull and baffling. I hated the assignments to turn out "compositions," and went at them like heavy labor, turning out leaden, lackluster paragraphs that were agonies for teachers to read and for me to write. The classics thrust on me to read seemed as deadening as chloroform.[1] 1

When our class was assigned to Mr. Fleagle for third-year English I anticipated another grim year in that dreariest of subjects. Mr. Fleagle was notorious among City students for dullness and inability to inspire. He was said to be stuffy, dull, and hopelessly out of date. To me he looked to be sixty or seventy and prim to a fault. He wore primly severe eyeglasses, his wavy hair was primly cut and primly combed. He wore prim vested suits with neckties blocked primly against the collar buttons of his primly starched white shirts. He had a primly pointed jaw, a primly straight nose, and a prim manner of speaking that was so correct, so gentlemanly, that he seemed a comic antique. 2

I anticipated a listless, unfruitful year with Mr. Fleagle and for a long time was not disappointed. We read *Macbeth*. Mr. Fleagle loved *Macbeth* and wanted us to love it too, but he lacked the gift of infecting others with his own passion. He tried to convey the murderous ferocity of Lady Macbeth one day by reading aloud the passage that concludes 3

> . . . I have given suck, and know
> How tender 'tis to love the babe that milks me.
> I would, while it was smiling in my face,
> Have plucked my nipple from his boneless gums . . .

The idea of prim Mr. Fleagle plucking his nipple from boneless gums was too much for the class. We burst into gasps of irrepressible[2] snickering. Mr. Fleagle stopped.

"There is nothing funny, boys, about giving suck to a babe. It is the—the very essence of motherhood, don't you see." 4

He constantly sprinkled his sentences with "don't you see." It wasn't a question but an exclamation of mild surprise at our ignorance. "Your pronoun needs an antecedent, don't you see," he would say, 5

[1]*chloroform:* a chemical that puts one to sleep.
[2]*irrepressible:* unable to be restrained or controlled.

very primly. "The purpose of the Porter's scene, boys, is to provide comic relief from the horror, don't you see."

Late in the year we tackled the informal essay. "The essay, don't you see, is the . . ." My mind went numb. Of all forms of writing, none seemed so boring as the essay. Naturally we would have to write informal essays. Mr. Fleagle distributed a homework sheet offering us a choice of topics. None was quite so simpleminded as "What I Did on My Summer Vacation," but most seemed to be almost as dull. I took the list home and dawdled until the night before the essay was due. Sprawled on the sofa, I finally faced up to the grim task, took the list out of my notebook, and scanned it. The topic on which my eye stopped was "The Art of Eating Spaghetti." 6

This title produced an extraordinary sequence of mental images. Surging up from the depths of memory came a vivid recollection of a night in Belleville when all of us were seated around the supper table—Uncle Allen, my mother, Uncle Charlie, Doris, Uncle Hal—and Aunt Pat served spaghetti for supper. Spaghetti was an exotic treat in those days. Neither Doris nor I had ever eaten spaghetti, and none of the adults had enough experience to be good at it. All the good humor of Uncle Allen's house reawoke in my mind as I recalled the laughing arguments we had that night about the socially respectable method for moving spaghetti from plate to mouth. 7

Suddenly I wanted to write about that, about the warmth and good feeling of it, but I wanted to put it down simply for my own joy, not for Mr. Fleagle. It was a moment I wanted to recapture and hold for myself. I wanted to relive the pleasure of an evening at New Street. To write it as I wanted, however, would violate all the rules of formal composition I'd learned in school, and Mr. Fleagle would surely give it a failing grade. Never mind. I would write something else for Mr. Fleagle after I had written this thing for myself. 8

When I finished it the night was half gone and there was no time left to compose a proper, respectable essay for Mr. Fleagle. There was no choice next morning but to turn in my private reminiscence of Belleville. Two days passed before Mr. Fleagle returned the graded papers, and he returned everyone's but mine. I was bracing myself for a command to report to Mr. Fleagle immediately after school for discipline when I saw him lift my paper from his desk and rap for the class's attention. 9

"Now, boys," he said, "I want to read you an essay. This is titled 'The Art of Eating Spaghetti.' " 10

And he started to read. My words! He was reading *my words* out loud to the entire class. What's more, the entire class was listening. Listening attentively. Then somebody laughed, then the entire class was laughing, and not in contempt and ridicule, but with open-hearted enjoyment. Even Mr. Fleagle stopped two or three times to repress a small prim smile. 11

I did my best to avoid showing pleasure, but what I was feeling was pure ecstasy at this startling demonstration that my words had the power to make people laugh. In the eleventh grade, at the eleventh hour as it were, I had discovered a calling. It was the happiest moment of my entire school career. When Mr. Fleagle finished he put the final seal on my happiness by saying, "Now that, boys, is an essay, don't you see. It's—don't you see—it's of the very essence of the essay, don't you see. Congratulations, Mr. Baker." 12

For the first time, light shone on a possibility. It wasn't a very heartening possibility, to be sure. Writing couldn't lead to a job after high school, and it was hardly honest work, but Mr. Fleagle had opened a door for me. After that I ranked Mr. Fleagle among the finest teachers in the school. 13

Thinking Critically about This Reading

In paragraph 11, Baker states, "And he started to read. My words! He was reading *my words* out loud to the entire class. What's more, the entire class was listening. Listening attentively." Why was this episode so key to Baker's decision to become a writer? Why did it lead him to rank "Mr. Fleagle among the finest teachers in the school" (13)?

Questions for Study and Discussion

1. Baker makes good use of transitional expressions, repetition of words and ideas, and pronoun references in paragraphs 1 and 2. Carefully reread the paragraphs, and identify where he employs these techniques.
2. Examine the transitions Baker uses between paragraphs from paragraph 4 to the end of the essay. Explain how these transitions work to make the paragraphs flow from one to another.
3. How does Baker describe his English teacher, Mr. Fleagle, in the second paragraph? (Glossary: *Description*) Why does he repeat the

word *prim* throughout the paragraph? Why is the vivid description important to the essay as a whole?

4. What does Baker write about in his informal essay for Mr. Fleagle? Why does he write about this subject? Why doesn't he want to turn the essay in?
5. What door does Mr. Fleagle open for Baker? Why is Baker reluctant to pursue the opportunity?

Classroom Activity Using Transitions

Read the following three paragraphs from a student's narrative essay. Provide transitions between sentences and paragraphs so that the narrative flows smoothly.

> Last year, I got lost on a hike during an extended camping trip in Oregon. I lost the path where a storm had washed it out and could not find my way back. I walked in the rain all day, desperate to find a road that would lead me to some sign of humanity. I tried not to panic, but I was cold and exhausted, and I had no extra clothes or any gear with me to make camp for the night.
>
> I picked a direction and hoped it would lead me before long to a gas station or a restaurant—anyplace where I could get something hot to drink. After about twenty minutes I came to a little diner, but I could tell from first sight that it was closed. The sign wasn't lit, and it looked like the lights were off inside, too.
>
> One of the workers let me in through the kitchen and gave me the last of a pot of coffee, which wasn't that hot anymore, but I was not feeling picky by that point. I had not had cell phone reception since the morning, but she let me use the diner's phone to call my friends. She had to lock up and leave before they arrived, but she sent me out to wait under the front awning with a piece of pie in a napkin and a wool scarf that she said had been sitting in the lost-and-found box for months.

Suggested Writing Assignments

1. Using Baker's inspiration writing about eating spaghetti as a model, write something from your own experience that you would like to record for yourself, not necessarily for the teacher. Don't worry about writing a formal essay. Simply use language with which you are comfortable to convey why the event or experience is important to you.

2. Write an essay in which you describe how your perception of someone important in your life changed. How did you feel about the person at first? How do you feel now? What brought about the change? What effect did the transition have on you? Make sure that your essay is coherent and flows well: use transitional expressions to help the reader follow the story of *your* transition.

The Magic of the Family Meal

■ Nancy Gibbs

Larry Busacca/Getty Images

Born in 1960 in New York City, Nancy Gibbs graduated with honors in history from Yale University in 1982. She continued her studies at Oxford University as a Marshall scholar, earning a master's degree in politics and philosophy in 1984. She went to work at Time *magazine in 1985 and became a feature writer in 1988. In 1991, she was named a senior editor and later became chief political writer. In that capacity, she wrote more than twenty cover stories about the 1996 and 2000 presidential campaigns and elections. In 2002,* Time *appointed her editor-at-large. In her years at* Time, *she has authored more than 130 cover stories, including the one for September 11, 2001, for which she received the National Magazine Award in 2002, and another entitled "Faith, God, and the Oval Office," about the role of religion in the 2004 George W. Bush–John Kerry presidential campaign. Gibbs also coauthored* Preacher and the Presidents: Billy Graham in the White House *(2007) with Michael Duffy. She lives in Westchester, New York, with her husband and two daughters.*

In "The Magic of the Family Meal," an essay first published in the June 12, 2006, issue of Time, *Gibbs reports on the current status of family dining in the United States and the ways that this dying tradition has shown a resurgence in recent years. Because research shows that children who eat with their parents are healthier, happier, and better students than children who don't, Gibbs advises that families should "make meals together a priority." As you read Gibbs's essay, notice how she achieves unity and coherence by using repeated words and phrases, transitional expressions, pronouns with specific antecedents, and repeated key ideas to connect one paragraph to another.*

Reflecting on What You Know

What was dinnertime like in your house while you were growing up? How many times a week did you eat dinner with your family? What activities and obligations made it difficult to eat together as a family? For you, what is the value of the so-called family meal?

Close your eyes and picture Family Dinner. June Cleaver is in an apron and pearls, Ward[1] in a sweater and tie. The napkins are linen, the children are scrubbed, steam rises from the green-bean casserole, and even the dog listens intently to what is being said. This is where the tribe comes to transmit wisdom, embed expectations, confess, conspire, forgive, repair. The idealized version is as close to a regular worship service, with its litanies and lessons and blessings, as a family gets outside a sanctuary. 1

That ideal runs so strong and so deep in our culture and psyche that when experts talk about the value of family dinners, they may leave aside the clutter of contradictions. Just because we eat together does not mean we eat right: Domino's alone delivers a million pizzas on an average day. Just because we are sitting together doesn't mean we have anything to say: children bicker and fidget and daydream; parents stew over the remains of the day. Often the richest conversations, the moments of genuine intimacy, take place somewhere else, in the car, say, on the way back from soccer at dusk, when the low light and lack of eye contact allow secrets to surface. 2

Yet for all that, there is something about a shared meal—not some holiday blowout, not once in a while but regularly, reliably—that anchors a family even on nights when the food is fast and the talk cheap and everyone has someplace else they'd rather be. And on those evenings when the mood is right and the family lingers, caught up in an idea or an argument explored in a shared safe place where no one is stupid or shy or ashamed, you get a glimpse of the power of this habit and why social scientists say such communion acts as a kind of vaccine, protecting kids from all manner of harm. 3

In fact, it's the experts in adolescent development who wax most emphatic about the value of family meals, for it's in the teenage years that this daily investment pays some of its biggest dividends. Studies 4

[1]*June and Ward Cleaver:* the parents in the classic family sitcom *Leave It to Beaver*, which aired from 1957 to 1963.

show that the more often families eat together, the less likely kids are to smoke, drink, do drugs, get depressed, develop eating disorders, and consider suicide, and the more likely they are to do well in school, delay having sex, eat their vegetables, learn big words, and know which fork to use. "If it were just about food, we would squirt it into their mouths with a tube," says Robin Fox, an anthropologist who teaches at Rutgers University in New Jersey, about the mysterious way that family dinner engraves our souls. "A meal is about civilizing children. It's about teaching them to be a member of their culture."

The most probing study of family eating patterns was published 5
last year by the National Center on Addiction and Substance Abuse (CASA) at Columbia University and reflects nearly a decade's worth of data gathering. The researchers found essentially that family dinner gets better with practice; the less often a family eats together, the worse the experience is likely to be, the less healthy the food, and the more meager the talk. Among those who eat together three or fewer times a week, 45 percent say the TV is on during meals (as opposed to 37 percent of all households), and nearly one-third say there isn't much conversation. Such kids are also more than twice as likely as those who have frequent family meals to say there is a great deal of tension among family members, and they are much less likely to think their parents are proud of them.

The older that kids are, the more they may need this protected 6
time together, but the less likely they are to get it. Although a majority of twelve-year-olds in the CASA study said they had dinner with a parent seven nights a week, only a quarter of seventeen-year-olds did. Researchers have found all kinds of intriguing educational and ethnic patterns. The families with the least educated parents, for example, eat together the most; parents with less than a high school education share more meals with their kids than do parents with high school diplomas or college degrees. That may end up acting as a generational corrective; kids who eat most often with their parents are 40 percent more likely to say they get mainly As and Bs in school than kids who have two or fewer family dinners a week. Foreign-born kids are much more likely to eat with their parents. When researchers looked at ethnic and racial breakdowns, they found that more than half of Hispanic teens ate with a parent at least six times a week, in contrast to 40 percent of black teens and 39 percent of whites.

Back in the really olden days, dinner was seldom a ceremonial 7
event for U.S. families. Only the very wealthy had a separate dining room. For most, meals were informal, a kind of rolling refueling; often

only the men sat down. Not until the mid-nineteenth century did the day acquire its middle-class rhythms and rituals; a proper dining room became a Victorian aspiration. When children were eight or nine, they were allowed to join the adults at the table for instruction in proper etiquette. By the turn of the century, restaurants had appeared to cater to clerical workers, and in time, eating out became a recreational sport. Family dinner in the Norman Rockwell mode had taken hold by the 1950s: Mom cooked, Dad carved, son cleared, daughter did the dishes.

All kinds of social and economic and technological factors then 8
conspired to shred that tidy picture to the point that the frequency of family dining fell about a third over the next thirty years. With both parents working and the kids shuttling between sports practices or attached to their screens at home, finding a time for everyone to sit around the same table, eating the same food and listening to one another, became a quaint kind of luxury. Meanwhile, the message embedded in the microwave was that time spent standing in front of a stove was time wasted.

But something precious was lost, anthropologist Fox argues, when 9
cooking came to be cast as drudgery and meals as discretionary. "Making food is a sacred event," he says. "It's so absolutely central—far more central than sex. You can keep a population going by having sex once a year, but you have to eat three times a day." Food comes so easily to us now, he says, that we have lost a sense of its significance. When we had to grow the corn and fight off predators, meals included a serving of gratitude. "It's like the American Indians. When they killed a deer, they said a prayer over it," says Fox. "That is civilization. It is an act of politeness over food. Fast food has killed this. We have reduced eating to sitting alone and shoveling it in. There is no ceremony in it."

Or at least there wasn't for many families until researchers in the 10
1980s began looking at the data and doing all kinds of regression analyses that showed how a shared pot roast could contribute to kids' success and health. What the studies could not prove was what is cause and what is effect. Researchers speculate that maybe kids who eat a lot of family meals have less unsupervised time and thus less chance to get into trouble. Families who make meals a priority also tend to spend more time on reading for pleasure and homework. A whole basket of values and habits, of which a common mealtime is only one, may work together to ground kids. But it's a bellwether, and baby boomers who won't listen to their instincts will often listen to the experts: the 2005 CASA study found that the number of adolescents eating with their family most nights has increased 23 percent since 1998.

That rise may also reflect a deliberate public-education campaign, including public-service announcements on TV Land and Nick at Nite that are designed to convince families that it's worth some inconvenience or compromise to make meals together a priority. The enemies here are laziness and leniency: "We're talking about a contemporary style of parenting, particularly in the middle class, that is overindulgent of children," argues William Doherty, a professor of family social science at the University of Minnesota at Minneapolis and author of *The Intentional Family: Simple Rituals to Strengthen Family Ties.* "It treats them as customers who need to be pleased." By that, he means the willingness of parents to let dinner be an individual improvisation—no routine, no rules, leave the television on, everyone eats what they want, teenagers take a plate to their room so they can keep IMing their friends. 11

The food-court mentality—Johnny eats a burrito, Dad has a burger, and Mom picks pasta—comes at a cost. Little humans often resist new tastes; they need some nudging away from the salt and fat and toward the fruits and fiber. A study in the *Archives of Family Medicine* found that more family meals tends to mean less soda and fried food and far more fruits and vegetables. 12

Beyond promoting balance and variety in kids' diets, meals together send the message that citizenship in a family entails certain standards beyond individual whims. This is where a family builds its identity and culture. Legends are passed down, jokes rendered, eventually the wider world examined through the lens of a family's values. In addition, younger kids pick up vocabulary and a sense of how conversation is structured. They hear how a problem is solved, learn to listen to other people's concerns, and respect their tastes. "A meal is about sharing," says Doherty. "I see this trend where parents are preparing different meals for each kid, and it takes away from that. The sharing is the compromise. Not everyone gets their ideal menu every night." 13

Doherty heard from a YMCA camp counselor about the number of kids who arrive with a list of foods they won't eat and who require basic instruction from counselors on how to share a meal. "They have to teach them how to pass food around and serve each other. The kids have to learn how to eat what's there. And they have to learn how to remain seated until everyone else is done." The University of Kansas and Michigan State offer students coaching on how to handle a business lunch, including what to do about food they don't like ("Eat it anyway") and how to pass the salt and pepper ("They're married. They never take separate vacations"). 14

15 When parents say their older kids are too busy or resistant to come to the table the way they did when they were seven, the dinner evangelists produce evidence to the contrary. The CASA study found that a majority of teens who ate three or fewer meals a week with their families wished they did so more often. Parents sometimes seem a little too eager to be rejected by their teenage sons and daughters, suggests Miriam Weinstein, a freelance journalist who wrote *The Surprising Power of Family Meals*. "We've sold ourselves on the idea that teenagers are obviously sick of their families, that they're bonded to their peer group," she says. "We've taken it to an extreme. We've taken it to mean that a teenager has no need for his family. And that's just not true." She scolds parents who blame their kids for undermining mealtime when the adults are coconspirators. "It's become a badge of honor to say, 'I have no time. I am so busy,'" she says. "But we make a lot of choices, and we have a lot more discretion than we give ourselves credit for," she says. Parents may be undervaluing themselves when they conclude that sending kids off to every conceivable extracurricular activity is a better use of time than an hour spent around a table, just talking to Mom and Dad.

16 The family-meal crusaders offer lots of advice to parents seeking to recenter their household on the dinner table. Groups like Ready, Set, Relax!, based in Ridgewood, New Jersey, have dispensed hundreds of kits to towns from Kentucky to California, coaching communities on how to fight overscheduling and carve out family downtime. More schools are offering basic cooking instruction. It turns out that when kids help prepare a meal, they are much more likely to eat it, and it's a useful skill that seems to build self-esteem. Research on family meals does not explore whether it makes a difference if dinner is with two parents or one or even whether the meal needs to be dinner. For families whose schedules make evenings together a challenge, breakfast or lunch may have the same value. So pull up some chairs. Lose the TV. Let the phone go unanswered. And see where the moment takes you.

Thinking Critically about This Reading

In paragraph 6, Gibbs states that "researchers have found [that] all kinds of intriguing educational and ethnic patterns" surround family dining. Did any of the statistical patterns cited in that paragraph surprise you? How well do these statistical findings fit your own experiences and observations? What conclusions, if any, can you draw from them?

Questions for Study and Discussion

1. According to Gibbs, what happens at the "idealized" family dinner? What do you think she means when she says, "The idealized version is as close to a regular worship service, with its litanies and lessons and blessings, as a family gets outside a sanctuary" (paragraph 1)?
2. What are the dividends for teenagers who grow up in a family that eats together? In what ways do family dinners act "as a kind of vaccine, protecting kids from all manner of harm" (3)?
3. Do you agree with Gibbs when she says, "The older that kids are, the more they may need this protected time [family meals] together" (6)? Explain why or why not.
4. Gibbs cites a number of surveys, studies, and experts in her essay to both explain and support the points she makes. Which information did you find most interesting? Most convincing?
5. Identify the strategies Gibbs uses to transition between paragraphs 1 and 2, 7 and 8, 8 and 9, 10 and 11, 11 and 12, and 12 and 13. How does each strategy work? Explain.
6. What cultural factors during the 1960s, 1970s, and 1980s undermined and helped destroy the ritual of family dining? According to Gibbs, what has happened since then to reinvigorate the idea of family meals?
7. According to Robin Fox, with the advent of fast food "we have reduced eating to sitting alone and shoveling it in. There is no ceremony in it" (9). What nutritional, social, and family values does a "shared pot roast" (10) offer children? Do you think that "it's worth some inconvenience or compromise to make meals together a priority" (11)? Explain.

Classroom Activity Using Transitions

The following sentences, which make up the first paragraph of E. B. White's essay "Once More to the Lake," have been rearranged. Place the sentences in what seems to you to be a coherent sequence by relying on language signals like transitions, repeated words, pronouns, and temporal references. Be prepared to explain your reasons for the placement of each sentence.

1. I have since become a salt-water man, but sometimes in summer there are days when the restlessness of the tides and the fearful cold of the sea water and the incessant wind which blows across the afternoon and into the evening make me wish for the placidity of a lake in the woods.
2. We all got ringworm from some kittens and had to rub Pond's Extract on our arms and legs night and morning, and my father rolled over in a canoe with all his clothes on; but outside of that the vacation was a success and from then on none of us ever thought there was any place in the world like that lake in Maine.
3. A few weeks ago this feeling got so strong I bought myself a couple of bass hooks and a spinner and returned to the lake where we used to go for a week's fishing and to revisit old haunts.
4. One summer, along about 1904, my father rented a camp on a lake in Maine and took us all there for the month of August.
5. We returned there summer after summer—always on August 1st for one month.

Suggested Writing Assignments

1. In paragraph 4, Gibbs quotes anthropologist Robin Fox: "A meal is about civilizing children. It's about teaching them to be a member of their culture." What exactly is Fox claiming here? What do children learn from eating meals with their family on a regular basis? Write an essay in which you agree or disagree with Fox's claim. Be sure to use examples from your own family experiences or observations of other families to illustrate and support your position. Be sure to relate your examples using adequate transitions, so that your essay is coherent.
2. Looking back on your own childhood and adolescence, how would you assess your family's mealtime experiences? Was mealtime in your house a family time, or did a "food-court mentality" (12) prevail? Was mealtime a place where your family built "its identity and culture" (13)? What did your parents do really well? What could they have done better? Based on your own experiences and observations, write an essay in which you offer advice to today's young parents. What insights can you offer parents to help them "recenter their household on the dinner table"(16)?

CHAPTER **9**

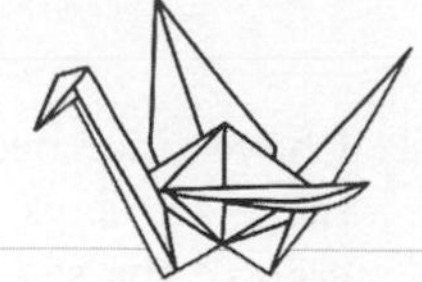

Effective Sentences

Each of the following paragraphs describes the Canadian city of Vancouver, British Columbia. Although the content of both paragraphs is essentially the same, the first paragraph is written in sentences of nearly the same length and pattern, whereas the second paragraph uses sentences of varying length and pattern.

Unvaried Sentences

Water surrounds Vancouver on three sides. The snow-crowned Coast Mountains ring the city on the northeast. Vancouver has a floating quality of natural loveliness. There is a curved beach at English Bay. This beach is in the shape of a half moon. Residential high-rises stand behind the beach. They are in pale tones of beige, blue, and ice-cream pink. Turn-of-the-century houses of painted wood frown upward at the glitter of office towers. Any urban glare is softened by folds of green lawns, flowers, fountains, and trees. Such landscaping appears to be unplanned. It links Vancouver to her ultimate treasure of greenness. That treasure is thousand-acre Stanley Park. Surrounding stretches of water dominate. They have image-evoking names like False Creek and Lost Lagoon. Sailboats and pleasure craft skim blithely across Burrard Inlet. Foreign freighters are out in English Bay. They await their turn to take on cargoes of grain.

Varied Sentences

Surrounded by water on three sides and ringed to the northeast by the snow-crowned Coast Mountains, Vancouver has a floating quality of natural loveliness. At English Bay, the half-moon curve of beach is backed by high-rises in pale tones of beige, blue, and ice-cream pink. Turn-of-the-century houses of painted wood frown upward at the glitter of office towers. Yet any urban glare is quickly softened by folds of green lawns, flowers, fountains, and trees that in

> a seemingly unplanned fashion link Vancouver to her ultimate treasure of greenness—thousand-acre Stanley Park. And always it is the surrounding stretches of water that dominate, with their image-evoking names like False Creek and Lost Lagoon. Sailboats and pleasure craft skim blithely across Burrard Inlet, while out in English Bay foreign freighters await their turn to take on cargoes of grain.

The difference between these two paragraphs is dramatic. The first is monotonous because of the sameness of the sentence structure and because the ideas are not related to one another in a meaningful way. The second paragraph is much more interesting and readable; its sentences vary in length and are structured to clarify the relationships among the ideas. Sentence variety, an important aspect of all good writing, should be used to express ideas precisely and to emphasize the most important ideas within each sentence. Sentence variety includes the use of *subordination, periodic and loose sentences, dramatically short sentences, active and passive voice, coordination,* and *parallelism.*

■ SENTENCE VARIETY

Subordination

Subordination, the process of giving one idea less emphasis than another in a sentence, is one of the most important characteristics of an effective sentence and a mature prose style. Writers subordinate ideas by introducing them either with subordinating conjunctions (*because, if, as though, while, when, after*) or with relative pronouns (*that, which, who, whomever, what*). Subordination not only deemphasizes some ideas but also highlights others that the writer believes are more important.

There is nothing about an idea—*any* idea—that automatically makes it primary or secondary in importance. The writer decides what to emphasize, and he or she may choose to emphasize the less profound or noteworthy of two ideas. Consider, for example, the following sentence: "Melissa was reading a detective story while the national election results were being televised." Everyone, including the author of the sentence, knows that the national election is a more noteworthy event than that Melissa was reading a detective story. But the sentence concerns Melissa, not the election, and so her reading is stated in the main clause, while the election news is subordinated in a dependent clause.

Generally, writers place the ideas they consider important in main clauses, and other ideas go into dependent clauses. Consider the following examples:

> When she was thirty years old, she made her first solo flight across the Atlantic.

> When she made her first solo flight across the Atlantic, she was thirty years old.

The first sentence emphasizes the solo flight; in the second sentence, the emphasis is on the pilot's age.

Periodic and Loose Sentences

Another way to achieve emphasis is to place the most important words, phrases, and clauses at the beginning or end of a sentence. The ending is the most emphatic part of a sentence, the beginning is less emphatic, and the middle is the least emphatic of all. The two preceding sentences about the thirty-year-old pilot put the main clause at the end, achieving special emphasis. The same thing occurs in a much longer kind of sentence, called a *periodic sentence,* in which the main idea is placed at the end, closest to the period. Here is an example from the *New Yorker*'s Talk of the Town feature:

> On the afternoon of the first day of spring, when the gutters were still heaped high with Monday's snow but the sky itself had been swept clean, we put on our galoshes and walked up the sunny side of Fifth Avenue to Central Park.
>
> –John Updike

By holding the main clause back, Updike keeps his readers in suspense and so puts the most emphasis possible on his main idea.

A *loose sentence,* on the other hand, states its main idea at the beginning and then adds details in subsequent phrases and clauses. Rewritten as a loose sentence, Updike's sentence might read like this:

> We put on our galoshes and walked up the sunny side of Fifth Avenue to Central Park on the afternoon of the first day of spring, when the gutters were still heaped high with Monday's snow but the sky itself had been swept clean.

The main idea still gets plenty of emphasis, since it is contained in a main clause at the beginning of the sentence. A loose sentence resembles the way people talk: it flows naturally and is easy to understand.

Dramatically Short Sentences

Another way to create emphasis is to use a *dramatically short sentence.* Especially when following a long and involved sentence, a short declarative sentence helps drive a point home. Here are two examples:

> The qualities that Barbie promotes (slimness, youth, and beauty) allow no tolerance of gray hair, wrinkles, sloping posture, or failing eyesight and hearing. Barbie's perfect body is eternal.
>
> –Danielle Kuykendall, student

> Be specific. Don't say "fruit." Tell what kind of fruit—"It is a pomegranate." Give things the dignity of their names. Just as with human beings, it is rude to say, "Hey, girl, get in line." That "girl" has a name. (As a matter of fact, if she's at least twenty years old, she's a woman, not a "girl" at all.) Things, too, have names. It is much better to say "the geranium in the window" than "the flower in the window." "Geranium"—that one word gives us a much more specific picture. It penetrates more deeply into the beingness of that flower. It immediately gives us the scene by the window—red petals, green circular leaves, all straining toward sunlight.
>
> –Natalie Goldberg, "Be Specific," pp. 309–10

Active and Passive Voice

Finally, since the subject of a sentence is automatically emphasized, writers may choose to use the *active voice* when they want to emphasize the doer of an action and the *passive voice* when they want to downplay or omit the doer completely. Here are two examples:

> High winds pushed our sailboat onto the rocks, where the force of the waves tore it to pieces.

> Our sailboat was pushed by high winds onto the rocks, where it was torn to pieces by the force of the waves.
>
> –Liz Coughlan, student

The first sentence emphasizes the natural forces that destroyed the boat, whereas the second sentence focuses attention on the boat itself. The passive voice may be useful in placing emphasis, but it has important disadvantages. As the examples show, and as the terms suggest, active-voice verbs are more vigorous and vivid than the same verbs in the passive voice. Then, too, some writers use the passive voice to hide or evade responsibility. "It has been decided" conceals who did the deciding, whereas "I have decided" makes it all clear. So the passive voice should be used only when necessary, as it is in this sentence.

SENTENCE EMPHASIS

Coordination

Often a writer wants to place equal emphasis on several facts or ideas. One way to do so is to give each its own sentence. For example, consider these three sentences about golfer Michelle Wie.

> Michelle Wie selected her club. She lined up her shot. She chipped the ball to within a foot of the pin.

But a long series of short, simple sentences quickly becomes tedious. Many writers would combine these three sentences by using **coordination**. The coordinating conjunctions *and, but, or, nor, for, so,* and *yet* connect words, phrases, and clauses of equal importance:

> Michelle Wie selected her club, lined up her shot, and chipped the ball to within a foot of the pin.
>
> –Will Briggs, student

By coordinating three sentences into one, the writer makes the same words easier to read and also shows that Wie's three actions are equally important parts of a single process.

Parallelism

When parts of a sentence are not only coordinated but also grammatically the same, they are parallel. **Parallelism** in a sentence is created by balancing a word with a word, a phrase with a phrase, or a clause with a clause. Here is a humorous example from the beginning of Mark Twain's *Adventures of Huckleberry Finn:*

> Persons attempting to find a motive in this narrative will be prosecuted; persons attempting to find a moral in it will be banished; persons attempting to find a plot in it will be shot.
>
> –Mark Twain

Parallelism is often found in speeches. For example, in the last sentence of the Gettysburg Address, Lincoln proclaims his hope that "government of the people, by the people, for the people, shall not perish from the earth." (See the Classroom Activity on pp. 318–19, for the complete text of Lincoln's Gettysburg Address.)

Thirty-Eight Who Saw Murder Didn't Call Police

■ Martin Gansberg

Reporter Martin Gansberg (1920–1995) was born in Brooklyn, New York, and graduated from St. John's University. Gansberg was an experienced copy editor completing one of his first reporting assignments when he wrote the following essay for the New York Times *in 1964, two weeks after the events he poignantly narrates. Once you've finished reading the essay, you will understand why it has been reprinted often and why the name Kitty Genovese is still invoked whenever questions of public apathy arise.*

Notice how Gansberg uses dialogue effectively in this essay to emphasize his point. Pay attention to how he constructs the sentences that incorporate dialogue and to how subordination and coordination often determine where quoted material appears.

Reflecting on What You Know

Have times changed? Are people more willing to jump in and help today, or are they simply taking more videos and posting on social media about what they see happening. How do you think you would react if you witnessed a crime?

For more than half an hour thirty-eight respectable, law-abiding citizens in Queens[1] watched a killer stalk and stab a woman in three separate attacks in Kew Gardens. 1

Twice their chatter and the sudden glow of their bedroom lights interrupted him and frightened him off. Each time he returned, sought her out, and stabbed her again. Not one person telephoned the police during the assault; one witness called after the woman was dead. 2

That was two weeks ago today. 3

Still shocked is Assistant Chief Inspector Frederick M. Lussen, in charge of the borough's detectives and a veteran of twenty-five years of 4

[1]*Queens:* one of New York City's five boroughs.

homicide investigations. He can give a matter-of-fact recitation on many murders. But the Kew Gardens slaying baffles him—not because it is a murder, but because the "good people" failed to call the police.

"As we have reconstructed the crime," he said, "the assailant had 5
three chances to kill this woman during a thirty-five-minute period. He returned twice to complete the job. If we had been called when he first attacked, the woman might not be dead now."

This is what the police say happened beginning at 3:20 a.m. in 6
the staid, middle-class, tree-lined Austin Street area:

Twenty-eight-year-old Catherine Genovese, who was called Kitty 7
by almost everyone in the neighborhood, was returning home from her job as manager of a bar in Hollis. She parked her red Fiat in a lot adjacent to the Kew Gardens Long Island Rail Road Station, facing Mowbray Place. Like many residents of the neighborhood, she had parked there day after day since her arrival from Connecticut a year ago, although the railroad frowns on the practice.

She turned off the lights of her car, locked the door, and started to 8
walk the one hundred feet to the entrance of her apartment at 82-70 Austin Street, which is in a Tudor building, with stores in the first floor and apartments on the second.

The entrance to the apartment is in the rear of the building 9
because the front is rented to retail stores. At night the quiet neighborhood is shrouded in the slumbering darkness that marks most residential areas.

Miss Genovese noticed a man at the far end of the lot, near a seven- 10
story apartment house at 82-40 Austin Street. She halted. Then, nervously, she headed up Austin Street toward Lefferts Boulevard, where there is a call box to the 102nd Police Precinct in nearby Richmond Hill.

She got as far as a street light in front of a bookstore before 11
the man grabbed her. She screamed. Lights went on in the ten-story apartment house at 82-67 Austin Street, which faces the bookstore. Windows slid open and voices punctuated the early-morning stillness.

Miss Genovese screamed: "Oh, my God, he stabbed me! Please 12
help me! Please help me!"

From one of the upper windows in the apartment house, a man 13
called down: "Let that girl alone!"

The assailant looked up at him, shrugged, and walked down Austin 14
Street toward a white sedan parked a short distance away. Miss Genovese struggled to her feet.

15 Lights went out. The killer returned to Miss Genovese, now trying to make her way around the side of the building by the parking lot to get to her apartment. The assailant stabbed her again.

16 "I'm dying!" she shrieked. "I'm dying!"

17 Windows were opened again, and lights went on in many apartments. The assailant got into his car and drove away. Miss Genovese staggered to her feet. A city bus, Q-10, the Lefferts Boulevard line to Kennedy International Airport, passed. It was 3:35 a.m.

18 The assailant returned. By then, Miss Genovese had crawled to the back of the building, where the freshly painted brown doors to the apartment house held out hope for safety. The killer tried the first door; she wasn't there. At the second door, 82-62 Austin Street, he saw her slumped on the floor at the foot of the stairs. He stabbed her a third time—fatally.

19 It was 3:50 by the time the police received their first call, from a man who was a neighbor of Miss Genovese. In two minutes they were at the scene. The neighbor, a seventy-year-old woman, and another woman were the only persons on the street. Nobody else came forward.

20 The man explained that he had called the police after much deliberation. He had phoned a friend in Nassau County for advice and then he had crossed the roof of the building to the apartment of the elderly woman to get her to make the call.

21 "I didn't want to get involved," he sheepishly told the police.

22 Six days later, the police arrested Winston Moseley, a twenty-nine-year-old business-machine operator, and charged him with homicide. Moseley had no previous record. He is married, has two children and owns a home at 133-19 Sutter Avenue, South Ozone Park, Queens. On Wednesday, a court committed him to Kings County Hospital for psychiatric observation.

23 When questioned by the police, Moseley also said that he had slain Mrs. Annie May Johnson, twenty-four, of 146-12 133d Avenue, Jamaica, on February 29 and Barbara Kralik, fifteen, of 174-17 140th Avenue, Springfield Gardens, last July. In the Kralik case, the police are holding Alvin L. Mitchell, who is said to have confessed to that slaying.

24 The police stressed how simple it would have been to have gotten in touch with them. "A phone call," said one of the detectives, "would have done it." The police may be reached by dialing "O" for operator or SPring 7-3100.[2]

---

[2] *SPring 7-3100:* a mid-twentieth-century phone number that used a combination of both letters (the *SP* of *spring*) and numbers.

Today witnesses from the neighborhood, which is made up of one-family homes in the $35,000 to $60,000 range with the exception of the two apartment houses near the railroad station, find it difficult to explain why they didn't call the police. 25

A housewife, knowingly if quite casually, said, "We thought it was a lovers' quarrel." A husband and wife both said, "Frankly, we were afraid." They seemed aware of the fact that events might have been different. A distraught woman, wiping her hands in her apron, said, "I didn't want my husband to get involved." 26

One couple, now willing to talk about that night, said they heard the first screams. The husband looked thoughtfully at the bookstore where the killer first grabbed Miss Genovese. 27

"We went to the window to see what was happening," he said, "but the light from our bedroom made it difficult to see the street." The wife, still apprehensive, added: "I put out the light and we were able to see better." 28

Asked why they hadn't called the police, she shrugged and replied: "I don't know." 29

A man peeked out from a slight opening in the doorway to his apartment and rattled off an account of the killer's second attack. Why hadn't he called the police at the time? "I was tired," he said without emotion. "I went back to bed." 30

It was 4:25 a.m. when the ambulance arrived to take the body of Miss Genovese. It drove off. "Then," a solemn police detective said, "the people came out." 31

Thinking Critically about This Reading

How does Gansberg reveal his attitude about the lack of response to the attack on Kitty Genovese, even though he writes in the third-person point of view and interjects no opinions of his own?

Questions for Study and Discussion

1. What is Gansberg's purpose? (Glossary: *Purpose*) What are the advantages or disadvantages in using narration to accomplish this purpose? Explain.
2. Where does the narrative actually begin? What is the function of the material that precedes the beginning of the narrative?

3. Analyze Gansberg's sentences in paragraphs 7–9. How does he use subordination to highlight what he believes is essential information? (Glossary: *Subordination*)
4. Gansberg uses a number of two- and three-word sentences in his narrative. Identify several of these sentences, and explain how they serve to punctuate and add drama to this story. Which short sentences have the greatest impact on you? Why?
5. Gansberg uses dialogue throughout his essay. (Glossary: *Dialogue*) How many people does he quote? What does he accomplish by using dialogue?
6. How would you describe Gansberg's tone? (Glossary: *Tone*) Is it appropriate for the story he narrates? Explain.
7. Reflect on Gansberg's ending. (Glossary: *Beginnings and Endings*) What would be lost or gained by adding a paragraph that analyzes the meaning of the narrative for readers?

Classroom Activity Using Effective Sentences

Repetition can be an effective writing device to emphasize important points and to enhance coherence. Unless it is handled carefully, however, it can often result in a tedious piece of writing. Rewrite the following paragraph, either eliminating repetition or reworking the repetitions to improve coherence and to emphasize important information.

> Daycare centers should be available to all women who work and have no one to care for their children. Daycare centers should not be available only to women who are raising their children alone or to families whose income is below the poverty level. All women who work should have available to them care for their children that is reliable, responsible, convenient, and does not cost an exorbitant amount. Women who work need and must demand more daycare centers. No woman should be prevented from working because of the lack of convenient and reliable facilities for child care.

Suggested Writing Assignments

1. Gansberg's essay is about public apathy and fear. What reasons did Kitty Genovese's neighbors give for not calling the police when they first heard her calls for help? How do these reasons reflect on human nature, particularly as it manifests itself in contemporary American society? Modeling your essay after Gansberg's,

narrate another event or series of events you know about that demonstrates either public involvement or public apathy. (Glossary: *Narration*)

2. It is common when using narration to tell about firsthand experience and to tell the story in the first person. (Glossary: *Narration; Point of View*) It is good practice, however, to try writing a narrative essay on something you don't know about firsthand but must learn about, much as a newspaper reporter gathers information for a story. For several days, be attentive to events occurring around you—in your neighborhood, school, community, region—events that would be appropriate for a narrative essay. Interview the principal characters involved in your story, take detailed notes, and then write your narration.
3. Gansberg's essay illustrates how people often choose to let someone else take care of a situation instead of taking action themselves. Reflect on the essay, and write your own essay in which you explore the reasons some people in dangerous or life-threatening situations choose to act while so many others do not. In your opinion, when should bystanders involve themselves in a situation such as the attack on Kitty Genovese? How involved should a bystander become? What advice do you think Gansberg would give? Why?

Salvation

■ Langston Hughes

CORBIS

Born in Joplin, Missouri, Langston Hughes (1902–1967) became an important figure in the African American cultural movement of the 1920s known as the Harlem Renaissance. He wrote poetry, fiction, and plays, and contributed columns to the New York Post *and an African American weekly, the* Chicago Defender. *He is best known for* The Weary Blues *(1926) and other books of poetry that express his racial pride, his familiarity with African American traditions, and his understanding of blues and jazz rhythms. In his memory, New York City designated his residence at 20 East 127th Street in Harlem as a landmark, and his street was renamed Langston Hughes Place.*

In the following selection from his autobiography, The Big Sea *(1940), notice how, for the sake of emphasis, Hughes varies the length and types of sentences he uses. The effect of the dramatically short sentence in paragraph 12, for instance, derives from the variety of sentences preceding it.*

Reflecting on What You Know

What role does religion play in your family? Do you consider yourself a religious person? Have you ever felt pressure from others to participate in religious activities? How did that make you feel?

I was saved from sin when I was going on thirteen. But not really saved. It happened like this. There was a big revival at my Auntie Reed's church. Every night for weeks there had been much preaching, singing, praying, and shouting, and some very hardened sinners had been brought to Christ, and the membership of the church had grown by leaps and bounds. Then just before the revival ended, they held a special meeting for children, "to bring the young lambs to the fold." My aunt spoke of it for days ahead. That night I was escorted to the 1 front row and placed on the mourners' bench with all the other young sinners, who had not yet been brought to Jesus.

My aunt told me that when you were saved you saw a light, and something happened to you inside! And Jesus came into your life! And God was with you from then on! She said you could see and hear and feel Jesus in your soul. I believed her. I had heard a great many old people say the same thing and it seemed to me they ought to know. So I sat there calmly in the hot, crowded church, waiting for Jesus to come to me. 2

The preacher preached a wonderful rhythmical sermon, all moans and shouts and lonely cries and dire pictures of hell, and then he sang a song about the ninety and nine safe in the fold, but one little lamb was left out in the cold. Then he said: "Won't you come? Won't you come to Jesus? Young lambs, won't you come?" And he held out his arms to all us young sinners there on the mourners' bench. And the little girls cried. And some of them jumped up and went to Jesus right away. But most of us just sat there. 3

A great many old people came and knelt around us and prayed, old women with jet-black faces and braided hair, old men with work-gnarled hands. And the church sang a song about the lower lights are burning, some poor sinners to be saved. And the whole building rocked with prayer and song. 4

Still I kept waiting to *see* Jesus. 5

Finally all the young people had gone to the altar and were saved, but one boy and me. He was a rounder's son named Westley. Westley and I were surrounded by sisters and deacons praying. It was very hot in the church, and getting late now. Finally Westley said to me in a whisper: "God damn! I'm tired o' sitting here. Let's get up and be saved." So he got up and was saved. 6

Then I was left all alone on the mourners' bench. My aunt came and knelt at my knees and cried, while prayers and songs swirled all around me in the little church. The whole congregation prayed for me alone, in a mighty wail of moans and voices. And I kept waiting serenely for Jesus, waiting, waiting—but he didn't come. I wanted to see him, but nothing happened to me. Nothing! I wanted something to happen to me, but nothing happened. 7

I heard the songs and the minister saying: "Why don't you come? My dear child, why don't you come to Jesus? Jesus is waiting for you. He wants you. Why don't you come? Sister Reed, what is this child's name?" 8

"Langston," my aunt sobbed. 9

"Langston, why don't you come? Why don't you come and be 10
saved? Oh, Lamb of God! Why don't you come?"

Now it was really getting late. I began to be ashamed of myself, 11
holding everything up so long. I began to wonder what God thought about Westley, who certainly hadn't seen Jesus either, but who was now sitting proudly on the platform, swinging his knickerbockered legs and grinning down at me, surrounded by deacons and old women on their knees praying. God had not struck Westley dead for taking his name in vain or for lying in the temple. So I decided that maybe to save further trouble, I'd better lie, too, and say that Jesus had come, and get up and be saved.

So I got up. 12

Suddenly the whole room broke into a sea of shouting, as they 13
saw me rise. Waves of rejoicing swept the place. Women leaped in the air. My aunt threw her arms around me. The minister took me by the hand and led me to the platform.

When things quieted down, in a hushed silence, punctuated by a 14
few ecstatic "Amens," all the new young lambs were blessed in the name of God. Then joyous singing filled the room.

That night, for the last time in my life but one—for I was a big 15
boy twelve years old—I cried. I cried, in bed alone, and couldn't stop. I buried my head under the quilts, but my aunt heard me. She woke up and told my uncle I was crying because the Holy Ghost had come into my life, and because I had seen Jesus. But I was really crying because I couldn't bear to tell her that I had lied, that I had deceived everybody in the church, that I hadn't seen Jesus, and that now I didn't believe there was a Jesus any more, since he didn't come to help me.

Thinking Critically about This Reading

Why does Hughes cry on the night of his being "saved"? What makes the story of his being saved so ironic? (Glossary: *Irony*)

Questions for Study and Discussion

1. What is salvation? Is it important to young Hughes that he be saved? Why does he expect to be saved at the revival meeting?

2. Hughes varies the length and structure of his sentences throughout the essay. How does this variety capture and reinforce the rhythms and drama of the evening's events? Explain.
3. What would be gained or lost if the essay began with the first two sentences combined as follows: "I was saved from sin when I was going on thirteen, but I was not really saved"?
4. Identify the coordinating conjunctions in paragraph 3. (Glossary: *Coordination*) Rewrite the paragraph without them. Compare your paragraph with the original, and explain what Hughes gains by using coordinating conjunctions.
5. Identify the subordinating conjunctions in paragraph 15. (Glossary: *Subordination*) What is it about the ideas in this last paragraph that makes it necessary for Hughes to use subordinating conjunctions?
6. How does Hughes's choice of words, or diction, help establish a realistic atmosphere for a religious revival meeting? (Glossary: *Diction*)

Classroom Activity Using Effective Sentences

Using coordination or subordination, rewrite each set of short sentences as a single sentence. Here is an example:

ORIGINAL: This snow is good for Colorado's economy. Tourists are now flocking to ski resorts.

REVISED: This snow is good for Colorado's economy because tourists are now flocking to ski resorts.

1. I can take the 6:30 express train. I can catch the 7:00 bus.
2. Miriam worked on her research paper. She interviewed five people for the paper. She worked all weekend. She was tired.
3. Juan's new job kept him busy every day. He did not have time to work out at the gym for over a month.
4. The Statue of Liberty welcomes newcomers to the United States. It was a gift of the French government. It was completely restored for the nation's two hundredth birthday. It is more than 120 years old.
5. Carla is tall. She is strong. She is a team player. She is the starting center on the basketball team.
6. Betsy loves Bach's music. She also likes Scott Joplin.

Suggested Writing Assignments

1. Like the young Hughes, we sometimes find ourselves in situations in which, for the sake of conformity, we do things we do not believe in. Consider one such experience you have had, and write an essay about it. What in human nature makes us occasionally act in ways that contradict our inner feelings? As you write, pay attention to your sentence variety.
2. In the end of his essay, Langston Hughes suffers alone. He cannot bring himself to talk about his dilemma with his aunt or uncle or other people in the church. Have you ever found yourself in a predicament with no one to turn to for advice or help? Why can it be so difficult for us to seek the help of others? Write an essay in which you explore answers to this question. Consider examples from your own experience and what you have seen and read about other people. Look for opportunities where your sentence variety can enhance the interest and drama of your essay.

Disconnected Urbanism

■ **Paul Goldberger**

Paul Goldberger is the Joseph Urban Chair in Design and Architecture at the New School and an influential architecture critic. After attending Yale University, he began his career at the New York Times, *and in 1984 he won a Pulitzer Prize for his architecture criticism for the paper. He later wrote the "Sky Line" column for the* New Yorker. *He is currently a contributing editor at* Vanity Fair. *Goldberger is the author of several books on the importance of architecture to modern life, including* Up from Zero: Politics, Architecture, and the Rebuilding of New York *(2004),* Why Architecture Matters *(2009), and* Building Up and Tearing Down: Reflections on the Age of Architecture *(2009).*

In "Disconnected Urbanism," Goldberger uses carefully constructed sentences to direct readers' attention to the heart of the problem cell phones pose for public life. As you read the essay, make note of the places where he mentions other issues related to modern life and then puts those issues aside to focus on his main point.

Reflecting on What You Know

Do you feel that cell phones are a disruptive presence in your life? Under what circumstances? When does technology make you feel connected, and when does it feel more like a distraction?

There is a connection between the idea of place and the reality of cellular telephones. It is not encouraging. Places are unique—or at least we like to believe they are—and we strive to experience them as a kind of engagement with particulars. Cell phones are precisely the opposite. When a piece of geography is doing what it is supposed to do, it encourages you to feel a connection to it that, as in marriage, forsakes 1 all others. When you are in Paris you expect to wallow in its Parisness, to feel that everyone walking up the Boulevard Montparnasse is as totally and completely there as the lampposts, the kiosks, the facade of the Brasserie Lipp—and that they could be no place else. So we want it to be in every city, in every kind of place. When you are in a forest, you want to experience its woodsiness; when you are on the beach, you want to feel connected to sand and surf.

This is getting harder to do, not because these special places don't exist or because urban places have come to look increasingly alike. 2
They have, but this is not another rant about the monoculture and sameness of cities and the suburban landscape. Even when you are in a place that retains its intensity, its specialness, and its ability to confer a defining context on your life, it doesn't have the all-consuming effect these places used to. You no longer feel that being in one place cuts you off from other places. Technology has been doing this for a long time, of course—remember when people communicated with Europe by letter and it took a couple of weeks to get a reply? Now we're upset if we have to send a fax because it takes so much longer than e-mail.

But the cell phone has changed our sense of place more than 3
faxes and computers and e-mail because of its ability to intrude into every moment in every possible place. When you walk along the street and talk on a cell phone, you are not on the street sharing the communal experience of urban life. You are in some other place—someplace at the other end of your phone conversation. You are there, but you are not there. It reminds me of the title of Lillian Ross's memoir of her life with William Shawn, *Here but Not Here*. Now that is increasingly true of almost every person on almost every street in almost every city. You are either on the phone or carrying one, and the moment it rings you will be transported out of real space into a virtual realm.

This matters because the street is the ultimate public space and 4
walking along it is the defining urban experience. It is all of us—different people who lead different lives—coming together in the urban mixing chamber. But what if half of them are elsewhere, there in body but not in any other way? You are not on Madison Avenue if you are holding a little object to your ear that pulls you toward a person in Omaha.

The great offense of the cell phone in public is not the intrusion 5
of its ring, although that can be infuriating when it interrupts a tranquil moment. It is the fact that even when the phone does not

ring at all, and is being used quietly and discreetly, it renders a public place less public. It turns the boulevardier into a sequestered individual, the flaneur into a figure of privacy. And suddenly the meaning of the street as a public place has been hugely diminished.

I don't know which is worse—the loss of the sense that walking 6
along a great urban street is a glorious shared experience or the blurring of distinctions between different kinds of places. But these cultural losses are related, and the cell phone has played a major role in both. The other day I returned a phone call from a friend who lives in Hartford. He had left a voice-mail message saying he was visiting his son in New Orleans, and when I called him back on his cell phone—area code 860, Hartford—he picked up the call in Tallahassee. Once the area code actually meant something in terms of geography: it outlined a clearly defined piece of the earth; it became a form of identity. Your telephone number was a badge of place. Now the area code is really not much more than three digits; and if it has any connection to a place, it's just the telephone's home base. An area code today is more like a car's license plate. The downward spiral that began with the end of the old telephone exchanges that truly did connect to a place—RHinelander 4 and BUtterfield 8 for the Upper East Side, or CHelsea 3 downtown, or UNiversity 4 in Morningside Heights—surely culminates in the placeless area codes such as 917 and 347 that could be anywhere in New York—or anywhere at all.

It's increasingly common for cell-phone conversations to begin 7
with the question, "Where are you?" and for the answer to be anything from "out by the pool" to "Madagascar." I don't miss the age when phone charges were based on distance, but that did have the beneficial effect of reinforcing a sense that places were distinguishable from one another. Now calling across the street and calling from New York to California or even Europe are precisely the same thing. They cost the same because to the phone they are the same. Every place is exactly the same as every other place. They are all just nodes on a network—and so, increasingly, are we.

Thinking Critically about This Reading

Goldberger's argument depends on the view that people want to experience place as "a kind of engagement with particulars" (paragraph 1). Do you think this is still true? Do you want to feel that the places you go are different from one another, each with its own special character?

Questions for Study and Discussion

1. Goldberger suggests that a place "encourages you to feel a connection to it that, as in marriage, forsakes all others" (1). What does he mean when he describes that connection as a marriage? Why do you think he echoes the language of a wedding vow? (Glossary: *Allusion*)
2. How might the title of the memoir Goldberger mentions in paragraph 3, *Here but Not Here*, function as an alternate title for his essay? How is it connected to his idea about modern life?
3. Notice how Goldberger uses subordination (especially dependent clauses that begin with "when") in his first paragraph. How does this sentence construction underscore his point about how we want to experience different places?
4. In the first sentence of paragraph 3, Goldberger uses active construction to identify what he sees as an important source of disconnection. Try rewriting that sentence in the passive voice. How would it change the tone of the paragraph?
5. At the end of the essay, Goldberger suggests that both cell phones and their users are "just nodes on a network" (7). What does he mean by this? Do you feel, like Goldberger does, that this trend is "not encouraging" (1)?
6. Goldberger sees cell phones as presenting an even greater problem than have other technologies in the past. Discuss why he feels this way, and then think about future innovations. How are cell phones changing? What other technologies do you see on the horizon? How might these add to the problem Goldberger describes?

Classroom Activity Using Effective Sentences

Rewrite the following sets of sentences to combine short, simple sentences and to reduce repetition wherever possible. Here is an example:

ORIGINAL: Angelo's team won the championship. He pitched a two-hitter. He struck out ten batters. He hit a home run.

REVISED: Angelo's team won the championship because he pitched a two-hitter, struck out ten batters, and hit a home run.

1. Bonnie wore shorts. The shorts were red. The shorts had pockets.
2. The deer hunter awoke at 5 A.M. He ate a quick breakfast. The breakfast consisted of coffee, juice, and cereal. He was in the woods before the sun came up.
3. My grandparents played golf every weekend for years. Last year they stopped playing. They miss the game now.
4. Fly over any major city. Look out the airplane's window. You will be appalled at the number of tall smokestacks you will see.
5. It did not rain for more than three months. Most crops in the region failed. Some farmers were on the brink of declaring bankruptcy.
6. Every weekday I go to work. I exercise. I shower and relax. I eat a light, low-fat dinner.

Suggested Writing Assignments

1. Write an essay based on one of the points Goldberger makes but sets aside. For example, in paragraph 2, he writes, "this is not another rant about the monoculture and sameness of cities and the suburban landscape," though he admits that sameness does exist. In paragraph 5, he claims, "The great offense of the cell phone in public is not the intrusion of its ring, although that can be infuriating when it interrupts a tranquil moment." Following his lead, use clear sentences to outline the exact nature of the problem you are addressing and to indicate what lies outside the boundaries of your current discussion.
2. Have you ever dreamed of something only to be disappointed when your dream came true? For example, have you ever fantasized about taking a trip someplace only to be disappointed when you actually visited that place? Perhaps you hoped to attend a particular college or university and it turned out not to be what you expected it to be. Write an essay about an experience in which reality falls short of a dream. Be sure to use a variety of sentence structures—active and passive, subordinated and coordinated, loose and periodic—as well as sentences demonstrating parallelism to create an essay with a lively and varied style.

CHAPTER **10**

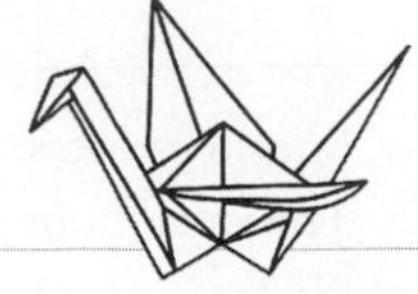

Writing with Sources

Some of the writing you do in college will be experiential (that is, based on your personal experiences), but many of your college assignments will ask you to do some research—to write with sources. Although most of us can do basic research—locate and evaluate print and online sources, take notes from those sources, and document those sources—we have not necessarily learned how to integrate these sources effectively and purposefully into our essays. (For more information on basic research and documentation practices, see Chapter 22.) Your purpose in writing with sources is not to present quotations that report what others have said about your topic. Your goal is to take ownership of your topic by analyzing, evaluating, and synthesizing the materials you have researched. By learning how to view the results of research from your own perspective, you can arrive at an informed opinion of your topic. In short, you become a participant in a conversation with your sources about your topic.

To help you on your way, this chapter provides advice on (1) using outside sources in your writing; (2) summarizing, paraphrasing, and quoting sources; (3) integrating summaries, paraphrases, and direct quotations into the text of your essay using signal phrases; (4) synthesizing sources; and (5) avoiding plagiarism when writing with sources. In addition, one student essay and two professional essays model different ways of engaging meaningfully with outside sources and of reflecting that engagement in writing.

■ USE OUTSIDE SOURCES IN YOUR WRITING

Each time you introduce an outside source into your essay, be sure that you are using that source in a purposeful way. Outside sources can be used to

- support your thesis,
- support your points with statements from noted authorities,

- offer memorable wording of key terms or ideas,
- extend your ideas by introducing new information, and
- articulate opposing positions for you to argue against.

Consider Don Peck's use of an outside source in the following passage from his essay "They're Watching You at Work," published in the December 2013 issue of the *Atlantic*.

> Ever since we've had companies, we've had managers trying to figure out which people are best suited to working for them. The techniques have varied considerably. Near the turn of the 20th century, one manufacturer in Philadelphia made hiring decisions by having its foremen stand in front of the factory and toss apples into the surrounding scrum of jobseekers. Those quick enough to catch the apples and strong enough to keep them were put to work.
>
> In those same times, a different (and less bloody) Darwinian process governed the selection of executives. Whole industries were being consolidated by rising giants like U.S. Steel, DuPont, and GM. Weak competitors were simply steamrolled, but the stronger ones were bought up, and their founders typically were offered high-level jobs within the behemoth. The approach worked pretty well. As Peter Cappelli, a professor at the Wharton School, has written, "Nothing in the science of predictions and selection beats observing actual performance in an equivalent role."

Here Peck quotes Peter Cappelli, a business school professor, to support his point that observations of workers in action have often been used to make hiring decisions.

The following passage comes from "Nature in the Suburbs," an essay that first appeared in *A Guide to Smart Growth: Shattering Myths, Providing Solutions*. The essay was adapted and published separately by the Heritage Foundation in 2004. Here environmentalist Jane S. Shaw uses several sources to substantiate her belief that "there is no reason to be pessimistic about the ability of wildlife to survive and thrive in the suburbs."

> This new ecology is different, but it is often friendly to animals, especially those that University of Florida biologist Larry Harris calls "meso-mammals," or mammals of medium size. They do not need broad territory for roaming to find food, as moose and grizzly bears do. They can find places in the suburbs to feed, nest, and thrive, especially where gardens flourish.

> One example of the positive impact of growth is the rebound of the endangered Key deer, a small white-tailed deer found only in Florida and named for the Florida Keys. According to *Audubon* magazine, the Key deer is experiencing a "remarkable recovery." The news report continues: "Paradoxically, part of the reason for the deer's comeback may lie in the increasing development of the area." Paraphrasing the remarks of a university researcher, the reporter says that human development "tends to open up overgrown forested areas and provide vegetation at deer level—the same factors fueling deer population booms in suburbs all over the country."

Note that in the last sentence of the second paragraph, Shaw is careful to say that she is quoting the *Audubon* reporter's paraphrase of a university researcher's thoughts and not the reporter's.

Sometimes source material is too long and detailed to be quoted directly in its entirety. In such cases, a writer will choose to summarize or paraphrase the material in his or her own words before introducing it in an essay. For example, notice how Scott Barry Kaufman, PhD, summarizes a lengthy creative-achievement study for use in his essay "Dreams of Glory," which appeared in the March 2014 issue of *Psychology Today*.

> Imagining future selves pays dividends long after school ends. In one of the longest and most comprehensive studies of creative achievement ever conducted, psychologist E. Paul Torrance followed a group of elementary school children for more than 30 years. He collected a wide variety of indicators of creative and scholastic promise. Strikingly, he found that the best predictor of lifelong personal and publicly recognized creative achievement—even better than academic indicators such as school grades and IQ scores—was the extent to which children had a clear future-focused image of themselves.

Here Kaufman introduces his summary by citing Torrance's name and giving his professional credentials (research psychologist). After briefly identifying the subjects and the length of the study as well as the data collected, Kaufman concludes with a pointed statement of Torrance's conclusion.

Finally, in the following passage from *The Way We Really Are: Coming to Terms with America's Changing Families* (1998), Stephanie

Coontz uses outside sources to present the position that she will argue against.

> The fallback position for those in denial about the socioeconomic transformation we are experiencing is to admit that many families are in economic stress but to blame their plight on divorce and unwed motherhood. Lawrence Mead of New York University argues that economic inequalities stemming from differences in wages and employment patterns "are now trivial in comparison to those stemming from family structure." David Blankenhorn claims that the "primary fault line" dividing privileged and nonprivileged Americans is no longer "race, religion, class, education, or gender" but family structure. Every major newspaper in the country has published editorials and opinion pieces along these lines. This "new consensus" produces a delightfully simple, inexpensive solution to the economic ills of America's families. From Republican Dan Quayle to the Democratic Party's Progressive Policy Institute, we hear the same words: "Marriage is the best anti-poverty program for children."
>
> Now I am as horrified as anyone by irresponsible parents who yield to the temptations of our winner-take-all society and abandon their family obligations. But we are kidding ourselves if we think the solution to the economic difficulties of America's children lies in getting their parents back together. Single-parent families, it is true, are five to six times more likely to be poor than two-parent ones. But correlations are not the same as causes. The association between poverty and single parenthood has several different sources, suggesting that the battle to end child poverty needs to be fought on a number of different fronts.

By letting the opposition articulate its own position, Coontz reduces the possibility of being criticized for misrepresenting her opponents while setting herself up to give strong voice to her thesis.

LEARN TO SUMMARIZE, PARAPHRASE, AND QUOTE FROM YOUR SOURCES

When taking notes from your print and online sources, you must decide whether to summarize, paraphrase, or quote directly. The approach you take is largely determined by the content of the source passage and the way that you envision using it in your essay. Each technique—summarizing, paraphrasing, and quoting—will help you incorporate source material into your essays. Making use of all three of these techniques rather than relying on only one or two will keep your text varied and interesting. All the examples and page numbers in the following discussion are taken from essays in *Models for Writers* unless otherwise noted.

Summary

When you **summarize** material from one of your sources, you capture in condensed form the essential idea of a passage, an article, or an entire chapter. Summaries are particularly useful when you are working with lengthy, detailed arguments or long passages of narrative or descriptive background information in which the details are not germane to the overall thrust of your essay. You simply want to capture the essence of the passage because you are confident that your readers will readily understand the point being made or do not need to be convinced of its validity. Because you are distilling information, a summary is always shorter than the original; often a chapter or more can be reduced to a paragraph, or several paragraphs to a sentence or two. Remember, in writing a summary you should use your own words.

Consider the following paragraphs, in which Richard Lederer compares big words with small words in some detail:

> When you speak and write, there is no law that says you have to use big words. Short words are as good as long ones, and short, old words—like *sun* and *grass* and *home*—are best of all. A lot of small words, more than you might think, can meet your needs with a strength, grace, and charm that large words do not have.
>
> Big words can make the way dark for those who read what you write and hear what you say. Small words cast their clear light on big things—night and day, love and hate, war and peace, and life and death. Big words at times seem strange to the eye and the ear and the mind and the heart. Small words are the ones we seem to have known from the time we were born, like the hearth fire that warms the home.
>
> –Richard Lederer, "The Case for Short Words," pp. 158–59

A student wishing to capture the gist of Lederer's point without repeating his detailed contrast created the accompanying summary note card.

Summary Note Card

> *Short Words*
>
> *Lederer favors short words for their clarity, familiarity, durability, and overall usefulness.*
>
> *Lederer, "The Case for Short Words," 158–59*

Paraphrase

When you **paraphrase** material from a source, you restate the information in your own words instead of quoting directly. Unlike a summary, which gives a brief overview of the essential information in the original, a paraphrase seeks to maintain the same level of detail as the original, to aid readers in understanding or believing the information presented. Your paraphrase should closely parallel the presentation of ideas in the original, but it should not use the same words or sentence structure as the original. Even though you are using your own words in a paraphrase, it's important to remember that you are borrowing ideas and therefore must acknowledge the source of these ideas with a citation.

How would you paraphrase the following passage from "The Ways of Meeting Oppression" by Martin Luther King Jr.?

> If the American Negro and other victims of oppression succumb to the temptation of using violence in the struggle for freedom, future generations will be the recipients of a desolate night of bitterness, and our chief legacy to them will be an endless reign of meaningless chaos. Violence is not the way.
>
> –Martin Luther King Jr., "The Ways of Meeting Oppression," p. 469

See the accompanying note card for an example of how one student paraphrased the passage.

Paraphrase Note Card

Non-Violence

African Americans and other oppressed peoples must not resort to taking up arms against their oppressors because to do so would lead the country into an era of turmoil and confusion. Confrontation will not yield the desired results.

Martin Luther King Jr.,
"The Ways of Meeting Oppression," 469

In most cases, it is best to summarize or paraphrase material—which by definition means using your own words—instead of quoting verbatim (word for word). Capturing an idea in your own words demonstrates that you have thought about and understood what your source is saying.

Direct Quotation

With a **direct quotation**, you copy the words of your source exactly, putting all quoted material in quotation marks. When you make a direct quotation note card, check the passage carefully for accuracy, including punctuation and capitalization. Be selective about what you choose to quote. Reserve direct quotation for important ideas stated memorably, for especially clear explanations by authorities, and for arguments by proponents of a particular position in their own words.

Consider the accompanying direct quotation note card. It quotes a sentence from Myriam Marquez's "Why and When We Speak

Spanish in Public" (p. 528), emphasizing her belief that language should not be used as a litmus test of patriotism.

Direct Quotation Note Card

Anti-English Only

"Being an American has very little to do with what language we use during our free time in a free country."

Myriam Marquez,
"Why and When We Speak Spanish in Public," 528

On occasion you'll find a long, useful passage with some memorable wording in it. Avoid the temptation to quote the whole passage; instead, try combining summary or paraphrase with direct quotation. Consider the following paragraph from Mary Sherry's "In Praise of the F Word":

> Passing students who have not mastered the work cheats them and their employers who expect graduates to have basic skills. We excuse this dishonest behavior by saying kids can't learn if they come from terrible environments. No one seems to stop to think that—no matter what environments they come from—most kids don't put school first on their list unless they perceive something is at stake. They'd rather be sailing.
>
> –Mary Sherry, "In Praise of the F Word," p. 560

In the accompanying quotation and paraphrase note card, notice how the student is careful to put quotation marks around all words borrowed directly.

Quotation and Paraphrase Note Card

> *Passing Not the Answer*
>
> *Students and prospective employers are often deceived when students are passed through the school system, even if their work doesn't merit passing. The public "excuse[s] this dishonest behavior by saying kids can't learn if they come from terrible environments." But has anyone ever questioned the fact that "most kids," in spite of environment, "don't put school first on their list unless they perceive something is at stake"? Without an incentive, students will choose most anything over school.*
>
> *Mary Sherry, "In Praise of the F Word," 560*

Some students prefer to keep notes in word processing files on the computer instead of on note cards. This is an acceptable practice, but you must be especially careful when taking notes this way. You will need to avoid the temptation to simply copy and paste in an unorganized fashion from online sources, a practice that will undoubtedly lead to unintentional plagiarism (see pp. 254–57). It is important to stay organized and be methodical when it comes to note taking. Keep careful track of the sources you are working with for each of your notes.

INTEGRATE BORROWED MATERIAL INTO YOUR TEXT

Whenever you want to use borrowed material (such as a summary, a paraphrase, or a direct quotation), your goal is to integrate these sources smoothly and logically and not disrupt the flow of your essay or confuse your readers. It is best to introduce borrowed material with a **signal phrase**, which alerts readers that borrowed information is about to be presented.

A signal phrase consists of at least the author's name and a verb (such as "Stephen King contends"). Signal phrases help readers follow your train of thought. When you integrate a summary, paraphrase, or quotation into your essay, vary your signal phrases and choose verbs for the signal phrases that accurately convey the tone and intent of the writer you are citing. (A signal phrase offers an opportunity to introduce the writer's bias, perspective, or expertise on the issue. See pp. 618–19 for more on bias.) If a writer is arguing, use the verb *argues* (or *asserts, claims,* or *contends*); if a writer is contesting a particular position or fact, use the verb *contests* (or *denies, disputes, refutes,* or *rejects*). Verbs that are specific to the situation in your essay will bring your readers into the intellectual debate (and avoid the monotony of all-purpose verbs like *says* or *writes*). The following examples show how you can vary signal phrases to add precision to your essay:

> Ellen Goodman, Pulitzer Prize–winning columnist for the *Boston Globe*, asserts that . . .
>
> To summarize Amy Tan's observations about the English language, . . .
>
> Social activist and nutrition guru Dick Gregory demonstrates that . . .
>
> Mary Sherry, a literacy teacher and educational writer, advocates . . .
>
> Mark Pfeifle rejects the widely held belief that "slacktivism" . . .
>
> Bharati Mukherjee, an immigrant who chose to embrace United States citizenship, exposes . . .

Other verbs to keep in mind when constructing signal phrases include the following:

acknowledges	compares	grants	reasons
adds	confirms	implies	reports
admits	declares	insists	responds
believes	endorses	points out	suggests

Well-chosen signal phrases help you integrate summaries, paraphrases, and quotations into the flow of your essay. Besides, signal phrases let your reader know who is speaking and, in the case of summaries and paraphrases, exactly where your ideas end and someone else's begin. Never confuse your reader with a quotation that appears suddenly, with no introduction. Unannounced quotations leave your reader wondering how the quoted material relates to the point you are trying to make. Look at the following student example. The quotation is from Nancy Gibbs's "The Magic of the Family Meal," appearing on pages 210–15.

Unannounced Quotation

Older Americans love to reminisce about the value of family dinners that they enjoyed during their childhoods, the ones that Norman Rockwell immortalized in his cover illustrations for the *Saturday Evening Post*. These dinners were times when family members caught up with one another, exchanged ideas, got to know each other. It was there at the dining table that children learned their family's values, history, and culture. But family dinners gradually became less frequent as parents got caught up in careers and children became involved in more and more activities. As more people caught meals on the run, some began to realize that something was now missing. Not surprisingly, family dinners are now back in the news. "[T]he more often families eat together, the less likely kids are to smoke, drink, do drugs, get depressed, develop eating disorders, and consider suicide, and the more likely they are to do well in school, delay having sex, eat their vegetables, learn big words, and know which fork to use" (Gibbs 212). When was the last time you ate dinner with your family?

In the following revision, the student integrates the quotation into the text by means of a signal phrase, in which she gives the writer's name and position, as well as a brief description of the article in which the quotation appeared. The student provides this context so that the reader can better understand how the quotation fits into the discussion.

Announced Quotation

Older Americans love to reminisce about the value of family dinners that they enjoyed during their childhoods, the ones that Norman Rockwell immortalized in his cover illustrations for the *Saturday Evening Post*. These dinners were times when family members caught up with one another, exchanged ideas, got to know each other. It was there at the dining table that children learned their family's values, history, and culture. But family dinners gradually became less frequent as parents got caught up in careers and children became involved in more and more activities. As more people caught meals on the run, some began to realize that something was now missing. Not surprisingly, family dinners are now back in the news. *Time* magazine editor Nancy Gibbs, in her report on the resurgence in family dining, emphasizes that "the more often families eat together, the less likely kids are to smoke, drink, do drugs, get depressed, develop eating disorders, and consider suicide, and the more likely they are to do well in school, delay having sex, eat their vegetables, learn big words, and know which fork to use" (212). When was the last time you ate dinner with your family?

SYNTHESIZE SEVERAL SOURCES TO DEEPEN YOUR DISCUSSION

Synthesis enables you to weave together your own ideas with the ideas of others—the sources you have researched for your essay—in the same paragraph, so as to deepen your discussion or to arrive at a new interpretation or conclusion. By learning how to synthesize the results of your research from your own perspective, you can arrive at an informed opinion of your topic.

When you synthesize several sources in your writing, you create a conversation among your sources in which you take an active role. Sometimes you will find yourself discussing two or three sources together to show a range of views regarding a particular topic or issue—this is called *informational* or *explanatory synthesis*. At other times you will have opportunities to play your sources against one another so as to delineate the opposing positions—this is called *persuasive* or *argument synthesis*.

In the following example from her essay "The Qualities of Good Teachers," student Marah Britto uses informational synthesis to combine her own thoughts about good teachers with the thoughts of three other writers whose essays appear in *Models for Writers* (parenthetical citations refer to pages in this text). In doing so, she explains the range of attributes that distinguish good teachers from their peers.

> We have all experienced a teacher who in some way stands out from all the others we have had, a teacher who has made an important difference in each of our lives. While most of us can agree on some of the character traits — dedication, love for students, patience, passion for his/her subject — that such teachers have in common, we cannot agree on that special something that sets them apart, that distinguishes them from the crowd. For me, it was my sixth-grade teacher Mrs. Engstrom, a teacher who motivated with her example. She never asked me to do anything that she was not willing to do herself. How many teachers show their love of ornithology by taking a student out

> for a bird walk at 5:30 in the morning, on a school day no less? For Thomas L. Friedman, it was his high school journalism teacher, Hattie M. Steinberg. In "My Favorite Teacher," he relates how her insistence upon the importance of "fundamentals" (103) made a lifelong impression on him, so much so that he never had to take another journalism course. For Carl T. Rowan, it was his high school English, history, and civics teacher, Miss Bessie Taylor Gwynn, whose influence he captures in "Unforgettable Miss Bessie." Miss Bessie taught Rowan to hold himself to high standards, to refuse "to lower [his] standards to those of the crowd" (411). And for Russell Baker, it was Mr. Fleagle, his high school English teacher. He recalls how prim and proper and predictable Mr. Fleagle was in the classroom. But that all changed after Mr. Fleagle read one of Baker's essays aloud. In doing that, his teacher had opened Baker's eyes to "a calling" and had given him "the happiest moment of [his] entire school career" (207). Interestingly, isn't it mutual respect and appreciation that is at the heart of any memorable student-teacher bond?

This second example is taken from student Bonnie Sherman's essay "Should Shame Be Used as Punishment?" Here she uses argument synthesis deftly to combine Hawthorne's use of shame in *The Scarlet Letter* with two opposing essays about shame as punishment, both of which appear in this text. Notice how Sherman uses her own reading of *The Scarlet Letter* as evidence to side ultimately with Professor Kahan's position.

> Shame has long been used as an alternative punishment to more traditional sentences of corporeal punishment, jail time, or community service. American colonists used the stocks to publicly humiliate citizens for their transgressions. In *The Scarlet Letter,* for example, Nathaniel Hawthorne recounts the story of how the community of Boston punished Hester Prynne for her adulterous affair by having her wear a scarlet letter "A" on her breast as a badge of shame. Such punishments were controversial then and continue to spark heated debate in the world of

> criminal justice today. Like June Tangney, psychology professor at George Mason University, many believe that shaming punishments — designed to humiliate offenders — are unusually cruel and should be abandoned. In her article "Condemn the Crime, Not the Person," she argues that "shame serves to escalate the very destructive patterns of behavior we aim to curb" (577). Interestingly, Hester Prynne's post-punishment life of community service and charitable work does not seem to bear out Tangney's claim. In contrast, Yale Law School professor Dan M. Kahan believes that Tangney's "anxieties about shame . . . seem overstated," and he persuasively supports this position in his essay "Shame Is Worth a Try" by citing a study showing that the threat of public humiliation generates more compliance than does the threat of jail time (583).

Instead of simply presenting your sources in a quotation here and a summary there in your essay, look for opportunities to use synthesis—to go beyond an individual source by relating several of your sources to one another and to your own thesis. Use the following checklist to help you with synthesis in your writing.

Checklist for Writing a Synthesis

1. Start by writing a brief summary of each source that you will be referring to in your synthesis.
2. Explain in your own words how your sources are related to one another and to your own ideas. For example, what assumptions do your sources share? Do your sources present opposing views? Do your sources illustrate a range or diversity of opinions? Do your sources support or challenge your ideas?
3. Have a clear idea or topic sentence for each paragraph before starting to write.
4. Combine information from two or more sources with your own ideas to support or illustrate your main idea.
5. Use signal phrases and parenthetical citations to show your readers the source of your borrowed materials.
6. Have fresh interpretations or conclusions as a goal each time you synthesize sources.

AVOID PLAGIARISM

Honesty and accuracy with sources are essential. Any material that you have borrowed word for word must be placed within quotation marks and be properly cited. Any idea, explanation, or argument that you have paraphrased or summarized must be documented, and you must show clearly where the paraphrased or summarized material begins and ends. In short, to use someone else's idea—whether in its original form or in an altered form—without proper acknowledgment is to be guilty of **plagiarism**.

You must acknowledge and document the source of your information whenever you do any of the following:

- Quote a source word for word
- Refer to information and ideas from another source that you present in your own words as either a paraphrase or a summary
- Cite statistics, tables, charts, graphs, or other visuals

You do not need to document the following types of information:

- Your own observations, experiences, ideas, and opinions
- Factual information available in many sources (information known as *common knowledge*)
- Proverbs, sayings, or familiar quotations

For a discussion of MLA style for in-text documentation practices, see pages 623–24 of Chapter 22. For a discussion of APA style, see pages 639–41 of Chapter 22.

The Council of Writing Program Administrators offers the following helpful definition of *plagiarism* in academic settings for administrators, faculty, and students: "In an instructional setting, plagiarism occurs when a writer deliberately uses someone else's language, ideas, or other (not common knowledge) material without acknowledging its source." Accusations of plagiarism can be substantiated even if plagiarism is accidental. A little attention and effort at the note-taking stage can go a long way toward eliminating inadvertent plagiarism. Check all direct quotations against the wording of the original, and double-check your paraphrases to be sure that you have not used the writer's wording or sentence structure. It is easy to forget to put quotation marks around material taken verbatim or to use the same sentence structure and most of the same words—substituting a synonym here and there—and treat it as a paraphrase. In working closely with the ideas and words of others, intellectual honesty demands that we distinguish between what we borrow—acknowledging it in a citation—and what is our own.

While writing, be careful whenever you incorporate one of your notes into your paper. Make sure that you put quotation marks around material taken verbatim, and double-check your text against your note card—or, better yet, against the original if you have it on hand—to make sure that your quotation is accurate. When paraphrasing or summarizing, make sure you do not inadvertently borrow key words or sentence structures from the original.

Using Quotation Marks for Language Borrowed Directly

When you use another person's exact words or sentences, you must enclose the borrowed language in quotation marks. Without quotation marks, you give your reader the impression that the wording is your own. Even if you cite the source, you are guilty of plagiarism if you fail to use quotation marks. The following examples demonstrate both plagiarism and a correct citation for a direct quotation.

Original Source

> So Grant and Lee were in complete contrast, representing two diametrically opposed elements in American life. Grant was the modern man emerging; beyond him, ready to come on the stage, was the great age of steel and machinery, of crowded cities and a restless burgeoning vitality.
>
> –Bruce Catton, "Grant and Lee: A Study in Contrasts," p. 513

Plagiarism

> So Grant and Lee were in complete contrast, according to Civil War historian Bruce Catton, representing two diametrically opposed elements in American life. Grant was the modern man emerging; beyond him, ready to come on the stage, was the great age of steel and machinery, of crowded cities and a restless burgeoning vitality (513).

Correct Citation of Borrowed Words in Quotation Marks

> "So Grant and Lee were in complete contrast," according to Civil War historian Bruce Catton, "representing two diametrically opposed elements in American life. Grant was the modern man emerging; beyond him, ready to come on the stage, was the great age of steel and machinery, of crowded cities and a restless burgeoning vitality" (513).

Using Your Own Words and Word Order When Summarizing and Paraphrasing

When summarizing or paraphrasing a source, you must use your own language. Pay attention to word choice and word order, especially if you are paraphrasing. Remember that it is not enough simply to use a synonym here or there and think that you have paraphrased the source; you *must* restate the original idea in your own words, using your own style and sentence structure. In the following examples, notice how plagiarism can occur when care is not taken in the wording or sentence structure of a paraphrase. Notice that in the acceptable paraphrase, the student writer uses her own language and sentence structure.

Original Source

Stereotypes are a kind of gossip about the world, a gossip that makes us prejudge people before we ever lay eyes upon them. Hence it is not surprising that stereotypes have something to do with the dark world of prejudice. Explore most prejudices (note that the word means prejudgment) and you will find a cruel stereotype at the core of each one.

–Robert L. Heilbroner, "Don't Let Stereotypes Warp Your Judgments," *Think* magazine, June 1961, p. 43

Unacceptably Close Wording

According to Heilbroner, we prejudge other people even before we have seen them when we think in stereotypes. That stereotypes are related to the ugly world of prejudice should not surprise anyone. If you explore the heart of most prejudices, beliefs that literally prejudge, you will discover a mean stereotype lurking (43).

Unacceptably Close Sentence Structure

Heilbroner believes that stereotypes are images of people, images that enable people to prejudge other people before they have seen them. Therefore, no one should find it surprising that stereotypes are somehow related to the ugly world of prejudice. Examine most prejudices (the word literally means prejudgment) and you will uncover a vicious stereotype at the center of each (43).

Acceptable Paraphrase

Heilbroner believes that there is a link between stereotypes and the hurtful practice of prejudice. Stereotypes make for easy

> conversation, a kind of shorthand that enables us to find fault with people before ever meeting them. If you were to dissect most human prejudices, you would likely discover an ugly stereotype lurking somewhere inside them (43).

Review the following Avoiding Plagiarism box as you proofread your final draft and check your citations one last time. If at any time while you are taking notes or writing your essay you have a question about plagiarism, consult your instructor for clarification and guidance before proceeding.

Avoiding Plagiarism

Questions to Ask about Direct Quotations
- Do quotation marks clearly indicate the language that I borrowed verbatim?
- Is the language of the quotation accurate, with no missing or misquoted words or phrases?
- Do the brackets or ellipsis marks clearly indicate any changes or omissions I have introduced?
- Does a signal phrase naming the author introduce each quotation?
- Does the verb in the signal phrase help establish a context for each quotation?
- Does a parenthetical page citation follow each quotation?

Questions to Ask about Summaries and Paraphrases
- Is each summary or paraphrase written in my own words and style?
- Does each summary or paraphrase accurately represent the opinion, position, or reasoning of the original writer?
- Does each summary or paraphrase start with a signal phrase so that readers know where my borrowed material begins?
- Does each summary or paraphrase conclude with a parenthetical page citation?

Questions to Ask about Facts and Statistics
- Do I use a signal phrase or some other marker to introduce each fact or statistic that is not common knowledge so that readers know where the borrowed material begins?
- Is each fact or statistic that is not common knowledge clearly documented with a parenthetical page citation?

The Case for Censoring Hate Speech

■ **Sean McElwee**

Sean McElwee grew up in Connecticut and graduated from King's College. He writes about current events and economics for print and online publications including The Day, Alternet.org, Salon.com, *and* Reason.com. *He works as a research assistant for Comeback America, a foundation that promotes fiscal responsibility.*

In "The Case for Censoring Hate Speech," McElwee answers the objections of free-speech advocates. According to McElwee, the idea for this essay came from "reading about the experiences of women, minorities and LGBT youth who had been harassed on websites like Twitter and Reddit." His goal was to "show that by allowing racism, homophobia and misogyny, these websites don't make speech more free, but rather, more constrained." McElwee did a lot of research in preparation for writing this essay, reading articles, conducting interviews, and gathering information on worldwide hate-speech laws. As you read, pay attention to how McElwee integrates quotations from various sources into his writing.

Reflecting on What You Know

The First Amendment to the Constitution states that "Congress shall make no law . . . abridging the freedom of speech." When or how do you think we should, for the public good, place restrictions on this right?

For the past few years speech has moved online, leading to fierce debates about its regulation. Most recently, feminists have led the charge to purge Facebook of misogyny that clearly violates its hate speech code. Facebook took a small step two weeks ago, creating a 1 feature that will remove ads from pages deemed "controversial." But such a move is half-hearted; Facebook and other social networking websites should not tolerate hate speech and, in the absence of a government mandate, adopt a European model of expunging offensive material.

Stricter regulation of Internet speech will not be popular with the libertarian-minded citizens of the United States, but it's necessary. A typical view of the case for expunging hate speech comes from Jeffrey Rosen, who argues in *The New Republic* that, 2

> given their tremendous size and importance as platforms for free speech, companies like Facebook, Google, Yahoo, and Twitter shouldn't try to be guardians of what Waldron calls a "well-ordered society"; instead, they should consider themselves the modern version of Oliver Wendell Holmes's fractious marketplace of ideas—democratic spaces where all values, including civility norms, are always open for debate.

This image is romantic and lovely but it's worth asking what this actually looks like. Rosen forwards one example: 3

> Last year, after the French government objected to the hash tag "#unbonjuif"—intended to inspire hateful riffs on the theme "a good Jew . . ."—Twitter blocked a handful of the resulting tweets in France, but only because they violated French law. Within days, the bulk of the tweets carrying the hash tag had turned from anti-Semitic to denunciations of anti-Semitism, confirming that the Twittersphere is perfectly capable of dealing with hate speech on its own, without heavy-handed intervention.

It's interesting to note how closely this idea resembles free market fundamentalism: simply get rid of any coercive rules and the "marketplace of ideas" will naturally produce the best result. Humboldt State University compiled a visual map that charts 150,000 hateful insults aggregated over the course of 11 months in the U.S. by pairing Google's Maps API with a series of the most homophobic, racist and otherwise prejudiced tweets. The map's existence draws into question the notion that the "Twittersphere" can organically combat hate speech; hate speech is not going to disappear from Twitter on its own. 4

The negative impacts of hate speech cannot be mitigated by the responses of third-party observers, as hate speech aims at two goals. 5

First, it is an attempt to tell bigots that they are not alone. Frank Collins—the neo-Nazi prosecuted in *National Socialist Party of America v. Skokie* (1977)—said, "We want to reach the good people, get the fierce anti-Semites who have to live among the Jews to come out of the woodwork and stand up for themselves."

The second purpose of hate speech is to intimidate the targeted minority, leading them to question whether their dignity and social status is secure. In many cases, such intimidation is successful. Consider the number of rapes that go unreported. Could this trend possibly be impacted by Reddit threads like /r/rapingwomen or /r/mensrights? Could it be due to the harassment women face when they even suggest the possibility they were raped? The rape culture that permeates Facebook, Twitter and the public dialogue must be held at least partially responsible for our larger rape culture. 6

Reddit, for instance, has become a veritable potpourri of hate speech; consider Reddit threads like /r/nazi, /r/killawoman, /r/misogny, /r/killingwomen. My argument is not that these should be taken down because they are offensive, but rather because they amount to the degradation of a class that has been historically oppressed. Imagine a Reddit thread for /r/lynchingblacks or /r/assassinatingthepresident. We would not argue that we should sit back and wait for this kind of speech to be "outspoken" by positive speech, but that it should be entirely banned. 7

American free speech jurisprudence relies upon the assumption that speech is merely the extension of a thought, and not an action. If we consider it an action, then saying that we should combat hate speech with more positive speech is an absurd proposition; the speech has already done the harm, and no amount of support will defray the victim's impression that they are not truly secure in this society. We don't simply tell the victim of a robbery, "Hey, it's okay, there are lots of other people who aren't going to rob you." Similarly, it isn't incredibly useful to tell someone who has just had their race/gender/sexuality defamed, "There are a lot of other nice people out there." 8

Those who claim to "defend free speech" when they defend the right to post hate speech online are in truth backwards. Free speech isn't an absolute right; no right is weighed in a vacuum. The court has imposed numerous restrictions on speech. Fighting words, libel and child pornography are all banned. Other countries merely go one step further by banning speech intended to intimidate vulnerable groups. The truth is that such speech does not democratize speech, it monopolizes speech. 9

Women, LGBTQ individuals and racial or religious minorities feel intimidated and are left out of the public sphere. On Reddit, for example, women have left or changed their usernames to be more male-sounding lest they face harassment and intimidation for speaking on Reddit about even the most gender-neutral topics. Even outside of the intentionally offensive sub-reddits (i.e., /r/imgoingtohellforthis) misogyny is pervasive. I encountered this when browsing /r/funny.

Those who try to remove this hate speech have been criticized from left and right. At *Slate*, Jillian York writes, "While the campaigners on this issue are to be commended for raising awareness of such awful speech on Facebook's platform, their proposed solution is ultimately futile and sets a dangerous precedent for special interest groups looking to bring their pet issue to the attention of Facebook's censors." 10

It hardly seems right to qualify a group fighting hate speech as an "interest group" trying to bring their "pet issue" to the attention of Facebook censors. The "special interest" groups she fears might apply for protection must meet Facebook's strict community standards, which state: 11

> While we encourage you to challenge ideas, institutions, events, and practices, we do not permit individuals or groups to attack others based on their race, ethnicity, national origin, religion, sex, gender, sexual orientation, disability or medical condition.

If anything, the groups to which York refers are nudging Facebook towards actually enforcing its own rules.

People who argue against such rules generally portray their opponents as standing on a slippery precipice, tugging at the question "what next?" We can answer that question: Canada, England, France, Germany, The Netherlands, South Africa, Australia and India all ban hate speech. Yet, none of these countries have slipped into totalitarianism. In many ways, such countries are more free when you weigh the negative liberty to express harmful thoughts against the positive liberty that is suppressed when you allow for the intimidation of minorities. 12

As Arthur Schopenhauer said, "the freedom of the press should be governed by a very strict prohibition of all and every anonymity." However, with the Internet the public dialogue has moved online, where hate speech is easy and anonymous. 13

Jeffrey Rosen argues that norms of civility should be open to discussion, but, in today's reality, this issue has already been decided; impugning someone because of their race, gender or orientation is not acceptable in a civil society. Banning hate speech is not a mechanism to further this debate because the debate is over. 14

As Jeremy Waldron argues, hate speech laws prevent bigots from "trying to create the impression that the equal position of members of vulnerable minorities in a rights-respecting society is less secure than implied by the society's actual foundational commitments." 15

Some people argue that the purpose of laws that ban hate speech is merely to avoid offending prudes. No country, however, has mandated that anything be excised from the public square merely because it provokes offense, but rather because it attacks the dignity of a group—a practice the U.S. Supreme Court called in *Beauharnais v. Illinois* (1952) "group libel." Such a standard could easily be applied to Twitter, Reddit and other social media websites. While Facebook's policy as written should be a model, its enforcement has been shoddy. Again, this isn't an argument for government intervention. The goal is for companies to adopt a European-model hate speech policy, one not aimed at expunging offense, but rather hate. Such a system would be subject to outside scrutiny by users. If this is the standard, the Internet will surely remain controversial, but it can also be free of hate and allow everyone to participate. A true marketplace of ideas must coexist with a multi-racial society open to people of all genders, orientations and religions, and it can. 16

Thinking Critically about This Reading

What does McElwee mean by calling Americans "libertarian-minded" (paragraph 2)? Compare that attitude with what he tells us about countries like Canada, England, and France.

Questions for Study and Discussion

1. Identify some places in the essay where McElwee synthesizes his sources. For example, how does he bring Jeffrey Rosen and Jeremy Waldron into conversation with each other?
2. Near the beginning of the essay, McElwee uses direct quotations from Rosen. Later, he summarizes Rosen's argument, using his

own language. How do these different uses of the source serve different purposes?

3. Which websites does McElwee think have the worst problems with hate speech, and why? What does he suggest websites could do to improve the situation?
4. In this essay, McElwee responds to an argument by Jeffrey Rosen. Why does he object to Rosen's position on free speech? What, for example, does he think is wrong with the evidence Rosen cites about how Twitter reacted to the hashtag #unbonjuif?
5. What does McElwee believe are the two goals of hate speech? Do you agree or disagree, and why?
6. How does he answer the concern that limiting hate speech is like "standing on a slippery precipice"(12)? What does he say to the charge that restricting hate speech is just about avoiding giving offense to people who are overly sensitive?
7. Who do you believe is the audience for McElwee's article? Cite places in the text that give you clues about what audience he has in mind.

Classroom Activity Using Writing with Sources

Use the examples of signal phrases and parenthetical citations on pages 248–51 as models for integrating the quotation into the flow of the discussion in each of the following two paragraphs. The quotation in the first example comes from page 100 of William L. Rathje's article "Rubbish!" in the December 1989 issue of the *Atlantic Monthly*. Rathje teaches at the University of Arizona, where he directs the Garbage Project.

> Most Americans think that we are producing more trash per person than ever, that plastic is a huge problem, and that paper biodegrades quickly in landfills. "The biggest challenge we will face is to recognize that the conventional wisdom about garbage is often wrong."

The quotation in the second example comes from page 99 of Rita Dove's essay "Loose Ends" from her 1995 book *The Poet's World*. Dove is a former poet laureate of the United States and teaches at the University of Virginia.

> Television, it could be argued, presents life in tidy almost predictable thirty- and sixty-minute packages. As any episode of

Friends, House, or *Law and Order* demonstrates, life on television, though exciting, is relatively easy to follow. Humor, simultaneous action, and special effects cannot overshadow the fact that each show has a beginning, a middle, and an end. "Life . . . is ragged. Loose ends rule." For many Americans, television provides an escape from their disjointed day-to-day lives.

Compare your signal phrases with those of your classmates, and discuss how smoothly each integrates the quotation into the passage.

Suggested Writing Assignments

1. Although McElwee works with many sources, the disagreement between Jeffrey Rosen and Jeremy Waldron seems to be the catalyst of this essay. Choose a subject you would like to write about, and find articles stating two opposing views. Write an essay summarizing the points these two authors make. Make sure to include a thesis that clearly states your position in the debate.
2. Look up the law banning hate speech in one of the countries McElwee mentions in paragraph 12. Write an essay analyzing the language of the law. How does it compare with our own First Amendment? Be deliberate in your decisions of when to summarize, to paraphrase, and to quote directly from the law. (Glossary: *Comparison and Contrast*)

The English-Only Movement: Can America Proscribe Language with a Clear Conscience?

■ **Jake Jamieson**

Courtesy of Jake Jamieson

An eighth-generation Vermonter, Jake Jamieson was born in Berlin, Vermont, and grew up in nearby Waterbury. He graduated from the University of Vermont in 1996 with a degree in elementary education and a focus in English. After graduation, he "bounced around" California and Colorado before landing in the Boston area, where he directed the product innovation and training department at iProspect, a search-engine marketing company. Recently Jamieson moved back to Montpelier, Vermont, where he started his own web design company.

Jamieson wrote the following essay while he was a student at the University of Vermont and has updated it for inclusion in this book. As a believer in the old axiom "If it isn't broken, don't fix it," Jamieson thinks that the official-English crowd wants to fix a system that seems to be working just fine. In this essay, he tackles the issue of legislating English as the official language of the United States. As you read, notice how he uses outside sources to present various pieces of the English-only position. He then tries to undercut that position by using his own thinking and examples as well as the opinions of experts who support him. Throughout his essay, Jamieson uses MLA style for his in-text citations and his list of works cited.

Reflecting on What You Know

It is now possible to visit many countries and be understood in English, regardless of other languages that are spoken in the host country. If you were to emigrate, how hard would you work to learn the predominant language of your chosen country? What advantages would you gain by learning that language, even if you could get by in English? How would you feel if the country had a law that required you to use its language in its schools and businesses? Write down your thoughts about these questions.

Many people think of the United States as a giant cultural "melting pot" where people from other countries come together and bathe in the warm waters of assimilation. In this scenario, the newly arrived immigrants readily adopt American cultural ways and learn to speak English. For others, however, this serene picture of the melting pot analogy does not ring true. These people see the melting pot as a giant cauldron into which immigrants are tossed; here their cultures, values, and backgrounds are boiled away in the scalding waters of discrimination. At the center of the discussion about immigrants and assimilation is language: should immigrants be required to learn English, or should accommodations be made so they can continue to use their native languages? 1

Those who argue that the melting pot analogy is valid believe that immigrants who come to America do so willingly and should be expected to become a part of its culture instead of hanging on to their past. For them, the expectation that immigrants will celebrate this country's holidays, dress as Americans dress, embrace American values, and most importantly speak English is not unreasonable. They believe that assimilation offers the only way for everyone in this country to live together in harmony and the only way to dissipate the tensions that inevitably arise when cultures clash. A major problem with this argument, however, is that there is no agreement on what exactly constitutes the "American way" of doing things. 2

Not everyone in America is of the same religious persuasion or has the same set of values, and different people affect vastly different styles of dress. There are so many sets of variables that it would be hard to defend the argument that there is only one culture in the United States. Currently, the one common denominator in America is that the majority of us speak English, and because of this a major movement is being staged in favor of making English the country's "official" language while it is still the country's national and common language. Making English America's "official" language would change the ground rules and expectations surrounding immigrant assimilation. According to the 3 columnist and social commentator Charles Krauthammer, making English the "official" language has important implications:

> "Official" means the language of the government and its institutions. "Official" makes clear our expectations of acculturation. "Official" means that every citizen, upon entering America's most sacred political space, the voting booth, should minimally be able to identify the words *president* and *vice president* and *county commissioner* and *judge*. The immigrant, of course, has the right to speak whatever he wants. But he must understand that when he comes to the United States, swears allegiance, and accepts its bounty, he undertakes to join its civic culture. In English. (112)

Many reasons are given to support the notion that making English the official language of the land is a good idea and that it is exactly what this country needs, especially in the face of the growing diversity of languages in metropolitan areas. Indeed, in a recent survey one Los Angeles school reported sixty different languages spoken in the homes of its students (National Education Association, par. 4).

Supporters of English-only contend that all government communication must be in English. Because communication is absolutely necessary for democracy to survive, they believe that the only way to ensure the existence of our nation is to make sure a common language exists. Making English official would ensure that all government business, from ballots to official forms to judicial hearings, would have to be conducted in English. According to former senator and presidential candidate Bob Dole, "Promoting English as our national language is not an act of hostility but a welcoming act of inclusion." He goes on to state that while immigrants are encouraged to continue speaking their native languages, "thousands of children [are] failing to learn the language, English, that is the ticket to the 'American Dream'" (qtd. in Donegan 51). Political and cultural commentator Greg Lewis echoes Dole's sentiments when he boldly states, "To succeed in America ... it's important to speak, read, and understand English as most Americans speak it. There's nothing cruel or unfair in that; it's just the way it is" (par. 5). 4

For those who do not subscribe to this way of thinking, however, this type of legislation is anything but the "welcoming act of inclusion" that it is described to be. Many of them, like Myriam Marquez, readily acknowledge the importance of English but fear that "talking in Spanish—or any other language, for that matter—is some sort of 5 litmus test used to gauge American patriotism" ("Why and When" 528). Others suggest that anyone attempting to regulate language is treading dangerously close to the First Amendment and must have a hidden agenda of some type. Why, it is asked, make a language official when it is already firmly entrenched and widely used in this country without legislation to mandate it? According to language diversity advocate James Crawford, the answer is plain and simple: "discrimination." He states that "it is certainly more respectable to discriminate by language than by race" or ethnicity. He points out that "most people are not sensitive to language discrimination in this nation, so it is easy to argue that you're doing someone a favor by making them speak English" (qtd. in Donegan 51). English-only legislation has been criticized as bigoted, anti-immigrant, mean-spirited, and steeped in nativism by those who oppose it, and some go so far as to say that this type of legislation will not foster better communication, as is the claim, but will instead encourage a "fear of being subsumed by a growing 'foreignness' in our midst" (Underwood 65).

For example, when a judge in Texas ruled that a mother was abusing her five-year-old girl by speaking to her only in Spanish, an uproar ensued. This ruling was accompanied by the statement that by talking to her daughter in a language other than English, the mother was "abusing that child and . . . relegating her to the position of house maid." The National Association for Bilingual Education (NABE) condemned this statement for "labeling the Spanish language as abuse." The judge, Samuel C. Kiser, subsequently apologized to the housekeepers of the country, adding that he held them "in the highest esteem," but stood firm on his ruling (qtd. in Donegan 51). One might notice that he went out of his way to apologize to the housekeepers he might have offended but saw no need to apologize to the millions of Spanish speakers whose language had just been belittled in a nationally publicized case. 6

This tendency of official-English proponents to put down other languages is one that shows up again and again, even though they maintain that they have nothing against other languages or the people who speak them. If there is no malice intended toward other languages, why is the use of any language other than English tantamount to lunacy according to an almost constant barrage of literature and editorial opinion? In a recent listing of the "New Year's Resolutions" of various conservative organizations, a group called U.S. English, Inc., stated that the U.S. government was not doing its job of convincing immigrants that they "must learn English to succeed in this country." Instead, 7 according to Stephen Moore and his associates, "in a bewildering display of irrationality, the U.S. government makes it possible to vote, file a tax return, get married, obtain a driver's license, and become a U.S. citizen in many languages" (46).

Now, according to this mindset, not only is speaking any language other than English abusive, but it is also irrational and bewildering. What is this world coming to when people want to speak and make transactions in their native language? Why do they refuse to change and become more like us? Why can't immigrants see that speaking English is quite simply the right way to go? These and many other questions like them are implied by official-English proponents when they discuss the issue. 8

Conservative attorney David Price argues that official-English legislation is a good idea because most English-speaking Americans prefer "out of pride and convenience to speak their native language on the job" (A13). This statement implies not only that the pride and convenience of non-English-speaking Americans is unimportant but that their native tongues are not as important as English. The scariest prospect of all is that this opinion is quickly gaining popularity all around the country. It appears to be most prevalent in areas with high concentrations of Spanish-speaking residents. 9

To date, a number of official-English bills and one amendment to the Constitution have been proposed in the House and Senate. There are more than twenty-seven states—including Missouri, North Dakota, Florida, Massachusetts, California, Virginia, and New Hampshire—that have made English their official language, and more are debating the issue every day. An especially disturbing fact about this debate—and it was front and center in 2007 during the discussions and protests about what to do with America's 12.5 million illegal immigrants—is that official-English laws always seem to be linked to anti-immigration legislation, such as proposals to limit immigration or to restrict government benefits to immigrants. 10

Although official-English proponents maintain that their bid for language legislation is in the best interest of immigrants, the facts tend to show otherwise. University of Texas Professor Robert D. King strongly believes that "language does not threaten American unity." He recommends that "we relax and luxuriate in our linguistic richness and our traditional tolerance of language differences" (64). A decision has to be made in this country about what kind of message we will send to the rest of the world. Do we plan to allow everyone in this 11 country the freedom of speech that we profess to cherish, or will we decide to reserve it only for those who speak English? Will we hold firm to our belief that everyone is deserving of life, liberty, and the pursuit of happiness in this country? Or will we show the world that we believe in these things only when they pertain to ourselves and people like us? "The irony," as Hispanic columnist Myriam Marquez observes, "is that English-only laws directed at government have done little to change the inevitable multicultural flavor of America" ("English-Only Laws" A10).

Works Cited

Donegan, Craig. "Debate over Bilingualism: Should English Be the Nation's Official Language?" *CQ Researcher* 19 Jan. 1996: 51–71. Print.

King, Robert D. "Should English Be the Law?" *Atlantic Monthly* Apr. 1997: 55–64. Print.

Krauthammer, Charles. "In Plain English: Let's Make It Official." *Time* 12 June 2006: 112. Print.

Lewis, Greg. "An Open Letter to Diversity's Victims." *WashingtonDispatch.com*. N.p., 12 Aug. 2003. Web. 15 Nov. 2011.

Marquez, Myriam. "English-Only Laws Serve to Appease Those Who Fear the Inevitable." *Orlando Sentinel* 10 July 2000: A10. Print.

---. "Why and When We Speak Spanish in Public." *Models for Writers*. 12th ed. Ed. Alfred Rosa and Paul Eschholz. Boston: Bedford, 2015. 527–29. Print.

Moore, Stephen, et al. "New Year's Resolutions." *National Review* 29 Jan. 1996: 46–48. Print.

National Education Association. "NEA Statement on the Debate over English Only." Teacher's College, U of Nebraska, Lincoln, 27 Sept. 1999. Web. 15 Nov. 2011.

Price, David. "English-Only Rules: EEOC Has Gone Too Far." *USA Today* 28 Mar. 1996, final ed.: A13. Print.

Underwood, Robert L. "At Issue: Should English Be the Official Language of the United States?" *CQ Researcher* 19 Jan. 1996: 65. Print.

Thinking Critically about This Reading

Jamieson claims that "there are so many sets of variables that it would be hard to defend the argument that there is only one culture in the United States" (paragraph 3). Do you agree with him, or do you see a dominant American culture with many regional variations? Explain.

Questions for Study and Discussion

1. What question does Jamieson seek to answer in his essay? How does he answer this question?
2. How does Jamieson respond to the people who argue that the melting pot analogy is valid? Do you agree with his counterargument?
3. Former senator Bob Dole believes that English "is the ticket to the 'American Dream'" (4). In what ways can it be considered the ticket?
4. For what purpose does Jamieson quote Greg Lewis in paragraph 4? What would have been lost had he dropped the Lewis quotation? Explain.
5. James Crawford believes that official-English legislation is motivated by "discrimination" (5). What do you think he means? Do you think that Crawford would consider Bob Dole's remarks in paragraph 4 discriminatory? Explain.
6. In paragraph 6, Jamieson presents the example of the Texas judge who ruled that speaking to a child only in Spanish constituted abuse. What point does this example help Jamieson make?
7. Jamieson is careful to use signal phrases to introduce each of his quotations and paraphrases. How do these signal phrases help readers follow the flow of the argument in his essay?
8. In his concluding paragraph, Jamieson leaves his readers with three important questions. How do you think he would answer each one? How would you answer them?

Classroom Activity Using Writing with Sources

Using the examples on pages 245–46 as a model, write a paraphrase for each of the following paragraphs—that is, restate the original ideas in your own words, using your own style and sentence structure.

> The great offense of the cell phone in public is not the intrusion of its ring, although that can be infuriating when it interrupts a tranquil moment. It is the fact that even when the phone does not ring at all, and is being used quietly and discreetly, it renders a public place less public. It turns the boulevardier into a sequestered individual, the flaneur into a figure of privacy. And suddenly the meaning of the street as a public place has been hugely diminished.
>
> –Paul Goldberger, "Disconnected Urbanism," pp. 236–37

> The history of a nation is more often the result of the unexpected than of the planned. In many cases it turns on momentous events. In 1968, American history was determined by a garbage men's strike. As Martin Luther King Jr. and the members of the SCLC commenced planning the Poor Peoples' March on Washington, the garbage men of Memphis, Tennessee, were embroiled in a wage dispute with Mayor Henry Loeb. On February 12th, the garbage men, most of whom were black, went on strike. What began as a simple dispute over wages soon developed into a full-fledged racial battle between the predominantly black union, local 1733, and the white power structure of the City of Memphis.
>
> –Robert L. Walsh and Leon F. Burrell, *The Other America*

Compare your paraphrases with those of your classmates.

Suggested Writing Assignments

1. It's no secret that English is the common language of the United States, but few of us know that the country has been cautious about promoting a government-mandated official language. Why do you suppose the federal government has chosen to take a hands-off position on the language issue? If it has not been necessary to mandate English in the past, why do you think people now feel a need to declare English the "official language" of the United States? Do you think this need is real? Write an essay in which you articulate your position on the English-only issue. Support your position with your own experiences and observations as well as with several outside sources.
2. Before writing an essay about assimilating non-English-speaking immigrants into American society, consider the following three statements:
   a. At this time, it is highly unlikely that Congress will pass a law saying that English is the official language of the United States.
   b. Immigrants should learn English as quickly as possible after arriving in the United States.
   c. The cultures and languages of immigrants should be respected and valued to reduce bitterness and resentment as immigrants are assimilated into American society.

   In your opinion, what is the best way to assimilate non-English-speaking immigrants into our society? Write an essay in which you propose how the United States, as a nation, can make statements (b) and (c) a reality without resorting to an English-only solution. How can we help immigrants become Americans without provoking ill will?

3. Is the English-only debate a political issue, a social issue, an economic issue, or some combination of the three? In this context, what do you see as the relationship between language and power? Write an essay in which you explore the relationship between language and power as it pertains to non-English-speaking immigrants living and functioning within an English-speaking culture.

The Clan of One-Breasted Women

■ Terry Tempest Williams

Lynn Goldsmith/CORBIS

American author, naturalist, conservationist, and activist Terry Tempest Williams was born in Corona, California, in 1955 and grew up in Utah, where she is descended from six generations of Mormon pioneers. Williams received a degree in English and biology in 1978 and an MS in environmental education in 1984 from the University of Utah. After graduation, she taught on a Navajo reservation in Montezuma Creek, Utah; she has also been naturalist-in-residence at the Utah Museum of Natural History. A prolific writer, her essays have appeared in the New Yorker, *the* Nation, Orion, *the* New York Times, *and* The Best American Essays *(2000). Williams is best known for her award-winning* Refuge: An Unnatural History of Family and Place *(1991), a book that interweaves memoir with a chronicle of the flooding of the Bear River Migratory Bird Refuge in 1983. Williams's other books include* Pieces of White Shell: A Journey to Navajoland *(1984),* An Unspoken Hunger *(1994),* Desert Quartet: An Erotic Landscape *(1995),* Red: Patience and Passion in the Desert *(2001),* The Open Space of Democracy *(2004),* Finding Beauty in a Broken World *(2008), and* When Women Were Birds (2012). *She has also written two books for children,* The Secret Language of Snow *(1984) and* Cattails *(1985). In 2009, Williams was featured in Ken Burns's PBS series* The National Parks: America's Best Idea. *Currently, she is the Annie Clark Tanner Scholar in Environmental Humanities at the University of Utah.*

"The Clan of One-Breasted Women" first appeared as the epilogue to her acclaimed Refuge. *This essay has since been published worldwide. In it, Williams explores the connection between radioactive fallout from aboveground nuclear testing on the Nevada desert during the 1950s and early 1960s and the high incidence of cancer occurring not only in her own family but in other Utah families as well.*

Reflecting on What You Know

> Today people are much more aware of the health risks caused by radiation and chemicals lurking in our environment than they were, say, fifty or sixty years ago. What do you know about the potential dangers of nuclear energy facilities, chemical fertilizers and pesticides, exhaust from the cars we drive, and preservatives and other additives in the foods we eat? Are you aware of any environmental contamination issues in the area where you grew up? Explain.

I belong to a Clan of One-Breasted Women. My mother, my grandmothers, and six aunts have all had mastectomies. Seven are dead. The two who survive have just completed rounds of chemotherapy and radiation. 1

I've had my own problems: two biopsies for breast cancer and a small tumor between my ribs diagnosed as "a border-line malignancy." 2

This is my family history. 3

Most statistics tell us breast cancer is genetic, hereditary, with rising percentages attached to fatty diets, childlessness, or becoming pregnant after thirty. What they don't say is living in Utah may be the greatest hazard of all. 4

We are a Mormon family with roots in Utah since 1847. The word-of-wisdom, a religious doctrine of health, kept the women in my family aligned with good foods: no coffee, no tea, tobacco, or alcohol. For the most part, these women were finished having their babies by the time they were thirty. And only one faced breast cancer prior to 1960. Traditionally, as a group of people, Mormons have a low rate of cancer. 5

Is our family a cultural anomaly? The truth is we didn't think about it. Those who did, usually the men, simply said, "bad genes." The women's attitude was stoic. Cancer was part of life. On February 16, 1971, the eve before my mother's surgery, I accidently picked up the telephone and overheard her ask my grandmother what she could expect. 6

"Diane, it is one of the most spiritual experiences you will ever encounter." 7

I quietly put down the receiver. 8

Two days later, my father took my three brothers and me to the hospital to visit her. She met us in the lobby in a wheelchair. No 9 bandages were visible. I'll never forget her radiance, the way she held herself in a purple velour robe and how she gathered us around her.

"Children, I am fine. I want you to know I felt the arms of God 10
around me."

We believed her. My father cried. Our mother, his wife, was 11
thirty-eight years old.

Two years ago, after my mother's death from cancer, my father and 12
I were having dinner together. He had just returned from St. George where his construction company was putting in natural gas lines for towns in southern Utah. He spoke of his love for the country: the sandstoned landscape, bare-boned and beautiful. He had just finished hiking the Kolob trail in Zion National Park. We got caught up in reminiscing, recalling with fondness our walk up Angel's Landing on his fiftieth birthday and the years our family had vacationed there. This was a remembered landscape where we had been raised.

Over dessert, I shared a recurring dream of mine. I told my father 13
that for years, as long as I could remember, I saw this flash of light in the night in the desert. That this image had so permeated my being, I could not venture south without seeing it again, on the horizon, illuminating buttes and mesas.

"You did see it," he said. 14

"Saw what?" I asked, a bit tentative. 15

"The bomb. The cloud. We were driving home from Riverside, 16
California. You were sitting on your mother's lap. She was pregnant. In fact, I remember the date, September 7, 1957. We had just gotten out of the Service. We were driving north, past Las Vegas. It was an hour or so before dawn, when this explosion went off. We not only heard it, but felt it. I thought the oil tanker in front of us had blown up. We pulled over and suddenly, rising from the desert floor, we saw it, clearly, this golden-stemmed cloud, the mushroom. The sky seemed to vibrate with an eerie pink glow. Within a few minutes, a light ash was raining on the car."

I stared at my father. This was new information to me. 17

"I thought you knew that," my father said. "It was a common oc- 18
currence in the fifties."

It was at this moment I realized the deceit I had been living under. 19
Children growing up in the American Southwest, drinking contaminated milk from contaminated cows, even from the contaminated breasts of their mother, my mother—members, years later, of the Clan of One-Breasted Women.

It is a well-known story in the Desert West, "The Day We Bombed Utah," or perhaps, "The Years We Bombed Utah."[1] Above ground atomic testing in Nevada took place from January 27, 1951, through July 11, 1962. Not only were the winds blowing north, covering "low use segments of the population" with fallout and leaving sheep dead in their tracks, but the climate was right. The United States of the 1950s was red, white, and blue. The Korean War was raging. McCarthyism was rampant. Ike was it and the Cold War was hot. If you were against nuclear testing, you were for a Communist regime. 20

Much has been written about this "American nuclear tragedy." Public health was secondary to national security. The Atomic Energy Commissioner, Thomas Murray, said, "Gentlemen, we must not let anything interfere with this series of tests, nothing."[2] 21

Again and again, the American public was told by its government, in spite of burns, blisters, and nausea, "It has been found that the tests may be conducted with adequate assurance of safety under conditions prevailing at the bombing reservations."[3] Assuaging public fears was simply a matter of public relations. "Your best action," an Atomic Energy Commission booklet read, "is not to be worried about fallout." A news release typical of the times stated, "We find no basis for concluding that harm to any individual has resulted from radioactive fallout."[4] 22

On August 30, 1979, during Jimmy Carter's presidency, a suit was filed entitled "Irene Allen vs. the United States of America." Mrs. Allen was the first to be alphabetically listed with twenty-four test cases, representative of nearly 1200 plaintiffs seeking compensation from the United States government for cancers caused from nuclear testing in Nevada. 23

Irene Allen lived in Hurricane, Utah. She was the mother of five children and had been widowed twice. Her first husband with their two oldest boys had watched the tests from the roof of the local high school. He died of leukemia in 1956. Her second husband died of pancreatic cancer in 1978. 24

[1]John G. Fuller, *The Day We Bombed Utah* (New York: New American Library, 1984). [All notes are Williams's.]

[2]Ferenc M. Szasz, "Downwind from the Bomb," *Nevada Historical Society Quarterly*, Fall 1987 Vol. XXX, No. 3, p. 185.

[3]Philip L. Fradkin, *Fallout* (Tucson: University of Arizona Press, 1989), 98.

[4]Ibid., 109.

In a town meeting conducted by Utah Senator Orrin Hatch, shortly before the suit was filed, Mrs. Allen said, "I am not blaming the government, I want you to know that, Senator Hatch. But I thought if my testimony could help in any way so this wouldn't happen again to any of the generations coming up after us . . . I am really happy to be here this day to bear testimony of this."[5] 25

God-fearing people. This is just one story in an anthology of thousands. 26

On May 10, 1984, Judge Bruce S. Jenkins handed down his opinion. Ten of the plaintiffs were awarded damages. It was the first time a federal court had determined that nuclear tests had been the cause of cancers. For the remaining fourteen test cases, the proof of causation was not sufficient. In spite of the split decision, it was considered a landmark ruling.[6] It was not to remain so for long. 27

In April 1987, the 10th Circuit Court of Appeals overturned Judge Jenkins' ruling on the basis that the United States was protected from suit by the legal doctrine of sovereign immunity, the centuries-old idea from England in the days of absolute monarchs.[7] 28

In January 1988, the Supreme Court refused to review the Appeals Court decision. To our court system, it does not matter whether the United States government was irresponsible, whether it lied to its citizens or even that citizens died from the fallout of nuclear testing. What matters is that our government is immune. "The King can do no wrong." 29

In Mormon culture, authority is respected, obedience is revered, and independent thinking is not. I was taught as a young girl not to "make waves" or "rock the boat." 30

"Just let it go—" my mother would say. "You know how you feel, that's what counts." 31

For many years, I did just that—listened, observed, and quietly formed my own opinions within a culture that rarely asked questions because they had all the answers. But one by one, I watched the women in my family die common, heroic deaths. We sat in waiting rooms hoping for good news, always receiving the bad. I cared for them, bathed their scarred bodies and kept their secrets. I watched 32

[5]Town meeting held by Senator Orrin Hatch in St. George, Utah, April 17, 1979, transcript, 26–28.

[6]Fradkin, op. cit., 228.

[7]*U.S. v. Allen*, 816 Federal Reporter, 2d/1417 (10th Circuit Court 1987), cert. denied, 108 S. Ct. 694 (1988).

beautiful women become bald as cytoxan, cisplatin, and adriamycin were injected into their veins. I held their foreheads as they vomited green-black bile and I shot them with morphine when the pain became inhuman. In the end, I witnessed their last peaceful breaths, becoming a midwife to the rebirth of their souls. But the price of obedience became too high.

The fear and inability to question authority that ultimately killed rural communities in Utah during atmospheric testing of atomic weapons was the same fear I saw being held in my mother's body. Sheep. Dead sheep. The evidence is buried. 33

I cannot prove that my mother, Diane Dixon Tempest, or my grandmothers, Lettie Romney Dixon and Kathryn Blackett Tempest, along with my aunts contracted cancer from nuclear fallout in Utah. But I can't prove they didn't. 34

My father's memory was correct, the September blast we drove through in 1957 was part of Operation Plumbbob, one of the most intensive series of bomb tests to be initiated. The flash of light in the night in the desert I had always thought was a dream developed into a family nightmare. It took fourteen years, from 1957 to 1971, for cancer to show up in my mother—the same time Howard L. Andrews, an authority on radioactive fallout at the National Institutes of Health, says radiation cancer requires to become evident.[8] The more I learn about what it means to be a "downwinder," the more questions I drown in. 35

What I do know, however, is that as a Mormon woman of the fifth generation of "Latter-Day-Saints," I must question everything, even if it means losing my faith, even if it means becoming a member of a border tribe among my own people. Tolerating blind obedience in the name of patriotism or religion ultimately takes our lives. 36

When the Atomic Energy Commission described the country north of the Nevada Test Site as "virtually uninhabited desert terrain," my family members were some of the "virtual uninhabitants." 37

One night, I dreamed women from all over the world circled a blazing fire in the desert. They spoke of change, of how they hold the moon in their bellies and wax and wane with its phases. They mocked at the presumption of even-tempered beings and made promises that they would never fear the witch inside themselves. The women danced 38

[8]Fradkin, op. cit., 116.

wildly as sparks broke away from the flames and entered the night sky as stars.

And they sang a song given to them by Shoshone grandmothers: 39

Ah ne nah, nah
nin nah nah—
Ah ne nah, nah
nin nah nah—
Nyaga mutzi
oh ne nay—
Nyaga mutzi
oh ne nay—[9]

The women danced and drummed and sang for weeks, preparing themselves for what was to come. They would reclaim the desert for the sake of their children, for the sake of the land. 40

A few miles downwind from the fire circle, bombs were being tested. Rabbits felt the tremors. Their soft leather pads on paws and feet recognized the shaking sands while the roots of mesquite and sage were smoldering. Rocks were hot from the inside out and dust devils hummed unnaturally. And each time there was another nuclear test, ravens watched the desert heave. Stretch marks appeared. The land was losing its muscle. 41

The women couldn't bear it any longer. They were mothers. They had suffered labor pains but always under the promise of birth. The red hot pains beneath the desert promised death only as each bomb became a stillborn. A contract had been broken between human beings and the land. A new contract was being drawn by the women who understood the fate of the earth as their own. 42

Under the cover of darkness, ten women slipped under the barbed wire fence and entered the contaminated country. They were trespassing. They walked toward the town of Mercury in moonlight, taking their cues from coyote, kit fox, antelope squirrel, and quail. They moved quietly and deliberately through the maze of Joshua trees. When a hint of daylight appeared they rested, drinking tea and sharing their rations of food. The women closed their eyes. The time 43

---

[9]This song was sung by the Western Shoshone women as they crossed the line at the Nevada Test Site on March 18, 1988, as part of their "Reclaim the Land" action. The translation they gave was: "Consider the rabbits how gently they walk on the earth. Consider the rabbits how gently they walk on the earth. We remember them. We can walk gently also. We remember them. We can walk gently also."

had come to protest with the heart, that to deny one's genealogy with the earth was to commit treason against one's soul.

At dawn, the women draped themselves in mylar, wrapping long streamers of silver plastic around their arms to blow in the breeze. They wore clear masks that became the faces of humanity. And when they arrived on the edge of Mercury, they carried all the butterflies of a summer day in their wombs. They paused to allow their courage to settle. 44

The town which forbids pregnant women and children to enter because of radiation risks to their health was asleep. The women moved through the streets as winged messengers, twirling around each other in slow motion, peeking inside homes and watching the easy sleep of men and women. They were astonished by such stillness and periodically would utter a shrill note or low cry just to verify life. 45

The residents finally awoke to what appeared as strange apparitions. Some simply stared. Others called authorities, and in time, the women were apprehended by wary soldiers dressed in desert fatigues. They were taken to a white, square building on the other edge of Mercury. When asked who they were and why they were there, the women replied, "We are mothers and we have come to reclaim the desert for our children." 46

The soldiers arrested them. As the ten women were blindfolded and handcuffed, they began singing: 47

You can't forbid us everything
You can't forbid us to think—
You can't forbid our tears to flow
And you can't stop the songs that we sing.

The women continued to sing louder and louder, until they heard the voices of their sisters moving across the mesa. 48

Ah ne nah, nah
nin nah nah—
Ah ne nah, nah
nin nah nah—
Nyaga mutzi
oh ne nay—
Nyaga mutzi
oh ne nay—

"Call for re-enforcement," one soldier said. 49

"We have," interrupted one woman. "We have—and you have 50
no idea of our numbers."

On March 18, 1988, I crossed the line at the Nevada Test Site and 51
was arrested with nine other Utahns for trespassing on military lands. They are still conducting nuclear tests in the desert. Ours was an act of civil disobedience. But as I walked toward the town of Mercury, it was more than a gesture of peace. It was a gesture on behalf of the Clan of One-Breasted Women.

As one officer cinched the handcuffs around my wrists, another 52
frisked my body. She found a pen and a pad of paper tucked inside my left boot.

"And these?" she asked sternly. 53

"Weapons," I replied. 54

Our eyes met. I smiled. She pulled the leg of my trousers back 55
over my boot.

"Step forward, please," she said as she took my arm. 56

We were booked under an afternoon sun and bussed to Tonapah, 57
Nevada. It was a two-hour ride. This was familiar country to me. The Joshua trees standing their ground had been named by my ancestors who believed they looked like prophets pointing west to the promised land. These were the same trees that bloomed each spring, flowers appearing like white flames in the Mojave. And I recalled a full moon in May when my mother and I had walked among them, flushing out mourning doves and owls.

The bus stopped short of town. We were released. The officials 58
thought it was a cruel joke to leave us stranded in the desert with no way to get home. What they didn't realize is that we were home, soul-centered and strong, women who recognized the sweet smell of sage as fuel for our spirits.

Thinking Critically about This Reading

In paragraph 20, Williams tells us that "the United States of the 1950s was red, white, and blue. The Korean War was raging. McCarthyism was rampant. Ike was it and the Cold War was hot. If you were against nuclear testing, you were for a Communist regime." Why do you think that Williams thought it was important for readers to know what the United States was like during these years? Explain.

Questions for Study and Discussion

1. How did you respond to Williams's opening three paragraphs? Together, did they work well as a beginning for you? Explain why or why not.
2. What "new information" (paragraph 17) does Williams learn while talking with her father over dinner shortly after her mother had died from cancer? Of what importance is this new information?
3. How does Williams use outside sources to support the idea that "public health was secondary to national security" (21)?
4. In paragraph 35, Williams paraphrases Howard L. Andrews. How does Williams signal where the paraphrase begins and ends? For what purpose does Williams bring Andrews into the discussion at this point?
5. Why did Williams remain silent about her suspicions about the nuclear testing for so long? What ultimately convinced her that she should speak out?
6. Williams has organized her essay into three sections—paragraphs 1–19, 20–29, and 30–58. How are the three sections related? Why do you think Williams ordered her essay in this way? (Glossary: *Organization*)
7. Why did the Shoshone women cross the line at the Nevada Test Site and enter the "contaminated country"? Why did Williams join them? What did Williams mean when she told the soldier frisking her that her pen and pad of paper were "weapons" (54)?

Classroom Activity Using Writing with Sources

For each of the following quotations, write an acceptable paraphrase and then a paraphrase with a partial quotation that avoids plagiarism (see pp. 245–48 and 256–57). Pay careful attention to the word choice and sentence structure of the original.

> The sperm whale is the largest of the toothed whales. Moby Dick was a sperm whale. Generally, male toothed whales are larger than the females. Female sperm whales may grow thirty-five to forty feet in length, while the males may reach sixty feet.
>
> –Richard Hendrick, *The Voyage of the Mimi*

> Astronauts from over twenty nations have gone into space, and they all come back, amazingly enough, saying the very same thing: the earth is a small, blue place of profound beauty that we must take care of. For each, the journey into space, whatever its original intents and purposes, became above all a spiritual one.
>
> –Al Reinhert, *For All Mankind*

> One of the usual things about education in mathematics in the United States is its relatively impoverished vocabulary. Whereas the student completing elementary school will already have a vocabulary for most disciplines of many hundreds, even thousands of words, the typical student will have a mathematics vocabulary of only a couple of dozen words.
>
> –Marvin Minsky, *The Society of Mind*

Suggested Writing Assignments

1. In paragraph 36, Williams emphatically states, "Tolerating blind obedience in the name of patriotism or religion ultimately takes our lives." Using examples from your own experience, observation, and reading, write an essay in which you agree or disagree with Williams's position.
2. Poet and environmentalist Wendell Berry has said that "it is impossible to care more or differently for each other than we care for the land." What do you think he means? Like the Western Shoshone women who crossed the government line at the Nevada Test Site as part of their "Reclaim the Land" action, we are all stewards of the earth. What responsibilities do you think we have toward the land? Toward one another? How can humans work in partnership with the land? Using your own experiences as well as research in the library and on the Internet, write an argumentative essay that answers these questions.
3. In 1962, Rachel Carson charged, in her landmark book *Silent Spring*, that "we have put poisonous and biologically potent chemicals indiscriminately into the hands of persons largely or wholly ignorant of their potential for harm." The validity of her charge is everywhere evident today. Write an essay about chemical and nuclear abuses using specific examples that have been brought to the public's attention since *Silent Spring* first appeared.

part three

The Language of the Essay

CHAPTER 11

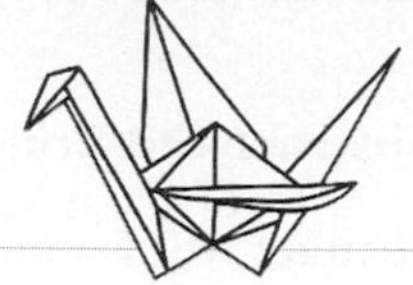

Diction and Tone

DICTION

Diction refers to a writer's choice and use of words. Good diction is precise and appropriate: the words mean exactly what the writer intends, and the words are well suited to the writer's subject, purpose, and intended audience.

Careful writers do not merely come close to saying what they want to say; they select words that convey their exact meaning. Perhaps Mark Twain put this idea best when he said, "The difference between the right word and the almost right word is the difference between lightning and the lightning bug." Inaccurate, imprecise, or inappropriate diction fails to convey the writer's intended meaning and may cause confusion and misunderstanding for the reader.

Connotation and Denotation

Both **connotation** and **denotation** refer to the meanings of words. Denotation is the dictionary meaning of a word—its literal meaning. Connotative meanings are the associations or emotional overtones that words have acquired. For example, the word *home* denotes a place where someone lives, but it connotes warmth, security, family, comfort, affection, and other more private thoughts and images. The word *residence* also denotes a place where someone lives, but its connotations are legal, colder, and more formal.

Many words in English have synonyms, or words with very similar denotations—for example, *mob, crowd, multitude,* and *bunch.* Deciding which to use depends largely on the connotations of each synonym and the context in which the word is to be used. For example, you might say, "There was a crowd at the lecture," but not "There was a mob at the lecture." Good writers are sensitive to both the denotations and the connotations of words.

Abstract and Concrete Words

Abstract words name ideas, conditions, emotions—things nobody can touch, see, or hear. Some abstract words are *love, wisdom, cowardice, beauty, fear,* and *liberty.* People often disagree about abstract things. You might find a forest beautiful, whereas someone else might find it frightening—and neither of you would be wrong. Beauty and fear are ideas; they exist in your mind. **Concrete** words refer to things we can touch, see, hear, smell, and taste, such as *sandpaper, soda, birch tree, smog, cow, sailboat, rocking chair,* and *pancake.* If you disagree with someone on a concrete issue—for example, you claim that the forest is mostly birch trees, whereas the other person says it is mostly pine—only one of you can be right, and both of you can be wrong; the kinds of trees that grow in the forest is a concrete fact, not an abstract idea.

Good writing balances ideas and facts, and it also balances abstract and concrete diction. If the writing is too abstract and has too few concrete facts and details, it will be unconvincing and tiresome. If the writing is too concrete and devoid of abstract ideas and emotions, it will seem mundane and dry.

General and Specific Words

General and **specific** do not necessarily refer to opposites. The same word can often be either general or specific, depending on the context: *Dessert* is more specific than *food* but more general than *chocolate cream pie.* Being specific is like being concrete: chocolate cream pie is something you can see and taste. Being general, on the other hand, is like being abstract. Food, dessert, and even pie are large classes of things that bring to mind only general tastes or images.

Good writing moves back and forth from the general to the specific. Without specific words, generalities can be unconvincing and even confusing: the writer's idea of "good food" may be very different from the reader's. But writing that does not connect its specific details to each other through generalization often lacks focus and direction.

Clichés

A word, phrase, or expression that has become trite through overuse is called a **cliché**. Let's assume your roommate has just returned from an evening out. You ask her, "How was the concert?" She responds, "The concert was okay, but they had us *packed in* there *like sardines.*

How was your evening?" And you reply, "Well, I finished my term paper, but the noise here is enough to *drive me crazy*. The dorm is a real *zoo*." The italicized expressions were once vivid and colorful, but through constant use they have grown stale and ineffective. Experienced writers always try to avoid such clichés as *believe it or not, doomed to failure, hit the spot, let's face it, sneaking suspicion, step in the right direction*, and *went to great lengths*. They strive to use fresh language.

Jargon

Jargon, or technical language, is the special vocabulary of a trade or profession. Writers use jargon with an awareness of their audience. If their audience is a group of co-workers or professionals, jargon may be used freely. If the audience is general, jargon should be used sparingly and carefully so that readers can understand it. Jargon becomes inappropriate when it is overused, used out of context, or used pretentiously. For example, computer terms like *input, output,* and *feedback* are sometimes used in place of *contribution, result,* and *response* in other fields, especially in business. If you think about it, these terms suggest that people are machines that receive and process information according to a program imposed by someone else.

Formal and Informal Diction

Diction is appropriate when it suits the occasion for which it is intended. If the situation is informal—a friendly e-mail, for example—the writing may be colloquial; that is, its words may be chosen to suggest the way people talk with one another. If, on the other hand, the situation is formal—an academic paper or a research report, for example—the words should reflect this formality. Informal writing tends to be characterized by slang, contractions, references to the reader, and concrete nouns. Formal writing tends to be impersonal, abstract, and free of contractions and references to the reader. Formal writing and informal writing are the extremes. Most writing falls between these two extremes and is a blend of the formal and informal elements that best fit the context.

■ TONE

Tone is the attitude a writer takes toward the subject and the audience. Tone is conveyed by the voice we use to express ourselves in our writing. The tone may be friendly, hostile, bitter, sarcastic, angry, serious, mocking, whimsical, humorous, enthusiastic, skeptical, indifferent, facetious, sad, and so on.

As you read the following paragraphs, notice how each writer creates a different tone and how that tone is supported by the diction—the writer's particular choice and use of words.

Nostalgic

When I was six years old, I thought I knew a lot. How to jump rope, how to skip a rock across a pond, and how to color and stay between the lines—these were all things I took great pride in. Nothing was difficult, and my days were carefree. That is, until the summer when everything became complicated and I suddenly realized I didn't know that much.

–Heather C. Blue, student

Angry

That man over there says that women need to be helped into carriages, and lifted over ditches, and to have the best place everywhere. Nobody ever helps me into carriages, or over mud-puddles, or gives me any best place! And ain't I a woman? Look at me! Look at my arm! I have ploughed and planted, and gathered into barns, and no man could head me! And ain't I a woman? I could work as much and eat as much as a man—when I could get it—and bear the lash as well! And ain't I a woman? I have borne thirteen children, and seen them most all sold off to slavery, and when I cried out with my mother's grief, none but Jesus heard me! And ain't I a woman?

–Sojourner Truth, "Ain't I a Woman?"

Sarcastic

Ultimately, the plutocratic takeover of rural America has a downside for the wealthy too. The more expensive a resort town gets, the farther its workers have to commute to keep it functioning. And if your heart doesn't bleed for the dishwasher or landscaper who commutes two to four hours a day, at least shed a tear for the wealthy vacationer who gets stuck in the ensuing traffic. It's bumper to bumper westbound out of Telluride, Colorado, every day at 5, or eastbound on Route 1 out of Key West, for the Lexuses as well as the beat-up old pickup trucks.

–Barbara Ehrenreich, "This Land Is Their Land"

Objective or Academic

In 2006 an American big-game hunter from Idaho shot and killed the first documented wild polar-grizzly bear hybrid, a mostly white male covered in patches of brown fur with long grizzly-like claws, a humped back, and eyes ringed by black skin. Four years later a second-generation "pizzly" or "grolar" was shot. After hearing reports of the bears, Brendan Kelly, then an Alaska-based biologist with the National Oceanic and Atmospheric Administration, started to wonder which other species might be interbreeding as a result of a changing Arctic landscape.

–Katherine Bagley, "Climate Change Is Causing Some Mixed-Up Wildlife"

Business or Professional

The renovation of the County Courthouse is progressing on schedule and within budget. Although the cost of certain materials is higher than our original bid indicated, we expect to complete the project without exceeding the estimated costs because the speed with which the project is being completed will reduce overall labor expenses.

–Tran Nuguélen, project engineer

Dramatic

Every day you walk on it, your baby crawls across it, and your dog rolls around on it. Your child may accidentally drop a piece of candy on it and eat the candy anyway. All the while you are unaware that your floor is made with a toxic chemical that has proven to cause various types of cancer and other serious health risks. Vinyl flooring—one of today's most affordable, durable, and easily installed flooring options—is manufactured using vinyl chloride.

–Mina Raine, student, "The Real Dangers of Vinyl Chloride"

Ironic

Once upon a time there was a small, beautiful, green and graceful country called Vietnam. It needed to be saved. (In later years no one could remember exactly what it needed to be saved from, but that is another story.) For many years Vietnam was in the process of being saved by France, but the French eventually tired of their labors and left. Then America took on the job. America was well equipped for country saving. It was the richest

> and most powerful nation on earth. It had, for example, nuclear explosives on hand and ready to use equal to six tons of TNT for every man, woman, and child in the world. It had huge and very efficient factories, brilliant and dedicated scientists, and most (but not everybody) would agree, it had good intentions. Sadly, America had one fatal flaw—its inhabitants were in love with technology and thought it could do no wrong. A visitor to America during the time of this story would probably have guessed its outcome after seeing how its inhabitants were treating their own country. The air was mostly foul, the water putrid, and most of the land was either covered with concrete or garbage. But Americans were never much on introspection, and they didn't foresee the result of their loving embrace on the small country. They set out to save Vietnam with the same enthusiasm and determination their forefathers had displayed in conquering the frontier.
>
> –The Sierra Club, "Vietnam Defoliation: A Fable for Our Times"

The diction and tone of an essay are subtle forces, but they exert a tremendous influence on readers. They are instrumental in determining how we will feel while reading an essay and what attitude we will have toward its argument or the points it makes. Readers react in a variety of ways. An essay written informally but with a largely angry tone may make one reader defensive and unsympathetic; another may believe that the author is being unusually honest and courageous and may admire these qualities and feel moved by them. Either way, the diction and tone of the piece have made a strong emotional impression. As you read the essays in this chapter and throughout this book, see if you can analyze how the diction and tone shape your reactions.

How Do Plants Know Which Way Is Up and Which Way Is Down?

■ **Robert Krulwich**

Alan Klein

Robert Krulwich earned a BA in history from Oberlin College and a JD from Columbia Law School, but he left the path toward a law career to cover the Watergate hearings for Pacifica Radio. He went on to work as a journalist for a number of publications and news programs, including Rolling Stone, 48 Hours, Nightline, *and* NOVA. *Krulwich has won Emmy Awards for his reports on computers and privacy, savings and loan bailouts, and the history of Barbie dolls.* TV Guide *called him "the most inventive network reporter in television." He is currently a correspondent for National Public Radio and cohost of the Peabody Award–winning show* Radiolab.

In this essay for NPR, Krulwich uses writing and illustrations to answer a simple question, leading to a rather complex series of scientific hypotheses. As you read, pay attention to how he avoids jargon, translating the scientists' research findings into language easy for general readers to understand.

Reflecting on What You Know

What do you know about the scientific method, which researchers employ to answer their questions about the world? What would you hypothesize about how plants grow right side up?

Think of a seed buried in a pot. Like this one: 1

It's dark down there in the potting soil. There's no light, no sunshine. So how does it know which way is up and which way is down? It *does know.* Seeds routinely send shoots up toward the sky, and roots the other way. Darkness doesn't confuse them. Somehow, they get it right . . . 2

More intriguing, if you turn a seedling (or a whole bunch of seedlings) upside down, as Thomas Andrew Knight of the British Royal Society did around 200 years ago, the tips and roots of the plant will sense, "Hey, I'm upside down," and will wiggle their way to the right direction, doing a double U-turn, like this: 3

How do they know? According to botanist Daniel Chamovitz, Thomas Knight 200 years ago assumed that plants must sense gravity. They feel the pull of the Earth. Knight proved it with a crazy experiment involving a spinning plate. 4

He attached a bunch of plant seedlings onto a disc (think of a 78 rpm record made of wood). The plate was then turned by a water wheel powered by a local stream, "at a nauseating speed of 150 revolutions per minute for several days." 5

If you've ever been at an amusement park in a spinning tea cup, you know that because of centrifugal force you get pushed *away from the* center of the spinning object toward the outside. 6

Knight wondered, would the plants respond to the centrifugal pull of gravity and point their roots to the outside of the spinning plate? When he looked . . . 7

. . . that's what they'd done. Every plant on the disc had responded to the pull of gravity, and pointed its roots to the outside. The roots pointed out, the shoots pointed in. So Thomas Knight proved that plants can and do sense gravitational pull.

But he couldn't explain how. 8

We humans have teeny crystalline stones floating in our ear cavities that literally sink in response to gravity, telling us what's up and what's down. What do plants have? 9

Strangely, this is a real puzzle. We still don't know for sure how plants do it. There is a team of botanists, John Kiss and his colleagues at Miami University in Ohio, who have a promising idea, but at the moment it's just a very educated guess. 10

Plants have special cells right down at the tip—the very bottom—of their roots. And if you look closely, inside these cells there are dense, little ball like structures called "statoliths"—which comes from the Greek, meaning "stationary stone." You can see them here. 11

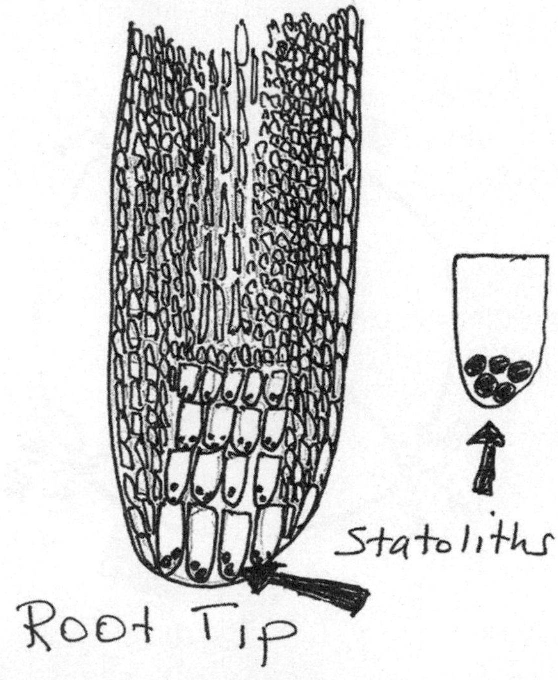

I think of them as pebbles inside a jar. If the jar is upright, the pebbles, naturally, fall to the bottom. 12

If I put the jar on its side, the pebbles will roll to the side of the 13
jar, the new bottom, and lie there.

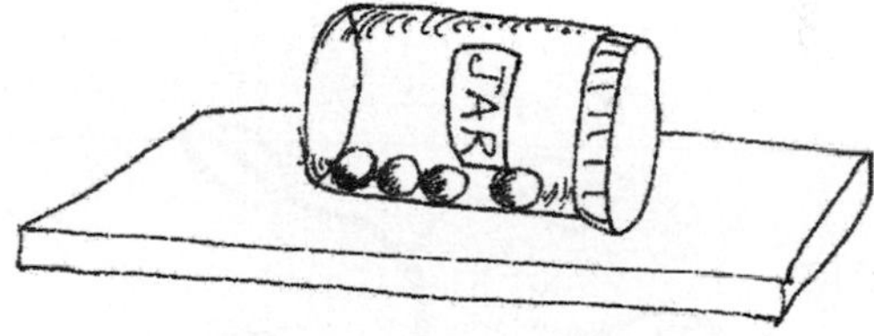

If I turn the jar upside down, the pebbles will drop into the cap, 14
which used to be the top but is now the bottom.

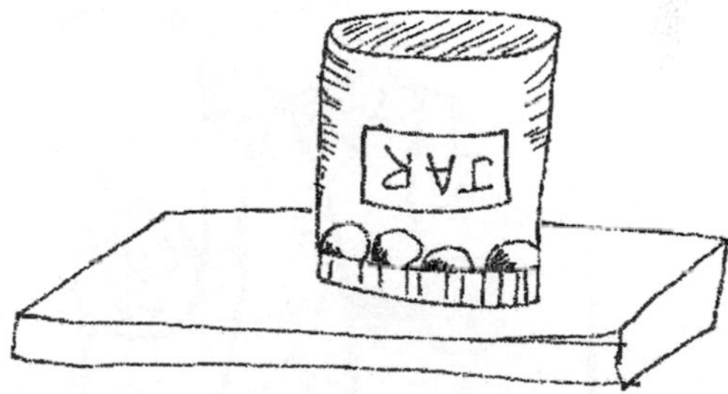

Basically these little pebbly things *respond to gravity.* In a plant 15
cell, gravity pulls them to the "bottom," and once they find a resting place, they can send signals to neighboring cells in the plant essentially saying, "OK guys! We now know where Down is. Those of you

that need to go down (root cells), go this way! Those of you who need to go up (the shoot on top), go the other way!"

This, suggests Professor Kiss, is how plants figure out where 16
"down" is. They use little statolith balls as gravity receptors.

His idea got a boost when he sent some seedlings into space (to 17
the space station) where the pull of gravity is close to zero, figuring if the statoliths just float randomly and don't drop to the bottom of their cells, the plants won't know which way is down. And sure enough, he reported that plants growing in space did not send their roots in any specific direction. The roots just went every which way.

So the next time you pass a tree, a flower, a grapevine, grasses, 18
bushes, vegetables, any plant that seems to be reaching for the sky, that plant may be going up not just because it wants to be kissed by the sun, but also because down at its bottom, in cells rooted in the Earth, it's got itty bitty rocks telling it, "go thattaway!"

Thinking Critically about This Reading

What role do the illustrations play in Krulwich's explanation? What do they add to his writing? Which do you find most effective?

Questions for Study and Discussion

1. How would you describe the tone of this essay? What is Krulwich's attitude toward the question he poses?
2. The first researcher Krulwich mentions is Thomas Andrew Knight, who performed his experiments on plants around two hundred years ago. What have scientists been able to determine about how plants grow since then? What do they still not know for sure?
3. How does Krulwich use analogies to illustrate the scientists' findings? For example, see the analogy of the record album in paragraph 5. Can you find other places where he helps readers visualize his subject?
4. Krulwich uses active verbs to convey the lively, even dramatic process of experimentation. The researchers he writes about *wonder*, *assume*, and *prove*. Identify other strong verb choices throughout the essay. What do they contribute to Krulwich's explanation of the science?
5. One of the few scientific terms Krulwich uses in his essay is "statolith." How would you define this word? What information does Krulwich offer to help you form this definition?
6. How does the behavior of plants in the space station support the current understanding of how these statoliths work?

Classroom Activity Using Diction and Tone

Writers create and control tone in their writing in part through the words they choose. For example, the words *laugh, cheery, dance,* and *melody* help create a tone of celebration. Make a list of the words that come to mind when considering each of the following tones:

humorous	authoritative	tentative
angry	triumphant	repentant

Compare your lists of words with those of others in the class. What generalizations can you make about the connotations associated with each of these tones?

Suggested Writing Assignments

1. Choose a subject on which you have some expertise—an adventurous favorite food, a cult comic series, or an uncommon job experience, for example. Write an introduction to your subject for a general audience, "translating" any specialized terminology for the reader.
2. Write an exploratory essay on a question you feel is unsolved, something that is, as Krulwich writes of the gravitational sense of plants, "a real puzzle." Using Krulwich's essay as a model, allow your essay to follow your mental process as you think about this question. What information can you gather, and from what sources? In what areas do you feel you have adequate knowledge, and where does that knowledge end? What leaves you wondering?

Me Talk Pretty One Day

David Sedaris

Ralph Orlowski/Getty Images

David Sedaris was born in 1956 in Binghamton, New York, and grew up in Raleigh, North Carolina. He briefly attended Western Carolina University and Kent State University but ultimately graduated from the Art Institute of Chicago in 1987. Before becoming a writer, Sedaris worked as a mover, an office temp, a housekeeper, and an elf in a department store Christmas display—an experience he wrote about in his celebrated essay "Santaland Diaries." He is a regular contributor to National Public Radio, Harper's, Details, *the* New Yorker, *and* Esquire *and has won several awards, including the James Thurber Prize for American Humor. Sedaris often writes about his quirky Greek family and his travels with his partner, Hugh Hamrick, with whom he currently lives in London. His essays and stories have been collected in several best-selling books, including* Barrel Fever *(1994),* Holidays on Ice *(1997),* Naked *(1997),* Dress Your Family in Corduroy and Denim *(2004),* When You Are Engulfed in Flames *(2008),* Squirrel Seeks Chipmunk: A Modest Bestiary *(2010), and* Let's Explore Diabetes with Owls *(2013).*

The following essay about taking French lessons in Paris first appeared in Esquire *in March 1999 and later became the title piece for Sedaris's fourth book,* Me Talk Pretty One Day *(2000). As you read, pay attention to how he uses his words to play with the ideas of language, understanding, and belonging.*

Reflecting on What You Know

Have you ever been in a situation in which you did not speak the prevalent language—for example, in a foreign country, in a language class, or among a group of people who spoke a language other than yours? How did you feel about not being able to communicate? How, if at all, did you get your thoughts across to others?

At the age of forty-one, I am returning to school and having to think of myself as what my French textbook calls "a true debutant." After paying my tuition, I was issued a student ID, which allows me a discounted entry fee at movie theaters, puppet shows, and Festyland, a far-flung amusement park that advertises with billboards picturing a cartoon stegosaurus sitting in a canoe and eating what appears to be a ham sandwich. 1

I've moved to Paris in order to learn the language. My school is the Alliance Française, and on the first day of class, I arrived early, watching as the returning students greeted one another in the school lobby. Vacations were recounted, and questions were raised concerning mutual friends with names like Kang and Vlatnya. Regardless of their nationalities, everyone spoke what sounded to me like excellent French. Some accents were better than others, but the students exhibited an ease and confidence I found intimidating. As an added discomfort, they were all young, attractive, and well dressed, causing me to feel not unlike Pa Kettle[1] trapped backstage after a fashion show. 2

I remind myself that I am now a full-grown man. No one will ever again card me for a drink or demand that I weave a floor mat out of newspapers. At my age, a reasonable person should have completed his sentence in the prison of the nervous and the insecure—isn't that the great promise of adulthood? I can't help but think that, somewhere along the way, I made a wrong turn. My fears have not vanished. Rather, they have seasoned and multiplied with age. I am now twice as frightened as I was when, at the age of twenty, I allowed a failed nursing student to inject me with a horse tranquilizer, and eight times more anxious than I was the day my kindergarten teacher pried my fingers off my mother's ankle and led me screaming toward my desk. "You'll get used to it," the woman had said. 3

I'm still waiting. 4

The first day of class was nerve-racking because I knew I'd be expected to perform. That's the way they do it here—everyone into the language pool, sink or swim. The teacher marched in, deeply tanned from a recent vacation, and rattled off a series of administrative announcements. I've spent some time in Normandy,[2] and I took a monthlong French class last summer in New York. I'm not completely in the dark, yet I understood only half of what this teacher was saying. 5

[1]*Pa Kettle:* someone who is simple or unsophisticated; the name of a character in a series of comic movies popular in the 1950s.

[2]*Normandy:* a province in northwestern France.

"If you have not *meismslsxp* by this time, you should not be in this room. Has everybody *apzkiubjxow*? Everyone? Good, we shall proceed." She spread out her lesson plan and sighed, saying, "All right, then, who knows the alphabet?" 6

It was startling because a) I hadn't been asked that question in a while, and b) I realized, while laughing, that I myself did not know the alphabet. They're the same letters, but they're pronounced differently. 7

"Ahh." The teacher went to the board and sketched the letter *A*. "Do we have anyone in the room whose first name commences with an ahh?" 8

Two Polish Annas raised their hands, and the teacher instructed them to present themselves, giving their names, nationalities, occupations, and a list of things they liked and disliked in this world. The first Anna hailed from an industrial town outside of Warsaw and had front teeth the size of tombstones. She worked as a seamstress, enjoyed quiet times with friends, and hated the mosquito. 9

"Oh, really," the teacher said. "How very interesting. I thought that everyone loved the mosquito, but here, in front of all the world, you claim to detest him. How is it that we've been blessed with someone as unique and original as you? Tell us, please." 10

The seamstress did not understand what was being said, but she knew that this was an occasion for shame. Her rabbity mouth huffed for breath, and she stared down at her lap as though the appropriate comeback were stitched somewhere alongside the zipper of her slacks. 11

The second Anna learned from the first and claimed to love sunshine and detest lies. It sounded like a translation of one of those Playmate of the Month data sheets, the answers always written in the same loopy handwriting: "Turn-ons: Mom's famous five-alarm chili! Turnoffs: Insincerity and guys who come on too strong!!!" 12

The two Polish women surely had clear notions of what they liked and disliked, but, like the rest of us, they were limited in terms of vocabulary, and this made them appear less than sophisticated. The teacher forged on, and we learned that Carlos, the Argentine bandoneon[3] player, loved wine, music, and, in his words, "Making sex with the women of the world." Next came a beautiful young Yugoslavian who identified herself as an optimist, saying that she loved everything life had to offer. 13

The teacher licked her lips, revealing a hint of the sadist[4] we would later come to know. She crouched low for her attack, placed her hands 14

[3]*bandoneon:* a small accordion popular in South America.
[4]*sadist:* one who finds pleasure in being cruel to others.

on the young woman's desk, and said, "Oh, yeah? And do you love your little war?"[5]

While the optimist struggled to defend herself, I scrambled to think of an answer to what had obviously become a trick question. How often are you asked what you love in this world? More important, how often are you asked and then publicly ridiculed for your answer? I recalled my mother, flushed with wine, pounding the table late one night, saying, "Love? I love a good steak cooked rare. I love my cat, and I love . . ." My sisters and I leaned forward, waiting to hear our names. "Tums," our mother said. "I love Tums." The teacher killed some time accusing the Yugoslavian girl of masterminding a program of genocide, and I jotted frantic notes in the margins of my pad. While I can honestly say that I love leafing through medical textbooks devoted to severe dermatological conditions, it is beyond the reach of my French vocabulary, and acting it out would only have invited unwanted attention. 15

When called upon, I delivered an effortless list of things I detest: blood sausage, intestinal paté, brain pudding. I'd learned these words the hard way. Having given it some thought, I then declared my love for IBM typewriters, the French word for "bruise," and my electric floor waxer. It was a short list, but still I managed to mispronounce IBM and afford the wrong gender to both the floor waxer and the typewriter. Her reaction led me to believe that these mistakes were capital crimes in the country of France. 16

"Were you always this *palicmkrexjs*?" she asked. "Even a *fiuscrzsws tociwegixp* knows that a typewriter is feminine." 17

I absorbed as much of her abuse as I could understand, thinking, but not saying, that I find it ridiculous to assign a gender to an inanimate object incapable of disrobing and making an occasional fool of itself. Why refer to Lady Flesh Wound or Good Sir Dishrag when these things could never deliver in the sack? 18

The teacher proceeded to belittle everyone from German Eva, who hated laziness, to Japanese Yukari, who loved paintbrushes and soap. Italian, Thai, Dutch, Korean, Chinese—we all left class foolishly believing that the worst was over. We didn't know it then, but the coming months would teach us what it is like to spend time in the presence of a wild animal. We soon learned to dodge chalk and to cover our heads and stomachs whenever she approached us with a question. She 19

[5] "*. . . your little war*": the Balkan War (1991–2001), which consisted of armed conflict and genocide in the territory of the former Yugoslavia.

hadn't yet punched anyone, but it seemed wise to prepare ourselves against the inevitable.

20 Though we were forbidden to speak anything but French, the teacher would occasionally use us to practice any of her five fluent languages.

21 "I hate you," she said to me one afternoon. Her English was flawless. "I really, really hate you." Call me sensitive, but I couldn't help taking it personally.

22 Learning French is a lot like joining a gang in that it involves a long and intensive period of hazing. And it wasn't just my teacher; the entire population seemed to be in on it. Following brutal encounters with my local butcher and the concierge[6] of my building, I'd head off to class, where the teacher would hold my corrected paperwork high above her head, shouting, "Here's proof that *David* is an ignorant and uninspired *ensigiejsokhjx*."

23 Refusing to stand convicted on the teacher's charges of laziness, I'd spend four hours a night on my homework, working even longer whenever we were assigned an essay. I suppose I could have gotten by with less, but I was determined to create some sort of an identity for myself. We'd have one of those "complete the sentence" exercises, and I'd fool with the thing for hours, invariably settling on something like, "A quick run around the lake? I'd love to. Just give me a minute to strap on my wooden leg." The teacher, through word and action, conveyed the message that, if this was my idea of an identity, she wanted nothing to do with it.

24 My fear and discomfort crept beyond the borders of my classroom and accompanied me out onto the wide boulevards, where, no matter how hard I tried, there was no escaping the feeling of terror I felt whenever anyone asked me a question. I was safe in any kind of a store, as, at least in my neighborhood, one can stand beside the cash register for hours on end without being asked something so trivial as, "May I help you?" or "How would you like to pay for that?"

25 My only comfort was the knowledge that I was not alone. Huddled in the smoky hallways and making the most of our pathetic French, my fellow students and I engaged in the sort of conversation commonly overheard in refugee camps.

26 "Sometimes me cry alone at night."

27 "That is common for me also, but be more strong, you. Much work, and someday you talk pretty. People stop hate you soon. Maybe tomorrow, okay?"

[6]*concierge:* a doorman in a French apartment building.

Unlike other classes I have taken, here there was no sense of competition. When the teacher poked a shy Korean woman in the eyelid with a freshly sharpened pencil, we took no comfort in the fact that, unlike Hyeyoon Cho, we all knew the irregular past tense of the verb "to defeat." In all fairness, the teacher hadn't meant to hurt the woman, but neither did she spend much time apologizing, saying only, "Well, you should have been paying more attention." 28

Over time, it became impossible to believe that any of us would ever improve. Fall arrived, and it rained every day. It was mid-October when the teacher singled me out, saying, "Every day spent with you is like having a cesarean section." And it struck me that, for the first time since arriving in France, I could understand every word that someone was saying. 29

Understanding doesn't mean that you can suddenly speak the language. Far from it. It's a small step, nothing more, yet its rewards are intoxicating and deceptive. The teacher continued her diatribe, and I settled back, bathing in the subtle beauty of each new curse and insult. 30

"You exhaust me with your foolishness and reward my efforts with nothing but pain, do you understand me?" 31

The world opened up, and it was with great joy that I responded, "I know the thing what you speak exact now. Talk me more, plus, please, plus." 32

Thinking Critically about This Reading

Sedaris's French teacher tells him that "every day spent with you is like having a cesarean section" (paragraph 29). Why is Sedaris's ability to recount this insult significant? What does the teacher's "cesarean section" metaphor mean?

Questions for Study and Discussion

1. Sedaris's tone is humorous. (Glossary: *Tone*) What words in particular help him create this tone? Did you find yourself smiling or laughing out loud as you read his essay? If so, what specific passages affected you this way?
2. What is your impression of Sedaris and his classmates? What words and phrases does he use to describe himself and them?

3. Why do you think Sedaris uses nonsense jumbles of letters—*meismslsxp* and *palicmkrexjs*, for example—in several places? How would his essay be different had he used the real words instead?
4. What does Sedaris realize in the final four paragraphs? What evidence does he provide of this realization?

Classroom Activity Using Diction and Tone

Good writers rely on strong verbs—verbs that contribute significantly to what is being said. Sportswriters, for example, are acutely aware of the need for strong action verbs because they must repeatedly describe similar situations. It is not enough for them to say that a team wins or loses; they must describe the type of win or loss more precisely. As a result, verbs such as *beat*, *bury*, *edge*, *shock*, and *trounce* are common in sports headlines. In addition to describing the act of winning, each of these verbs makes a statement about the quality of the victory. Like sportswriters, we all write about actions that are performed daily. If we were restricted to using only the verbs *eat*, *drink*, *sleep*, and *work* for each of these activities, our writing would be repetitious, monotonous, and most likely wordy. List as many verbs as you can that could be used in place of these four. What connotative differences do you find in your lists of alternatives? What is the importance of these connotative differences for you as a writer?

Suggested Writing Assignments

1. Write a narrative essay recounting a humorous incident in your life. (Glossary: *Narration*) Use the following questions to start thinking about the incident: Where were you? What happened? Who witnessed the incident? Did you think it was humorous at the time? Do you view it differently now? Why or why not? Choose words and phrases for your narrative that convey a humorous tone. (Glossary: *Tone*)
2. "Refusing to stand convicted on the teacher's charges of laziness," Sedaris explains, "I'd spend four hours a night on my homework, working even longer whenever we were assigned an essay" (23). Write an essay in which you evaluate Sedaris's teacher. Given that she inspired Sedaris to apply himself to his work, do you think she was an effective teacher? Would her methods have the same effect on you? Why or why not? (Glossary: *Cause and Effect*)

3. As Sedaris's essay illustrates, fitting in often depends on our ability to communicate with authenticity—using the appropriate pronunciation, terminology, or slang—to a particular audience. (Glossary: *Audience; Slang*) Have you ever felt alienated by a group because you didn't use its lingo appropriately, or have you ever alienated someone else for the same reason? Write a narrative essay in which you recount one such event. (Glossary: *Narration*) Be sure to use diction and tone creatively to convey your meaning. Before you begin, you might find it helpful to refer to your response to the Reflecting on What You Know prompt for this selection.

Be Specific

■ Natalie Goldberg

Ritch Davidson

Born in 1948, Natalie Goldberg has made a specialty of writing about writing. Her first and best-known work, Writing Down the Bones: Freeing the Writer Within, *was published in 1986. Goldberg's advice to would-be writers is, on the one hand, practical and pithy; on the other, it is almost mystical in its call to know and appreciate the world. Her other books about writing include* Wild Mind: Living the Writer's Life *(1990),* Living Color *(1996),* Thunder and Lightning: Cracking Open the Writer's Craft *(2000), and* Old Friend from Far Away: The Practice of Writing Memoir *(2008). Goldberg has also written fiction. Her first novel,* Banana Rose, *was published in 1994. She is also a painter whose work is exhibited in Taos, New Mexico.* Living Color: A Writer Paints Her World *(1997) is about painting as her second art form, and* Top of My Lungs *(2002) is a collection of poetry and paintings.*

In "Be Specific," a chapter from Writing Down the Bones, *Goldberg argues for precise diction, which brings us out of abstract ideas and "close to the ground."*

Reflecting on What You Know

Suppose someone says to you, "I walked in the woods." What do you envision? Write down what you see in your mind's eye. Now suppose someone says, "I walked in the redwood forest." Again, write down what you see. How are the two descriptions different, and why?

Be specific. Don't say "fruit." Tell what kind of fruit—"It is a pomegranate." Give things the dignity of their names. Just as with human beings, it is rude to say, "Hey, girl, get in line." That "girl" has a name. (As a matter of fact, if she's at least twenty 1 years old, she's a woman, not a "girl" at all.) Things, too, have names. It is much better to say "the geranium in the window" than "the flower in the window." "Geranium"—that one word gives us a much more specific picture. It penetrates more deeply into the beingness of that flower. It immediately gives us the scene by the window—red petals, green circular leaves, all straining toward sunlight.

About ten years ago I decided I had to learn the names of plants and flowers in my environment. I bought a book on them and walked down the tree-lined streets of Boulder,[1] examining leaf, bark, and seed, trying to match them up with their descriptions and names in the book. Maple, elm, oak, locust. I usually tried to cheat by asking people working in their yards the names of the flowers and trees growing there. I was amazed how few people had any idea of the names of the live beings inhabiting their little plot of land. 2

When we know the name of something, it brings us closer to the ground. It takes the blur out of our mind; it connects us to the earth. If I walk down the street and see "dogwood," "forsythia," I feel more friendly toward the environment. I am noticing what is around me and can name it. It makes me more awake. 3

If you read the poems of William Carlos Williams,[2] you will see how specific he is about plants, trees, flowers—chicory, daisy, locust, poplar, quince, primrose, black-eyed Susan, lilacs—each has its own integrity. Williams says, "Write what's in front of your nose." It's good for us to know what is in front of our nose. Not just "daisy," but how the flower is in the season we are looking at it—"The days-eye hugging the earth / in August . . . brownedged, / green and pointed scales / armor his yellow."* Continue to hone your awareness: to the name, to the month, to the day, and finally to the moment. 4

Williams also says: "No idea, but in things." Study what is "in front of your nose." By saying "geranium" instead of "flower," you are penetrating more deeply into the present and being there. The closer we can get to what's in front of our nose, the more it can teach us everything. "To see the World in a Grain of Sand, and a heaven in a Wild Flower . . ."** 5

In writing groups and classes too, it is good to quickly learn the names of all the other group members. It helps to ground you in the group and make you more attentive to each other's work. 6

---

[1]*Boulder:* a city in Colorado.

[2]*William Carlos Williams* (1883–1963): American poet.

*William Carlos Williams, "Daisy," in *The Collected Earlier Poems* (New York: New Directions, 1938). [Goldberg's note]

**William Blake, "The Auguries of Innocence." [Goldberg's note]

Learn the names of everything: birds, cheese, tractors, cars, buildings. A writer is all at once everything—an architect, French cook, farmer—and at the same time, a writer is none of these things. 7

Thinking Critically about This Reading

What does Goldberg mean when she states, "Give things the dignity of their names" (paragraph 1)? Why, according to Goldberg, should writers refer to things by their specific names?

Questions for Study and Discussion

1. Goldberg claims that knowing the plants in her environment by name keeps her "more awake" (3). Do you think her diction does the same for a reader?
2. How does Goldberg "specifically" follow the advice she gives writers in this essay?
3. Goldberg makes several lists of the names of things. What purpose do these lists serve? (Glossary: *Purpose*)
4. Throughout the essay, Goldberg instructs the reader to be specific and to be aware of the physical world. Of what besides names is the reader advised to be aware? Why?
5. In paragraphs 3, 5, and 6, Goldberg cites a number of advantages to be gained by knowing the names of things. What are these advantages? Do they ring true to you?
6. What specific audience does Goldberg address? (Glossary: *Audience*) How do you know?

Classroom Activity Using Diction and Tone

A useful exercise in learning to be specific is to see the words we use for people, places, things, and ideas as being positioned somewhere on a "ladder of abstraction." In the following chart, notice how the words progress from more general to more specific.

More General	*General*	*Specific*	*More Specific*
Organism	Plant	Flower	Alstroemeria
Vehicle	Car	Chevrolet	1958 Chevrolet Impala

Try to fill in the missing parts of the following ladder of abstraction:

More General	*General*	*Specific*	*More Specific*
Writing instrument	__________	Fountain pen	Waterman fountain pen
__________	Sandwich	Corned beef sandwich	Reuben
American	__________	Pueblo	Laguna Pueblo
Book	Reference book	Dictionary	__________
School	High school	Technical high school	__________
Medicine	Oral medicine	Gel capsule	__________

Suggested Writing Assignments

1. Goldberg likes William Carlos Williams's statement, "No idea, but in things" (5). What does this statement mean to you? Using this line as both a title and a thesis, write your own argument for the use of the specific over the general in a certain field—news reporting, writing poetry, or making music, for example. (Glossary: *Argumentation*) Be sure to support your argument with specific examples and diction that is precise and appropriate.
2. Write a brief essay advising your readers of something they should do. Title your essay, as Goldberg does, with a directive ("Be Specific"). Tell your readers how they can improve their lives by taking your advice, and give strong examples of the behavior you are recommending. Be sure that your tone is appropriate and that your diction is persuasive.

No, I Do Not Want to Pet Your Dog

Farhad Manjoo

Helen Bailey

Farhad Manjoo was born in South Africa in 1978 and moved with his family to the United States when he was a young boy. He graduated from Cornell University, where he served as the editor of the student paper, the Cornell Daily Sun. *He has worked as a staff writer for* Slate *and has been a regular contributor to NPR. He currently writes a technology column for the* Wall Street Journal. *He is the author of* True Enough: Learning to Live in a Post-Fact Society *(2008), in which he discusses the ascendance of opinion and punditry in the news media.*

"No, I Do Not Want to Pet Your Dog" first appeared in Slate *magazine in May 2013. Manjoo says of his writing process, "I write whatever moves me. I spend a lot of time thinking about column ideas—whatever seems off in life, whatever needs commenting on, I write that." In this piece, Manjoo responds to an everyday irritation by describing an America in which dogs have "achieved dominion" over spaces from which they were once barred. As you read, note how his ironic language pokes fun at the way dog owners talk about and treat their beloved pets.*

Reflecting on What You Know

Where do you feel comfortable encountering dogs or other pets? In what places is their presence acceptable? From what spaces should they be excluded?

The other day I walked into my gym and saw a dog. A half-dozen people were crowding around him, cooing and petting. He was a big dog, a lean and muscular Doberman with, I later 1 learned, the sort of hair-trigger bark you'd prize if you wanted to protect a big stash of gold bullion.

"This is Y.," the dog's owner said. No explanation was offered for the pooch's presence, as if it were the most natural thing in the world to have a dog in a place usually reserved for human beings. *Huh*, I thought. 2

The dog came up to me, because in my experience that's what dogs do when you don't want them to come up to you. They get up real close, touching you, licking you, theatrically begging you to respond. The dog pushed his long face toward my hand, the canine equivalent of a high five. And so—in the same way it's rude to leave a high-fiver hanging, especially if the high-fiver has big teeth and a strong jaw—I was expected to pet him. I ran my hand across his head half-heartedly. I guess I was fairly sure he wouldn't snap and bite me, but stranger things have happened—for instance, dogs snapping and biting people all the time. 3

Anyway, happily, I survived. 4

But wait a second. Come on! Why was this dog here? And why was no one perturbed that this dog was here? When this beast was barking at a passersby through the window as we were all working out, why did no one go, *Hey, just throwing this out there, should we maybe not have this distracting, possibly dangerous animal by the free weights?* 5

No one was asking because no one could ask. Sometime in the last decade, dogs achieved dominion over urban America. They are everywhere now, allowed in places that used to belong exclusively to humans, and sometimes only to human adults: the office, restaurants, museums, buses, trains, malls, supermarkets, barber shops, banks, post offices. Even at the park and other places where dogs belong, they've been given free rein. Dogs are frequently allowed to wander off leash, to run toward you and around you, to run across the baseball field or basketball court, to get up in your grill. Even worse than the dogs are the owners, who seem never to consider whether there may be people in the gym/office/restaurant/museum who do not care to be in close proximity to their dogs. After all, what kind of monster would have a problem with a poor innocent widdle doggie? It's a dog's world. We just live in it. And it's awful. Bad dogs! 6

Not everyone agrees with me on this issue. Some people—or maybe even most people, since dogs, like zombies, have an insidious way of turning opponents into allies—love that dogs abound. If you 7 adore dogs but aren't able to keep one, the world is now your dog park, with pooches everywhere to pet and nuzzle and otherwise brighten your day.

I am not a dog person. (Could you tell?) It's not that I actively despise mutts; I just don't have much time for them, in the same way I don't have time for crossword puzzles or Maroon 5. Now imagine if, everywhere you went, whatever you did, Maroon 5 was always playing and everyone pretended it was totally normal—that this permanent new situation was not in any way offensive, distracting, dirty, and potentially dangerous. 8

OK, bad example. 9

But here's my problem: There's now a cultural assumption that everyone must love dogs. Dog owners are rarely forced to reckon with the idea that there are people who aren't enthralled by their furry friends, and that taking their dogs everywhere might not be completely pleasant for these folks. 10

Example: If you're in the office and someone has brought her dog in for the day—because, *fun*!—the dog is sure to come around you, get between your legs, rub against your thigh, take a nap on your feet, or do some other annoying thing. 11

If the dog's owner notices these antics, I can promise you she won't apologize for the imposition. Nor will she ask you if you mind her dog doing what he's doing. Nor will she pull on its leash, because there won't be a leash, this being an office, where dogs are as welcome as Wi-Fi and free coffee. 12

Instead, if the owner says anything, it will be on the order of, "Don't worry, he loves people!" Oh, OK then! I guess I'll just take your word for it, and forget for the moment that 1,000 Americans a day go to emergency rooms because of dog bites. More Americans seek medical attention for dog bites than for choking or falls. You're more likely to have to go to a doctor for a bite than to call the fire department for a home fire. Like it or not, American dog owner, your pet is a hazard. 13

But let's leave aside the possibility that I'm scared (maybe legitimately!) of your dog, since you've assured me your dog loves people, and there's no chance you could be wrong. What if I'm allergic? Or what if I just plain hate your dog? What if I think he's dirty, since after all he did just put his nose in another dog's butt? And what if I just want to go through my workday without being slobbered on by an animal? 14

I know this sounds curmudgeonly. You want to shake me and tell 15
me to snap out of it, to get over myself and just love dogs already. But that's because you like dogs and don't see anything but good in them. For you, a dog is like ice cream. What churl doesn't like ice cream? Well, I'm that churl—I'm canine intolerant.

To give you a sense of how I feel when I'm accosted by your dog, 16
let's replace that animal with my 2½-year-old son. Now, I love my son, but on any objective scale of socially acceptable behavior, he is the worst. He's loud. He's inconsiderate of people's personal space—if he's left free he won't watch where he's walking and will run into you, either on purpose or accidentally. He's jumpy and fidgety in confined spaces; in an airplane it is physically impossible to restrain him from kicking the seat in front of him. He scratches himself often, sometimes picks his nose, sometimes offers to pick yours. He will constantly say inappropriate things. The other day at Target, he noticed a little person and commented, for pretty much everyone to hear, "That lady is short!" On top of all this, he may be packing a diaper full of urine and feces.

Weirdly, irrationally, despite all this, I feel the same way about 17
my son as you do about your dog: I love him unconditionally and just don't understand why even strangers wouldn't want him around all the time. Indeed, I think almost everything he does, even the inappropriate things, is the cutest behavior ever exhibited in human history.

And yet, still, I rein him in. I realize that, although he's impossibly 18
cute, it's possible he might aggravate some people. For this reason, whenever I go into public spaces with my toddler, I treat him as if I were handling nuclear waste or a dangerous animal. I keep him confined. I shush him. If he does anything out of turn—screams, touches people—I make a show of telling him to quit it and I apologize profusely. And, finally, there are some places that are completely off-limits to my son: nice restaurants, contemplative adult spaces like grown-up museums and coffee shops, the gym, and the office. Especially the office.

Yes, there are parents who don't act this way, awful parents who 19
let their terrible kids run free. The rest of us hate those people because they give all parents a bad name. But I'll submit there are many more such dog owners than there are overindulgent parents. Most parents I know are mortified by the thought that their children might be causing anguish for others. This is evident in the world around you: It's why your co-workers rarely bring their toddlers to work. It's

why 2-year-olds don't approach you in the park and lick your leg or ask you whether you need to visit the potty. It's why, when a child is being unruly in a supermarket or restaurant, you'll usually see his parents strive to get him to knock it off.

But dog owners? They seem to suffer few qualms about their ani- 20
mals' behavior. That's why there are so many dogs running around at the park, jumping up on the bench beside you while you're trying to read a book, the owner never asking if it's OK with you. That's why, when you're at a café, the dog at the neighboring table feels free to curl up under your seat. That's why there's a dog at your office right at this moment and you're having to pretend that he's just the cutest.

Well, no more, my fellow doggie skeptics. Let's take back the 21
peace we're owed. The next time your young, happy co-worker brings in his dog for the day, tell him the office is not a canine playpen. It's time to take that dog home.

Thinking Critically about This Reading

Why does Manjoo compare dogs in public spaces with small children? Do you agree with his argument that there should be some adults-only places, free from both dogs and children?

Questions for Study and Discussion

1. In this essay, Manjoo uses informal, colloquial diction. Why do you think he chooses this approach instead of making a more formal argument? How would more formal diction change the effect of his piece?
2. In several instances, Manjoo portrays dogs as acting like people, demanding "the canine equivalent of a high five" (paragraph 3), or getting "up in your grill" (6). Besides adding humor to the essay, what is the point of these characterizations?
3. How does Manjoo use rhetorical questions to emphasize the problem? (See paragraph 5 for some examples of questions he raises to make a point rather than to elicit an answer.)
4. How does Manjoo present the opposing views of dog lovers and those who are "canine intolerant" (15)? Do you think the two will ever agree on this issue?

5. Though his tone is humorous, Manjoo includes some serious points about the potential danger of bringing dogs into public places. Identify these places in the essay. What source does he draw on?
6. How does the behavior of dog owners compare with the behavior of parents? Why does Manjoo think parents have a better approach to dealing with public places? (Glossary: *Comparison and Contrast*)
7. What does Manjoo hope to achieve with this essay? What call to action does he make at the end? (Glossary: *Purpose*)

Classroom Activity Using Diction and Tone

Writers of all sorts have to match their language to the occasion for writing. In the Gettysburg Address, the text of which follows, President Abraham Lincoln was presented with the grave and monumental occasion of commemorating lives lost in war. He declares it "fitting and proper" that the nation designate part of the battlefield as a memorial. Read the speech and then discuss how Lincoln finds a similarly "fitting and proper" diction for his speech. Which words or phrases best reflect the seriousness of the occasion?

> Four score and seven years ago our fathers brought forth on this continent, a new nation, conceived in Liberty, and dedicated to the proposition that all men are created equal.
>
> Now we are engaged in a great civil war, testing whether that nation, or any nation so conceived and so dedicated, can long endure. We are met on a great battle-field of that war. We have come to dedicate a portion of that field, as a final resting place for those who here gave their lives that that nation might live. It is altogether fitting and proper that we should do this.
>
> But, in a larger sense, we can not dedicate—we can not consecrate—we can not hallow—this ground. The brave men, living and dead, who struggled here, have consecrated it, far above our poor power to add or detract. The world will little note, nor long remember what we say here, but it can never forget what they did here. It is for us the living, rather, to be dedicated here to the unfinished work, which they who fought here have thus far so nobly advanced. It is rather for us to be here dedicated to the great task remaining before us—that from these honored dead we take increased devotion to that cause for which they gave the last full measure of

devotion—that we here highly resolve that these dead shall not have died in vain—that this nation, under God, shall have a new birth of freedom—and that government of the people, by the people, for the people, shall not perish from the earth.

Suggested Writing Assignments

1. Following Manjoo's lead, write about a pet peeve or an irritation you encounter in everyday life. Though your complaint might be serious, take a humorous tone to gain your reader's sympathy. Title your essay "No, I Do Not ______."
2. Write a dog lover's response to Manjoo, defending the presence of animals in public places. Choose your language wisely, with the goal of poking fun at but not harshly mocking those who hold an opposing viewpoint.

CHAPTER **12**

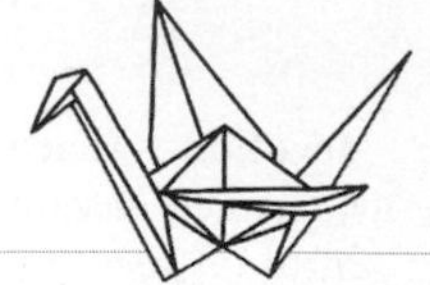

Figurative Language

Figurative language is language used in an imaginative rather than a literal sense. Although it is most often associated with poetry, figurative language is used widely in our daily speech and in our writing. Prose writers have long known that figurative language brings freshness and color to writing and also helps clarify ideas. For example, when asked by his teacher to explain the concept of brainstorming, one student replied, "Well, brainstorming is like having a tornado in your head." This figurative language helps others imagine the whirl of ideas in this young writer's head as he brainstorms a topic for writing.

The two most common **figures of speech** are the simile and the metaphor. A **simile** compares two essentially different ideas or things and uses *like* or *as* to link them.

> I was taught that candles are like house cats—domesticated versions of something wild and dangerous.
>
> –Sloane Crosley, *I Was Told There'd Be Cake*

> I walked toward her and hailed her as a visitor to the moon might salute a survivor of a previous expedition.
>
> –John Updike, *Assorted Prose*

A **metaphor** compares dissimilar ideas or things without using *like* or *as*.

> She was very old and small and she walked slowly in the dark pine shadows, moving a little from side to side in her steps, with the balanced heaviness and lightness of a pendulum in a grandfather clock.
>
> –Eudora Welty, *A Worn Path*

> Charm is the ultimate weapon, the supreme seduction, against which there are few defenses.
>
> –Laurie Lee, *I Can't Stay Long*

To expand the richness of a particular comparison, writers sometimes use several sentences or even a whole paragraph to develop a metaphor. Such a comparison is called an *extended metaphor*.

> The point is that you have to strip down your writing before you can build it back up. You must know what the essential tools are and what job they were designed to do. If I may belabor the metaphor on carpentry, it is first necessary to be able to saw wood neatly and to drive nails. Later you can bevel the edges or add elegant finials, if that is your taste. But you can never forget that you are practicing a craft that is based on certain principles. If the nails are weak, your house will collapse. If your verbs are weak and your syntax is rickety, your sentences will fall apart.
>
> –William Zinsser, *On Writing Well*

Another frequently used figure of speech is **personification**. In personification, the writer attributes human qualities to ideas or objects.

> The moon bathed the valley in a soft, golden light.
>
> –Corey Davis, student

> Blond October comes striding over the hills wearing a crimson shirt and faded green trousers.
>
> –Hal Borland, *Borland Country*

> Procrastination is the thief of time. Collar him.
>
> –Charks Dickens, *David Copperfield*

In all the preceding examples, notice how the writers' use of figurative language enlivens their prose and emphasizes their ideas. Each vividly communicates an idea or the essence of an object by comparing it to something concrete and familiar. In each case, too, the figurative language grows out of the writer's thinking, reflecting the way he or she sees the material. Be similarly honest in your use of figurative language, keeping in mind that figures of speech should never be used merely to dress up your writing. Above all, use them to develop your ideas and clarify your meaning for the reader.

The Barrio

■ Robert Ramirez

Courtesy of Robert Ramirez

Robert Ramirez was born in Edinburg, Texas, in 1949. After graduating from the University of Texas–Pan American, he taught writing and held the positions of cameraman, reporter, anchor, and producer for the local news on KGBT-TV, the CBS affiliate in Harlingen, Texas. He currently works as an alumni fund-raiser for the University of Texas–Pan American.

The following essay first appeared in Pain and Promise: The Chicano Today *(1972), edited by Edward R. Simmen. Notice how Ramirez uses figurative language, particularly metaphors, to awaken the reader's senses to the sights, sounds, and smells that are the essence of the barrio.*

Reflecting on What You Know

Where did you grow up? What do you remember most about your childhood neighborhood? How did it feel as a young person to live in this world? Do you still call this neighborhood "home"? Explain.

The train, its metal wheels squealing as they spin along the silvery tracks, rolls slower now. Through the gaps between the cars blinks a streetlamp, and this pulsing light on a barrio streetcorner beats slower, like a weary heartbeat, until the train shudders to a halt, the light goes out, and the barrio is deep asleep. 1

Throughout Aztlán[1] (the Nahuatl term meaning "land to the north"), trains grumble along the edges of a sleeping people. From Lower California, through the blistering Southwest, down the Rio Grande[2] to the muddy Gulf, the darkness and mystery of dreams engulf 2

[1]*Aztlán:* the mythical place of origin of the Aztec peoples.
[2]*Rio Grande:* a river flowing from southwest Colorado to Texas and Mexico and into the Gulf of Mexico.

communities fenced off by railroads, canals, and expressways. Paradoxical[3] communities, isolated from the rest of the town by concrete columned monuments of progress, and yet stranded in the past. They are surrounded by change. It eludes their reach, in their own backyards, and the people, unable and unwilling to see the future, or even touch the present, perpetuate the past.

Leaning from the expressway or jolting across the tracks, one enters a different physical world permeated by a different attitude. The physical dimensions are impressive. It is a large section of town which extends for fifteen blocks north and south along the tracks, and then advances eastward, thinning into nothingness beyond the city limits. Within the invisible (yet sensible) walls of the barrio are many, many people living in too few houses. The homes, however, are much more numerous than on the outside. 3

Members of the barrio describe the entire area as their home. It is a home, but it is more than this. The barrio is a refuge from the harshness and the coldness of the Anglo world. It is a forced refuge. The leprous people are isolated from the rest of the community and contained in their section of town. The stoical pariahs of the barrio accept their fate, and from the angry seeds of rejection grow the flowers of closeness between outcasts, not the thorns of bitterness and the mad desire to flee. There is no want to escape, for the feeling of the barrio is known only to its inhabitants, and the material needs of life can also be found here. 4

The *tortillería* [tortilla factory] fires up its machinery three times a day, producing steaming, round, flat slices of barrio bread. In the winter, the warmth of the tortilla factory is a wool *sarape* [blanket] in the chilly morning hours, but in the summer, it unbearably toasts every noontime customer. 5

The *panadería* [bakery] sends its sweet messenger aroma down the dimly lit street, announcing the arrival of fresh, hot sugary *pan dulce* [sweet rolls]. 6

The small corner grocery serves the meal-to-meal needs of customers, and the owner, a part of the neighborhood, willingly gives credit to people unable to pay cash for foodstuffs. 7

The barbershop is a living room with hydraulic chairs, radio, and television, where old friends meet and speak of life as their salted hair falls aimlessly about them. 8

[3]*paradoxical:* seemingly contradictory.

The pool hall is a junior level country club where *'chucos* [young men], strangers in their own land, get together to shoot pool and rap, while veterans, unaware of the cracking, popping balls on the green felt, complacently play dominoes beneath rudely hung *Playboy* foldouts. 9

The *cantina* [canteen or snackbar] is the night spot of the barrio. It is the country club and the den where the rites of puberty are enacted. Here the young become men. It is in the taverns that a young dude shows his *machismo* through the quantity of beer he can hold, the stories of *rucas* [women] he has had, and his willingness and ability to defend his image against hardened and scarred old lions. 10

No, there is no frantic wish to flee. It would be absurd to leave the familiar and nervously step into the strange and cold Anglo community when the needs of the Chicano[4] can be met in the barrio. 11

The barrio is closeness. From the family living unit, familial relationships stretch out to immediate neighbors, down the block, around the corner, and to all parts of the barrio. The feeling of family, a rare and treasurable sentiment, pervades and accounts for the inability of the people to leave. The barrio is this attitude manifested on the countenances[5] of the people, on the faces of their homes, and in the gaiety of their gardens. 12

The color-splashed homes arrest your eyes, arouse your curiosity, and make you wonder what life scenes are being played out in them. The flimsy, brightly colored, wood-frame houses ignore no neon-brilliant color. Houses trimmed in orange, chartreuse, lime-green, yellow, and mixtures of these and other hues beckon the beholder to reflect on the peculiarity of each home. Passing through this land is refreshing like Brubeck,[6] not narcoticizing like revolting rows of similar houses, which neither offend nor please. 13

In the evenings, the porches and front yards are occupied with men calmly talking over the noise of children playing baseball in the unpaved extension of the living room, while the women cook supper or gossip with female neighbors as they water the *jardines* [gardens]. The gardens mutely echo the expressive verses of the colorful houses. The denseness of multicolored plants and trees gives the house the appearance of an oasis or a tropical island hideaway, sheltered from the rest of the world. 14

---

[4]*Chicano:* an American of Mexican descent.

[5]*countenances:* facial expressions that indicate mood or character.

[6]*Dave Brubeck* (1920–2012): pianist, composer, and conductor of "cool" modern jazz.

15 Fences are common in the barrio, but they are fences and not the walls of the Anglo community. On the western side of town, the high wooden fences between houses are thick, impenetrable walls, built to keep the neighbors at bay. In the barrio, the fences may be rusty, wire contraptions or thick green shrubs. In either case you can see through them and feel no sense of intrusion when you cross them.

16 Many lower-income families of the barrio manage to maintain a comfortable standard of living through the communal action of family members who contribute their wages to the head of the family. Economic need creates interdependence and closeness. Small barefooted boys sell papers on cool, dark Sunday mornings, deny themselves pleasantries, and give their earnings to *mamá*. The older the child, the greater the responsibility to help the head of the household provide for the rest of the family.

17 There are those, too, who for a number of reasons have not achieved a relative sense of financial security. Perhaps it results from too many children too soon, but it is the homes of these people and their situation that numbs rather than charms. Their houses, aged and bent, oozing children, are fissures[7] in the horn of plenty. Their wooden homes may have brick-pattern asbestos tile on the outer walls, but the tile is not convincing.

18 Unable to pay city taxes or incapable of influencing the city to live up to its duty to serve all the citizens, the poorer barrio families remain trapped in the nineteenth century and survive as best they can. The backyards have well-worn paths to the outhouses, which sit near the alley. Running water is considered a luxury in some parts of the barrio. Decent drainage is usually unknown, and when it rains, the water stands for days, an incubator of health hazards and an avoidable nuisance. Streets, costly to pave, remain rough, rocky trails. Tires do not last long, and the constant rattling and shaking grind away a car's life and spread dust through screen windows.

19 The houses and their *jardines,* the jollity of the people in an adverse world, the brightly feathered alarm clock pecking away at supper and cautiously eyeing the children playing nearby, produce a mystifying sensation at finding the noble savage[8] alive in the twentieth century. It is easy to look at the positive qualities of life in the barrio, and look at them with a distantly envious feeling. One wishes to experience the

[7]*fissures:* narrow openings or cracks.
[8]*noble savage:* in literature, an idealized concept of uncivilized man.

feelings of the barrio and not the hardships. Remembering the illness, the hunger, the feeling of time running out on you, the walls, both real and imagined, reflecting on living in the past, one finds his envy becoming more elusive, until it has vanished altogether.

Back now beyond the tracks, the train creaks and groans, the cars 20
jostle each other down the track, and as the light begins its pulsing, the barrio, with all its meanings, greets a new dawn with yawns and restless stretchings.

Thinking Critically about This Reading

What evidence does Ramirez give to support the following claim: "Members of the barrio describe the entire area as their home. It is a home, but it is more than this" (paragraph 4)?

Questions for Study and Discussion

1. What is the barrio? Where is it? What does Ramirez mean when he states, "There is no want to escape, for the feeling of the barrio is known only to its inhabitants, and the material needs of life can also be found here" (4)?
2. Ramirez uses Spanish phrases throughout his essay. Why do you suppose he uses them? What is their effect on the reader? He also uses the words *home, refuge, closeness*, and *family.* What do they connote in the context of this essay? (Glossary: *Connotation/ Denotation*) In what ways, if any, are they essential to the writer's purpose? (Glossary: *Purpose*)
3. Identify several metaphors and similes that Ramirez uses in his essay, and explain why they are particularly appropriate.
4. In paragraph 6, Ramirez uses personification when he refers to the aroma of freshly baked sweet rolls as a "messenger." Cite other words or phrases that Ramirez uses to give human characteristics to the barrio.
5. Explain Ramirez's use of the imagery of walls and fences to describe a sense of cultural isolation. What might this imagery symbolize? (Glossary: *Symbol*)
6. Ramirez begins with a relatively positive picture of the barrio but ends on a more disheartening note. (Glossary: *Beginnings and Endings*) Why does he organize his essay in this way? What might the effect have been had he reversed these images?

Classroom Activity Using Figurative Language

Create a metaphor or simile that would be helpful in describing each item in the following list. To illustrate the process, the first one has been completed for you.

1. Skyscraper: The skyscraper sparkled like a huge glass needle.
2. Sound of an explosion
3. Intelligent student
4. Crowded bus
5. Slow-moving car
6. Pillow
7. Narrow alley
8. Greasy french fries
9. Hot sun
10. Dull knife

Compare your metaphors and similes with those written by other members of your class. Which metaphors and similes seem to work best for each item on the list? Why? Do any seem tired or clichéd?

Suggested Writing Assignments

1. In paragraph 19, Ramirez states, "One wishes to experience the feelings of the barrio and not the hardships." Explore his meaning in light of what you have just read and any experience or knowledge you may have of "ghetto" living. In what way can it be said that the hardships of such living are a necessary part of its "feelings"? How might barrio life change, for better or for worse, if the city were to "live up to its duty to serve all the citizens" (18)?
2. Write a brief essay in which you describe your own neighborhood. (Glossary: *Description*) You may find it helpful to review what you wrote in response to the Reflecting on What You Know prompt for this selection.

The Flight of the Eagles

■ N. Scott Momaday

N. Scott Momaday was born in Lawton, Oklahoma, in 1934 and lived on the Kiowa reservation with his parents and grandparents. After a year, his family moved to Arizona, where he lived most of his life. Both of his parents worked as teachers on Indian reservations, which exposed Momaday to the cultures and languages of the tribes of the Southwest United States, particularly the Navajo, Apache, and Pueblo. Momaday eventually taught on a Pueblo reservation himself before moving to California to complete MA and PhD degrees at Stanford University. In 1969, his novel House Made of Dawn *won a Pulitzer Prize and initiated what critic Kenneth Lincoln called a Native American renaissance in literature. Since that time, Momaday has published numerous books, including* The Way to Rainy Mountain *(1969),* The Ancient Child *(1989),* The Man Made of Words: Essays, Stories, Passages *(1997), and* Again the Far Morning: New and Selected Poems *(2011).*

In this excerpt from House Made of Dawn, *Momaday uses dense, inventive language—including figures of speech—to paint a precise picture of two birds in flight. As you read, notice how Momaday's similes help you visualize the scene.*

Reflecting on What You Know

Seeing birds in flight is a relatively common experience, so we might take it for granted. Close your eyes and visualize a bird flying. How would you describe the way it moves through the air?

They were golden eagles, a male and a female, in their mating flight. They were cavorting, spinning and spiraling on the cold, clear columns of air, and they were beautiful. They swooped and hovered, leaning on the air, and swung close together, feinting and screaming with delight. The female was full-grown, and the span of her broad wings was greater than any man's height. There was a fine flourish to her motion; she was deceptively, incredibly fast, and her pivots and wheels were wide and full blown. But her great weight was streamlined and perfectly controlled. She carried a rattlesnake; it hung shining from her feet, limp and curving out in the trail of her flight. Suddenly her wings and tail fanned, catching full on the wind, and for an instant she was still, widespread and spectral in the blue, while her mate flared past and away, turning around in the distance to look for her. Then she began to beat upward at an angle from the rim until she was small in the sky, and she let go of the snake. It fell slowly, writhing and rolling, floating out like a bit of silver thread against the wide backdrop of the land. She held still above, buoyed up on the cold current, her crop and hackles gleaming like copper in the sun. The male swerved and sailed. He was younger than she and a little more than half as large. He was quicker, tighter in his moves. He let the carrion drift by; then suddenly he gathered himself and swooped, sliding down in a blur of motion to the strike. He hit the snake in the head, with not the slightest deflection of his course or speed, cracking its long body like a whip. Then he rolled and swung upward in a great pendulum arc, riding out his momentum. At the top of his glide he let go of the snake in turn, but the female did not go for it. Instead she soared out over the plain, nearly out of sight, like a mote receding into the haze of the far mountain. The male followed.

Thinking Critically about This Reading

Why does Momaday pay such careful attention to what others might ignore—the intricate movements of two birds? What meaning does he find in their paired flight?

Questions for Study and Discussion

1. Near the beginning of the passage, Momaday personifies the birds as "screaming with delight." What does this seemingly human emotion add to the scene he depicts? Do you notice any other instances of personification?
2. Circle all of the active verbs in the first three sentences of the paragraph. Why does Momaday choose these words? What picture do they paint in your mind?

3. How would you describe Momaday's tone in this passage? What words or phrases do you think best convey his attitude toward the eagles?
4. Discuss how the two birds contrast with each other. How does Momaday describe the differences in their appearance?
5. The interaction that Momaday witnesses between the birds centers on the rattlesnake. How does he use similes to help readers picture their movements?
6. How does Momaday begin the paragraph? How does he end it? How do these sentences shape the very short story he tells about the eagles?

Classroom Activity Using Figurative Language

What is the most unusual event you have witnessed? Using the figures of speech you have learned (simile, metaphor, and personification), write six sentences that describe the event so that your readers can appreciate it. First state what the event was, then present your sentences in either a connected paragraph or a series of separate sentences. Share your description with your classmates to determine how effectively you have conveyed the dominant impression you wished to create.

Suggested Writing Assignments

1. Write a single carefully crafted paragraph in which you describe in detail your close observations of some small event in nature—the movement of trees in the wind, a bee buzzing around a flower, or a person feeding pigeons in a park. Use similes, metaphors, or personification to communicate what you observed to a reader.
2. Momaday pays careful attention in this passage to the way the birds move. For example, he uses the metaphor of a pendulum to convey the shape of the bird's flight. Write a personal essay about something that requires movement—for example, walking or cycling to school, cooking dinner, or playing a sport. Think about how those movements feel to you as you perform them and how they might look to an outside observer. As you compose your essay, focus on metaphors or other figures of speech that add a sense of motion.

Polaroids

■ Anne Lamott

Born in San Francisco in 1954, Anne Lamott is a graduate of Goucher College in Baltimore and the author of seven novels; Imperfect Birds *(2010) is the most recent of them. She has also written a food-review column for* California *magazine and a book-review column for* Mademoiselle. *In 1993, she published* Operating Instructions: A Journal of My Son's First Year, *in which she describes her own adventures as a single parent. Lamott has also written four books about her thoughts on faith:* Traveling Mercies: Some Thoughts on Faith *(1999),* Plan B: Further Thoughts on Faith *(2005),* Help, Thanks, Wow: The Three Essential Prayers *(2012), and* Stitches: A Handbook on Meaning, Hope and Repair *(2013).*

Anne Lamott. Mark Richards

The following selection is a chapter from Lamott's popular book about writing, Bird by Bird *(1994). The entire essay is built around the metaphor of a developing Polaroid photograph. Notice how effectively Lamott weaves in references to the Polaroid to clarify points she wishes to make about the process of writing.*

Reflecting on What You Know

Do you or does someone in your family enjoy taking photographs? Do the pictures always come out just the way you expected (or hoped) they would, or do they sometimes contain surprises? Perhaps they made you laugh, or disappointed you, or revealed something of value—some new insight into a familiar person, scene, or relationship. Comment on several memorable photographs.

Writing a first draft is very much like watching a Polaroid develop. 1
You can't—and, in fact, you're not supposed to—know exactly what the picture is going to look like until it has finished developing. First you just point at what has your attention and take the picture. In the last chapter, for instance, what had my attention were the contents

of my lunch bag. But as the picture developed, I found I had a really clear image of the boy against the fence. Or maybe *your* Polaroid was supposed to be a picture of that boy against the fence, and you didn't notice until the last minute that a family was standing a few feet away from him. Now, maybe it's his family, or the family of one of the kids in his class, but at any rate these people are going to be in the photograph, too. Then the film emerges from the camera with a grayish green murkiness that gradually becomes clearer and clearer, and finally you see the husband and wife holding their baby with two children standing beside them. And at first it all seems very sweet, but then the shadows begin to appear, and then you start to see the animal tragedy, the baboons baring their teeth. And then you see a flash of bright red flowers in the bottom left quadrant that you didn't even know were in the picture when you took it, and these flowers evoke a time or a memory that moves you mysteriously. And finally, as the portrait comes into focus, you begin to notice all the props surrounding these people, and you begin to understand how props define us and comfort us, and show us what we value and what we need, and who we think we are.

You couldn't have had any way of knowing what this piece of work would look like when you first started. You just knew that there was something about these people that compelled you, and you stayed with that something long enough for it to show you what it was about. 2

Watch this Polaroid develop: 3

Six or seven years ago I was asked to write an article on the Special Olympics. I had been going to the local event for years, partly because a couple of friends of mine compete. Also, I love sports, and I love to watch athletes, special or otherwise. So I showed up this time with a great deal of interest but no real sense of what the finished article might look like. 4

Things tend to go very, very slowly at the Special Olympics. It is not like trying to cover the Preakness. Still, it has its own exhilaration, and I cheered and took notes all morning. 5

The last track-and-field event before lunch was a twenty-five-yard race run by some unusually handicapped runners and walkers, many of whom seemed completely confused. They lumped and careened along, one man making a snail-slow break for the stands, one heading out toward the steps where the winners receive their medals; both of them were shepherded back. The race took just about forever. And here it was nearly noon and we were all so hungry. Finally, though, 6 everyone crossed over the line, and those of us in the stands got up to go—when we noticed that way down the track, four or five yards from the starting line, was another runner.

She was a girl of about sixteen with a normal-looking face above a wracked and emaciated body. She was on metal crutches, and she was just plugging along, one tiny step after another, moving one crutch forward two or three inches, then moving a leg, then moving the other crutch two or three inches, then moving the other leg. It was just excruciating. Plus, I was starving to death. Inside I was going, Come on, come on, come on, swabbing at my forehead with anxiety, while she kept taking these two- or three-inch steps forward. What felt like four hours later, she crossed the finish line, and you could see that she was absolutely stoked, in a shy, girlish way. 7

A tall African American man with no front teeth fell into step with me as I left the bleachers to go look for some lunch. He tugged on the sleeve of my sweater, and I looked up at him, and he handed me a Polaroid someone had taken of him and his friends that day. "Look at us," he said. His speech was difficult to understand, thick and slow as a warped record. His two friends in the picture had Down's syndrome. All three of them looked extremely pleased with themselves. I admired the picture and then handed it back to him. He stopped, so I stopped, too. He pointed to his own image. "That," he said, "is one cool man." 8

And this was the image from which an article began forming, although I could not have told you exactly what the piece would end up being about. I just knew that something had started to emerge. 9

After lunch I wandered over to the auditorium, where it turned out a men's basketball game was in progress. The African American man with no front teeth was the star of the game. You could tell that he was because even though no one had made a basket yet, his teammates almost always passed him the ball. Even the people on the *other* team passed him the ball a lot. In lieu of any scoring, the men stampeded in slow motion up and down the court, dribbling the ball thunderously. I had never heard such a loud game. It was all sort of crazily beautiful. I imagined describing the game for my article and then for my students: the loudness, the joy. I kept replaying the scene of the girl on crutches making her way up the track to the finish line—and all of a sudden my article began to appear out of the grayish green murk. And I could see that it was about tragedy transformed 10 over the years into joy. It was about the beauty of sheer effort. I could see it almost as clearly as I could the photograph of that one cool man and his two friends.

The auditorium bleachers were packed. Then a few minutes later, still with no score on the board, the tall black man dribbled slowly from one end of the court to the other, and heaved the ball up into the air, and it dropped into the basket. The crowd roared, and all the men on both teams looked up wide-eyed at the hoop, as if it had just burst into flames. 11

You would have loved it, I tell my students. You would have felt like you could write all day. 12

Thinking Critically about This Reading

In what way does the African American man's perception of himself in the Polaroid picture help Lamott with her writing assignment?

Questions for Study and Discussion

1. This entire essay is based on an extended metaphor or analogy. (Glossary: *Analogy*) What is the metaphor? How does it serve to clarify Lamott's central idea?
2. Besides the extended metaphor, Lamott uses several figures of speech in this essay. Find at least one metaphor and one simile. How does each contribute to the effect of the piece on the reader?
3. Lamott uses the phrase "grayish green murkiness" in the first paragraph and refers again to "grayish green murk" near the end of the essay, in paragraph 10. Why does she repeat these words? What does this phrase mean to a photographer? To a writer? For which of them does it function as a metaphor?
4. In paragraph 1, Lamott identifies four elements in "*your* Polaroid" that you didn't expect to find. What are they? Why does she include them?
5. Although the diction of this essay is simple and informal (Glossary: *Diction*), the structure is quite complicated. It is almost like an essay within an essay. What purpose is served by the long embedded narrative about the Special Olympics? (Glossary: *Example*) How does Lamott succeed in achieving unity? (Glossary: *Unity*)

Classroom Activity Using Figurative Language

Imagine each of the following abstract nouns as a character. What would each character look like? How would it act or talk? Choose one of these characters, and write a substantial descriptive paragraph, developing your ideas. What does this imaginative leap to personification reveal about the abstraction?

1. Friendship
2. Jealousy
3. Justice
4. Frustration
5. Perfection

Suggested Writing Assignments

1. With sudden insight, Lamott understands what the Special Olympics meant to her: "It was about tragedy transformed over the years into joy. It was about the beauty of sheer effort" (paragraph 10). Everyone has experiences in life that take on special meaning. Look back on a significant event you have witnessed or in which you took part, one that has come to represent to you some important truth about life. Write a narrative essay describing the event. Wait until you are at or approaching the end of your narrative to reveal explicitly your insight into its meaning.
2. When we think about our daily activities, we often clarify our understanding of some aspect of them by seeing one activity in terms of another. Not everyone's perceptions will be the same: A good horseback rider, for example, might come back from a relaxing day on the trail thinking, "Riding a horse is a form of meditation," while the novice bumping around in the saddle thinks, "Riding a horse is a form of torture." A computer expert finds that surfing the web is like traveling on a magic carpet, while someone else might find it more like being lost in a labyrinth. Choose an activity in your daily life that suggests such a simile or metaphor. Write an essay about the activity that begins with a figure of speech and explores its implications.

part ■ four

Types of Essays

CHAPTER **13**

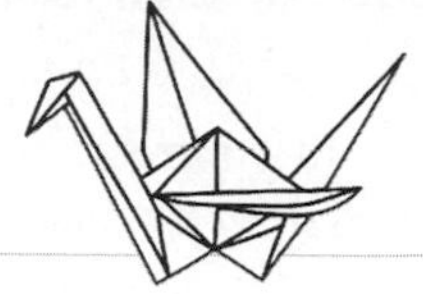

Illustration

Illustration is the use of **examples**—facts, opinions, samples, and anecdotes or stories—to make ideas more concrete and to make generalizations more specific and detailed. Examples enable writers not just to tell but also to show what they mean. The more specific the example, the more effective it is. For instance, in an essay about alternative sources of energy, a writer might offer an example of how a local architecture firm designed a home heated by solar collectors instead of by a conventional oil, gas, or electric system.

A writer uses examples to clarify or support the thesis in an essay and the main ideas in paragraphs. Sometimes a single striking example suffices; at other times a whole series of related examples is necessary. The following paragraph presents a single extended example—an explanation of weather as a chaotic system:

> The weather provides the most familiar example of a chaotic system. Meteorologists make thousands upon thousands of measurements of wind speed, air temperature, and barometric pressure in their efforts to predict the weather. They do pretty well with 24- and 48-hour forecasts, and sometimes they even get the seven-day predictions right. But no matter how fancy the measurements and the computer simulations, there is no way to predict what the weather will be a year from now. The chaotic nature of atmospheric motion is sometimes dramatized as the "butterfly effect," which says that in a chaotic system an effect as small as a butterfly's flapping its wings in Singapore may eventually make it rain in Texas.
>
> –Robert M. Hazen and James Trefil, *Science Matters: Achieving Scientific Literacy*

This single example is effective because it is familiar to many readers. Hazen and Trefil explain the idea of a chaotic system in a simple manner and using an example familiar to all so readers better understand the point they are trying to make.

In contrast, another writer supports his topic sentence about the growth of the fast-food industry with several examples:

> The extraordinary growth of the fast food industry has been driven by fundamental changes in American society. Adjusted for inflation, the hourly wage of the average U.S. worker peaked in 1973 and then steadily declined for the next twenty-five years. During that period, women entered the workforce in record numbers, often motivated less by a feminist perspective than by a need to pay the bills. In 1975, about one-third of American mothers with young children worked outside the home; today almost two-thirds of such mothers are employed. As the sociologists Cameron Lynne Macdonald and Carmen Sirianni have noted, the entry of so many women into the workforce has greatly increased demand for the types of services that housewives traditionally perform: cooking, cleaning, and child care. A generation ago, three-quarters of the money used to buy food in the United States was spent to prepare meals at home. Today about half of the money used to buy food is spent at restaurants—mainly at fast food restaurants.
>
> –Eric Schlosser, *Fast Food Nation*

Schlosser uses numerous examples to support his topic sentence with adequate supporting evidence. By citing specific examples of key changes in American society that have led to tremendous growth in the fast-food industry, Schlosser makes his point strong and convincing to the reader.

To use illustration effectively, begin by thinking of ideas and generalizations about your topic that you can make clearer and more persuasive by illustrating them with facts, anecdotes, or specific details. You should focus primarily on your main point—the central generalization that you will develop in your essay. Also be alert for other statements or references that may benefit from illustration. Points that are already clear and uncontroversial and that your readers will understand and immediately agree with can stand on their own as you pass along quickly to your next idea; belaboring the obvious wastes your time and energy, as well as your reader's. Often, however, you will find that examples add clarity, color, and weight to what you say.

Consider the following generalization:

> Americans are a pain-conscious people who would rather get rid of pain than seek and cure its root causes.

This assertion is broad and general; it raises the following questions: How so? What does this mean exactly? Why does the writer think so?

The statement could be the topic sentence of a paragraph or perhaps even the thesis of an essay or of an entire book. As a writer, you could make the generalization stronger and more meaningful through illustrations. You might support this statement by citing specific situations or specific cases in which Americans have gone to the drugstore instead of to a doctor, as well as by supplying sales figures per capita of painkillers in the United States as compared with other countries.

Illustration is so useful and versatile a strategy that it is found in all kinds of writing. It is essential, for example, in writing a successful argument essay. In an essay arguing that non-English-speaking students starting school in the United States should be taught English as a second language, one writer supports her argument with the following illustration, drawn from her own experience as a Spanish-speaking child in an English-only school:

> Without the use of Spanish, unable to communicate with the teacher or students, for six long weeks we guessed at everything we did. When we lined up to go anywhere, neither my sister nor I knew what to expect. Once, the teacher took the class on a bathroom break, and I mistakenly thought we were on our way to the cafeteria for lunch. Before we left, I grabbed our lunch money, and one of the girls in line began sneering and pointing. Somehow she figured out my mistake before I did. When I realized why she was laughing, I became embarrassed and threw the money into my sister's desk as we walked out of the classroom.
>
> –Hilda Alvarado, student

Alvarado could have summarized her point in the preceding paragraph in fewer words:

> Not only are non-English-speaking students in English-only schools unable to understand the information they are supposed to be learning, but they are also subject to frequent embarrassment and teasing from their classmates.

By offering an illustration, however, Alvarado makes her point more vividly and effectively.

macmillanhighered.com/mfw12e
e-readings > Peace Corps, *What Are Some Ways Peace Corps Volunteers Grow During Service?* [video]

A Crime of Compassion

■ Barbara Huttmann

Barbara Huttmann was born in Oakland in 1935 and now lives in the San Francisco Bay area. She received her nursing degree in 1976. After obtaining a master's degree in nursing administration, she cofounded a healthcare consulting firm for hospitals, nursing organizations, and consumers. Her interest in patients' rights is clearly evident in her two books, The Patient's Advocate *(1981) and* Code Blue: A Nurse's True-Life Story *(1982).*

In the following essay, which first appeared in Newsweek *in 1983, Huttmann narrates the final months of the life of Mac, one of her favorite patients. By using emotional and graphic details, Huttmann hopes that Mac's example will convince her audience of the need for new legislation that would permit terminally ill patients to choose to die rather than suffer great pain and indignity. As you read about Mac, consider the degree to which his experience seems representative of what patients often endure because medical technology is now able to keep them alive longer than they would be able to survive on their own.*

Reflecting on What You Know

For most people, being sick is at best an unpleasant experience. Reflect on an illness you have had, whether a simple common cold or an affliction that required you to be hospitalized. What were your concerns and fears? For what were you most thankful?

"Murderer," a man shouted. "God help patients who get *you* for a nurse." 1

"What gives you the right to play God?" another one asked. 2

It was the *Phil Donahue Show*[1] where the guest is a fatted calf and the audience a 200-strong flock of vultures hungering to pick at 3

[1]*Phil Donahue Show:* the first daytime TV talk show that involved the audience. It aired from 1970 to 1996.

the bones. I had told them about Mac, one of my favorite cancer patients. "We resuscitated him fifty-two times in just one month. I refused to resuscitate him again. I simply sat there and held his hand while he died."

There wasn't time to explain that Mac was a young, witty, macho cop who walked into the hospital with thirty-two pounds of attack equipment, looking as if he could single-handedly protect the whole city, if not the entire state. "Can't get rid of this cough," he said. Otherwise, he felt great. 4

Before the day was over, tests confirmed that he had lung cancer. And before the year was over, I loved him, his wife, Maura, and their three kids as if they were my own. All the nurses loved him. And we all battled his disease for six months without ever giving death a thought. Six months isn't such a long time in the whole scheme of things, but it was long enough to see him lose his youth, his wit, his macho, his hair, his bowel and bladder control, his sense of taste and smell, and his ability to do the slightest thing for himself. It was also long enough to watch Maura's transformation from a young woman into a haggard, beaten old lady. 5

When Mac had wasted away to a sixty-pound skeleton kept alive by liquid food we poured down a tube, IV solutions we dripped into his veins, and oxygen we piped to a mask on his face, he begged us: "Mercy . . . for God's sake, please just let me go." 6

The first time he stopped breathing, the nurse pushed the button that calls a "code blue" throughout the hospital and sends a team rushing to resuscitate the patient. Each time he stopped breathing, sometimes two or three times in one day, the code team came again. The doctors and technicians worked their miracles and walked away. The nurses stayed to wipe the saliva that drooled from his mouth, irrigate the big craters of bedsores that covered his hips, suction the lung fluids that threatened to drown him, clean the feces that burned his skin like lye,[2] pour the liquid food down the tube attached to his stomach, put pillows between his knees to ease the bone-on-bone pain, turn him every hour to keep the bedsores from getting worse, and change his gown and linen every two hours to keep him from being soaked in perspiration. 7

At night I went home and tried to scrub away the smell of decaying flesh that seemed woven into the fabric of my uniform. It was in 8

[2]*lye:* a chemical that is used in cleaning products and that can burn skin.

my hair, the upholstery of my car—there was no washing it away. And every night I prayed that Mac would die, that his agonized eyes would never again plead with me to let him die.

Every morning I asked his doctor for a "no-code" order. Without that order, we had to resuscitate every patient who stopped breathing. His doctor was one of several who believe we must extend life as long as we have the means and knowledge to do it. To not do it is to be liable for negligence, at least in the eyes of many people, including some nurses. I thought about what it would be like to stand before a judge, accused of murder, if Mac stopped breathing and I didn't call a code. 9

And after the fifty-second code, when Mac was still lucid enough to beg for death again, and Maura was crumbled in my arms again, and when no amount of pain medication stilled his moaning and agony, I wondered about a spiritual judge. Was all this misery and suffering supposed to be building character or infusing us all with the sense of humility that comes from impotence? 10

Had we, the whole medical community, become so arrogant that we believed in the illusion of salvation through science? Had we become so self-righteous that we thought meddling in God's work was our duty, our moral imperative, and our legal obligation? Did we really believe that we had the right to force "life" on a suffering man who had begged for the right to die? 11

Such questions haunted me more than ever early one morning when Maura went home to change her clothes and I was bathing Mac. He had been still for so long, I thought he at last had the blessed relief of coma. Then he opened his eyes and moaned, "Pain . . . no more . . . Barbara . . . do something . . . God, let me go." 12

The desperation in his eyes and voice riddled me with guilt. "I'll stop," I told him as I injected the pain medication. 13

I sat on the bed and held Mac's hands in mine. He pressed his bony fingers against my hand and muttered, "Thanks." Then there was one soft sigh and I felt his hands go cold in mine. "Mac?" I whispered, as I waited for his chest to rise and fall again. 14

A clutch of panic banded my chest, drew my finger to the code button, urged me to do something, anything . . . but sit there alone with death. I kept one finger on the button, without pressing it, as a waxen pallor[3] slowly transformed his face from person to empty 15

---

[3]*pallor:* extreme paleness.

shell. Nothing I've ever done in my forty-seven years has taken so much effort as it took *not* to press that code button.

Eventually, when I was as sure as I could be that the code team would fail to bring him back, I entered the legal twilight zone and pushed the button. The team tried. And while they were trying, Maura walked into the room and shrieked, "No . . . don't let them do this to him . . . for God's sake . . . please, no more." 16

Cradling her in my arms was like cradling myself, Mac, and all those patients and nurses who had been in this place before, who do the best they can in a death-denying society. 17

So a TV audience accused me of murder. Perhaps I am guilty. If a doctor had written a no-code order, which is the only *legal* alternative, would he have felt any less guilty? Until there is legislation making it a criminal act to code a patient who has requested the right to die, we will all of us risk the same fate as Mac. For whatever reason, we developed the means to prolong life, and now we are forced to use it. We do not have the right to die. 18

Thinking Critically about This Reading

In the rhetorical question "Did we really believe that we had the right to force 'life' on a suffering man who had begged for the right to die?" (paragraph 11), why do you think Huttmann places the word *life* in quotation marks?

Questions for Study and Discussion

1. Why do you think Huttman chooses Mac's story to illustrate this problem with the healthcare industry? How does his experience support her thesis?
2. Why do people in the audience of the *Phil Donahue Show* call Huttmann a "murderer"? Is their accusation justified? In what ways do you think Huttmann might agree with them?
3. In paragraph 15, Huttmann states, "Nothing I've ever done in my forty-seven years has taken so much effort as it took *not* to press that code button." How effectively does she describe her struggle against pressing the code button? What steps led to her ultimate decision not to press the button?

4. What, according to Huttmann, is "the only *legal* alternative" (18) to her action? What does she find hypocritical about that choice?
5. Huttmann makes a powerfully emotional appeal for a patient's right to die. Some readers might find some of her story shocking or offensive. Cite examples of some of the graphic scenes Huttmann describes, and discuss their impact on you as a reader. (Glossary: *Example*) Do they help persuade you to Huttmann's point of view, or do you find them overly unnerving? What would have been gained or lost had she left them out?
6. Huttmann's story covers a period of six months. In paragraphs 4–6, she describes the first five months of Mac's illness; in paragraphs 7–10, the sixth month; and in paragraphs 12–17, the final morning. What important point about narration does her use of time in this sequence demonstrate? (Glossary: *Narration*)
7. Huttmann concludes her essay with the statement "We do not have the right to die" (18). What does she mean by this? In your opinion, is she exaggerating or simply stating a fact? Does her example of Mac adequately illustrate her concluding point? Explain.

Classroom Activity Using Illustration

Huttmann illustrates her thesis by using the single example of Mac's experience in the hospital. Using the model statement and example that follows, find a single example that might be used to best illustrate each of the following potential thesis statements:

MODEL: Seat belts save lives. (*Possible example:* Your aunt was in an automobile accident but she survived because she was wearing her seat belt.)

Friends can be very handy.

Having good study skills can improve a student's grades.

Loud music can damage your hearing.

Reading the directions for a new product you have just purchased can save time and aggravation.

Humor can often make a bad situation more tolerable.

U.S. manufacturers can make their products safer.

Suggested Writing Assignments

1. Write a letter to the editor of *Newsweek* in response to Huttmann's essay. Are you for or against legislation that would give terminally ill patients the right to die? Give examples from your personal experience or from your reading to support your opinion. You may find it helpful to read the student paper on pages 72–76, an argument for the rights of the terminally ill to die, before beginning your letter.
2. Using one of the following sentences as your thesis statement, write an essay giving examples from your personal experience or from your reading to support your opinion.
   - Consumers have more power than they realize.
   - Most products do (or do not) measure up to the claims of their advertisements.
   - Religion is (or is not) alive and well in the United States.
   - The U.S. government works far better than its critics claim.
   - Being able to write well is more than a basic skill.
   - The seasons for professional sports are too long.
   - Today's college students are (or are not) serious-minded when it comes to academics.

The Bluе Marble

■ Gregory Petsko

Gregory Petsko was born in Washington, D.C., in 1948. He earned his BA from Princeton University and studied on a Rhodes Scholarship at Oxford University, where he earned his DPhil. He taught for over ten years at the Massachusetts Institute of Technology before moving to Brandeis University in Waltham, MA, where he is currently a professor emeritus of biochemistry and chemistry. Petsko is a member of the National Academy of Sciences and the recipient of awards from the American Chemical Society and the Max Planck Society. He studies protein structures and how they affect health, particularly neurological health.

In "The Blue Marble," first published in the journal Genome Biology *in April 2001, Petsko calls for scientists to find a new image that will inspire interest at a time when "science is at an historically low ebb in public estimation." As you read, pay attention to the way he describes and discusses the famous photograph of Earth from space, as well as other memorable images, to exemplify the way a picture can "galvanize an entire generation."*

Reflecting on What You Know

What famous photographs are most vivid in your mind? Why do these images stick with you? What do you think they represent?

It is one of the most iconic images—not just of our time, but of all time. The picture of the earth as seen from 28,000 miles (45,000 km) out in space—often called "the blue marble" because it resembles the spherical agates we used to play with as children—was taken on 7 December 1972 by the crew of the spacecraft *Apollo 17*. The Arabian 1

Peninsula is clearly visible at the top, with the east coast of Africa extending down towards Antarctica, the white mass at the bottom. . . . For those who care about such things, the photo was taken with a 70 mm Hasselblad camera with an 80 mm lens. *Apollo 17* was the last manned lunar mission, so no human beings have since been far enough out into space to take another picture that shows the whole globe. Because of the National Aeronautics and Space Administration's (NASA's) insistence on de-emphasizing the role of any one crew member in space missions, the photograph is credited to the entire flight team: Eugene Cernan, Ronald Evans and Jack Schmit. It is still not known for certain who actually took what might be the most famous photograph in the history of the medium.

The timing of the picture was auspicious, to say the least. The early 1970s marked the beginning of an era of environmental activism in the US, and the blue marble Earth photo, being the first ever taken of an illuminated face of the entire planet, rapidly became a symbol of the movement. It's easy to see why. Our whole planet suddenly, in this image, seemed tiny, vulnerable, and incredibly lonely against the vast blackness of the cosmos. It also seemed *whole* in a way that no map could illustrate. Regional conflict and petty differences could be dismissed as trivial compared with environmental dangers that threatened all of humanity, traveling together through the void on this fragile-looking marble. 2

I had occasion to use this picture in a talk I gave recently, and it got me thinking about the power of images. 3

The word "iconic" is often used for pictures like this one, and it fits. The word means, of course, to be like an icon, which is a symbol that perfectly represents something other than just itself. The blue marble was an iconic image because it perfectly represented the human condition of living on an island in the universe, with all the frailty an island ecosystem is prey to. People are particularly moved by images, in part because we have evolved to have our visual system as our primary sensory input, but also because an image can be retained easily in the mind's eye, and so forms the stuff of memory. The right image, offered at the right time, can have effects far greater than those imagined by the one creating it. 4

Consider another picture that changed the world: the famous photograph of the German dirigible *Hindenburg* bursting into flames on 6 May 1937, in the skies over the Lakehurst Naval Air Station in New Jersey. It was that photo, more than the scale of the 5 disaster—36 people were killed, mostly from jumping to escape the fire, but 62 survived by staying on board as the burning blimp floated to the ground—that spelled doom for the graceful zeppelins that almost filled the skies during the period between the two world wars. Even nowadays, when the substitution of helium for hydrogen would mean that a similar conflagration would be impossible, the power of that picture has prevented the revival of lighter-than-air craft as passenger carriers, relegating them to advertising vehicles hovering over sporting events despite their environmental friendliness.

Another iconic image comes from a time of great turbulence, 6
when student protests over the Vietnam war erupted into violence on many college campuses. On 4 May 1970, in the city of Kent, Ohio, a group of Ohio National Guard soldiers opened fire on a group of unarmed students from Kent State University. Four students were killed and nine wounded, one of whom was paralyzed for life. The photograph that came to symbolize the entire student movement and the official overreaction to it was taken moments later by John Filo, a photojournalism student. It shows a 14-year-old runaway from Florida, Mary Ann Vecchio, who had joined the protests that day, kneeling over the body of 20-year-old Jeffrey Glenn Miller, who had been shot dead. Vecchio is screaming in anguish, her arms flung outwards like a figure in a Victorian mezzotint.

That picture won John Filo the Pulitzer Prize. He eventually be- 7
came a picture editor at the weekly news magazine *Newsweek*, and is now on the staff of the communications department of CBS television network. Mary Ann Vecchio went back to Florida (involuntarily), married, and later moved to Las Vegas where she currently works as a respiratory therapist. In 1995, at an event at Emerson College in Boston, Massachusetts, commemorating the 25th anniversary of what became known as the Kent State Massacre largely because of that photograph, she met John Filo for the first time.

I'm sure you can think of many more examples of images that 8
have the power to alter events (there's even a website for many of them: http://www.famouspictures.org). I'll just mention one more, another Pulitzer winner: the photograph, taken by Associated Press photojournalist Eddie Adams, on 1 February 1968, of South Vietnamese General Nguyen Ngoc Loan in the act of executing Vietcong operative Nguyen Van Lem by a pistol shot to the head. That picture drove home to millions of Americans, in a way that no words had been able to do, the stark brutality of that war.

9 Ironically, despite being demonized around the world because of that image, General Loan—who was acting legally according to the laws of South Vietnam in executing an enemy who had been captured not wearing a uniform—was considered a hero by his people. Later that year he was wounded in action, and after the war ended in 1975, Loan settled in the US and became a pizza cook in northern Virginia.

10 Eddie Adams, who died of Lou Gehrig's Disease in 2004, had this to say about the photograph that made him famous: "The general killed the Viet Cong; I killed the general with my camera. Still photographs are the most powerful weapon in the world. People believe them, but photographs do lie, even without manipulation. They are only half-truths. What the photograph didn't say was, 'What would you do if you were the general at that time and place on that hot day, and you caught the so-called bad guy after he blew away one, two or three American soldiers?' General Loan was what you would call a real warrior, admired by his troops. I'm not saying what he did was right, but you have to put yourself in his position." When Nguyen Ngoc Loan died of cancer in 1998, Eddie Adams sent flowers.

11 Science, of course, has its own icons. The mushroom cloud that came to stand for the atomic age, with all its potential horror. Any picture or caricature of Einstein, with that halo of hair and casual appearance he so carefully cultivated (he once wrote "photographer's model" for "occupation" on a form, perhaps not in jest), which has become synonymous with the very idea of genius. But perhaps the most interesting one comes from the dawn of genomics: the double helix. I don't know if Watson and Crick understood from the beginning that the symmetrical beauty of the structure of DNA was almost certain to make them far more famous than many other people who had made equally important discoveries that could not be understood so easily, but that's certainly the way it turned out.

12 Unfortunately, none of these science-related images will do for us what the blue marble did for environmentalists—galvanize an entire generation. Right now, science is at an historically low ebb in public estimation. Years of carefully orchestrated attacks by the religious right and other anti-science organizations, combined with public-relations and ethical blunders on the part of some scientists, have led to science being regarded by many lay people as just another collection of self-serving, commercially oriented egoists. We haven't had a universal triumph along the lines of Jonas Salk's polio vaccine in quite some time, and the ones we have had (for example,

AIDS and many cancers are no longer inevitably fatal diseases, at least in the developed world) have not been publicized the way they should have.

There are many things we can and should do to fight this trend, but one of the most effective is one I haven't heard talked about: finding our own, new iconic image, one that would serve to capture, and make obvious, the enormous value that science brings to the human condition. It ought to be possible: biology is becoming very visualization-oriented, with new imaging techniques offering undreamed-of resolution into the inner workings of the cell. Genomics has led to a plethora of metaphors (the genome as Rosetta Stone or encyclopedia, for instance) that conceivably could serve as the basis for a powerful symbol. And the world is filled with people who are alive today only because of the discoveries of basic researchers and the efforts of physicians and pharmaceutical/biotechnology companies to translate those discoveries into treatments and cures. 13

The problem is that all of the images I've talked about in this essay were unplanned. They were not intended to be iconic; they came about purely by chance. Either the right person was there at the right time and the moment had so much power that symbolism instantly became attached to the picture, or else the image itself had a power all its own (born of simplicity, perhaps, as in the case of the double helix) that made iconic status inevitable, even when not immediate. 14

Maybe that's the way it has to be. Maybe people have become so cynical and media-savvy that they can only be moved by something possessing the authenticity of accident. Probably we can't—and shouldn't—just design the image we think we need and try to foist it on the public. But we can still be on the lookout for the right image to come along, for our big blue marble, so that when it does, we will know it. 15

Thinking Critically about This Reading

The "blue marble" photograph that Petsko discusses at the beginning of his essay is "credited to the entire flight team" (paragraph 1). Why is it important that no one knows for certain who took this famous picture? What do you think it has to do with Petsko's argument?

Questions for Study and Discussion

1. Why do you think Petsko chooses the "blue marble" photo as the most iconic of all the famous images he discusses in this essay? Why does it have such lasting power?
2. Why were the 1970s an "auspicious" time for this photograph to appear (2)? How did it fit into the political and social concerns of that decade?
3. The "blue marble" photo is just one example of how "the right image, offered at the right time, can have effects far greater than those imagined by the one creating it" (4). What other iconic photos does Petsko offer to illustrate this point?
4. Several photos that Petsko describes have surprising backstories. Why does he tell us about the meeting of Mary Ann Vecchio and photographer John Filo, or the reaction of Eddie Adams to the death of the general he had photographed, Nguyen Ngoc Loan? What do these stories tell us about the way iconic images work?
5. Why does Petsko think that present-day scientists are in a good position to find their own iconic image? What examples does he give to illustrate the photogenic nature of science?
6. What is Petsko's purpose in writing this essay? What fact about the iconic images he discusses complicates his call to action?

Classroom Activity Using Illustration

Read the following application letter for a summer internship. In addition to directing the recipient's attention to her résumé, the writer highlights relevant experience in her second paragraph. Identify the point she makes about her skills, then discuss how the examples she chooses help support that point.

Dear Ms. Crandal:

I have learned from your website that you are hiring undergraduates for summer internships. An internship with Abel's buyer training program interests me because I have learned that your program is one of the best in the industry.

The professional and analytical qualities that my attached résumé describes match the job description on your website. My experience with the Alumni Relations Program and the University Center Committee have enhanced my communication and persuasive abilities as well as my understanding of negotiation and compromise. For example, in the alumni program, I persuaded both uninvolved and active alumni to become more engaged with the direction of the university. On the University Center Committee, I balanced students' demands with the financial and structural constraints of the administration. With these skills, I can ably assist the buyers in your department with their summer projects and successfully juggle multiple responsibilities.

I would appreciate the opportunity to meet with you to discuss your summer internship program further. If you have questions or would like to speak with me, please contact me at (412) 863-2289 any weekday after 3 p.m., or you can e-mail me at msparker@ubi.edu. Thank you for your consideration.

Sincerely,

Marsha S. Parker

Marsha S. Parker

Suggested Writing Assignments

1. Choose a photo you think is representative of the current decade. Write an essay in which you describe the photo and explain why you think it is significant. What issues or concerns does it suggest? Find other photos that illustrate your point, and discuss what they have in common.
2. Petsko believes that the power of the images he discusses in "The Blue Marble" owe a great deal to "the authenticity of accident" (15). Write an essay arguing for the importance of accident in another area of life. What can people plan for, and when does chance play a crucial role? Illustrate your thesis with evidence from personal experience or from research.

Incivility Crisis of Politics Is Just a Symptom of Division

Cornell W. Clayton

Washington State University

Cornell W. Clayton graduated from the University of Utah before earning master's and doctoral degrees from Oxford University. In 1992, he joined the faculty of Washington State University, where he serves as the director of the Thomas S. Foley Institute for Public Policy and Public Service, and is the Claudius O. Johnson Distinguished Professor of Political Science. Clayton is the author of The Politics of Justice: The Attorney General and the Making of Legal Policy *(1992) and* Government Lawyers: The Federal Legal Bureaucracy and Presidential Politics *(1995). His new book,* The Supreme Court and the Political Regime, *will be published by the University of Chicago Press.*

Clayton wrote this essay as a guest columnist for the Seattle Times. *He acknowledges that incivility in politics is distasteful but urges readers to see it not as a cause of problems but as an effect of the divisions that occur at "critical elections or junctures in American democracy." As you read, notice how Clayton puts our current political climate in context by discussing examples of past misbehavior in American politics.*

Reflecting on What You Know

What do you think makes the current political climate so contentious? What behavior do you expect from politicians and commentators, and what lines do you think they should not cross?

1 Calling a young coed a "slut" on the radio is uncivil, as Rush Limbaugh recently did in disagreeing with Sandra Fluke over reproductive rights for women. So too is hollering "You lie!" at the

president during his speech, as South Carolina Congressman Joe Wilson did in disagreeing with Obama's health-care bill. Occupy Wall Street loudmouths, tea-party crazies, vitriolic campaign ads . . . What has happened to civil discourse in America?

The rude, unruly nature of today's political debate is a common lament heard from politicians, pundits and academics alike. The "incivility crisis," as it is labeled, is blamed for partisan gridlock and the failure of our democratic institutions to address the nation's most pressing challenges. 2

I dislike uncivil behavior, and I believe it says more about the louts who engage in it than those they seek to insult. But before concluding incivility threatens American democracy, let's consider how the two are related. 3

To begin with, nostalgia for the kinder, gentler politics of the past is based on myth. Many previous periods in America were far worse than today. During the election of 1800, the partisan press called John Adams a "hideous hermaphroditical character" and Thomas Jefferson "a mean-spirited, low-lived fellow, the son of a half-breed Indian squaw." Opponents called John Quincy Adams a "pimp" during the election of 1828 and referred to Andrew Jackson as "Andrew Jackass" (which is how the Democratic Party came to adopt the donkey as its symbol). 4

During the run-up to the Civil War, Sen. Preston Brooks of South Carolina attacked Charles Sumner of Massachusetts, beating him with a cane on the Senate floor for a speech he gave against the Kansas-Nebraska Act. President Abraham Lincoln was dehumanized in the Southern press but also by Copperheads in the North; one Wisconsin newspaper opined, "Mr. Lincoln is fungus from the corrupt womb of bigotry and fanaticism," adding "the man who votes for Lincoln now is a traitor and murderer." 5

During the 1930s, President Franklin Roosevelt was regularly accused of being "un-American," a "communist" or worse by opponents of the New Deal. Father Charles Coughlin, the forerunner to today's bombastic radio talk-show hosts, laced his attacks on FDR with anti-Semitic conspiracy theories. 6

American politics, the turn-of-the-century fictional character Mr. Dooley once quipped, "ain't never been 'beanbag.' " 7

What can we learn from past periods of incivility? First, incivility is a symptom, not the cause of political division. Previous periods 8 were nearly always associated with what historians identify as critical elections or junctures in American democracy: periods that produced new political parties (the Democratic Party in the 1820s or the GOP in the 1860s) or major social movements advancing rights of the oppressed (working-class immigrants during the New Deal or women and African Americans during the 1960s). Impassioned, angry debate during such periods reflected deep divisions over the country's future and what it meant to be American.

What are the causes of division today? For starters, wealth and income is more unequally distributed than at any time since 1932. That growing inequality accompanies a dramatic decline in social mobility. Americans born in low-income families today are less likely to move up the social ladder than at any time in the past 50 years, and less able to do so than counterparts in most other developed democracies around the world. The growing inequality in American wealth and opportunity drives bitter debates over taxation, government spending and social programs. 9

Changing demographics also cause deep divisions. The percentage of the foreign-born population in the U.S. has risen from 5 percent in 1970 to nearly 14 percent today, the highest level since the 1930s. And we are becoming a nation of minorities. Non-Hispanic whites now make up only 63 percent of the total population in the U.S. and will become a minority within a few decades. These demographic shifts create anxieties about the nature of American culture and identity, which in turn fuel angry debates over immigration, language, religion and other issues. 10

The polarization of wealth and the demographic transformations closely mirror the partisan polarization index used by political scientists to measure ideological division between political parties. In other words, these changes correlate closely with Republicans becoming more conservative and Democrats more liberal over the past 50 years. 11

There are other sources of division, too: ideological polarization caused by partisan reapportionment and the role of special interests in campaigns; the fragmentation and polarization of the media; and the replacement of traditional communities with lifestyle enclaves where Americans interact only with those of similar social class and belief systems. Addressing these substantive sources of political conflict will ultimately do far more to restore a more productive public discourse than worrying about the manners of our debates. 12

Worries about polite or acceptable political discourse also raise 13
questions about context and power. In the past, uncivil behavior has often advanced democratic causes. Those who lack power often have no other way to press their rights. At a time when it was thought unfitting for women to speak publicly about politics, the suffragists of the 19th century were certainly uncivil. Fanny Wright was shouted down at Tammany Hall in 1836 by men who thought her very presence inappropriate.

Similarly, leaders of the modern civil-rights movement challenged 14
Southern segregation with lunch-counter sit-ins, boycotts and violation of state laws. That was uncivil. Other groups lacking power—labor organizers, Native Americans, gays and others—have faced similar dilemmas: Either wait patiently for others to press for their rights within existing frameworks of proper behavior, or seek democratic reform themselves by challenging those frameworks.

Incivility also can be undemocratic. The Know Nothing Party 15
during the 1850s, the Ku Klux Klan in the early 20th century, Eugene "Bull" Connor in the 1960s, all used tactics that were uncivil and undemocratic because they sought to exclude others from participation in American democracy.

Some forms of behavior are undemocratic by nature: silencing 16
others through threats, intimidation or acts of violence; delegitimizing others by casting doubts on their citizenship or rights (i.e., labeling them "un-American"); or misleading and dishonest debate. These behaviors threaten democracy more than the occasional insult or angry outburst because they betray a core democratic responsibility. The willingness to engage in honest debate and lose on issues you care deeply about reaffirms your commitment to common citizenship.

It would be nice if we could all just get along. Democratic com- 17
promise is more easily achieved when we refrain from insulting and demonizing those we disagree with.

But American democracy has survived past periods of incivility. It 18
will survive this, if we remain clear-eyed in addressing the substantive challenges dividing the country and reaffirm that what unites us as Americans is stronger than what divides us.

Thinking Critically about This Reading

Clayton argues that rather than addressing incivility, we should focus on the "substantive sources of political conflict." How would this change the tone of the conversation? Do you agree that incivility is a symptom, not a cause?

Questions for Study and Discussion

1. Clayton begins this essay with recent examples of uncivil behavior. What do his examples have in common? What do they tell us about the political climate he is describing?
2. Later in the essay, Clayton turns to examples from earlier in American politics. From what eras does he draw these examples? What is significant about these times in our history?
3. Clayton asks readers to rethink the assumption that incivility is destructive to American democracy. How does he think the two are related?
4. List Clayton's reasons for why politics are currently so divisive. Do you agree with his assessment?
5. In what situations can incivility be a useful tool? When does Clayton think adhering to rules about polite discourse might hamper democracy?
6. When does incivility go beyond being distasteful and pose a real threat to democracy? What examples does Clayton give of "undemocratic" incivility?

Classroom Activity Using Illustration

Think of a problem you believe is characteristic of our time (for example, cell phone overuse or obsessive selfies). Then, working with classmates, list some examples that help you trace the behavior over several years. You may want to do some research into historical precedents for this type of phenomenon. Once you have gathered your examples, discuss what they reveal. Do they illustrate a dramatic shift, or do they, like the examples Clayton cites, suggest that not as much has changed as you initially guessed?

Suggested Writing Assignments

1. In this essay, Clayton attempts to shift our understanding of the problem and make us rethink whether incivility is a cause or an

effect. Choose a subject on which you would like to encourage readers to change their thinking. What do people generally misunderstand about it, causing them to miss the root cause of a problem? Write an essay that attempts to convince readers to change their view of the problem.

2. Often a writer searches for examples to illustrate a point that he or she wants to make, but you might also work in the other direction. Choose several examples of the way students at your school behave. Write down your examples, paying attention to accuracy and detail. Then use these examples to build an argument. When viewed together, what do these examples suggest about the culture of your school?

In Defense of Dangerous Ideas

Steven Pinker

David Levenson/Getty Images

Internationally recognized language and cognition scholar and researcher Steven Pinker was born in Montreal, Quebec, Canada, in 1954. He immigrated to the United States shortly after receiving his BA from McGill University in 1976. After earning a doctorate from Harvard University in 1979, Pinker taught psychology at Stanford University and the Massachusetts Institute of Technology, where he directed the Center for Cognitive Neuroscience. Currently, he is the Johnstone Family Professor of Psychology at Harvard University. Pinker has written extensively on language development in children, starting with Language Learnability and Language Development *(1984). Pinker's books* The Language Instinct *(1994),* How the Mind Works *(1997),* Words and Rules: The Ingredients of Language *(1999),* The Blank Slate: The Modern Denial of Human Nature *(2002),* The Stuff of Thought: Language as a Window into Human Nature *(2007), and* The Better Angels of Our Nature *(2011) all attest to the public's interest in human language and the world of ideas.*

The following article was first published as the preface to What Is Your Dangerous Idea? Today's Leading Thinkers on the Unthinkable *(2006, edited by John Brockman) and later posted at* Edge *(www.edge.com). In this essay, Steven Pinker explores what makes an idea "dangerous" and argues that "important ideas [need to] be aired," especially in academia, no matter how discomfiting people find them. Notice how Pinker uses a number of examples from a wide range of academic disciplines to illustrate his points about dangerous ideas and the need to discuss them.*

Reflecting on What You Know

What did you think when you first read the title to Pinker's essay? For you, what would make an idea dangerous? Do any issues or questions make you uncomfortable or unwilling to discuss them? Explain.

In every age, taboo questions raise our blood pressure and threaten moral panic. But we cannot be afraid to answer them. 1

Do women, on average, have a different profile of aptitudes and emotions than men? 2

Were the events in the Bible fictitious—not just the miracles, but those involving kings and empires? 3

Has the state of the environment improved in the last fifty years? 4

Do most victims of sexual abuse suffer no lifelong damage? 5

Did Native Americans engage in genocide and despoil the landscape? 6

Do men have an innate tendency to rape? 7

Did the crime rate go down in the 1990s because two decades earlier poor women aborted children who would have been prone to violence? 8

Are suicide terrorists well-educated, mentally healthy, and morally driven? 9

Would the incidence of rape go down if prostitution were legalized? 10

Do African American men have higher levels of testosterone, on average, than white men? 11

Is morality just a product of the evolution of our brains, with no inherent reality? 12

Would society be better off if heroin and cocaine were legalized? 13

Is homosexuality the symptom of an infectious disease? 14

Would it be consistent with our moral principles to give parents the option of euthanizing newborns with birth defects that would consign them to a life of pain and disability? 15

Do parents have any effect on the character or intelligence of their children? 16

Have religions killed a greater proportion of people than Nazism? 17

Would damage from terrorism be reduced if the police could torture suspects in special circumstances? 18

Would Africa have a better chance of rising out of poverty if it hosted more polluting industries or accepted Europe's nuclear waste? 19

Is the average intelligence of Western nations declining because 20
duller people are having more children than smarter people?

Would unwanted children be better off if there were a market in 21
adoption rights, with babies going to the highest bidder?

Would lives be saved if we instituted a free market in organs for 22
transplantation?

Should people have the right to clone themselves, or enhance the 23
genetic traits of their children?

Perhaps you can feel your blood pressure rise as you read these 24
questions. Perhaps you are appalled that people can so much as think such things. Perhaps you think less of me for bringing them up. These are dangerous ideas—ideas that are denounced not because they are self-evidently false, nor because they advocate harmful action, but because they are thought to corrode the prevailing moral order.

Think about It

By "dangerous ideas" I don't have in mind harmful technologies, like 25
those behind weapons of mass destruction, or evil ideologies, like those of racist, fascist, or other fanatical cults. I have in mind statements of fact or policy that are defended with evidence and argument by serious scientists and thinkers but which are felt to challenge the collective decency of an age. The ideas listed above, and the moral panic that each one of them has incited during the past quarter century, are examples. Writers who have raised ideas like these have been vilified, censored, fired, threatened, and in some cases physically assaulted.

Every era has its dangerous ideas. For millennia, the monotheistic 26
religions have persecuted countless heresies, together with nuisances from science such as geocentrism, biblical archeology, and the theory of evolution. We can be thankful that the punishments have changed from torture and mutilation to the canceling of grants and the writing of vituperative reviews. But intellectual intimidation, whether by sword or by pen, inevitably shapes the ideas that are taken seriously in a given era, and the rear-view mirror of history presents us with a warning.

Time and again, people have invested factual claims with ethical 27
implications that today look ludicrous. The fear that the structure of our solar system has grave moral consequences is a venerable example, and the foisting of "intelligent design" on biology students is a contemporary one. These travesties should lead us to ask whether the contemporary intellectual mainstream might be entertaining

similar moral delusions. Are we enraged by our own infidels and heretics whom history may some day vindicate?

Unsettling Possibilities

Dangerous ideas are likely to confront us at an increasing rate, and we 28
are ill-equipped to deal with them. When done right, science (together with other truth-seeking institutions, such as history and journalism) characterizes the world as it is, without regard to whose feelings get hurt. Science in particular has always been a source of heresy, and today the galloping advances in touchy areas like genetics, evolution, and the environment sciences are bound to throw unsettling possibilities at us. Moreover, the rise of globalization and the Internet are allowing heretics to find one another and work around the barriers of traditional media and academic journals. I also suspect that a change in generational sensibilities will hasten the process. The term "political correctness" captures the 1960s conception of moral rectitude that we baby boomers brought with us as we took over academia, journalism, and government. In my experience, today's students—black and white, male and female—are bewildered by the idea, common among their parents, that certain scientific opinions are immoral or certain questions too hot to handle.

What makes an idea "dangerous"? One factor is an imaginable 29
train of events in which acceptance of the idea could lead to an outcome recognized as harmful. In religious societies, the fear is that if people ever stopped believing in the literal truth of the Bible they would also stop believing in the authority of its moral commandments. That is, if today people dismiss the part about God creating the earth in six days, tomorrow they'll dismiss the part about "Thou shalt not kill." In progressive circles, the fear is that if people ever were to acknowledge any differences between races, sexes, or individuals, they would feel justified in discrimination or oppression. Other dangerous ideas set off fears that people will neglect or abuse their children, become indifferent to the environment, devalue human life, accept violence, and prematurely resign themselves to social problems that could be solved with sufficient commitment and optimism.

All these outcomes, needless to say, would be deplorable. But none 30
of them actually follows from the supposedly dangerous idea. Even if it turns out, for instance, that groups of people are different in their averages, the overlap is certainly so great that it would be irrational and unfair to discriminate against individuals on that basis. Likewise, even if it turns out that parents don't have the power to shape their children's

personalities, it would be wrong on grounds of simple human decency to abuse or neglect one's children. And if currently popular ideas about how to improve the environment are shown to be ineffective, it only highlights the need to know what would be effective.

Another contributor to the perception of dangerousness is the intellectual blinkers that humans tend to don when they split into factions. People have a nasty habit of clustering in coalitions, professing certain beliefs as badges of their commitment to the coalition and treating rival coalitions as intellectually unfit and morally depraved. Debates between members of the coalitions can make things even worse, because when the other side fails to capitulate to one's devastating arguments, it only proves they are immune to reason. In this regard, it's disconcerting to see the two institutions that ought to have the greatest stake in ascertaining the truth—academia and government—often blinkered by morally tinged ideologies. One ideology is that humans are blank slates and that social problems can be handled only through government programs that especially redress the perfidy[1] of European males. Its opposite number is that morality inheres in patriotism and Christian faith and that social problems may be handled only by government policies that punish the sins of individual evildoers. New ideas, nuanced ideas, hybrid ideas—and sometimes dangerous ideas—often have trouble getting a hearing against these group-bonding convictions. 31

The conviction that honest opinions can be dangerous may even arise from a feature of human nature. Philip Tetlock and Alan Fiske have argued that certain human relationships are constituted on a basis of unshakable convictions. We love our children and parents, are faithful to our spouses, stand by our friends, contribute to our communities, and are loyal to our coalitions not because we continually question and evaluate the merits of these commitments but because we feel them in our bones. A person who spends too much time pondering whether logic and fact really justify a commitment to one of these relationships is seen as just not "getting it." Decent people don't carefully weigh the advantages and disadvantages of selling their children or selling out their friends or their spouses or their colleagues or their country. They reject these possibilities outright; they "don't go there." So the taboo on questioning sacred values makes sense in the context of personal relationships. It makes far less sense in the context of discovering how the world works or running a country. 32

[1]*perfidy:* disloyalty, infidelity, or unfaithfulness.

Explore All Relevant Ideas

Should we treat some ideas as dangerous? Let's exclude outright lies, 33 deceptive propaganda, incendiary conspiracy theories from malevolent crackpots, and technological recipes for wanton destruction. Consider only ideas about the truth of empirical claims or the effectiveness of policies that, if they turned out to be true, would require a significant rethinking of our moral sensibilities. And consider ideas that, if they turn out to be false, could lead to harm if people believed them to be true. In either case, we don't know whether they are true or false a priori,[2] so only by examining and debating them can we find out. Finally, let's assume that we're not talking about burning people at the stake or cutting out their tongues but about discouraging their research and giving their ideas as little publicity as possible. There is a good case for exploring all ideas relevant to our current concerns, no matter where they lead. The idea that ideas should be discouraged a priori is inherently self-refuting. Indeed, it is the ultimate arrogance, as it assumes that one can be so certain about the goodness and truth of one's own ideas that one is entitled to discourage other people's opinions from even being examined.

Also, it's hard to imagine any aspect of public life where igno- 34 rance or delusion is better than an awareness of the truth, even an unpleasant one. Only children and madmen engage in "magical thinking," the fallacy that good things can come true by believing in them or bad things will disappear by ignoring them or wishing them away. Rational adults want to know the truth, because any action based on false premises will not have the effects they desire. Worse, logicians tell us that a system of ideas containing a contradiction can be used to deduce any statement whatsoever, no matter how absurd. Since ideas are connected to other ideas, sometimes in circuitous and unpredictable ways, choosing to believe something that may not be true, or even maintaining walls of ignorance around some topic, can corrupt all of intellectual life, proliferating error far and wide. In our everyday lives, would we want to be lied to, or kept in the dark by paternalistic "protectors," when it comes to our health or finances or even the weather? In public life, imagine someone saying that we should not do research into global warming or energy shortages because if it found that they were serious the consequences for the economy would be extremely unpleasant. Today's leaders who tacitly take this position

[2]*a priori:* beforehand.

are rightly condemned by intellectually responsible people. But why should other unpleasant ideas be treated differently?

There is another argument against treating ideas as dangerous. Many of our moral and political policies are designed to preempt what we know to be the worst features of human nature. The checks and balances in a democracy, for instance, were invented in explicit recognition of the fact that human leaders will always be tempted to arrogate power to themselves. Likewise, our sensitivity to racism comes from an awareness that groups of humans, left to their own devices, are apt to discriminate and oppress other groups, often in ugly ways. History also tells us that a desire to enforce dogma and suppress heretics is a recurring human weakness, one that has led to recurring waves of gruesome oppression and violence. A recognition that there is a bit of Torquemada[3] in everyone should make us wary of any attempt to enforce a consensus or demonize those who challenge it. 35

"Sunlight is the best disinfectant," according to Justice Louis Brandeis's famous case for freedom of thought and expression. If an idea really is false, only by examining it openly can we determine that it is false. At that point we will be in a better position to convince others that it is false than if we had let it fester in private, since our very avoidance of the issue serves as a tacit acknowledgment that it may be true. And if an idea is true, we had better accommodate our moral sensibilities to it, since no good can come from sanctifying a delusion. This might even be easier than the ideaphobes fear. The moral order did not collapse when the earth was shown not to be at the center of the solar system, and so it will survive other revisions of our understanding of how the world works. 36

Dangerous to Air Dangerous Ideas?

In the best Talmudic[4] tradition of arguing a position as forcefully as possible and then switching sides, let me now present the case for discouraging certain lines of intellectual inquiry. . . . [Alison] Gopnik and [W. Daniel] Hillis offer as their "dangerous idea" the exact opposite of [Daniel] Gilbert's: they say that it's a dangerous idea for thinkers to air their dangerous ideas. How might such an argument play out? 37

First, one can remind people that we are all responsible for the foreseeable consequences of our actions, and that includes the 38

[3] *Torquemada:* Tomás de Torquemada (1420–1498), Spanish grand inquisitor.
[4] *Talmudic:* Jewish or Hebrew.

consequences of our public statements. Freedom of inquiry may be an important value, according to this argument, but it is not an absolute value, one that overrides all others. We know that the world is full of malevolent and callous people who will use any pretext to justify their bigotry or destructiveness. We must expect that they will seize on the broaching of a topic that seems in sympathy with their beliefs as a vindication of their agenda.

Not only can the imprimatur of scientific debate add legitimacy to toxic ideas, but the mere act of making an idea common knowledge can change its effects. Individuals, for instance, may harbor a private opinion on differences between genders or among ethnic groups but keep it to themselves because of its opprobrium. But once the opinion is aired in public, they may be emboldened to act on their prejudice—not just because it has been publicly ratified but because they must anticipate that everyone else will act on the information. Some people, for example, might discriminate against the members of an ethnic group despite having no pejorative opinion about them, in the expectation that their customers or colleagues will have such opinions and that defying them would be costly. And then there are the effects of these debates on the confidence of the members of the stigmatized groups themselves. 39

Of course, academics can warn against these abuses, but the qualifications and nitpicking they do for a living may not catch up with the simpler formulations that run on swifter legs. Even if they did, their qualifications might be lost on the masses. We shouldn't count on ordinary people to engage in the clear thinking—some would say the hair-splitting—that would be needed to accept a dangerous idea but not its terrible consequence. Our overriding precept, in intellectual life as in medicine, should be "First, do no harm." 40

We must be especially suspicious when the danger in a dangerous idea is to someone other than its advocate. Scientists, scholars, and writers are members of a privileged elite. They may have an interest in promulgating ideas that justify their privileges, that blame or make light of society's victims, or that earn them attention for cleverness and iconoclasm. Even if one has little sympathy for the cynical Marxist argument that ideas are always advanced to serve the interest of the ruling class, the ordinary skepticism of a tough-minded intellectual should make one wary of "dangerous" hypotheses that are no skin off the nose of their hypothesizers. (The mind-set that leads us to blind review, open debate, and statements of possible conflicts of interest.) 41

But don't the demands of rationality always compel us to seek the complete truth? Not necessarily. Rational agents often choose to be 42 ignorant. They may decide not to be in a position where they can receive a threat or be exposed to a sensitive secret. They may choose to avoid being asked an incriminating question, where one answer is damaging, another is dishonest, and a failure to answer is grounds for the questioner to assume the worst (hence the Fifth Amendment protection against being forced to testify against oneself). Scientists test drugs in double-blind studies in which they keep themselves from knowing who got the drug and who got the placebo, and they referee manuscripts anonymously for the same reason. Many people rationally choose not to know the gender of their unborn child, or whether they carry a gene for Huntington's disease, or whether their nominal father is genetically related to them. Perhaps a similar logic would call for keeping socially harmful information out of the public sphere.

Intolerance of Unpopular Ideas

As for restrictions on inquiry, every scientist already lives with them. 43
They accede, for example, to the decisions of committees for the protection of human subjects and to policies on the confidentiality of personal information. In 1975, biologists imposed a moratorium on research on recombinant DNA pending the development of safeguards against the release of dangerous microorganisms. The notion that intellectuals have carte blanche in conducting their inquiry is a myth.

Though I am more sympathetic to the argument that important 44
ideas be aired than to the argument that they should sometimes be suppressed, I think it is a debate we need to have. Whether we like it or not, science has a habit of turning up discomfiting thoughts, and the Internet has a habit of blowing their cover.

Tragically, there are few signs that the debates will happen in the 45
place where we might most expect it: academia. Though academics owe the extraordinary perquisite of tenure to the ideal of encouraging free inquiry and the evaluation of unpopular ideas, all too often academics are the first to try to quash them. The most famous recent example is the outburst of fury and disinformation that resulted when Harvard president Lawrence Summers gave a measured analysis of the multiple causes of women's underrepresentation in science and math departments in elite universities and tentatively broached the possibility that discrimination and hidden barriers were not the only cause.

But intolerance of unpopular ideas among academics is an old 46
story. Books like Morton Hunt's *The New Know-Nothings* and Alan

Kors and Harvey Silverglate's *The Shadow University* have depressingly shown that universities cannot be counted on to defend the rights of their own heretics and that it's often the court system or the press that has to drag them into policies of tolerance. In government, the intolerance is even more frightening, because the ideas considered there are not just matters of intellectual sport but have immediate and sweeping consequences. Chris Mooney, in *The Republican War on Science,* joins Hunt in showing how corrupt and demagogic legislators are increasingly stifling research findings they find inconvenient to their interests.

Thinking Critically about This Reading

What do you think is Pinker's purpose in defending "dangerous ideas"? What does he want his readers to do after reading this essay? Did he achieve his purpose with you? Explain.

Questions for Study and Discussion

1. Pinker starts his essay with a list of twenty-two questions, each an example of a dangerous idea. What were you thinking as you read Pinker's list? Which questions touched a sensitive nerve for you? Explain.
2. How does Pinker define *dangerous idea*? Do you agree with his definition?
3. According to Pinker, fear is one of the main factors that contributes to the perception of dangerousness. What examples of fears does Pinker use to illustrate this claim? What other factors contribute to the perception of dangerousness?
4. Do you believe that "the taboo on questioning sacred values makes sense in the context of personal relationships" (paragraph 32)? Why or why not? Why do you think Pinker believes that "it makes far less sense in the context of discovering how the world works or running a country" (32)?
5. What does Pinker mean when he says, "The idea that ideas should be discouraged a priori is inherently self-refuting" (33)?
6. According to Pinker, what is the "case for discouraging certain lines of intellectual inquiry" (37)? What evidence does he present to support this side of the issue?
7. How does Pinker support his claim that "intolerance of unpopular ideas among academics is an old story" (46)?

Classroom Activity Using Illustration

Consider the following paragraph from the rough draft of a student paper on Americans' obsession with losing weight. The student writer wanted to show the extreme actions people sometimes take to improve their appearance.

> Americans have long been obsessed with thinness—even at the risk of dying. In the 1930s, people took di-nitrophenol, an industrial poison, to lose weight. It boosted metabolism but caused blindness and some deaths. Since that time, dieters have experimented with any number of bizarre schemes that seem to work wonders in the short term but often end in disappointment or disaster in the long term. Some weight-loss strategies have even led to life-threatening eating disorders.
>
> –Harry Crouse, student

Try your hand at revising this paragraph, supplying specific examples of "bizarre schemes" or "weight-loss strategies" you have tried, observed, or read about. Share your examples with others in your class. Which examples best illustrate and support the central idea contained in the writer's topic sentence?

Suggested Writing Assignments

1. Reread the list of twenty-two questions at the beginning of Pinker's essay. After giving them some thought, select one to use as a central example in an essay about the need to debate important ideas no matter how uncomfortable those ideas might make us. Before you start writing, consider the following questions: What about the question I've chosen makes me or others uncomfortable? What are some of the idea's implications if we find it to be true? False? What would happen if we simply ignore this question?
2. In a case involving freedom of thought and expression, Justice Louis Brandeis said, "Sunlight is the best disinfectant" (36). What do you think he meant? How do you think Justice Brandeis would respond to the proposition that "it's a dangerous idea for thinkers to air their dangerous ideas" (37)? How do you respond to this proposition? Write an essay in which you present your position, making sure to support it with clear examples from your own experiences or reading.

CHAPTER **14**

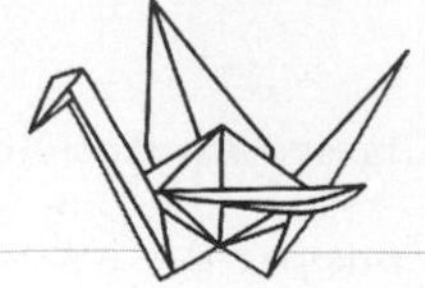

Narration

To *narrate* is to tell a story or to recount a series of events. Whenever you relate an incident or use an **anecdote** (a very brief story) to make a point, you use narration. In its broadest sense, **narration** is any account of any event or series of events. We all love to hear stories; some people believe that sharing stories is a part of what defines us as human beings. Good stories are interesting, sometimes suspenseful, and always instructive because they give us insights into the human condition. Although most often associated with fiction, narration is effective and useful in all kinds of writing. For example, in "A Crime of Compassion" (pp. 342–45), nurse Barbara Huttmann tells how she brought an end to one of her patient's long suffering as she argues against repeatedly using extraordinary measures to revive dying patients against their wishes.

Good narration has five essential features: a clear context; well-chosen and thoughtfully emphasized details; a logical, often chronological organization; an appropriate and consistent point of view; and a meaningful point or purpose. Consider, for example, the following narrative from a student essay titled "I Remember Love":

> I remember standing in my driveway that evening after we got back from dinner; her eyes sparkled in the dim light from my truck's interior as she stood beside it with the door open. I held her hands while we talked about spending Christmas morning with our families, and that we would not see each other until the evening. I told her that I had a Christmas gift for her so she did not have to wait until the following evening. I recall the excitement in her eyes when I handed her the wrapped present with a card attached to the top of the package. She asked me if she could open it right then, and I told her I didn't mind; however, I recommended that she at least save the card for Christmas morning. She

agreed, and she seemed so happy after opening the gift; she hugged me tightly, and we kissed as we held on to each other in the cold night air.

I remember when she was walking away, I wanted to yell out "I love you," but in that moment, I also remember thinking that there was no reason to rush it. I figured there would be plenty of time to tell her that I loved her, and I remember that she meant more to me than anyone or anything I had ever known. The few seconds it took her to leave my sight may have been the same few seconds in which I experienced the deepest thoughts of my life as I realized the woman of my dreams was right in front of me, and I finally found the person who made me feel complete. I thought about how she was all I wanted as I stood spellbound by everything from the kiss to her eyes. Even after she had driven out of view, I still stood there for several minutes in the cold of night, thinking that she would be the last girl I would ever kiss; I recall being completely all right with this idea, and I hoped she felt the same way. As I walked inside the house, I felt better than I ever had before or since.

–Skyler Waid, student

This story contains all the elements of good narration. The writer begins by establishing a clear context for his narrative by telling when, where, and to whom the action happened. He has chosen details well, including enough details so that we know what is happening but not so many that we become overwhelmed, confused, or bored. The writer organizes his narration logically with a beginning that sets the scene, a middle that relates an exchange between him and his girlfriend, and an end that makes his point, all arranged chronologically. He tells the entire story from the first-person point of view. Finally, he reveals the purpose of his narration: to recount his experience of the first time he fell in love.

The writer could have chosen to tell his story from the third-person point of view. In this point of view, the narrator is not a participant in the action and uses the pnonous *he* and *she* instead of *I*. In the following example, Carl T. Rowan tells a story of being scolded by a teacher, one whom he would grow to revere. Again we experience the event directly through the writer's eyes, but also through his ears, as he includes dialogue to make us feel as if we had been there with him that day.

I shall never forget the day she scolded me into reading *Beowulf*.

"But Miss Bessie," I complained, "I ain't much interested in it."

Her large brown eyes became daggerish slits. "Boy," she said, "how dare you say 'ain't' to me! I've taught you better than that."

"Miss Bessie," I pleaded, "I'm trying to make first-string end on the football team, and if I go around saying 'it isn't' and 'they aren't,' the guys are gonna laugh me off the squad."

"Boy," she responded, "you'll play football because you have guts. But do you know what *really* takes guts? Refusing to lower your standards to those of the crowd. It takes guts to say you've got to live and be somebody fifty years after all the football games are over."

I started saying "it isn't" and "they aren't," and I still made first-string end—and class valedictorian—without losing my buddies' respect.

–Carl T. Rowan, "Unforgettable Miss Bessie" (p. 411)

As you begin to write your own narration, take time to ask yourself why you are telling your story. Your purpose in writing will influence which events and details you include and which you leave out. You should include enough details about the action and its context so that your readers can understand what's going on. However, you should not get so carried away with details that your readers become confused or bored by an excess of information. In good storytelling, deciding what to leave out is as important as deciding what to include.

Be sure to give some thought to the organization of your narrative. Chronological organization is natural in narration because it is a reconstruction of the original order of events, but it is not always the most interesting. To add interest to your storytelling, try using a technique common in the movies and theater called *flashback*. Begin your narration midway through the story with an important or exciting event, and then use flashback to fill in what happened earlier. Notice how one student uses this very technique. She disrupts the chronological organization of her narrative by beginning in the recent past and then uses a flashback to take us back to when she was a youngster:

Essay opens in recent past

It was a Monday afternoon, and I was finally home from track practice. The coach had just told me that I had a negative attitude and should contemplate why I was on the team. My father greeted me in the living room.

"Hi, honey. How was practice?"

Dialogue creates historical present

"Not good, Dad. Listen, I don't want to do this anymore. I hate the track team."

"What do you mean *hate*?"

"The constant pressure is making me crazy."

"How so?"

"It's just not fun anymore."

"Well, I'll have to talk to the coach— "

"No! You're supposed to be my father, not my coach."

"I am your father, but I'm sure . . ."

"Just let me do what I want. You've had your turn."

He just let out a sigh and left the room. Later he told me that I was wasting my "God-given abilities." The funny part was that none of my father's anger hit me at first. All I knew was that I was free.

Essay returns in time to when troubles began

My troubles began the summer I was five years old. It was late June . . .

–Trena Isley, student, "On the Sidelines" (p. 64)

macmillanhighered.com/mfw12e
e-readings > Imam Khalid Latif, *Shattered Silence* [video]

What's in a Name?

■ Henry Louis Gates Jr.

The preeminent African American scholar of our time, Henry Louis Gates Jr. was born in West Virginia in 1950. He is the Alphonse Fletcher University Professor and director of the W. E. B. Du Bois Institute for African and African American Research at Harvard University. Among his impressive list of publications are The Signifying Monkey: A Theory of Afro-American Literary Criticism *(1988),* Loose Canons: Notes on Culture Wars *(1992),* Thirteen Ways of Looking at a Black Man *(1999),* Mr. Jefferson and Miss Wheatley *(2003), and* Black in Latin America *(2011). He is also the host of an acclaimed PBS documentary series,* The African Americans *(2013). His* Colored People: A Memoir *(1994) recollects his youth growing up in Piedmont, West Virginia, and his emerging sexual and racial awareness. Gates studied history at Yale University. Then, with the assistance of an Andrew W. Mellon Foundation Fellowship and a Ford Foundation Fellowship, he pursued advanced degrees in English at Clare College at the University of Cambridge. He has been honored with a MacArthur Foundation Fellowship, inclusion on* Time *magazine's "25 Most Influential Americans" list, a National Humanities Medal, and election to the American Academy of Arts and Letters.*

In this essay, excerpted from a longer article published in the fall 1989 issue of Dissent *magazine, Gates tells the story of an early encounter with the language of prejudice. In learning how one of the "bynames" used by white people to define African Americans robs them of their identity, he feels the sting of racism firsthand. Notice how Gates's use of dialogue gives immediacy and poignancy to his narration.*

Reflecting on What You Know

Reflect on the use of racially charged language. For example, has anyone ever used a racial epithet or name to refer to you?

When did you first become aware that such names existed? How do you feel about being characterized by your race? If you yourself have ever used such names, what was your intent in using them? What was the response of others?

The question of color takes up much space in these pages, but the question of color, especially in this country, operates to hide the graver questions of the self.

–James Baldwin, 1961

. . . blood, darky, Tar Baby, Kaffir, shine . . . moor, blackamoor, Jim Crow, spook . . . quadroon, meriney, red bone, high yellow . . . Mammy, porch monkey, home, homeboy, George . . . spearchucker, schwarze, Leroy, Smokey . . . mouli, buck, Ethiopian, brother, sistah . . .

–Trey Ellis, 1989

I had forgotten the incident completely, until I read Trey Ellis's essay, "Remember My Name," in a recent issue of the *Village Voice*[1] (June 13, 1989). But there, in the middle of an extended italicized list of the bynames of "the race" ("the race" or "our people" being the terms my parents used in polite or reverential discourse, "jigaboo" or "nigger" more commonly used in anger, jest, or pure disgust), it was: "George." Now the events of that very brief exchange return to mind so vividly that I wonder why I had forgotten it. 1

My father and I were walking home at dusk from his second job. He "moonlighted" as a janitor in the evenings for the telephone company. Every day but Saturday, he would come home at 3:30 from his regular job at the paper mill, wash up, eat supper, then at 4:30 head downtown to his second job. He used to make jokes frequently about a union official who moonlighted. I never got the joke, but he and his friends thought it was hilarious. All I knew was that my family always ate well, that my brother and I had new clothes to wear, and that all of the white people in Piedmont, West Virginia, treated my parents with an odd mixture of resentment and respect that even we understood at the time had something directly to do with a small but certain measure of financial security. 2

[1]*Village Voice:* a nationally distributed weekly newspaper published in New York City.

He had left a little early that evening because I was with him and I had to be in bed early. I could not have been more than five or six, and we had stopped off at the Cut-Rate Drug Store (where no black person in town but my father could sit down to eat, and eat off real plates with real silverware) so that I could buy some caramel ice cream, two scoops in a wafer cone, please, which I was busy licking when Mr. Wilson walked by. 3

Mr. Wilson was a very quiet man, whose stony, brooding, silent manner seemed designed to scare off any overtures of friendship, even from white people. He was Irish, as was one-third of our village (another third being Italian), the more affluent among whom sent their children to "Catholic School" across the bridge in Maryland. He had white straight hair, like my Uncle Joe, whom he uncannily resembled, and he carried a black worn metal lunch pail, the kind that Riley[2] carried on the television show. My father always spoke to him, and for reasons that we never did understand, he always spoke to my father. 4

"Hello, Mr. Wilson," I heard my father say. 5

"Hello, George." 6

I stopped licking my ice cream cone, and asked my Dad in a loud voice why Mr. Wilson had called him "George." 7

"Doesn't he know your name, Daddy? Why don't you tell him your name? Your name isn't George." 8

For a moment I tried to think of who Mr. Wilson was mixing Pop up with. But we didn't have any Georges among the colored people in Piedmont; nor were there colored Georges living in the neighboring towns and working at the mill. 9

"Tell him your name, Daddy." 10

"He knows my name, boy," my father said after a long pause. "He calls all colored people George." 11

A long silence ensued. It was "one of those things," as my Mom would put it. Even then, that early, I knew when I was in the presence of "one of those things," one of those things that provided a glimpse, through a rent[3] curtain, at another world that we could not affect but that affected us. There would be a painful moment of silence, and you 12

---

[2]*Riley:* Chester A. Riley, the lead character on the U.S. television show *The Life of Riley*, a blue-collar, ethnic sitcom popular in the 1950s.

[3]*rent:* torn.

would wait for it to give way to a discussion of a black superstar such as Sugar Ray[4] or Jackie Robinson.[5]

"Nobody hits better in a clutch than Jackie Robinson." 13

"That's right. Nobody." 14

I never again looked Mr. Wilson in the eye. 15

Thinking Critically about This Reading

What is "one of those things," as Gates's mom put it (paragraph 12)? In what ways is "one of those things" really Gates's purpose in telling this story?

Questions for Study and Discussion

1. Gates prefaces his essay with two quotations. What is the meaning of each quotation? Why do you suppose Gates uses both quotations? How does each relate to his purpose? (Glossary: *Purpose*)
2. Gates begins by explaining where he got the idea for his essay. How well does this approach work? Is it an approach you could see yourself using often? Explain.
3. In his first paragraph, Gates sets the context for his narrative. He also reveals that his parents used terms of racial abuse among themselves. Why does Gates make so much of Mr. Wilson's use of the word *George* when his own parents used words that were much more obviously offensive?
4. Gates describes and provides some background information about Mr. Wilson in paragraph 4. (Glossary: *Description*) What is Gates's purpose in providing this information? (Glossary: *Purpose*)

Classroom Activity Using Narration

Beginning at the beginning and ending at the end is not the only way to tell a story. Think of the events in a story that you would like to tell. Don't write the story, but simply list the events that need to be included. Be sure to include at least ten major events in your story.

[4]*Sugar Ray:* Walker Smith Jr. (1921–1989), American professional boxer and six-time world champion.

[5]*Jackie Robinson:* Jack Roosevelt Robinson (1919–1972), the first black baseball player in the major leagues in the modern era.

Now play with the arrangement of those events so as to avoid the chronological sequencing of them that would naturally come to mind. Try to develop as many patterns as you can, but be careful that you have a purpose in developing each sequence and that you do not create something that might confuse a listener or reader. Discuss your results with your classmates.

Suggested Writing Assignments

1. Using Gates's essay as a model, identify something that you have recently read that triggers in you a story from the past. Perhaps a newspaper article about how local high school students helped the community reminds you of a community project you and your classmates were involved in. Or perhaps reading about some act of heroism reminds you of a situation in which you performed (or failed to perform) a similar deed. Make sure that you have a purpose in telling the story, that you establish a clear context for it, and that you have enough supporting details to enrich your story. (Glossary: *Purpose; Details*) Also think about how to begin and end your story and which narrative sequence you will use. (Glossary: *Beginnings and Endings*)
2. How do you feel about your name? Do you like it? Does it sound pleasant? Do you think that your name shapes your identity in a positive or a negative way, or do you think that it has no effect on your sense of who you are? Write an essay about your name and the way it helps or fails to help you present yourself to the world. Be sure to develop your essay using narration by including several anecdotes or a longer story involving your name. (Glossary: *Anecdote*)

Momma, the Dentist, and Me

■ **Maya Angelou**

Syracuse Newspapers/Frank Ordonez/ The Image Works

Best-selling author and poet Maya Angelou (1928–2014) was an educator, historian, actress, playwright, civil rights activist, producer, and director. She is best known as the author of I Know Why the Caged Bird Sings *(1970), the first book in a series that constitutes her complete autobiography, and for "On the Pulse of the Morning," a characteristically optimistic poem on the need for personal and national renewal that she read at President Bill Clinton's inauguration in 1993. Starting with her beginnings in St. Louis in 1928, Angelou's autobiography presents a life of joyful triumph over hardships that tested her courage and threatened her spirit. It includes the titles* All God's Children Need Traveling Shoes *(1986),* The Heart of a Woman *(1997), and* A Song Flung Up to Heaven *(2002). Several volumes of her poetry were collected in* Complete Collected Poems of Maya Angelou *in 1994. Her most recent book is* Mom & Me & Mom *(2013), a memoir of her relationship with her mother. At the time of her death, Angelou was the Reynolds Professor of American Studies at Wake Forest University and had received more than fifty honorary degrees.*

In the following excerpt from I Know Why the Caged Bird Sings, *Angelou narrates what happened, and what might have happened, when her grandmother, the "Momma" of the story, took her to the local dentist. As you read, consider how vital first-person narration is to the essay's success, particularly as you gauge the effect of the italicized paragraphs.*

Reflecting on What You Know

When you were growing up, were you ever present when one or both of your parents were arguing with another adult about a matter concerning you? What were the circumstances? Narrate the events that brought about the controversy, and show how it was resolved. Were you embarrassed by your parents' actions, or were you happy that they stood up for you?

The angel of the candy counter had found me out at last, and was exacting excruciating penance for all the stolen Milky Ways, Mounds, Mr. Goodbars, and Hersheys with Almonds. I had two cavities that were rotten to the gums. The pain was beyond the bailiwick[1] of crushed aspirins or oil of cloves. Only one thing could help me, so I prayed earnestly that I'd be allowed to sit under the house and have the building collapse on my left jaw. Since there was no Negro dentist in Stamps, nor doctor either, for that matter, Momma had dealt with previous toothaches by pulling them out (a string tied to the tooth with the other end looped over her fist), pain killers, and prayer. In this particular instance the medicine had proved ineffective; there wasn't enough enamel left to hook a string on, and the prayers were being ignored because the Balancing Angel was blocking their passage. 1

I lived a few days and nights in blinding pain, not so much toying with as seriously considering the idea of jumping in the well, and Momma decided I had to be taken to a dentist. The nearest Negro dentist was in Texarkana, twenty-five miles away, and I was certain that I'd be dead long before we reached half the distance. Momma said we'd go to Dr. Lincoln, right in Stamps, and he'd take care of me. She said he owed her a favor. 2

I knew there were a number of whitefolks in town that owed her favors. Bailey and I had seen the books which showed how she had lent money to Blacks and whites alike during the Depression, and most still owed her. But I couldn't aptly remember seeing Dr. Lincoln's name, nor had I ever heard of a Negro's going to him as a patient. However, Momma said we were going, and put water on the stove for our baths. I had never been to a doctor, so she told me that after the bath (which would make my mouth feel better) I had to put on freshly starched and ironed underclothes from inside out. The ache failed to respond to the bath, and I knew then that the pain was more serious than that which anyone had ever suffered. 3

Before we left the Store, she ordered me to brush my teeth and then wash my mouth with Listerine. The idea of even opening my clamped jaws increased the pain, but upon her explanation that when you go to a doctor you have to clean yourself all over, but most especially the part that's to be examined, I screwed up my courage and unlocked my teeth. The cool air in my mouth and the jarring of my molars dislodged what little remained of my reason. I had frozen to the pain, 4

[1]*bailiwick:* a specific area of interest, skill, or authority.

my family nearly had to tie me down to take the toothbrush away. It was no small effort to get me started on the road to the dentist. Momma spoke to all the passers-by, but didn't stop to chat. She explained over her shoulder that we were going to the doctor and she'd "pass the time of day" on our way home.

Until we reached the pond the pain was my world, an aura that 5
haloed me for three feet around. Crossing the bridge into whitefolks' country, pieces of sanity pushed themselves forward. I had to stop moaning and start walking straight. The white towel, which was drawn under my chin and tied over my head, had to be arranged. If one was dying, it had to be done in style if the dying took place in whitefolks' part of town.

On the other side of the bridge the ache seemed to lessen as if a 6
whitebreeze blew off the whitefolks and cushioned everything in their neighborhood—including my jaw. The gravel road was smoother, the stones smaller, and the tree branches hung down around the path and nearly covered us. If the pain didn't diminish then, the familiar yet strange sights hypnotized me into believing that it had.

But my head continued to throb with the measured insistence of 7
a bass drum, and how could a toothache pass the calaboose,[2] hear the songs of the prisoners, their blues and laughter, and not be changed? How could one or two or even a mouthful of angry tooth roots meet a wagonload of powhitetrash children, endure their idiotic snobbery, and not feel less important?

Behind the building which housed the dentist's office ran a small 8
path used by servants and those tradespeople who catered to the butcher and Stamps's one restaurant. Momma and I followed that lane to the backstairs of Dentist Lincoln's office. The sun was bright and gave the day a hard reality as we climbed up the steps to the second floor.

Momma knocked on the back door and a young white girl 9
opened it to show surprise at seeing us there. Momma said she wanted to see Dentist Lincoln and to tell him Annie was there. The girl closed the door firmly. Now the humiliation of hearing Momma describe herself as if she had no last name to the young white girl was equal to the physical pain. It seemed terribly unfair to have a toothache and a headache and have to bear at the same time the heavy burden of Blackness.

[2]*calaboose:* a jail.

It was always possible that the teeth would quiet down and 10
maybe drop out of their own accord. Momma said we would wait. We leaned in the harsh sunlight on the shaky railings of the dentist's back porch for over an hour.

He opened the door and looked at Momma. "Well, Annie, what 11
can I do for you?"

He didn't see the towel around my jaw or notice my swollen face. 12

Momma said, "Dentist Lincoln. It's my grandbaby here. She got 13
two rotten teeth that's giving her a fit."

She waited for him to acknowledge the truth of her statement. He 14
made no comment, orally or facially.

"She had this toothache purt' near four days now, and today I 15
said, 'Young lady, you going to the Dentist.'"

"Annie?" 16

"Yes, sir, Dentist Lincoln." 17

He was choosing words the way people hunt for shells. "Annie, 18
you know I don't treat nigra, colored people."

"I know, Dentist Lincoln. But this here is just my little grandbaby, 19
and she ain't gone be no trouble to you . . ."

"Annie, everybody has a policy. In this world you have to have a 20
policy. Now, my policy is I don't treat colored people."

The sun had baked the oil out of Momma's skin and melted the 21
Vaseline in her hair. She shone greasily as she leaned out of the dentist's shadow.

"Seem like to me, Dentist Lincoln, you might look after her, she 22
ain't nothing but a little mite.[3] And seems like maybe you owe me a favor or two."

He reddened slightly. "Favor or no favor. The money has all been 23
repaid to you and that's the end of it. Sorry, Annie." He had his hand on the doorknob. "Sorry." His voice was a bit kinder on the second "Sorry," as if he really was.

Momma said, "I wouldn't press on you like this for myself but I 24
can't take No. Not for my grandbaby. When you come to borrow my money you didn't have to beg. You asked me, and I lent it. Now, it wasn't my policy. I ain't no moneylender, but you stood to lose this building and I tried to help you out."

"It's been paid, and raising your voice won't make me change my 25
mind. My policy . . ." He let go of the door and stepped nearer Momma.

---

[3]*mite:* a very small creature.

The three of us were crowded on the small landing. "Annie, my policy is I'd rather stick my hand in a dog's mouth than in a nigger's."

He had never once looked at me. He turned his back and went through the door into the cool beyond. Momma backed up inside herself for a few minutes. I forgot everything except her face which was almost a new one to me. She leaned over and took the doorknob, and in her everyday soft voice she said, "Sister, go on downstairs. Wait for me. I'll be there directly." 26

Under the most common of circumstances I knew it did no good to argue with Momma. So I walked down the steep stairs, afraid to look back and afraid not to do so. I turned as the door slammed, and she was gone. 27

Momma walked in that room as if she owned it. She shoved that silly nurse aside with one hand and strode into the dentist's office. He was sitting in his chair, sharpening his mean instruments and putting extra sting into his medicines. Her eyes were blazing like live coals and her arms had doubled themselves in length. He looked up at her just before she caught him by the collar of his white jacket. 28

"Stand up when you see a lady, you contemptuous scoundrel." Her tongue had thinned and the words rolled off well enunciated. Enunciated and sharp like little claps of thunder. 29

The dentist had no choice but to stand at R.O.T.C.[4] *attention. His head dropped after a minute and his voice was humble. "Yes, ma'am, Mrs. Henderson."* 30

"You knave, do you think you acted like a gentleman, speaking to me like that in front of my granddaughter?" She didn't shake him, although she had the power. She simply held him upright. 31

"No, ma'am, Mrs. Henderson." 32

"No, ma'am, Mrs. Henderson, what?" Then she did give him the tiniest of shakes, but because of her strength the action set his head and arms to shaking loose on the ends of his body. He stuttered much worse than Uncle Willie. "No, ma'am, Mrs. Henderson, I'm sorry." 33

With just an edge of her disgust showing, Momma slung him back in his dentist's chair. "Sorry is as sorry does, and you're about the sorriest dentist I ever laid my eyes on." (She could afford to slip into the vernacular[5] *because she had such eloquent command of English.)* 34

---

[4]*R.O.T.C.:* Reserve Officers Training Corps of the U.S. military.

[5]*vernacular:* the everyday language spoken by people of a particular country or region.

"I didn't ask you to apologize in front of Marguerite, because I don't want her to know my power, but I order you, now and herewith. Leave Stamps by sundown." 35

"Mrs. Henderson, I can't get my equipment . . ." He was shaking terribly now. 36

"Now, that brings me to my second order. You will never again practice dentistry. Never! When you get settled in your next place, you will be a veterinarian caring for dogs with the mange, cats with the cholera, and cows with the epizootic. Is that clear?" 37

The saliva ran down his chin and his eyes filled with tears. "Yes, ma'am. Thank you for not killing me. Thank you, Mrs. Henderson." 38

Momma pulled herself back from being ten feet tall with eight-foot arms and said, "You're welcome for nothing, you varlet,[6] *I wouldn't waste a killing on the likes of you."* 39

On her way out she waved her handkerchief at the nurse and turned her into a crocus sack of chicken feed. 40

Momma looked tired when she came down the stairs, but who wouldn't be tired if they had gone through what she had. She came close to me and adjusted the towel under my jaw (I had forgotten the toothache; I only knew that she made her hands gentle in order not to awaken the pain). She took my hand. Her voice never changed. "Come on, Sister." 41

I reckoned we were going home where she would concoct a brew to eliminate the pain and maybe give me new teeth too. New teeth that would grow overnight out of my gums. She led me toward the drugstore, which was in the opposite direction from the Store. "I'm taking you to Dentist Baker in Texarkana." 42

I was glad after all that I had bathed and put on Mum[7] and Cashmere Bouquet talcum powder. It was a wonderful surprise. My toothache had quieted to solemn pain, Momma had obliterated the evil white man, and we were going on a trip to Texarkana, just the two of us. 43

On the Greyhound she took an inside seat in the back, and I sat beside her. I was so proud of being her granddaughter and sure that some of her magic must have come down to me. She asked if I was scared. I only shook my head and leaned over on her cool brown upper arm. There was no chance that a dentist, especially a Negro 44

[6]*varlet:* a rascal; lowlife.
[7]*Mum:* a brand of deodorant.

dentist, would dare hurt me then. Not with Momma there. The trip was uneventful, except that she put her arm around me, which was very unusual for Momma to do.

The dentist showed me the medicine and the needle before he deadened my gums, but if he hadn't I wouldn't have worried. Momma stood right behind him. Her arms were folded and she checked on everything he did. The teeth were extracted and she bought me an ice cream cone from the side window of a drug counter. The trip back to Stamps was quiet, except that I had to spit into a very small empty snuff can which she had gotten for me and it was difficult with the bus humping and jerking on our country roads. 45

At home, I was given a warm salt solution, and when I washed out my mouth I showed Bailey the empty holes, where the clotted blood sat like filling in a pie crust. He said I was quite brave, and that was my cue to reveal our confrontation with the peckerwood dentist and Momma's incredible powers. 46

I had to admit that I didn't hear the conversation, but what else could she have said than what I said she said? What else done? He agreed with my analysis in a lukewarm way, and I happily (after all, I'd been sick) flounced into the Store. Momma was preparing our evening meal and Uncle Willie leaned on the door sill. She gave her version. 47

"Dentist Lincoln got right uppity. Said he'd rather put his hand in a dog's mouth. And when I reminded him of the favor, he brushed it off like a piece of lint. Well, I sent Sister downstairs and went inside. I hadn't never been in his office before, but I found the door to where he takes out teeth, and him and the nurse was in there thick as thieves. I just stood there till he caught sight of me." Crash bang the pots on the stove. "He jumped just like he was sitting on a pin. He said, 'Annie, I done tole you, I ain't gonna mess around in no niggah's mouth.' I said, 'Somebody's got to do it then,' and he said, 'Take her to Texarkana to the colored dentist' and that's when I said, 'If you paid me my money I could afford to take her.' He said, 'It's all been paid.' I tole him everything but the interest been paid. He said, ''Twasn't no interest.' I said, ''Tis now. I'll take ten dollars as payment in full.' You know, Willie, it wasn't no right thing to do, 'cause I lent that money without thinking about it. 48

"He tole that little snippety nurse of his'n to give me ten dollars and make me sign a 'paid in full' receipt. She gave it to me and I 49 signed the papers. Even though by rights he was paid up before, I figger, he gonna be that kind of nasty, he gonna have to pay for it."

Momma and her son laughed and laughed over the white man's evilness and her retributive[8] sin. 50

I preferred, much preferred, my version. 51

Thinking Critically about This Reading

What does Angelou mean when she states, "On the other side of the bridge the ache seemed to lessen as if a whitebreeze blew off the white-folks and cushioned everything in their neighborhood—including my jaw" (paragraph 6)? How long did Angelou's pain relief last? Why?

Questions for Study and Discussion

1. What is Angelou's purpose? (Glossary: *Purpose*)
2. Compare and contrast the content and style of the interaction between Momma and the dentist that is given in italics with the one given at the end of the narrative. (Glossary: *Comparison and Contrast*)
3. Angelou tells her story chronologically and in the first person. (Glossary: *Point of View*) What are the advantages of first-person narration?
4. Identify three similes Angelou uses in her narrative. (Glossary: *Figure of Speech*) Explain how each simile serves her purpose. (Glossary: *Purpose*)
5. Why do you suppose Angelou says she prefers her own version of the episode to that of her grandmother?
6. This is a story of pain—and not just the pain of a toothache. How does Angelou describe the pain of the toothache? What other pain does she tell of in this autobiographical piece?

Classroom Activity Using Narration

One of Angelou's themes in "Momma, the Dentist, and Me" is that cruelty, whether racial, social, professional, or personal, is difficult to

[8]*retributive:* demanding something in repayment, especially punishment.

endure and leaves a lasting impression on a person. As a way of practicing chronological order, consider a situation in which an unthinking or insensitive person made you feel inferior. Rather than write a draft of an essay at this point, simply list the sequence of events that occurred, in chronological order. Once you have completed this step, consider whether there is a more dramatic order you might use if you were actually to write an essay.

Suggested Writing Assignments

1. Using Angelou's essay as a model, give two versions of an actual event—one the way you thought or wished it had happened and the other the way events actually took place. You may want to refer to your answers to the Reflecting on What You Know prompt for this selection before you begin writing.
2. Every person who tells a story puts his or her signature on it in some way—by the sequencing of events, the amount and type of details used, and the tone the teller employs. (Glossary: *Tone*) Consider a time when you and a relative or friend experienced the same interesting sequence of events, then tell the story of those events from your unique perspective. (Glossary: *Point of View*) Once you have done so, try telling the story from what you imagine the other person's perspective to be. Perhaps you even heard the other person actually tell the story. What is the same in both versions? How do the renditions differ?

Listening to My Father

■ Michael Dirda

Julia Ewan/The Washington Post/Getty Images

Michael Dirda was born in Lorain, Ohio, in 1948. He was the recipient of a Fulbright Scholarship, and he studied at Oberlin College, where he graduated with highest honors in English, and at Cornell University, where he earned a PhD in comparative literature. Dirda is currently a Pulitzer Prize–winning book critic for the Washington Post *and a regular contributor to the* New York Review of Books *and the* Times Literary Supplement. *In his own words, though, Dirda thinks of himself "as more bookman and essayist than critic," with an aim to "excite others to try the books I review or the older works and authors that I love." He is also the author of a memoir,* An Open Book: Chapters from a Reader's Life, *and four collections of essays, including* Classics for Pleasure *(2007) and* On Conan Doyle *(2011), which was the winner of the Mystery Writers of America's Edgar Allan Poe Award for a biographical or critical work.*

"Listening to My Father" was published in Dirda's Readings: Essays and Literary Entertainments *(2000). It was originally published, on Father's Day, as an essay for a monthly column called "Readings." As you read, note how Dirda narrates his father's life as a reader, and reflect on how that aspect of his life affected a son with an "incomprehensible passion for reading."*

Reflecting on What You Know

What did your parents like—or not like—to read? Did you grow up to have similar tastes, or do you read very differently?

My father, a soul ravaged by discontent, always prey to righteous 1
indignation and of a brooding temperament, daydreamed that his children, especially his only son, would accomplish great things in

the world. He yearned to see my name—his name, too—metaphorically or even actually in lights, and was constantly urging me from an early age to better myself. I should learn to handle tools. I should sell newspapers door to door. I should invest my pocket money in stocks. I should jog each night around the block and build up my muscles by lifting weights. We are talking here about a pudgy, shy little boy, with thick glasses, bowed legs, and an incomprehensible passion for reading.

I never saw my dad read a book in his life. When he arrived home 2
from National Tube, he would open the screen door without a word, and merely grimace or grunt as my mother gave him a quick peck on the cheek and a cheery "Hi, hon." As soon as my sisters and I heard his footsteps, we would immediately switch off the television—even if Zorro was just about to be unmasked or the Lone Ranger blown up in the abandoned silver mine. Dad would drop his big grocery bag, filled with dirty work clothes, by the back door and then sit down, without a word, at his place at the head of the dining-room table. The newspaper would be there waiting, next to his plate, and my mother would instantly bring him a fifth of Seagram's and a cold Stroh's beer, along with a bottle opener. Dad would glance at the front page, unscrew the cap from the whiskey bottle, and measure one shot. After knocking that back, he would open the beer and carefully pour half the bottle into a glass, then take a sip. Meanwhile, my mother would produce some breaded Lake Erie perch, a mound of scalloped potatoes, a serving of canned corn, maybe a couple of rolls, a little salad of lettuce, cucumber, and tomato. My father would spend at least half an hour at the table, slowly eating his dinner, sipping his beer, reading his paper.

In the summer he would often take the *Lorain Journal* outside 3
and relax under the oak trees in one of the big Adirondack-style lawn chairs he had built. Sometimes he would chew on a toothpick as he folded and unfolded the paper. My dad could make a couple dozen pages of newsprint last half an afternoon or most of an evening. He particularly loved to read about the discomfiture of the rich, whom he passionately hated and envied. He was convinced that politics was simply a means for the upper classes to protect their wealth and to get more of it. What could be more obvious? In particular, he came to loathe John Kennedy and could never quite understand why his death received such extravagant attention. "The man was only doing his job. He knew the risks. On the same day Kennedy was shot, three

autoworkers in Detroit were killed when a crane collapsed on them. Why don't they get a fancy funeral? They were killed doing their job. What's the difference?" And he would wave his hand with disgust, dismissing an invisible crowd of political hypocrites and toadies. For a long time he kept a news clipping that appeared a week or so after Kennedy had been buried. A group of Catholic school kids had come to pay their respects to the dead president. As a priest or nun started to bless the grave, the container of holy water broke open, snuffing out the eternal flame. "God has spoken," intoned my father.

Sometimes, while my mother put my three sisters to bed, Dad 4
would invite me to scrunch down next to him in the cream-colored recliner (with special Magic Fingers vibrating action) and look through the pages of an old illustrated encyclopedia or a Sears catalogue. One evening when I was perhaps 7 or 8, I sat next to him while he slowly read aloud a highly abbreviated kids' version, with smudgy watercolors, of *Don Quixote*. Now, forty years later, I remember how close I felt that night to my father, strong and handsome with his aquiline nose and curly black hair, as he described the misadventures of the deluded knight. Perhaps even then I suspected that this quick-witted, unhappy man, troubled by a fierce but unfocused desire for material success, had much of Don Quixote in him: He never ceased wanting the world, his children, his own life, to be better than they were or were ever likely to be.

Long before I could read, my father introduced me to the beauty 5
and evocative power of words. When I'd ask him for a story, he would tell me about Ulysses and the Cyclops, chuckling at the Greek hero's ingenuity and applauding the comeuppance of an oppressor. Sometimes he would chant the tall-tale ballad of Abdul Abulbul Amir and Ivan Skavinsky Skavar: The two great warriors embark on an epic duel after Ivan treads on Abdul's toe. "They fought all that night neath the pale yellow moon / The din it was heard of afar / Great multitudes came so great was the fame / Of Abdul and Ivan Skavar." In the end both die, leaving comrades to mourn and a Circassian maiden heartbroken. Often as we rode down the highway in our old green Chevy, Dad would break out in song. "Old Dan and I our throats are dry / for the taste of water / cool water." At other times he would recite the lyrics to a then-current hit about Mary Ann "down by the seashore sifting sand." "Even little children love Mary Ann," he would repeat to himself, "down by the seashore sifting sand." Once, I remember, I was sick with the flu when Dad suddenly arrived home

and, hearing of my illness, rushed to the blue davenport where I had been shivering under mounds of covers. He stroked my fevered brow and then began to recite: "'Twas many and many a year ago / In a kingdom by the sea / That a maiden there lived / Whom you may know / By the name of Annabel Lee." I was enchanted by the music of the sounds, a sing-song melodiousness that my father took pains to emphasize, "She was a child and I was a child / In this kingdom by the sea," he went on but soon stalled, not knowing much more of the poem than this. I've sometimes wondered how he knew it at all.

My dad had dropped out of school at 16 when his own father died, leaving him the support of a mother, two sisters, and a brother. 6
Naturally, he went to work in the same steel mill that had killed my Russian-immigrant grandfather, and where he himself proceeded to labor for the next forty-odd years, despising every minute. There were many such stories in the Depression: My mother's mother was a widow with ten children; my mother-in-law raised her younger siblings. These people were tough customers. Though their own lives might be desperate, they were nevertheless convinced that their sons and daughters would dance in the sunshine, live in big houses on hilltops. "Get rich," my dad used to tell me, "and vote Republican."

Thinking Critically about This Reading

Dirda's father dropped out of school, and Dirda claims to never have seen him read a book. Yet the father seems to have had a deep impact on Dirda as a reader and writer. What values does Dirda's father instill in his son, both in his advice and through his example?

Questions for Study and Discussion

1. One of the essential features of good narration is well-chosen detail. What details does Dirda use to portray his father's character and habits?
2. Dirda uses repetition in the first paragraph to emphasize his father's constant advice. How does this repetition capture the father's voice? The son's feelings about the advice?
3. Narration often moves back and forth between summary and scene—between discussing broad swaths of time and focusing

on a specific moment. Identify some places where Dirda summarizes his father's habitual actions and other places where he writes about specific days. How does he balance these two approaches to time?

4. How does the story of Dirda's father resemble the stories of other people in his generation? Why do you think Dirda uses the word "naturally" (paragraph 6) in reference to his father's entry into the steel mill where his own father died?
5. At the beginning of the essay, Dirda describes his father as a "soul ravaged by discontent, always prey to righteous indignation and of a brooding temperament." How does the rest of the essay bear this out? How do the examples of his father's behavior support this characterization? [Glossary: *Illustration*]

Classroom Activity Using Narration

Read the following report by the National Transportation Safety Board about an accident on a rail line. As you read, mark words or phrases that help establish the chronological progression of events. Discuss how these signal phrases help you follow the narration of the accident.

The Accident

On the morning of the accident, two night-shift signal maintainers were repairing a switch at tower 18. Between 4:00 and 4:30 A.M., two day-shift maintainers joined them.[1] As the two crews conferred about the progress of the repair, Green Line train run 1 approached the tower. A trainee was operating the train, and a train operator/line instructor[2] was observing. Both crew members on the train later stated that they had not heard the control center's radioed advisory that workers were on the track structure at tower 18. The line instructor said that as the train approached the tower with a proceed (green) signal, he observed wayside maintenance personnel

[1]All times referred to in this report are central standard time.

[2]Line instructors are working train operators who provide on-the-job training to operator trainees.

Source: National Transportation Safety Board, "Railroad Accident Brief: Chicago Transit Authority, DCA-02-FR-005, Chicago, Illinois, February 26, 2002." www.ntsb.gov/publictn/2003/RAB0304.htm

from about 150 feet away and told the trainee to stop the train, which he did. One of the maintainers gave the train a hand signal to proceed, and the train continued on its way. Shortly after the train left, the night-shift maintainers also left.

The day-shift maintainers continued to work. Just before the accident, they removed a defective part and started to install a replacement. According to both men, they were squatting over the switch machine. One was facing the center of the track and attaching wires, while the other was facing the Loop with his back to the normal direction of train movements. He was shining a flashlight on the work area.

The accident train approached the tower on the proceed signal. One maintainer later said that he remembered being hit by the train, while the other said that he was hit by "something." A train operator/line instructor was operating the train, and a trainee was observing. Both later said that they had not seen any wayside workers. They said that they had heard noise that the student described as a "thump" in the vicinity of the accident and caught a "glimpse" of something.

Both maintainers later stated that they had not seen or heard the train as it approached. After being struck, one of the maintainers fell from the structure. The other fell to the deck of the platform on the outside of the structure. He used his radio to tell the control center that he and another maintainer had been "hit by the train." Emergency medical personnel were dispatched to the scene, and an ambulance took both men to a local hospital.

In the meantime, the accident train continued past the tower and stopped at the next station, Clark and Lake, where the crew members inspected the train from the platform and found no damage. They continued on their way until they heard the radio report that workers had been struck by a train. They stopped their train at the next station and reported to a supervisor.

According to the operator of the accident train, nothing had distracted her from her duties, and she had been facing forward and watching the track before the train arrived at tower 18. The trainee supported her account. Both crew members said that they had not heard the control center's radioed advisory that workers were on the track structure at tower 18.

Writing Suggestions

1. Write about a memory from your childhood. Using Dirda's paragraphs as a model, begin with habitual actions, describing the

way things usually were, then narrate a specific incident that stands out in your mind.

2. Narrate a brief story in which one or both of your parents gives you advice. Did you appreciate the advice at the time? Did you act on it? How do you feel about the value of the advice now, in hindsight? As you write, think about the usual demands of narration—especially the requirement that your story have some meaningful point or purpose.

The Story of an Hour

■ Kate Chopin

The Granger Collection, NY

Kate Chopin (1851–1904) was born in St. Louis of Creole Irish descent. Following her marriage, she lived in Louisiana, where she acquired the intimate knowledge of Creole Cajun culture that provided the impetus for much of her work and earned her a reputation as a writer who captured the ambience of the bayou region. When her first novel, The Awakening *(1899), was published, however, it generated scorn and outrage for its explicit depiction of a southern woman's sexual awakening. Only recently has Chopin been recognized for her literary talent and originality. Besides* The Awakening, *her works include two collections of short fiction,* Bayou Folk *(1894) and* A Night in Acadie *(1897). In 1969,* The Complete Works of Kate Chopin *was published by Louisiana State University Press, and the Library of America published* Kate Chopin: Complete Novels and Stories *in 2002.*

As you read the following story, first published as "The Dream of an Hour" in Vogue *magazine in 1894, try to gauge how your reactions to Mrs. Mallard are influenced by Chopin's use of third-person narration.*

Reflecting on What You Know

How do you react to the idea of marriage—committing to someone for life? What are the advantages of such a union? What are the disadvantages?

Knowing that Mrs. Mallard was afflicted with a heart trouble, great 1
care was taken to break to her as gently as possible the news of her husband's death.

It was her sister Josephine who told her, in broken sentences; 2
veiled hints that revealed in half concealing. Her husband's friend

Richards was there, too, near her. It was he who had been in the newspaper office when intelligence of the railroad disaster was received, with Brently Mallard's name leading the list of "killed." He had only taken the time to assure himself of its truth by a second telegram, and had hastened to forestall any less careful, less tender friend in bearing the sad message.

She did not hear the story as many women have heard the same, 3
with a paralyzed inability to accept its significance. She wept at once, with sudden, wild abandonment, in her sister's arms. When the storm of grief had spent itself she went away to her room alone. She would have no one follow her.

There stood, facing the open window, a comfortable, roomy arm- 4
chair. Into this she sank, pressed down by a physical exhaustion that haunted her body and seemed to reach into her soul.

She could see in the open square before her house the tops of trees 5
that were all aquiver with the new spring life. The delicious breath of rain was in the air. In the street below a peddler was crying his wares. The notes of a distant song which someone was singing reached her faintly, and countless sparrows were twittering in the eaves.

There were patches of blue sky showing here and there through 6
the clouds that had met and piled one above the other in the west facing her window.

She sat with her head thrown back upon the cushion of the chair, 7
quite motionless, except when a sob came up into her throat and shook her, as a child who has cried itself to sleep continues to sob in its dreams.

She was young, with a fair, calm face, whose lines bespoke repres- 8
sion and even a certain strength. But now there was a dull stare in her eyes, whose gaze was fixed away off yonder on one of those patches of blue sky. It was not a glance of reflection, but rather indicated a suspension of intelligent thought.

There was something coming to her and she was waiting for it, 9
fearfully. What was it? She did not know; it was too subtle and elusive to name. But she felt it, creeping out of the sky, reaching toward her through the sounds, the scents, the color that filled the air.

Now her bosom rose and fell tumultuously. She was beginning to 10
recognize this thing that was approaching to possess her, and she was striving to beat it back with her will—as powerless as her two white slender hands would have been.

When she abandoned herself a little whispered word escaped her 11
slightly parted lips. She said it over and over under her breath: "free, free, free!" The vacant stare and the look of terror that had followed it went from her eyes. They stayed keen and bright. Her pulses beat fast, and the coursing blood warmed and relaxed every inch of her body.

She did not stop to ask if it were or were not a monstrous joy that 12
held her. A clear and exalted perception enabled her to dismiss the suggestion as trivial.

She knew that she would weep again when she saw the kind, tender 13
hands folded in death; the face that had never looked save with love upon her, fixed and gray and dead. But she saw beyond that bitter moment a long procession of years to come that would belong to her absolutely. And she opened and spread her arms out to them in welcome.

There would be no one to live for her during those coming years; 14
she would live for herself. There would be no powerful will bending hers in that blind persistence with which men and women believe they have a right to impose a private will upon a fellow-creature. A kind intention or a cruel intention made the act seem no less a crime as she looked upon it in that brief moment of illumination.

And yet she had loved him—sometimes. Often she had not. 15
What did it matter! What could love, the unsolved mystery, count for in face of this possession of self-assertion which she suddenly recognized as the strongest impulse of her being!

"Free! Body and soul free!" she kept whispering. 16

Josephine was kneeling before the closed door with her lips to the 17
keyhole, imploring for admission. "Louise, open the door! I beg; open the door—you will make yourself ill. What are you doing, Louise? For heaven's sake open the door."

"Go away. I am not making myself ill." No; she was drinking in a 18
very elixir of life through that open window.

Her fancy was running riot along those days ahead of her. Spring 19
days, and summer days, and all sorts of days that would be her own. She breathed a quick prayer that life might be long. It was only yesterday she had thought with a shudder that life might be long.

She arose at length and opened the door to her sister's importuni- 20
ties.[1] There was a feverish triumph in her eyes, and she carried herself unwittingly like a goddess of Victory. She clasped her sister's waist,

[1] *importunities:* urgent requests or demands.

and together they descended the stairs. Richards stood waiting for them at the bottom.

Some one was opening the front door with a latchkey. It was Brently Mallard who entered, a little travel-stained, composedly carrying his grip-sack and umbrella. He had been far from the scene of the accident, and did not even know there had been one. He stood amazed at Josephine's piercing cry; at Richards' quick motion to screen him from the view of his wife. 21

But Richards was too late. 22

When the doctors came they said she had died of heart disease— of joy that kills. 23

Thinking Critically about This Reading

Chopin describes Mrs. Mallard as "beginning to recognize this thing that was approaching to possess her, and she was striving to beat it back with her will—as powerless as her two white slender hands would have been" (paragraph 10). Why does Mrs. Mallard fight her feeling of freedom, however briefly? How does she come to accept it?

Questions for Study and Discussion

1. What assumptions do Mrs. Mallard's sister and acquaintances make about her feelings toward her husband? What are her true feelings?
2. Reread paragraphs 5–9. What is Chopin's purpose in this section? (Glossary: *Purpose*) Do these paragraphs add to the story's effectiveness? Explain.
3. All the events of Chopin's story take place in an hour. Would the story be as poignant if they had taken place over the course of a day or even several days? Explain. Why do you suppose the author selected the time frame as a title for her story? (Glossary: *Title*)
4. Chopin could have written an essay detailing the oppression of women in marriage, but she chose instead to write a fictional narrative. This allows her to show readers the type of situation that can arise in an outwardly happy marriage rather than tell them about it. Why else do you think she chose to write a fictional narrative? What other advantages does it give her over nonfiction?

5. Why do you think Chopin narrates her story in the third person? (Glossary: *Point of View*)

Classroom Activity Using Narration

Using cues in the following sentences, rearrange them in chronological order.

1. The sky was gray and gloomy for as far as she could see, and sleet hissed off the glass.
2. "Oh, hi. I'm glad you called," she said happily, but her smile dimmed when she looked outside.
3. As Betty crossed the room, her phone rang, startling her.
4. "No, the weather's awful, so I don't think I'll get out to visit you today," she said, disappointed.
5. "Hello," she said, and she wandered over to the window.

Write five sentences of your own that cover a progression of events. Try to include dialogue. (Glossary: *Dialogue*) Then scramble them, and see if a classmate can put them back in the correct order.

Suggested Writing Assignments

1. Write a narrative essay in which you describe your reaction to a piece of news you once received—good or bad—that provoked a strong emotional response. What were your emotions? What did you do in the couple of hours after you received the news? How did your perceptions of the world around you change? What made the experience memorable?
2. Write an anecdote about a married couple you know—perhaps your grandparents or a pair of friends. Choose a specific story to narrate to readers, and choose your details well to illustrate the scene as you saw it. Then use the anecdote as the foundation for an essay that explores your current views on marriage. Are you married, or have you been? Do you look forward to marriage hopefully, or do you intend to avoid it? How does the story you narrate make you think about marriage?

CHAPTER **15**

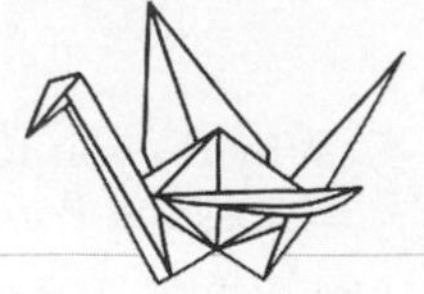

Description

To describe is to create a verbal picture. A person, a place, a thing—even an idea or a state of mind—can be made vividly concrete through **description**. In the following passage, Mark Twain describes the Mississippi River in the late afternoon:

> I still kept in mind a certain wonderful sunset which I witnessed when steamboating was new to me. A broad expanse of the river was turned to blood; in the middle distance the red hue brightened into gold, through which a solitary log came floating, black and conspicuous; in one place a long, slanting mark lay sparkling upon the water; in another the surface was broken by boiling, tumbling rings that were as many tinted as an opal; where the ruddy flush was faintest was a smooth spot that was covered with graceful circles and radiating lines, ever so delicately traced; the shore on our left was densely wooded, and the somber shadow that fell from this forest was broken in one place by a long, ruffled trail that shone like silver; and high above the forest wall a clean-stemmed dead tree waved a single leafy bough that glowed like a flame in the unobstructed splendor that was flowing from the sun. There were graceful curves, reflected images, woody heights, soft distances, and over the whole scene, far and near, the dissolving lights drifted steadily, enriching it every passing moment with new marvels of coloring.
>
> –Mark Twain, "Two Ways of Seeing a River," p. 494

Writing any description requires, first of all, that the writer gather many details about a subject, relying not only on what the eyes see but on the other sense impressions—touch, taste, smell, and hearing—as well. From this catalog of details, the writer selects those that will most effectively create a **dominant impression**—the single quality, mood, or atmosphere the writer wishes to emphasize.

Consider, for example, the details Cherokee Paul McDonald uses to evoke the dominant impression in the following passage, and contrast them with those in the subsequent example by student Dan Bubany:

> I was coming up on the little bridge in the Rio Vista neighborhood of Fort Lauderdale, deepening my stride and my breathing to negotiate the slight incline without altering my pace. And then, as I neared the crest, I saw the kid.
>
> He was a lumpy little guy with baggy shorts, a faded T-shirt and heavy sweat socks falling down over old sneakers.
>
> Partially covering his shaggy blond hair was one of those blue baseball caps with gold braid on the bill and a sailfish patch sewn onto the peak. Covering his eyes and part of his face was a pair of those stupid-looking '50s-style wrap-around sunglasses.
>
> He was fumbling with a beat-up rod and reel, and he had a little bait bucket by his feet. I puffed on by, glancing down into the empty bucket as I passed.
>
> –Cherokee Paul McDonald, "A View from the Bridge," pp. 127–28

> For this particular Thursday game against Stanford, Fleming wears white gloves, a maroon sport coat with brass buttons, and gray slacks. Shiny silver-framed bifocals match the whistle pressed between the lips on his slightly wrinkled face, and he wears freshly polished black shoes so glossy that they reflect the grass he stands on. He is not fat, but his coat neatly conceals a small, round pot belly.
>
> –Dan Bubany, student

The dominant impression that McDonald creates of the young boy is one of a scruffy little urchin. There is nothing about the boy's appearance that suggests any thought was given to what he is wearing. Bubany, on the other hand, creates a dominant impression of a neat, polished, kindly man.

Writers must also carefully plan the order in which to present their descriptive details. The pattern of organization must fit the subject of the description logically and naturally and must be easy to follow. For example, visual details can be arranged spatially—from left to right, top to bottom, near to far—or in any other logical order. Other patterns include smallest to largest, softest to loudest, least significant to most significant, and most unusual to least unusual.

How much detail is enough? There is no fixed answer. A good description includes enough vivid details to create a dominant impression and to bring a scene to life but not so many that readers are distracted, confused, or bored. In an essay that is purely descriptive, there is room for much detail. Usually, however, writers use description to create the setting for a story, to illustrate ideas, to help clarify a definition or a comparison, or to make the complexities of a process more understandable. Such descriptions should be kept short and should include just enough detail to make them clear and helpful.

macmillanhighered.com/mfw12e
e-readings > Peter Aguero, *Me & Her & It* [audio]

The Corner Store

■ **Eudora Welty**

Philip Gould/CORBIS

One of the most honored and respected writers of the twentieth century, Eudora Welty was born in 1909 in Jackson, Mississippi, where she lived most of her life and where she died in 2001. Her first book, A Curtain of Green *(1941), is a collection of short stories. Although she went on to become a successful writer of novels, essays, and book reviews, among other genres (as well as a published photographer), she is most often remembered as a master of the short story. In 1980, Welty was awarded the prestigious Presidential Medal of Freedom.* The Collected Stories of Eudora Welty *was published in 1982. Her other best-known works include a collection of essays,* The Eye of the Story *(1975); her autobiography,* One Writer's Beginnings *(1984); and a collection of book reviews and essays,* The Writer's Eye *(1994). Welty's novel* The Optimist's Daughter *won the Pulitzer Prize for Fiction in 1973. In 1999, the Library of Congress published two collections of her work:* Welty: Collected Novels *and* Welty: Collected Essays and Memoirs.

Welty's description of the corner store, taken from an essay in The Eye of the Story *about growing up in Jackson, recalls for many readers the neighborhood store in the town or city where they grew up. As you read, pay attention to the effect Welty's spatial arrangement of descriptive details has on the dominant impression of the store.*

Reflecting on What You Know

Write about a store you frequented as a child. Maybe it was the local supermarket, the hardware store, or the corner convenience store. Using your five senses (sight, smell, taste, touch, and hearing), describe what you remember about the place.

Our Little Store rose right up from the sidewalk; standing in a street of family houses, it alone hadn't any yard in front, any tree or flower bed. It was a plain frame building covered over with brick. Above the door, a little railed porch ran across on an upstairs level and four windows with shades were looking out. But I didn't catch on to those. 1

Running in out of the sun, you met what seemed total obscurity inside. There were almost tangible smells—licorice recently sucked in a child's cheek, dill pickle brine[1] that had leaked through a paper sack in a fresh trail across the wooden floor, ammonia-loaded ice that had been hoisted from wet croker sacks[2] and slammed into the icebox[3] with its sweet butter at the door, and perhaps the smell of still untrapped mice. 2

Then through the motes of cracker dust, cornmeal dust, the Gold Dust of the Gold Dust Twins that the floor had been swept out with, the realities emerged. Shelves climbed to high reach all the way around, set out with not too much of any one thing but a lot of things—lard, molasses, vinegar, starch, matches, kerosene, Octagon soap (about a year's worth of octagon-shaped coupons cut out and saved brought a signet ring[4] addressed to you in the mail). It was up to you to remember what you came for, while your eye traveled from cans of sardines to tin whistles to ice-cream salt to harmonicas to flypaper (over your head, batting around on a thread beneath the blades of the ceiling fan, stuck with its testimonial catch). 3

Its confusion may have been in the eye of its beholder. Enchantment is cast upon you by all those things you weren't supposed to have need for, to lure you close to wooden tops you'd outgrown, boys' marbles and agates in little net pouches, small rubber balls that wouldn't bounce straight, frail, frazzly kite string, clay bubble pipes that would snap off in your teeth, the stiffest scissors. You could contemplate those long narrow boxes of sparklers gathering dust while you waited for it to be the Fourth of July or Christmas, and noisemakers in the shape of tin frogs for somebody's birthday party you hadn't been invited to yet, and see that they were all marvelous. 4

You might not have even looked for Mr. Sessions when he came around his store cheese (as big as a doll's house) and in front of the counter looking for you. When you'd finally asked him for, and 5

[1]*brine:* salty water used to preserve or pickle food.

[2]*croker sacks:* sacks or bags made of burlap—a coarse, woven fabric.

[3]*icebox:* a wooden box or cupboard that held ice in a lower compartment to cool a second compartment above it, which was used for storing perishable food.

[4]*signet ring:* a ring bearing an official-looking seal.

received from him in its paper bag, whatever single thing it was that you had been sent for, the nickel that was left over was yours to spend.

Down at a child's eye level, inside those glass jars with mouths in their sides through which the grocer could run his scoop or a child's hand might be invited to reach for a choice, were wineballs, all-day suckers, gumdrops, peppermints. Making a row under the glass of a counter were the Tootsie Rolls, Hershey bars, Goo Goo Clusters, Baby Ruths. And whatever was the name of those pastilles that came stacked in a cardboard cylinder with a cardboard lid? They were thin and dry, about the size of tiddledy-winks,[5] and in the shape of twisted rosettes. A kind of chocolate dust came out with them when you shook them out in your hand. Were they chocolate? I'd say, rather, they were brown. They didn't taste of anything at all, unless it was wood. Their attraction was the number you got for a nickel. 6

Making up your mind, you circled the store around and around, around the pickle barrel, around the tower of Crackerjack boxes; Mr. Sessions had built it for us himself on top of a packing case like a house of cards. 7

If it seemed too hot for Crackerjacks, I might get a cold drink. Mr. Sessions might have already stationed himself by the cold-drinks barrel, like a mind reader. Deep in ice water that looked black as ink, murky shapes—that would come up as Coca-Colas, Orange Crushes, and various flavors of pop—were all swimming around together. When you gave the word, Mr. Sessions plunged his bare arm in to the elbow and fished out your choice, first try. I favored a locally bottled concoction called Lake's Celery. (What else could it be called? It was made by a Mr. Lake out of celery. It was a popular drink here for years but was not known universally, as I found out when I arrived in New York and ordered one in the Astor bar.) You drank on the premises, with feet set wide apart to miss the drip, and gave him back his bottle and your nickel. 8

But he didn't hurry you off. A standing scale was by the door, with a stack of iron weights and a brass slide on the balance arm, that would weigh you up to three hundred pounds. Mr. Sessions, whose hands were gentle and smelled of carbolic,[6] would lift you up and set your feet on the platform, hold your loaf of bread for you, and taking his time while you stood still for him, he would make certain of what 9

[5]*tiddledy-winks:* playing pieces from the game Tiddledy-Winks, flat and round in shape, the size of quarters (tiddledies) and dimes (winks).

[6]*carbolic:* a sweet, musky-smelling chemical once used in soap.

you weighed today. He could even remember what you weighed the last time, so you could subtract and announce how much you'd gained. That was goodbye.

Thinking Critically about This Reading

What does Mr. Sessions himself contribute to the overall experience of Welty's store? What does Welty's store contribute to the community?

Questions for Study and Discussion

1. Which of the three patterns of organization does Welty use in this essay—chronological, spatial, or logical? If she uses more than one, where precisely does she use each type?
2. In paragraph 2, Welty describes the smells that a person encountered when entering the corner store. Why do you think she presents these smells before giving any visual details of the inside of the store?
3. What dominant impression does Welty create in her description of the corner store? (Glossary: *Dominant Impression*) How does she create this dominant impression?
4. What impression of Mr. Sessions does Welty create? What details contribute to this impression? (Glossary: *Details*)
5. Why does Welty place certain pieces of information in parentheses? What, if anything, does this information add to your understanding of the corner store? Might this information be left out? Explain.
6. Comment on Welty's ending. (Glossary: *Beginnings and Endings*) Is it too abrupt? Why or why not?

Classroom Activity Using Description

Make a long list of the objects and people in your classroom as well as the physical features of the room—desks, windows, chalkboard, students, professor, dirty walls, burned-out lightbulb, a clock that is always ten minutes fast, and so on. Determine a dominant impression that you would like to create in describing the classroom. Now choose from your list those items that would best illustrate the dominant impression you have chosen. Your instructor may wish you to compare your response with those of other students.

Suggested Writing Assignments

1. Using Welty's essay as a model, describe your neighborhood store or supermarket. Gather a large quantity of detailed information from memory and from an actual visit to the store if that is still possible. You may find it helpful to reread what you wrote in response to the Reflecting on What You Know prompt for this selection. Once you have gathered your information, try to select those details that will help you create a dominant impression of the store. Finally, organize your examples and illustrations according to a clear organizational pattern.
2. Write a short essay about a special event at your school—or choose a normal day to capture. Consider the feeling of the day you're describing: celebratory, anxious, sleepy, bustling, and so on. Using Welty's essay as a model, write a description of the scene from your memory, choosing details that capture the dominant impression you identified.

Unforgettable Miss Bessie

■ Carl T. Rowan

In addition to being a popular syndicated newspaper columnist, Carl T. Rowan (1925–2000) was an ambassador to Finland and director of the U.S. Information Agency. Born in Ravenscroft, Tennessee, he received degrees from Oberlin College and the University of Minnesota. He worked as a columnist for the Minneapolis Tribune *and the* Chicago Sun-Times *before moving to Washington, D.C. In 1996, Washington College awarded Rowan an honorary doctor of letters degree in recognition of his achievements as a writer and his contributions to minority youth, most notably through the organization he founded in 1987, Project Excellence. In 1991, Rowan published* Breaking Barriers: A Memoir. *He is also the author of two biographies, one of baseball great Jackie Robinson and the other of former Supreme Court justice Thurgood Marshall. His last book,* The Coming Race War in America, *was published in 1996.*

In the following essay, first published in the March 1985 issue of Reader's Digest, *Rowan describes a high school teacher whose lessons went far beyond the subjects she taught. Through telling details about Miss Bessie's background, behavior, and appearance, Rowan creates a dominant impression of her—the one he wants to leave readers with. Notice how he begins with some factual information about Miss Bessie and concludes by showing why she was "so vital to the minds, hearts, and souls" of her students.*

Reflecting on What You Know

Perhaps you have at some time taught a friend or a younger brother or sister how to do something—tie a shoe, hit a ball, read, solve a puzzle, drive a car—but you never thought of yourself as a teacher. Did you enjoy the experience of sharing what you know with someone else? Would you consider becoming a teacher someday?

She was only about five feet tall and probably never weighed more than 110 pounds, but Miss Bessie was a towering presence in the classroom. She was the only woman tough enough to make me read *Beowulf*[1] and think for a few foolish days that I liked it. From 1938 to 1942, when I attended Bernard High School in McMinnville, Tennessee, she taught me English, history, civics—and a lot more than I realized. 1

I shall never forget the day she scolded me into reading *Beowulf*. 2

"But Miss Bessie," I complained, "I ain't much interested in it." 3

Her large brown eyes became daggerish slits. "Boy," she said, "how dare you say 'ain't' to me! I've taught you better than that." 4

"Miss Bessie," I pleaded, "I'm trying to make first-string end on the football team, and if I go around saying 'it isn't' and 'they aren't,' the guys are gonna laugh me off the squad." 5

"Boy," she responded, "you'll play football because you have guts. But do you know what *really* takes guts? Refusing to lower your standards to those of the crowd. It takes guts to say you've got to live and be somebody fifty years after all the football games are over." 6

I started saying "it isn't" and "they aren't," and I still made first-string end—and class valedictorian—without losing my buddies' respect. 7

During her remarkable 44-year career, Mrs. Bessie Taylor Gwynn taught hundreds of economically deprived black youngsters—including my mother, my brother, my sisters, and me. I remember her now with gratitude and affection—especially in this era when Americans are so wrought-up about a "rising tide of mediocrity"[2] in public education and the problems of finding competent, caring teachers. Miss Bessie was an example of an informed, dedicated teacher, a blessing to children, and an asset to the nation. 8

Born in 1895, in poverty, she grew up in Athens, Alabama, where there was no public school for blacks. She attended Trinity School, a private institution for blacks run by the American Missionary Association, and in 1911 graduated from the Normal School (a "super" high school) at Fisk University in Nashville. Mrs. Gwynn, the essence of pride and privacy, never talked about her years in Athens; only in the months before her death did she reveal that she had never attended Fisk University itself because she could not afford the four-year course. 9

---

[1]*Beowulf:* an epic poem written in Old English by an anonymous author in the early eighth century.

[2]*mediocrity:* state of being second-rate; not outstanding.

10 At Normal School she learned a lot about Shakespeare, but most of all about the profound importance of education—especially, for a people trying to move up from slavery. "What you put in your head, boy," she once said, "can never be pulled out by the Ku Klux Klan,[3] the Congress, or anybody."

11 Miss Bessie's bearing of dignity told anyone who met her that she was "educated" in the best sense of the word. There was never a discipline problem in her classes. We didn't dare mess with a woman who knew about the Battle of Hastings, the Magna Carta, and the Bill of Rights—and who could also play the piano.

12 This frail-looking woman could make sense of Shakespeare, Milton, Voltaire, and bring to life Booker T. Washington and W. E. B. Du Bois. Believing that it was important to know who the officials were that spent taxpayers' money and made public policy, she made us memorize the names of everyone on the Supreme Court and in the President's Cabinet. It could be embarrassing to be unprepared when Miss Bessie said, "Get up and tell the class who Frances Perkins[4] is and what you think about her."

13 Miss Bessie knew that my family, like so many others during the Depression,[5] couldn't afford to subscribe to a newspaper. She knew we didn't even own a radio. Still, she prodded me to "look out for your future and find some way to keep up with what's going on in the world." So I became a delivery boy for the Chattanooga *Times*. I rarely made a dollar a week, but I got to read a newspaper every day.

14 Miss Bessie noticed things that had nothing to do with schoolwork, but were vital to a youngster's development. Once a few classmates made fun of my frayed, hand-me-down overcoat, calling me "Strings." As I was leaving school, Miss Bessie patted me on the back of that old overcoat and said, "Carl, never fret about what you *don't* have. Just make the most of what you *do* have—a brain."

15 Among the things that I did not have was electricity in the little frame house that my father had built for $400 with his World War I

[3]*Ku Klux Klan:* a secret organization in the United States hostile toward African Americans (and eventually other groups as well), founded in 1915 and continuing to the present.

[4]*Frances Perkins* (1882–1965): U.S. secretary of labor during the presidency of Franklin D. Roosevelt and the first woman appointed to a cabinet post.

[5]*Depression:* the longest and most severe modern economic slump in North America, Europe, and other industrialized areas of the world so far; it began in 1929 and ended around 1939. Also called the Great Depression.

bonus. But because of her inspiration, I spent many hours squinting beside a kerosene lamp reading Shakespeare and Thoreau, Samuel Pepys and William Cullen Bryant.

No one in my family had ever graduated from high school, so there was no tradition of commitment to learning for me to lean on. Like millions of youngsters in today's ghettos and barrios, I needed the push and stimulation of a teacher who truly cared. Miss Bessie gave plenty of both, as she immersed me in a wonderful world of similes, metaphors and even onomatopoeia. She led me to believe that I could write sonnets as well as Shakespeare, or iambic-pentameter verse to put Alexander Pope to shame. 16

In those days the McMinnville school system was rigidly "Jim Crow,"[6] and poor black children had to struggle to put anything in their heads. Our high school was only slightly larger than the once-typical little red schoolhouse, and its library was outrageously inadequate—so small, I like to say, that if two students were in it and one wanted to turn a page, the other one had to step outside. 17

Negroes, as we were called then, were not allowed in the town library, except to mop floors or dust tables. But through one of those secret Old South arrangements between whites of conscience and blacks of stature, Miss Bessie kept getting books smuggled out of the white library. That is how she introduced me to the Brontës, Byron, Coleridge, Keats and Tennyson. "If you don't read, you can't write, and if you can't write, you might as well stop dreaming," Miss Bessie once told me. 18

So I read whatever Miss Bessie told me to, and tried to remember the things she insisted that I store away. Forty-five years later, I can still recite her "truths to live by," such as Henry Wadsworth Longfellow's lines from "The Ladder of St. Augustine": 19

The heights by great men reached and kept
Were not attained by sudden flight.
But they, while their companions slept,
Were toiling upward in the night.

Years later, her inspiration, prodding, anger, cajoling, and almost osmotic infusion of learning finally led to that lovely day when Miss Bessie dropped me a note saying, "I'm so proud to read your column in the Nashville *Tennessean.*" 20

[6] *"Jim Crow":* a term referring to the racial segregation laws in the U.S. South between the late 1800s and the mid-1900s.

Miss Bessie was a spry 80 when I went back to McMinnville and visited her in a senior citizens' apartment building. Pointing out proudly that her building was racially integrated, she reached for two glasses and a pint of bourbon. I was momentarily shocked, because it would have been scandalous in the 1930s and '40s for word to get out that a teacher drank, and nobody had ever raised a rumor that Miss Bessie did. 21

I felt a new sense of equality as she lifted her glass to mine. Then she revealed a softness and compassion that I had never known as a student. 22

"I've never forgotten that examination day," she said, "when Buster Martin held up seven fingers, obviously asking you for help with question number seven, 'Name a common carrier.' I can still picture you looking at your exam paper and humming a few bars of 'Chattanooga Choo Choo.' I was so tickled, I couldn't punish either of you." 23

Miss Bessie was telling me, with bourbon-laced grace, that I never fooled her for a moment. 24

When Miss Bessie died in 1980, at age 85, hundreds of her former students mourned. They knew the measure of a great teacher: love and motivation. Her wisdom and influence had rippled out across generations. 25

Some of her students who might normally have been doomed to poverty went on to become doctors, dentists, and college professors. Many, guided by Miss Bessie's example, became public-school teachers. 26

"The memory of Miss Bessie and how she conducted her classroom did more for me than anything I learned in college," recalls Gladys Wood of Knoxville, Tennessee, a highly respected English teacher who spent 43 years in the state's school system. "So many times, when I faced a difficult classroom problem, I asked myself, *How would Miss Bessie deal with this?* And I'd remember that she would handle it with laughter and love." 27

No child can get all the necessary support at home, and millions of poor children get *no* support at all. This is what makes a wise, educated, warm-hearted teacher like Miss Bessie so vital to the minds, hearts, and souls of this country's children. 28

Thinking Critically about This Reading

Rowan states that Miss Bessie "taught me English, history, civics—and a lot more than I realized" (paragraph 1). Aside from the standard school subjects, what did Miss Bessie teach Rowan? What role did she play in his life?

Questions for Study and Discussion

1. Throughout the essay, Rowan offers details of Miss Bessie's physical appearance. What specific details does he give, and in what context does he give them? (Glossary: *Details*) Do Miss Bessie's physical characteristics match the quality of her character? Explain.
2. At what point in the essay does Rowan give us the details of Miss Bessie's background? Why do you suppose he delays giving us this important information?
3. Do you think Rowan's first few paragraphs make for an effective introduction? Explain.
4. Does Miss Bessie's drinking influence your opinion of her? Why or why not? Why do you think Rowan mentions this aspect of her behavior in his essay?
5. How does dialogue serve Rowan's purpose? (Glossary: *Dialogue; Purpose*)
6. How would you sum up the character of Miss Bessie? Make a list of the key words Rowan uses that you believe best describe her.

Classroom Activity Using Description

Important advice for writing well is to show rather than tell. Your task with this activity is to reveal a person's character. For example, to indicate that someone is concerned about current events without coming out and saying so, you might show her reading the morning newspaper. Or you might show a character's degree of formality by including his typical greeting: *How ya doing?* In other words, the things a person says and does are often important indicators of personality. Choose one of the following traits, and make a list of at least four ways to show that someone possesses that trait. Share your list with the class, and discuss the "show-not-tell" strategies you have used.

plain and uncomplicated	thoughtful	independent
reckless	politically involved	quick witted
artistic	irresponsible	public spirited
a sports lover	conversationalist	loyal

Suggested Writing Assignments

1. In paragraph 18, Rowan writes the following: "'If you don't read, you can't write, and if you can't write, you might as well stop dreaming,' Miss Bessie once told me." Write an essay in which you explore this theme (which, in essence, is also the theme of *Models for Writers*).
2. Think of all the teachers you have had, and then write a description of the one who has had the greatest influence on you. (Glossary: *Description*) Remember to give some consideration to the balance you want to achieve between physical attributes and personality traits.

My Rosetta

■ Judith Ortiz Cofer

Miriam Berkley

Judith Ortiz Cofer was born in 1952 in Hormigueros, Puerto Rico. As a young girl, she moved with her family to Paterson, New Jersey, and when she was fifteen, the family settled in Augusta, Georgia. Cofer earned a BA in English from Augusta College and an MA from Florida Atlantic University. She is the author of numerous books, including A Love Story Beginning in Spanish *(2005), a collection of poems;* The Meaning of Consuelo *(2003), a novel;* The Latin Deli: Prose and Poetry *(1993); and* Silent Dancing *(1990), a collection of poetry and essays. Cofer writes in several genres and for audiences of varied ages, but her writing is unified by the influence of oral storytelling, commentary on how immigrants negotiate dual identities, and concern with gender issues and the empowerment of women. Cofer has been honored for her writing with grants and awards from the National Endowment for the Arts, the Georgia Council for the Arts, and the Witter Bynner Foundation. She is currently the Franklin Professor of English and Creative Writing at the University of Georgia.*

In this essay from her book Woman in Front of the Sun: On Becoming a Writer *(2000), Cofer remembers a woman who played a small but significant role in her life. As you read, pay attention to how she describes what is unexpected about Sister Rosetta by using humorous comparisons to capture her teacher's unique qualities.*

Reflecting on What You Know

What adults outside of your family have most influenced your life? What do you think made them so important you? How did they help you grow?

Sister Rosetta came into my life in 1966, at exactly the right moment. I was fourteen, beginning to stretch my bones after the long sleep of childhood, and the whole nation seemed to be waking up along with me. Each day the transistor radio I took everywhere informed me that the streets were alive with rebellion. Rock and roll filled the airwaves with throbbing sounds like those the heart makes when you are young and still listening to it—sounds that made me want to dance, yell, break out of my parents' cocoon of an apartment, sprout wings, and fly away from my predictable life and (what I feared most) a predictable future as a good Catholic barrio woman. Instead I was signed up for classes leading to my confirmation in the Catholic Church, spiritual preparation for the bishop's symbolic slap in the face: turn the other cheek, girl, you are now one of us humble followers of Christ. But my teacher in the ways of Christian humility, Sister Rosetta, was anything but the docile bride of Jesus I had expected. 1

She was not an attractive woman. Her face, although bright with wit, belonged on an Irish guy with a tough job, perhaps a construction foreman or a cop. If a nun's coif had not framed those features—the slightly bulbous nose, plump red-veined cheeks, and close-set eyes—this could have been the face of a heavy drinker or a laborer. She walked without grace but with a self-assured step we could hear approaching on the hardwood floors of the church basement where our lessons were held after school on cold winter afternoons in Paterson, New Jersey. Her rosary swinging from side to side on her habit's skirts, she strode in and slammed on the desktop whatever she was carrying that day. Then she'd lift herself onto the desk and face us, hands on hips as if to say, *What a shit job this is*. 2

And it was. Common knowledge had it that Sister Rosetta was assigned all the routine work of the convent by the Mother Superior to keep her busy and out of trouble. There was a rumor among us public school kids that Sister Rosetta had been arrested for taking part in a civil rights demonstration. And that she had been sent to our mainly Puerto Rican parish so that Father Jones, our saintly missionary pastor, could keep her under his wing. We found it funny to think of the shy, skinny man standing up to Sister Rosetta. 3

"OK, my little dumplings," Sister Rosetta would greet us, squinting like a coach about to motivate her team. "Today we are going to get in touch with our souls through music. Now listen carefully. You've never heard anything like this." Out of curiosity at first, then 4 in near rapture, that day I listened to the exotic music of Ravi Shankar emerge from the old turntable Sister Rosetta had dragged in. The celestial notes of his sitar enveloped me in a gauzy veil of sound, stirring me in a new way. Sister had tacked the album cover on the corkboard, and as I looked deeply into Shankar's onyx eyes he seemed to look back: in his gaze there were answers to questions I was almost ready to ask.

5 She must have noticed my enchantment, because Sister Rosetta handed me that record album as I was walking out of her overheated classroom. All she said was, "Bring it back without a scratch." Much to my mother's annoyance, I played Shankar's music every day after school in my room while I did my homework. She called it *los gatos peleando*, the cat-fight album; but to me the high, lingering notes were an alarm clock bringing me out of myself, out of ignorance and into the realm of the senses. For my thirteenth birthday I had received my own turntable and a Felipe Rodriguez album of Puerto Rican *boleros*, the romantic ballads my parents danced to at parties. I played the record occasionally for their sake, but Rodriguez's deep-throated laments about lost loves and weak women in tears did not appeal much to me. I liked the leaping, acrobatic images that Shankar's music induced, replacing my childhood dreams of flight.

Thinking Critically about This Reading

At the beginning of "My Rosetta," Cofer claims that Sister Rosetta appeared in her life "at exactly the right moment." What was special about this time in her life? Find passages from the essay that show how Cofer was feeling at this moment in time.

Questions for Study and Discussion

1. Cofer describes herself coming out of the "long sleep of childhood" (paragraph 1), awoken by the "alarm clock" of Ravi Shankar's music (5). Discuss the metaphor of sleep and waking in this essay. How does it help to convey the fourteen-year-old student's sense of the world?
2. Why does Cofer fear being a "good Catholic barrio woman" (1)? Explain this vision of her future, and discuss why she rejects it.

3. Cofer sets up the first appearance of Sister Rosetta by telling us she is "anything but the docile bride of Jesus" (1). How does the description of her in paragraph 2 contradict that stereotypical picture of a nun?
4. In addition to describing Sister Rosetta's appearance, Cofer vividly portrays her actions. Highlight places in the text that describe Sister Rosetta's way of moving or gesturing. What impressions do these passages give you about her character?
5. What is Sister Rosetta's reputation among the public school students? Do you see any connections between her situation and Cofer's?
6. Explain the difference of opinion between Cofer and her mother over the Ravi Shankar album. How does the music Cofer's parents prefer compare to it?

Classroom Activity Using Description

One of the best ways to make a description of a person memorable is to use a simile (making a comparison using *like* or *as*, such as "Her feet floated like a feather in a breeze") or a metaphor (making a comparison without the use of *like* or *as*, such as "His fists were iron"). Think of a time when you were one of a group of people assembled to do something most or all of you didn't really want to do. People in such a situation behave in various ways, showing their discomfort. One might stare steadily at the ground, for example. A writer describing the scene could use a metaphor to make this more vivid for the reader: "With his gaze he drilled a hole in the ground between his feet." Other people in an uncomfortable situation might fidget, lace their fingers together, breathe rapidly, squirm, or tap an object, such as a pen or a key. Create a simile or a metaphor to describe each of these behaviors. Compare your metaphors and similes with those of your classmates. Discuss which ones work best for each behavior.

Suggested Writing Assignments

1. Choose someone close to you, and write an essay describing him or her to a stranger. Using "My Rosetta" as a model, use both physical appearance and characteristic gestures as a way to communicate personality.

2. Write a personal essay about a time in your life when your view of the world was changing. Rather than stating this change up front, focus on first describing your surroundings—as Cofer does with her neighborhood and her parents' "coçoon of an apartment" (1). How much can you convey through well-chosen details about the environment to which you were reacting?

Hunting Your Own Dinner

■ **Bill Heavey**

Bill Heavey is originally from Bethesda, Maryland, and currently lives in the suburbs of Washington, D.C. He attended George Washington University and is an editor-at-large for Field & Stream *magazine. Heavey is the author of* If You Didn't Bring Jerky, What Did I Just Eat? *(2008) and* It's Only Slow Food Until You Try to Eat It: Misadventures of a Suburban Hunter-Gatherer *(2013), from which this selection was excerpted.*

On his website Heavey writes, "Hunting and fishing are too important and too much fun to be left to the experts." In "Hunting Your Own Dinner," he recounts the first time he killed a deer with a bow and arrow. As you read, consider how his descriptions of the deer and the surrounding forest convey the feelings of the amateur hunter.

Reflecting on What You Know

Have you ever been hunting? Would you ever try it? Why or why not?

As the buck rises from its bed in the underbrush 40 yards away, every cell in my body decides to attempt a jailbreak. I'm in my hunting stand, 24 feet up a tulip poplar, where I've been concealed for four hours waiting for a deer to pass. And this one has been right in front of me the whole time. I would like to come to my feet, but my legs are shaking too hard. 1

This is my third autumn spent trying to kill a deer with a bow and arrow, and this is the closest I've come. At 40 yards, I see the nap of its hair lying in one direction along its back, the opposite along its shoulder. The buck, a five-pointer, standing now, drops its antlered head almost to the ground and stretches its entire body. And then it freezes. It becomes a lawn statue. A minute later, when it reanimates 2 and ambles out of sight, I'm devastated. But in hunting, you don't move without a good reason. And a broken heart doesn't qualify.

What I love about hunting, despite my lack of success, is how it 3
makes everything matter in a way it didn't before. Wind—to which I was indifferent—becomes a matter of life and death. A deer downwind of you will scent you—"bust you" is the hunter's term—and be gone before you ever see it. Conversely, if the deer is upwind, you're still in business. Unless, of course, the wind shifts.

Likewise, every sound matters. The woods are a spider web, and 4
you enter as a fly hitting that web. The animals—seen and unseen—register and alert one another to your arrival. All you can do is sit quiet and still. Do this, and within 15 or 20 minutes the woods will absorb you. Sit still enough and a goldfinch, mistaking you for a tree, will light on your chest, fluff itself for a few seconds and fly off.

Sitting motionless but present, alert to the wind on your skin and 5
the intermittent patter of acorns falling, you may hear a sudden uptick in chatter among the birds and squirrels. Another fly has hit the web. Now you are among the animals alerted. It could be anything, including a deer.

You enter a state of relaxed but heightened awareness, a kind of 6
active meditation. But entry into this world comes at a price. You have to be hunting—I do, anyway.

My legs, although still shaking hard, are once again taking re- 7
quests from my brain. I stand and take my bow in hand. Fifteen minutes later, I hear footfalls in the leaves behind me. A doe walks calmly right beneath my stand. Right under the doe's raised tail is a buck, following its nose.

The doe makes a wide circle, the buck dogging her every step. 8
They are all of eight yards away. I draw and aim, noting the burrs in the buck's coat just below where I want my arrow to go. I release the arrow. The doe shudders reflexively at the sound but doesn't alter stride. The buck, his nose still right under her tail, shows no reaction. They exit stage left. I can't have missed. It's impossible. But there's no other explanation.

It's growing dark by the time I lower my bow on a rope and qui- 9
etly climb down. I find my arrow sticking out of the dirt at precisely the angle I shot, as if having penetrated nothing more solid than air. But when I pull it, I find that the shaft is slick with blood. A few feet away there is a dark medallion of blood in the leaves. Then another. Then, 15 yards from where I shot it, the downed buck. My arrow

passed right through him. He never even knew he'd been shot. It's as clean a kill as you can hope to make.

I start to cry out, "Yes!" but my voice instantly sounds wrong 10
here, a transgression, and I swallow the word before it escapes my lips. I had wondered and worried how it would feel to kill an animal, and now I know. It feels—in both the modern and archaic senses—awesome. I'm flooded, overwhelmed, seized by interlocking feelings of euphoria and contrition, pride and humility, reverence and, yes, fear. The act of killing an innocent being feels—and will always feel—neither wholly wrong nor wholly right. I stroke the buck's flank. I apologize for taking its life. I murmur, "Thank you."

That night I broil the buck's tenderloin. It's fantastic, wild rather 11
than gamy. What ran in the woods now sits on my plate, without the benefit of an inspector's stamp or the supermarket's sanctifying fluorescence. What I've done feels subversive, almost illicit. I have stolen food. And it is good.

Thinking Critically about This Reading

How does Heavey contrast hunting with buying meat at a supermarket? How are the two different? Why does he call his way of eating "subversive" (paragraph 11)?

Questions for Study and Discussion

1. Heavey's descriptions in this selection appeal to several of the senses, not just to the sense of sight. Highlight places where he focuses on the sounds or smells of the woods. What effect do these passages have on you as a reader?
2. Heavey begins with a moment of high drama, when he first sees a buck. How do the details he chooses in describing the buck add to the tension of this opening?
3. Heavey's ability to kill his prey depends heavily on his ability to observe and anticipate its movements. How do Heavey's descriptions display this attention to how the buck moves?
4. In paragraph 4, Heavey relates an anecdote about a goldfinch perching on a hunter's chest, "mistaking [him] for a tree." How does this anecdote encapsulate Heavey's relationship with nature?

5. In paragraph 10, Heavey discusses the complex emotions he feels after killing the buck. What are the two definitions of "awesome" to which he refers? How do they both apply to his feelings at this moment?
6. This selection ends with the provocative statement, "I have stolen food. And it is good." In what way is killing the buck a theft? What makes it good?

Classroom Activity Using Description

The verbs you use in writing a description can themselves convey much descriptive information. Take, for example, the verb *walk*. This word actually tells us little more than "to move on foot" in the most general sense. Using more precise and descriptive alternatives—*hike*, *slink*, *saunter*, *stalk*, *step*, *stride*, *stroll*, *tramp*, *wander*—enhances your descriptive powers and enlivens your writing. For each of the following verbs, make a list of at least four descriptive alternatives. Then compare your lists with those of others in the class.

go	throw	exercise
see	take	study
say	drink	sleep

Suggested Writing Assignments

1. Sometimes we take for granted the details that can make for powerful description. Choose a familiar object, one that you see all the time, and write a page of very close observation—"noting the burrs in the buck's coat," so to speak. What does this description reveal that you didn't know or forgot about the object? Use what you've written to craft a concise paragraph describing the object to someone else, choosing from among your observations those details you deem most important for conveying the character of the object.
2. Most descriptive writing is primarily visual—that is, it appeals to our sense of sight. Good description, however, often goes beyond the visual by appealing to one or more of the other senses: hearing, smell, taste, and touch. One way to heighten your awareness of these other senses is to purposefully deemphasize the visual

impressions you receive. For example, while standing on a busy street corner, sitting in a small Chinese restaurant, or walking into a movie theater after the show has started, carefully note what you hear, smell, taste, and feel. (It may help if you close your eyes to eliminate visual distractions as you carry out this experiment.) Use these sense impressions to write a brief description of the street corner, the Chinese restaurant, the movie theater, or another spot of your choosing.

CHAPTER **16**

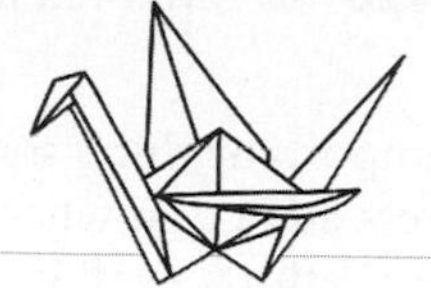

Process Analysis

When you give someone directions to your home, tell how to make ice cream, or explain how a president is elected, you are using **process analysis**. Process analysis usually arranges a series of events in order and relates them to one another, as narration and cause and effect do, but process analysis has a different emphasis. Whereas narration tells mainly *what* happens and cause and effect focuses on *why* it happens, process analysis tries to explain—in detail—*how* it happens.

There are two types of process analysis—directional and informational. The *directional* type provides instructions on how to do something. These instructions can be as brief as the directions for making instant coffee printed on the label or as complex as the directions in a manual for assembling a new gas grill. The purpose of directional process analysis is to give the reader directions to follow that will lead to the desired results.

Consider these directions for performing the Heimlich maneuver:

> Stand behind the victim, wrap your arms around the victim's waist, and make a fist. Place the thumb side of your fist against the victim's upper abdomen, below the ribcage and above the navel. Grasp your fist with your other hand and press into her upper abdomen with a quick upward thrust. Do not squeeze the ribcage. Repeat until the stuck object is expelled.
>
> –Joshua Piven and David Borgenicht,
> *The Worst-Case Scenario Survival Handbook: Life*

Piven and Borgenicht present clear, step-by-step directions for performing the Heimlich maneuver on a choking victim, being careful to present enough detail and instruction so that any person would be able to perform the maneuver.

After explaining in two previous paragraphs the first two steps involved in learning how to juggle, a student writer moves to the important third step. Notice here how he explains the third step, offers advice on what to do if things go wrong, and encourages his readers' efforts—all useful in directional process analysis:

> Step three is merely a continuum of "the exchange" with the addition of the third ball. Don't worry if you are confused—I will explain. Hold two balls in your right hand and one in your left. Make a perfect toss with one of your balls in your right hand and then an exchange with the one in your left hand. The ball coming from your left hand should now be exchanged with the, as of now, unused ball in your right hand. This process should be continued until you find yourself reaching under nearby chairs for bouncing tennis balls. It is true that many persons' backs and legs become sore when learning how to juggle because they've been picking up balls that they've inadvertently tossed around the room. Try practicing over a bed; you won't have to reach down so far. Don't get too upset if things aren't going well; you're probably keeping the same pace as everyone else at this stage.
>
> –William Peterson, student

The *informational* type of process analysis, on the other hand, tells how something works, how something is made, or how something occurs. You would use informational process analysis if you wanted to explain how the human heart functions, how an atomic bomb works, how hailstones are formed, how you selected the college you are attending, or how the polio vaccine was developed. Rather than giving specific directions, informational process analysis explains and informs.

In the illustration by Nigel Holmes on page 429, Jim Collins uses informational process analysis to explain a basic legislative procedure—how a bill becomes a law.

Clarity is crucial for successful process analysis. The most effective way to explain a process is to divide it into steps and to present those steps in a clear (usually chronological) sequence. Transitional words and phrases such as *first, next, after,* and *before* help to connect steps to one another. Naturally, you must be sure that no step is omitted or given out of order. Also, you may sometimes have to explain *why* a certain step is necessary, especially if it is not obvious. With intricate, abstract, or particularly difficult steps, you might use analogy or comparison to clarify the steps for your reader.

e macmillanhighered.com/mfw12e
e-readings > Sustainable America, *How to Compost in Your Apartment* [infographic]

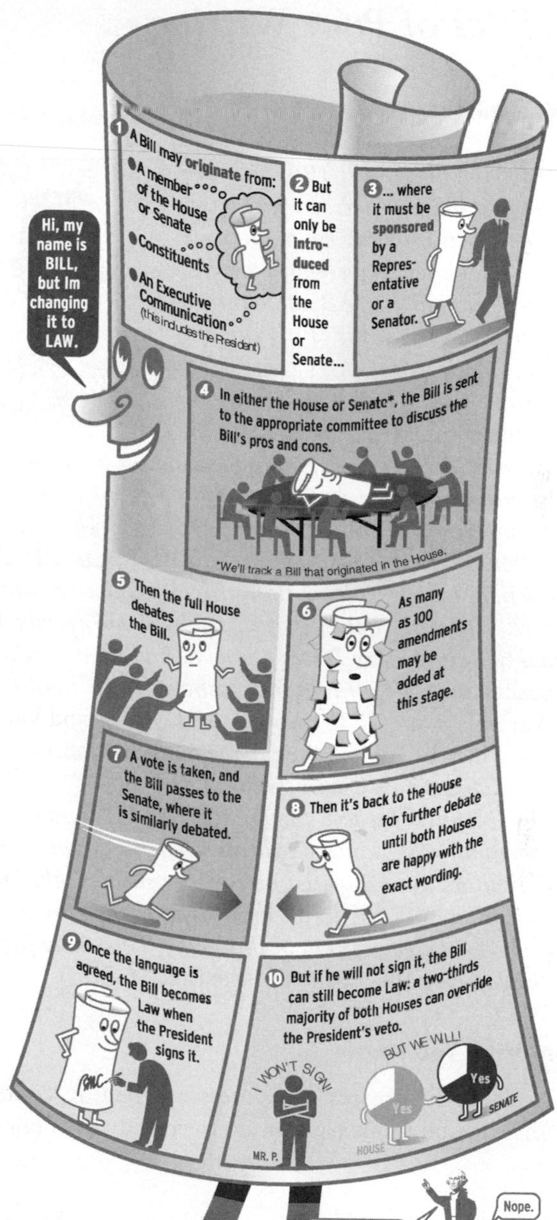

Graphic by Nigel Holmes

The Principles of Poor Writing

■ **Paul W. Merrill**

Rick Friedman

Paul Willard Merrill (1887–1961) was a noted astronomer whose specialty was spectroscopy—the measurement of a quantity as a function of either wavelength or frequency. Merrill earned his AB at Stanford University in 1908 and his PhD at the University of California in 1913. After spending three years at the University of Michigan, Merrill went to work at the National Bureau of Standards, concentrating on aerial photography in the visible and infrared spectra. He was the first to propose doing infrared astronomy from airplanes. In 1919, he joined the Mt. Wilson Observatory, located near Pasadena, California, where he spent more than three decades researching peculiar stars, especially long-period variables. He received the Bruce Medal and the Henry Draper Medal, had an asteroid and a lunar crater named after him, and authored four books: The Nature of Variable Stars *(1938),* Spectra of Long-Period Variable Stars *(1940),* Lines of the Chemical Elements in Astronomical Spectra *(1956), and* Space Chemistry *(1963).*

As Merrill states in the beginning of this essay, "Poor writing is so common that every educated person ought to know something about it." As a scientist himself, he suspects that many scientists who write poorly do so more by ear than by a set of principles, which he freely offers in this essay. This essay first appeared in the January 1947 issue of Scientific Monthly.

Reflecting on What You Know

Describe your three greatest weaknesses when it comes to writing. What do you think you can do to remedy each one?

Books and articles on good writing are numerous, but where can you find sound, practical advice on how to write poorly? Poor writing is so common that every educated person ought to know 1 something about it. Many scientists actually do write poorly, but they probably perform by ear without perceiving clearly how their results are achieved. An article on the principles of poor writing might help. The author considers himself well qualified to prepare such an article; he can write poorly without half trying.

The average student finds it surprisingly easy to acquire the usual tricks of poor writing. To do a consistently poor job, however, one must grasp a few essential principles: 2

1. Ignore the reader.
2. Be verbose, vague, and pompous.
3. Do not revise.

Ignore the Reader

The world is divided into two great camps: yourself and others. A little obscurity or indirection in writing will keep the others at a safe distance. Write as if for a diary. Keep your mind on a direct course between yourself and the subject; don't think of the reader—he makes a bad triangle. This is fundamental. Constant and alert consideration of the probable reaction of the reader is a serious menace to poor writing; moreover, it requires mental effort. A logical argument is that if you write poorly enough, your readers will be too few to merit any attention whatever. 3

Ignore the reader wherever possible. If the proposed title, for example, means something to you, stop right there; think no further. If the title baffles or misleads the reader, you have won the first round. Similarly, all the way through you must write for yourself, not for the reader. Practice a dead-pan technique, keeping your facts and ideas all on the same level of emphasis with no telltale hints of relative importance or logical sequence. Use long sentences containing many ideas loosely strung together. *And* is the connective most frequently employed in poor writing because it does not indicate cause and effect, nor does it distinguish major ideas from subordinate ones. *Because* seldom appears in poor writing, nor does the semicolon—both are replaced by *and*. 4

Camouflage transitions in thought. Avoid such connectives as *moreover, nevertheless, on the other hand*. If unable to resist the temptation to give some signal for a change in thought, use *however*. A poor sentence may well begin with *however* because to the reader, with no idea what comes next, *however* is too vague to be useful. A good sentence begins with the subject or with a phrase that needs emphasis. 5

The "hidden antecedent" is a common trick of poor writing. Use a pronoun to refer to a noun a long way back, or to one decidedly subordinate in thought or syntax; or the pronoun may refer to something not directly expressed. If you wish to play a little game with the reader, offer him the wrong antecedent as bait; you may be astonished how easy it is to catch the poor fish. 6

In ignoring the reader, avoid parallel constructions which give the thought away too easily. I need not elaborate, for you probably employ inversion frequently. It must have been a naive soul who said, "When the thought is parallel, let the phrases be parallel." 7

In every technical paper omit a few items that most readers need to know. You had to discover these things the hard way; why make it easy for the reader? Avoid defining symbols: never specify the units in which data are presented. Of course it will be beneath your dignity to give numerical values of constants in formulae. With these omissions, some papers may be too short; lengthen them by explaining things that do not need explaining. In describing tables, give special attention to self-explanatory headings; let the reader hunt for the meaning of *Pr*. 8

Be Verbose, Vague, and Pompous

The cardinal sin of poor writing is to be concise and simple. Avoid being specific: it ties you down. Use plenty of deadwood: include many superfluous words and phrases. Wishful thinking suggests to a writer that verbosity somehow serves as a cloak or even as a mystic halo by which an idea may be glorified. A cloud of words may conceal defects in observation or analysis, either by opacity or by diverting the reader's attention. Introduce abstract nouns at the drop of a hat—even in those cases where the magnitude of the motion in a downward direction is inconsiderable. Make frequent use of the words *case, character, condition, former* and *latter, nature, such, very*. 9

Poor writing, like good football, is strong on razzle-dazzle, weak on information. Adjectives are frequently used to bewilder the reader. It isn't much trouble to make them gaudy or hyperbolic; at least they can be flowery and inexact. 10

Deadwood

BIBLE: Render to Caesar the things that are Caesar's.

POOR: In the case of Caesar it might well be considered appropriate from a moral or ethical point of view to render to that potentate all of those goods and materials of whatever character or quality which can be shown to have had their original source in any portion of the domain of the latter.

SHAKESPEARE: I am no orator as Brutus is.

POOR: The speaker is not, what might be termed as adept in the profession of public speaking, as might be properly stated of Mr. Brutus. (Example from P. W. Swain. *Amer. J. Physics,* 13, 318, 1945.)

CONCISE: The dates of several observations are in doubt.

POOR: It should be mentioned that in the case of several observations there is room for considerable doubt concerning the correctness of the dates on which they were made.

REASONABLE: Exceptionally rapid changes occur in the spectrum.

POOR: There occur in the spectrum changes which are quite exceptional in respect to the rapidity of their advent.

REASONABLE: Formidable difficulties, both mathematical and observational, stand in the way.

POOR: There are formidable difficulties of both a mathematical and an observational nature that stand in the way.

Case

REASONABLE: Two sunspots changed rapidly.

POOR: There are two cases where sunspots changed with considerable rapidity.

REASONABLE: Three stars are red.

POOR: In three cases the stars are red in color.

Razzle-Dazzle

Immaculate precision of observation and extremely delicate calculations . . .

It would prove at once a world imponderable, etherealized. Our actions would grow gradific.

Well for us that the pulsing energy of the great life-giving dynamo in the sky never ceases. Well, too, that we are at a safe distance from the flame-licked whirlpools into which our earth might drop like a pellet of waste fluff shaken into the live coals of a grate fire.

Do Not Revise

Write hurriedly, preferably when tired. Have no plan; write down items as they occur to you. The article will thus be spontaneous and poor. Hand in your manuscript the moment it is finished. Rereading a few days later might lead to revision—which seldom, if ever, makes the writing worse. If you submit your manuscript to colleagues (a bad practice), pay no attention to their criticisms or comments. Later, resist firmly any editorial suggestion. Be strong and infallible; don't let anyone break down your personality. The critic may be trying to help you or he may have an ulterior motive, but the chance of his causing improvement in your writing is so great that you must be on guard. 11

Thinking Critically about This Reading

Why do you think Merrill might have written "The Principles of Poor Writing"? What special motivation do you think his career as a scientist might have provided him? Explain.

Questions for Study and Discussion

1. *Irony* is the use of words to suggest something different from their meaning. At what point in the essay did you realize that Merrill is being ironic? (Glossary: *Irony*) Did his title, introduction, or actual advice tip you off? Explain.
2. Is the author's process analysis the directional type or the informational type? What leads you to this conclusion?
3. Why has Merrill ordered his three process steps in this particular way? Could he have used a different order? (Glossary: *Organization*) Explain.
4. How useful are the author's examples in helping you understand his principles? Do you agree with all his examples? (Glossary: *Example*) Explain.
5. Why do you suppose Merrill chose to use irony to show his readers that they needed to improve their writing? (Glossary: *Irony*)

What do you see as the potential advantages and disadvantages to such a strategy?

6. In what types of writing situations is irony especially useful?

Classroom Activity Using Process Analysis

Most do-it-yourself jobs require that you follow a set process to achieve results. Make a list of the steps involved in doing one of the following household activities:

cleaning windows
repotting a plant
making burritos
changing a flat tire
unclogging a drain
doing laundry

Have at least one other person read your list of steps, checking for both the order of the steps and any omitted steps.

Suggested Writing Assignments

1. Write a process analysis in which you explain the steps you usually follow when deciding to make a purchase of some importance or expense to you. Hint: It's best to analyze your process with a specific product in mind. Do you compare brands, store prices, and so on? What are your priorities—that the item be stylish or durable, offer good overall value, or give high performance?
2. Try writing a process analysis essay in which you are ironic about the steps that need to be followed. For example, in an essay on how to lose weight by changing your diet or increasing your exercise, you might cast in a positive light all the things that absolutely should not be done. These might include parking as close as you can to your destination to avoid walking or buying a half gallon of your favorite ice cream instead of a pint because the half gallons are on sale.

Guacamole Is a Cruel Mistress

■ Marion Winik

Chris Hartlove

Marion Winik is an essayist and memoirist. She was born in 1958 in New York City and grew up on the New Jersey shore. A graduate of Brown University in 1978, she earned her MFA from Brooklyn College in 1983. Her first literary efforts were two books of poetry published by small presses: Nonstop *(1981) and* BoyCrazy *(1986). After being contacted by a literary agent, Winik published* Telling *(1994), her first collection of essays, some of which were previously published in* Texas Quarterly, Parenting, American Way, *the* Austin Chronicle, *and the* Houston Chronicle. *She wrote about her marriage to her husband Tony, who died of AIDS, in* First Comes Love *(1996), which became a New York Times Notable Book for that year. She followed it with an account of life as a single mom,* The Lunch-Box Chronicles: Notes from the Parenting Underground *(1998), and a book of advice,* Rules for the Unruly: Living an Unconventional Life *(2001). Among her other books are another collection of her essays,* Above Us Only Sky *(2005), and a book of very short essays in which she remembers people important in her life,* The Glen Rock Book of the Dead *(2008). Her most recent publications are* Highs in the Low Fifties *(2013) and an e-book titled* Guesswork. *She is an assistant professor at the University of Baltimore.*

In this essay, she describes how to make a favorite food, one she perfected during her years living in Texas. Could you follow these instructions to make her "famous" guacamole?

Reflecting on What You Know

Do you have a cooking "specialty"? What food would you most want to perfect? Why?

A couple of weeks ago in *The New York Times Book Review* "How to" issue, novelist Kate Christensen, who has recently moved to Maine, had a wonderful essay about making clam chowder. The theme of embracing a new place through its ingredients and dishes is a sweet one to me. It was the story of me and Texas, where I lived for 20 years. 1

The Tex-Mex food I am and always will be obsessed with is divided into two categories: things you can make at home, and things you should go to Texas to eat in a restaurant, like cheese enchiladas or huevos rancheros with fresh tortillas and refried beans. I won't dwell on the latter; it will just make us sad. Fortunately, in the do-at-home group is guacamole. 2

I first ate guacamole at a happy hour in Austin when I was 18. Guacamole was the sexiest word I had ever heard, especially as pronounced by the smoldering Chicano waiter: *wah-ka-molay*. Then I scooped it onto a tortilla chip and put it in my mouth—50 shades of rich avocado, piquant with garlic and tangy with citrus. It looked like money and tasted like sex. It was the perfect foil for the fire of the chiles in the salsa, the jalapeño slices on the nacho, the heat of the Texas sun. 3

These days guacamole is everywhere, including ready-made in tubs at the grocery store and prepared by hand in a molcajete at your table in an upscale Mexican restaurant. Some of this guacamole is okay, some is not. None is better than you can make yourself at home if you do it right. Right is a method I have come to after decades of experimentation, with my sons, who were born and raised in Texas, as a critical audience. Emphasis on the critical, as we shall see. 4

There are many ingredients commonly put in guacamole that should not be there. You will not need limes, cilantro, onion, tomatoes, salsa, or jalapeño. I love these things, but I save them for my salsa, which I make in the food processor to go with the guacamole. Or if I am feeling energetic, I chop them by hand. 5

The ideal guacamole has only four components: avocado, salt, lemon, and garlic. Lime is traditional, I know, but I believe lemon does more to bring out the other flavors. You might add a shot of Tabasco or other bottled pepper sauce. It's not that it will be inedible if you add the stuff I listed above, but it won't be as perfect in color, texture or taste. Like a picky six-year-old, I don't like little things in my guacamole. I certainly don't like the color it turns when you add tomatoes or grocery-store salsa. It should be an almost electric green. 6

I have not mentioned sour cream or mayonnaise. These no more belong in your guacamole than in your coffee. 7

Do not consider making guacamole if you do not have ripe avocados. An avocado is ripe when you can indent it slightly with your thumb, but it is still a little firm. It is overripe when it is soft and loose in its shell. These overripe avocados will be brown inside and taste nasty. If you can find only rock-hard avocados, put them in a paper bag on top of your refrigerator for a few days. If you want guacamole on Friday, the best bet is to buy avocados early in the week. Once they are ripe, move them to the fridge. There they will be fine for several days. 8

You should not prepare the guacamole much in advance of your guests' arrival or it will not be the right color. You can even wait until they get there. Hand them a cold Bohemia or a margarita on the rocks, and they will wait happily. (To make margaritas, mix in a pitcher one cup good silver tequila, one-quarter cup Triple Sec, the juice of two limes, two tablespoons Minute Maid frozen limeade. Pour over ice in glasses rimmed with salt.) If you have made salsa, you can put that out with chips while you whip up the guac. 9

Cut the avocado in half lengthwise with a knife. Pull the halves apart, remove the pit, and slip a spoon between the shell and the fruit to pry it out, then drop it into a bowl. It will probably come out whole, but if it doesn't, scrape out every last bit. 10

For every two avocados, use the juice of half a lemon (if the lemons are small or dry, maybe a whole one), and one or two cloves of garlic, put through a press. Mash these together with a fork. Add salt to taste. The salt is indispensable but too much will wreck it, and I am not the kind of girl to get out the measuring spoons. 11

Here as elsewhere, pride goeth before a fall. 12

My kids and I spent the Fourth of July with our old best friends from Texas, Jim and Jessica, who now live in DC. Jim was doing his famous barbecue and I was doing my famous guacamole. I saw that Jim had some kind of fancy salt sitting by his stove in a little dish. For some reason I thought it would be less salty than regular salt, so I put several generous pinches into the bowl, mixed it up, and almost spit out what I sampled. I had totally wrecked it and I had no more avocados. Trying to hide my error, I gaily chopped up a tomato and an onion, threw them in, and acted like nothing was wrong when I put the slightly brownish and soupy concoction on the table. 13

"What happened to the guacamole, Mom?" asked my son Hayes, staring at it dubiously. 14

I mumbled something about variety being the spice of life. I later 15
heard that Jim spoke privately to Hayes about the matter.

"What's the deal with your mom's guacamole?" he asked. 16

"Tomatoes," said Hayes grimly. "I know. I already talked to her 17
about it."

Well, they ate it—some of it. I ate most, actually, as one some- 18
times does in this situation.

The final pitfall to avoid is over-mashing. You don't want a ho- 19
mogeneous creamy texture. Part chunky, part smooth is good. And the chips make a difference too. The finest in Baltimore are homemade at Tortilleria Sinaloa on Eastern Avenue. Serve them warm if possible. Once you've got a famous guacamole on your hands, you have to give it its due.

Thinking Critically about This Reading

How does guacamole tie the author to the years she lived in Texas? What does her recipe remind her about "embracing a new place through its ingredients and dishes" (paragraph 1)?

Questions for Study and Discussion

1. Winik begins her process analysis by listing ingredients, like many recipes do. What does she include in her ideal guacamole? What ingredients does she exclude? What advice does she offer about selecting the ingredients?
2. What are the proper conditions for making guacamole? When and how is it best accomplished?
3. What are the steps for actually assembling the guacamole? How does Winik use directional process analysis to make her steps easy for a cook to reproduce?
4. Notice that Winik embeds a smaller process analysis in paragraph 9. How does her margarita recipe accomplish, on a smaller scale, the same tasks as her guacamole instructions?
5. Near the end of the essay, Winik includes a scene from a party for which she was supposed to produce her famous guacamole. What do you think this adds to the essay?

Classroom Activity Using Process Analysis

Review the following illustrations detailing the process of making an origami crane, like the ones depicted on the cover of this book. Try to make one yourself. Then, working with your classmates, try writing instructions to supplement these visual directions. Discuss what the written instructions add to the visual ones. Do they make the process easier?

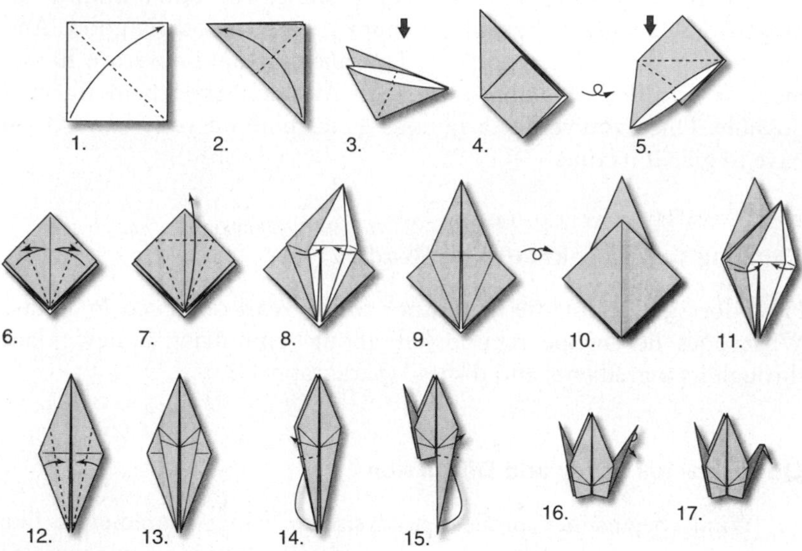

Suggested Writing Assignments

1. Winik takes her failed guacamole at the party as evidence of the saying "pride goeth before a fall" (12). Think of an episode from your own life that illustrates this maxim. You could choose a lighthearted subject, like Winik's, or address a more serious one. Write an essay about this episode, using informational process analysis to break down the series of events that led to your "fall."
2. Think about a familiar process that you believe needs improvement. After choosing your topic, do some background research. In your own words, write a process analysis in which you argue for a revision of the existing process. (Glossary: *Argumentation*) For example, are you happy with the process for dealing with recyclables where you live, the procedure for registering for classes, or the way dorm rooms are assigned on campus?

Why Leaves Turn Color in the Fall

Diane Ackerman

Ulf Andersen/Getty Images

Born in Waukegan, Illinois, in 1948, Diane Ackerman received degrees from Pennsylvania State University and Cornell University. She has written several books of poetry, a prose memoir, a play, and several collections of essays, including The Moon by Whale Light, and Other Adventures among Bats, Penguins, Crocodilians, and Whales *(1991);* A Natural History of Love *(1994);* The Rarest of the Rare: Vanishing Animals, Timeless Worlds *(1995);* The Curious Naturalist *(1998);* Deep Play *(1999);* Cultivating Delight *(2002);* An Alchemy of Mind: The Marvel and Mystery of the Brain *(2004);* The Zookeeper's Wife: A War Story *(2007);* Dawn Light: Dancing with Cranes and Other Ways to Start the Day *(2009); and* One Hundred Names for Love: A Stroke, a Marriage, and the Language of Healing *(2011). Ackerman has worked as a writer-in-residence at several major universities, has directed the Writers' Program at Washington University in St. Louis, and has been a staff writer at the* New Yorker. *She currently lives in upstate New York.*

Every October, residents of the northeastern United States are dazzled by a spectacular color show that sets them to wondering, "Where do the colors come from?" In the following selection from Ackerman's acclaimed A Natural History of the Senses *(1990), she lets us in on one of nature's secrets. Notice the way Ackerman shares her enthusiasm for the natural world as she explains the process by which autumn leaves assume their brilliant colors.*

Reflecting on What You Know

What is your favorite season? What about this season makes it your favorite—the weather, the activities and memories, the time of year, or a combination of these and other factors?

The stealth of autumn catches one unaware. Was that a goldfinch perching in the early September woods, or just the first turning leaf? A red-winged blackbird or a sugar maple closing up shop for the winter? Keen-eyed as leopards, we stand still and squint hard, looking for signs of movement. Early-morning frost sits heavily on the grass, and turns barbed wire into a string of stars. On a distant hill, a small square of yellow appears to be a lighted stage. At last the truth dawns on us: Fall is staggering in, right on schedule, with its baggage of chilly nights, macabre holidays, and spectacular, heart-stoppingly beautiful leaves. Soon the leaves will start cringing on the trees, and roll up in clenched fists before they actually fall off. Dry seedpods will rattle like tiny gourds. But first there will be weeks of gushing color so bright, so pastel, so confetti-like, that people will travel up and down the East Coast just to stare at it—a whole season of leaves. 1

Where do the colors come from? Sunlight rules most living things with its golden edicts. When the days begin to shorten, soon after the summer solstice on June 21, a tree reconsiders its leaves. All summer it feeds them so they can process sunlight, but in the dog days of summer the tree begins pulling nutrients back into its trunk and roots, pares down, and gradually chokes off its leaves. A corky layer of cells forms at the leaves' slender petioles, then scars over. Undernourished, the leaves stop producing the pigment chlorophyll, and photosynthesis ceases. Animals can migrate, hibernate, or store food to prepare for winter. But where can a tree go? It survives by dropping its leaves, and by the end of autumn only a few fragile threads of fluid-carrying xylem hold leaves to their stems. 2

A turning leaf stays partly green at first, then reveals splotches of yellow and red as the chlorophyll gradually breaks down. Dark green seems to stay longest in the veins, outlining and defining them. During the summer, chlorophyll dissolves in the heat and light, but it is also being steadily replaced. In the fall, on the other hand, no new pigment is produced, and so we notice the other colors that were always there, right in the leaf, although chlorophyll's shocking green hid them from view. With their camouflage gone, we see these colors for the first time all year, and marvel, but they were always there, hidden like a vivid secret beneath the hot glowing greens of summer. 3

The most spectacular range of fall foliage occurs in the northeastern United States and in eastern China, where the leaves are robustly colored, thanks in part to a rich climate. European maples don't achieve the same flaming reds as their American relatives, which 4 thrive on cold nights and sunny days. In Europe, the warm, humid weather turns the leaves brown or mildly yellow. Anthocyanin, the pigment that gives apples their red and turns leaves red or red-violet, is produced by sugars that remain in the leaf after the supply of nutrients dwindles. Unlike the carotenoids, which color carrots, squash, and corn, and turn leaves orange and yellow, anthocyanin varies from year to year, depending on the temperature and amount of sunlight. The fiercest colors occur in years when the fall sunlight is strongest and the nights are cool and dry (a state of grace scientists find vexing to forecast). This is also why leaves appear dizzyingly bright and clear on a sunny fall day: The anthocyanin flashes like a marquee.

Not all leaves turn the same colors. Elms, weeping willows, 5
and the ancient ginkgo all grow radiant yellow, along with hickories, aspens, bottlebrush buckeyes, cottonweeds, and tall, keening poplars. Basswood turns bronze, birches bright gold. Water-loving maples put on a symphonic display of scarlets. Sumacs turn red, too, as do flowering dogwoods, black gums, and sweet gums. Though some oaks yellow, most turn a pinkish brown. The farmlands also change color, as tepees of cornstalks and bales of shredded-wheat-textured hay stand drying in the fields. In some spots, one slope of a hill may be green and the other already in bright color, because the hillside facing south gets more sun and heat than the northern one.

An odd feature of the colors is that they don't seem to have any 6
special purpose. We are predisposed to respond to their beauty, of course. They shimmer with the colors of sunset, spring flowers, the tawny buff of a colt's pretty rump, the shuddering pink of a blush. Animals and flowers color for a reason—adaptation to their environment—but there is no adaptive reason for leaves to color so beautifully in the fall any more than there is for the sky or ocean to be blue. It's just one of the haphazard marvels the planet bestows every year. We find the sizzling colors thrilling, and in a sense they dupe us. Colored like living things, they signal death and disintegration. In time, they will become fragile and, like the body, return to dust. They are as we hope our own fate will be when we die: Not to vanish, just to sublime from one beautiful state into another. Though leaves lose their green life, they bloom with urgent colors, as the woods grow mummified day by day, and Nature becomes more carnal, mute, and radiant.

We call the season "fall," from the Old English *feallan,* to fall, which leads back through time to the Indo-European *phol,* which also means to fall. So the word and the idea are both extremely ancient, and haven't really changed since the first of our kind needed a name for fall's leafy abundance. As we say the word, we're reminded of that other Fall, in the garden of Eden, when fig leaves never withered and scales fell from our eyes. Fall is the time when leaves fall from the trees, just as spring is when flowers spring up, summer is when we simmer, and winter is when we whine from the cold. 7

Children love to play in piles of leaves, hurling them into the air like confetti, leaping into soft unruly mattresses of them. For children, leaf fall is just one of the odder figments of Nature, like hailstones or snowflakes. Walk down a lane overhung with trees in the never-never land of autumn, and you will forget about time and death, lost in the sheer delicious spill of color. Adam and Eve concealed their nakedness with leaves, remember? Leaves have always hidden our awkward secrets. 8

But how do the colored leaves fall? As a leaf ages, the growth hormone, auxin, fades, and cells at the base of the petiole divide. Two or three rows of small cells, lying at right angles to the axis of the petiole, react with water, then come apart, leaving the petioles hanging on by only a few threads of xylem. A light breeze, and the leaves are airborne. They glide and swoop, rocking in invisible cradles. They are all wing and may flutter from yard to yard on small whirlwinds or updrafts, swiveling as they go. Firmly tethered to earth, we love to see things rise up and fly—soap bubbles, balloons, birds, fall leaves. They remind us that the end of a season is capricious, as is the end of life. We especially like the way leaves rock, careen, and swoop as they fall. Everyone knows the motion. Pilots sometimes do a maneuver called a "falling leaf," in which the plane loses altitude quickly and on purpose, by slipping first to the right, then to the left. The machine weighs a ton or more, but in one pilot's mind it is a weightless thing, a falling leaf. She has seen the motion before, in the Vermont woods where she played as a child. Below her the trees radiate gold, copper, and red. Leaves are falling, although she can't see them fall, as she falls, swooping down for a closer view. 9

At last the leaves leave. But first they turn color and thrill us for weeks on end. Then they crunch and crackle underfoot. They *shush,* as children drag their small feet through leaves heaped along the curb. Dark, slimy mats of leaves cling to one's heels after a rain. 10

A damp, stuccolike mortar of semidecayed leaves protects the tender shoots with a roof until spring, and makes a rich humus. An occasional bulge or ripple in the leafy mounds signals a shrew or a field mouse tunneling out of sight. Sometimes one finds in fossil stones the imprint of a leaf, long since disintegrated, whose outlines remind us how detailed, vibrant, and alive are the things of this earth that perish.

Thinking Critically about This Reading

In paragraphs 2 and 6, Ackerman attributes some human qualities to nature and to the trees. What effect does her personification have on you as a reader? Why do you think she chose to use these figures of speech in a process analysis essay? (Glossary: *Figure of Speech*)

Questions for Study and Discussion

1. According to Ackerman, exactly what causes leaves to change color? What particular conditions cause the brightest colors in autumn leaves?
2. Briefly summarize the steps of the process by which leaves change color.
3. Not only does Ackerman describe the process by which leaves change color, but she includes other information as well. For example, she uses cause-and-effect analysis to explain why leaves are particularly bright some years, why trees turn color at different rates, and why leaves lose their grip and fall from the trees. (Glossary: *Cause and Effect*) Did you find this information useful? What, if anything, did it add to your appreciation of Ackerman's process analysis?
4. How has Ackerman organized her essay? (Glossary: *Organization*) Explain why this organization seems most appropriate for her subject.
5. Identify several figures of speech—simile, metaphor, and personification—that Ackerman uses, and explain how each functions in the context of her essay. (Glossary: *Figure of Speech*)
6. Reread Ackerman's concluding sentence. What does she mean? Why do you suppose she chose to end her essay this way? In

what ways, if any, is it a particularly appropriate ending for her essay? (Glossary: *Beginnings and Endings*)

Classroom Activity Using Process Analysis

To give another person clear directions on how to do something, you need to have a thorough understanding of the process yourself. Analyze one of the following activities by listing any materials you might need and the steps you would follow in completing it:

studying for an exam
determining miles per gallon for an automobile
finding a person's contact information on the Internet
beginning an exercise program
getting from where your writing class meets to where you normally have lunch
installing new software on your computer
writing an essay
adding or dropping a class from your course schedule

Have at least one other person read your list of materials and the steps involved, checking for anything you may have omitted.

Suggested Writing Assignments

1. Our world is filled with hundreds of natural processes—for example, the cycle of the moon, the rising and setting of the sun, the germination of a seed, the movement of the tides, the formation of a tornado, the transformation of a caterpillar into a butterfly or moth, and the flowering of a tree. Using Ackerman's essay as a model, write an informational process analysis explaining one such natural process.
2. Select one of the tasks listed in the Classroom Activity, and write a brief essay in which you give directions for successfully performing the task.

CHAPTER **17**

Definition

Definition allows you to communicate precisely what you want to say. At its most basic level, you will frequently need to define key words. Your reader needs to know just what you mean when you use unfamiliar words (such as *accoutrement*), words that are open to various interpretations (such as *liberal*), or familiar words that are used in a particular sense. Important terms that are not defined or that are defined inaccurately confuse readers and hamper communication.

Consider the opening paragraph from a student essay titled "Secular Mantras":

> Remember *The Little Engine That Could*? That's the story about the tiny locomotive that hauled the train over the mountain when the big, rugged locomotives wouldn't. Remember how the Little Engine strained and heaved and chugged, "I think I can—I think I can—I think I can" until she reached the top of the mountain? That's a perfect example of a secular mantra in action. You have probably used a secular mantra (pronounce it "mantruh") already today. It's any word or group of words that helps you use your energy when you consciously repeat it to yourself. You must understand two qualities about secular mantras to be able to recognize one.
>
> –Keith Eldred, student

Eldred engages his readers with the story of the Little Engine and then uses that example to lead into a definition of *secular mantra*. He concludes the paragraph with a sentence that tells readers what is coming next.

There are three basic ways to define a word, and each is useful in its own way. The first method is to give a *synonym*—that is, to use a word that has nearly the same meaning as the word you wish to define (*face* for *countenance, nervousness* for *anxiety*). No two words have exactly the same meaning, but you can nevertheless pair an unfamiliar word with a familiar one and thereby clarify your meaning.

Another way to define a word quickly, often within a single sentence, is to give a *formal definition*—that is, to place the term in a general class and then distinguish it from other members of that class by describing its particular characteristics, as in the following examples:

Word	*Class*	*Characteristics*
A watch	is a mechanical device	that is used for telling time and is usually carried or worn.
Semantics	is an area of linguistics	that is concerned with the study of the meaning of words.

The third method of defining a word is to give an *extended definition*—that is, to use one or more paragraphs (or even an entire essay) to define a new or difficult term or to rescue a controversial word from misconceptions that may obscure its meaning. In an essay-length extended definition, you provide your readers with information about the meaning of a single word, a concept, or an object. You must consider what your readers already know, or think they know, about your topic. Are there popular misconceptions that need to be corrected? Are some aspects of the topic seldom considered? Have particular experiences helped you understand the topic? You can use synonyms or formal definitions in an extended definition, but you must convince readers to accept your particular understanding of the word, concept, or object.

In the following two-paragraph sequence, the writers provide an extended definition of *restorative justice,* an important concept in the field of criminal justice:

> When an individual meets a violent death through crime, the entire community suffers. The victim's family members and friends lose not only their loved one and the future they planned to share but also a sense of security and trust in other people. Community members are shocked and disheartened when a murder occurs in their neighborhood, and they respond with sadness, fear, anger, and distrust. The criminal justice response focuses on arresting, convicting, and punishing the offender for his actions. During such tragedies, the losses suffered by the offender and his family members typically are overlooked. Restorative justice, by recognizing the connections and relationships (whether healthy, strained, or contemptuous) among offenders, victims, their family members, and

> the community seeks to address crime in a more holistic manner. It seeks to heal and strengthen communities by providing a restorative process for everyone affected by a serious crime.
>
> Howard Zehr, a pioneer in restorative justice theory, practice, and scholarship, outlines the key principles of restorative justice: "1) crime is a violation of people and of interpersonal relationships; 2) violations create obligations; 3) the central obligation is to put right the wrongs." Too often the criminal justice system loses sight of human nature, causing it to ignore many of the emotional consequences of the entire process. Even though the present criminal justice system leads to a verdict and a judgment that purports to right the scales of justice, the collateral damage can be staggering. The offender is often encouraged by his lawyers to deny or minimize responsibility. Though punished, the offender is rarely held personally accountable by publicly acknowledging his guilt, facing his victims, and offering an apology or the truth. In fact, the traditional justice system encourages many offenders to continue to deny responsibility, even in prison, and to blame others for their own actions. Restorative justice encourages offender accountability by stressing dialogue and truth-telling as central to putting things right and repairing personal relationships.
>
> –Elizabeth Beck, Sarah Britto, and Arlene Andrews, *In the Shadow of Death*

Another term that illustrates the need for extended definition is *obscene*. What is obscene? Books that are banned in one school system are considered perfectly acceptable in another. Movies that are shown in one town cannot be shown in a neighboring town. The meaning of *obscene* has been clouded by contrasting personal opinions as well as by conflicting social norms. Therefore, if you use the term *obscene* (and especially if you tackle the issue of obscenity itself), you must define clearly and thoroughly what you mean by that term—that is, you have to give an extended definition. There are a number of methods you might use to develop such a definition. You could define *obscene* by explaining what it does not mean. You could also make your meaning clear by narrating an experience, by comparing and contrasting it to related terms (such as *pornographic* or *erotic*), by citing specific examples, or by classifying the various types of obscenity. Any of these methods could help you develop an effective definition.

e **macmillanhighered.com/mfw12e**
e-readings > National Science Foundation, *The Tragedy of the Commons* [animation]

What Is Crime?

■ **Lawrence M. Friedman**

Courtesy of Lawrence M. Friedman

Born in 1930 in Chicago, Lawrence M. Friedman is currently Marion Rice Kirkwood Professor of Law at Stanford University. He earned his undergraduate degree in 1948 and his law degree in 1951, both from the University of Chicago. After serving a two-year stint in the military, he practiced law in Chicago before embarking on his long and distinguished teaching and writing career. He taught law at St. Louis University and the University of Wisconsin before settling at Stanford in 1968. A prize-winning expert on U.S. legal history, Friedman is perhaps best known for A History of American Law *(1973) and its sequel,* American Law in the Twentieth Century *(2002). His other books include* The Republic of Choice: Law, Authority, and Culture *(1990),* The Horizontal Society *(1999), and* Law in America: A Short History *(2002). In 2011, he wrote* Inside the Castle: Law and the Family in 20th Century America. *He has been president of the American Society for Legal History, the Law and Society Association, and the Research Committee on Sociology of Law.*

The following selection is taken from the introduction to Crime and Punishment in American History *(1993), a book in which Friedman traces the response to crime throughout U.S. history. Here he explains what it takes for a certain behavior or act to be considered a crime.*

Reflecting on What You Know

How would you answer the question "What is crime?" For you, what makes some acts criminal and others not? Explain.

There is no real answer to the question, What is crime? There are popular ideas about crime: crime is bad behavior, antisocial behavior, blameworthy acts, and the like. But in a very basic sense, crime is a *legal* concept: what makes some conduct criminal, and 1 other conduct not, is the fact that some, but not others, are "against the law."*

2 Crimes, then, are forbidden acts. But they are forbidden in a special way. We are not supposed to break contracts, drive carelessly, slander people, or infringe copyrights; but these are not (usually) criminal acts. The distinction between a *civil* and a *criminal* case is fundamental in our legal system. A civil case has a life cycle entirely different from that of a criminal case. If I slander somebody, I might be dragged into court, and I might have to open my checkbook and pay damages; but I cannot be put in prison or executed, and if I lose the case, I do not get a criminal "record." Also, in a slander case (or a negligence case, or a copyright-infringement case), the injured party pays for, runs, and manages the case herself. He or she makes the decisions and hires the lawyers. The case is entirely voluntary. Nobody forces anybody to sue. I can have a good claim, a valid claim, and simply forget it, if I want.

3 In a criminal case, in theory at least, society is the victim, along with the "real" victim—the person robbed or assaulted or cheated. The crime may be punished without the victim's approval (though, practically speaking, the complaining witness often has a crucial role to play). In "victimless crimes" (gambling, drug dealing, certain sex offenses), there is nobody to complain; both parties are equally guilty (or innocent). Here the machine most definitely has a mind of its own. In criminal cases, moreover, the state pays the bills. It should be pointed out, however, that the further back in history one goes, the more this pat[1] distinction between "civil" and "criminal" tends to blur. In some older cultures, the line between private vengeance and public prosecution was indistinct or completely absent. Even in our own history, we shall see some evidence that the cleavage between "public" and "private" enforcement was not always deep and pervasive.

4 All sorts of nasty acts and evil deeds are not against the law, and thus not crimes. These include most of the daily events that anger or irritate us, even those we might consider totally outrageous. Ordinary lying is not a crime; cheating on a wife or husband is not a crime in

*Most criminologists, but not all, would agree with this general formulation; for an exception see Michael R. Gottfredson and Travis Hirschi, *A General Theory of Crime* (1990). [Friedman's note]

[1]*pat:* seemingly precise.

most states (at one time it was, almost everywhere); charging a huge markup at a restaurant or store is not, in general, a crime; psychological abuse is (mostly) not a crime.

Before some act can be isolated and labeled as a crime, there must be 5
a special, solemn, social, and *political* decision. In our society, Congress, a state legislature, or a city government has to pass a law or enact an ordinance adding the behavior to the list of crimes. Then this behavior, like a bottle of poison, carries the proper label and can be turned over to the heavy artillery of law for possible enforcement.

We repeat: crime is a *legal* concept. This point, however, can lead 6
to a misunderstanding. The law, in a sense, "creates" the crimes it punishes; but what creates criminal law? Behind the law, and above it, enveloping it, is society; before the law made the crime a crime, some aspect of social reality transformed the behavior, culturally speaking, into a crime; and it is the social context that gives the act, and the legal responses, their real meaning. Justice is supposed to be blind, which is to say impartial. This may or may not be so, but justice is blind in one fundamental sense: justice is an abstraction.[2] It cannot see or act on its own. It cannot generate its own norms, principles, and rules. Everything depends on society. Behind every *legal* judgment of criminality is a more powerful, more basic *social* judgment; a judgment that this behavior, whatever it is, deserves to be outlawed and punished.

Thinking Critically about This Reading

What does Friedman mean when he states, "Behind every *legal* judgment of criminality is a more powerful, more basic *social* judgment; a judgment that this behavior, whatever it is, deserves to be outlawed and punished" (paragraph 6)? According to Friedman, what must happen before any offensive behavior can be deemed criminal?

Questions for Study and Discussion

1. What general definition of *crime* do most criminologists agree on, according to Friedman?
2. What are the major differences between a criminal case and a civil case? Why does Friedman make this distinction? Explain.

[2]*abstraction:* a theoretical concept.

3. In what sense is society the "victim" in a criminal case (3)? Do you believe that it is important for society to join with the "real" victim in prosecuting a criminal case? Explain.
4. Friedman states that "all sorts of nasty acts and evil deeds are not against the law, and thus not crimes" (4). What examples does he provide to illustrate this point? (Glossary: *Example*) Do any of his examples surprise you? Explain.
5. What does Friedman mean by "crime is a *legal* concept" (1)? Why do you think he repeats this statement in paragraph 6? According to Friedman, what misunderstanding can the statement lead to?

Classroom Activity Using Definition

Define one of the following terms formally by putting it in a class and then differentiating it from other words in the class. (See p. 448.)

potato chips	tenor saxophone	sociology	Monopoly (the game)
love	physical therapy	chickadee	Buddhism

Suggested Writing Assignments

1. Write an essay recounting a time when you were the victim of somebody's outrageous behavior. What were the circumstances of the incident? How did you respond at the time? What action, if any, did you take at a later time? According to Friedman's definition, was the behavior criminal?
2. Some of the most pressing social issues in American life today are further complicated by imprecise definitions of critical terms. Various medical cases, for example, have brought worldwide attention to the legal and medical definitions of the word *death*. Debates continue about the meanings of other controversial words. Using one of the following controversial terms or another of your choosing, write an essay in which you discuss its definitions and the problems associated with defining it.

minority (ethnic)	theft	equality
monopoly (business)	lying	success
morality	addiction	pornography
cheating	life	marriage

The Company Man

■ Ellen Goodman

Mikki Ansin

Ellen Goodman, American journalist and Pulitzer Prize–winning columnist, was born in Boston in 1941. After graduating cum laude from Radcliffe College in 1963, she worked as a reporter and researcher for Newsweek. *In 1967, she began working at the* Boston Globe *and in 1974 became a full-time columnist. Her regular column, "At Large," was syndicated by the* Washington Post *Writers Group and appeared in nearly four hundred newspapers across the country. She wrote her last column on January 1, 2010. In addition, her writing has appeared in* McCall's, Harper's Bazaar, *and* Family Circle, *and her commentaries have been broadcast on radio and television. Several collections of Goodman's columns have been published as books, including* Close to Home *(1979),* At Large *(1981),* Keeping in Touch *(1985),* Value Judgments *(1995),* Making Sense *(1999), and* Paper Trail: Common Sense in Uncommon Times *(2004).*

In the following essay, taken from Close to Home, *Goodman defines* workaholic *by offering a poignant example.*

Reflecting on What You Know

Many jobs have regular hours, but some—like journalism, medicine, and high-level management—are less predictable and may require far more time. Think about your career goals. Do you think that you will emphasize your work life more than your home life? How much time beyond the standard forty work hours per week are you willing to spend to advance your career or support your family? Has this issue influenced your choice of career in any way, or do you anticipate that it will? Explain.

He worked himself to death, finally and precisely, at 3:00 A.M. Sunday morning. 1

The obituary didn't say that, of course. It said that he died of a coronary thrombosis—I think that was it—but everyone among his friends and acquaintances knew it instantly. He was a perfect Type A, a workaholic, a classic, they said to each other and shook their heads—and thought for five or ten minutes about the way they lived. 2

This man who worked himself to death finally and precisely at 3:00 A.M. Sunday morning—on his day off—was fifty-one years old and a vice-president. He was, however, one of six vice-presidents, and one of three who might conceivably—if the president died or retired soon enough—have moved to the top spot. Phil knew that. 3

He worked six days a week, five of them until eight or nine at night, during a time when his own company had begun the four-day week for everyone but the executives. He worked like the Important People. He had no outside "extracurricular interests," unless, of course, you think about a monthly golf game that way. To Phil, it was work. He always ate egg salad sandwiches at his desk. He was, of course, overweight, by twenty or twenty-five pounds. He thought it was okay, though, because he didn't smoke. 4

On Saturdays, Phil wore a sports jacket to the office instead of a suit, because it was the weekend. 5

He had a lot of people working for him, maybe sixty, and most of them liked him most of the time. Three of them will be seriously considered for his job. The obituary didn't mention that. 6

But it did list his "survivors" quite accurately. He is survived by his wife, Helen, forty-eight years old, a good woman of no particular marketable skills, who worked in an office before marrying and mothering. She had, according to her daughter, given up trying to compete with his work years ago, when the children were small. A company friend said, "I know how much you will miss him." And she answered, "I already have." 7

"Missing him all these years," she must have given up part of herself which had cared too much for the man. She would be "well taken care of." 8

His "dearly beloved" eldest of the "dearly beloved" children is a hard-working executive in a manufacturing firm down South. In the day and a half before the funeral, he went around the neighborhood researching his father, asking the neighbors what he was like. They were embarrassed. 9

His second child is a girl, who is twenty-four and newly married. She lives near her mother and they are close, but whenever she was 10 alone with her father, in a car driving somewhere, they had nothing to say to each other.

The youngest is twenty, a boy, a high-school graduate who has spent the last couple of years, like a lot of his friends, doing enough odd jobs to stay in grass and food. He was the one who tried to grab at his father, and tried to mean enough to him to keep the man at home. He was his father's favorite. Over the last two years, Phil stayed up nights worrying about the boy. 11

The boy once said, "My father and I only board here." 12

At the funeral, the sixty-year-old company president told the forty-eight-year-old widow that the fifty-one-year-old deceased had meant much to the company and would be missed and would be hard to replace. The widow didn't look him in the eye. She was afraid he would read her bitterness and, after all, she would need him to straighten out the finances—the stock options and all that. 13

Phil was overweight and nervous and worked too hard. If he wasn't at the office, he was worried about it. Phil was a Type A, a heart-attack natural. You could have picked him out in a minute from a lineup. 14

So when he finally worked himself to death, at precisely 3:00 A.M. Sunday morning, no one was really surprised. 15

By 5:00 P.M. the afternoon of the funeral, the company president had begun, discreetly of course, with care and taste, to make inquiries about his replacement. One of three men. He asked around: "Who's been working the hardest?" 16

Thinking Critically about This Reading

What is the significance of Phil's youngest son's statement, "My father and I only board here" (paragraph 12)? What does it convey about Phil's relationship with his family?

Questions for Study and Discussion

1. After reading Goodman's essay, how would you define *company man*? As you define the term, consider what such a man is not, as well as what he is. Is *company man* synonymous with *workaholic*? Explain.
2. In paragraph 4, Goodman says that Phil worked like "the Important People." How would you define that term in the context of the essay? (Glossary: *Definition*)

3. What is Goodman's purpose? (Glossary: *Purpose*) Explain.
4. Do you think Goodman's unemotional tone is appropriate for her purpose? (Glossary: *Tone; Purpose*) Why or why not?
5. Goodman repeats the day and time that Phil worked himself to death. Why are those facts important enough to bear repetition? What about them is ironic? (Glossary: *Irony*)

Classroom Activity Using Definition

The connotation of the term *workaholic* depends on the context. For Phil's employers—and at his workplace in general—the term had a positive connotation. For those who knew Phil outside the workplace, it had a negative one. Choose one of the following terms, and provide two definitions—one positive and one negative—that could apply to the term in different contexts.

go-getter	overachiever
party animal	mover and shaker

Suggested Writing Assignments

1. A procrastinator—a person who continually puts off responsibilities—is very different from a workaholic. Write an essay, modeled on Goodman's, that uses an extended example to define this personality type.
2. One issue Goodman does not raise is how a person becomes a workaholic. Write an essay in which you speculate about how someone might develop workaholism. How does a desirable trait like a strong work ethic begin to affect someone adversely? How might workaholism be avoided?
3. What insights does Goodman's essay give you about work in the corporate world? What do you think a worker like Phil owes to his company, and what does the company owe to him? Write an essay in which you describe the ideal relationship between work and personal life. For support, use examples from Goodman's essay or your own work experiences and observations.

What Happiness Is

■ Eduardo Porter

Miriam Berkley

Eduardo Porter was born in 1963, in Phoenix, Arizona, of a Mexican mother and an American father. When he was six, his family moved to Mexico City, where he lived until he graduated from the Universidad Nacional Autónoma de México in 1987 with a degree in physics. Later he earned an MSc from the Imperial College of Science and Technology in London, England. Porter started his career in journalism at Notimex, a Mexican news agency, where he wrote mostly in Spanish about the stock market and the financial world. From 1996 to 2000, he worked for America Economia, *a business magazine for Latin America. In 2000, he moved to the Los Angeles bureau of the* Wall Street Journal, *where he covered issues related to the Hispanic community. Porter joined the* New York Times *in 2004, first as an economics writer in the newsroom and later as a member of the editorial board. Once at the* Times, *he had the opportunity to explore his long-standing interest in the ubiquity of prices. "Slowly," he shared, "the broader idea that prices are involved in every one of our decisions, that economics affect people's behavior gelled for me." His research resulted in* The Price of Everything: Solving the Mystery of Why We Pay What We Do, *published in 2011.*

In the following selection, taken from the "The Price of Happiness" chapter in The Price of Everything, *Porter sheds some light on the "slippery concept" of happiness. As you read his essay, notice how he explores many different perspectives—from Gandhi, Lincoln, and Kennedy to Freud and even Snoopy—on the meaning of happiness, the pursuit of which is guaranteed in the U.S. Constitution, before settling on a broad definition from the world of economics.*

Reflecting on What You Know

What makes you happy—a good relationship? A delicious meal? Satisfying or rewarding work? Money? Is *happiness* a term that's easy for you to define, or do you find it somewhat elusive? Explain.

Happiness is a slippery concept, a bundle of meanings with no precise, stable definition. Lots of thinkers have taken a shot at it. "Happiness is when what you think, what you say, and what you do are in harmony," proposed Gandhi. Abraham Lincoln argued "most people are about as happy as they make up their minds to be." Snoopy, the beagle-philosopher in *Peanuts*, took what was to my mind the most precise stab at the underlying epistemological problem. "My life has no purpose, no direction, no aim, no meaning, and yet I'm happy. I can't figure it out. What am I doing right?" 1

Most psychologists and economists who study happiness agree that what they prefer to call "subjective well-being" comprises three parts: satisfaction, meant to capture how people judge their lives measured up against their aspirations; positive feelings like joy; and the absence of negative feelings like anger. 2

It does exist. It relates directly to objective measures of people's quality of life. Countries whose citizens are happier on average report lower levels of hypertension in the population. Happier people are less likely to come down with a cold. And if they get one, they recover more quickly. People who are wounded heal more quickly if they are satisfied with their lives. People who say they are happier smile more often, sleep better, report themselves to be in better health, and have happier relatives. And some research suggests happiness and suicide rates move in opposite directions. Happy people don't want to die. 3

Still, this conceptual mélange[1] can be difficult to measure. Just ask yourself how happy you are, say, on a scale of one to three, as used by the General Social Survey. Then ask yourself what you mean by that. Answers wander when people are confronted with these questions. We entangle gut reactions with thoughtful analysis, and confound sensations of immediate pleasure with evaluations of how life meshes with our long-term aspirations. We might say we know what will make us happy in the future—fame, fortune, or maybe a partner. But when we get to the future, it rarely does. While we do seem to know how to tell the difference between lifelong satisfaction and immediate well-being, the immediate tends to contaminate the ontological. 4

During an experiment in the 1980s, people who found a dime on top of a Xerox machine before responding to a happiness survey 5

[1]*mélange:* a mixture of often incongruous elements.

reported a much higher sense of satisfaction with life than those who didn't. Another study found that giving people a chocolate bar improved their satisfaction with their lives. One might expect that our satisfaction with the entire span of our existence would be a fairly stable quantity—impervious to day-to-day joys and frustrations. Yet people often give a substantially different answer to the same question about lifetime happiness if it is asked again one month later.

Sigmund Freud argued that people "strive after happiness; they want to become happy and to remain so." Translating happiness into the language of economics as "utility," most economists would agree. This simple proposition gives them a powerful tool to resist Bobby Kennedy's proposal to measure not income but something else. For if happiness is what people strive for, one needn't waste time trying to figure out what makes people happy. One must only look at what people do. The fact of the matter is that people mostly choose to work and make money. Under this optic, economic growth is the outcome of our pursuit of well-being. It is what makes us happy. 6

This approach has limitations. We often make puzzling choices that do not make us consistently happier. We smoke despite knowing about cancer and emphysema. We gorge on chocolate despite knowing it will make us unhappy ten pounds down the road. Almost two thirds of Americans say they are overweight, according to a recent Gallup poll. But only a quarter say they are seriously trying to lose weight. In the 1980s a new discipline called Prospect Theory—also known as behavioral economics—deployed the tools of psychology to analyze economic behavior. It found all sorts of peculiar behaviors that don't fit economics' standard understanding of what makes us happy. For instance, losing something reduces our happiness more than winning the same thing increases it—a quirk known as loss aversion. We are unable to distinguish between choices that have slightly different odds of making us happy. We extrapolate from a few experiences to arrive at broad, mostly wrong conclusions. We herd, imitating successful behaviors around us. 7

Still, it remains generally true that we pursue what we think makes us happy—and though some of our choices may not make us happy, some will. Legend has it that Abraham Lincoln was riding in a carriage one rainy evening, telling a friend that he agreed with economists' theory that people strove to maximize their happiness, when he caught sight of a pig stuck in a muddy riverbank. He ordered the carriage to stop, got out, and pulled the pig out of the muck to safety. 8

When the friend pointed out to a mud-caked Lincoln that he had just disproved his statement by putting himself through great discomfort to save a pig, Lincoln retorted: "What I did was perfectly consistent with my theory. If I hadn't saved that pig I would have felt terrible."

So perhaps the proper response to Bobby Kennedy's angst is to agree that pursuing economic growth often has negative side effects—carbon emissions, environmental degradation—that are likely to make us unhappy down the road. Still, it remains true that American citizens—and the citizens of much of the world—expend enormous amounts of time and energy pursuing more money and a bigger GDP because they think it will improve their well-being. And that will make them happy. 9

Thinking Critically about This Reading

What do you think Porter means when he says, "While we do seem to know how to tell the difference between lifelong satisfaction and immediate well-being, the immediate tends to contaminate the ontological" (paragraph 4). Do you agree with Porter?

Questions for Study and Discussion

1. Porter opens his essay with the statement, "Happiness is a slippery concept, a bundle of meanings with no precise, stable definition." How does he illustrate this generalization? (Glossary: *Example*) How effective did you find this beginning? (Glossary: *Beginnings and Endings*)
2. According to Porter, what are the three parts of what psychologists and economists call "subjective well-being" (2)? Why is it useful to have this information when discussing the meaning of happiness? Explain.
3. In what ways is happiness related to a person's "quality of life" (3)? What character traits, according to Porter, do happy people possess?
4. What point does Porter make with the story about Abraham Lincoln and the pig?
5. How does Porter use economics to explain what he thinks happiness is? What are the limitations, if any, of his economic model?

Classroom Activity Using Definition

Definitions often depend on perspective, as Porter illustrates in his essay with the word *happiness*. Discuss with your classmates other words or terms (*competition*, *wealth*, *success*, *jerk*, *superstar*, *failure*, *poverty*, *luxury*, *beauty*) whose definitions depend on one's perspective. Choose several of these words, and write brief definitions for each of them from your perspective. Share your definitions with your classmates, and discuss how perspective affects the way we define things in our world differently.

Suggested Writing Assignments

1. Using Porter's essay or Asimov's "Intelligence" (pp. 54–55) as a model, write a short essay in which you define one of the following abstract terms or another similar term of your choosing. Before beginning to write, you may find it helpful to review what you and your classmates discovered in the Classroom Activity for this selection.

friendship	freedom	trust
commitment	love	hate
peace	liberty	charm
success	failure	beauty

2. How much stock do you put in Porter's claim that "people mostly choose to work and make money. . . . It is what makes us happy" (6)? Or do you side with Bobby Kennedy's "proposal to measure not income but something else"? Write an essay in which you present your position in this debate on what happiness is.

CHAPTER **18**

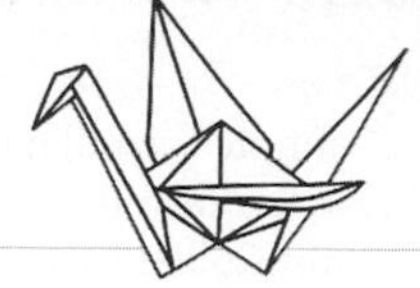

Division and Classification

A writer practices **division** by separating a class of things or ideas into categories following a clear principle or basis. In the following paragraph, journalist Robert MacNeil establishes categories of speech according to their level of formality:

> It fascinates me how differently we all speak in different circumstances. We have levels of formality, as in our clothing. There are very formal occasions, often requiring written English: the job application or the letter to the editor—the darksuit, serious-tie language, with everything pressed and the lint brushed off. There is our less formal out-in-the-world language—a more comfortable suit, but still respectable. There is language for close friends in the evenings, on weekends—bluejeans-and-sweat-shirt language, when it's good to get the tie off. There is family language, even more relaxed, full of grammatical short cuts, family slang, echoes of old jokes that have become intimate shorthand—the language of pajamas and uncombed hair. Finally, there is the language with no clothes on; the talk of couples—murmurs, sighs, grunts—language at its least self-conscious, open, vulnerable, and primitive.
>
> –Robert MacNeil, *Wordstruck: A Memoir*

With **classification**, on the other hand, a writer groups individual objects or ideas into already established categories. Division and classification can operate separately but often accompany each other. Here, for example, is a passage about levers in which the writer first discusses generally how levers work. In the second paragraph, the writer uses division to establish three categories of levers and then uses classification to group individual levers into those categories:

> Every lever has one fixed point called the "fulcrum" and is acted on by two forces—the "effort" (exertion of hand muscles) and the "weight" (object's resistance). Levers work according to a

> simple formula: the effort (how hard you push or pull) multiplied by its distance from the fulcrum (effort arm) equals the weight multiplied by its distance from the fulcrum (weight arm). Thus two pounds of effort exerted at a distance of four feet from the fulcrum will raise eight pounds located one foot from the fulcrum.
>
> There are three types of levers, conventionally called "first kind," "second kind," and "third kind." Levers of the first kind have the fulcrum located between the effort and the weight. Examples are a pump handle, an oar, a crowbar, a weighing balance, a pair of scissors, and a pair of pliers. Levers of the second kind have the weight in the middle and magnify the effort. Examples are the handcar crank and doors. Levers of the third kind, such as a power shovel or a baseball batter's forearm, have the effort in the middle and always magnify the distance.

The following paragraph introduces a classification of the kinds of decisions one has to make when purchasing a smartphone:

> When you are shopping for a smartphone, you have a great number of options from which to choose. Among these are manufacturer, model, price, carrier, and phone features. In the area of features alone, one has to consider the different kinds of operating systems, battery, screen sizes and resolutions, storage capacities, and types of cameras that are available.
>
> –Freddy Chessa, student

In writing, division and classification are affected directly by the writer's practical purpose—what the writer wants to explain or prove. That purpose determines the class of things or ideas being divided and classified. For instance, a writer might divide television programs according to their audiences (adults, families, or children) and then classify individual programs into each category to show that television networks value certain audiences more than others. A writer who is concerned about violence in television programming would divide programs into those with and without fights and murders and then classify various programs into those categories. Writers with other purposes would divide television programs differently (by the day and time of broadcast, for example, or by the number of women featured in prominent roles) and then classify individual programs accordingly.

Another example may help clarify how division and classification work hand in hand in writing. Suppose a sociologist wants to determine whether income level influences voting behavior in a particular neighborhood. The sociologist chooses as her subject the fifteen families living on Maple Street. Her goal then becomes to group these families in a way that is relevant to her purpose. She knows that she wants to divide the neighborhood in two ways—according to (1) income level (low, middle, and high) and (2) voting behavior (voters and nonvoters)—but her process of division won't be complete until she can classify the fifteen families into her five groupings.

In confidential interviews with each family, the sociologist learns what the family's income is and whether any member of the household voted in a state or federal election in the last four years. Based on this information, she classifies each family according to her established categories and at the same time divides the neighborhood into the subclasses that are crucial to her study. Her work leads her to construct the following diagram of her divisions and classifications.

Purpose: To group 15 families according to income and voting behavior and to study the relationships between the two.

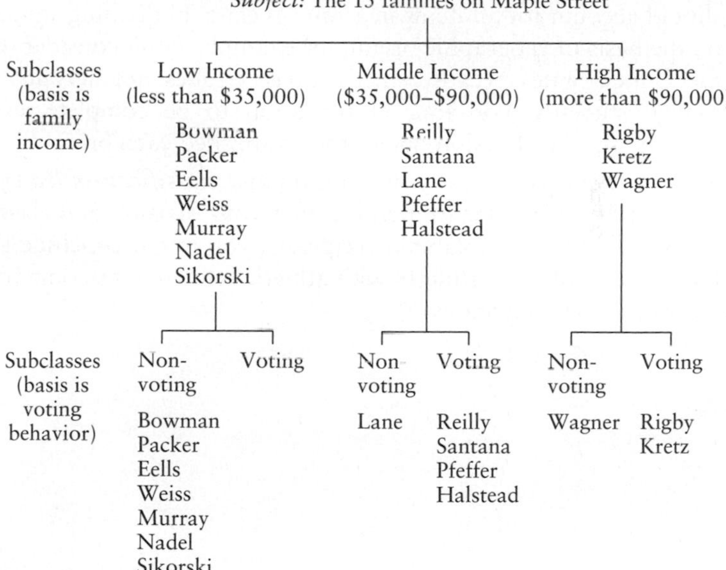

Conclusion: On Maple Street, there seems to be a relationship between income level and voting behavior: the low-income families are nonvoters.

The diagram on page 465 allows the sociologist to visualize her division and classification system and its essential components—subject, basis or principle of division, subclasses or categories, and conclusion. Her ultimate conclusion depends on her ability to work back and forth among divisions, subclasses, and the actual families to be classified.

The following guidelines can help you use division and classification in your writing:

1. *Identify a clear purpose, and use a principle of division that is appropriate to that purpose.* If you want to examine the common characteristics of four-year athletic scholarship recipients at your college or university, you might consider the following principles of division: program of study, sport, place of origin, or gender. In this case, it would not be useful to divide students on the basis of their favorite type of music because that seems irrelevant to your purpose.
2. *Divide your subject into unique categories.* An item can belong to only one category. For example, don't divide students as men, women, and athletes.
3. *Make your division and classification complete.* Your categories should account for all items in a subject class. In dividing students on the basis of geographic origin, for example, don't consider only the United States because such a division does not account for foreign students. For your classification to be complete, every student must be placed in one of the established categories.
4. *State the conclusion that your division and classification lead you to draw.* For example, after conducting your division and classification of athletic scholarship recipients, you might conclude that the majority of male athletes with athletic scholarships come from the western United States.

macmillanhighered.com/mfw12e
e-readings > WIRED, *What's Inside Coffee* [video]

The Ways of Meeting Oppression

■ Martin Luther King Jr.

© Bettmann/CORBIS

Martin Luther King Jr. (1929–1968) was the leading spokesman for the rights of African Americans during the 1950s and 1960s. He established the Southern Christian Leadership Conference, organized many civil rights demonstrations, and opposed the Vietnam War and the draft. Beginning in 1960, King was a pastor at the Ebenezer Baptist Church in Atlanta, where both his father and his grandfather had served. In 1964, he was awarded the Nobel Peace Prize for his resistance to racial oppression and discrimination. King was assassinated at the age of thirty-nine in Memphis, Tennessee, where he had traveled to provide leadership and support to striking sanitation workers. In 1983, President Ronald Reagan signed a bill creating a national holiday to honor King's life and legacy.

In the following essay, taken from his book Strive toward Freedom *(1958), King classifies the three ways that oppressed people throughout history have reacted to their oppressors. As you read, pay particular attention to how King orders his discussion of the three types of oppression to support his argument and the conclusion he presents in paragraph 8.*

Reflecting on What You Know

Isaac Asimov once said, "Violence is the last refuge of the incompetent." What are your thoughts on the reasons for violent behavior on either a personal or a national level? Is violence ever justified? If so, under what circumstances?

Oppressed people deal with their oppression in three characteristic ways. One way is acquiescence: the oppressed resign themselves to their doom. They tacitly adjust themselves to oppression, and thereby become conditioned to it. In every movement toward freedom some of 1 the oppressed prefer to remain oppressed. Almost 2800 years ago Moses[1] set out to lead the children of Israel from the slavery of Egypt to the freedom of the promised land. He soon discovered that slaves do not always welcome their deliverers. They become accustomed to being slaves. They would rather bear those ills they have, as Shakespeare pointed out, than flee to others that they know not of. They prefer the "fleshpots of Egypt" to the ordeals of emancipation.

There is such a thing as the freedom of exhaustion. Some people 2
are so worn down by the yoke of oppression that they give up. A few years ago in the slum areas of Atlanta, a Negro guitarist used to sing almost daily: "Been down so long that down don't bother me."[2] This is the type of negative freedom and resignation that often engulfs the life of the oppressed.

But this is not the way out. To accept passively an unjust system 3
is to cooperate with that system; thereby the oppressed become as evil as the oppressor. Noncooperation with evil is as much a moral obligation as is cooperation with good. The oppressed must never allow the conscience of the oppressor to slumber. Religion reminds every man that he is his brother's keeper. To accept injustice or segregation passively is to say to the oppressor that his actions are morally right. It is a way of allowing his conscience to fall asleep. At this moment the oppressed fails to be his brother's keeper. So acquiescence—while often the easier way—is not the moral way. It is the way of the coward. The Negro cannot win the respect of his oppressor by acquiescing; he merely increases the oppressor's arrogance and contempt. Acquiescence is interpreted as proof of the Negro's inferiority. The Negro cannot win the respect of the white people of the South or the peoples of the world if he is willing to sell the future of his children for his personal and immediate comfort and safety.

A second way that oppressed people sometimes deal with oppres- 4
sion is to resort to physical violence and corroding hatred. Violence often brings about momentary results. Nations have frequently won their independence in battle. But in spite of temporary victories, violence never brings permanent peace. It solves no social problem; it merely creates new and more complicated ones.

[1] *Moses:* a Hebrew prophet, teacher, and leader in the fourteenth to thirteenth centuries B.C.E.

[2] *"Been down . . . bother me":* lyric possibly adapted from "Stormy Blues" by American jazz singer Billie Holiday (1915–1959).

Violence as a way of achieving racial justice is both impractical and immoral. It is impractical because it is a descending spiral ending in destruction for all. The old law of an eye for an eye leaves everybody blind. It is immoral because it seeks to humiliate the opponent rather than win his understanding; it seeks to annihilate rather than to convert. Violence is immoral because it thrives on hatred rather than love. It destroys community and makes brotherhood impossible. It leaves society in monologue rather than dialogue. Violence ends by defeating itself. It creates bitterness in the survivors and brutality in the destroyers. A voice echoes through time saying to every potential Peter, "Put up your sword."[3] History is cluttered with the wreckage of nations that failed to follow this command. 5

If the American Negro and other victims of oppression succumb to the temptation of using violence in the struggle for freedom, future generations will be the recipients of a desolate night of bitterness, and our chief legacy to them will be an endless reign of meaningless chaos. Violence is not the way. 6

The third way open to oppressed people in their quest for freedom is the way of nonviolent resistance. Like the synthesis in Hegelian[4] philosophy, the principle of nonviolent resistance seeks to reconcile the truths of two opposites—acquiescence and violence—while avoiding the extremes and immoralities of both. The nonviolent resister agrees with the person who acquiesces that one should not be physically aggressive toward his opponent; but he balances the equation by agreeing with the person of violence that evil must be resisted. He avoids the nonresistance of the former and the violent resistance of the latter. With nonviolent resistance, no individual or group need submit to any wrong, nor need anyone resort to violence in order to right a wrong. 7

It seems to me that this is the method that must guide the actions of the Negro in the present crisis in race relations. Through nonviolent resistance the Negro will be able to rise to the noble height of opposing the unjust system while loving the perpetrators of the system. The Negro must work passionately and unrelentingly for full stature as a citizen, but he must not use inferior methods to gain it. He must never come to terms with falsehood, malice, hate, or destruction. 8

---

[3]*"Put up your sword":* the apostle Peter had drawn his sword to defend Jesus from arrest; the voice was Jesus's, who surrendered himself for trial and crucifixion (John 18:11).

[4]*Georg Wilhelm Friedrich Hegel* (1770–1831): German philosopher.

Nonviolent resistance makes it possible for the Negro to remain in the South and struggle for his rights. The Negro's problem will not be solved by running away. He cannot listen to the glib suggestion of those who would urge him to migrate en masse to other sections of the country. By grasping his great opportunity in the South he can make a lasting contribution to the moral strength of the nation and set a sublime example of courage for generations yet unborn. 9

By nonviolent resistance, the Negro can also enlist all men of good will in his struggle for equality. The problem is not a purely racial one, with Negroes set against whites. In the end, it is not a struggle between people at all, but a tension between justice and injustice. Nonviolent resistance is not aimed against oppressors but against oppression. Under its banner consciences, not racial groups, are enlisted. 10

Thinking Critically about This Reading

King states "There is such a thing as the freedom of exhaustion" (paragraph 2). Why, according to King, is this type of freedom "negative"?

Questions for Study and Discussion

1. What is King's thesis? (Glossary: *Thesis*)
2. How does classifying the three types of resistance to oppression help him develop his thesis?
3. Why do you suppose King discusses acquiescence, violence, and nonviolent resistance in that order? What organizational principle does he use to rank them?
4. How does King's organizational pattern help him build his argument and support his thesis? Would his argument work as well if he had changed the order of his discussion? Why or why not?
5. King states that he favors nonviolent resistance over the other two ways of meeting oppression. What disadvantages does he see in meeting oppression with acquiescence or with violence?

Classroom Activity Using Division and Classification

Be prepared to discuss in class why you believe that division and classification are important ways of thinking about everyday life. Give examples of how you use the two complementary strategies when you use a computer search engine, shop on the web, select items in your local supermarket, or look for textbooks in your college bookstore.

Suggested Writing Assignments

1. Using King's essay as a model, write an essay on various solutions to a current social or personal problem. Organize your ideas according to a rational scheme relying on the principles of division and classification. Be sure that you have a clear thesis statement and that the division and classification you employ to develop your essay help convince your reader of your ideas and beliefs.
2. King's use of division and classification in "The Ways of Meeting Oppression" is simple, logical, and natural. He knows that the oppressed can't give in to their oppressors, can't answer violence with violence, and therefore must take a third path of nonviolent resistance to rise above their enemies. Using King's essay as a model, write an essay in which you discuss how to respond to prejudice, hatred, competition, greed, aggression, or some other social force that we all find difficult to overcome.

Doubts about Doublespeak

■ William Lutz

Robert J. Laramie

Born in Racine, Wisconsin, in 1940, William Lutz is best known for Doublespeak: From "Revenue Enhancement" to "Terminal Living": How Government, Business, Advertisers, and Others Use Language to Deceive You *(1990) and* The New Doublespeak: Why No One Knows What Anyone's Saying Anymore *(1996). His book* Doublespeak Defined: Cut through the Bull**** and Get the Point! *was published in 1999. (The term* doublespeak *was coined by George Orwell in his novel* Nineteen Eighty-Four. *It refers to speech or writing that presents two or more contradictory ideas in a way that deceives an unsuspecting audience.) As chair of the National Council of Teachers of English's Committee on Public Doublespeak, Lutz has been a watchdog of public officials who use language to "mislead, distort, deceive, inflate, circumvent, and obfuscate." Each year, the committee presents the Orwell Awards to recognize outrageous uses of doublespeak in government and business. Lutz is a professor emeritus of English at Rutgers University–Camden and was the editor of the* Quarterly Review of Doublespeak *for fourteen years.*

The following essay first appeared in the July 1993 issue of State Government News. *As you read, notice how Lutz organizes his essay by naming and defining four categories of doublespeak, describing each one's function or consequences, and giving examples of each type. This organizational pattern is simple, practical, and easy to follow.*

Reflecting on What You Know

Imagine that you work for a manufacturing plant in your town and that your boss has just told you that you are on the list of people who will be "dehired" or that you are part of a program of "negative employee retention." What would you think was happening to you? Would you be happy about it? What would you think of the language your boss used to describe your situation?

During the past year, we learned that we can shop at a "unique 1
retail biosphere" instead of a farmers' market, where we can buy items made of "synthetic glass" instead of plastic, or purchase a "high velocity, multipurpose air circulator," or electric fan. A "waste-water conveyance facility" may "exceed the odor threshold" from time to time due to the presence of "regulated human nutrients," but that is not to be confused with a sewage plant that stinks up the neighborhood with sewage sludge. Nor should we confuse a "resource development park" with a dump. Thus does doublespeak continue to spread.

Doublespeak is language which pretends to communicate but 2
doesn't. It is language which makes the bad seem good, the negative seem positive, the unpleasant seem attractive, or at least tolerable. It is language which avoids, shifts, or denies responsibility; language which is at variance with its real or purported meaning. It is language which conceals or prevents thought.

Doublespeak is all around us. We are asked to check our packages 3
at the desk "for our convenience" when it's not for our convenience at all but for someone else's convenience. We see advertisements for "pre-owned," "experienced," or "previously distinguished" cars, not used cars, and for "genuine imitation leather," "virgin vinyl," or "real counterfeit diamonds." Television offers not reruns but "encore telecasts." There are no slums or ghettos, just the "inner city" or "substandard housing" where the "disadvantaged" or "economically nonaffluent" live and where there might be a problem with "substance abuse." Nonprofit organizations don't make a profit, they have "negative deficits" or experience "revenue excesses." With doublespeak it's not dying but "terminal living" or "negative patient care outcome."

There are four kinds of doublespeak. The first kind is the euphe- 4
mism, a word or phrase designed to avoid a harsh or distasteful reality. Used to mislead or deceive, the euphemism becomes doublespeak. In 1984 the U.S. State Department's annual reports on the status of human rights around the world ceased using the word "killing." Instead the State Department used the phrase "unlawful or arbitrary deprivation of life," thus avoiding the embarrassing situation of government-sanctioned killing in countries supported by the United States.

A second kind of doublespeak is jargon, the specialized language 5
of a trade, profession, or similar group, such as doctors, lawyers, plumbers, or car mechanics. Legitimately used, jargon allows members of a group to communicate with each other clearly, efficiently, and quickly. Lawyers and tax accountants speak to each other of an

"involuntary conversion" of property, a legal term that means the loss or destruction of property through theft, accident, or condemnation. But when lawyers or tax accountants use unfamiliar terms to speak to others, then the jargon becomes doublespeak.

In 1978 a commercial 727 crashed on takeoff, killing three passengers, injuring twenty-one others, and destroying the airplane. The insured value of the airplane was greater than its book value, so the airline made a profit of $1.7 million, creating two problems: the airline didn't want to talk about one of its airplanes crashing, yet it had to account for that $1.7 million profit in its annual report to its stockholders. The airline solved both problems by inserting a footnote in its annual report which explained that the $1.7 million was due to "the involuntary conversion of a 727." 6

A third kind of doublespeak is gobbledygook or bureaucratese. Such doublespeak is simply a matter of overwhelming the audience with words—the more the better. Alan Greenspan, a polished practitioner of bureaucratese, once testified before a Senate committee that "it is a tricky problem to find the particular calibration in timing that would be appropriate to stem the acceleration in risk premiums created by falling incomes without prematurely aborting the decline in the inflation-generated risk premiums." 7

The fourth kind of doublespeak is inflated language, which is designed to make the ordinary seem extraordinary, to make everyday things seem impressive, to give an air of importance to people or situations, to make the simple seem complex. Thus do car mechanics become "automotive internists," elevator operators become "members of the vertical transportation corps," grocery store checkout clerks become "career associate scanning professionals," and smelling something becomes "organoleptic analysis." 8

Doublespeak is not the product of careless language or sloppy thinking. Quite the opposite. Doublespeak is language carefully designed and constructed to appear to communicate when in fact it doesn't. It is language designed not to lead but mislead. Thus, it's not a tax increase but "revenue enhancement" or "tax-base broadening." So how can you complain about higher taxes? Those aren't useless, billion dollar pork barrel projects; they're really "congressional projects of national significance," so don't complain about wasteful government spending. That isn't the Mafia in Atlantic City; those are just "members of a career-offender cartel," so don't worry about the influence of organized crime in the city. 9

New doublespeak is created every day. The Environmental Protection Agency once called acid rain "poorly-buffered precipitation," then dropped that term in favor of "atmospheric deposition of anthropogenically-derived acidic substances," but recently decided that acid rain should be called "wet deposition." The Pentagon, which has in the past given us such classic doublespeak as "hexiform rotatable surface compression unit" for steel nut, just published a pamphlet warning soldiers that exposure to nerve gas will lead to "immediate permanent incapacitation." That's almost as good as the Pentagon's official term "servicing the target," meaning to kill the enemy. Meanwhile, the Department of Energy wants to establish a "monitored retrievable storage site," a place once known as a dump for spent nuclear fuel. 10

Bad economic times give rise to lots of new doublespeak designed to avoid some very unpleasant economic realities. As the "contained depression" continues so does the corporate policy of making up even more new terms to avoid the simple, and easily understandable, term "layoff." So it is that corporations "reposition," "restructure," "reshape," or "realign" the company and "reduce duplication" through "release of resources" that involves a "permanent downsizing" or a "payroll adjustment" that results in a number of employees being "involuntarily terminated." 11

Other countries regularly contribute to doublespeak. In Japan, where baldness is called "hair disadvantaged," the economy is undergoing a "severe adjustment process," while in Canada there is an "involuntary downward development" of the work force. For some government agencies in Canada, wastepaper baskets have become "user friendly, space effective, flexible, deskside sortation units." Politicians in Canada may engage in "reality augmentation," but they never lie. As part of their new freedom, the people of Moscow can visit "intimacy salons," or sex shops as they're known in other countries. When dealing with the bureaucracy in Russia, people know that they should show officials "normal gratitude," or give them a bribe. 12

The worst doublespeak is the doublespeak of death. It is the language, wrote George Orwell in 1946, that is "largely the defense of the indefensible . . . designed to make lies sound truthful and murder respectable, and to give an appearance of solidity to pure wind." In the doublespeak of death, Orwell continued, "defenseless villages are bombarded from the air, the inhabitants driven out into the countryside, the cattle machine-gunned, the huts set on fire with incendiary bullets. This is called pacification. Millions of peasants are 13 robbed of their farms and sent trudging along the roads with no more than they can carry. This is called transfer of population or rectification of frontiers." Today, in a country once called Yugoslavia, this is called "ethnic cleansing."[1]

It's easy to laugh off doublespeak. After all, we all know what's going on, so what's the harm? But we don't always know what's going on, and when that happens, doublespeak accomplishes its ends. It alters our perception of reality. It deprives us of the tools we need to develop, advance, and preserve our society, our culture, our civilization. It breeds suspicion, cynicism, distrust, and, ultimately, hostility. It delivers us into the hands of those who do not have our interests at heart. As Samuel Johnson[2] noted in eighteenth-century England, even the devils in hell do not lie to one another, since the society of hell could not subsist without the truth, any more than any other society. 14

Thinking Critically about This Reading

According to Lutz, doublespeak "alters our perception of reality. . . . It breeds suspicion, cynicism, distrust, and, ultimately, hostility" (paragraph 14). What is Lutz's plan for combating doublespeak and its negative effects?

Questions for Study and Discussion

1. What is Lutz's thesis? (Glossary: *Thesis*)
2. The author divides doublespeak into four categories. What are they?
3. For what purpose has Lutz used division and classification? (Glossary: *Purpose*)
4. Why might Lutz have ordered the categories as he has? (Glossary: *Organization*)
5. Are Lutz's illustrative examples good ones? (Glossary: *Example*) Why or why not? Should he have used fewer examples? More examples? Explain.
6. Could the order of Lutz's first two paragraphs be reversed? (Glossary: *Beginnings and Endings*) What would be gained or lost if they were?

---

[1] *"ethnic cleansing":* Lutz is referring to the breakup of the Federal Republic of Yugoslavia in the Balkan region of southeastern Europe in the early 1990s and the 1992–1995 genocide centered in the cities of Sarajevo and Srebrenica.

[2] *Samuel Johnson (1709–1784):* an important English writer.

7. Reread Lutz's last paragraph, in which he makes some serious claims about the importance of doublespeak. Is such seriousness on his part justified by what he has written about doublespeak in the body of his essay? Why or why not?

Classroom Activity Using Division and Classification

Examine the following lists of hobbies, books, and buildings. Determine at least three principles that could be used to divide the items listed in each group. Finally, classify the items in each group according to one of the principles you have established.

Hobbies

watching sports on TV	surfing the web
stamp collecting	hiking
scuba diving	dancing

Books

The Adventures of Huckleberry Finn	*Guinness Book of World Records*
American Heritage Dictionary	*To Kill a Mockingbird*
The Joy of Cooking	*Gone with the Wind*

Buildings

Empire State Building	Taj Mahal
White House	Library of Congress
the Alamo	Buckingham Palace

Suggested Writing Assignments

1. Write an essay in which you consider the effects of doublespeak. Is it always a form of lying? Is it harmful to our society, and if so, how? How can we measure its effects? Be sure to cite instances of doublespeak that are not included in Lutz's essay. You can uncover these through your reading, web browsing, or library research.
2. College is a time of stress for many students. In an essay, use division and classification to discuss the different kinds of pressure students experience at your school.

Mother Tongue

■ Amy Tan

Mark Mainz/Getty Images for AFI

Amy Tan was born in 1952 in Oakland, California, to parents who had emigrated from China. Though her mother and teachers encouraged her to pursue a career in math or science, she found an irrepressible interest in literature, and in her first year at college, she changed her major from pre-med to English. She earned bachelor's and master's degrees from San Jose State University, but she did not begin writing fiction until she was thirty-three. Her first book, The Joy Luck Club *(1987), was published two years later to great acclaim and was later adapted into a successful film. Her other novels include* The Kitchen God's Wife *(1991),* The Hundred Secret Senses *(1995),* The Bonesetter's Daughter *(2000), and, most recently,* The Valley of Amazement *(2013).*

This essay, "Mother Tongue," is born out of Tan's realization that she speaks not one but many "Englishes." As you read, pay careful attention to how she divides these forms of the language into categories, and consider how multiple Englishes make her writing richer.

Reflecting on What You Know

How different is the language you speak at home from the one you speak at school? Do you talk differently with your mother than you do with your friends or your boss? How many different languages do you speak on any given day?

I am not a scholar of English or literature. I cannot give you much more than personal opinions on the English language and its variations in this country or others. 1

I am a writer. And by that definition, I am someone who has always loved language. I am fascinated by language in daily life. I spend a great deal of my time thinking about the power of language—the 2 way it can evoke an emotion, a visual image, a complex idea, or a simple truth. Language is the tool of my trade. And I use them all—all the Englishes I grew up with.

3 Recently, I was made keenly aware of the different Englishes I do use. I was giving a talk to a large group of people, the same talk I had already given to half a dozen other groups. The nature of the talk was about my writing, my life, and my book, *The Joy Luck Club.* The talk was going along well enough, until I remembered one major difference that made the whole talk sound wrong. My mother was in the room. And it was perhaps the first time she had heard me give a lengthy speech, using the kind of English I have never used with her. I was saying things like, "The intersection of memory upon imagination" and "There is an aspect of my fiction that relates to thus-and-thus"—a speech filled with carefully wrought grammatical phrases, burdened, it suddenly seemed to me, with nominalized forms, past perfect tenses, conditional phrases, all the forms of standard English that I had learned in school and through books, the forms of English I did not use at home with my mother.

4 Just last week, I was walking down the street with my mother, and I again found myself conscious of the English I was using, the English I do use with her. We were talking about the price of new and used furniture and I heard myself saying this: "Not waste money that way." My husband was with us as well, and he didn't notice any switch in my English. And then I realized why. It's because over the twenty years we've been together I've often used that same kind of English with him, and sometimes he even uses it with me. It has become our language of intimacy, a different sort of English that relates to family talk, the language I grew up with.

5 So you'll have some idea of what this family talk I heard sounds like, I'll quote what my mother said during a recent conversation which I videotaped and then transcribed. During this conversation, my mother was talking about a political gangster in Shanghai who had the same last name as her family's, Du, and how the gangster in his early years wanted to be adopted by her family, which was rich by comparison. Later, the gangster became more powerful, far richer than my mother's family, and one day showed up at my mother's wedding to pay his respects. Here's what she said in part: "Du Yusong having business like fruit stand. Like off the street kind. He is Du like Du Zong—but not Tsung-ming Island people. The local people call putong, the river east side, he belong to that side local people. That

man want to ask Du Zong father take him in like become own family. Du Zong father wasn't look down on him, but didn't take seriously, until that man big like become a mafia. Now important person, very hard to inviting him. Chinese way, came only to show respect, don't stay for dinner. Respect for making big celebration, he shows up. Mean gives lots of respect. Chinese custom. Chinese social life that way. If too important won't have to stay too long. He come to my wedding. I didn't see, I heard it. I gone to boy's side, they have YMCA dinner. Chinese age I was nineteen."

You should know that my mother's expressive command of English belies how much she actually understands. She reads the *Forbes* report, listens to *Wall Street Week*, converses daily with her stockbroker, reads all of Shirley MacLaine's books with ease—all kinds of things I can't begin to understand. Yet some of my friends tell me they understand 50 percent of what my mother says. Some say they understand 80 to 90 percent. Some say they understand none of it, as if she were speaking pure Chinese. But to me, my mother's English is perfectly clear, perfectly natural. It's my mother tongue. Her language, as I hear it, is vivid, direct, full of observation and imagery. That was the language that helped shape the way I saw things, expressed things, made sense of the world. 6

Lately, I've been giving more thought to the kind of English my mother speaks. Like others, I have described it to people as "broken" or "fractured" English. But I wince when I say that. It has always bothered me that I can think of no way to describe it other than "broken," as if it were damaged and needed to be fixed, as if it lacked a certain wholeness and soundness. I've heard other terms used, "limited English," for example. But they seem just as bad, as if everything is limited, including people's perceptions of the limited English speaker. 7

I know this for a fact, because when I was growing up, my mother's "limited" English limited my perception of her. I was ashamed of her English. I believed that her English reflected the quality of what she had to say. That is, because she expressed them imperfectly her thoughts were imperfect. And I had plenty of empirical evidence to support me: the fact that people in department stores, at banks, and at restaurants did not take her seriously, did not give her good service, pretended not to understand her, or even acted as if they did not hear her. 8

My mother has long realized the limitations of her English as well. When I was fifteen, she used to have me call people on the phone to pretend I was she. In this guise, I was forced to ask for information or even to complain and yell at people who had been rude to her. One time it was a call to her stockbroker in New York. She had cashed out her small portfolio and it just so happened we were going to go to New York the next week, our very first trip outside California. I had to get on the phone and say in an adolescent voice that was not very convincing, "This is Mrs. Tan." 9

And my mother was standing in the back whispering loudly, "Why he don't send me check, already two weeks late. So mad he lie to me, losing me money." 10

And then I said in perfect English, "Yes, I'm getting rather concerned. You had agreed to send the check two weeks ago, but it hasn't arrived." 11

Then she began to talk more loudly. "What he want, I come to New York tell him front of his boss, you cheating me?" And I was trying to calm her down, make her be quiet, while telling the stockbroker, "I can't tolerate any more excuses. If I don't receive the check immediately, I am going to have to speak to your manager when I'm in New York next week." And sure enough, the following week there we were in front of this astonished stockbroker, and I was sitting there red-faced and quiet, and my mother, the real Mrs. Tan, was shouting at his boss in her impeccable broken English. 12

We used a similar routine just five days ago, for a situation that was far less humorous. My mother had gone to the hospital for an appointment, to find out about a benign brain tumor a CAT scan had revealed a month ago. She said she had spoken very good English, her best English, no mistakes. Still, she said, the hospital did not apologize when they said they had lost the CAT scan and she had come for nothing. She said they did not seem to have any sympathy when she told them she was anxious to know the exact diagnosis, since her husband and son had both died of brain tumors. She said they would not give her any more information until the next time and she would have to make another appointment for that. So she said she would not leave until the doctor called her daughter. She wouldn't budge. And when the doctor finally called her daughter, me, who spoke in perfect English—lo and behold—we had assurances the CAT scan would be found, promises that a conference call on Monday would be held, 13 and apologies for any suffering my mother had gone through for a most regrettable mistake.

I think my mother's English almost had an effect on limiting my possibilities in life as well. Sociologists and linguists probably will tell you that a person's developing language skills are more influenced by peers. But I do think that the language spoken in the family, especially in immigrant families which are more insular, plays a large role in shaping the language of the child. And I believe that it affected my results on achievement tests, I.Q. tests, and the SAT. While my English skills were never judged as poor, compared to math, English could not be considered my strong suit. In grade school I did moderately well, getting perhaps B's, sometimes B-pluses, in English and scoring perhaps in the sixtieth or seventieth percentile on achievement tests. But those scores were not good enough to override the opinion that my true abilities lay in math and science, because in those areas I achieved A's and scored in the ninetieth percentile or higher. 14

This was understandable. Math is precise; there is only one correct answer. Whereas, for me at least, the answers on English tests were always a judgment call, a matter of opinion and personal experience. Those tests were constructed around items like fill-in-the-blank sentence completion, such as, "Even though Tom was ______, Mary thought he was ______." And the correct answer always seemed to be the most bland combinations of thoughts, for example, "Even though Tom was shy, Mary thought he was charming," with the grammatical structure "even though" limiting the correct answer to some sort of semantic opposites, so you wouldn't get answers like, "Even though Tom was foolish, Mary thought he was ridiculous." Well, according to my mother, there were very few limitations as to what Tom could have been and what Mary might have thought of him. So I never did well on tests like that. 15

The same was true with word analogies, pairs of words in which you were supposed to find some sort of logical, semantic relationship—for example, "*Sunset* is to *nightfall* as ______ is to ______." And here you would be presented with a list of four possible pairs, one of which showed the same kind of relationship: *red* is to *stoplight*, *bus* is to *arrival*, *chills* is to *fever*, *yawn* is to *boring*: Well, I could never think that way. I knew what the tests were asking, but I could not block out of my mind the images already created by the first pair, "*sunset* is to *nightfall*"—and I would see a burst of colors against a darkening sky, the moon rising, the lowering of a curtain of stars. 16

And all the other pairs of words—*red, bus, stoplight, boring*—just threw up a mass of confusing images, making it impossible for me to sort out something as logical as saying: "A sunset precedes nightfall" is the same as "a chill precedes a fever." The only way I would have gotten that answer right would have been to imagine an associative situation, for example, my being disobedient and staying out past sunset, catching a chill at night, which turns into feverish pneumonia as punishment, which indeed did happen to me.

17 I have been thinking about all this lately, about my mother's English, about achievement tests. Because lately I've been asked, as a writer, why there are not more Asian Americans represented in American literature. Why are there few Asian Americans enrolled in creative writing programs? Why do so many Chinese students go into engineering? Well, these are broad sociological questions I can't begin to answer. But I have noticed in surveys—in fact, just last week—that Asian students, as a whole, always do significantly better on math achievement tests than in English. And this makes me think that there are other Asian American students whose English spoken in the home might also be described as "broken" or "limited." And perhaps they also have teachers who are steering them away from writing and into math and science, which is what happened to me.

18 Fortunately, I happen to be rebellious in nature and enjoy the challenge of disproving assumptions made about me. I became an English major my first year in college, after being enrolled as pre-med. I started writing nonfiction as a freelancer the week after I was told by my former boss that writing was my worst skill and I should hone my talents toward account management.

19 But it wasn't until 1985 that I finally began to write fiction. And at first I wrote using what I thought to be wittily crafted sentences, sentences that would finally prove I had mastery over the English language. Here's an example from the first draft of a story that later made its way into *The Joy Luck Club*, but without this line: "That was my mental quandary in its nascent state." A terrible line, which I can barely pronounce.

20 Fortunately, for reasons I won't get into today, I later decided I should envision a reader for the stories I would write. And the reader I decided upon was my mother, because these were stories about mothers. So with this reader in mind—and in fact she did read my early drafts—I began to write stories using all the Englishes I grew up with: the English I spoke to my mother, which for lack of a better

term might be described as "simple"; the English she used with me, which for lack of a better term might be described as "broken"; my translation of her Chinese, which could certainly be described as "watered down"; and what I imagined to be her translation of her Chinese if she could speak in perfect English, her internal language, and for that I sought to preserve the essence, but neither an English nor a Chinese structure. I wanted to capture what language ability tests can never reveal: her intent, her passion, her imagery, the rhythms of her speech and the nature of her thoughts.

Apart from what any critic had to say about my writing, I knew I 21
had succeeded where it counted when my mother finished reading my book and gave me her verdict: "So easy to read."

Thinking Critically about This Reading

How does Tan's essay play on the phrase "mother tongue"? What does this term mean in common usage, and how does Tan add to or alter this definition?

Questions for Study and Discussion

1. How does Tan's profession affect her discussion of language in this essay? How does she describe a writer's special relationship to language?
2. Where and how does Tan use the English she learned in school? Besides this "standard English" (paragraph 3), what other categories does her language fit into?
3. Tan describes her mother's English as "vivid, direct, full of observation and imagery" (6). Reread the transcript of Tan's mother's side of the conversation in paragraph 5, and note places where you see these qualities in her speech.
4. As she tries to classify her mother's English, Tan finds all of the terms she can think of unsatisfying. What is wrong with "broken" and "limited" as descriptors?
5. There is an apparent contradiction in the scene with the stockbroker when Tan describes her mother's "impeccable broken English" (12). What does she mean by this? How would you explain the contradiction?

6. What is "terrible" about the line Tan quotes from an early draft of a story that became part of *The Joy Luck Club* (19)? How does she find a solution to this problem with her writing?

Classroom Activity Using Division and Classification

The drawing on page 486 is a basic exercise in classification. By determining the features all the figures have in common, establish the general class to which they belong. Next, establish subclasses by determining the distinctive features that distinguish one subclass from another. Finally, place each figure in an appropriate subclass within your classification system. You may wish to compare your system with those developed by other members of the class, and discuss any differences that exist.

Suggested Writing Assignments

1. Think back to your response to the Reflecting on What You Know prompt, and create a set of classifications for the kinds of language you speak. Then write versions of the same brief story (you might choose a family legend like the one Tan's mother recounts) in each of these languages. How is the telling of the story different when you write with different audiences in mind? (Glossary: *Audience*)
2. Music can be classified into many different types (jazz, country, pop, rock, soul, rap, classical, big band, western, blues, gospel). Each of these large classifications has a lot of variety within it. Write an essay in which you identify your favorite type of music as well as at least three subclassifications of that music. Explain the characteristics of each category, and use two or three artists and their songs as examples.

a
b
c
d
e
f
g
h
i
j
k
l
m
n
o

CHAPTER **19**

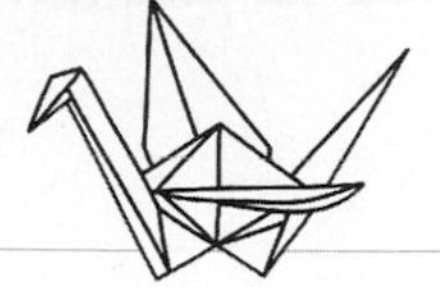

Comparison and Contrast

A **comparison** points out the ways that two or more people, places, or things are alike. A **contrast** points out how they differ. The subjects of a comparison or contrast should be in the same class or general category; if they have nothing in common, there is no good reason for setting them side by side.

The function of any comparison or contrast is to clarify and explain. The writer's purpose may be simply to inform or to make readers aware of similarities or differences that are interesting and significant in themselves. Or the writer may explain something unfamiliar by comparing it with something very familiar, perhaps explaining the game of squash by comparing it with tennis. Finally, the writer can point out the superiority of one thing by contrasting it with another—for example, showing that one product is the best by contrasting it with all its competitors.

As a writer, you have two main options for organizing a comparison or contrast: the subject-by-subject pattern or the point-by-point pattern. For a short essay comparing and contrasting Philadelphia, Pennsylvania, and San Diego, California, as vacation destinations, you would probably follow the *subject-by-subject* pattern of organization. With this pattern, you first discuss the points you wish to make about one city and then discuss the corresponding points for the other city. An outline of the body of your essay might look like this:

Subject-by-Subject Pattern

I. Philadelphia
   A. Climate
   B. Public transportation
   C. Tourist attractions (museums, zoos, theme parks)
   D. Accommodations

II. San Diego
   A. Climate
   B. Public transportation
   C. Tourist attractions (museums, zoos, theme parks)
   D. Accommodations

The subject-by-subject pattern presents a unified discussion of each city by emphasizing the cities and not the four points of comparison. Because these points are relatively few, readers should easily remember what you said about Philadelphia's climate when you later discuss San Diego's climate and should be able to make the appropriate connections between them.

For a somewhat longer essay comparing and contrasting solar energy and wind energy, however, you should consider using the *point-by-point* pattern of organization. With this pattern, your essay is organized according to the various points of comparison. Discussion alternates between solar and wind energy for each point of comparison. An outline of the body of your essay might look like this:

Point-by-Point Pattern

I. Installation expenses
   A. Solar
   B. Wind
II. Efficiency
   A. Solar
   B. Wind
III. Operating costs
   A. Solar
   B. Wind
IV. Convenience
   A. Solar
   B. Wind
V. Maintenance
   A. Solar
   B. Wind
VI. Safety
   A. Solar
   B. Wind

With the point-by-point pattern, the writer makes immediate comparisons between solar and wind energy so that readers can consider each similarity and difference separately.

Each organizational pattern has its advantages. In general, the subject-by-subject pattern is useful in short essays, in which few points are being considered; and the point-by-point pattern is preferable in long essays, in which numerous points are being considered.

A good essay of comparison and contrast tells readers something significant that they do not already know—that is, it must do more than merely point out the obvious. As a rule, therefore, writers tend to draw contrasts between things that are usually perceived as being similar or comparisons between things usually perceived as being different. In fact, comparison and contrast often go together. For example, an essay about the twin cities of Minneapolis and St. Paul might begin by showing how much they are alike but end with a series of contrasts revealing how much they differ. A consumer magazine might report the contrasting claims made by six car manufacturers and then go on to demonstrate that all the cars actually do much the same thing in the same way.

The following student essay about hunting and photography explores the increasing popularity of photographic safaris. After first pointing out the obvious differences between hunting with a gun and hunting with a camera, the writer focuses on the similarities between the two activities, which make many hunters willing to trade their guns for cameras. Notice how she successfully uses the subject-by-subject organizational plan in the body of her essay to explore three key similarities between hunters and photographers.

Guns and Cameras

The hunter has a deep interest in the apparatus he uses to kill his prey. He carries various types of guns, different kinds of ammunition, and special sights and telescopes to increase his chances of success. He knows the mechanics of his guns and understands how and why they work. This fascination with the hardware of his sport is practical—it helps him achieve his goal—but it frequently becomes an end, almost a hobby in itself.

Not until the very end of the long process of stalking an animal does a game hunter use his gun. First he enters into the animal's world. He studies his prey, its habitat, its daily habits, its watering holes and feeding areas, its migration patterns, its enemies and allies, its diet and food chain. Eventually the hunter himself becomes animal-like, instinctively sensing the habits and moves of his prey. Of course, this instinct gives the hunter a better chance of killing the animal; he knows where and when he will get the best shot. But it gives him more than that. Hunting is not just pulling the trigger and killing the prey. Much of it is a multifaceted and ritualistic identification with nature.

After the kill, the hunter can do a number of things with his trophy. He can sell the meat or eat it himself. He can hang the animal's head on the wall or lay its hide on the floor or even sell these objects. But any of these uses is a luxury, and its cost is high. An animal has been destroyed; a life has been eliminated.

Like the hunter, the photographer has a great interest in the tools he uses. He carries various types of cameras, lenses, and film to help him get the picture he wants. He understands the way cameras work, the uses of telephoto and micro lenses, and often the technical procedures of printing and developing. Of course, the time and interest a photographer invests in these mechanical aspects of his art allow him to capture and produce the image he wants. But as with the hunter, these mechanics can and often do become fascinating in themselves.

The wildlife photographer also needs to stalk his "prey" with knowledge and skill in order to get an accurate "shot." Like the hunter, he has to understand the animal's patterns, characteristics, and habitat; he must become animal-like in order to succeed. And like the hunter's, his pursuit is much more prolonged and complicated than the shot itself. The stalking processes are almost identical and give many of the same satisfactions.

The successful photographer also has something tangible to show for his efforts. A still picture of an animal can be displayed in a home, a gallery, a shop; it can be printed in a publication, as a postcard, or as a poster. In fact, a single photograph can be used in all these ways at once; it can be reproduced countless times. And despite all these ways of using his "trophies," the photographer continues to preserve his prey.

–Barbara Bowman, student

Analogy is a special form of comparison. When a subject is unobservable, complex, or abstract—when it is so unfamiliar that readers may have trouble understanding it—analogy can be effective. By pointing out certain similarities between a difficult subject and a more familiar or concrete subject, writers can help their readers grasp the difficult subject. Unlike a true comparison, though, which analyzes items that belong to the same class (breeds of dogs or types of engines), analogy pairs things from different classes that have nothing in common except through the imagination of the writer. In addition, whereas comparison seeks to illuminate specific features of both subjects, the primary purpose of analogy is to clarify the one subject that is complex or unfamiliar. For example, to explore the similarities (and differences) between short stories and novels (two forms of fiction), you would probably choose comparison. Short stories and novels belong to the same class (fiction), and your purpose is to reveal something about both. If, however, your purpose is to explain the craft of fiction writing, you might note its similarities to the craft of carpentry. In this case you would be drawing an analogy because the two subjects clearly belong to different classes. Carpentry is the more concrete subject and the one more people will have direct experience with. If you use your imagination, you will easily see many ways that the tangible work of the carpenter can be used to help readers understand the abstract work of the novelist.

Depending on its purpose, an analogy can be made in a sentence or in several paragraphs to clarify a particular aspect of the larger topic being discussed or it can provide the organizational strategy for an entire essay. Consider the following analogies:

> People are like stained-glass windows. They sparkle and shine when the sun is out, but when the darkness sets in, their true beauty is revealed only if there is a light from within.
>
> Elisabeth Kübler-Ross

> Writing a first draft is very much like watching a Polaroid develop. You can't—and, in fact, you're not supposed to—know exactly what the picture is going to look like until it has finished developing. First you just point at what has your attention and take the picture. In the last chapter, for instance, what had my attention were the contents of my lunch bag. But as the picture developed, I found I had a really clear image of the boy against the fence. Or maybe *your* Polaroid was supposed to be a picture of that boy against the fence, and you didn't notice until the last minute that a family was standing a few feet away from him. Now, maybe it's his family, or the family of one of the kids in his class, but at any rate these people are going to be in the photograph, too. Then the film emerges from the camera with a grayish green murkiness that gradually becomes clearer and clearer, and finally you see the husband and wife holding their baby with two children standing beside them. And at first it all seems very sweet, but then the shadows begin to appear, and then you start to see the animal tragedy, the baboons baring their teeth. And then you see a flash of bright red flowers in the bottom left quadrant that you didn't even know were in the picture when you took it, and these flowers evoke a time or a

macmillanhighered.com/mfw12e
e-readings > CDC, *Screen Time vs. Lean Time* [infographic]

memory that moves you mysteriously. And finally, as the portrait comes into focus, you begin to notice all the props surrounding these people, and you begin to understand how props define us and comfort us, and show us what we value and what we need, and who we think we are.

You couldn't have had any way of knowing what this piece of work would look like when you first started. You just knew that there was something about these people that compelled you, and you stayed with that something long enough for it to show you what it was about.

–Anne Lamott, "Polaroids" (pp. 331–32)

Two Ways of Seeing a River

■ Mark Twain

Copyright by A.F. Bradley, N.Y./Library of Congress

Samuel L. Clemens (1835–1910), who wrote under the pen name of Mark Twain, was born in Florida, Missouri, and raised in Hannibal, Missouri. He wrote the novels Tom Sawyer *(1876),* The Prince and the Pauper *(1882),* Huckleberry Finn *(1884), and* A Connecticut Yankee in King Arthur's Court *(1889), as well as many other works of fiction and nonfiction. One of America's most popular writers, Twain is generally regarded as the most important practitioner of the realistic school of writing, a style that emphasizes observable details.*

The following passage is taken from Life on the Mississippi *(1883), Twain's study of the great river and his account of his early experiences learning to be a river steamboat pilot. As you read the passage, notice how Twain makes use of figurative language in describing two very different ways of seeing the Mississippi River.*

Reflecting on What You Know

As we age and gain experience, our interpretation of the same memory—or how we view the same scene—can change. For example, the way we view our own appearance changes all the time, and photos from our childhood or teenage years may surprise us in the decades that follow. Perhaps something we found amusing in our younger days may make us feel uncomfortable or embarrassed now, or perhaps the house we grew up in later seems smaller or less appealing than it used to. Write about a memory that has changed for you over the years. How does your interpretation of it now contrast with how you experienced it earlier?

Now when I had mastered the language of this water and had come to know every trifling feature that bordered the great river as familiarly as I knew the letters of the alphabet, I had made a valuable acquisition. But I had lost something, too. I had lost something which 1 could never be restored to me while I lived. All the grace, the beauty, the poetry, had gone out of the majestic river! I still kept in mind a certain wonderful sunset which I witnessed when steamboating was new to me. A broad expanse of the river was turned to blood; in the middle distance the red hue brightened into gold, through which a solitary log came floating, black and conspicuous; in one place a long, slanting mark lay sparkling upon the water; in another the surface was broken by boiling, tumbling rings that were as many tinted as an opal;[1] where the ruddy flush was faintest was a smooth spot that was covered with graceful circles and radiating lines, ever so delicately traced; the shore on our left was densely wooded, and the somber shadow that fell from this forest was broken in one place by a long, ruffled trail that shone like silver; and high above the forest wall a clean-stemmed dead tree waved a single leafy bough that glowed like a flame in the unobstructed splendor that was flowing from the sun. There were graceful curves, reflected images, woody heights, soft distances, and over the whole scene, far and near, the dissolving lights drifted steadily, enriching it every passing moment with new marvels of coloring.

I stood like one bewitched. I drank it in, in a speechless rapture. The 2
world was new to me and I had never seen anything like this at home. But as I have said, a day came when I began to cease from noting the glories and the charms which the moon and the sun and the twilight wrought upon the river's face; another day came when I ceased altogether to note them. Then, if that sunset scene had been repeated, I should have looked upon it without rapture and should have commented upon it inwardly after this fashion: "This sun means that we are going to have wind tomorrow; that floating log means that the river is rising, small thanks to it; that slanting mark on the water refers to a bluff reef which is going to kill somebody's steamboat one of these nights, if it keeps on stretching out like that; those tumbling 'boils' show a dissolving bar and a changing channel there; the lines and circles in the slick water over yonder are a warning that that troublesome place is shoaling up dangerously; that silver streak in the shadow of the forest is the 'break' from a new snag and he has located himself in the very best place he could have found to fish for steamboats; that tall dead tree, with a single living branch, is not going to last long, and then how is a body ever going to get through this blind place at night without the friendly old landmark?"

[1]*opal:* a multicolored, iridescent gemstone.

No, the romance and beauty were all gone from the river. All the value any feature of it had for me now was the amount of usefulness it could furnish toward compassing the safe piloting of a steamboat. Since those days, I have pitied doctors from my heart. What does the lovely flush in a beauty's cheek mean to a doctor but a "break" that ripples above some deadly disease? Are not all her visible charms sown thick with what are to him the signs and symbols of hidden decay? Does he ever see her beauty at all, or doesn't he simply view her professionally and comment upon her unwholesome condition all to himself? And doesn't he sometimes wonder whether he has gained most or lost most by learning his trade? 3

Thinking Critically about This Reading

In the opening paragraph, Twain exclaims, "All the grace, the beauty, the poetry, had gone out of the majestic river!" What is "the poetry," and why was it lost for him?

Questions for Study and Discussion

1. What method of organization does Twain use in this selection? (Glossary: *Organization*) What alternative methods might he have used? What would have been gained or lost?
2. Explain the analogy Twain uses in paragraph 3. (Glossary: *Analogy*) What is his purpose in using this analogy?
3. Twain uses a number of similes and metaphors in this selection. (Glossary: *Figure of Speech*) Identify three of each, and explain what Twain is comparing in each case. What do these figures of speech add to Twain's writing?
4. Now that he has learned the trade of steamboating, does Twain believe that he has "gained most or lost most" (paragraph 3)? What has he gained, and what has he lost?
5. Twain points to a change of attitude he underwent as a result of seeing the river from a new perspective, that of a steamboat pilot. What role does knowledge play in Twain's inability to see the river as he once did?

Classroom Activity Using Comparison and Contrast

Using the sample outlines on pages 487–88 as models, prepare both subject-by-subject and point-by-point outlines for one of the following topics:

dogs and cats as pets
Facebook and Twitter
an SUV and a hybrid car
your local newspaper and the *New York Times* or *USA Today*
a high school–level course and a college-level course
the San Antonio Spurs and the Miami Heat basketball teams

Before starting your outline, determine the key points you wish to compare and contrast. Be prepared to explain any advantages you see of one organizational plan over the other.

Suggested Writing Assignments

1. Twain's essay contrasts the perception of one person before and after acquiring a particular body of knowledge. Different people also usually perceive the same scene or event differently, even if they are experiencing it simultaneously. To use an example from Twain's writing, a poet and a doctor might perceive a rosy-cheeked young woman in entirely different ways. Write a comparison and contrast essay in which you show how two people with different experiences might perceive the same subject. It can be a case of profound difference (such as a musician and an electrician at the same pyrotechnic rock concert) or one more subtle (such as a novelist and a screenwriter seeing the same lovers' quarrel in a restaurant). Add a short postscript in which you explain your choice of subject-by-subject comparison or point-by-point comparison for your essay.
2. Learning how to drive a car may not be as involved as learning how to pilot a steamboat on the Mississippi River, but it has a tremendous effect on how we function and on how we perceive our surroundings. Write an essay about short trips you took as a passenger and as a driver. Compare and contrast your perceptions and actions. What is most important to you as a passenger?

What is most important to you as a driver? How do your perceptions shift between the two roles? What changes in terms of what you notice around you and the way you notice it?

3. Is it possible for two people to have two completely different views of something? How might experience or perspective change how they view something? Write an essay modeled on Twain's in which you offer two different views of an event. You might consider a reporter's view compared with a victim's view, a teacher's view compared with a student's view, or a customer's view compared with a salesperson's view.

Taking My Son to College, Where Technology Has Replaced Serendipity

■ **Christina Baker Kline**

Photograph by Karin Diana

Christina Baker Kline was born in Cambridge, England, and grew up in Maine. She is a graduate of Yale University, where she majored in English, and received graduate degrees from Cambridge University and the University of Virginia. She is the author of many novels, including Sweet Water *(1993),* Desire Lines *(1999),* The Way Life Should Be *(2007),* Bird in Hand *(2009), and the* New York Times *best-seller* Orphan Train *(2013). She is also the coeditor, with Anne Burt, of* About Face: Women Write about What They See When They Look in the Mirror *(2008). Kline was a writer-in-residence at Fordham University from 2007 to 2011, and she has been the recipient of several fellowships from the Geraldine R. Dodge Foundation. She is currently at work on a new novel, inspired by Andrew Wyeth's famous painting* Christina's World. *She lives in Montclair, New Jersey.*

In this essay, which first appeared in the New Jersey Star-Ledger, *Kline drops her son off at college and looks back on memories of her own freshman year. As you read, note the ways Kline thinks her son's time in college will contrast with what she experienced.*

Reflecting on What You Know

How does technology affect the way you experience college? In what ways does it make the experience better? Do you think you lose anything by having more technology available than did previous generations of students?

My son Hayden started college last week. Like many parents of freshmen, my husband and I drove him to school together, the back of the car filled with essentials like extra-long twin sheets, a clip-on light for his bunk bed and a random mix of extension cords. 1

The milk crates, shower caddy and three-ring binders we helped him carry up the stairs flashed me back to my own first days of college—but they weren't the only reason this experience felt so familiar. 2

Three decades ago I was a freshman at the same university. Unlike Hayden, who grew up outside of New York and attended a competitive suburban high school, I was the only student from my small town in Maine to go to Yale, one of the few to even venture out of state. And I had no idea what I was getting into. 3

I was lucky, in a way, to be so naive; I didn't know what I didn't know. I floated through my first year obliviously unaware of the social currencies being exchanged around me, only dimly perceiving markers of wealth and status. 4

When a fellow student bragged about his Alfa Romeo, I thought he meant a Camaro, the fanciest car I'd ever seen. When a classmate casually mentioned that she was meeting her parents in Gstaad for the long weekend, I assumed it was a town in Connecticut. Imagine my surprise when I realized that actual Vanderbilts lived in Vanderbilt Hall. 5

But it wasn't just my relative lack of sophistication that made my experience so vastly different from my son's. Typewriters and carbon paper, telephones with curly cords, TVs with a few channels and no remotes, cassette tapes; compared with the tools Hayden has at his disposal, I went to college in the Stone Age. 6

Without even thinking about it, my son uses technology in almost everything he does, large and small. He installed Yale-specific apps on his phone that provide information about when the washers and dryers in the basement of his dorm are available, the daily menus of each dining hall, ratings of local restaurants, student contact information, the entire list of classes, and an interactive campus map that shows you where you are and where you're going. 7

Within minutes of learning his three suitemates' names this summer, he knew an incredible amount about them: They friended and followed each other on Facebook and Twitter and Instagram and immediately had access to each other's prom pictures, family vacation shots, performance videos, philosophical musings. They established an ongoing group text, exchanging information such as who was 8 bringing an Xbox and who had a coffeemaker. Soon after arriving on campus, Hayden made a spreadsheet of potential classes, vetting them in advance by using teacher rating sites and watching videos of potential professors on YouTube.

There's no question that my son is better prepared for college 9
than I was. He manages his time better, is more efficient and more directed, and spends less time in lines and more time doing exactly what he sets out to do.

But I wonder what may be lost. I suspect it's unlikely that he will 10
ever, as I did, trek all the way across campus on a snowy day to a friend's dorm room, only to find that person gone but another roommate available, and making a new friend in the process. He won't have to type and retype his papers—using Wite-Out, no less!—to make revisions, finding in that process new insights into what he's written. I doubt that he'll make his way to a common room at 9 p.m. every Sunday to watch a specific TV show (*L.A. Law*, I'm thinking of you), bonding with a hearty group of loyalists.

I think fondly of the rabbit holes I disappeared down when I re- 11
searched papers for history and English because I couldn't find quite what I was looking for, or because I had to go through so much material to find examples for my thesis. When you can type a few words into a search engine and land on your topic—or when you can scan a Shakespeare play for specific words or symbols—what opportunities might you miss to expand your thinking in unexpected ways?

I worry that students today are more connected and more frag- 12
mented, learning more about one another from afar but watching programs on their iPads in their rooms. The knowledge they have at their fingertips may make them more productive, but it may also blunt the thrill of unanticipated discovery.

Sometime in my first week on that long-ago campus, I found my- 13
self hopelessly lost, scrutinizing an indecipherable map, when a freshman boy came up to me. "Can I help you with that?" he asked, and though he didn't know his way around any better than I did, we figured it out together. Twenty-three years of marriage later, we're still figuring it out.

As Hayden navigates his own journey, I wish for him the satisfac- 14
tion of productivity and the joy of tapping his potential. But I also hope for him at least some of the wide-eyed wonder I felt as a freshman, the delight of discovering a world that was as remote and unknown to me as a foreign country.

And I hope he'll experience the unexpected pleasures of getting 15
lost, of chance encounters, and the incalculable benefits of time wasted for no good reason at all.

Thinking Critically about This Reading

Kline makes an argument for valuing what some might consider setbacks: "getting lost," "time wasted," and so on. Why? What benefits can come from these apparent problems?

Questions for Study and Discussion

1. Kline's essay focuses on the contrast between her son's freshman college experience and her own, but she sets up this series of contrasts by establishing what they have in common. How is his freshman year like hers?
2. Why does Kline say she was lucky to be naive when she first arrived at college? What sorts of things did she understand as a freshman?
3. In paragraphs 6 and 7, Kline contrasts the old technology she used as a student and the new technology available to Hayden. How do these two lists illustrate her point about what has changed? How foreign does her list of tools sound to you?
4. Notice that as she contrasts the two college experiences, Kline primarily uses a point-by-point organization. How does she think technology will change college students' social lives? Their intellectual work?
5. Find a definition for the word *serendipity,* which Kline uses in her title. Then choose examples from her essay that show what she means by this word. (Glossary: *Illustration*)
6. Near the end of the essay, Kline hopes that Hayden will benefit from technology but also put it aside at times. How does she imagine him finding a middle ground?

Classroom Activity Using Comparison and Contrast

Do you think that writing and speaking are contrasting skills? William Hazlitt argues that they are in his essay "On the Difference between Writing and Speaking." Read the following excerpt, paying attention to how Hazlitt uses parallel structure in his sentences to emphasize the direct contrast. How does each new point build on the last? Where do you think he makes the most convincing case for seeing writing and speaking as two very different modes of communication?

> The great leading distinction between writing and speaking is, that more time is allowed for the one than the other; and hence different faculties are required for, and different objects attained by, each. He is properly the best speaker who can collect together the greatest number of apposite ideas at a moment's warning: he is properly the best writer who can give utterance to the greatest quantity of valuable knowledge in the course of his whole life. The chief requisite for the one, then, appears to be quickness and facility of perception—for the other, patience of soul, and a power increasing with the difficulties it has to master. He cannot be denied to be an expert speaker, a lively companion, who is never at a loss for something to say on every occasion or subject that offers: he, by the same rule, will make a respectable writer, who, by dint of study, can find out anything good to say upon any one point that has not been touched upon before, or who, by asking for time, can give the most complete and comprehensive view of any question. The one must be done off-hand, at a single blow: the other can only be done by a repetition of blows, by having time to think and do better. In speaking, less is required of you, if you only do it at once, with grace and spirit: in writing, you stipulate for all that you are capable of, but you have the choice of your own time and subject. You do not expect from the manufacturer the same despatch in executing an order that you do from a shopman or warehouseman. The difference of quicker and slower, however, is not all: that is merely a difference of comparison in doing the same thing. But the writer and speaker have to do things essentially different. Besides habit, and greater or less facility, there is also a certain reach of capacity, a certain depth or shallowness, grossness or refinement of intellect, which marks out the distinction between those whose chief ambition is to shine by producing an immediate effect, or who are thrown back, by a natural bias, on the severer researches of thought and study.

Suggested Writing Assignments

1. How might this essay look different if it were written from Hayden's perspective instead of his mother's? Write an essay in which you contrast some aspect of your life (in school or otherwise)

with what your parents experienced. You will probably want to start with what you share before discussing how your experiences are different.

2. How did you decide on the college you would attend? Think about the important factors that influenced your decision, then write a point-by-point comparison of your school with another you considered or another nearby.

Two Ways to Belong in America

Bharati Mukherjee

Marty Lederhandler/AP Photo

Bharati Mukherjee was born into an aristocratic family in Calcutta (now Kolkata), India, in 1940. She earned bachelor's and master's degrees from the University of Calcutta, and in 1961, she pursued her long-held desire to become a writer by earning an MFA at the University of Iowa and eventually a PhD in English and comparative literature. She lived in Canada for fourteen years, until legislation against South Asians prompted her to move with her American husband back to the United States. Mukherjee has taught at McGill University; Skidmore College; and Queens College, City University of New York and is now on the faculty at the University of California–Berkeley. She has published seven novels, including The Tiger's Daughter *(1971),* Jasmine *(1989),* The Holder of the World *(1993), and* Miss New India *(2011); two collections of short stories,* Darkness *(1985) and* The Middleman and Other Stories *(1988), for which she won the National Book Critics Circle Award; and two works of nonfiction,* Political Culture and Leadership in India *(1991) and* Regionalism in Indian Perspective *(1992).*

The following essay was first published in the New York Times *in 1996 in response to legislation that gave expedited citizenship for legal immigrants living in the United States. As you read Mukherjee's essay, notice how she has organized her presentation of the different views that she and her sister hold toward citizenship.*

Reflecting on What You Know

The word *immigrant* has many connotations. If you have moved to the United States from another country, what associations does the word have for you and your family? If you were born in the United States, what associations does the word have for you? Discuss the word *immigrant* with your classmates. How does one's perspective affect the associations that this word has for them? Explain.

This is a tale of two sisters from Calcutta, Mira and Bharati, who have lived in the United States for some thirty-five years, but who find themselves on different sides in the current debate over the status of immigrants. I am an American citizen and she is not. I am moved that thousands of long-term residents are finally taking the oath of citizenship. She is not. 1

Mira arrived in Detroit in 1960 to study child psychology and preschool education. I followed her a year later to study creative writing at the University of Iowa. When we left India, we were almost identical in appearance and attitude. We dressed alike, in saris; we expressed identical views on politics, social issues, love and marriage in the same Calcutta convent-school accent. We would endure our two years in America, secure our degrees, then return to India to marry the grooms of our father's choosing. 2

Instead, Mira married an Indian student in 1962 who was getting his business administration degree at Wayne State University. They soon acquired the labor certifications necessary for the green card of hassle-free residence and employment. 3

Mira still lives in Detroit, works in the Southfield, Michigan, school system, and has become nationally recognized for her contributions in the fields of preschool education and parent-teacher relationships. After thirty-six years as a legal immigrant in this country, she clings passionately to her Indian citizenship and hopes to go home to India when she retires. 4

In Iowa City in 1963, I married a fellow student, an American of Canadian parentage. Because of the accident of his North Dakota birth, I bypassed labor-certification requirements and the race-related "quota" system that favored the applicant's country of origin over his or her merit. I was prepared for (and even welcomed) the emotional strain that came with marrying outside my ethnic community. In thirty-three years of marriage, we have lived in every part of North America. By choosing a husband who was not my father's selection, I was opting for fluidity, self-invention, blue jeans and T-shirts, and renouncing three thousand years (at least) of caste-observant, "pure 5 culture" marriage in the Mukherjee family. My books have often been read as unapologetic (and in some quarters overenthusiastic) texts for cultural and psychological "mongrelization." It's a word I celebrate.

Mira and I have stayed sisterly close by phone. In our regular 6
Sunday morning conversations, we are unguardedly affectionate. I am her only blood relative on this continent. We expect to see each other through the looming crises of aging and ill health without being asked. Long before Vice President Gore's "Citizenship USA" drive, we'd had our polite arguments over the ethics of retaining an overseas citizenship while expecting the permanent protection and economic benefits that come with living and working in America.

Like well-raised sisters, we never said what was really on our 7
minds, but we probably pitied one another. She, for the lack of structure in my life, the erasure of Indianness, the absence of an unvarying daily core. I, for the narrowness of her perspective, her uninvolvement with the mythic depths or the superficial pop culture of this society. But, now, with the scapegoating of "aliens" (documented or illegal) on the increase, and the targeting of long-term legal immigrants like Mira for new scrutiny and new self-consciousness, she and I find ourselves unable to maintain the same polite discretion. We were always unacknowledged adversaries, and we are now, more than ever, sisters.

"I feel used," Mira raged on the phone the other night. "I feel 8
manipulated and discarded. This is such an unfair way to treat a person who was invited to stay and work here because of her talent. My employer went to the INS and petitioned for the labor certification. For over thirty years, I've invested my creativity and professional skills into the improvement of *this* country's preschool system. I've obeyed all the rules, I've paid my taxes, I love my work, I love my students, I love the friends I've made. How dare America now change its rules in midstream? If America wants to make new rules curtailing benefits of legal immigrants, they should apply only to immigrants who arrive after those rules are already in place."

To my ears, it sounded like the description of a long-enduring, 9
comfortable yet loveless marriage, without risk or recklessness. Have we the right to demand, and to expect, that we be loved? (That, to me, is the subtext of the arguments by immigration advocates.) My sister is an expatriate, professionally generous and creative, socially courteous and gracious, and that's as far as her Americanization can go. She is here to maintain an identity, not to transform it.

I asked her if she would follow the example of others who have decided to become citizens because of the anti-immigration bills in Congress. And here, she surprised me. "If America wants to play the manipulative game, I'll play it too," she snapped. "I'll become a U.S. citizen for now, then change back to Indian when I'm ready to go home. I feel some kind of irrational attachment to India that I don't to America. Until all this hysteria against legal immigrants, I was totally happy. Having my green card meant I could visit any place in the world I wanted to and then come back to a job that's satisfying and that I do very well." 10

In one family, from two sisters alike as peas in a pod, there could not be a wider divergence of immigrant experience. America spoke to me—I married it—I embraced the demotion from expatriate aristocrat to immigrant nobody, surrendering those thousands of years of "pure culture," the saris, the delightfully accented English. She retained them all. Which of us is the freak? 11

Mira's voice, I realize, is the voice not just of the immigrant South Asian community but of an immigrant community of the millions who have stayed rooted in one job, one city, one house, one ancestral culture, one cuisine, for the entirety of their productive years. She speaks for greater numbers than I possibly can. Only the fluency of her English and the anger, rather than fear, born of confidence from her education, differentiate her from the seamstresses, the domestics, the technicians, the shop owners, the millions of hardworking but effectively silenced documented immigrants as well as their less fortunate "illegal" brothers and sisters. 12

Nearly twenty years ago, when I was living in my husband's ancestral homeland of Canada, I was always well-employed but never allowed to feel part of the local Quebec or larger Canadian society. Then, through a Green Paper that invited a national referendum on the unwanted side effects of "nontraditional" immigration, the Government officially turned against its immigrant communities, particularly those from South Asia. 13

I felt then the same sense of betrayal that Mira feels now. I will never forget the pain of that sudden turning, and the casual racist outbursts the Green Paper elicited. That sense of betrayal had its desired effect and drove me, and thousands like me, from the country. 14

Mira and I differ, however, in the ways in which we hope to interact with the country that we have chosen to live in. She is happier to live in America as an expatriate Indian than as an immigrant American. 15

I need to feel like a part of the community I have adopted (as I tried to feel in Canada as well). I need to put roots down, to vote and make the difference that I can. The price that the immigrant willingly pays, and that the exile avoids, is the trauma of self-transformation.

Thinking Critically about This Reading

What do you think Mukherjee's sister means when she says in paragraph 10, "If America wants to play the manipulative game, I'll play it too"? How do you react to her decision and her possible plans if and when she eventually returns to India?

Questions for Study and Discussion

1. What is Mukherjee's thesis? (Glossary: *Thesis*)
2. Mukherjee has used comparison and contrast as her organizing principle. What type of comparison and contrast has she used?
3. Why is the pattern of organization that Mukherjee used appropriate for her subject and her purpose?
4. Why might Mukherjee have ordered her points of discussion in the way that she has? Explain.
5. What arguments does Mukherjee make for becoming a U.S. citizen? What arguments does her sister make for retaining her Indian citizenship?
6. Why does Mukherjee's sister feel "used" by attempts to change U.S. laws regarding benefits for noncitizens?
7. What does Mukherjee mean when she says in paragraph 15, "The price that the immigrant willingly pays, and that the exile avoids, is the trauma of self-transformation"?

Classroom Activity Using Comparison and Contrast

In preparation for writing an essay of comparison and contrast on two world leaders (or popular singers, actors, or sports figures), write out answers to the following questions:

1. Who could I compare and contrast?
2. What is my purpose?

3. Which are more interesting—their similarities or their differences?
4. What specific points should I discuss?
5. What organizational pattern will best suit my purpose: subject-by-subject or point-by-point?

Suggested Writing Assignments

1. Mukherjee writes about the relationship she had with her sister in paragraph 7 by saying that "we never said what was really on our minds, but we probably pitied one another." These types of differences are played out on a larger scale when immigrants who have transformed themselves into Americans are confronted by those who have chosen to retain their ethnic identity, and these tensions often lead to name-calling and aggressive prejudice. Similar situations also exist within the Latino, African American, and Southeast Asian American communities and perhaps among all immigrant groups. Write an essay comparing and contrasting the choices of lifestyle that members of an ethnic or cultural community you are familiar with make as they try to find a comfortable place in American society.
2. Mukherjee presents her sister's reasons for not becoming a citizen and supports them with statements her sister has made. Imagine that you are Mira Mukherjee. Write a counterargument to the one presented by your sister that gives your reasons for remaining an Indian citizen. Consider that you have already broken with tradition by marrying a man not of your father's choosing but also that the "trauma of self-transformation" that your sister raises in the conclusion of her essay is much deeper and more complicated than she has represented it. Can you say that you are holding to tradition when you are not? Can you engage in a challenging self-transformation if it is not genuinely motivated?

Grant and Lee: A Study in Contrasts

■ Bruce Catton

Katherine Young/Library of Congress

Bruce Catton (1897–1978) grew up in Petoskey, Michigan. As a young man, he left his studies at Oberlin College to serve in World War I and never returned to complete his degree. He became a journalist and a historian, publishing several books of popular history on the Civil War, including the Pulitzer Prize–winning A Stillness at Appomattox *(1953) and* Two Roads to Sumter *(1963).*

In this essay, Catton compares the two generals who met to negotiate the terms for the surrender of the Confederate Army. As you read, notice how Catton masterfully shows the "complete contrast" between Ulysses S. Grant and Robert E. Lee as well as the fact that "these two great soldiers had much in common."

Reflecting on What You Know

April 2015 marks the 150th anniversary of the end of the devastating Civil War. What do you know about the causes of this war? How would you explain the contrast between the North and the South?

When Ulysses S. Grant and Robert E. Lee met in the parlor of a modest house at Appomattox Court House, Virginia, on April 9, 1865, to work out the terms for the surrender of Lee's Army of Northern Virginia, a great chapter in American life came to a close, and a great new chapter began. 1

These men were bringing the Civil War to its virtual finish. To be sure, other armies had yet to surrender, and for a few days the fugitive Confederate government would struggle desperately and vainly, 2 trying to find some way to go on living now that its chief support was gone. But in effect it was all over when Grant and Lee signed the papers. And the little room where they wrote out the terms was the scene of one of the poignant, dramatic contrasts in American history.

They were two strong men, these oddly different generals, and they represented the strengths of two conflicting currents that, through them, had come into final collision. 3

Back of Robert E. Lee was the notion that the old aristocratic concept might somehow survive and be dominant in American life. 4

Lee was tidewater Virginia, and in his background were family, culture, and tradition . . . the age of chivalry transplanted to a New World which was making its own legends and its own myths. He embodied a way of life that had come down through the age of knighthood and the English country squire. America was a land that was beginning all over again, dedicated to nothing much more complicated than the rather hazy belief that all men had equal rights and should have an equal chance in the world. In such a land Lee stood for the feeling that it was somehow of advantage to human society to have a pronounced inequality in the social structure. There should be a leisure class, backed by ownership of land; in turn, society itself should be keyed to the land as the chief source of wealth and influence. It would bring forth (according to this ideal) a class of men with a strong sense of obligation to the community; men who lived not to gain advantage for themselves, but to meet the solemn obligations which had been laid on them by the very fact that they were privileged. From them the country would get its leadership; to them it could look for the higher values—of thought, of conduct, of personal deportment—to give it strength and virtue. 5

Lee embodied the noblest elements of this aristocratic ideal. Through him, the landed nobility justified itself. For four years, the Southern states had fought a desperate war to uphold the ideals for which Lee stood. In the end, it almost seemed as if the Confederacy fought for Lee; as if he himself was the Confederacy . . . the best thing that the way of life for which the Confederacy stood could ever have to offer. He had passed into legend before Appomattox. Thousands of tired, underfed, poorly clothed Confederate soldiers, long since past the simple enthusiasm of the early days of the struggle, somehow considered Lee the symbol of everything for which they had been willing to die. But they could not quite put this feeling into words. If the Lost 6

Cause, sanctified by so much heroism and so many deaths, had a living justification, its justification was General Lee.

Grant, the son of a tanner on the Western frontier, was everything Lee was not. He had come up the hard way and embodied nothing in particular except the eternal toughness and sinewy fiber of the men who grew up beyond the mountains. He was one of a body of men who owed reverence and obeisance to no one, who were self-reliant to a fault, who cared hardly anything for the past but who had a sharp eye for the future. 7

These frontier men were the precise opposites of the tidewater aristocrats. Back of them, in the great surge that had taken people over the Alleghenies and into the opening Western country, there was a deep, implicit dissatisfaction with a past that had settled into grooves. They stood for democracy, not from any reasoned conclusion about the proper ordering of human society, but simply because they had grown up in the middle of democracy and knew how it worked. Their society might have privileges, but they would be privileges each man had won for himself. Forms and patterns meant nothing. No man was born to anything, except perhaps to a chance to show how far he could rise. Life was competition. 8

Yet along with this feeling had come a deep sense of belonging to a national community. The Westerner who developed a farm, opened a shop, or set up in business as a trader, could hope to prosper only as his own community prospered—and his community ran from the Atlantic to the Pacific and from Canada down to Mexico. If the land was settled, with towns and highways and accessible markets, he could better himself. He saw his fate in terms of the nation's own destiny. As its horizons expanded, so did his. He had, in other words, an acute dollars-and-cents stake in the continued growth and development of his country. 9

And that, perhaps, is where the contrast between Grant and Lee becomes most striking. The Virginia aristocrat, inevitably, saw himself in relation to his own region. He lived in a static society which could endure almost anything except change. Instinctively, his first loyalty would go to the locality in which that society existed. He would fight to the limit of endurance to defend it, because in defending it he was defending everything that gave his own life its deepest meaning. 10

The Westerner, on the other hand, would fight with an equal tenacity for the broader concept of society. He fought so because everything he lived by was tied to growth, expansion, and a constantly 11 widening horizon. What he lived by would survive or fall with the nation itself. He could not possibly stand by unmoved in the face of an attempt to destroy the Union. He would combat it with everything he had, because he could only see it as an effort to cut the ground out from under his feet.

So Grant and Lee were in complete contrast, representing two diametrically opposed elements in American life. Grant was the modern man emerging; beyond him, ready to come on the stage, was the great age of steel and machinery, of crowded cities and a restless burgeoning vitality. Lee might have ridden down from the old age of chivalry, lance in hand, silken banner fluttering over his head. Each man was the perfect champion of his cause, drawing both his strengths and his weaknesses from the people he led. 12

Yet it was not all contrast, after all. Different as they were—in background, in personality, in underlying aspiration—these two great soldiers had much in common. Under everything else, they were marvelous fighters. Furthermore, their fighting qualities were really very much alike. 13

Each man had, to begin with, the great virtue of utter tenacity and fidelity. Grant fought his way down the Mississippi Valley in spite of acute personal discouragement and profound military handicaps. Lee hung on in the trenches at Petersburg after hope itself had died. In each man there was an indomitable quality . . . the born fighter's refusal to give up as long as he can still remain on his feet and lift his two fists. 14

Daring and resourcefulness they had, too; the ability to think faster and move faster than the enemy. These were the qualities which gave Lee the dazzling campaigns of Second Manassas and Chancellorsville and won Vicksburg for Grant. 15

Lastly, and perhaps greatest of all, there was the ability, at the end, to turn quickly from war to peace once the fighting was over. Out of the way these two men behaved at Appomattox came the possibility of a peace of reconciliation. It was a possibility not wholly realized, in the years to come, but which did, in the end, help the two sections to become one nation again . . . after a war whose bitterness might have seemed to make such a reunion wholly impossible. No part of either man's life became him more than the part he played in their brief meeting in the McLean house at Appomattox. Their behavior there put all succeeding generations of Americans in their debt. Two great Americans, Grant and Lee—very different, yet under 16 everything very much alike. Their encounter at Appomattox was one of the great moments of American history.

Thinking Critically about This Reading

Catton says that although there were a few days in which the Confederates continued to struggle against the Union forces, the war was effectually "all over when Grant and Lee signed the papers" (paragraph 2). Is this true not only for the military action but also for the cultural conflict, which Catton describes in his essay? Why or why not?

Questions for Study and Discussion

1. In paragraphs 5 and 6, Catton discusses Robert E. Lee at length. Which of Lee's characteristics does he emphasize? What does he represent in this contrast?
2. The following paragraphs, 7–9, focus on Ulysses S. Grant. What are his most salient characteristics? How are his values in opposition to Lee's?
3. After making broad comparisons of these two men, Catton focuses in on the point at which he thinks "the contrast between Grant and Lee becomes most striking" (10). Explain how the two generals understand the society to which each belongs. How do they believe they are responsible to this society?
4. Discuss the imagery Catton uses in paragraph 12 to suggest that Lee is a representative of the past whereas Grant looks forward to the future. How does he help readers picture this contrast?
5. Although the two men are fundamentally different, toward the end of the essay, Catton turns to consider what they have in common. What qualities of "marvelous fighters" (13) do Grant and Lee share?

Classroom Activity Using Comparison and Contrast

The following passage is taken from the late Stephen E. Ambrose's book *Crazy Horse and Custer: The Parallel Lives of Two American Warriors* (1975). Carefully read and analyze the passage, in which

Ambrose compares and contrasts Chief Crazy Horse and General George Armstrong Custer. Then answer the questions that follow.

> It was bravery, above and beyond all other qualities, that Custer and Crazy Horse had in common. Each man was an outstanding warrior in war-mad societies. Thousands upon thousands of Custer's fellow whites had as much opportunity as he did to demonstrate their courage, just as all of Crazy Horse's associates had countless opportunities to show that they equaled him in bravery. But no white warrior, save his younger brother, Tom, could outdo Custer, just as no Indian warrior, save his younger brother, Little Hawk, could outdo Crazy Horse. And for both white and red societies, no masculine virtue was more admired than bravery. To survive, both societies felt they had to have men willing to put their lives on the line. For men who were willing to do so, no reward was too great, even though there were vast differences in the way each society honored its heroes.
>
> Beyond their bravery, Custer and Crazy Horse were individualists, each standing out from the crowd in his separate way. Custer wore outlandish uniforms, let his hair fall in long, flowing golden locks across his shoulders, surrounded himself with pet animals and admirers, and in general did all he could to draw attention to himself. Crazy Horse's individualism pushed him in the opposite direction—he wore a single feather in his hair when going into battle, rather than a war bonnet. Custer's vast energy set him apart from most of his fellows; the Sioux distinguished Crazy Horse from other warriors because of Crazy Horse's quietness and introspection. Both men lived in societies in which drugs, especially alcohol, were widely used, but neither Custer nor Crazy Horse drank. Most of all, of course, each man stood out in battle as a great risk taker.

What is Ambrose's point in these two paragraphs? How does he use comparison and contrast to make this point? How has he organized his paragraphs? How else might he have organized them? Explain.

Suggested Writing Assignments

1. Think of two historical figures you believe are in direct opposition, and write a "study in contrasts," organizing your ideas about the two figures to highlight how they differ. Following Catton's model, you might want to use the conclusion of your essay to consider any common ground these two figures share.

2. Catton convinces readers that the contrast between these two men is not only stark but also "poignant" because each man represents a larger trend in American society. Choose someone who you think represents an important current trend in public life, and write an essay analyzing what he or she stands for. Like Catton, you can use both strict facts (Lee is from tidewater Virginia) and more figurative characterizations (Lee is like a knight out of the age of chivalry) to capture the person's essence.

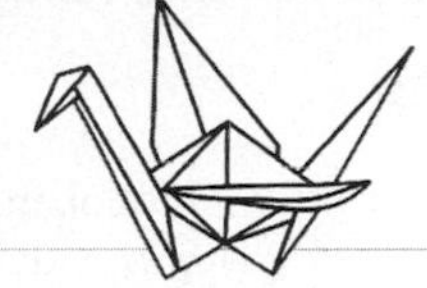

CHAPTER **20**

Cause and Effect

Every time you answer a question that asks *why*, you engage in the process of *causal analysis*—that is, you try to determine a *cause* or series of causes for a particular *effect*. When you answer a question that asks *what if*, you try to determine what *effect* will result from a particular *cause*. You will have many opportunities to use **cause and effect** in the writing you will do in college. For example, in history, you might be asked to determine the causes for the 1991 breakup of the former Soviet Union; in political science, you might be asked to determine the critical issues in the 2008 presidential election; in sociology, you might be asked to analyze the effects that the AIDS epidemic has had on sexual-behavior patterns among Americans; and in economics, you might be asked to predict what will happen to our country if we enact large tax cuts.

Fascinated by the effects that private real estate development was having on his neighborhood, a student writer decided to find out what was happening in the older sections of cities across the country. In his first paragraph, Kevin Cunningham describes three possible effects (or fates) of a city's aging. In his second paragraph, he singles out one effect—redevelopment—and discusses in detail the effect it has had on Hoboken, New Jersey.

Effect: decay

Effect: urban renewal

Effect: redevelopment

Effects of redevelopment

One of three fates awaits the aging neighborhood. Decay may continue until the neighborhood becomes a slum. It may face urban renewal, with old buildings being razed and ugly new apartment houses taking their place. Or it may undergo redevelopment, in which government encourages the upgrading of existing housing stock by offering low-interest loans or outright grants; thus, the original character of the neighborhood may be retained or restored, allowing the city to keep part of its identity.

> An example of redevelopment at its best is Hoboken, New Jersey. In the early 1970s, Hoboken was a dying city, with rundown housing and many abandoned buildings. However, low-interest loans enabled some younger residents to refurbish their homes, and soon the area began to show signs of renewed vigor. Even outsiders moved in and rebuilt some of the abandoned houses. Today, whole blocks have been restored, and neighborhood life is active again. The city does well, too, because property values are higher and so are property taxes.
>
> –Kevin Cunningham, student

In the following example, popular author Bill Bryson explains why the transition from being hunter-gatherers to farmers and city dwellers did not have a beneficial effect on us as humans:

> It is not as if farming brought a great improvement in living standards either. A typical hunter-gatherer enjoyed a more varied diet and consumed more protein and calories than settled people, and took in five times as much vitamin C as the average person today. Even in the bitterest depths of the ice ages, we now know, nomadic people ate surprisingly well—and surprisingly healthily. Settled people, by contrast, became reliant on a much smaller range of foods, which all but ensured dietary insufficiencies. The three great domesticated crops of prehistory were rice, wheat, and maize, but all had significant drawbacks as staples. As the journalist John Lanchester explains: "Rice inhibits the activity of Vitamin A; wheat has a chemical that impedes the action of zinc and can lead to stunted growth; maize is deficient in essential amino acids and contains phytates, which prevent the absorption of iron." The average height of people actually fell by almost six inches in the early days of farming in the Near East. Even on Orkney, where prehistoric life was probably as good as it could get, an analysis of 340 ancient skeletons showed that hardly any people lived beyond their twenties.
>
> What killed the Orcadians was not dietary deficiency but disease. People living together are vastly more likely to spread illness from household to

household, and the close exposure to animals through domestication meant that flu (from pigs or fowl), smallpox and measles (from cows and sheep), and anthrax (from horses and goats, among others) could become part of the human condition, too. As far as we can tell, virtually all of the infectious diseases have become endemic only since people took to living together. Settling down also brought a huge increase in "human commensals"—mice, rats, and other creatures that live with and off us—and these all too often acted as disease vectors.

So sedentism meant poorer diets, more illness, lots of toothache and gum disease, and earlier deaths. What is truly extraordinary is that these are all still factors in our lives today. Out of the thirty thousand types of edible plants thought to exist on Earth, just eleven—corn, rice, wheat, potatoes, cassava, sorghum, millet, beans, barley, rye, and oats—account for 93 percent of all that humans eat, and every one of them was first cultivated by our Neolithic ancestors. Exactly the same is true of husbandry. The animals we raise for food today are eaten not because they are notably delectable or nutritious or a pleasure to be around, but because they were the ones first domesticated in the Stone Age.

We are, in the most fundamental way, Stone Age people ourselves. From a dietary point of view, the Neolithic period is still with us. We may sprinkle our dishes with bay leaves and chopped fennel, but underneath it all is Stone Age food. And when we get sick, it is Stone Age diseases we suffer.

–Bill Bryson, *At Home: A Short History of Private Life*

Determining causes and effects is usually a complex process. One reason is that *immediate causes* are readily apparent (because they are closest to the effect) and *ultimate causes* are not as apparent (because they are somewhat removed and even hidden). Furthermore, ultimate causes may bring about effects that themselves become immediate causes, thus creating a *causal chain.* Consider the following causal chain: Sally, a computer salesperson, prepared extensively for a meeting with an important client (ultimate cause), impressed the client (immediate cause), and made a very large sale (effect). The chain did not stop there: the large sale caused her to be promoted by her employer (effect). For a detailed example of a causal chain, read Barry Commoner's analysis of the near disaster at the Three Mile Island nuclear facility in Chapter 5 (pp. 123–24).

A second reason causal analysis can be complex is that an effect may have several possible or actual causes, and a cause may have several possible or actual effects. An upset stomach may be caused by eating spoiled food, but it may also be caused by overeating, flu, allergy, nervousness, pregnancy, or any combination of factors. Similarly, the high cost of electricity may have multiple effects—higher profits for utility companies, fewer sales of electrical appliances, higher prices for other products, and the development of alternative sources of energy.

Sound reasoning and logic are present in all good writing, but they are central to any causal analysis. Writers of believable causal analysis examine their material objectively and develop their essays carefully. They examine all causes and effects methodically and then evaluate them. They are convinced by their own examination of the material but are not afraid to admit that other causes and effects might exist. Above all, they do not let their own prejudices interfere with the logic of their analyses and presentations.

Because people are accustomed to thinking of causes with their effects, they sometimes commit an error in logic known as the "after this, therefore because of this" fallacy (in Latin, *post hoc, ergo propter hoc*). This **logical fallacy** leads people to believe that one event somehow caused a second event, just because the second event followed the first—that is, they sometimes make causal connections that are not proven. For example, if students perform better after a free breakfast program is instituted at their school, one cannot assume that the improvement was caused by the breakfast program. There could be any number of other causes for this effect, and a responsible writer would analyze and consider them all before suggesting a cause.

e macmillanhighered.com/mfw12e
e-readings > U.S. Department of State, *Help Protect Our Ocean* [video]

Why We Crave Horror Movies

■ Stephen King

Jon Ragel/CORBIS

Stephen King's name is synonymous with horror stories. Born in 1947, King is a 1970 graduate of the University of Maine. He worked as a janitor in a knitting mill, a laundry worker, and a high school English teacher before he struck it big with his writing. Many consider King to be the most successful writer of modern horror fiction today. To date, he has written dozens of novels, collections of short stories and novellas, and screenplays, among other works. His books have sold well over 250 million copies worldwide, and many of his novels have been made into popular motion pictures, including Stand by Me, Misery, The Green Mile, *and* Dreamcatcher. *His books, starting with* Carrie *in 1974, include* Salem's Lot *(1975),* The Shining *(1977),* The Dead Zone *(1979),* Christine *(1983),* Pet Sematary *(1983),* The Dark Half *(1989),* The Girl Who Loved Tom Gordon *(1999),* From a Buick 8 *(2002),* Under the Dome *(2009), and* Doctor Sleep *(2013). His other works include* Danse Macabre *(1980), a nonfiction look at horror in the media, and* On Writing: A Memoir of the Craft *(2000). The widespread popularity of horror books and films shows that many people share King's fascination with the macabre.*

In the following selection, originally published in Playboy *in 1982—a variation on "The Horror Movie as Junk Food" chapter in* Danse Macabre*—King analyzes the reasons we flock to horror movies.*

Reflecting on What You Know

What movies have you seen recently? Do you prefer watching any one particular kind of movie—comedy, drama, science fiction, or horror, for example—over others? How do you explain your preference?

I think that we're all mentally ill; those of us outside the asylums only hide it a little better—and maybe not all that much better, after all. We've all known people who talk to themselves, people who sometimes squinch their faces into horrible grimaces when they believe no one is watching, people who have some hysterical fear—of snakes, the dark, the tight place, the long drop . . . and, of course, those final worms and grubs that are waiting so patiently underground. 1

When we pay our four or five bucks and seat ourselves at tenth-row center in a theater showing a horror movie, we are daring the nightmare. 2

Why? Some of the reasons are simple and obvious. To show that we can, that we are not afraid, that we can ride this roller coaster. Which is not to say that a really good horror movie may not surprise a scream out of us at some point, the way we may scream when a roller coaster twists through a complete 360 or plows through a lake at the bottom of the drop. And horror movies, like roller coasters, have always been the special province of the young; by the time one turns forty or fifty, one's appetite for double twists or 360-degree loops may be considerably depleted. 3

We also go to reestablish our feelings of essential normality; the horror movie is innately conservative, even reactionary. Freda Jackson as the horrible melting woman in *Die, Monster, Die!* confirms for us that no matter how far we may be removed from the beauty of a Robert Redford or a Diana Ross, we are still light-years from true ugliness. 4

And we go to have fun. 5

Ah, but this is where the ground starts to slope away, isn't it? Because this is a very peculiar sort of fun, indeed. The fun comes from seeing others menaced—sometimes killed. One critic has suggested that if pro football has become the voyeur's[1] version of combat, then the horror film has become the modern version of the public lynching. 6

It is true that the mythic, "fairy-tale" horror film intends to take away the shades of gray. . . . It urges us to put away our more civilized and adult penchant for analysis and to become children again, seeing things in pure blacks and whites. It may be that horror movies provide psychic relief on this level because this invitation to lapse into simplicity, irrationality, and even outright madness is extended so rarely. We are told we may allow our emotions a free rein . . . or no rein at all. 7

[1]*voyeur:* one who observes from a distance.

If we are all insane, then sanity becomes a matter of degree. If your insanity leads you to carve up women like Jack the Ripper or the Cleveland Torso Murderer,[2] we clap you away in the funny farm (but neither of those two amateur-night surgeons was ever caught, heh-heh-heh); if, on the other hand, your insanity leads you only to talk to yourself when you're under stress or to pick your nose on your morning bus, then you are left alone to go about your business . . . though it is doubtful that you will ever be invited to the best parties. 8

The potential lyncher is in almost all of us (excluding saints, past and present; but then, most saints have been crazy in their own ways), and every now and then, he has to be let loose to scream and roll around in the grass. Our emotions and our fears form their own body, and we recognize that it demands its own exercise to maintain proper muscle tone. Certain of these emotional muscles are accepted—even exalted—in civilized society; they are, of course, the emotions that tend to maintain the status quo of civilization itself. Love, friendship, loyalty, kindness—these are all the emotions that we applaud, emotions that have been immortalized in the couplets of Hallmark cards and in the verses (I don't dare call it poetry) of Leonard Nimoy.[3] 9

When we exhibit these emotions, society showers us with positive reinforcement; we learn this even before we get out of diapers. When, as children, we hug our rotten little puke of a sister and give her a kiss, all the aunts and uncles smile and twit and cry, "Isn't he the sweetest little thing?" Such coveted treats as chocolate-covered graham crackers often follow. But if we deliberately slam the rotten little puke of a sister's fingers in the door, sanctions follow—angry remonstrance from parents, aunts, and uncles; instead of a chocolate-covered graham cracker, a spanking. 10

But anticivilization emotions don't go away, and they demand periodic exercise. We have such "sick" jokes as, "What's the difference between a truckload of bowling balls and a truckload of dead babies?" (You can't unload a truckload of bowling balls with a pitchfork . . . a joke, by the way, that I heard originally from a ten-year-old.) Such a joke may surprise a laugh or a grin out of us even as we recoil, a possibility that confirms the thesis: if we share a brotherhood of 11

[2]*Jack the Ripper or the Cleveland Torso Murderer:* serial murderers who were active in the 1880s and the 1930s, respectively.

[3]*Leonard Nimoy* (b. 1931): an actor famous for playing Mr. Spock on the U.S. television series *Star Trek,* which aired from 1966 to 1969.

man, then we also share an insanity of man. None of which is intended as a defense of either the sick joke or insanity but merely as an explanation of why the best horror films, like the best fairy tales, manage to be reactionary, anarchistic,[4] and revolutionary all at the same time.

The mythic horror movie, like the sick joke, has a dirty job to do. It deliberately appeals to all that is worst in us. It is morbidity unchained, our most base instincts let free, our nastiest fantasies realized . . . and it all happens, fittingly enough, in the dark. For those reasons, good liberals often shy away from horror films. For myself, I like to see the most aggressive of them—*Dawn of the Dead,* for instance—as lifting a trap door in the civilized forebrain and throwing a basket of raw meat to the hungry alligators swimming around in that subterranean river beneath. 12

Why bother? Because it keeps them from getting out, man. It keeps them down there and me up here. It was Lennon and McCartney who said that all you need is love, and I would agree with that. 13

As long as you keep the gators fed. 14

Thinking Critically about This Reading

What does King mean when he states that "the horror movie is innately conservative, even reactionary" (paragraph 4)?

Questions for Study and Discussion

1. What, according to King, causes people to crave horror movies? What other reasons can you add to King's list?
2. Identify the analogy King uses in paragraph 3, and explain how it works. (Glossary: *Analogy*)
3. What emotions does society applaud? Why? Which ones does King label "anticivilization emotions" (11)?
4. In what ways is a horror movie like a sick joke? What is the "dirty job," or effect, that the two have in common (12)?
5. King starts his essay with the attention-grabbing sentence, "I think that we're all mentally ill." How does he develop this idea of

[4]*anarchistic:* against any authority; favoring anarchy.

insanity in his essay? What does King mean when he says, "The potential lyncher is in almost all of us" (9)? How does King's last line relate to the theme of mental illness?

6. What is King's tone? (Glossary: *Tone*) Point to particular words or sentences that lead you to this conclusion.

Classroom Activity Using Cause and Effect

Use the following test, developed by William V. Haney, to determine your ability to accurately analyze evidence that is presented to you. After completing Haney's test, discuss your answers with other members of your class.

The Uncritical Inference Test

Directions

1. You will read a brief story. Assume that all of the information presented in the story is definitely accurate and true. Read the story carefully. You may refer back to the story whenever you wish.
2. You will then read statements about the story. Answer them in numerical order. *Do not go back* to fill in answers or to change answers. This will only distort your test score.
3. After you read each statement carefully, determine whether the statement is:
   a. "T"—meaning: On the basis of the information presented in the story the statement is *definitely true.*
   b. "F"—meaning: On the basis of the information presented in the story the statement is *definitely false.*
   c. "?"—The statement *may* be true (or false) but on the basis of the information presented in the story you cannot be definitely certain. (If any part of the statement is doubtful, mark the statement "?".)
4. Indicate your answer by circling either "T" or "F" or "?" opposite the statement.

The Story

Babe Smith has been killed. Police have rounded up six suspects, all of whom are known gangsters. All of them are known to have been near the scene of the killing at the approximate time that it occurred. All had substantial motives for wanting Smith killed. However, one of these suspected gangsters, Slinky Sam, has positively been cleared of guilt.

Statements about the Story

1. Slinky Sam is known to have been near the scene of the killing of Babe Smith. T F ?
2. All six of the rounded-up gangsters were known to have been near the scene of the murder. T F ?
3. Only Slinky Sam has been cleared of guilt. T F ?
4. All six of the rounded-up suspects were near the scene of Smith's killing at the approximate time that it took place. T F ?
5. The police do not know who killed Smith. T F ?
6. All six suspects are known to have been near the scene of the foul deed. T F ?
7. Smith's murderer did not confess of his own free will. T F ?
8. Slinky Sam was not cleared of guilt. T F ?
9. It is known that the six suspects were in the vicinity of the cold-blooded assassination. T F ?

Suggested Writing Assignments

1. Write an essay in which you analyze, in light of King's remarks about the causes of our cravings for horror movies, a horror movie you've seen. In what ways did the movie satisfy your "anticivilization emotions" (11)? How did you feel before going to the theater? How did you feel when leaving?
2. Write an essay in which you analyze the most significant reasons (or causes) for your going to college. You may wish to discuss such matters as your high school experiences, people and events that influenced your decision, and your goals in college as well as in later life.
3. Horror films offer many haunting images—the shower scene in Hitchcock's *Psycho,* the man chasing his son with an axe in *The Shining,* or the girl crawling out of the TV in *The Ring*. Choose a scary movie scene you think is iconographic—an unforgettable symbol of the essence of terror. Write an essay examining the scene, considering the causes of your fright.

Why and When We Speak Spanish in Public

■ Myriam Marquez

Patrick Farrell/Miami Herald/MCT

An award-winning columnist for the Orlando Sentinel, *Myriam Marquez was born in Havana, Cuba, in 1954 and grew up in southern Florida. After graduating from the University of Maryland in 1983 with a degree in journalism and a minor in political science, she worked for United Press International in Washington, D.C., and Maryland, covering the Maryland legislature as statehouse bureau chief. Marquez joined the editorial board of the* Sentinel *in 1987 and, beginning in 1990, wrote three weekly columns. Her commentaries focused on state and national politics, the human condition, civil liberties, and issues important to women and Hispanics. The Florida Society of Newspaper Editors awarded her its highest award for commentary in 2003. In 2005, she joined the* Miami Herald, *where she served for several years as the editorial page editor. She is currently the executive director of* El Nuevo Herald, *the nation's largest Spanish-language daily newspaper.*

Marquez grew up bilingual and recognizes that English is the "common language" in the United States but knows that being American has little if anything to do with what language one speaks. In this article, which first appeared in the Orlando Sentinel *on July 5, 1999, Marquez explains why she and her parents continue to speak Spanish when they are together, even though they have lived in the United States for many years.*

Reflecting on What You Know

When you are in public and hear people around you speaking a foreign language, what is your immediate reaction? Are you intrigued? Do you feel uncomfortable? How do you regard people who speak a language other than English in public? Why?

When I'm shopping with my mother or standing in line with my stepdad to order fast food or anywhere else we might be together, we're going to speak to one another in Spanish. 1

That may appear rude to those who don't understand Spanish and overhear us in public places. 2

Those around us may get the impression that we're talking about them. They may wonder why we would insist on speaking in a foreign tongue, especially if they knew that my family has lived in the United States for forty years and that my parents do understand English and speak it, albeit with difficulty and a heavy accent. 3

Let me explain why we haven't adopted English as our official family language. For me and most of the bilingual people I know, it's a matter of respect for our parents and comfort in our cultural roots. 4

It's not meant to be rude to others. It's not meant to alienate anyone or to Balkanize[1] America. 5

It's certainly not meant to be un-American—what constitutes an "American" being defined by English speakers from North America. 6

Being an American has very little to do with what language we use during our free time in a free country. From its inception,[2] this country was careful not to promote a government-mandated official language. 7

We understand that English is the common language of this country and the one most often heard in international business circles from Peru to Norway. We know that, to get ahead here, one must learn English. 8

But that ought not mean that somehow we must stop speaking in our native tongue whenever we're in a public area, as if we were ashamed of who we are, where we're from. As if talking in Spanish—or any other language, for that matter—is some sort of litmus test[3] used to gauge American patriotism. 9

Throughout this nation's history, most immigrants—whether from Poland or Finland or Italy or wherever else—kept their language through the first generation and, often, the second. I suspect that they spoke among themselves in their native tongue—in public. Pennsylvania even provided voting ballots written in German during much of the 1800s for those who weren't fluent in English. 10

In this century, Latin American immigrants and others have fought for this country in U.S.-led wars. They have participated fully in this 11

[1]*Balkanize:* to divide a region or territory into small, often hostile units.

[2]*inception:* the beginning of something.

[3]*litmus test:* a test that uses a single indicator to prompt a decision.

nation's democracy by voting, holding political office, and paying taxes. And they have watched their children and grandchildren become so "American" that they resist speaking in Spanish.

You know what's rude? 12

When there are two or more people who are bilingual and another 13
person who speaks only English and the bilingual folks all of a sudden start speaking Spanish, which effectively leaves out the English-only speaker. I don't tolerate that.

One thing's for sure. If I'm ever in a public place with my mom or 14
dad and bump into an acquaintance who doesn't speak Spanish, I will switch to English and introduce that person to my parents. They will respond in English, and do so with respect.

Thinking Critically about This Reading

Marquez states that "being an American has very little to do with what language we use during our free time in a free country" (paragraph 7). What activities does Marquez suggest truly make someone an American?

Questions for Study and Discussion

1. What is Marquez's thesis? (Glossary: *Thesis*)
2. Against what ideas does she seem to be arguing? How do you know?
3. What effect do you think Marquez was trying to achieve by beginning paragraph 9, with the word *but*?
4. Is this essay one of causes, effects, or both? What details lead you to this conclusion?
5. Do you agree with Marquez that our patriotism should not be gauged by whether we speak English in public? Or do you think that people living in this country ought to affirm their patriotism by speaking only English in public? Explain.

Classroom Activity Using Cause and Effect

Develop a causal chain in which you examine the ramifications of an action you took in the past. Identify each part in the chain. For example, you decided that you wanted to do well in a course (ultimate cause), so you got started on a research project early (immediate cause), which enabled you to write several drafts of your paper (immediate cause), which earned you an A for the project (effect), which led to an excellent grade for the class (effect), which enabled you to take the advanced seminar you wanted (effect).

Suggested Writing Assignments

1. Marquez's essay is set against the backdrop of a larger language-based controversy currently taking place in the United States called the English-only movement. Research the controversy in your school library or on the Internet, and write a cause-and-effect essay exploring why the movement began and what is keeping it alive.
2. There is often more than one cause for an event. List at least six possible causes for one of the following events:

an upset victory in a competition	a change in your major
an injury you suffered	a quarrel with a friend

   Examine your list, and identify the causes that seem most probable. Which of these are immediate causes, and which are ultimate causes? Using this material, write a short cause-and-effect essay on one of the topics.

Does Trying to Be Happy Make Us Unhappy?

■ **Adam Grant**

Adam Grant was born in 1981 and grew up in the suburbs of Detroit. He is a professor of management at the Wharton School of the University of Pennsylvania—the youngest faculty member to achieve tenure and the recipient of many accolades for his teaching. He has received awards for his scholarly achievements from the American Psychological Association, the Academy of Management, and the Society for Industrial and Organizational Psychology. Grant earned a BA from Harvard as well as an MA and a PhD in organizational psychology from the University of Michigan. He is the author of Give and Take: A Revolutionary Approach to Success, *one of Amazon's Best Books of 2013.*

Grant wrote "Does Trying to Be Happy Make Us Unhappy?" for LinkedIn, as one of the site's "influencers." Focusing on the efforts of one acquaintance, Tom, to find happiness, Grant asks readers to question their assumptions about how we achieve that elusive state. As you read, pay attention to the life changes Tom believes will lead him to greater happiness. Grant suggests that these efforts are actually causes of unhappiness.

Reflecting on What You Know

How would you define the "pursuit of happiness" granted to us by the Declaration of Independence? How do you find happiness in your own life?

As we muddle through our days, the quest for happiness looms large. In the U.S., citizens are granted three inalienable rights: life, liberty, and the pursuit of happiness. In the kingdom of Bhutan, 1 there's a national index to measure happiness. But what if searching for happiness actually prevents us from finding it? There's reason to believe that the quest for happiness might be a recipe for misery.

In a series of new studies led by the psychologist Iris Mauss, the more value people placed on happiness, the less happy they became. I saw it happen to Tom, a savant who speaks half a dozen languages, from Chinese to Welsh. In college, Tom declared a major in computer science, but found it dissatisfying. He became obsessed with happiness, longing for a career and a culture that would provide the perfect match for his interests and values. Within two years of graduating from college, he had bounced from working at the United Nations to an Internet startup in New York, applied for jobs as a supermarket manager, consultant and venture capitalist, and considered moving to Puerto Rico, Trinidad, Colombia, or Canada. 2

These careers and countries didn't fulfill him. After another year, he was doing stand-up comedy, contemplating a move to London to pursue an advanced degree in education, philosophy of science, management, or psychology. But none of these paths made him happy. Dissatisfied with his own lack of progress toward happiness, he created an online tool to help people develop more productive habits. That wasn't satisfying either, so he moved to Beijing. He lasted two years there, but didn't find the right cultural fit, so he moved to Germany and considered starting a college dorm for adults and a bar for nerds. In the next two years, he was off to Montreal and Pittsburgh, then back to Germany working on a website to help couples spend more quality time together. Still not happy, he abandoned that plan and returned to Beijing to sell office furniture. One year and two more moves across two continents later, he admitted to his friends, "I'm harder to find than Carmen Sandiego." 3

Tom made four mistakes that are all too common on the road to happiness. The first blunder was in trying to figure out if he was happy. When we pursue happiness, our goal is to experience more joy and contentment. To find out if we're making progress, we need to compare our past happiness to our current happiness. This creates a problem: the moment we make that comparison, we shift from an experiencing mode to an evaluating mode. Consider several decades of research by the psychologist Mihaly Csikszentmihalyi on flow, a state of complete absorption in an activity. Think of being engrossed in a Harry Potter book, playing a sport you love, or catching up with a good friend you haven't seen in years. You're in the zone: you're so 4 immersed in the task that you lose track of time and the outside world.

Csikszentmihalyi finds that when people are in a flow state, they 5
don't report being happy, as they're too busy concentrating on the activity or conversation. But afterward, looking back, they describe flow as the optimal emotional experience. By looking everywhere for happiness, Tom disrupted his ability to find flow. He was so busy assessing each new job and country that he never fully engaged in his projects and relationships. Instead, he became depressed and entered a vicious cycle documented by psychologists Katariina Salmela-Aro and Jari-Erik Nurmi: depression leads people to evaluate their daily projects as less enjoyable, and ruminating about why they're not fun makes the depression worse.

The second error was in overestimating the impact of life circum- 6
stances on happiness. As psychologist Dan Gilbert explains in *Stumbling on Happiness*, we tend to overestimate the emotional impact of positive life events. We think a great roommate or a major promotion will make us happier, overlooking the fact that we'll adapt to the new circumstances. For example, in a classic study, winning the lottery didn't appear to yield lasting gains in happiness. Each time Tom moved to a new job and country, he was initially excited to be running on a new treadmill, but within a matter of months, the reality of the daily grind set in: he was still running on a treadmill.

The third misstep was in pursuing happiness alone. Happiness is 7
an individual state, so when we look for it, it's only natural to focus on ourselves. Yet a wealth of evidence consistently shows that self-focused attention undermines happiness and causes depression. In one study, Mauss and colleagues demonstrated that the greater the value people placed on happiness, the more lonely they felt every day for the next two weeks. In another experiment, they randomly assigned people to value happiness, and found that it backfired: these people reported feeling lonelier and also had a progesterone drop in their saliva, a hormonal response linked to loneliness. As Tom changed jobs and countries alone, he left behind the people who made him happy.

The final mistake was in looking for intense happiness. When we 8
want to be happy, we look for strong positive emotions like joy, elation, enthusiasm, and excitement. Unfortunately, research shows that this isn't the best path to happiness. Research led by the psychologist Ed Diener reveals that happiness is driven by the frequency, not the intensity, of positive emotions. When we aim for intense positive

emotions, we evaluate our experiences against a higher standard, which makes it easier to be disappointed. Indeed, Mauss and her colleagues found that when people were explicitly searching for happiness, they experienced less joy in watching a figure skater win a gold medal. They were disappointed that the event wasn't even more jubilating. And even if they themselves had won the gold medal, it probably wouldn't have helped. Studies indicate that an intense positive experience leads us to frame ordinary experiences as less positive. Once you've landed a gold medal or won the lottery, it's hard to take pleasure in finding a great parking spot or winning a video game. Tom was looking so hard for the perfect job and the ideal country that he failed to appreciate an interesting task and a great restaurant.

Today, for the first time in more than a decade, Tom reports being—and appears to be—happy. Instead of pursuing happiness alone, he fell in love and got married. Rather than evaluating his happiness daily and hunting for his dream job, he's finding flow and experiencing daily satisfaction in helping his wife set up a company. He's no longer bouncing around from one continent to another, following the advice of psychologists Ken Sheldon and Sonja Lyubomirsky: "Change your actions, not your circumstances." 9

In *Obliquity,* John Kay argues that the best things in life can only be pursued indirectly. I believe this is true for happiness: if you truly want to experience joy or meaning, you need to shift your attention away from joy or meaning, and toward projects and relationships that bring joy and meaning as by-products. As the great philosopher John Stuart Mill once wrote, "Those only are happy who have their minds fixed on some object other than their own happiness." 10

Thinking Critically about This Reading

Why does Grant turn to psychologists as sources for this essay? How does their research challenge assumptions about happiness?

Questions for Study and Discussion

1. What is Tom's understanding of the causal chain that will lead to happiness? What kinds of things does he try in his pursuit of happiness?
2. Grant is describing a common psychological phenomenon in this essay, so why does he focus on the experiences of one man? Why

might he have chosen Tom in particular? What effect does Tom's story have on you as a reader?

3. In his analysis of why Tom's attempts to find happiness failed, Grant states that Tom made four mistakes. List these mistakes, and explain why each is a barrier to happiness.
4. Near the end, Grant writes that Tom "reports being—and appears to be—happy" (paragraph 9). What changed for Tom? Does his new attitude support the conclusions of the psychologists about how people find happiness?
5. In this essay, Grant asks readers to adjust their sense of the causal chain that leads to happiness. What does it mean to think of happiness not as an effect but as a "by-product"?

Classroom Activity Using Cause and Effect

Read the following excerpt from an internal proposal to manage a business's health-care costs. In the introduction, the memo writer outlines increases to health-care expenses in recent years. How does she explain the causes of the increases? Can you separate the immediate causes from the ultimate causes? Discuss the proposed action for reducing costs.

ABO, Inc.
Interoffice Memo

To: Joan Marlow, Director, Human Resources Division

From: Leslie Galusha, Chief, Employee Benefits Department

Date: June 16, 2014

Subject: Employee Fitness and Health-Care Costs

Health-care and workers' compensation insurance costs at ABO, Inc., have risen 100 percent over the last five years. In 2005, costs were $5,675 per employee per year; in 2011, they have reached $11,560 per employee per year. This doubling of costs mirrors a national trend, with health-care costs anticipated to continue to rise at the same rate for the next ten years. Controlling these escalating expenses will be essential. They are eating into ABO's profit margin because the company currently pays 70 percent of the costs for employee coverage.

Healthy employees bring direct financial benefits to companies in the form of lower employee insurance costs, lower absenteeism rates, and reduced turnover. Regular physical exercise promotes fit, healthy people by reducing the risk of coronary heart disease, diabetes, osteoporosis, hypertension, and stress-related problems. I propose that to promote regular, vigorous physical exercise for our employees, ABO implement a health-care program that focuses on employee fitness. . . .

Problem of Health-Care Costs

The U.S. Department of Health and Human Services (HHS) recently estimated that health-care costs in the United States will triple by the year 2020. Corporate expenses for health care are rising at such a fast rate that if unchecked, in seven years they will significantly erode corporate profits.

According to HHS, people who do not participate in a regular and vigorous exercise program incur double the health-care costs and are hospitalized 30 percent more days than people who exercise regularly. Nonexercisers are also 41 percent more likely to submit medical claims over $10,000 at some point during their careers than are those who exercise regularly.

These figures are further supported by data from independent studies. A model created by the National Institutes of Health (NIH) . . .

Suggested Writing Assignments

1. Write a personal essay about a time when you did something for the wrong reasons. What, at the time, did you believe would be the effects of your actions? How do you understand the causal chain differently now, with the benefit of hindsight?
2. Write an essay in which you assess the effects of the Internet on you and your peers' happiness. How does it help people connect with one another, become more productive, or follow their interests? How does it isolate people, distort the way we view others' experiences, or make us dependent on technology? Would you say the net effect on happiness is positive or negative?

Black Men and Public Space

■ Brent Staples

Courtesy of Brent Staples

Brent Staples was born in Chester, Pennsylvania, in 1951, the oldest of nine children. He earned a BA at Widener University and a PhD at the University of Chicago. He worked for the New York Times *as an assistant editor for metropolitan news and as editor of the book review before he joined the paper's editorial board in 1990. His writing, focusing on the areas of education, criminal justice, and economics, appears frequently in the opinion pages. He is also the author of a memoir,* Parallel Time: Growing Up in Black and White *(1994), winner of the Anisfield-Wolf Book Award.*

In "Black Men and Public Space," first published in Ms. *magazine, Staples describes his nighttime experiences on city streets. He tries to understand the effects he has on other pedestrians, even as he recognizes that the ultimate causes of the tension in these encounters are persistent and damaging stereotypes about African American men.*

Reflecting on What You Know

Have you ever felt scared or intimidated when you were out in public? Have you ever sensed that someone felt scared or intimidated by you? What do you think causes these anxieties?

My first victim was a woman—white, well dressed, probably in her late twenties. I came upon her late one evening on a deserted street in Hyde Park, a relatively affluent neighborhood in an otherwise mean, impoverished section of Chicago. As I swung onto the avenue behind her, there seemed to be a discreet, uninflammatory distance between us. Not so. She cast back a worried glance. To her, 1 the youngish black man—a broad six feet two inches with a beard and billowing hair, both hands shoved into the pockets of a bulky military jacket—seemed menacingly close. After a few more quick glimpses, she picked up her pace and was soon running in earnest. Within seconds, she disappeared into a cross street.

That was more than a decade ago. I was twenty-two years old, a graduate student newly arrived at the University of Chicago. It was in the echo of that terrified woman's footfalls that I first began to know the unwieldy inheritance I'd come into—the ability to alter public space in ugly ways. It was clear that she thought herself the quarry of a mugger, a rapist, or worse. Suffering a bout of insomnia, however, I was stalking sleep, not defenseless wayfarers. As a softy who is scarcely able to take a knife to a raw chicken—let alone hold one to a person's throat—I was surprised, embarrassed, and dismayed all at once. Her flight made me feel like an accomplice in tyranny. It also made it clear that I was indistinguishable from the muggers who occasionally seeped into the area from the surrounding ghetto. The first encounter, and those that followed, signified that a vast, unnerving gulf lay between nighttime pedestrians—particularly women—and me. And I soon gathered that being perceived as dangerous is a hazard in itself. I only needed to turn a corner into a dicey situation, or crowd some frightened, armed person in a foyer somewhere, or make an errant move after being pulled over by a policeman. Where fear and weapons meet—and they often do in urban America—there is always the possibility of death. 2

In that first year, my first away from my hometown, I was to become thoroughly familiar with the language of fear. At dark, shadowy intersections, I could cross in front of a car stopped at a traffic light and elicit the *thunk, thunk, thunk, thunk* of the driver—black, white, male, or female—hammering down the door locks. On less traveled streets after dark, I grew accustomed to but never comfortable with people crossing to the other side of the street rather than pass me. Then there were the standard unpleasantries with policemen, doormen, bouncers, cabdrivers, and others whose business it is to screen out troublesome individuals *before* there is any nastiness. 3

I moved to New York nearly two years ago and I have remained an avid night walker. In central Manhattan, the near-constant crowd cover minimizes tense one-on-one street encounters. Elsewhere—in SoHo, for example, where sidewalks are narrow and tightly spaced buildings shut out the sky—things can get very taut indeed. 4

After dark, on the warrenlike streets of Brooklyn where I live, I often see women who fear the worst from me. They seem to have set their faces on neutral, and with their purse straps strung across their chests bandolier-style, they forge ahead as though bracing themselves against being tackled. I understand, of course, that the danger they perceive is not a hallucination. Women are particularly vulnerable to street violence, and young black males are drastically overrepresented among the perpetrators of that violence. Yet these truths are no solace against the kind of alienation that comes of being ever the suspect, a fearsome entity with whom pedestrians avoid making eye contact. 5

It is not altogether clear to me how I reached the ripe old age of twenty-two without being conscious of the lethality nighttime pedestrians attributed to me. Perhaps it was because in Chester, Pennsylvania, the small, angry industrial town where I came of age in the 1960s, I was scarcely noticeable against a backdrop of gang warfare, street knifings, and murders. I grew up one of the good boys, had perhaps a half-dozen fistfights. In retrospect, my shyness of combat has clear sources. 6

As a boy, I saw countless tough guys locked away; I have since buried several, too. They were babies, really—a teenage cousin, a brother of twenty-two, a childhood friend in his mid-twenties—all gone down in episodes of bravado played out in the streets. I came to doubt the virtues of intimidation early on. I chose, perhaps unconsciously, to remain a shadow—timid, but a survivor. 7

The fearsomeness mistakenly attributed to me in public places often has a perilous flavor. The most frightening of these confusions occurred in the late 1970s and early 1980s, when I worked as a journalist in Chicago. One day, rushing into the office of a magazine I was writing for with a deadline story in hand, I was mistaken for a burglar. The office manager called security and, with an ad hoc posse, pursued me through the labyrinthine halls, nearly to my editor's door. I had no way of proving who I was. I could only move briskly toward the company of someone who knew me. 8

Another time I was on assignment for a local paper and killing time before an interview. I entered a jewelry store on the city's affluent Near North Side. The proprietor excused herself and returned with an enormous red Doberman pinscher straining at the end of a leash. She stood, the dog extended toward me, silent to my questions, her eyes bulging nearly out of her head. I took a cursory look around, nodded, and bade her good night. 9

Relatively speaking, however, I never fared as badly as another black male journalist. He went to nearby Waukegan, Illinois, a couple of summers ago to work on a story about a murderer who was born there. Mistaking the reporter for the killer, police officers hauled him from his car at gunpoint and but for his press credentials would probably have tried to book him. Such episodes are not uncommon. Black men trade tales like this all the time. 10

Over the years, I learned to smother the rage I felt at so often being taken for a criminal. Not to do so would surely have led to madness. I now take precautions to make myself less threatening. I move about with care, particularly late in the evening. I give a wide berth to nervous people on subway platforms during the wee hours, particularly when I have exchanged business clothes for jeans. If I happen to be entering a building behind some people who appear skittish, I may walk by, letting them clear the lobby before I return, so as not to seem to be following them. I have been calm and extremely congenial on those rare occasions when I've been pulled over by the police. 11

And on late-evening constitutionals I employ what has proved to be an excellent tension-reducing measure: I whistle melodies from Beethoven and Vivaldi and the more popular classical composers. Even steely New Yorkers hunching toward nighttime destinations seem to relax, and occasionally they even join in the tune. Virtually everybody seems to sense that a mugger wouldn't be warbling bright, sunny selections from Vivaldi's *Four Seasons*. It is my equivalent of the cowbell that hikers wear when they know they are in bear country. 12

Thinking Critically about This Reading

Staples finds that he has "the ability to alter public space in ugly ways" (paragraph 2). What does he mean by "ugly" in this sentence? What is ugly about the encounters he describes in the rest of the essay?

Questions for Study and Discussion

1. One of the challenges Staples takes up in this essay is to recognize himself as a cause. What effects does he have on other people? How does he explain those reactions?

2. Discuss Staples's word choice in the first paragraph. How does the language contribute to the feeling of the scene? Which words do you find most telling? (Glossary: *Diction*)
3. How does Staples see himself? How does he believe others see him? Discuss the contrast between these two views. (Glossary: *Comparison and Contrast*)
4. How does Staples describe the complex emotions he felt after the encounter with his "first victim"? Discuss the mix of feelings he mentions in paragraph 2.
5. Learning that others fear him becomes, in turn, a source of fear for Staples. Why? Why is causing fear "a hazard in itself" (2)?
6. What technique does Staples come up with for diminishing the tension in these public encounters? Why does he think it works? What do you think of this solution?
7. Staples ends with a metaphor that likens him to a hiker in "bear country." Discuss the implications of this comparison. (Glossary: *Figure of Speech*)

Classroom Activity Using Cause and Effect

In preparation for writing a cause-and-effect essay, list four effects (two on society and two on personal behavior) for one of the following items: television, cell phones, e-mail, microwave ovens, DVD technology, the Internet, or an item of your choice. For example, the automobile could be said to have had the following effects:

Society

A national highway system developed, based on asphalt roads.

The petroleum and insurance industries expanded in size and influence.

Personal Behavior

People with cars can live far from public transportation.

Suburban and rural drivers walk less than urban dwellers.

Suggested Writing Assignments

1. Twenty-five years after Staples published his essay, a young black man, Trayvon Martin, was shot on a street in Sanford, Florida.

First, consider your opinions about the Martin case and the verdict. If you aren't familiar with this case or don't remember much about it, do a little research to familiarize yourself with the case and to be sure you have the facts. (Refer to Evaluating Your Print and Online Sources in Chapter 22, to ensure that you consult credible, unbiased sources.) Then, consider whether you agree with some or all of the ideas Staples presents in his essay and why. Finally, write an essay applying Staples's cause-and-effect analysis to the Martin case. What might his experiences have to tell us about Martin's death? You might also look up, and incorporate into your discussion, the editorial in which Staples addresses the Trayvon Martin case ("Young, Black, Male, and Stalked by Bias," published in the *New York Times* on April 14, 2012).

2. One way to think of ourselves is in terms of the influences that have caused us to be who we are. What contributed to making you who you are—parents, teachers, or coaches? Your neighborhood or cultural heritage? Friends you identify with or heroes you look up to? Write an essay in which you discuss two or three of your most important influences, considering the effects they have had on your life.

CHAPTER **21**

Argument

The word *argument* probably brings to mind a verbal disagreement of the sort that nearly everyone has participated in. Such disputes are satisfying when you convert someone to your point of view. More often, though, verbal arguments are inconclusive and frustrating because you might fail to make your position understood or may believe that your opponent has been stubborn and unreasonable. Because verbal arguments generally arise spontaneously, they cannot be thoughtfully planned or researched. Indeed, it is often not until later that the convincing piece of evidence or the forcefully phrased assertion finally comes to mind.

Also known as **argumentation**, written arguments share common goals with spoken ones: they attempt to convince a reader to agree with a particular point of view, to make a particular decision, or to pursue a particular course of action. Written arguments, however, involve the presentation of well-chosen evidence and the artful control of language. Writers of arguments must imagine their probable audience and predict the sorts of objections that may be raised. Writers must choose in advance a specific, sufficiently detailed thesis or proposition. There is a greater need to be organized; to choose the most effective types of evidence from all that is available; and to determine the strategies of rhetoric, language, and style that will best suit the argument's subject, purpose, and thesis and ensure its effect on the intended audience. In the end, such work can be far more satisfying than spontaneous oral argument.

Most people who specialize in the study of arguments identify two essential categories: persuasion and logic. *Persuasive appeals* are directed at readers' emotions, at their subconscious, even at their biases and prejudices. These appeals involve diction, slanting, figurative language, analogy, rhythmic patterns of speech, and the establishment of a tone that will encourage a positive response. Persuasion very often attempts to get the audience to take action. Examples of persuasive argument are found in the exaggerated claims of advertisers and the speech making of political and social activists.

Logical appeals, on the other hand, are directed primarily at the audience's intellectual faculties, understanding, and knowledge. Such appeals depend on the reasoned movement from assertion to evidence to conclusion and on an almost mathematical system of proof and counterproof. Logical argument, unlike persuasion, does not normally impel its audience to action. Logical argument is commonly found in scientific or philosophical articles, legal decisions, and technical proposals.

Most arguments are neither purely persuasive nor purely logical. A well-written editorial, for example, will present a logical arrangement of assertions and evidence, but it will also employ striking diction and other persuasive patterns of language to reinforce its effectiveness. Thus, the kinds of appeals a writer emphasizes depend on the nature of the topic, the thesis or proposition of the argument, the writer's purpose, the various kinds of support (evidence, opinions, examples, facts, statistics) offered, and a thoughtful consideration of the audience. Knowing the differences between persuasive and logical appeals is essential in learning both to read and to write arguments.

True arguments make assertions about which there is a legitimate and recognized difference of opinion. Readers probably do not need to be convinced that falling in love is a beautiful and intense experience, that crime rates should be reduced, or that computers are changing the world; most everyone would agree with such assertions. But not everyone would agree that women experience love more intensely than men, that the death penalty reduces the incidence of crime, or that computers are changing the world for the worse; these assertions are arguable and admit of differing perspectives. Similarly, a leading heart specialist might argue in a popular magazine that too many doctors are advising patients to have pacemakers implanted when the devices are not necessary; a writer for a small-town newspaper might write an editorial urging that a local agency supplying food to poor families be given a larger percentage of the town's budget; and a foreign-policy specialist might produce a long and complex book attempting to prove that the current administration exhibits no consistent policy in its relationship with other countries and that the Department of State needs to be overhauled. No matter what its forum or its structure, an argument has as its chief purpose the detailed setting forth of a particular point of view and the rebuttal of any opposing views.

Argumentation frequently uses the other rhetorical strategies covered in Chapters 13 to 20. In your efforts to argue convincingly, you may find it necessary to define, to compare and contrast, to analyze causes and effects, to classify, to describe, or to narrate. Nevertheless, it is the writer's attempt to convince, not explain, that is of primary importance in an argumentative essay. In this respect, it is helpful to keep in mind that there are two basic patterns of thinking and presenting our thoughts that are followed in argumentation: **induction** and **deduction**.

Inductive reasoning, the more common type of reasoning, moves from a set of specific examples to a general statement. In doing so, the writer makes an *inductive leap* from the evidence to the generalization. For example, after examining enrollment statistics, we can conclude that students do not like to take courses offered early in the morning or late in the afternoon.

Deductive reasoning, in contrast, moves from a general statement to a specific conclusion. It works on the model of the **syllogism**, a three-part argument that consists of a major premise, a minor premise, and a conclusion, as in the following example:

a. All women are mortal. *(Major premise)*
b. Jeanne is a woman. *(Minor premise)*
c. Jeanne is mortal. *(Conclusion)*

A syllogism will fail to work if either of the premises is untrue:

a. All living creatures are mammals. *(Major premise)*
b. A butterfly is a living creature. *(Minor premise)*
c. A butterfly is a mammal. *(Conclusion)*

The problem is immediately apparent. The major premise is false: many living creatures are not mammals, and a butterfly happens to be one of the nonmammals. Consequently, the conclusion is invalid.

WRITING ARGUMENTS

Writing an argument is a challenging assignment that can be very rewarding. By nature, an argument must be carefully reasoned and thoughtfully structured to have maximum effect. Therefore, allow yourself enough time to think about your thesis; to gather the evidence you need; and to draft, revise, edit, and proofread your essay. Fuzzy thinking, confused expression, and poor organization will be immediately evident to your reader and will diminish your chances for completing the assignment successfully. The following seven steps will remind you of some key features of arguments and help you sequence your activities as you research and write.

1. Determine the Thesis or Proposition

Begin by deciding on a topic that interests you and that has some significant differences of opinion or some points that you have questions about. Find out what's in the news about your topic, what people are saying about it, and what authors and instructors are emphasizing as important intellectual arguments. As you pursue your research, consider what assertion or assertions you can make about your topic. The more specific you make the thesis or proposition, the more directed your research can become and the more focused your ultimate argument will be. Don't hesitate to modify or even reject an initial thesis as your research warrants.

A thesis can be placed anywhere in an argument, but while learning to write arguments, you should place the statement of your controlling idea near the beginning of your composition. Explain the importance of the thesis, and make clear to your reader that you share a common concern or interest in this issue. State your central assertion directly in your first or second paragraph so that your reader will have no doubt or confusion about your position. You may also wish to lead off with a striking piece of evidence to capture your reader's interest.

2. Take Account of Your Audience

In no other type of writing is the question of audience more important than in argumentation. The tone you establish, the type of diction you choose, the kinds of evidence you select to buttress your assertions, and the organizational pattern you follow can influence your audience to trust you and believe your assertions. If you judge the nature of your audience accurately; respect its knowledge of the subject; and correctly envision whether it is likely to be hostile, neutral, complacent, or receptive, you will be able to tailor the various aspects of your argument appropriately. (For more on audience, refer to the discussion of ethos, pathos, and logos on pp. 551–52.)

3. Gather the Necessary Supporting Evidence

For each point of your argument, be sure to provide appropriate and sufficient evidence: verifiable facts and statistics, illustrative examples and narratives, or quotations from authorities. Don't overwhelm your reader with evidence, but don't skimp, either. Demonstrate your command of the topic and control of the thesis by choosing carefully from all the evidence at your disposal.

4. Settle on an Organizational Pattern

Once you think that you have sufficient evidence to make your assertion convincing, consider how best to organize your argument. To some extent, your organization will depend on your method of reasoning—inductive, deductive, or a combination of the two. For example, is it necessary to establish a major premise before moving on to discuss a minor premise? Should most of your evidence precede your direct statement of an assertion or follow it? Will induction work better with the particular audience you have targeted? As you present your primary points, you may find it effective to move from least important to most important or from most familiar to least familiar. A scratch outline can help, but often a writer's most crucial revisions in an argument involve rearranging its components into a sharper, more coherent order. Often it is difficult to tell what that order should be until the revision stage of the writing process.

5. Consider Refutations to Your Argument

As you proceed with your argument, you may wish to take into account well-known and significant opposing arguments. To ignore opposing views would be to suggest to your reader any one of the following: you don't know about the opposing views, you know about them and are obviously and unfairly weighting the arguments in your favor, or you know about them and have no reasonable answers for them. Grant the validity of opposing arguments or refute them, but respect your reader's intelligence by addressing the objections to your assertion. Your reader will in turn respect you for doing so.

6. Avoid Faulty Reasoning

Have someone read your argument for errors in judgment and for faulty reasoning. Sometimes others can more easily see problems because they aren't intimately tied to your assertion. These errors are typically called **logical fallacies**. Review the Logical Fallacies box below, making sure that you have not committed any of these errors in reasoning.

Logical Fallacies

Oversimplification: A simple solution to what is clearly a complex problem or a simple solution to a problem that the writer does not fully understand: *We have a balance-of-trade deficit because foreigners make better products than we do.* This fallacy often occurs when the writer attempts to offer a cause for an event—such as a fire, a natural disaster, or a mechanical failure—and doesn't consider other possibilities.

Hasty generalization: A fallacy often found in inductive reasoning (reasoning from the particular to the general) wherein the writer uses too little evidence or evidence that is not representative to reach a conclusion: *My grandparents, like most older folks, don't understand their Social Security benefits.*

Post hoc, ergo propter hoc: (Latin for "After this, therefore because of this.") Confusing chance with causation. Just because one event comes after another in time does not mean the first event caused the second: *I went swimming yesterday, and the next thing I knew, I had a cold. Every time I wear my orange sweater to a basketball game, we win.* Swimming may or may not be the cause of the cold, and one fan's clothing is not the reason a team wins or loses.

Begging the question: Arriving at a conclusion based on a premise (a statement used as the basis of an argument) that does not have adequate support: *Gambling is wrong because people should stay away from games of chance. Lying is wrong because it's always best to tell the truth.* The first example describes gambling as a game of chance but does not offer proof of what is wrong with it. In the second example, the arguer has failed to provide proof of anything.

False analogy: An analogy compares something unfamiliar to something familiar with the hope that the unfamiliar becomes more clearly understood. False analogies ignore important dissimilarities between the items being compared and therefore do not serve as proof: *If we can put a man on the moon, we should be able to cure* *the common cold.* Although the two tasks are scientifically complex, there is no reason to believe that accomplishing them involves the same knowledge, skills, or processes.

Either/or thinking: The fallacy of seeing only two alternatives in a situation when, in fact, there may be other possibilities. During the greatest protest era of the 1960s, many citizens demonstrated against the government. Those who were opposed to the demonstrators simplified the problems our country was facing at the time with posters and bumper stickers reading: *America: Love it or leave it!* This either/or thinking ignores the many possibilities for thought and action that lie between the two extremes of loving the country or leaving it.

Non sequitur: (Latin for "It does not follow.") The writer uses an inference or a conclusion that is not clearly related to the established premises or evidence: *The witness was very sincere and convincing. Her testimony was reliable.* Showing sincerity or being convincing does not necessarily prove the witness's reliability. One can be sincere and convincing but also inaccurate.

If you are having difficulty identifying various kinds of logical fallacies, you are not alone. Whereas they are sometimes easier to identify in the writing of others, they are often difficult to identify in your own writing. Logical fallacies sometimes occur because the argument is based on premises that are not true, the evidence is insufficient for the claims, and erroneous conclusions are drawn. One way to identify logical fallacies in your own writing is to take the position of someone arguing against you. What would you find wrong with your argument and for what reasons? Becoming your own adversary will help you detect and avoid errors in reasoning and strengthen your arguments. Complete the activity in the box below to practice identifying and correcting logical fallacies.

Detecting Logical Fallacies

Each of the following may contain one or more examples of faulty reasoning. Analyze each to determine what, if anything, is wrong with it. If you find an error in logic, determine which of the logical fallacies is occurring and do your best to correct it.

1. Don't lend books to friends. They never return them.
2. I am not in favor of his argument for a new school because he's so liberal and likes to spend money.
3. Don't ever invest in the stock market. You could lose a ton of money.
4. Osama bin Laden has been killed, so we don't need to be afraid of terrorism any longer.
5. Larry the Cable Guy said to take the medicine he was advertising and not "get heartburn in the first place."
6. He'll make a great coach. He was an excellent quarterback when he played.
7. We ought to close the pool at the hotel because too many people have drowned there.
8. The juror was released from the drunk-driving case because he had been a binge drinker in college.
9. Reducing the number of unemployment checks a person can receive will result in more people finding jobs.
10. Exit exams for college seniors will improve the quality of instruction.

7. Conclude Forcefully

In the conclusion of your essay, be sure to restate your position in new language, at least briefly. Besides persuading your reader to accept your point of view, you may also want to encourage some specific course of action. Above all, your conclusion should not introduce new information that may surprise your reader. It should seem to follow naturally, almost seamlessly, from the series of points that you have carefully established in the body of the essay. Don't overstate your case, but at the same time don't qualify your conclusion with the use of too many words or phrases like *I think, in my opinion, maybe, sometimes,* and *probably.* These words can make you sound indecisive and fuzzy headed rather than rational and sensible.

THINKING CRITICALLY ABOUT ARGUMENT

Take a Stand

Even though you have chosen a topic, gathered information about it, and established a thesis statement or proposition, you need to take a stand—to fully commit yourself to your beliefs and ideas about the issue before you. If you attempt to work with a thesis that you have not clearly thought through or are confused about, or if you take a position you do not fully believe in or care about, it will show in your writing. Your willingness to research, to dig up evidence, to find the most effective organizational pattern for your material, to construct strong paragraphs and sentences, and to find just the right diction to convey your argument is a direct reflection of just how strongly you take a stand—and how much you believe in that stand. With a strong stand, you can argue vigorously and convincingly.

Consider Ethos, Pathos, and Logos

Classical thinkers believed that there are three key components in all rhetorical communication: the *speaker* (or writer) who comments on a *subject* to an *audience*. For purposes of discussion, we can isolate each of these entities, but in actual rhetorical situations they are inseparable, and each inextricably influences the other two. The ancients also recognized the importance of three elements of argumentation: ethos, which is related to the speaker/writer; logos, which is related to the subject; and pathos, which is related to the audience.

Ethos (the Greek word for "character") has to do with the authority, credibility, and, to a certain extent, morals of the speaker/writer. The classical rhetoricians believed that it was important for the speaker/writer to be credible and to argue for a worthwhile cause. Putting one's argumentative skills in the service of a questionable cause was simply not acceptable. But how does one establish credibility? Sometimes it is gained through achievements outside the rhetorical arena—that is, the speaker has had experience with an issue, has argued the subject before, and has been judged to be honest and sincere. In the case of your own writing, establishing such credentials is not always possible, so you will need to be more concerned than usual with presenting your argument reasonably, sincerely, and in language untainted by excessive emotionalism. Finally, you should always respect your audience in your writing.

Logos (Greek for "word") is related to the subject and is the effective presentation of the argument itself. Is the thesis or claim worthwhile? Is it logical, consistent, and well buttressed by supporting evidence? Is the evidence itself factual, reliable, and convincing? Finally, is the argument so thoughtfully organized and clearly presented that it will affect the audience? This aspect of argumentation is at once the most difficult to accomplish and the most rewarding.

Pathos (Greek for "emotion") has most to do with the audience. How does the speaker/writer present an argument to maximize its appeal for a given audience? One way is through artful and strategic use of well-crafted language. Certain buzzwords, slanted diction, or loaded language may become either rallying cries or causes of resentment in an argument. Remember that audiences can range from friendly and sympathetic to hostile and resistant, with myriad possibilities in between. A friendly audience will welcome new information and support your position; a hostile audience will look for flaws in your logic and examples of dishonest manipulation. Caution, subtlety, and critical thinking must be applied to an uncommitted audience.

macmillanhighered.com/mfw12e
e-readings > Intelligence Squared, *Should College Football Be Banned?* [video]

A Farm Boy Reflects

■ **Nicholas D. Kristof**

Rebecca Sapp/WireImage/Getty Images

Born in 1959, Nicholas D. Kristof was raised on a farm in Yamhill, Oregon. He graduated from Harvard University and won a Rhodes Scholarship to study law at Oxford University. He has traveled to over 150 countries and served as a correspondent in Hong Kong, Beijing, and Tokyo. Since 2001, he has been a columnist for the New York Times, *often using his writing to call attention to human rights abuses around the world. He is the winner of two Pulitzer Prizes, one for his coverage of the democracy movement in China's Tiananmen Square and the other, of the genocide in Darfur. He is also a coauthor with his wife, Sheryl WuDunn, of* China Wakes: The Struggle for the Soul of a Rising Power *(1994),* Thunder from the East: Portrait of a Rising Asia *(2000), and* Half the Sky: Turning Oppression into Opportunity for Women Worldwide *(2009).*

In "A Farm Boy Reflects," originally published on July 31, 2008, in the New York Times, *Kristof argues that even meat eaters should "draw the line at animals being raised in cruel conditions." As you read, consider how he uses examples from his personal experience to persuade readers.*

Reflecting on What You Know

Do you eat meat? If not, why not? If so, have you ever asked yourself where you would "draw the line"?

In a world in which animal rights are gaining ground, barbecue season should make me feel guilty. My hunch is that in a century or two, our descendants will look back on our factory farms with uncomprehending revulsion. But in the meantime, I love a good burger. 1

This comes up because the most important election this November that you've never heard of is a referendum on animal rights in 2

California, the vanguard state for social movements. Proposition 2[1] would ban factory farms from raising chickens, calves or hogs in small pens or cages.

Livestock rights are already enshrined in the law in Florida, Arizona, Colorado and here in Oregon, but California's referendum would go further and would be a major gain for the animal rights movement. And it's part of a broader trend. Burger King announced last year that it would give preference to suppliers that treat animals better, and when a hamburger empire expostulates tenderly about the living conditions of cattle, you know public attitudes are changing. 3

Harvard Law School now offers a course on animal rights. Spain's Parliament has taken a first step in granting rights to apes, and Austrian activists are campaigning to have a chimpanzee declared a person. Among philosophers, a sophisticated literature of animal rights has emerged. 4

I'm a farm boy who grew up here in the hills outside Yamhill, Ore., raising sheep for my F.F.A. and 4-H projects. At various times, my family also raised modest numbers of pigs, cattle, goats, chickens and geese, although they were never tightly confined. 5

Our cattle, sheep, chickens and goats certainly had individual personalities, but not such interesting ones that it bothered me that they might end up in a stew. Pigs were more troubling because of their unforgettable characters and obvious intelligence. To this day, when tucking into a pork chop, I always feel as if it is my intellectual equal. 6

Then there were the geese, the most admirable creatures I've ever met. We raised Chinese white geese, a common breed, and they have distinctive personalities. They mate for life and adhere to family values that would shame most of those who dine on them. 7

While one of our geese was sitting on her eggs, her gander would go out foraging for food—and if he found some delicacy, he would rush back to give it to his mate. Sometimes I would offer males a dish of corn to fatten them up—but it was impossible, for they would take it all home to their true loves. 8

Once a month or so, we would slaughter the geese. When I was 10 years old, my job was to lock the geese in the barn and then rush and grab one. Then I would take it out and hold it by its wings on the chopping block while my dad or someone else swung the ax. 9

[1]*Proposition 2:* a 2008 ballot proposition in California that sought to regulate the confinement of farm animals. The ballot passed in November 2008 with over 63 percent approval.

The 150 geese knew that something dreadful was happening and would cower in a far corner of the barn, and run away in terror as I approached. Then I would grab one and carry it away as it screeched and struggled in my arms. 10

Very often, one goose would bravely step away from the panicked flock and walk tremulously toward me. It would be the mate of the one I had caught, male or female, and it would step right up to me, protesting pitifully. It would be frightened out of its wits, but still determined to stand with and comfort its lover. 11

We eventually grew so impressed with our geese—they had virtually become family friends—that we gave the remaining ones to a local park. (Unfortunately, some entrepreneurial thief took advantage of their friendliness by kidnapping them all—just before the next Thanksgiving.) 12

So, yes, I eat meat (even, hesitantly, goose). But I draw the line at animals being raised in cruel conditions. The law punishes teenage boys who tie up and abuse a stray cat. So why allow industrialists to run factory farms that keep pigs almost all their lives in tiny pens that are barely bigger than they are? 13

Defining what is cruel is, of course, extraordinarily difficult. But penning pigs or veal calves so tightly that they cannot turn around seems to cross that line. 14

More broadly, the tide of history is moving toward the protection of animal rights, and the brutal conditions in which they are sometimes now raised will eventually be banned. Someday, vegetarianism may even be the norm. 15

Perhaps it seems like soggy sentimentality as well as hypocrisy to stand up for animal rights, particularly when I enjoy dining on these same animals. But my view was shaped by those days in the barn as a kid, scrambling after geese I gradually came to admire. 16

So I'll enjoy the barbecues this summer, but I'll also know that every hamburger patty has a back story, and that every tin of goose liver pâté could tell its own rich tale of love and loyalty. 17

Thinking Critically about This Reading

What makes the referendum on animal rights such an important election in Kristof's mind? What is at issue? To what larger changes might it lead?

Questions for Study and Discussion

1. How does Kristof appeal to *ethos* in his essay? How does his background contribute to the argument he makes?
2. Why does Kristof think future generations will feel differently about eating meat? How much does this matter to his argument?
3. Kristof lists several examples of cultural change surrounding the consumption of meat. Discuss these examples. Why do you think he identifies them as part of a "broader trend" (paragraph 3)?
4. Kristof includes a relatively long discussion of goose behavior in this short essay. What is remarkable about that behavior? How does it challenge Kristof's ideas about animals?
5. The essay ends on a fanciful note, imagining the compelling life stories of the animals we eat. What do you think of this ending? How does it connect with Kristof's stories about the geese?
6. Kristof admits that he continues to eat goose, even though he does so "hesitantly"(3). What position does he ultimately take on eating animals? Does his argument convince you of this view?

Classroom Activity Using Argument

Write a paragraph that makes an argument about how people should eat. Use one of the following quotes to support your argument:

> In America we eat, collectively, with a glum urge for food to fill us. We are ignorant of flavor. We are as a nation taste-blind.
>
> –M.F.K. Fisher, *Serve It Forth*

> Don't eat anything your great-great-grandmother wouldn't recognize as food.
>
> –Michael Pollan, "Unhappy Meals"

> Choosing leaf or flesh, factory farm or family farm, does not in itself change the world, but teaching ourselves, our children, our local communities, and our nation to choose conscience over ease can.
>
> –Jonathan Safran Foer, *Eating Animals*

Compare your paragraph with a classmate's, and discuss why you chose the quote you did. How did you integrate it into your paragraph?

Suggested Writing Assignments

1. Extend Kristof's essay by making an argument of your own, calling for specific action on the issue of animal cruelty. Make a proposal for how farms could avoid crossing the line Kristof draws between acceptable practices and cruelty. For example, you may wish to look up the regulations outlined by California's Proposition 2, which passed after Kristof wrote his column.
2. Respond to Kristof's essay with a counterargument; keep in mind that a good argument resists either/or thinking. Rather than arguing for or against eating meat, think about which of Kristof's propositions you would want to challenge or rethink. On what points would you agree with him, and where do your ideas diverge?

In Praise of the F Word

■ Mary Sherry

Courtesy of Mary Sherry

Mary Sherry was born in Bay City, Michigan. She received a BA from Dominican University and an MBA from the University of St. Thomas. She later founded a research and publishing company specializing in information for economic and development organizations. About her early writing career, Sherry comments: "My interest in writing began in high school. I wrote for the school paper and wound up as editor my senior year. I started out majoring in math in college but found my writing skills were stronger, so I switched, thinking I would be good at writing technical materials. That eventually happened, but my first nationally published work was based on an experience at a church meeting. I have been observing events, writing about them and getting such essays published ever since." Sherry has taught in adult-literacy programs and has written essays on educational problems for various newspapers, including the Wall Street Journal *and* America *magazine. She also serves on the city council in her current home of Burnsville, Minnesota.*

In the following essay, originally published in Newsweek *in 1991, Sherry takes a provocative stance—that the threat of flunking is a "positive teaching tool." She believes students would be better off if they had a "healthy fear of failure," and she marshals a series of logical appeals to both clarify and support her argument.*

Reflecting on What You Know

Comment on what you see as the relationship between learning and grades. Do teachers and students pay too much attention to grades at the expense of learning? Or are grades not seen as that important?

Tens of thousands of eighteen-year-olds will graduate this year and be handed meaningless diplomas. These diplomas won't look any different from those awarded their luckier classmates. Their validity will be questioned only when their employers discover that these graduates are semiliterate. 1

Eventually a fortunate few will find their way into educational-repair shops—adult-literacy programs, such as the one where I teach basic grammar and writing. There, high-school graduates and high-school dropouts pursuing graduate-equivalency certificates will learn the skills they should have learned in school. They will also discover they have been cheated by our educational system. 2

As I teach, I learn a lot about our schools. Early in each session I ask my students to write about an unpleasant experience they had in school. No writers' block here! "I wish someone would have made me stop doing drugs and made me study." "I liked to party and no one seemed to care." "I was a good kid and didn't cause any trouble, so they just passed me along even though I didn't read well and couldn't write." And so on. 3

I am your basic do-gooder, and prior to teaching this class I blamed the poor academic skills our kids have today on drugs, divorce, and other impediments to concentration necessary for doing well in school. But, as I rediscover each time I walk into the classroom, before a teacher can expect students to concentrate, he has to get their attention, no matter what distractions may be at hand. There are many ways to do this, and they have much to do with teaching style. However, if style alone won't do it, there is another way to show who holds the winning hand in the classroom. That is to reveal the trump card[1] of failure. 4

I will never forget a teacher who played that card to get the attention of one of my children. Our youngest, a world-class charmer, did little to develop his intellectual talents but always got by. Until Mrs. Stifter. 5

Our son was a high-school senior when he had her for English. "He sits in the back of the room talking to his friends," she told me. "Why don't you move him to the front row?" I urged, believing the embarrassment would get him to settle down. Mrs. Stifter looked at me steely-eyed over her glasses. "I don't move seniors," she said. "I flunk them." I was flustered. Our son's academic life flashed before my eyes. 6

[1]*trump card:* a secret weapon; hidden advantage.

No teacher had ever threatened him with that before. I regained my composure and managed to say that I thought she was right. By the time I got home I was feeling pretty good about this. It was a radical approach for these times, but, well, why not? "She's going to flunk you," I told my son. I did not discuss it any further. Suddenly English became a priority in his life. He finished out the semester with an A.

I know one example doesn't make a case, but at night I see a parade of students who are angry and resentful for having been passed along until they could no longer even pretend to keep up. Of average intelligence or better, they eventually quit school, concluding they were too dumb to finish. "I should have been held back" is a comment I hear frequently. Even sadder are those students who are high-school graduates who say to me after a few weeks of class, "I don't know how I ever got a high-school diploma." 7

Passing students who have not mastered the work cheats them and the employers who expect graduates to have basic skills. We excuse this dishonest behavior by saying kids can't learn if they come from terrible environments. No one seems to stop to think that—no matter what environments they come from—most kids don't put school first on their list unless they perceive something is at stake. They'd rather be sailing. 8

Many students I see at night could give expert testimony on unemployment, chemical dependency, abusive relationships. In spite of these difficulties, they have decided to make education a priority. They are motivated by the desire for a better job or the need to hang on to the one they've got. They have a healthy fear of failure. 9

People of all ages can rise above their problems, but they need to have a reason to do so. Young people generally don't have the maturity to value education in the same way my adult students value it. But fear of failure, whether economic or academic, can motivate both. 10

Flunking as a regular policy has just as much merit today as it did two generations ago. We must review the threat of flunking and see it as it really is—a positive teaching tool. It is an expression of confidence by both teachers and parents that the students have the ability to learn the material presented to them. However, making it work again would take a dedicated, caring conspiracy between teachers and parents. It would mean facing the tough reality that passing kids who haven't learned the material—while it might save them grief for the short term—dooms them to long-term illiteracy. It would mean that teachers would have to follow through on their threats, and parents would have to stand 11 behind them, knowing their children's best interests are indeed at stake. This means no more doing Scott's assignments for him because he might fail. No more passing Jodi because she's such a nice kid.

This is a policy that worked in the past and can work today. A wise teacher, with the support of his parents, gave our son the opportunity to succeed—or fail. It's time we return this choice to all students. 12

Thinking Critically about This Reading

According to Sherry, "We must review the threat of flunking and see it as it really is—a positive teaching tool. It is an expression of confidence by both teachers and parents that the students have the ability to learn the material presented to them" (paragraph 11). How can flunking students be "an expression of confidence" in them?

Questions for Study and Discussion

1. What is Sherry's thesis? (Glossary: *Thesis*) What evidence does she use to support her argument?
2. Sherry uses dismissive language to characterize objections to flunking—*cheats* and *dooms*. In your opinion, does she do enough to acknowledge the other side of the argument? Explain.
3. What is the "F word" discussed in the essay? Does referring to it in this way increase the effectiveness of the essay? Why?
4. Who makes up Sherry's audience? (Glossary: *Audience*) Are they receptive to the "F word"? Explain your answer.
5. In what way is Sherry qualified to comment on the potential benefits of flunking students? Do you think her induction is accurate?

Classroom Activity Using Argument

A first-year composition student, Marco Schmidt, is preparing to write an essay in which he will argue that music should be a required course for all public high school students. He has compiled the following pieces of evidence:

- Informal interviews with four classmates. Three of the classmates stated that they would have enjoyed and benefited from taking a music course in high school, and the fourth stated that she would not have been interested in taking music.

- An article from a professional journal for teachers comparing the study habits of students who were involved in music and those who were not. The author, a psychologist, found that students who play an instrument or sing regularly have better study habits than students who do not.
- A brief article from a national newsmagazine praising an inner-city high school's experimental curriculum, in which music classes play a prominent part.
- The personal website of a high school music teacher who posts information about the successes and achievements of her former students.

Discuss these pieces of evidence with your classmates. Which are most convincing? Which provide the least support for Marco's argument? Why? What other types of evidence might Marco find to support his argument?

Suggested Writing Assignments

1. Write an essay in which you argue against Sherry's thesis. (Glossary: *Thesis*) In what ways is flunking bad for students? Are there techniques more positive than a "fear of failure" that can be used to motivate students?
2. Think of something that involves short-term pain or sacrifice but that can be beneficial in the long run. For example, exercising requires exertion, but it may help prevent health problems. Studying and writing papers when you'd rather be having fun or even sleeping may seem painful, but earning a college degree leads to personal growth and development. Even if the benefits are obvious, imagine a skeptical audience, and write an argument in favor of the short-term sacrifice over the long-term consequences of avoiding it. (Glossary: *Audience*)

Lincoln's Call to Service—and Ours

■ **Stanley McChrystal**

Stanley McChrystal was born in Fort Leavenworth, Kansas, to a family with a long history in the military. He followed in his father's footsteps by graduating from West Point and went on to complete Special Forces training to become a Green Beret. McChrystal became known for his ascetic lifestyle, running a dozen miles a day and eating only one meal. He attained the rank of fourstar general and served as commander of both the Joint Special Operations Command—a unit responsible for counterterrorism efforts around the world—and U.S. Forces–Afghanistan. He retired from the military in 2010.

In this essay from the Wall Street Journal, *McChrystal argues for new opportunities for civilian service to the nation. As you read, look for places where he anticipates objections or answers opposing views.*

Reflecting on What You Know

Have you ever been involved in community service, either on your own or with a school or church group? How did the experience affect you? How do you think it contributed to your neighbors, your city, or your country?

My father first took me to Gettysburg when I was 12 years old. He was a lieutenant colonel in the Army, home from the first of two tours in Vietnam. I remember in particular the hundreds of obelisks poking over the berms, the oxidized plaques attached to rocks and the statues lining the roadways. All spoke for the thousands of men and boys who had died in the grass and dirt serving their nation. 1

I was young, but I recognized the gravity of the place. 2

Though I went on to have a career in the military, the visits to Gettysburg with my father were not preparation for soldiering as much as they were early lessons in citizenship—a particular understanding of citizenship that President Lincoln defined and challenged us to fulfill when he delivered his famous address there. It's a citizenship that does not simply reflect upon the sacrifices of others, but that honors their sacrifice through action: "It is for us the living, rather, to be dedicated to the unfinished work which they who fought here have thus far so nobly advanced." 3

Today, as ever, the task is unfinished. Yet the duties of citizenship have fallen from the national agenda. Talk of service is largely confined to buoyant commencement ceremonies. And too often it is just that: talk. 4

Less than 1% of Americans serve in the military—a historic low during wartime—leading to a broad, complacent assumption that serving the nation is someone else's job. As we've allowed our understanding of service to be so narrowly limited to the uniform, we've forgotten Lincoln's audience: with the armies still fighting, the president exhorted a crowd of civilians on their duty to carry forward the nation's work. 5

It is right that we send off the young Americans graduating this month from high school, college and professional schools with speeches. They should be congratulated for completing the many exams now behind them. But we must remember another test—Lincoln's test of citizenship—and begin to mark these important junctures in life not just with words, but with real-world commitment. 6

Universal national service should become a new American rite of passage. Here is a specific, realistic proposal that would create one million full-time civilian national-service positions for Americans ages 18–28 that would complement the active-duty military—and would change the current cultural expectation that service is only the duty of those in uniform. 7

At age 18, every young man and woman would receive information on various options for national service. Along with the five branches of the military, graduates would learn about new civilian service branches organized around urgent issues like education, health care and poverty. The positions within these branches would be offered through AmeriCorps as well as through certified nonprofits. Service would last at least a year. 8

9 Returning military veterans would be treated as the civic assets they are and permitted to use a portion of their GI Bill benefits to support a period of civilian national service, since such service helps them transition to life back home.

10 The new service opportunities would be created in accordance with the smart rules that have guided AmeriCorps since its founding in 1994, which allow that program to field tens of thousands of service members without displacing workers and who fill vital niches their paid colleagues do not.

11 Serving full-time for a year or two needs to be a realistic option for all young Americans, regardless of their family's finances. So civilian service positions would be modestly paid, as AmeriCorps positions are now. (Most AmeriCorps service members receive a $12,100 stipend for the year, and if they complete their term of service, a $5,550 scholarship to help cover tuition or to pay off student loans.) Government agencies focused on the challenges that these service members address, as well as the corporations that will benefit from employing Americans whose leadership will be cultivated by service, should step up to fund these efforts.

12 Instead of making national service legally mandatory, corporations and universities, among other institutions, could be enlisted to make national service socially obligatory. Schools can adjust their acceptance policies and employers their hiring practices to benefit those who have served—and effectively penalize those who do not.

13 More than most Americans realize, the demand to serve already exists. In 2011, there were nearly 600,000 applications to AmeriCorps—a program with only 80,000 positions, only half of which are full time. The Peace Corps received 150,000 requests for applications but has funding for only 4,000 new positions each year. This gap represents democratic energy wasted and a generation of patriotism needlessly squandered.

14 Some, particularly after having just observed Memorial Day, might think that only war is capable of binding a generation and instilling true civic pride. But you don't have to hear the hiss of bullets to develop a deeper claim to the nation. In my nearly four decades in the military, I saw young men and women learn the meaning and responsibilities of citizenship by wearing the uniform in times of both peace and war. They were required to work with people of different backgrounds, introduced to teamwork and discipline, unified by

common tests, and brought even closer by sacrifice. Some discovered, often to their surprise, that they were leaders.

This transformation is not exclusive to the military. Those who 15
disagree need only visit young teachers working 18-hour days together in the Ninth Ward of New Orleans. In rural Colorado health clinics, in California's forests, or Midwest neighborhoods devastated by tornadoes, skeptics would see teams of young people—affluent and poor, college-educated and not—devoting their days to a singular, impactful mission.

Universal national service would surely face obstacles. But 16
America is too big, and our challenges too expansive, for small ideas. To help stem the high-school dropout crisis, to conserve rivers and parks, to prepare for and respond to disasters, to fight poverty and, perhaps most important, to instill in all Americans a sense of civic duty, the nation needs all its young people to serve.

Whatever the details of a specific plan, the objective must be a 17
cultural shift that makes service an expected rite of citizenship. Anything less fails Lincoln's test.

Thinking Critically about This Reading

How does Lincoln's Gettysburg Address support this argument? Discuss how McChrystal's proposal responds to what he understands as a "call to service" in that speech. (You can read the full speech in Chapter 11, pp. 318–19.)

Questions for Study and Discussion

1. What sentence would you identify as McChrystal's thesis? (Glossary: *Thesis*) Where does he state his argument most directly?
2. What problem is McChrystal responding to in this essay? Find a sentence or two that explains the problem this new model for civilian service would solve.
3. Though Gettysburg is a famous battlefield, McChrystal writes that his visits were "not preparation for soldiering as much as they were early lessons in citizenship" (paragraph 3). What did he learn there about being a citizen?
4. McChrystal lays out many details of his plan in this essay. What does he tell us about how this new civilian force would be organized, funded, and so on?

5. Though McChrystal is primarily focused on service as a duty, he also believes it has benefits for the individuals who undertake it. What are these benefits? Do you find them a persuasive reason to serve?
6. What big problems does McChrystal think this civilian force could help solve? Can you imagine others?

Classroom Activity Using Argumentation

An excellent way to gain experience in formulating an argument on an issue and establishing your own thesis is to engage in a debate with someone who is on the other side of the question. When we listen to arguments and think of refutations and counterarguments, we have a chance to rehearse and revise our position before we put it in written form. It is especially important to carefully consider others' arguments, so that you can respond to them thoughtfully rather than ignoring or dismissing them.

To practice this technique, use McChrystal's argument for universal service to the country as the subject of your debate, or choose another topic on which class opinion is divided. Each side should select a spokesperson to present that group's argument before the class. Begin with one group, which will offer its argument. Before making a counterargument, the other side should summarize the points they have just heard to their opponents' satisfaction, to show that they have really listened to and considered the argument. Both groups should have the opportunity to rebut several times, as class time allows. Finally, come together as a class to discuss the success of each side in (1) articulating its position, (2) presenting ideas and evidence to support that position, and (3) responding to the other side. This exercise should give you a good idea of the kind of work involved in preparing a written argument.

Suggested Writing Assignments

1. Though McChrystal argues passionately for a civilian service corps, he stops short of proposing that service become "legally mandatory." Research some arguments for mandatory service—that is, conscription. Write an essay comparing an argument for conscription with McChrystal's argument for "socially obligatory" service.

2. How would you improve the country if you had a force of energetic, dedicated young people at your disposal? Compose an argument for which problem most urgently needs to be addressed. To make your argument effective, include evidence to convince your reader of the importance of the issue as well as specific proposals for how members of the civilian service could help.

The Declaration of Independence

■ Thomas Jefferson

Library of Congress

President, governor, statesman, lawyer, architect, philosopher, and writer, Thomas Jefferson (1743–1826) is one of the most important figures in U.S. history. He was born in Albemarle County, Virginia, in 1743 and attended the College of William and Mary. After being admitted to law practice in 1767, he began a long and illustrious career of public service to the colonies and, later, the new republic. In 1809, after two terms as president, Jefferson retired to Monticello, a home he had designed and helped build. Ten years later, he founded the University of Virginia. Jefferson died at Monticello on July 4, 1826, the fiftieth anniversary of the signing of the Declaration of Independence.

Jefferson drafted the Declaration in 1776. Although it was revised by Benjamin Franklin and his colleagues at the Continental Congress, the Declaration retains in its sound logic and forceful, direct style the unmistakable qualities of Jefferson's prose.

Reflecting on What You Know

In your mind, what is the meaning of democracy? Where do your ideas about democracy come from?

When in the course of human events, it becomes necessary for one people to dissolve the political bands which have connected them with another, and to assume among the Powers of the earth, the separate and equal station to which the Laws of Nature and of Nature's God entitle them, a decent respect to the opinions of mankind requires that they should declare the causes which impel them to the separation. 1

We hold these truths to be self-evident, that all men are created equal, that they are endowed by their Creator with certain unalienable 2

Rights, that among these are Life, Liberty and the pursuit of Happiness. That to secure these rights, Governments are instituted among Men deriving their just powers from the consent of the governed. That whenever any Form of Government becomes destructive of these ends, it is the Right of the People to alter or to abolish it, and to institute new Government, laying its foundation on such principles and organizing its powers in such form, as to them shall seem most likely to effect their Safety and Happiness. Prudence, indeed, will dictate that Governments long established should not be changed for light and transient[1] causes; and accordingly all experience hath shown, that mankind are more disposed to suffer, while evils are sufferable, than to right themselves by abolishing the forms to which they are accustomed. But when a long train of abuses and usurpations pursuing invariably the same Object evinces a design to reduce them under absolute Despotism, it is their right, it is their duty, to throw off such government, and to provide new Guards for their future security. Such has been the patient sufferance of these Colonies; and such is now the necessity which constrains them to alter their former Systems of Government. The history of the present King of Great Britain[2] is a history of repeated injuries and usurpations, all having in direct object the establishment of an absolute Tyranny over these States. To prove this, let Facts be submitted to a candid world.

He has refused his Assent to Laws, the most wholesome and necessary for the public good. 3

He has forbidden his Governors to pass Laws of immediate and pressing importance, unless suspended in their operation till his Assent should be obtained; and when so suspended, he has utterly neglected to attend to them. 4

He has refused to pass other Laws for the accommodation of large districts of people, unless those people would relinquish the right of Representation in the Legislature, a right inestimable to them and formidable to tyrants only. 5

He has called together legislative bodies at places unusual, uncomfortable, and distant from the depository of their Public Records, for the sole purpose of fatiguing them into compliance with his measures. 6

He has dissolved Representative Houses repeatedly, for opposing with manly firmness his invasions on the rights of the people. 7

[1]*transient:* not lasting; not permanent.

[2]*King of Great Britain:* King George III (1738–1820), who ruled the British Empire from 1760 to 1820.

He has refused for a long time, after such dissolutions, to cause 8
others to be elected; whereby the Legislative Powers, incapable of Annihilation, have returned to the People at large for their exercise; the State remaining in the mean time exposed to all the dangers of invasion from without, and convulsions within.

He has endeavoured to prevent the population of these States; for 9
that purpose obstructing the Laws of Naturalization of Foreigners; refusing to pass others to encourage their migration hither, and raising the conditions of new Appropriations of Lands.

He has obstructed the Administration of Justice, by refusing his 10
Assent to Laws for establishing Judiciary Powers.

He has made Judges dependent on his Will alone, for the tenure of 11
their offices, and the amount and payment of their salaries.

He has erected a multitude of New Offices, and sent hither swarms 12
of Officers to harass our People, and eat out their substance.

He has kept among us, in time of peace, Standing Armies without 13
the Consent of our Legislature.

He has affected to render the Military independent of and superior 14
to the Civil Power.

He has combined with others to subject us to jurisdictions foreign 15
to our constitution, and unacknowledged by our laws; giving his Assent to their acts of pretended Legislation:

For quartering large bodies of armed troops among us: 16

For protecting them, by a mock Trial, from Punishment for 17
any Murders which they should commit on the Inhabitants of these States:

For cutting off our Trade with all parts of the world: 18

For imposing Taxes on us without our Consent: 19

For depriving us in many cases, of the benefits of Trial by Jury: 20

For transporting us beyond Seas to be tried for pretended offenses: 21

For abolishing the free System of English Laws in a Neighbouring 22
Province, establishing therein an Arbitrary government, and enlarging its boundaries so as to render it at once an example and fit instrument for introducing the same absolute rule into these Colonies:

For taking away our Charters, abolishing our most valuable Laws, 23
and altering fundamentally the Forms of our Governments:

For suspending our own Legislatures, and declaring themselves 24
invested with Power to legislate for us in all cases whatsoever.

He has abdicated Government here, by declaring us out of his 25
Protection and waging War against us.

He has plundered our seas, ravaged our Coasts, burnt our towns and destroyed the Lives of our people. 26

He is at this time transporting large Armies of foreign Mercenaries to compleat works of death, desolation and tyranny, already begun with circumstances of Cruelty & perfidy scarcely paralleled in the most barbarous ages, and totally unworthy the Head of a civilized nation. 27

He has constrained our fellow Citizens taken Captive on the high Seas to bear Arms against their Country, to become the executioners of their friends and Brethren, or to fall themselves by their Hands. 28

He has excited domestic insurrections amongst us, and has endeavoured to bring on the inhabitants of our frontiers, the merciless Indian Savages, whose known rule of warfare is an undistinguished destruction of all ages, sexes and conditions. 29

In every stage of these Oppressions We Have Petitioned for Redress in the most humble terms: Our repeated petitions have been answered only by repeated injury. A Prince, whose character is thus marked by every act which may define a Tyrant, is unfit to be the ruler of a free People. 30

Nor have We been wanting in attention to our British brethren. We have warned them from time to time of attempts by their legislature to extend an unwarrantable jurisdiction over us. We have reminded them of the circumstances of our emigration and settlement here. We have appealed to their native justice and magnanimity[3] and we have conjured them by the ties of our common kindred to disavow these usurpations, which would inevitably interrupt our connections and correspondence. They too have been deaf to the voice of justice and of consanguinity. We must, therefore, acquiesce[4] in the necessity, which denounces our Separation, and hold them, as we hold the rest of mankind, Enemies in War, in Peace Friends. 31

We, therefore, the Representatives of the United States of America, in General Congress, Assembled, appealing to the Supreme Judge of the world for the rectitude of our intentions, do, in the Name, and by Authority of the good People of these Colonies, solemnly publish and declare, That these United Colonies are, and of Right ought to be Free and Independent States; that they are Absolved from all Allegiance to the British Crown, and that all political connection between them and the State of Great Britain, is and ought to be totally dissolved; and that 32

[3]*magnanimity:* quality of being calm, generous, upstanding.
[4]*acquiesce:* comply; accept.

as Free and Independent States, they have full power to levy War, conclude Peace, contract Alliances, establish Commerce, and to do all other Acts and Things which Independent States may of right do. And for the support of this Declaration, with a firm reliance on the protection of Divine Providence, we mutually pledge to each other our Lives, our Fortunes and our sacred Honor.

Thinking Critically about This Reading

What, according to the Declaration of Independence, is the purpose of government?

Questions for Study and Discussion

1. In paragraph 2, Jefferson presents certain "self-evident" truths. What are these truths, and how are they related to his argument? Do you consider them self-evident?
2. The Declaration of Independence is a deductive argument; therefore, it can be presented in the form of a syllogism. (Glossary: *Syllogism*) Identify the major premise, the minor premise, and the conclusion of Jefferson's argument.
3. The list of charges against the king is given as evidence in support of Jefferson's minor premise. (Glossary: *Evidence*) Does Jefferson offer any evidence in support of his major premise?
4. How does Jefferson refute the possible charge that the colonists should have tried to solve their problems by less drastic means?
5. Where in the Declaration does Jefferson use parallel structure? (Glossary: *Parallelism*) What does he achieve by using it?
6. Although the basic structure of the Declaration reflects sound deductive reasoning, Jefferson's language, particularly when he lists the charges against the king, tends to be emotional. (Glossary: *Diction*) Identify as many examples of this emotional language as you can, and discuss possible reasons for why Jefferson uses this kind of language.

Classroom Activity Using Argument

Choose one of the following controversial subjects, and think about how you would write an argument for or against it. Write three sentences that summarize three important points, two based on logic and one based on persuasion/emotion. Then write one sentence that acknowledges the opposing point of view. For example, if you were to argue for stricter enforcement of a leash law and waste-pickup ordinance for dog owners in your town, you might write the following:

Logic	Dogs allowed to run free can be a menace to joggers and local wildlife.
Logic	Dog waste poses a health risk, particularly in areas where children play.
Emotion	How would you feel if you hit an unleashed dog with your car?
Counterargument	Dogs need fresh air and exercise, too.

Gun control
The effectiveness of standardized testing
Women in combat
Paying college athletes
Assisted suicide for the terminally ill
Government surveillance programs

Suggested Writing Assignments

1. The issue of human rights is often discussed. Review the arguments for and against the U.S. government's active and outspoken promotion of the human rights issue as reported in the press. Then write an argument of your own in favor of a continued strong human rights policy on the part of U.S. governmental leaders.

2. Using one of the subjects listed below, develop a thesis, and then write an essay in which you argue in support of that thesis:

   Minimum wage
   Social Security
   Capital punishment
   Erosion of individual rights
   Welfare
   Separation of church and state
   First Amendment rights

CRIME: FINDING AN EFFECTIVE PUNISHMENT

The authors of the three essays in this mini-casebook on punishment are concerned with the role that shame and guilt should play, if any, in discouraging nonviolent crimes. Their interest in this topic is instigated by several recent trends in our society, namely public-shaming sentences that have been imposed by judges and the emergence of social media, which has allowed the public to anonymously engage in the public humiliation of offenders as a kind of hoped-for retribution. Oddly enough, both these attempts at justice fail to consider the unintended negative consequences of such actions.

Although recent judicial practices and a social environment fashioned by technological innovation have put a new face on shaming, the practice is nothing new. Remember that shaming lies at the heart of one of our most artistically brilliant and psychologically complicated classical novels, *The Scarlet Letter* by Nathaniel Hawthorne. Written in the nineteenth century but set in a seventeenth-century Puritanical New England village, the novel examines the life of young Hester Prynne, who has borne a child out of wedlock and is punished by being made to wear an elaborately embroidered red letter A on the bosom of her dress as an ever-present sign of her crime and humiliation, or so it is intended. How all this plays out is another matter. Suffice it to say that shame and guilt and the public's need for retribution are ageless impulses and need to be recognized and tended to, if not always resolved.

June Tangney in "Condemn the Crime, Not the Person" emphasizes the need to understand the difference between shame and guilt and what contemporary research reveals about the way each emotion plays itself out in the public arena of punishment. Dan M. Kahan, a prominent professor of law, advocates in "Shame Is Worth a Try" that we not reject using shame in our judicial practices, as has been urged, but that we use it wisely and appropriately as a low-cost form of punishment. Finally, Cole Stryker in "The Problem with Public Shaming" looks more deeply into the role of online networks in carrying out shaming and asks whether such activities do much to advance society or are simply attempts at making us feel better. In sum, these essays provide ideas to ponder and material to substantiate our own views about how best to make the punishment fit the crime.

Condemn the Crime, Not the Person

June Tangney

George Mason University

*Psychology educator and researcher June Tangney was born in Buffalo, New York, in 1958. After graduating from the State University of New York at Buffalo in 1979, she attended the University of California–Los Angeles, where she earned a master's degree in 1981 and a doctorate in 1985. Tangney taught briefly at Bryn Mawr College and held a research position at the Regional Center for Infants and Young Children in Rockville, Maryland. Since 1988 she has been a professor of psychology at George Mason University, where she was recognized with a Teaching Excellence Award. She is the coauthor of five books—*Self-Conscious Emotions: The Psychology of Shame, Guilt, Embarrassment, and Pride *(1995), with Kurt W. Fisher;* Shame and Guilt *(2002), with Rhonda L. Dearing;* Handbook of Self and Identity *(2005), with Mark R. Leary;* Social Psychological Foundations of Clinical Psychology *(2010), with James E. Maddux; and* Shame in the Therapy Hour *(2011), with Rhonda L. Dearing—and is an associate editor of the journal* Self and Identity.

In the following essay, first published in the Boston Globe *on August 5, 2001, Tangney argues against the use of public humiliation as punishment. She bases her position on recent scientific evidence, much of which comes from her own work on shame and guilt.*

Reflecting on What You Know

For you, what is the difference between *shame* and *guilt*? Provide an example from your own experience to illustrate your understanding of each concept.

1 As the costs of incarceration mount and evidence of its failure as a deterrent grows, judges understandably have begun to search for creative alternatives to traditional sentences. One recent trend is the use of "shaming" sentences—sanctions explicitly designed to induce feelings of shame.

2 Judges across the country are sentencing offenders to parade around in public carrying signs broadcasting their crimes, to post signs on their front lawns warning neighbors of their vices, and to display "drunk driver" bumper stickers on their cars.

3 A number of social commentators have urged America to embrace public shaming and stigmatization as cheaper and effective alternatives for curbing a broad range of nonviolent crimes. Punishments aimed at public humiliation certainly appeal to our sense of moral righteousness. They do indeed appear fiscally attractive when contrasted with the escalating costs of incarceration.

4 But recent scientific evidence suggests that such attempts at social control are misguided. Rather than fostering constructive change, shame often makes a bad situation worse.

5 The crux[1] of the matter lies in the distinction between shame and guilt. Recent research has shown that shame and guilt are distinct emotions with very different implications for subsequent moral and interpersonal behavior. Feelings of shame involve a painful focus on the self—the humiliating sense that "I am a bad person."

6 Such humiliation is typically accompanied by a sense of shrinking, of being small, worthless, and powerless, and by a sense of being exposed. Ironically, research has shown that such painful and debilitating feelings of shame do not motivate constructive changes in behavior.

7 Shamed individuals are no less likely to repeat their transgressions (often more so), and they are no more likely to attempt reparation[2] (often less so). Instead, because shame is so intolerable, people in the midst of the experience often resort to any one of a number of defensive tactics.

8 They may seek to hide or escape the shameful feeling, denying responsibility. They may seek to shift the blame outside, holding others responsible for their dilemma. And not infrequently, they become irrationally angry with others, sometimes resorting to overtly aggressive and destructive actions. In short, shame serves to escalate the very destructive patterns of behavior we aim to curb.

[1]*crux:* the essential or deciding point.
[2]*reparation:* a making of amends; repayment.

Contrast this with feelings of guilt which involve a focus on a specific behavior—the sense that "I did a bad thing" rather than "I am a bad person." 9

Feelings of guilt involve a sense of tension, remorse, and regret over the "bad thing done." 10

Research has shown that this sense of tension and regret typically motivates reparative action (confessing, apologizing, or somehow repairing the damage done) without engendering[3] all the defensive and retaliative responses that are the hallmark of shame. 11

Most important, feelings of guilt are much more likely to foster constructive changes in future behavior because what is at issue is not a bad, defective self, but a bad, defective behavior. And, as anyone knows, it is easier to change a bad behavior (drunken driving, slumlording, thievery) than to change a bad, defective self. 12

How can we foster constructive feelings of guilt among America's offenders? Well, one way is to force offenders to focus on the negative consequences of their behavior, particularly on the painful negative consequences for others. 13

Community service sentences can do much to promote constructive guilt when they are tailored to the nature of the crime. What is needed are imposed activities that underscore the tangible destruction caused by the offense and that provide a path to redemption by ameliorating[4] similar human misery. 14

Drunk drivers, for example, could be sentenced to help clear sites of road accidents and to assist with campaigns to reduce drunken driving. Slumlords could be sentenced to assist with nuts and bolts repairs in low-income housing units. In this way, offenders are forced to see, first-hand, the potential or actual destructiveness of their infractions and they become actively involved in constructive solutions. 15

Some critics have rejected community service as an alternative to incarceration, suggesting that such community-based sentences somehow cheapen an otherwise honorable volunteer activity while at the same time not adequately underscoring the criminal's disgrace. 16

Scientific research, however, clearly indicates that public shaming and humiliation is not the path of choice. Such efforts are doomed to provoke all sorts of unintended negative consequences. 17

---

[3]*engendering:* causing or producing.

[4]*ameliorating:* improving or making better.

In contrast, thoughtfully constructed guilt-oriented community service sentences are more likely to foster changes in offenders' future behaviors, while contributing to the larger societal good. My guess is that any honorable community service volunteer would welcome such constructive changes. 18

Thinking Critically about This Reading

Tangney states, "A number of social commentators have urged America to embrace public shaming and stigmatization as cheaper and effective alternatives for curbing a broad range of nonviolent crimes" (paragraph 3). What evidence does she present to counter these arguments?

Questions for Study and Discussion

1. What is a "shaming" sentence (1)? According to Tangney, why do judges use such sentences in place of more traditional ones?
2. What is Tangney's position on using sentences intended to shame offenders? Briefly state her thesis in your own words. (Glossary: *Thesis*)
3. What for Tangney is the key difference between shame and guilt? Why does she believe that guilt works better than shame as a form of punishment?
4. Paragraph 13 begins with a rhetorical question: "How can we foster constructive feelings of guilt among America's offenders?" (Glossary: *Rhetorical Question*) How does Tangney answer this question? What suggestions would you add to her solution?
5. How does Tangney counter the critics of community service? Do you find her counterarguments convincing? Why or why not?

Classroom Activity Using Argument

The effectiveness of a writer's argument depends in large part on the writer's awareness of audience. For example, a writer arguing that there is too much violence portrayed on television might present different kinds of evidence, reasoning, and diction for different audiences, such as parents, lawmakers, or television producers and writers.

Review several of the argument essays you have read in this chapter. In your opinion, for what primary audience is each essay intended? List the evidence you found in each essay that helped you determine your answer. (Glossary: *Evidence*)

Suggested Writing Assignments

1. Write an essay in which you tell the story of a childhood punishment that you received or witnessed. (Glossary: *Narration*) How did you feel about the punishment? Was it justified? Appropriate? Effective? Why or why not? In retrospect, did the punishment shame or humiliate you, or did it bring out feelings of guilt? What did you learn from this experience? Before beginning to write, read or review Dick Gregory's "Shame" (pp. 163–67).
2. Tangney writes, "As the costs of incarceration mount and evidence of its failure as a deterrent grows, judges understandably have begun to search for creative alternatives to traditional sentences" (1). Ideally, knowing what the punishment will be should deter people from doing the wrong thing in the first place, but do punishments really act as deterrents? Are certain punishments more effective as deterrents than others? What are the deterrent benefits of both shame and guilt punishments? Conduct library and Internet research to answer these questions, and then report your findings and conclusions in an essay.

Shame Is Worth a Try

■ **Dan M. Kahan**

Courtesy of Dan M. Kahan

Dan M. Kahan was born in 1963 and graduated from Middlebury College in 1986 and Harvard Law School in 1989, where he served as president of the Harvard Law Review. *He clerked for Judge Harry Edwards of the U.S. Court of Appeals for the District of Columbia circuit in 1989–1990 and for Justice Thurgood Marshall of the U.S. Supreme Court in 1990–1991. After practicing law for two years in Washington, D.C., Kahan launched his teaching career, first at the University of Chicago Law School and later at Yale Law School, where since 2003 he has been the Elizabeth K. Dollard Professor of Law. From 2005 to 2006, he served as deputy dean of Yale Law School. His teaching and research interests include criminal law, risk perception, punishment, and evidence. Kahan, who has written widely in legal journals on current social issues including gun control, is coauthor, with Tracey Meares, of* Urgent Times: Policing and Rights in Inner-City Communities *(1999).*

In the following essay, first published in the Boston Globe *on August 5, 2001, Kahan argues in favor of the use of shame as "an effective, cheap, and humane alternative to imprisonment."*

Reflecting on What You Know

Think about the times you were punished as a child. Who punished you—parents, teachers, or other authority figures? What kinds of bad behavior were you punished for? What type of punishment worked best to deter you from behaving badly later on? Explain.

Is shame an appropriate criminal punishment? Many courts and legislators around the country think so. Steal from your employer in Wisconsin and you might be ordered to wear a sandwich board proclaiming your offense. Drive drunk in Florida or Texas and you 1 might be required to place a conspicuous "DUI" bumper sticker on your car. Refuse to make your child-support payments in Virginia and you will find that your vehicle has been immobilized with an appropriately colored boot (pink if the abandoned child is a girl, blue if a boy).

Many experts, however, are skeptical of these new shaming punishments. Some question their effectiveness as a deterrent. Others worry that the new punishments are demeaning and cruel. 2

Who's right? As is usually the case, both sides have their points. But what the shame proponents seem to be getting, and the critics ignoring, is the potential of shame as an effective, cheap, and humane alternative to imprisonment. 3

There's obviously no alternative to imprisonment for murderers, rapists, and other violent criminals. But they make up less than half the American prison population. 4

Liberal and conservative reformers alike have long believed that the remainder can be effectively punished with less severe "alternative sanctions," like fines and community service. These sanctions are much cheaper than jail. They also allow the offender to continue earning an income so he can compensate his victim, meet his child-support obligations, and the like. 5

Nevertheless, courts and legislators have resisted alternative sanctions—not so much because they won't work, but because they fail to express appropriate moral condemnation of crime. Fines seem to say that offenders may buy the privilege of breaking the law; and we can't very well condemn someone for purchasing what we are willing to sell. 6

Nor do we condemn offenders to educate the retarded, install smoke detectors in nursing homes, restore dilapidated low income housing, and the like. Indeed, saying that such community service is punishment for criminals insults both those who perform such services voluntarily and those whom the services are supposed to benefit. 7

There's no confusion about the law's intent to condemn, however, when judges resort to public shaming. As a result, judges, legislators, and the public at large generally do accept shame as a morally appropriate punishment for drunken driving, nonaggravated assaults, embezzlement,[1] small-scale drug distribution, larceny,[2] toxic waste dumping, perjury, and a host of other offenses that ordinarily would result in a short jail term. 8

[1]*embezzlement:* stealing money or goods entrusted to one's care.
[2]*larceny:* theft.

The critics' anxieties about shame, moreover, seem overstated. Clearly, shame hurts. People value their reputations for both emotional and financial reasons. In fact, a series of studies by Harold Grasmick, a sociologist at the University of Oklahoma, suggests that the prospect of public disgrace exerts greater pressure to comply with the law than does the threat of imprisonment and other formal punishments. 9

There's every reason to believe, then, that shaming penalties will be an effective deterrent, at least for nonviolent crimes. Indeed, preliminary reports suggest that certain shaming punishments, including those directed at deadbeat dads, are extraordinarily effective. 10

At the same time, shame clearly doesn't hurt as much as imprisonment. Individuals who go to jail end up just as disgraced as those who are shamed, and lose their liberty to boot. Those who've served prison time are also a lot less likely to regain the respect and trust of their law-abiding neighbors—essential ingredients of rehabilitation. Given all this, it's hard to see shame as cruel. 11

Consider the case of a Florida mother sentenced to take out a newspaper ad proclaiming "I purchased marijuana with my kids in the car." 12

The prospect that her neighbors would see the ad surely caused her substantial embarrassment. But the alternative was a jail sentence, which would not only have humiliated her more but could also have caused her to lose custody of her children. Not surprisingly, the woman voluntarily accepted the shaming sanction in lieu of[3] jail time, as nearly all offenders do. 13

Shame, like any other type of criminal punishment, can definitely be abused. Some forms of it, like the public floggings imposed by authoritarian states abroad, are pointlessly degrading. 14

In addition, using shame as a supplement rather than a substitute for imprisonment only makes punishment more expensive for society and destructive for the offender. Accordingly, requiring sex offenders to register with local authorities is harder to defend than are other types of shaming punishments, which are true substitutes for jail. 15

These legitimate points, however, are a reason to insist that shaming be carried out appropriately, not to oppose it across the board. 16

In short, shame is cheap and effective and frees up scarce prison space for the more serious offenses. Why not at least give it a try? 17

[3]*in lieu of:* in place of; instead of.

Thinking Critically about This Reading

What does Kahan mean when he states that "requiring sex offenders to register with local authorities is harder to defend than are other types of shaming punishments" (paragraph 15)?

Questions for Study and Discussion

1. What is Kahan's thesis? (Glossary: *Thesis*) Where does he state it most clearly?
2. What examples of shaming punishments does Kahan provide? For you, do these punishments seem to fit the crime? Explain.
3. How does Kahan handle the opposition argument that public shaming is cruel?
4. According to Kahan, why have courts and legislators resisted alternative punishments such as fines and community service?
5. What evidence does Kahan present to show that shaming punishments work? (Glossary: *Evidence*)
6. How convincing is Kahan's argument? What is the strongest part of his argument? The weakest part? Explain.

Classroom Activity Using Argument

Is public shaming justifiable? Hold a class debate, dividing into teams that will argue for and against such punishment. Team members should divide themselves among different aspects of their position (for example, psychological repercussions of the punishment, more traditional sentences it could replace, and examples of judges who have used shaming) and then do library and Internet research to develop ideas and evidence. The teams should be allowed equal time to present their assertions and the evidence they have to support them. Finally, the class as a whole should be prepared to discuss the effectiveness of the presentations on both sides of the question.

Suggested Writing Assignments

1. Write an essay in which you argue your position on the issue of using public shaming as a punishment. Is public shaming appropriate for some or all offenses that would otherwise result in

a short jail term? Explain. Support your argument with evidence from Kahan's essay, June Tangney's "Condemn the Crime, Not the Person" (pp. 576–79), and your own experiences and observations. (Glossary: *Evidence*) You may find it helpful to review your Reflecting on What You Know response for this selection.

2. Identify several current problems at your college or university involving violations of campus rules for parking, cheating on exams, plagiarizing papers, recycling waste, using drugs or alcohol, defacing school property, and so on. Select one of these problems, and write a proposal to treat violators with a shaming punishment of your own design. Address your proposal to your school's student government organization or administration office.
3. What is your position on the issue of whether convicted sex offenders should be required to register with local authorities? Should registration be required even though they have already served their sentences in prison? Should people have the right to know the identity of any sex offenders living in their neighborhoods, or is this an invasion of privacy? Conduct library and Internet research on the subject of sex offender registration, and write an essay arguing for or against the measure.

The Problem with Public Shaming

■ Cole Stryker

Cole Stryker was born in Pittsburgh, Pennsylvania, attended Grove City College, and currently works as a freelance writer and media consultant in New York. He is the author of Epic Win for Anonymous: How 4Chan's Army Conquered the Web *(2011) and* Hacking the Future: Privacy, Identity, and Anonymity on the Web *(2012). Stryker's writing has appeared in many publications, including* Salon, Vice, *the* New York Observer, *and* PopMatters.

Wesley Stringer

In this essay, which first appeared in the Nation, *Stryker argues against a form of public punishment facilitated by online networks. Though he says shaming is not new, he expresses concerns about tactics used by groups like Anonymous and, more recently, websites like Gawker and Jezebel. He writes, "I think journalists should be quick to condemn socially destructive behaviors, but give people more benefit of the doubt than one would think they might deserve. A lot of bloggers don't recognize the power they wield to ruin someone's life." As you read, consider how his analysis of the problem works to win readers over to his argument.*

Reflecting on What You Know

What methods do people use to point out or even punish questionable behavior online? How do you think Internet users should treat people who are thoughtless, rude, or even hateful?

Today most people would tell you that the stocks, pillory and other tools of public punishment are barbaric. We've moved past them, having figured out more humane ways to deal with crime. Why, then, the resurgence of public shaming, namely the mainstream acceptance 1 of the "dox," which, in its purest form, is the digging up of a target's personal information—name, phone number, address, Social Security number, familial relationships, financial history—and exposing it online to encourage harassment from others? This practice has gradually been popularized by Anonymous, the amorphous collective of trolls and "hacktivists" that alternately terrorize tween girls and disable government websites.

In 2012, this practice was broadly adopted by media outlets. In October, Gawker unmasked a creep, notorious for facilitating the sharing of sexualized images of women (underage and otherwise) taken without their consent. Gawker declared him "the biggest troll on the web." Its sister blog Jezebel called for the naming of names of such creeps, and later exposed a bunch of teenage Twitter users making racist remarks about Obama, going so far as to personally alert the administrators of their schools by phone. 2

This trend runs silly, as well—Buzzfeed ridiculed spoiled teens whining about their Christmas presents, while every media outlet covered Nice Guys of OK Cupid, a blog that ridicules clueless misogyny by sharing photos of hapless bros with regrettable stances on gender politics. Prepare to see a lot more of this sort of thing now that Facebook has released its Graph Search tool, which makes it possible to search for a controversial keyword or phrase (say, "I hate n—ers"), find people who've used that phrase on their profiles and grab some screenshots—you've got a ready-made outrage-baiting trend piece. 3

The dox phenomenon played out with unfortunate results last month, when on March 17, development evangelist Adria Richards tweeted a photo of two men who'd been making sophomoric jokes at a tech conference, leading to the removal of the offenders, and then the firing of one. A wave of backlash ensued against Richards; strangers sent her abusive, threatening messages, and Internet trolls conspired to get her fired, attacking her employer's website with dummy traffic. Her employer eventually did terminate her contract, citing Richards's divisive tactics. 4

The First Amendment protects a lot of abhorrent speech, but societies have always resorted to some form of vigilante justice to preserve widely known and observed rules of social conduct that don't result in a crime when they're broken. So we turn instead to public humiliation, an organic form of social control that never really went away completely, as evidenced by the occasional signboard-bearing 5 ne'er-do-well on the nightly news. Publicity-seeking judges occasionally will expose deadbeat dads, public urinators, drunk drivers and repeat drug offenders. But these are outliers. We don't prop people up in public, brand them with scarlet letters or hurl spoiled produce.

We didn't cease these punishments because we began to see them as barbaric. They simply stopped working. Historians point to the urbanization of impersonal cities with mobile, transient populations. It's difficult to encourage shame if they can easily disappear into the crowd or escape to the next town. Shame works in closed, small communities that share similar norms. As the New World opened up and expanded, public humiliation ceased to be an effective means of norm reinforcement. 6

American adjudicators typically look to five goals to justify a punishment: incapacitation, restitution, deterrence, rehabilitation and retribution. Neither incapacitation nor restitution apply to doxxing, since there are no legal enforcement mechanisms. To the extent that those who engage in public shaming think they are satisfying one of the remaining three, they faultily assume that deeply rooted social ills like racism, sexism and homophobia are personal failings that can be remedied through vicious public blowback and a permanent stain on their character. 7

It's common to argue that a perpetrator "deserves" to be shamed, but in fact human psychology doesn't work this way. Many pedophiles, for instance, recognize that they are inexorably—even biologically—bound to impulses that they themselves loathe. Does the shaming—through public registries for example—cause the pedophile to reform? Unlikely. Does it deter others from engaging in pedophilic acts, or does it drive them to darker corners and sneakier tactics? 8

Racism is not as tied to biology, but environment can be a powerful antibody to shame. Imagine you are a teenager living with white supremacist parents surrounded by white supremacist neighbors and you get suspended from school because you said something racist. Do you turn inward and examine your sense of shared humanity with brown people, or do you simply become resentful toward those who've punished you, perhaps even more sure of your sundry prejudices? Does it even deter you from vocalizing your racism, or do you simply channel it through a different medium where you're less likely to be caught? In March, a racist New York City EMT employee was outed by the *New York Post* for posting vile tweets. His online 9 supporters countered by violently threatening the reporter who broke the story, sometimes anonymously, sometimes not. These behaviors are symptoms of a systemic ideological cancer that is highly resistant to shaming because racists are typically proud of their hate.

Which leaves tit-for-tat as the lone valid criterion for public humiliation. But retribution, too, is problematic. Consider the announcement of the Sandy Hook episode and the ensuing media frenzy to name the shooter. He was first incorrectly identified as Ryan Lanza, who turned out to be the killer's brother. Other "Ryan Lanzas" and their friends and families were harassed during the confusion. Reporters are notoriously bad at getting the facts straight during the frenzied moments following a big story, let alone amateur detectives or doxxers. Things get especially hairy when big media publish the identity of alleged aggressors based on unverified claims from untrustworthy sources. Amateur detectives raced against the FBI to uncover the perpetrators behind the Boston bombings on social news site Reddit. They fingered the wrong person, resulting in a misguided witch hunt that prompted Reddit's general manager Erik Martin to publicly apologize. Such exposure can lead to misguided counterattacks from a faceless troll army. On an Internet where people can so deftly conceal their identities and impersonate strangers, we must be mindful of our propensity for error. 10

Then there is the permanence problem. Once embarrassing information about a person is online, it's never going to go away. Imagine, thirty years from now, some potential employer evaluating a candidate based on a thoughtless remark she made as a teenager. The permanence of uploaded information ensures that modern shamings, while obviously milder in severity, can far exceed the scope of the scarlet letter, the most extreme manifestation of which was at least branded on the chest, where it could be covered. Every modern system of punishment attempts to deal in proportionalities. Put simply, the punishment must fit the crime. 11

Finally, the angry mob problem. Unlike institutionalized forms of punishment, public shaming can spiral out of control, far beyond the imaginations of the media outlets who performed the initial exposure. Vigilante justice is a tricky thing, with online anonymity leading to harsher consequences from a host of far-flung strangers exercising psychopathic levels of schadenfreude. Whose norms are we to enforce? Would Jezebel's writers be comfortable knowing that the tactics it employed against racist teenagers have been used against abortion doctors? 12

The rise of the social web may be perceived as a re-villaging, where the permanence of one's digital footprint behaves as a deterrent, making it seem to some like an ideal time to reintroduce public shaming to reinforce norms. But considered through a historical lens, public shaming begins to look like a tool designed not to humanely punish the perp but rather to satisfy the crowd. 13

This explains its resurgence. When has the crowd ever been bigger, or more thirsty for vengeance? The faceless Internet, with its shadowy cyberbullies and infinite display of every social ill, is scary. And when it slithers its tentacles in a person's life, we become desperate for some way to fight back—to shine light into the darkness and counterattack those who would victimize behind the veil of anonymity. But doxxing, even just naming publicly available names to channel outrage (or worse) at someone who has violated your norms, is not only an ineffective way to deal, it risks causing more harm than the initial offense. Last year's trendy rise of media-sponsored shaming is self-righteousness masquerading as social justice. In many cases the targets deserve to be exposed and more, but public shaming does not drive social progress. It might make us feel better, but let's not delude ourselves into thinking we've made a positive difference. 14

Thinking Critically about This Reading

Why does Stryker think that 2012 was an important year in the history of public shaming? What events does he cite, and why are they significant?

Questions for Study and Discussion

1. Though Stryker calls his essay "The Problem with Public Shaming," his analysis carefully considers several interconnected problems. Make a list of the problems he identifies, and explain them as clearly as you can. What is the "permanence problem" (paragraph 11)? The "angry mob problem" (12)?
2. How does Stryker define *doxxing*, a new form of public shaming? How would you describe it in your own words? (Glossary: *Definition*)
3. Stryker suggests that this kind of "vigilante justice" is used not just for crimes but as a form of social control. Explain this distinction. What kinds of offenses have people used doxxing to punish?

4. Public shaming went out of fashion not because people found it "barbaric," Stryker argues, but because it "simply stopped working" (6). Why? What societal changes led to the comeback of shaming?
5. In paragraph 7, Stryker lists five potential goals American judges look to when deciding on a punishment. He quickly dismisses the first two, incapacitation and restitution, as impossible outcomes of online shaming. Why does he reject the other three, deterrence, rehabilitation, and retribution, as possible positive outcomes of the dox phenomenon?
6. How does Stryker summarize his argument in the concluding paragraph? Choose one sentence that you think makes his point most forcefully.

Classroom Activity Using Argument

Identify the fallacy in each of the following statements. (For more information on logical fallacies, see the box on pp. 548–49.)

a. Oversimplification
b. Hasty generalization
c. *Post hoc, ergo propter hoc*
d. Begging the question
e. False analogy
f. Either/or thinking
g. *Non sequitur*

1. America: Love it or leave it! ______
2. Two of my best friends who are overweight don't exercise at all. Overweight people are simply not getting enough exercise. ______
3. If we use less gasoline, the price of gasoline will fall. ______
4. Life is precious because we want to protect it at all costs. ______
5. Randy is a good mechanic, so he'll be a good race car driver. ______
6. Susan drank hot lemonade, and her cold went away. ______
7. Students do poorly in college because they do too much surfing on the web. ______
8. If we can eliminate pollution, we can cure cancer. ______
9. Such actions are illegal because they are prohibited by law. ______
10. Every time I have something important to do on my computer, it crashes. ______
11. We should either raise taxes or cut social programs. ______

12. Education ought to be managed the way a good business is managed. ______

Suggested Writing Assignments

1. Write an essay that makes an argument about public shaming based on this sentence in Stryker's piece: "But considered through a historical lens, public shaming begins to look like a tool designed not to humanely punish the perp but rather to satisfy the crowd" (13). To support your argument, research punishments that involve public shaming, focusing not on the effects on the offender but on the reaction of the audience to his or her shame.
2. In a *Wall Street Journal* piece entitled "Persuasion as the Cure for Incivility," John I. Jenkins argues that our current political culture involves too much fighting and not enough persuading:

> What if, instead of dealing with opponents by demonizing them and distorting their views, we were to take some steps to persuade them? I don't mean to suggest that one could persuade a stalwart partisan to switch parties, but perhaps one could persuade another that a particular policy or a position is "not as bad as you think."
>
> If I am trying to persuade others, I first have to understand their position, which means I have to listen to them. I have to appeal to their values, which means I have to show them respect. I have to find the best arguments for my position, which means I have to think about my values in the context of their concerns. I have to answer their objections, which means I have to work honestly with their ideas. I have to ask them to listen to me, which means I can't insult them.

Write an essay in which you argue for something you believe in passionately, trying honestly to persuade someone who has an opposing view. To perfect the tone, you might imagine a specific audience, perhaps a parent or sibling whom you care about deeply but with whom you sometimes disagree. What approach would you take if you wanted to convince that person that your opinion was correct, or maybe even "not as bad" as he or she thinks?

■ SLACKTIVISM: SOCIAL MEDIA MEETS ACTIVISM

Mark Pfeifle begins his article in this mini-casebook on slacktivism with a definition of the term drawn from the *Urban Dictionary*: Slacktivism is "the ideology for people who want to appear to be doing something for a particular cause without actually having to do anything." At the heart of the argument about this latest social trend is whether the definition of the term as generally accepted is, indeed, accurate. In other words, is it true in all—or even in most—cases that hitting the "like" or "share" button on a web page is all you need to do to be a social activist today? Has hitting a button taken the place of truly engaging with important issues and getting the job done? The term *slacktivist* is a recently invented label, a blend of the words *slacker* and *activist,* which are of course opposite in meaning. This raises the obvious question: How can you be a slacker (a procrastinator or a lazy person) and still be an activist (one who turns beliefs into actions)? In this way, the term is oxymoronic, harboring within itself contradictory meanings, and thus nicely points to the ironies inherent in the arguments against slacktivism.

However, the arguments surrounding the label are not as clear-cut as they might appear on the surface. Does holding a rally, organizing a charity run, or wearing a bracelet on behalf of a particular cause always simply end there? In other words, are these things merely a way for people to get together socially? They may be for some, but in the minds and hearts of others, they might be the starting point that spurs more concrete and visible action. Might a rally be an advertising strategy for spreading information about an issue that in turn attracts donations and volunteer participation and actually gets something done? Or is showing support, whether via a sign-up sheet or on your phone, a feel-good way of discharging your social responsibility when you already have too much on your schedule?

Heidi Schlumpf in "'Slacktivism' Makes the World a Better Place from the Couch" finds fault with slacktivism but also sees it as a potential entry point for further activist involvement. Gabriella Corvese in "Putting Action Back in Activism" offers an assessment based on her personal experience as a student at Brown University with One Billion Rising, a movement fighting violence against women worldwide. Finally, Mark Pfeifle in "Changing the Face(book) of Social Activism" offers his own firsthand account from inside the U.S. government on the power of social media to effect change around the world. Of the year 2009 he writes, "Social media had become the new soft weapon of democracy," and he provides compelling examples to support his argument.

"Slacktivism" Makes the World a Better Place from the Couch

■ **Heidi Schlumpf**

Courtesy of Heidi Schlumpf

Heidi Schlumpf studied journalism at the University of Notre Dame and earned a master's degree in theological studies from Garrett-Evangelical Theological Seminary at Northwestern University. She is a regular contributor to the National Catholic Reporter *and* U.S. Catholic, *and she interviews authors of books on religion for* Publishers Weekly. *Schlumpf currently teaches communications at Aurora University, outside of Chicago. She is the author of* While We Wait: Spiritual and Practical Advice for Those Trying to Adopt *(2009) and* The Notre Dame Book of Prayer *(2010).*

In this essay, Schlumpf argues that although slacktivism might not cause immediate change, it can be a good starting point for people who want to get involved in social issues. As she makes her argument, she carefully considers criticisms of social media activism, acknowledging its weaknesses in order to make a more nuanced argument for its benefits.

Reflecting on What You Know

Have you ever clicked "like" or posted an image to show your support for a cause on Facebook? Why or why not? How effective do you think social media campaigns are for addressing social issues?

This morning I did a little work on the global fight against HIV/AIDS. Then I joined an environmental protest against genetically modified food and another one supporting undocumented workers. And, of course, a little feminist consciousness-raising. 1

Man, are my fingers tired. 2

You see, all this activism was accomplished while sitting on the sofa, computer in my lap, sipping my morning coffee. I merely opened 3 my inbox and responded to various requests to sign online petitions or to like, share or re-tweet in favor of causes I support—or against those I oppose.

Who knew changing the world could be so easy? 4

It's called "slacktivism" (a combination of the words "slacker" and "activism") by critics and refers to any feel-good effort, usually online, that requires minimal effort or investment, whether financial or personal. 5

Old-fashioned activists tend to look down their protest signs at slacktivists, seeing them as a bunch of, well, slackers. 6

To them, slacktivism is activism "lite" that doesn't contribute to meaningful change and, even worse, is more about the activist's self-esteem or online image. 7

And it's not just secular causes that are appealing to the desire to "care by clicking"—especially among younger folks. A number of Catholic and other religious social justice organizations encourage slacktivism, too. Did you sign an online petition against the LCWR investigation? Or click to get a free "I support the nuns" bumper sticker? Or even "like" NCR's "Support Our Sisters" Facebook page? 8

Sure, "Support Our Sisters" has garnered more than 3,300 "likes," but high participation does not equal high commitment, argued Malcolm Gladwell in his 2010 *New Yorker* piece subtitled, "Why the revolution will not be tweeted." Unlike those who literally put their lives on the line in the 1960s, he said, today's online activists are not motivated enough for high-risk activism. 9

Or are they? 10

According to a 2010 study by researchers at Georgetown University's Center for Social Impact Communication and Ogilvy Public Relations, people who frequently engaged in "promotional social activity" (joining a cause group on Facebook, posting an icon on a social profile, blogging about a cause) were as likely as non-media social promoters to donate and twice as likely to volunteer their time and take part in events like charity walks. 11

"The presumption was that these individuals were replacing more 'meaningful' actions with simple clicks and shares," Denise Keyes, executive director of the Georgetown center, said in a press release announcing the study's findings. "But what we found is that they're actually supplementing—not replacing—actions like donating, volunteering and planning events." 12

So the Catholics who supported the sisters with a click were also 13
more likely to support them in the streets or by getting out their checkbooks?

It's debatable. Other critics of slacktivism point to the psychological 14
phenomenon of "social loafing," in which people are shown to put less effort into a task when other people are doing it with them. There's also the tendency for people to think they've done their part once they've done something, even if that "something" is only sharing a meme.

And some of the "causes" on sites such as change.org don't ad- 15
dress systemic change, but rather seek to help an individual: "Stop Segundo's deportation!" or "Free the Disney dolphins!" Don't underestimate the power of an individual story on slacktivists: More than $680,000 was raised for the bullied grandmother/bus monitor in New York this summer. What most homeless shelters or other nonprofits wouldn't give for that donation!

Also criticized as not "real" activism are corporate activism, like 16
buying a pink kitchen appliance to support breast cancer research; short-term boycotts, such as Earth Hour (in which people turn off their lights for one hour on March 31); and promoting a cause with identity markers like wristbands, car magnets or avatar adjustments.

The problem? Those actions are all about you: your pink toaster, 17
your bumper, your image, your need to feel like you're doing something.

But let's be honest: Plenty of old-fashioned activists also are moti- 18
vated by not-so-purely-selfless motives, and there have always been varying degrees of involvement in causes. When I was unmarried and child-free, I used to protest at the School of the Americas, even risking arrest. My sister, home with three children, baked me cookies for the trip. Now that I have two toddlers, I bake cookies, write checks and click "like."

It's true that amassing signatures does not necessarily result in 19
real change, but it may depend on the cause. I joined thousands of death penalty opponents in petitioning the governor of Mississippi, but he still refused to commute the sentence of a young man on death row.

But how different is amassing numbers online than amassing them 20
in a public place? If the purpose is to bring together like-minded folks, demonstrate power in numbers and get the attention of decision-makers and/or the media, "slacktivism" can make a difference. Awareness alone doesn't solve problems, but it's usually a good start.

21 And if people contribute/create their online identities by associating themselves with various causes, is that so bad? I would argue it's better to tell the world who you are based on your values rather than where you shop, or who your favorite band is.

Thinking Critically about This Reading

Schlumpf opens her essay with a joke at the expense of slacktivists. Why do you think she begins this way? What effect does the joke have on you as a reader?

Questions for Study and Discussion

1. How does Schlumpf define *slacktivism*? Where does the word come from? How is it different from "old-fashioned" activism?
2. Summarize the criticisms of online activism that Schlumpf discusses. Does she consider these to be valid concerns?
3. How do research findings contribute to Schlumpf's thinking about slacktivism? (Note that the research cited in paragraphs 11–14 neither conclusively supports nor refutes the tactic.) What do you take away from these findings?
4. One critique Schlumpf considers is that online campaigns often fail to "address systemic change, but rather seek to help an individual" (paragraph 15). Why is this considered a problem? How do her examples illustrate the point?
5. Ultimately, why does Schlumpf argue in favor of online activism? In her opinion what positive effects can it have?

Classroom Activity Using Argument

Working as a class or in groups, collect a series of visuals to supplement Schlumpf's verbal argument. What images do you think would best encapsulate the criticism that slacktivism is "more about the activist's self-esteem or online image" (7)? What images could illustrate social media demonstrating "power in numbers" or getting media attention? Once you have gathered your visuals, discuss what they add to the argument of the essay.

Suggested Writing Assignments

1. At the end of her essay, Schlumpf argues that "it's better to tell the world who you are based on your values rather than where you shop, or who your favorite band is." Reflect on what you tell the world about who you are on social media, then write an essay that argues your own position on how people should represent themselves online.
2. Schlumpf suggests that social media has made a significant change to the way people become active in political or social causes. What other aspects of our lives or relationships have been changed by social media? Write an essay exploring how dating, attending school, traveling, or some other activity has changed with the rise of social media. Using Schlumpf's essay as a model, conclude by taking a position about whether the change is, on the whole, positive or negative.

Putting Action Back in Activism

■ Gabriella Corvese

Courtesy of Gabriella Corvese

Gabriella Corvese was born in Providence, Rhode Island. She studies public health at Brown University as a member of the class of 2015, and she writes for the Brown Daily Herald. *Her interests include creative nonfiction and screenwriting. When asked about her writing process, Corvese offered these comments: "I read quite a bit of online material from newspapers, magazines and blogs. In fact, this is probably the most important part of the process to me. Writing is great, but reading what other writers have to say is even more important. It really helps you get the big picture. Learning about the viewpoints of others—especially those who disagree with me—is a great way for me to formulate my thoughts."*

In this essay, Corvese reflects on a campus event organized by One Billion Rising. When she first heard about their visit, she decided to "critically look at the organization rather than just accept them for what they bring." As you read, pay attention to the questions she raises about the goals of One Billion Rising and the tactics it uses to approach the issue of violence against women.

Reflecting on What You Know

How do college students, with all the demands on their time, work to support causes they believe in? How do organizations try to harness the energy and enthusiasm of students? What do you think are the best ways for young people to get involved in political or social issues?

A pink ribbon. An inspirational YouTube video. A group of women dancing. What do these things have in common? While they are symbols of important movements, they are also symbols of a dangerous trend in activism: "slacktivism." 1

Slacktivism, as the name suggests, involves supporting a cause on an individual level without doing much to support the big picture. Fred Clark, a Christian blogger, claims to have invented the word, defining it in reference to small movements that can positively affect society. Though it is well-intentioned, its danger rests in the relegation of significant issues to a symbol, color or image. Symbolism can effectively raise awareness, but it does not directly help solve the problem itself and can ignore more serious aspects of an issue. Unfortunately, slacktivism and the instant gratification it provides are new and prominent trends for activist groups. 2

The vastness of social media makes these acts incredibly easy. You can share a picture to let your Facebook friends know you care. Twitter has a hashtag for every cause. But what is the actual effect of these actions? Though social networks allow the easy spread of information, a problem arises when the only support for a cause is a photo with a few thousand shares. While it is satisfying and convenient for the individual to show concern for an issue, those in need of support receive little benefit. 3

Not all slacktivism occurs online. On Valentine's Day, One Billion Rising came to Brown in an effort to end violence against women. The movement and its founder, Eve Ensler, intended for one billion women around the world to dance in support of the one in three women who will be victims of violence during their lives. It provided empowering opportunities to share stories and stand in solidarity against the abuse of women worldwide, and though I cannot speak for all women in judging its effectiveness, I believe it is a worthy and well-intentioned cause. 4

But it is here where One Billion Rising falls into the slacktivist trap—dancing does little to solve the issue of violence against women worldwide, and the symbol of dancing is not a response to some of the severe acts of brutality that affect them. While One Billion Rising effectively raises awareness of the violence many women face, awareness is only the beginning of the solution to a global problem—a truth that applies to many activist groups that rely on symbolism to address problems. 5

6 There are plenty of ways to provide more effective advocacy. Write letters to legislators and public officials who can put issues of public interest on the political table. Donate money to a cause rather than just talking about it, but only after researching where the money goes. V-Day, the organization that sponsors One Billion Rising, raises $4 million annually through college and community events for domestic violence and rape crisis centers. One Billion Rising at Brown took donations for the Sojourner House, a center for domestic violence victims in Rhode Island. Despite value in awareness and empowerment, the additional value of financial support cannot be ignored.

7 Throwing money at a problem is not always the solution, though, and some do not have the resources to donate. Education on a cause is another effective method of garnering support, as it allows people to make choices based on information rather than based on who is shouting the loudest. While slacktivism can inspire discourse on important issues, it often does not lead to conversation on how to take further steps of support. After dancing, what can participants in One Billion Rising do to further empower women and prevent violence? In the long run, informed commitment is more valuable than celebration and spectacle alone.

8 Activist groups like V-Day and One Billion Rising are vital parts of culture both here and outside of Brown. American society alone would not be the way it is without groups that fight for causes that impassion them. But to make the difference that many others have, activist groups should do more than promote symbolism. I support One Billion rising, but I also support taking action above and beyond passive acts. Since slacktivism and its convenience are probably not going anywhere any time soon, it should become the gateway into more direct, informative and effective forms of activism. Through dance alone, One Billion Rising will not solve a problem, but one billion educated and committed individuals have the potential to change the world.

Thinking Critically about This Reading

At the beginning of her essay, Corvese identifies slacktivism as a "dangerous trend." What is dangerous about it?

Questions for Study and Discussion

1. Corvese identifies symbolic actions as a key problem with slacktivism. What does she mean when she discusses symbolism? What examples does she give?
2. What is Corvese's definition of *slacktivism*? Where does she suggest the word comes from? (Glossary: *Definition*)
3. In her assessment of the effects of slacktivism, Corvese notes that "the vastness of social media" (paragraph 3) makes it easy for slacktivists to show their support but does little for the actual people in need. In what way can supporting causes on Facebook and Twitter have little overall effect? (Glossary: *Cause and Effect*)
4. What does Corvese think is the main goal of campaigns like One Billion Rising? How well do these campaigns achieve their goal?
5. What other actions does Corvese suggest to readers who want to support the cause of One Billion Rising? How can they move on from slacktivism to activism?

Classroom Activity Using Argument

Write an opinion piece or a letter to the editor of your school paper, making an argument about some problem you have identified or a change you would like to see implemented. Then share your work with a few classmates. Discuss where the arguments are most effective and where they could use more evidence or more persuasive writing. Consider actually revising and submitting your writing to the paper for consideration.

Suggested Writing Assignments

1. Browse the op-ed section of a local or national newspaper, and select a piece that interests you. Read it carefully, then write an essay in which you respond to its argument. Your own writing should make an argument, but it need not be simply pro or con. Determine what parts of the piece you want to expound on, question, or refute. Use this as the foundation for your argument.
2. Corvese writes, "I support One Billion Rising, but I also support taking action above and beyond passive acts" (8). How do you

think the organizers of One Billion Rising would answer Corvese's critique? Write an essay that addresses some of her questions and concerns about the movement, writing from the perspective of a One Billion Rising organizer. You might wish to take as your starting point a variation on her statement: "I support more direct forms of activism, but . . ."

Changing the Face(book) of Social Activism

■ **Mark Pfeifle**

The White House

A native of Wishek, North Dakota, Mark Pfeifle graduated from the University of North Dakota with a bachelor's degree in communications. He was a national security adviser to George W. Bush, serving as deputy assistant to the president and deputy national security adviser for Strategic Communication and Global Outreach, and he helped promote the president's "surge" of troops into Iraq. In 2009, he was awarded the army's Outstanding Civilian Service Award for his work on communications strategies supporting counterterrorism measures around the world. He is the founder and president of a Washington, D.C., public relations company, Off the Record Strategies, and writes regularly for the Huffington Post.

In "Changing the Face(book) of Social Activism," Pfeifle argues that social media has "successfully reinvented social activism." As you read, pay attention to the evidence he offers to show this dramatic change in the way people become politically involved.

Reflecting on What You Know

What role has social media played in recent political movements, both in the United States and abroad? Do you see Facebook, Twitter, and other sites as tools for political action?

1 The Urban Dictionary defines "Slacktivism" as "the ideology for people who want to appear to be doing something for a particular cause without actually having to do anything." It's an apt description of those who click the Facebook "like" and "share" buttons for everything from neutering pets to resolving the European debt crisis. No

need to spend a lot of time learning facts, mastering complex arguments, or organizing your friends and neighbors—and you can leave your money in your wallet. Just retweet a 140-character analysis of federal spending and you can move on to the ball scores.

That's been the argument, anyway, of critics of the so-called "social media revolution." They see our newfound global connectivity as a passing fad at best, or, at worst, as yet another sign of our divisiveness and narcissism—and to a large extent, they have a point. Much of the political expression on the Internet, if expressed "IRL" ("in real life"), would result in a punch in the nose, if not an arrest. Go to the "comments" section of most websites and it won't take long before you read the online equivalent of a drive-by shooting; the vicious, personal, and usually anonymous attack is the substitute for reasoned debate. There's also the practical question of how to mesh the political gears with social media. As one veteran politico once challenged me, "Explain how Twitter and Facebook gets somebody out of the Barcalounger and into the voting booth." 2

I'm living proof of the power of social media: On Jan. 20, 2009, it put me out of work. President Obama's 2008 campaign deftly utilized the emerging social media icons of the time—YouTube, MeetUp, Facebook, and Twitter—as means for millions of Americans to vent their frustration with the policies of my then-employer, President George W. Bush, and it played a central role in returning the Democrats to power. 3

From Cairo to Tripoli to Wall Street's Zuccotti Park, social media has reduced the cost and complexity of organizing mass numbers of individuals into a single, cohesive, political force. In the process it has redefined social activism. What's more, as it continues to evolve to develop new platforms, it creates new opportunities for political expression that become increasingly difficult for others to suppress. In 2009 the Iranian regime thought it could calm an increasingly rebellious populace by shutting down traditional media, but that was before the shooting of a 26-year-old female protester was captured on video, uploaded, and viewed by millions. At the height of the uproar, more than 221,000 Iran tweets were sent in just one hour. In one day, 3,000 Iranian videos were uploaded on YouTube, and 2.2 million blog entries were posted. The young woman, named Neda, had become the "cause," and social media, not traditional outlets, were providing the megaphone. 4

Later that year, a Tunisian fruit-stand owner named Mohamed 5
Bouazizi was accosted (not for the first time) by police thugs demanding a bribe. They confiscated his wares; he complained to the government, which, as usual, did nothing. Bouazizi, age 26, doused himself with gasoline and set himself on fire. The day of Bouazizi's self-immolation, no one—least of all Muammar Gaddafi, Hosni Mubarak, Bashar al-Assad, and Tunisia's Ali Abdullah Saleh—had any idea of the upheaval that would result from the ideas, voices, and actions that were soon to be unleashed through social media. As word of Mohamed Bouazizi's brazen act of protest spread across the Middle East and throughout the Horn of Africa, it caused an unprecedented wave of civil disobedience, public demonstrations, and strikes across the region. Social media had become the new soft weapon of democracy. Mubarak tried to pull the plug on the Internet, but repression couldn't keep up with the pace of technology as Google and Twitter deployed means to keep the Egyptian protesters' voices alive. Twitter introduced a new "voice-to-Twitter" service that allowed users to post by merely calling a dedicated phone number, and thanks to Google Translate, the messages from the teeming streets of Cairo soon became understandable across the planet. Social media may not have been the spark that set the fire, but it certainly provided the oxygen that caused it to spread.

While true that "slacktivism," online bullying, and unprecedented 6
threats to our privacy are challenges, few could argue that social media has not vastly facilitated political involvement. The results have been impressive, if not always as dramatic as the Arab Spring. Consider the phenomenon of Joseph Kony, the brutal Ugandan guerrilla leader who was the subject of an online video that was viewed by 100 million people worldwide. In the Kony case, 850,000 Facebook users clicked the "like" button. What resulted was the deployment of 100 U.S. advisers and 5,000 African Union troops whose mission was to hunt down Kony, achieving a goal that countless diplomats, non-government organizations, and journalists had failed to do in the previous 25 years.

People are using social media to hunt war criminals, win the 7
White House, defeat an American House Speaker, change banking regulations, and overthrow dictators in Libya, Tunisia, Egypt, and Yemen. In each instance it was social media that facilitated broad-based social activism and empowered the aspirations of millions. Its power has just begun to be tested, but the evidence so far indicates that social media has successfully reinvented social activism.

Thinking Critically about This Reading

Pfeifle writes that the power of social media has "just begun to be tested" (paragraph 7). What does his essay suggest about the future of online political action? How do you think users could or will expand the functions of social media to make a greater political impact?

Questions for Study and Discussion

1. Pfeifle uses a definition of *slacktivism* from the *Urban Dictionary*. Why does he start out by saying it is an appropriate term for what is happening on Facebook?
2. Pfeifle claims to be "living proof of the power of social media" (3). How does his own experience support his argument about changes to the landscape of political action?
3. Pfeifle strengthens his argument by considering possible problems with online organizing. How does he summarize the concerns of critics in paragraph 2? How does he go on to answer these concerns in the rest of his essay?
4. What is the value of social media? What does it allow activists and organizers to do that they would have found difficult or impossible before?
5. Pfeifle supports his argument with examples from the Arab Spring movement. How do these examples demonstrate the relationship between online and "IRL" activism? How do they reinforce each other?

Classroom Activity Using Argument

Pfeifle uses the metaphor of a megaphone to describe the way social media amplifies the voices of people who might not be heard in "traditional outlets." Later, he turns to another metaphor to describe an incidence of social media accelerating political change: it "may not have been the spark that set the fire, but it certainly provided the oxygen that caused it to spread" (5). Make a list of as many metaphors as you can think of that illuminate something about social media. Once you have finished brainstorming, go back through your list and consider the connotations of each. Which figures of speech would be useful if you were arguing that social media is a beneficial tool of progress? Which might be better at suggesting that users should approach social media with caution, or claiming that social media has little effect? Social media is a complex phenomenon; what aspects of it do your different metaphors help describe?

Suggested Writing Assignments

1. In 2009, Pfeifle received a good deal of attention for his argument in the *Christian Science Monitor* that Twitter should receive a Nobel Peace Prize. Look up this essay, and write an analysis of Pfeifle's argument. How does he support the idea of this unconventional choice for the prestigious prize?
2. Pfeifle mentions the online campaign to bring attention to Joseph Kony, a Ugandan warlord charged with abducting tens of thousands of children. Not everyone who saw this campaign, especially the video produced by the group Invisible Children, thought it treated the issue with sufficient accuracy or depth. Research the controversy around the Kony campaign, then write an essay in which you use it as a central example, either arguing for the power of social activism online or questioning its effectiveness.

BODY IMAGE: HOW WE SEE OURSELVES

In our culture today, there is a significant amount of social pressure to look physically attractive, and it is often the media that define what is considered "attractive." We are bombarded daily with descriptions and images of "ideal" bodies that set unrealistic expectations for both males and females to live up to. At the center of the current debate over body image are the detrimental effects these images and expectations can have on men's and women's perceptions of their own bodies, and how men and women may alter their bodies as a result. This casebook seeks to examine what negative effects, if any, these unrealistic portrayals of men's and women's bodies have on people's self-image. Some of the selections in this casebook highlight efforts being made to counter negative body image and promote healthier attitudes about the body.

This selection of online videos, audio recordings, blog posts, and infographics calls attention to the different ways men and women perceive bodies, and points out varying causes and effects of these (often negative) perceptions. Also included are a few examples of positive campaign efforts designed to counter the negative effects that media can have on young women's body image, along with critical questions that evaluate these campaigns' effectiveness. It is worth noting that although the focus of these movements and arguments is often reserved for the plight that women and young girls face, members of both genders deal with norms and expectations of how they ought to look. While viewing this casebook, consider why our culture tends to view body image as a "women's issue." For instance, does it seem less "manly" to be concerned about one's appearance or to feel bad about one's appearance? Do you think men struggle with body image pressures, and if so, what might be the cause of those pressures?

In the spoken-poetry video "Shrinking Women," Lily Myers eloquently narrates the pressure she faces from her mother and her frustration with the particular pressures women face as opposed to men, like her father. In the infographic "Women Are Dying to Be Thin," the group Rader Programs hints at the connection between the fashion industry and negative body image by presenting statistics that compare and contrast actual women with those in the fashion industry. Additionally, an infographic by the National Eating Disorders Association, "A Silent Epidemic?" takes a look at traditionally overlooked cases of eating disorders among males. On the other side of the debate, Carrie Arnold in her blog post "What's Photoshop Got to Do with It?" questions the connection between the media and eating disorders, and argues for a distinction between eating disorders and what she calls "disordered eating." Additionally, Dr. Kelly Flanagan's letter "Words from a Father to His Daughter (from the Makeup Aisle)" and an advertisement video from the "I'm a Girl" campaign in New York City present positive attempts to combat negative body image and empower young girls to feel good about themselves and their bodies. Together, these online resources take a close look at how both men and women struggle with body image issues, examine the possible causes for negative self-image, and present some efforts to promote positive body image and self-worth.

macmillanhighered.com/mfw12e
e-readings > Lily Myers, *Shrinking Women* [video]
Rader Programs, *Women Are Dying to Be Thin* [infographic]
Carrie Arnold, *What's Photoshop Got to Do with It?* [blog]
Kelly Flanagan, *Words from a Father to His Daughter (from the Makeup Aisle)* [audio]
NEDA, *A Silent Epidemic?* [infographic]

CHAPTER **22**

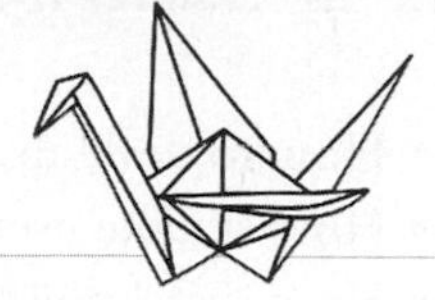

A Brief Guide to Writing a Research Paper

The research paper is an important part of a college education—and for good reason. In writing a research paper, you acquire a number of indispensable skills that you can adapt to other college assignments and to situations after graduation.

The real value of writing a research paper, however, goes beyond acquiring basic skills; it is a unique hands-on learning experience. The purpose of a research paper is not to present a collection of quotations that show you can report what others have said about your topic. Rather, your goal is to **analyze, evaluate**, and **synthesize** the materials you research and thereby learn how to do so with any topic. You learn how to view the results of research from your own perspective and to arrive at an informed opinion of a topic.

Writing a research paper is not very different from the other writing you will be doing in your college writing course. You will find yourself drawing heavily on what you learned from the four student essays in the first two chapters of this text. First you determine what you want to write about. Then you decide on a purpose, consider your audience, develop a thesis, collect your evidence, write a first draft, revise and edit, and prepare a final copy. What differentiates the research paper from other kinds of papers is your use of outside sources and how you acknowledge them. Your research will involve working with print and electronic sources. Your aim is to select the most appropriate sources for your research from the many that are available on your topic. (See also Chapter 10, Writing with Sources.)

In this chapter, you will learn some valuable research techniques:

- How to establish a realistic schedule for your research project
- How to conduct research on the Internet using keyword searches
- How to evaluate sources
- How to analyze sources

- How to develop a working bibliography
- How to take useful notes
- How to acknowledge your sources using either Modern Language Association (MLA) style in-text citations and a list of works cited or American Psychological Association (APA) style in-text citations and a list of references
- How to present/format your research paper

ESTABLISHING A REALISTIC SCHEDULE

A research project easily spans several weeks. To avoid losing track of time and finding yourself facing an impossible deadline at the last moment, establish a realistic schedule for completing key tasks. By thinking of the research paper as a multistage process, you avoid becoming overwhelmed by the size of the whole undertaking.

Your schedule should allow at least a few days to accommodate unforeseen needs and delays. Use the following template, which lists the essential steps in writing a research paper, to plan your research schedule.

Research Paper Schedule

Task	Completion Date
1. Choose a research topic, and pose a worthwhile question.	___/___/___
2. Locate print and electronic sources.	___/___/___
3. Develop a working bibliography.	___/___/___
4. Evaluate and analyze your sources.	___/___/___
5. Read your sources, taking complete and accurate notes.	___/___/___
6. Develop a preliminary thesis, and make a working outline.	___/___/___
7. Write a draft of your paper, including sources that you have summarized, paraphrased, and quoted.	___/___/___
8. Visit your college writing center for help with your revision.	___/___/___
9. Decide on a final thesis, and modify your outline.	___/___/___
10. Revise your paper, and properly cite all borrowed materials.	___/___/___
11. Prepare a list of works cited.	___/___/___
12. Prepare the final manuscript, and proofread.	___/___/___
13. Submit your research paper.	___/___/___

FINDING AND USING SOURCES

You should use materials found through a search of your school library's holdings—including books, newspapers, journals, magazines, encyclopedias, pamphlets, brochures, and government documents—as your primary tools for research. Print sources, unlike many Internet sources, are often reviewed by experts in the field before they are published, are generally overseen by a reputable publishing company or organization, and are examined by editors and fact checkers for accuracy and reliability. Unless you are instructed otherwise, you should try to use print sources in your research.

The best place to start any search for print and online sources is your college library's home page. There you will find links to the computerized catalog of book holdings, online reference works, periodical databases, and electronic journals, as well as a list of full-text databases. You'll also find links for subject study guides and for help conducting your research.

To get started, decide on some likely keyword search terms and try them out. You might have to try a number of different terms related to your topic to generate the best results. (For tips on refining your keyword searches, see pp. 614–15.) Your goal is to create a preliminary listing of books, magazine and newspaper articles, public documents and reports, and other sources that may be helpful in exploring your topic. At this early stage, it is better to err on the side of listing too many sources so that, later on, you will not have to relocate sources you discarded too hastily.

You will find that Internet sources can be informative and valuable additions to your research. The Internet is especially useful in providing recent data, stories, and reports. For example, you might find a just-published article from a university laboratory or a news story in your local newspaper's online archives. Generally, however, Internet sources should be used alongside other sources and not as a replacement for them. The Internet offers a vast number of useful and carefully maintained resources, but it also contains much unreliable information. It is your responsibility to determine whether a given Internet source should be trusted. (For advice on evaluating sources, see pp. 615–17.)

macmillanhighered.com/mfw12e
Tutorials > Digital Writing > Online Research

If you need more instruction on conducting Internet searches, go to your campus computer center or consult one of the many books written for Internet beginners. You can also access valuable information for searching the Internet at Diana Hacker and Barbara Fister's Research and Documentation Online at macmillanhighered .com/resdoc.

CONDUCTING KEYWORD SEARCHES

When searching for sources about your topic in an electronic database, in the library's computerized catalog, or on the Internet, you should start with a keyword search. To make the most efficient use of your time, you will want to know how to conduct a keyword search that is likely to yield solid sources and leads for your research project. As obvious or simple as it may sound, the key to a successful keyword search is the quality of the keywords you generate about your topic. You might find it helpful to start a list of potential keywords as you begin your search and add to it as your work proceeds. Often you will discover meaningful combinations of keywords that will lead you directly to the sources you need.

Databases and library catalogs index sources by author, title, year of publication, and subject headings (which are assigned by a cataloger who has previewed the source). The object here is to find a keyword that matches one of the subject headings. Once you begin to locate sources on your topic, be sure to note the subject headings that are listed for each source. You can use these subject headings as keywords to lead you to additional book sources. They can also lead you to articles that are gathered in full-text databases (such as InfoTrac, LexisNexis, Expanded Academic ASAP, and JSTOR) to which your library subscribes.

The keyword search process is somewhat different—more wide open—when you are searching on the Internet. It is always a good idea to look for search tips on the help screens or advanced search instructions for the search engine you are using before initiating a keyword search. When you type a keyword in the "Search" box on a search engine's home page, the search engine electronically scans Internet sites to match your keyword to titles and texts. On the Internet, the quality of the search terms (the keywords) is determined by the relevance of the hits on the first page that comes up. A search on the Internet might yield a million hits, but the search engine's

Refining Keyword Searches on the Web

Command terms and characters vary somewhat among electronic databases and popular Internet search engines, but the following functions are almost universally accepted. You can click on the site's "Help" or "Advanced Search" links to ask questions about refining your keyword search.

- Use quotation marks or parentheses when you are searching for words in exact sequence—for example, "whooping cough"; (Supreme Court).
- Use AND or a plus sign (+) between words to narrow your search by specifying that all words need to appear in a document—for example, tobacco AND cancer; Shakespeare + sonnet.
- Use NOT or a minus sign (–) between words to narrow your search by eliminating unwanted words—for example, monopoly NOT game; cowboys - Dallas.
- Use an asterisk (*) to indicate that you will accept variations of a term—for example, "food label*" for food labels, food labeling, and so forth.

algorithm puts the best sources up front. After you scan the first couple of pages of results, you can decide whether these sites seem on topic. If they seem off topic, you will need to refine your search terms to narrow or broaden your search (for tips, see the box above).

■ EVALUATING YOUR PRINT AND ONLINE SOURCES

You will not have to spend much time in the library to realize that you cannot read every print and online source that appears relevant. Given the abundance of print and Internet sources, the key to successful research is identifying those books, articles, websites, and other online sources that will help you the most. You must evaluate your potential sources to determine which materials you will read, which you will skim, and which you will simply eliminate. (See pp. 616–17 for some evaluation strategies and questions to assist you in identifying your most promising sources.)

You can also find sources on the Internet itself that offer useful guidelines for evaluating electronic sources. One excellent example

Strategies for Evaluating Print and Online Sources

Evaluating a Book

- Read the dust jacket or cover copy for insights into the book's coverage, its currency, and the author's expertise.
- Scan the copyright page to check the publication year.
- Scan the table of contents, and identify any promising chapters.
- Read the author's preface, looking for his or her thesis and purpose. Do the thesis and purpose clearly relate to your topic?
- Check the index for key words or key phrases related to your research topic.
- Read the opening and concluding paragraphs of any promising chapters. If you are unsure about a chapter's usefulness, skim the whole chapter.
- Ask yourself: Does the source appear to be too general or too technical for my needs or audience?

Evaluating an Article

- Ask yourself what you know about the journal or magazine publishing the article:
    - Is the publication scholarly or popular? Scholarly journals (*American Economic Review, Journal of Marriage and the Family, Wilson Quarterly*) publish articles representing original research written by authorities in the field. Such articles always cite their sources in notes, reference lists, or works cited, which means that you can check their accuracy and delve deeper into the topic by locating these sources. Popular news and general-interest magazines (*National Geographic, Smithsonian, Time, Ebony*), on the other hand, publish informative, entertaining, and easy-to-read articles written by editorial staff or freelance writers. Popular essays sometimes cite sources but often do not, making them somewhat less authoritative and less helpful in terms of extending your research.
    - What is the reputation of the journal or magazine? Determine the publisher or sponsor. Is it an academic institution, a commercial enterprise, or an individual? Does the publisher or publication have a reputation for accuracy and objectivity?
    - Who are the readers of this journal or magazine?
- Try to determine the author's credentials. Is he or she an expert?
- Consider the title or headline of the article, the opening paragraph or two, and the conclusion. Does the source appear to be too general or too technical for your needs and audience?
- For articles in journals, read the abstract (a summary of the main points), if there is one.

- Examine any photographs, charts, graphs, or other illustrations that accompany the article. Determine how useful they might be for your research purposes.

Evaluating a Website

- Consider the type of website. Is this site a personal blog or professional publication? Often the URL, especially the top-level domain name, can give you a clue about the kinds of information provided and the type of organization behind the site. Common suffixes include:

  .com — business, commercial, or personal
  .edu — educational institution
  .gov — government sponsored
  .int — international organization
  .mil — U.S. military
  .net — various types of networks
  .org — nonprofit organization, but also some commercial or personal

  Be advised that *.org* is not regulated like *.edu* and *.gov*, for example. Most nonprofits use *.org*, but many commercial and personal sites do as well.
- Examine the home page of the site:
  - Does the content appear to be related to your research topic?
  - Is the home page well maintained and professional in appearance?
  - Is there an *About* link on the home page that takes you to background information on the site's sponsor? Is there a mission statement, history, or statement of philosophy? Can you verify whether the site is official—that is, is it actually sanctioned by the organization or company?
- Identify the author of the site. What are the author's qualifications for writing on this subject?
- Determine whether a print equivalent is available. If so, is the web version identical to the print version, or is it altered in some way?
- Determine when the site was last updated. Is the content current enough for your purposes?

was created by reference librarians at the Wolfgram Memorial Library of Widener University. Type *wolfgram evaluate web pages* into a search engine to access that site.

On the basis of your evaluation, select the most promising books, articles, and websites to pursue in depth for your research project.

ANALYZING YOUR SOURCES FOR POSITION AND BIAS

Before beginning to take notes, analyze each source carefully. Look for the writer's main ideas, key examples, strongest arguments, and conclusions. How would you summarize the writer's position? Does the writer have a discernible bias? In what ways, if any, has the writer's bias colored his or her claims and evidence? It is important to ask yourself where each writer stands relative to the other writers as well as to your own position on the subject. You'll need to read critically; it is easy to become absorbed in sources that support your beliefs. Ask yourself whether these like-minded sources consider the possible merits of alternative points of view. If only to test your own position, you should always seek out several independent sources with

Checklist for Analyzing a Writer's Position and Bias

- What is the writer's thesis or claim?
- How does the writer support this thesis? Does the **evidence** seem reasonable and representative, or is it mainly vague, anecdotal, or sensational?
- What is the writer's attitude toward the subject (tone)?
- Is the author's **purpose** to inform? Or is it to argue for a particular position? If it's to argue, is the writer's appeal logical and reasoned, or is it largely emotional?
- Does the writer consider opposing viewpoints?
- What are the writer's basic assumptions? Which of these are stated, and which are implied? Are they acceptable?
- Does the writer have any discernible cultural, political, religious, or gender biases? Is the writer associated with a special-interest group, such as the American Medical Association, the National Organization for Women, the American Immigration Council, the Sierra Club, the National Education Association, the National Rifle Association, or Amnesty International?
- Is the writer an expert on the subject? Do other writers on the subject mention this author in their work?
- Does the publisher or publication have a reputation for accuracy and objectivity? Or does it have an inclination for a particular viewpoint?
- Is important information documented in notes or links so that it can be verified or corroborated in other sources?
- Does the source reflect current thinking and research in the field?

opposing viewpoints. By knowing exactly where each of your sources is positioned, you can more effectively use them in the context of your research paper.

Look for information about the authors themselves—information like that provided in the writer headnote that accompanies each selection in *Models for Writers*. Such information will help you determine the writer's authority and perspective or bias on the issue. You should also consider the reputation and special interests of book publishers and magazines, because you are likely to get different views—conservative, liberal, international, feminist—on the same topic depending on which publication you read. Use the checklist on page 618 to assist you in analyzing each of your print and online sources for the writer's position and bias.

■ DEVELOPING A WORKING BIBLIOGRAPHY FOR YOUR SOURCES

As you discover books, journal and magazine articles, newspaper stories, and websites that you think might be helpful for writing your paper, you need to start maintaining a record of important information about each source. This record, called a *working bibliography*, will enable you to know where sources are located when it comes time to consult and acknowledge them in your paper and list of works cited (for MLA) or list of references (for APA). See pages 625–32 and 641–46 for an explanation of how to prepare these lists. In all likelihood, your working bibliography will contain more sources than you actually consult and include in your final list.

You may find it easy to make a separate bibliography card, using a three-by-five-inch index card, for each work that you think might be helpful to your research. As your collection of cards grows, alphabetize them by the authors' last names. By using a separate card for each book, article, or website, you can continually edit your working bibliography, dropping sources that do not prove helpful and adding new ones.

With the computerization of most library resources, you can copy bibliographic information from the library computer catalog and periodical indexes or from the Internet and paste it into a document on your computer. Then you can edit, add, delete, and search these sources throughout the research process. You can also track your project online with a citation manager like the Bedford Bibliographer, at macmillanhighered.com/bibliographer. One advantage of the copy/paste option over the index card method is accuracy, especially in punctuation, spelling, and capitalization—details that are essential when accessing Internet sites.

Checklist for a Working Bibliography

For Books

- Library call number
- Names of all authors, editors, and translators
- Title and subtitle
- Publication data:
  - Place of publication (city and state)
  - Publisher's name
  - Date of publication
- Edition number (if not the first) and volume number (if applicable)

For Periodical Articles

- Names of all authors
- Title and subtitle of article
- Title of journal, magazine, or newspaper
- Publication data:
  - Volume number and issue number
  - Date of issue
  - Page numbers

For Internet Sources

- Names of all authors, editors, compilers, or sponsoring agents
- Title and subtitle of the document
- Title of the longer work to which the document belongs (if applicable)
- Title of the site or discussion list name
- Author, editor, or compiler of the website or online database
- Date of release, online posting, or latest revision
- Name and vendor of database or name of online service or network
- Medium (online, CD-ROM)
- Format of online source (web page, e-mail)

Date of access
Electronic address (URL or network path)

For Other Sources
Name of author, government agency, organization, company, recording artist, personality
Title of the work
Format (pamphlet, unpublished diary, interview, television broadcast)
Publication or production data:
Name of publisher or producer
Date of publication, production, or release
Identifying codes or numbers (if applicable)

TAKING NOTES

As you read, take notes. You're looking for ideas, facts, opinions, statistics, examples, and other evidence that you think will be useful as you write your paper. As you read through books and articles, look for recurring themes, and notice where writers are in agreement and where they differ. Try to remember that the effectiveness of your paper is largely determined by the quality—not necessarily the quantity—of your notes. Your purpose is not to present a collection of quotes that show that you've read all the material and know what others have said about your topic. Your goal is to **analyze, evaluate,** and **synthesize** the information you collect—in other words, to enter into the discussion of the issues and thereby take ownership of your topic. You want to view the results of your research from your own perspective and arrive at an informed opinion of your topic. (For more on writing with sources, see Chapter 10.)

Now for some practical advice on taking notes. First, be systematic in your note taking. As a rule, write one note on a card and include the author's full name, the complete title of the source, and a page number indicating the origin of the note. Use cards of uniform size, preferably four-by-six-inch cards because they are large enough to accommodate even a long note on a single card and yet small enough to be easily handled and conveniently carried. If you keep notes electronically, consider creating a separate file for each topic or source, or using an electronic research manager like Zotero. If you keep your notes organized, when you get to the planning and writing stage you will be able to sequence them according to the plan you have envisioned for your paper. Furthermore, should you decide to alter your organizational plan, you can easily reorder your notes to reflect those revisions.

Be very careful, though, when taking notes electronically—especially if you are taking your notes from an online source. It is very easy and tempting to simply copy and paste phrases or whole paragraphs into your notes. This can get you into trouble, however, when you go to write your paper if you do not keep careful track of which words belong to the author and which are your own. For tips on avoiding plagiarism, see pages 254–57.

Second, try not to take too many notes. One good way to control your note taking is to ask yourself, "How exactly does this material help prove or disprove my thesis?" Try to envision where in your paper you could use the information. If it does not seem relevant to your thesis, don't bother to take a note.

Once you decide to take a note, you must decide whether to summarize, paraphrase, or quote directly. The approach you take should be determined by the content of the passage and the way you plan to use it in your paper. For detailed advice on summaries, paraphrases, and quotations, see Chapter 10, pages 243–48.

■ DOCUMENTING SOURCES

Whenever you summarize, paraphrase, or quote a person's thoughts and ideas and whenever you use facts or statistics that are not commonly known or believed, you must properly acknowledge the source of your information. If you do not properly acknowledge ideas and information created by someone else, you are guilty of **plagiarism**—of using someone else's material but making it look as if it were your own (see pp. 254–57). You must document the source of your information whenever you do the following:

- Quote a source word for word
- Refer to information and ideas from another source that you present in your own words as either a paraphrase or a summary
- Cite statistics, tables, charts, or graphs

You do not need to document these types of information:

- Your own observations, experiences, and ideas
- Factual information available in a number of reference works (known as "common knowledge")
- Proverbs, sayings, and familiar quotations

A reference to the source of your borrowed information is called a **citation**. There are many systems for making citations, and your citations must consistently follow one of these systems. The documentation style recommended by the Modern Language Association is commonly used in English and the humanities and is the style used throughout this book. Another common system is the American Psychological Association (APA) style, which is generally used in the social sciences. Your instructor will probably tell you which style to use. For more information on documentation styles, consult the appropriate manual or handbook, or go to Diana Hacker and Barbara Fister's Research and Documentation Online at macmillanhighered .com/resdoc.

MLA-Style Documentation

There are two components of MLA-style documentation. *In-text citations* are placed in the body of your paper, and the *list of works cited* provides complete publication data for your in-text citations and is placed at the end of your paper. Both of these components are necessary for complete documentation.

In-Text Citations

In-text citations, also known as *parenthetical citations*, give the reader citation information immediately, at the point at which it is most meaningful. Rather than having to find a footnote or an endnote, the reader sees the citation as part of the writer's text.

Most in-text citations consist of only the author's last name and a page reference. Usually the author's name is given in an introductory

e **macmillanhighered.com/mfw12e**
Tutorials > Documentation and Working with Sources > Do I Need to Cite That?

e **macmillanhighered.com/mfw12e**
LearningCurve > Working with Sources (MLA)

or signal phrase at the beginning of the borrowed material, and the page reference is given in parentheses at the end. If the author's name is not given in a signal phrase, put it in parentheses along with the page reference. (For more information on signal phrases, see pp. 248–51). When you borrow material from two or more works by the same author, you must include the title of the work in the signal phrase or parenthetically at the end. The parenthetical reference signals the end of the borrowed material and directs your readers to the list of works cited should they want to pursue a particular source. Treat electronic sources as you do print sources, keeping in mind that some electronic sources use paragraph numbers instead of page numbers. Consider the following examples of in-text citations, taken from the opening paragraph of student Charley Horton's paper "How Humans Affect Our Global Environment."

In-Text Citations (MLA Style)

Controversy has always shadowed public discussions of our environment and environmental policy. In her book *Silent Spring*, Rachel Carson first warned Americans about the dire consequences of the irresponsible use of herbicides and insecticides. As early as 1962, she clearly saw that "a grim specter has crept upon us almost unnoticed" (58). First decried as an alarmist, Carson is now revered as an early leader in the ecology movement. Today the debate is not limited to pesticides, where controversy still swirls around the use of certain lawn care products and their commercial agricultural counterparts. It has expanded to include often uncivil discussions about the causes of climate change. Audrey Schulman has written extensively on severe climatic events, and she concludes that human behavior has had a direct impact on global climate change. She knows that while "some human cultures, through their agriculture and hunting, have respected and adapted to ecological limits" (79), others have not. Like her predecessor Rachel Carson, Schulman believes that Americans must act to avoid an ecological tragedy: "We have the ability to shape our destiny" (79).

List of Works Cited (MLA Style)

Carson, Rachel. "Fable for Tomorrow." *Models for Writers*. 12th ed. Eds. Alfred Rosa and Paul Eschholz. Boston: Bedford, 2015. 56–58. Print.

Schulman, Audrey. "Fahrenheit 59: What a Child's Fever Might Tell Us about Climate Change." *Orion*. Orion Magazine, Jan./Feb. 2007: 78–79. Print.

In the preceding example, the student followed MLA style guidelines for his Works Cited list. When constructing the list of works cited page for your paper, consult the following MLA guidelines, based on the *MLA Handbook for Writers of Research Papers*, 7th edition (2009), where you will find model entries for periodical print publications, nonperiodical print publications, web publications, and other common sources.

List of Works Cited

In this section, you will find general MLA guidelines for creating a works cited list, followed by sample entries that cover the citation situations you will encounter most often. Make sure that you follow the formats as they appear on these pages. If you would like to compile your list of works cited online, go to **macmillanhighered.com /bibliographer.**

Periodical Print Publications: Journals, Magazines, and Newspapers

ARTICLE IN A SCHOLARLY JOURNAL

For all scholarly journals—whether they paginate continuously throughout a given year or not—provide the volume number, the issue number, the year, the page numbers, and the medium. Separate the volume number and the issue number with a period.

Masuzawa, Tomoko. "The Bible as Literature?—Note on a Litigious Ferment of the Concept 'Comparative Literature.'" *Comparative Literature* 65.3 (2013): 306–24. Print.

e **macmillanhighered.com/mfw12e**
Tutorials > Documentation and Working with Sources > How to Cite an Article in MLA Style

Guidelines for Constructing Your Works Cited Page

1. Begin the list on a fresh page following the last page of text.
2. Center the title *Works Cited* at the top of the page.
3. Double-space both within and between entries on your list.
4. Alphabetize your sources by the authors' last names. If you have two or more authors with the same last name, alphabetize first by last names and then by first names.
5. If you have two or more works by the same author, alphabetize by the first word of the titles, not counting *A*, *An*, or *The*. Use the author's name in the first entry and three unspaced hyphens followed by a period in subsequent entries:

   Quart, Alissa. *Branded: The Buying and Selling of Teenagers*. New York: Perseus, 2003. Print.

   ---. "Welcome to (Company Name Here) High (TM)." *New York Times* 1 July 2003, late ed.: A19. Print.
6. For more than one author, reverse only the name of the first author.
7. If no author is known, alphabetize by title.
8. Begin each entry at the left margin. If the entry is longer than one line, indent the second and subsequent lines five spaces or one-half inch.
9. Italicize the titles of books, journals, magazines, and newspapers. Use quotation marks with titles of periodical articles, chapters and essays within books, short stories, and poems.
10. Provide the medium of the source (*Print, Web, Film, Television, Performance*).

ARTICLE IN A MAGAZINE

When citing a weekly or biweekly magazine, give the complete date (day, month, year). Months less than five letters should be spelled out, all others abbreviated.

Von Drehle, David. "Broken Trust: Fifty Years after JFK's Assassination." *Time* 25 Nov. 2013: 40–49. Print.

When citing a magazine published every month or every two months, provide the month or months and year. If an article in a magazine is not printed on consecutive pages—for example, an article might begin on page 45 and then skip to page 48—include only the first page followed by a plus sign.

Mascarelli, Amanda Leigh. "Fall Guys." *Audubon* Nov.-Dec. 2009: 44+. Print.

ARTICLE IN A NEWSPAPER

Bilton, Nick. "Internet's Sad Legacy: No More Secrets." *New York Times* 16 Dec. 2013, national ed.: B8. Print.

Nonperiodical Print Publications: Books, Brochures, and Pamphlets

BOOK WITH ONE AUTHOR

Shlaes, Amity. *Coolidge*. New York: Harper, 2013. Print.

Feel free to use a shortened version of the publisher's name—for example, *Houghton* for Houghton Mifflin, or *Cambridge UP* for Cambridge University Press.

ANTHOLOGY

Eggers, Dave, ed. *The Best American Nonrequired Reading, 2002*. New York: Houghton, 2002. Print.

BOOK WITH TWO OR MORE AUTHORS

For a book with two or three authors, list the authors in the order in which they appear on the title page.

Courtney, Elizabeth, and Eric Zencey. *Greening Vermont: The Search for a Sustainable State*. Montpelier, VT: Vermont Natural Resources Council, 2012. Print.

For a book with four or more authors, list the first author in the same way for a single-author book, followed by a comma and the abbreviation *et al.* ("and others").

Beardsley, John, et al. *Gee's Bend: The Women and Their Quilts*. Atlanta: Tinwood, 2002. Print.

macmillanhighered.com/mfw12e
Tutorials > Documentation and Working with Sources > How to Cite a Book in MLA Style

WORK IN AN ANTHOLOGY

Smith, Seaton. "'Jiving' with Your Teen." *The Best American Nonrequired Reading, 2002*. Ed. Dave Eggers. New York: Houghton, 2002. 217–20. Print.

AN ILLUSTRATED BOOK OR GRAPHIC NOVEL

Clemens, Samuel L. *The Adventures of Huckleberry Finn*. Illus. Norman Rockwell. New York: Heritage, 1940. Print.

Neufeld, Josh, writer and artist. *A.D.: New Orleans after the Deluge*. New York: Pantheon, 2009. Print.

BOOK PUBLISHED IN A SECOND OR SUBSEQUENT EDITION

Phillipson, David W. *African Archaeology*. 3rd ed. New York: Cambridge UP, 2005. Print.

GOVERNMENT PUBLICATION

United States. Dept. of Health and Human Services. *Eat Healthy, Be Active, Community Workshops*. Washington: GPO, 2012. Print.

Give the government, the agency, and the title with a period and a space after each. The publisher is the Government Printing Office (GPO).

Web Publications

The following guidelines and models for citing information retrieved from the World Wide Web have been adapted from the most recent advice of the MLA, as detailed in the *MLA Handbook for Writers of Research Papers,* 7th ed. (2009), and from the "MLA Style" section on the MLA's website. You will quickly notice that citations of web publications have some features in common with both print publications and reprinted works, broadcasts, and live performances. Standard information for all citations of online materials includes the following:

1. Name of the author, editor, or compiler of the work. The guidelines for print sources for works with more than one author, a corporate author, or an unnamed author apply. For anonymous works, begin your entry with the title of the work.
2. Title of the work. Italicize the title, unless it is part of a larger work. Titles that are part of a larger work should be presented within quotation marks.
3. Title of the overall website in italics, if distinct from item 2.

4. Version or edition of the site, if relevant.
5. Publisher or sponsor of the site. This information is often found at the bottom of the web page. If this information is not available, use *N.p.* (for *no publisher*).
6. Date of publication (day, month, and year, if available). If no date is given, use *n.d.*
7. Medium of publication. For online sources, the medium is *Web*.
8. Date of access (day, month, and year).

MLA style does not require you to include URLs in works cited entries. If your instructor wants you to include URLs in your citations or if you believe readers will not be able to locate the source without the URL, insert the URL as the last item in an entry, immediately after the date of access. Enclose the URL in angle brackets, followed by a period. Include the page number, if any, after the year of publication; if no page number is given, use *n. pag*. The following example illustrates an entry with the URL included:

Reychler, Luc. "Peace Building Architecture." *Peace and Conflict Studies* 9.1 (2002): n. pag. Web. 17 July 2014. <www.gmu.edu/programs/icar/pcs/LR83PCS.htm>.

MLA style requires that you break URLs extending over more than one line only after a slash. Do *not* add spaces, hyphens, or any other punctuation to indicate the break.

ONLINE SCHOLARLY JOURNALS

To cite an article, a review, an editorial, or a letter to the editor in a scholarly journal existing only in electronic form on the web, provide the author, the title of the article, the title of the journal, the volume and issue, and the date of issue, followed by the page numbers (if available), the medium, and the date of access.

ARTICLE IN AN ONLINE SCHOLARLY JOURNAL

Rist, Thomas. "Religion, Politics, Revenge: The Dead in Renaissance Drama." *Early Modern Literary Studies* 9.1 (2003): n. pag. Web. 28 Feb. 2014.

macmillanhighered.com/mfw12e
Tutorials > Documentation and Working with Sources > How to Cite a Website in MLA Style

PERIODICAL PUBLICATIONS IN ONLINE DATABASES

Here are some model entries for periodical publications collected in online databases/subscription services.

JOURNAL ARTICLE FROM AN ONLINE DATABASE/SUBSCRIPTION SERVICE

Kauvar, Elaine M. "Warring Desires: The Future of Jewish-American Literature." *American Literary History* 21.4 (2009): 877–90. *Project Muse*. Web. 17 Feb. 2014.

MAGAZINE ARTICLE FROM AN ONLINE DATABASE/SUBSCRIPTION SERVICE

Keizer, Garret. "Sound and Fury: The Politics of Noise in a Loud Society." *Harper's Magazine*. Mar. 2001: 39–48. *Expanded Academic ASAP Plus*. Web. 27 Mar. 2014.

NEWSPAPER ARTICLE FROM AN ONLINE DATABASE/SUBSCRIPTION SERVICE

Sanders, Joshunda. "Think Race Doesn't Matter? Listen to Eminem." *San Francisco Chronicle* 20 July 2003. *LexisNexis*. Web. 18 Mar. 2014.

McEachern, William Ross. "Teaching and Learning in Bilingual Countries: The Examples of Belgium and Canada." *Education* 123.1 (2002): 103. *Expanded Academic ASAP Plus*. Web. 18 Dec. 2013.

NONPERIODICAL WEB PUBLICATIONS

Nonperiodical web publications include all web-delivered content that does not fit into one of the previous two categories—scholarly journal web publications and periodical publications from an online database/subscription service.

ARTICLE IN AN ONLINE MAGAZINE

Walsh, Joan. "Poverty Nation: How America Created a Low-Wage Work Swamp." *Salon.com*. Salon Media Group, 15 Dec. 2013. Web. 18 Dec. 2013.

Huang, Lily. "The Case of the Disappearing Rabbit." *Newsweek*. Newsweek, 25 July 2009. Web. 10 Jan. 2011.

e **macmillanhighered.com/mfw12e**
Tutorials > Documentation and Working with Sources > How to Cite a Database in MLA Style

ARTICLE IN AN ONLINE NEWSPAPER

Ritter, Malcolm. "Cat-Mouse Game Might Explain How Felines Got Tame." *Seattletimes.com*. Seattle Times, 16 Dec. 2013. Web. 18 Dec. 3013.

BOOK OR PART OF A BOOK ACCESSED ONLINE

For a book available online, provide the author, the title, the editor (if any), original publication information, the name of the database or website, the medium (*Web*), and the date of access.

Hawthorne, Nathaniel. *The Blithedale Romance*. Intro. George Parsons Lathrop. Salem Edition. Boston, 1894. Web. 28 Feb. 2014.

If you are citing only part of an online book, include the title or name of the part directly after the author's name.

Woolf, Virginia. "Kew Gardens." *Monday or Tuesday*. New York: Harcourt, 1921. *Bartleby.com: Great Books Online*. Web. 15 Nov. 2013.

SPEECH, ESSAY, POEM, OR SHORT STORY FROM AN ONLINE SITE

Faulkner, William. "On Accepting the Nobel Prize." 10 Dec. 1950. *The History Place: Great Speeches Collection*. Web. 12 Mar. 2014.

ARTICLES AND STORIES FROM ONLINE NEWS SERVICES

Pressman, Gabe. "Eminent Domain: Let the Public Beware!" *NBCNewYork.com*. NBC New York, 5 Dec. 2009. Web. 6 Mar. 2014.

"Iran Police Clash with Protesters." *CNN.com*. Cable News Network, 7 Dec. 2009. Web. 7 Mar. 2014.

ONLINE GOVERNMENT PUBLICATION

United States. Dept. of Treasury. Internal Revenue Service. *Your Rights as a Taxpayer*. Sept. 2012. Web. 4 Apr. 2014.

WIKI ENTRY

"C. S. Lewis." *Wikipedia*. Wikimedia Foundation, 12 Dec. 2013. Web. 15 Dec. 2013.

No author is listed for a Wiki entry because the content is written collaboratively.

ADDITIONAL COMMON SOURCES

TELEVISION OR RADIO BROADCAST

"Everyone's Waiting." *Six Feet Under*. Dir. Alan Ball. Perf. Peter Krause, Michael C. Hall, Frances Conroy, and Lauren Ambrose. Writ. Alan Ball. HBO. 21 Aug. 2005. Television.

FILM OR VIDEO RECORDING

Schindler's List. Dir. Steven Spielberg. Perf. Liam Neeson, Ralph Fiennes, and Ben Kingsley. Universal, 1993. DVD.

INTERVIEW

Handke, Peter. Interview. *New York Times Magazine* 2 July 2006: 13. Print.

For interviews that you conduct, provide the name of the person interviewed, the type of interview (personal, telephone, e-mail), and the date.

Mosher, Howard Frank. Telephone interview. 30 Jan. 2014.

CARTOON OR COMIC STRIP

Luckovich, Mike. Cartoon. *Atlanta Journal-Constitution* 24 Nov. 2009. Print.

ADVERTISEMENT

American Cruise Lines. Advertisement. *Smithsonian* Jan. 2013: 7. Print.

AN ANNOTATED STUDENT MLA-STYLE RESEARCH PAPER

Lesley Timmerman's assignment was to write an argument, and she was free to choose her own topic. After considering a number of possible topics and doing some preliminary research on several of them, she turned to a subject that she and her classmates had been discussing: the need for corporations to be socially responsible for their actions.

Timmerman began by brainstorming about her topic. She made lists of ideas, facts, issues, arguments, and opposing arguments. Once she was confident that she had amassed enough information to begin writing, she made a rough outline of an organizational plan she thought she could follow and ran it by her professor. With this plan in mind, she wrote a first draft of her essay. After taking a break from the draft for a day or two, Timmerman went back and examined it carefully, assessing how it could be improved.

After rereading her first draft, Timmerman saw that her organizational plan could be modified to emphasize the examples of PepsiCo and Walmart. She could then develop them as examples of the many socially responsible corporations that measure their success by the "triple bottom line" of "profit, planet, and people." And these two examples would lead naturally into her discussion of what socially responsible corporations mean to employees and consumers alike. Timmerman scoured her sources to make sure that she was using the materials that best either supported or illustrated the points she wanted to make about corporate responsibility as well as the opposition's argument.

The final draft of Timmerman's research paper illustrates that she has learned how the parts of a well-researched and well-written paper fit together and how to make revisions that emulate some of the qualities of the model essays she had read and studied in class. The following is the final draft of her paper, which demonstrates MLA-style documentation and format for research papers.

Timmerman 1

Lesley Timmerman

Professor Jennifer Wilson

English 102

17 April 2014

Title is focused and announces the thesis

An Argument for Corporate Responsibility

Double space between the title and the first paragraph—and throughout the essay

Opponents of corporate social responsibility (CSR) argue that a company's sole duty is to generate profits. According to them, by acting for the public good, corporations are neglecting their primary obligation to make money. However, as people are becoming more and more conscious of corporate impacts on society and the environment, separating profits from company practices and ethics does not make sense. Employees want to work for institutions that share their values, and consumers want to buy products from companies that are making an impact and improving people's lives. Furthermore, businesses exist in an

Brief statement of one side of the issue

interdependent world where the health of the environment and the well-being of society really do matter. For these reasons, corporations have to take responsibility for their actions, beyond making money for shareholders. For their own benefit as well as the public's, companies must strive to be socially responsible.

Summary of the opposing view clearly introduced with signal phrase

In his article "The Case against Corporate Responsibility," *Wall Street Journal* writer Aneel Karnani argues that CSR will never be able to solve the world's problems. Thinking it can, Karnani says, is a dangerous illusion. He recommends that instead of expecting corporate managers to act in the public interest, we should rely on philanthropy and government regulation. Karnani maintains that "Managers who sacrifice profit for the common good . . . are in effect imposing a tax on their shareholders and arbitrarily deciding how that money should be spent." In other words, according to Karnani, corporations should not be determining what constitutes socially responsible behavior; individual donors and the government should. Certainly, individuals should continue to make charitable gifts, and governments should maintain laws and regulations to protect the public interest. However, Karnani's reasoning for why corporations should be exempt from social responsibility is flawed. With very few exceptions, corporations' socially responsible actions are not arbitrary and do not sacrifice long-term profits.

Lead-in to quotation

1" margin on each side and at bottom

Essayist's response to the quotation

In fact, corporations have already proven that they can contribute profitably and meaningfully to solving significant global problems by integrating CSR into their standard practices and long-term visions. Rather than focusing on shareholders' short-term profits, many companies have begun measuring their success by "profit, planet, and people"—what is known as the "triple bottom line." Businesses operating under this principle consider their environmental and social impacts, as well as their financial impacts, and make responsible and compassionate decisions. For example, such businesses use resources efficiently,

Author concisely states her position

Timmerman 3

Transitions ("For example," "also") alert readers to where the writer is taking them

create healthy products, choose suppliers who share their ethics, and improve economic opportunities for people in the communities they serve. By doing so, companies often save money. They also contribute to the sustainability of life on earth and ensure the sustainability of their own businesses. In their book *The Triple Bottom Line: How Today's Best-Run Companies Are Achieving Economic, Social, and Environmental Success*, coauthors Savitz and Weber demonstrate that corporations need to become sustainable, in all ways. They argue that "the only way to succeed in today's interdependent world is to embrace sustainability" (xi). The authors go on to show that for the vast majority of companies, a broad commitment to sustainability enhances profitability (Savitz and Weber 39).

Signal phrase introduces both the direct quotation and the paraphrase directly following

For example, PepsiCo has been able to meet the financial expectations of its shareholders while demonstrating its commitment to the triple bottom line. In addition to donating over $16 million to help victims of natural disasters, Pepsi has woven concerns for people and for the planet into its company practices and culture (Bejou 4). For instance, because of a recent water shortage in an area of India where Pepsi runs a plant, the company began a project to build community wells (Savitz and Weber 160). Though Pepsi did not cause the water shortage nor was its manufacturing threatened by it, "Pepsi realizes that the well-being of the community is part of the company's responsibility" (Savitz and Weber 161). Ultimately, Pepsi chose to look beyond the goal of maximizing short term profits. By doing so, the company improved its relationship with this Indian community, improved people's daily lives and opportunities, and improved its own reputation. In other words, Pepsi embraced CSR and ensured a more sustainable future for everyone involved.

Parenthetical citations clearly document what the author has borrowed

Another example of a wide-reaching company that is working toward greater sustainability on all fronts is Walmart. The corporation has issued a CSR policy that includes three ambitious goals: "to be fully supplied by renewable energy, to create zero waste and to sell products that sustain people and the environment" ("From Fringe to Mainstream"). As Dr. Doug Guthrie, dean of George Washington University's School of Business, noted in a recent lecture, if a company as powerful as Walmart were to succeed in these goals, the impact would be huge. To illustrate Walmart's potential influence, Dr. Guthrie pointed out that the corporation's exports from China to the United States are equal to Mexico's total exports to the United States. In committing to CSR, the company's leaders are acknowledging how much their power depends on the earth's natural resources, as well as the communities who produce, distribute, sell, and purchase Walmart's products. The company is also well aware that achieving its goals will "ultimately save the company a great deal of money" ("From Fringe to Mainstream"). For good reason, Walmart, like other companies around the world, is choosing to act in *everyone's* best interest.

Author now introduces statistical evidence that might have turned the reader off if introduced earlier

Recent research on employees' and consumers' social consciousness offers companies further reason to take corporate responsibility seriously. For example, studies show that workers care about making a difference (Meister). In many cases, workers would even take a pay cut to work for a more responsible, sustainable company. In fact, 45 percent of workers said they would take a 15 percent reduction in pay "for a job that makes a social or environmental impact" (Meister). Even more said they would take a 15 percent cut in pay to work for a company with values that match their own (Meister). The numbers are most significant among Millennials (those born between, approximately, 1980 and the early 2000s). Eighty percent of Millennials said they "wanted to work for a company that cares about how it impacts and contributes to society," and over half said they would not work for an "irresponsible company" (Meister). Given this more socially conscious generation, companies are going to find it harder

Timmerman 5

and harder to ignore CSR. To recruit and retain employees, employers will need to earn the admiration, respect, and loyalty of their workers by becoming "good corporate citizen[s]" (qtd. in "From Fringe to Mainstream").

Similarly, studies clearly show that CSR matters to today's consumers. According to an independent report, 80 percent of Americans say they would switch brands to support a social cause. Eighty-eight percent say they approve of companies' using social or environmental issues in their marketing. And 83 percent say they "wish more of the products, services and retailers would support causes" (Cone Communications 5–6). Other independent surveys corroborate these results, confirming that today's customers, especially Millennials, care about more than just price ("From Fringe to Mainstream"). Furthermore, plenty of companies have seen what happens when they assume that consumers do not care about CSR. For example, in 1997, when Nike customers discovered that their shoes were manufactured by child laborers in Indonesia, the company took a huge financial hit (Guthrie). Today, information-age customers are even more likely to educate themselves about companies' labor practices and environmental records. Smart corporations will listen to consumer preferences, provide transparency, and commit to integrating CSR into their long-term business plans.

Author argues that it is in the companies' interest to be socially responsible

In this increasingly interdependent world, the case against CSR is becoming more and more difficult to defend. Exempting corporations and relying on government to be the world's conscience does not make good social, environmental, or economic sense. Contributors to a recent article in the online journal *Knowledge@ Wharton,* published by the Wharton School of Business, agree. Professor Eric Orts maintains that "it is an outmoded view to say that one must rely only on the government and regulation to police business responsibilities. What we need is re-conception of what the purpose of business is" (qtd. in "From Fringe to Mainstream"). The question is, what should the purpose of a business be in today's world? Professor of Business Administration David Bejou of Elizabeth City State University has a thoughtful and sensible answer to that question. He writes:

Author's lead-in to the quotation guides the readers' response to the quotation

> [I]t is clear that the sole purpose of a business is not merely that of generating profits for its owners. Instead, because compassion provides the necessary equilibrium between a company's purpose and the needs of its communities, it should be the new philosophy of business. (Bejou 1)

As Bejou implies, the days of allowing corporations to act in their own financial self-interest with little or no regard for their effects on others are over. None of us can afford such a narrow view of business. The world is far too interconnected. A seemingly small corporate decision — to buy coffee beans directly from local growers or to install solar panels — can affect the lives and livelihoods of many people and determine the environmental health of whole regions. A business, just like a government or an individual, therefore has an ethical responsibility to act with compassion for the public good.

Author ends on an upbeat note

Fortunately, corporations have many incentives to act responsibly. Customer loyalty, employee satisfaction, overall cost-savings, and long-term viability are just some of the advantages businesses can expect to gain by embracing comprehensive CSR policies. Meanwhile, companies have very little to lose by embracing a socially conscious view. These days, compassion is profitable. Corporations would be wise to recognize the enormous power, opportunity, and responsibility they have to effect positive change.

Timmerman 7

Works Cited

Alphabetical by author's last name

Hanging indent ½"

An article on a blog without a known author

A clip from YouTube

Bejou, David. "Compassion as the New Philosophy of Business." *Journal of Relationship Marketing* 10.1 (2011): 1–6. *Business Source Complete*. Web. 15 Mar. 2014.

Cone Communications. *2010 Cone Cause Evolution Study*. Cone, 2010. Web. 15 Mar. 2014.

"From Fringe to Mainstream: Companies Integrate CSR Initiatives into Everyday Business." *Knowledge@ Wharton*. The Wharton School of the University of Pennsylvania, 23 May 2012. Web. 14 Mar. 2014.

Guthrie, Doug. Keynote address. "Promoting a Comprehensive Approach to Corporate Social Responsibility (CSR)." 26 Apr. 2012. *YouTube*. Web. 11 Mar. 2014.

Karnani, Aneel. "The Case against Corporate Social Responsibility." *Wall Street Journal*. Dow Jones, 14 June 2012. Web. 12 Mar. 2014.

Meister, Jeanne. "Corporate Social Responsibility: A Lever for Employee Attraction & Engagement." *Forbes*. Forbes.com, 7 June 2012. Web. 12 Mar. 2014.

Savitz, Andrew W., with Karl Weber. *The Triple Bottom Line: How Today's Best-Run Companies Are Achieving Economic, Social, and Environmental Success*. San Francisco: Jossey-Bass, 2006. Print.

APA-Style Documentation

The American Psychological Association (APA) recommends a simple, two-part system for documenting sources. The system consists of a brief *in-text citation* at the point where words or ideas have been borrowed from a source, and a *list of references* at the end of the paper, which includes complete bibliographical information for all sources cited in the text. The following recommendations are based on the *Publication Manual of the American Psychological Association*, 6th edition (2010), as well as APA's website.

In-Text Citations

APA style recommends the author-date citation system for sources cited in the text. At the appropriate point in the text, give the author's last name and year of publication. For all direct quotations, you must also include the page number preceded by *p.* (page numbers are not required with paraphrases and summaries). You can present this information in several different ways—at the beginning of the borrowed material: *According to DeAngelus (2014)*; at the end of the borrowed material: *(DeAngelus, 2014)*; or divided between the beginning and the end of the borrowed material: *According to DeAngelus, cognitive development can vary greatly from one child to another even within the same family (2014)*. When presenting the information parenthetically, use commas to separate the author's last name, year, and page number: *(DeAngelus, 2014, p. 27)*. For a discussion of using signal phrases to integrate quotations, paraphrases, and summaries smoothly into your research paper, see pages 248–51.

Each in-text citation directs your readers to the list of references should they want to pursue a particular source. Treat electronic sources as you would print sources, keeping in mind that some electronic sources use paragraph numbers instead of page numbers. Consider the following examples of APA in-text citations found in the opening paragraph of student Nancy Magnusson's paper "The English-Only Controversy."

In-Text Citations (APA Style)

Many people are surprised to discover that English is not the official language of the United States. Today, even as English literacy becomes a necessity for people in many parts of the world, some people in the United States believe its primacy is being threatened right at home. Much of the current controversy focuses on Hispanic communities with large Spanish-speaking populations who may feel little or no pressure to learn English. Columnist and cultural critic Charles Krauthammer (2006) believes English should be America's official language. He notes that this country has been "blessed . . . with a linguistic unity that brings a critically needed cohesion to a nation as diverse, multiracial and multiethnic as America" and that communities such as these threaten the bond created by a common language (p. 112). There are others, however, who think that the threat has been sensationalized, that "language does not threaten American unity. Benign neglect is a good policy for any country when it comes to language, and it's a good policy for America" (King, 1997, p. 64). Let's revisit the arguments on both sides of the English-only debate to determine what options are available to best serve America's growing number of non-English-speaking residents.

References

King, R. D. (1997, April). Should English be the law? *Atlantic Monthly, 279,* 55–64.

Krauthammer, C. (2006, June 12). In plain English: Let's make it official. *Time, 174,* 112.

In the preceding example, the student followed APA style guidelines for her reference list. When constructing the reference page for your paper, consult the following APA guidelines, where you will find model entries for common print and online sources.

List of References

In this section, you will find general APA guidelines for creating a list of references, followed by model entries that cover the citation situations you will encounter most often. If you would like to compile your list of references online, go to **macmillanhighered.com/bibliographer**.

Guidelines for Constructing Your Reference Page

1. Place your list of sources on a separate page at the end of your paper.
2. Center the title *References* at the top of the page. (See the model on page 650.)
3. Double-space both within and between entries on your list.
4. Arrange your sources alphabetically by the authors' or editors' last names. If you have two or more authors with the same last name, alphabetize by the initials of the first name.
5. If you have two or more works by the same author, arrange them chronologically by year of publication, starting with the one published earliest. Arrange works published in the same year alphabetically by title, and use lowercase letters to differentiate them: (2013a), (2013b), (2013c). Include the author's name, including any initials, with all entries.

6. Reverse *all* authors' names within each entry, and use initials, not first and middle names (Burns, E. A.). Name up to seven authors, separating names and parts of names with commas. Use an ampersand (&) instead of *and* before the last author's name. If there are more than seven authors, use an ellipsis after the sixth author followed by the last author's name.
7. If no author or editor is known, alphabetize by the first word of the title, not counting *A*, *An*, or *The*.
8. Begin each entry at the left margin, and indent subsequent lines five spaces.
9. Give the date of publication in parentheses after the last author's name. For some journal, magazine, and newspaper articles, you will need to include the month and sometimes the day as well as the year (2014, December 2).
10. For book and article titles, capitalize the first word of the title, the first word of the subtitle if there is one, and any proper names. Begin all other words with lowercase letters. With titles of journals, capitalize all significant words (*Social Work with Groups: A Journal of Community and Clinical Practice*).
11. Italicize the titles of books, journals, magazines, and newspapers. Do not italicize or put quotation marks around article titles.
12. For book publications, provide the city of publication followed by a comma and the two-letter postal abbreviation of the state (Davenport, IA). Follow the city and state with a colon.
13. For book publications, provide the publisher's name after the place of publication. For many commercial publishers, use shortened names, such as *Houghton* for Houghton Mifflin. Provide the full name of university presses, corporations, and professional associations. Omit such terms as *Publishers, Co.,* and *Inc.* Retain the term *Books* and, for academic publishers, *Press*.
14. Use the abbreviations *p.* and *pp.* for page numbers of all newspaper articles and for chapters or articles in edited books. Do *not* use these abbreviations for articles in journals or magazines. When citing inclusive page numbers, give complete figures: 217–223.
15. For an online source, APA format stresses that you include the same elements, in the same order, as you would for a reference to a print source, and add as much electronic retrieval information as needed for others to locate each source. APA also recommends using a DOI (digital object identifier), when available, in place of a URL in references to electronic texts. The DOI is more permanent and consistent than a URL. No retrieval date is necessary if the content is not likely to be updated or changed.

16. When dividing a URL at the end of a line, never insert a hyphen to mark the break. Break line immediately *before* most marks of punctuation (an exception would be http://, which should never break). Do not italicize, underline, or use angle brackets with URLs, and do not add a period at the end of a URL.

Periodicals

JOURNAL ARTICLE WITH A DOI

Niedt, C. (2013). The politics of eminent domain: From false choices to community benefits. *Urban Geography, 34,* 1047–1069. doi:10.1080/02723638.2013.819683.

If the journal is paginated by volume, the issue number is not needed. When a journal is paginated by issue, APA requires that the issue number be given parenthetically after the volume number.

Nock, M. K. (2008). Actions speak louder than words: An elaborated theoretical model of the social functions of self-injury and other harmful behaviors. *Applied and Preventive Psychology, 12*(4), 159–168. doi:10.1016/j.appsy.22008.5.002.

JOURNAL ARTICLE WITH A DOI AND MULTIPLE AUTHORS

When an article has up to seven authors, present all the authors' names in your reference entry.

Brown, L. F., Rand, K. L., Bigatti, S. M., Stewart, J. C., Theobald, D. E., Wu, J., & Kroenke, K. (2013). Longitudinal relationships between fatigue and depression in cancer patients with depression and/or pain. *Health Psychology, 32,* 1199–1208. doi:10.1037/a0029773.

JOURNAL ARTICLE WITHOUT A DOI

Stephens, R. (2012). What if? Preparing schools and communities for the unthinkable. *Law Enforcement Executive Forum, 12*(4), 1–7.

If there is no DOI assigned and the article is retrieved online, provide the URL of the home page of the journal.

Nordhall, O., & Agerstrom, J. (2013). Future-oriented people show stronger moral concerns. *Current Research in Social Psychology, 18*, 52–63. Retrieved from http://www.uiowa.edu/-grpproc/crisp/crisp.html

MAGAZINE ARTICLE (MONTHLY OR WEEKLY)

Tucker, A. (2012, October). The great New England vampire panic. *Smithsonian, 43*, 58–65.

Abend, L. (2013, December 16). Boys won't be boys. *Time, 182,* 40–44.

ONLINE MAGAZINE ARTICLE

DeAngelis, T. (2013, December). When the conflict comes home. *Monitor on Psychology, 44*(11). Retrieved from http://www.apa.org/monitor/

NEWSPAPER ARTICLE (DAILY OR WEEKLY)

Broder, J. M. (2009, December 17). Poor and emerging states stall climate negotiations. *The New York Times*, p. A16.

Hall, K. L. (2003, June 20). The biggest barrier to college isn't race. *The Chronicle of Higher Education*, p. B20.

When the article appears on discontinuous pages, provide all page numbers.

Goode, E. (2013, December 16). Sheriffs refuse to enforce laws on gun control. *The New York Times*, pp. A1, A15.

ONLINE NEWSPAPER ARTICLE

Weeks, L. (2006, February 8). Burdens of the modern beast. *The Washington Post*. Retrieved from http://www.washingtonpost.com

Books, Reference Books, and Book Chapters

BOOK WITH ONE AUTHOR

Gladwell, M. (2013). *David and Goliath: Underdogs, misfits, and the art of battling giants*. New York, NY: Little, Brown.

BOOK WITH TWO TO SEVEN AUTHORS

Beck, E., Britto, S., & Andrews, A. (2007). *In the shadow of death: Restorative justice and death row families*. New York, NY: Oxford University Press.

ELECTRONIC VERSION OF A PRINT BOOK

Dewey, J. (1916). *Democracy and education: An introduction to the philosophy of education*. Retrieved from http://www.gutenberg.org/etext/852

BOOK WITH A GROUP OR AN INSTITUTIONAL AUTHOR

National Association for the Advancement of Colored People. (1994). *Beyond the Rodney King story: An investigation of police conduct in minority communities*. Boston, MA: Northeastern University Press.

EDITED BOOK

Clark, V., Eschholz, P., Rosa, A., & Simon, B. L. (Eds.). (2008). *Language: Introductory readings* (7th ed.). Boston, MA: Bedford.

EDITION OTHER THAN THE FIRST

Leopold, Aldo. (1989). *A Sand County almanac and other sketches here and there* (commemorative ed.). New York, NY: Oxford University Press.

ARTICLE OR CHAPTER IN AN EDITED BOOK OR ANTHOLOGY

Lawson, W. (2003). Remembering school. In M. Prior (Ed.), *Learning and behavior problems in Asperger syndrome* (pp. 177–193). New York, NY: Guilford.

ARTICLE IN A REFERENCE BOOK

Anagnost, G. T. (2005). Sandra Day O'Connor. In *The Oxford Companion to the Supreme Court* (2nd ed., pp. 701–704). New York, NY: Oxford University Press.

ENTRY IN AN ONLINE REFERENCE BOOK

Jaworska, A. (2009). Advance directives and substitute decision-making. In E. N. Zalta (Ed.), *The Stanford encyclopedia of philosophy* (Summer 2009 ed.). Retrieved from http://plato.stanford.edu/entries/advance-directives/

GOVERNMENT PUBLICATION, PRINT AND ONLINE

U.S. Department of Housing and Urban Development. (2000). *Welfare to work: Reaching a new workforce*. Washington, DC: Government Printing Office.

Federal Reserve Bank of Dallas Texas. (2008). *Building wealth: A beginners guide to securing your financial future*. Retrieved from http://www.dallasfed.org/educate/pfe.cfm

ADVERTISEMENT, PRINT AND ONLINE

Sprint. (2013, November 25). [Advertisement]. *Time, 182*, 5.

Ford Motor Company. (2013). 2014 Fusion [Advertisement]. Retrieved from http://www.ford.com/cars/fusion/

AN ANNOTATED STUDENT APA-STYLE RESEARCH PAPER

Laura DeVeau was free to choose her own topic when it came time to write a research paper for her English 102 class. After considering a number of possible topics and doing some preliminary research on several of them, she turned to a subject that interested her personally: the effects of religion and spirituality on the mental health of society.

DeVeau was particularly interested to learn that historically, psychology professionals saw little value in religion and spirituality and, in fact, viewed them as having a negative impact on the mental health of individuals and society in general. This jarred with her own experience, and DeVeau set out in her first draft to document the psychological benefits and value of spiritual and religious beliefs. Once finished with the draft, she put it aside for a day before reading it carefully in an effort to see how she could strengthen it. DeVeau reworked her opening two paragraphs. In the first paragraph, she clearly described her research dilemma: the wide variety of opinions about the impact of religion on a person's life. In the second paragraph, she focused the scope of her project on her disagreement with professionals in the field of

macmillanhighered.com/mfw12e
Tutorials > Documentation and Working with Sources > How to Cite a Website in APA Style; How to Cite a Database in APA Style

macmillanhighered.com/mfw12e
LearningCurve > Working with Sources (APA)

psychology who claim that religious feelings are not compatible with sound mental health. DeVeau then looked at all of her examples to make sure that they were well organized and persuasive. Finally, she scoured her sources to make sure that she was using the materials that best supported or illustrated the points she wanted to make about the value of spirituality and religion.

The final draft of DeVeau's research paper illustrates that she has learned how the parts of a well-researched and well-written paper fit together and how to make revisions that emulate some of the qualities of the model essays she has read and studied in class. On the following pages you will see the cover page (required for all APA-style research papers), first page, and list of references from DeVeau's paper. You can read her full essay online at **macmillanhighered.com/mfw12e**.

macmillanhighered.com/mfw12e
e-readings > Laura DeVeau, "The Role of Spirituality and Religion in Mental Health"

Running head

RELIGION IN MENTAL HEALTH 1

The APA-style cover page gives title, author, and course information

The Role of Spirituality and Religion
in Mental Health

Laura DeVeau
English 102
Professor Gardner
April 12, 2010

RELIGION IN MENTAL HEALTH 2

Short form of title and page number as running head

The Role of Spirituality and Religion in Mental Health

It has been called "a vestige of the childhood of mankind," "the feeling of something true, total and absolute," "an otherworldly answer as regards the meaning of life" (Jones, 1991, p. 1; Amaro, 1998; Kristeva, 1987, p. 27). It has been compared to medicine, described as a psychological cure for mental illness, and also referred to as the cause of a dangerous fanaticism. With so many differing opinions on the impact of religion in people's lives, where would one begin a search for the truth? Who has the answer: Christians, humanists, objectivists, atheists, psychoanalysts, Buddhists, philosophers, cults? This was my dilemma at the advent of my research into how religion and spirituality affect the mental health of society as a whole.

Citation of multiple works from references

In this paper, I explore the claims, widely accepted by professionals in the field of psychology, that religious and spiritual practices have a negative impact on mental health. In addition, though, I cannot help but reflect on how this exploration has changed my beliefs as well. Religion is such a personal experience that one cannot be dispassionate in reporting it. One can, however, subject the evidence provided by those who have studied the issue to critical scrutiny. Having done so, I find myself in disagreement with those who claim religious feelings are incompatible with sound mental health. There is a nearly limitless number of beliefs regarding spirituality. Some are organized and involve rituals like mass or worship. Many are centered around the existence of a higher being, while others focus on the self. I have attempted to uncover the perfect set of values that lead to a better lifestyle, but my research has pointed me in an entirely different direction, where no single belief seems to be adequate but where spiritual belief in general should be valued more highly than it is currently in mental health circles.

Acknowledgment of opposing viewpoints

Thesis explicitly introduced

RELIGION IN MENTAL HEALTH 7

References begin on a new page

References

An online source

A book

An article or a chapter in a book

An article in a journal

Anonymous source alphabetized by title

Amaro, J. (1998). *Psychology, psychoanalysis and religious faith. Nielsen's psychology of religion page*. Retrieved from http://www.psywww.com/psyrelig/amaro.html

Beyerman A. K. (1989). *The holistic health movement.* Tuscaloosa, AL: Alabama University Press.

Dein, S. (2010, January). Religion, spirituality, and mental health. *Psychiatric Times, 20*(1): 1–3. Retrieved from http://www.psychiatrictimes.com/articles/religion-spirituality-and-mental-health

Ellis, A. (1993). Dogmatic devotion doesn't help, it hurts. In B. Slife (Ed.), *Taking sides: Clashing views on controversial psychological issues* (pp. 297–301). New York, NY: Scribner.

Jones, J. W. (1991). *Contemporary psychoanalysis and religion: Transference and transcendence*. New Haven, CT: Yale University Press.

Kristeva, J. (1987). *In the beginning was love: Psychoanalysis and faith*. New York, NY: Columbia University Press.

Larson, D. (1998). Does religious commitment improve mental health? In B. Slife (Ed.), *Taking sides: Clashing views on controversial psychological issues* (pp. 292–296). New York, NY: Scribner.

Pargament, K. I., Smith, B. W., Koening, H. G., & Perez, L. (1998). Patterns of positive and negative religious coping with major life stressors. *Journal for the Scientific Study of Religion, 37*, 710–724.

"Psychological benefits." (1999). *Walking the labyrinth.* Retrieved April 3, 2000, from http://www.labyrinthway.com/html/benefits.html

Verghese, A. (2008). Spirituality and mental health. *Indian Journal of Psychiatry, 50*(4): 233–237. doi:10.4103/0019-5545.44742

Glossary of Useful Terms

Abstract See *Concrete/Abstract.*

Allusion An allusion is a passing reference to a familiar person, place, or thing, often drawn from history, the Bible, mythology, or literature. An allusion is an economical way for a writer to capture the essence of an idea, atmosphere, emotion, or historical era, as in "The scandal was his Watergate" or "He saw himself as a modern Job" or "The campaign ended not with a bang but with a whimper." An allusion should be familiar to the reader; if it is not, it will add nothing to the meaning.

Analogy Analogy is a special form of comparison in which the writer explains something unfamiliar by comparing it to something familiar: "A transmission line is simply a pipeline for electricity. In the case of a water pipeline, more water will flow through the pipe as water pressure increases. The same is true of electricity in a transmission line."

Analysis An analysis is an examination of a reading or a source to understand the writer's main point and to assess the piece of writing for its relevance, bias, overall argument, and reliability.

Anecdote An anecdote is a short narrative about an amusing or interesting event. Writers often use anecdotes to begin essays as well as to illustrate certain points.

Argumentation To argue is to attempt to persuade the reader to agree with a point of view, to make a given decision, or to pursue a particular course of action. There are two basic types of argumentation: logical and persuasive. See the introduction to Chapter 21 (pp. 543–52) for a detailed discussion of argumentation.

Attitude A writer's attitude reflects his or her opinion of a subject. The writer can think very positively or very negatively about a subject or have an attitude that falls somewhere in between. See also *Tone.*

Audience An audience is the intended readership for a piece of writing. For example, the readers of a national weekly news magazine come from all walks of life and have diverse interests, opinions, and educational backgrounds. In contrast, the readership of an organic chemistry journal is made up of people whose interests and education are quite similar. The essays in *Models for Writers* are intended for general readers, intelligent people who may lack specific information about the subject being discussed.

Beginnings and Endings A beginning is the sentence, group of sentences, or section that introduces an essay. Good beginnings usually identify the thesis or controlling idea, attempt to interest readers, and establish a tone.

An ending is the sentence or group of sentences that brings an essay to a close. Good endings are purposeful and well planned. They can be a summary, a concluding example, an anecdote, or a quotation. Endings satisfy readers when they are the natural outgrowths of the essays themselves and give readers a sense of finality or completion. Good essays do not simply stop; they conclude. See the introduction to Chapter 6 (pp. 144–52) for a detailed discussion of beginnings and endings.

Cause and Effect Cause-and-effect analysis explains the reasons for an occurrence or the consequences of an action. See the introduction to Chapter 20 (pp. 517–20) for a detailed discussion of cause and effect.

Citation A reference to a published or unpublished work that indicates that the material being referenced is not original with the present author. A citation allows a reader to examine the referenced material to verify its authenticity, accuracy, and appropriateness.

Classification See *Division and Classification.*

Cliché A cliché is an expression that has become ineffective through overuse. Expressions such as *quick as a flash, jump for joy,* and *slow as molasses* are clichés. Writers normally avoid such trite expressions and seek instead to express themselves in fresh and forceful language. See also *Diction.*

Coherence Coherence is a quality of good writing that results when all sentences, paragraphs, and longer divisions of an essay are naturally connected. Coherent writing is achieved through (1) a logical sequence of ideas (arranged in chronological order, spatial order, order of importance, or some other appropriate order), (2) the purposeful repetition of key words and ideas, (3) a pace suitable for your topic and your reader, and (4) the use of transitional words and expressions. Coherence should not be confused with unity. (See *Unity*.) See also *Transition*.

Colloquial Expression A colloquial expression is an expression that is characteristic of or appropriate to spoken language or to writing that seeks the effect of spoken language. Colloquial expressions are informal, as *chem, gym, come up with, be at wit's end, won't,* and *photo* illustrate. Thus, colloquial expressions are acceptable in formal writing only if they are used purposefully. See also *Diction*.

Combined Strategies By combining rhetorical strategies, writers are able to develop their ideas in interesting ways. For example, in writing a cause-and-effect essay about a major oil spill, the writer might want to describe the damage the spill caused as well as explain the cleanup process step by step.

Comparison and Contrast Comparison and contrast is used to point out the similarities and differences between two or more subjects in the same class or category. The function of any comparison and contrast is to clarify—to reach some conclusion about the items being compared and contrasted. See the introduction to Chapter 19 (pp. 487–92) for a detailed discussion of comparison and contrast.

Conclusions See *Beginnings and Endings*.

Concrete/Abstract A concrete word names a specific object, person, place, or action that can be directly perceived by the senses, such as *car, bread, building, book, John F. Kennedy, Chicago,* or *hiking*. An abstract word, in contrast, refers to general qualities, conditions, ideas, actions, or relationships that cannot be directly perceived by the senses, such as *bravery, dedication, excellence, anxiety, stress, thinking,* or *hatred*. See the introduction to Chapter 11 (p. 288) for more on abstract and concrete words.

Connotation/Denotation Both connotation and denotation refer to the meanings of words. Denotation is the dictionary meaning of a word, the literal meaning. Connotation, on the other hand, is the implied or suggested meaning of a word. For example, the denotation of *lamb* is "a young sheep." The connotations of *lamb* are numerous: *gentle, docile, weak, peaceful, blessed, sacrificial, blood, spring, frisky, pure, innocent,* and so on. See the introduction to Chapter 11 (p. 287) for more on connotation and denotation.

Controlling Idea See *Thesis*.

Coordination Coordination is the joining of grammatical constructions of the same rank (words, phrases, and clauses) to indicate that they are of equal importance. For example, "*They ate hot dogs,* and *we ate hamburgers.*" See the introduction to Chapter 9 (p. 222) for more on coordination. See also *Subordination*.

Deduction Deduction is the process of reasoning from stated premises to a conclusion that follows necessarily. This form of reasoning moves from the general to the specific. See the introduction to Chapter 21 (p. 545) for a discussion of deductive reasoning and its role in argumentation. See also *Syllogism*.

Definition Definition, a rhetorical pattern, is a statement of the meaning of a word. A definition may be either brief or extended, part of an essay or an entire essay itself. See the introduction to Chapter 17 (pp. 447–49) for a detailed discussion of definition.

Denotation See *Connotation/Denotation*.

Description Description tells how a person, place, or thing is perceived by the five senses. See the introduction to Chapter 15 (pp. 402–4) for a detailed discussion of description.

Details Details are the small elements that collectively contribute to the overall impression of a person, place, thing, or idea. For example, in the sentence "The *organic, whole-grain* dog biscuits were *reddish brown, beef flavored,* and in the *shape of a bone,*" the italicized words are details.

Dialogue Dialogue is the conversation of two or more people as represented in writing. Dialogue is what people say directly to one another.

Diction Diction refers to a writer's choice and use of words. Good diction is precise and appropriate: The words mean exactly what the writer intends, and the words are well suited to the writer's subject, intended audience, and purpose in writing. The word-conscious writer knows that there are differences among *aged, old,* and *elderly; blue, navy,* and *azure;* and *disturbed, angry,* and *irritated*. Furthermore, this writer knows in which situation to use each word. See the introduction to Chapter 11 (pp. 287–89) for a detailed discussion of diction. See also *Cliché, Colloquial Expression, Connotation/Denotation, Jargon,* and *Slang*.

Direct Quotation Material borrowed word for word that must be placed within quotation marks and properly cited.

Division and Classification Division and classification are rhetorical patterns used by the writer first to establish categories and then to arrange or sort people, places, or things into these categories according to their different characteristics, thus making them more manageable for the writer and more understandable and meaningful for the reader. See the introduction to Chapter 18 (pp. 463–66) for a detailed discussion of division and classification.

Documentation The act or the instance of supplying documents or references as to where they may be found.

Dominant Impression A dominant impression is the single mood, atmosphere, or quality a writer emphasizes in a piece of descriptive writing. The dominant impression is created through the careful selection of details and is, of course, influenced by the writer's subject, audience, and purpose. See the introduction to Chapter 15 (pp. 402–4) for more on dominant impression.

Emphasis Emphasis is the placement of important ideas and words within sentences and longer units of writing so that they have the greatest impact. In general, what comes at the end has the most impact, and at the beginning nearly as much; what comes in the middle gets the least emphasis.

Endings See *Beginnings and Endings.*

Evaluation An evaluation of a piece of writing is an assessment of its effectiveness or merit. In evaluating a piece of writing, one should ask the following questions: What is the writer's purpose? Is it a worthwhile purpose? Does the writer achieve the purpose? Is the writer's information sufficient and accurate? What are the strengths of the essay? What are its weaknesses? Depending on the type of writing and the purpose, more specific questions can also be asked. For example, with an argument one could ask: Does the writer follow the principles of logical thinking? Is the writer's evidence sufficient and convincing?

Evidence Evidence is the information on which a judgment or argument is based or by which proof or probability is established. Evidence usually takes the form of statistics, facts, names, examples or illustrations, and opinions of authorities.

Example An example illustrates a larger idea or represents something of which it is a part. An example is a basic means of developing or clarifying an idea. Furthermore, examples enable writers to show rather than simply tell readers what they mean. See the introduction to Chapter 13 (pp. 339–41) for more on example.

Facts Facts are pieces of information presented as having objective reality—that is, having actual existence. For example, water boils at 212°F, Katharine Hepburn died in 2003, and the USSR no longer exists—these are all facts.

Fallacy See *Logical Fallacy.*

Figure of Speech A figure of speech is a brief, imaginative comparison that highlights the similarities between things that are basically dissimilar. Figures of speech make writing vivid, interesting, and memorable. The most common figures of speech are:

Simile: An explicit comparison introduced by *like* or *as*. "The fighter's hands were like stone."

Metaphor: An implied comparison that makes one thing the equivalent of another. "All the world's a stage."

Personification: A special kind of figure of speech in which human traits are assigned to ideas or objects. "The engine coughed and then stopped."

See the introduction to Chapter 12 (pp. 320–21) for a detailed discussion of figurative language.

Focus Focus is the limitation a writer gives his or her subject. The writer's task is to select a manageable topic given the constraints of time, space, and purpose. For example, within the general subject of sports, a writer could focus on government support of amateur athletes or narrow the focus further to government support of Olympic athletes.

General See *Specific/General.*

Idiom An idiom is a word or phrase that is used habitually with special meaning. The meaning of an idiom is not always readily apparent to nonnative speakers of that language. For example, *catch a cold, hold a job, make up your mind,* and *give them a hand* are all idioms in English.

Illustration Illustration is the use of examples to explain, elucidate, or corroborate. Writers rely heavily on illustration to make their ideas both clear and concrete. See the introduction to Chapter 13 (pp. 339–41) for a detailed discussion of illustration.

Induction Induction is the process of reasoning to a conclusion about all members of a class through an examination of only a few members of the class. This form of reasoning moves from the particular to the general. See the introduction to Chapter 21 (p. 545) for a discussion of inductive reasoning and its role in argumentation.

Inductive Leap An inductive leap is the point at which a writer of an argument, having presented sufficient evidence, moves to a generalization or conclusion. See also *Induction.*

Introduction See *Beginnings and Endings.*

Irony Irony is the use of words to suggest something different from their literal meaning. For example, when Jonathan Swift suggested in "A Modest Proposal" that Ireland's problems could be solved if the people of Ireland fattened their babies and sold them to the English landlords for food, he meant that almost any other solution would be preferable. A writer can use irony to establish a special relationship with the reader and to add an extra dimension or twist to the meaning. See the introduction to Chapter 11 (pp. 291–92) for more on irony.

Jargon Jargon, or technical language, is the special vocabulary of a trade, profession, or group. Doctors, construction workers, lawyers, and teachers, for example, all have a specialized vocabulary that they use on the job. See also *Diction.*

Logical Fallacy A logical fallacy is an error in reasoning that renders an argument invalid. See the introduction to Chapter 21 (pp. 548–50) for a discussion of common logical fallacies.

Metaphor See *Figure of Speech.*

Narration To narrate is to tell a story, to relate what happened. Although narration is most often used in fiction, it is also important in expository writing, either by itself or in conjunction with other types of prose. See the introduction to Chapter 14 (pp. 372–75) for a detailed discussion of narration.

Opinion An opinion is a belief or conclusion, which may or may not be substantiated by positive knowledge or proof. (If not substantiated, an opinion is a prejudice.) Even when based on evidence and sound reasoning, an opinion is personal and can be changed and is therefore less persuasive than facts and arguments.

Organization Organization is the pattern or order the writer imposes on his or her material. Some often-used patterns of organization include time order, space order, and order of importance. See the introduction to Chapter 5 (pp. 121–26) for a detailed discussion of organization.

Paradox A paradox is a seemingly contradictory statement that is nonetheless true. For example, "We little know what we have until we lose it" is a paradoxical statement.

Paragraph The paragraph, the single most important unit of thought in an essay, is a series of closely related sentences. These sentences adequately develop the central or controlling idea of the paragraph. This central idea, usually stated in a topic sentence, is necessarily related to the purpose of the whole composition. A well-written paragraph has several distinguishing characteristics: a clearly stated or implied topic sentence, adequate development, unity, coherence, and an appropriate organizational strategy. See the introduction to Chapter 7 (pp. 169–72) for a detailed discussion of paragraphs.

Parallelism Parallel structure is the repetition of word order or grammatical form either within a single sentence or in several sentences that develop the same central idea. As a rhetorical device, parallelism can aid coherence and add emphasis. Franklin Roosevelt's statement "I see one-third of a nation ill-housed, ill-clad, and ill-nourished" illustrates effective parallelism. See the introduction to Chapter 9 (pp. 222–23) for more on parallelism.

Paraphrase A restatement of the information a writer is borrowing. A paraphrase closely parallels the presentation of ideas in the original, but it does not use the same words or sentence structure. See also *Direct Quotation*, *Plagiarism*, and *Summary*.

Perhapsing To use speculative material when the facts necessary to develop a work of nonfiction are not known or available to the writer. See Thinking Critically about This Reading following Erin Murphy's "White Lies" (p. 155).

Personification See *Figure of Speech*.

Persuasion Persuasion, or persuasive argument, is an attempt to convince readers to agree with a point of view, to make a decision, or to pursue a particular course of action. Persuasion appeals strongly to the emotions, whereas logical argument does not.

Plagiarism The use of someone else's ideas in their original form or in an altered form without proper documentation. Writers avoid plagiarism by (1) putting direct quotations within quotation marks and properly citing them, and (2) documenting any idea, explanation, or argument that is borrowed and presented in a summary or paraphrase, making it clear where the borrowed material begins and ends. See the introduction to Chapter 10, Writing with Sources (pp. 254–57).

Point of View Point of view refers to the grammatical person in an essay. For example, the first-person point of view uses the pronoun *I* and is commonly found in autobiography and the personal essay; the third-person point of view uses the pronouns *he, she,* or *it* and is commonly found in objective writing. See the introduction to Chapter 14 (pp. 372–75) for a discussion of point of view in narration.

Process Analysis Process analysis is a rhetorical strategy used to explain how something works or to give step-by-step directions for doing something. See the introduction to Chapter 16 (pp. 427–29) for a detailed discussion of process analysis.

Purpose Purpose is what the writer wants to accomplish in a particular piece of writing. Purposeful writing seeks to *tell* (narration), to *describe* (description), to *explain* (process analysis, definition, division and classification, comparison and contrast, and cause and effect), or to *convince* (argument).

Rhetorical Modes Spoken or written strategies for presenting subjects, the most common of which are argument, cause and effect, comparison and contrast, definition, description, division and classification, illustration, narration, and process analysis.

Rhetorical Question A rhetorical question is asked for its rhetorical effect but requires no answer from the reader. "When will nuclear proliferation end?" is such a question. Writers use rhetorical questions to introduce topics they plan to discuss or to emphasize important points. See the introduction to Chapter 6 (p. 149) for another example.

Sentence A sentence is a grammatical unit that expresses a complete thought. It consists of at least a subject (a noun) and a predicate (a verb). See the introduction to Chapter 9 (pp. 218–23) for a detailed discussion of effective sentences.

Signal Phrase A phrase alerting the reader that borrowed information follows. A signal phrase usually consists of an author's name and a verb (for example, "Coughlan argues" or "Yadav disagrees") and helps integrate direct quotations, paraphrases, and summaries into the flow of a paper. A signal phrase tells the reader who is speaking and indicates exactly where your ideas end and your source's begin.

Simile See *Figure of Speech.*

Slang Slang is the unconventional, informal language of particular subgroups in our culture. Slang terms, such as *bummed, sweat, dark,* and *cool,* are acceptable in formal writing only if used selectively for specific purposes.

Specific/General General words name groups or classes of objects, qualities, or actions. Specific words, on the other hand, name individual objects, qualities, or actions within a class or group. To some extent the terms *general* and *specific* are relative. For example, *clothing* is a class of things. *Shirt,* however, is more specific than *clothing* but more general than *T-shirt*. See also *Diction.*

Strategy A strategy is a means by which a writer achieves his or her purpose. Strategy includes the many rhetorical decisions the writer makes about organization, paragraph structure, sentence structure, and diction. In terms of the whole essay, strategy refers to the principal rhetorical mode a writer uses. If, for example, a writer wishes to explain how to make chocolate chip cookies, the most effective strategy would be process analysis. If it is the writer's purpose to analyze why sales of American cars have declined in recent years, the most effective strategy would be cause-and-effect analysis.

Style Style is the individual manner in which a writer expresses his or her ideas. Style is created by the author's particular choice of words, construction of sentences, and arrangement of ideas.

Subordination Subordination is the use of grammatical constructions to make one part of a sentence dependent on, rather than equal to, another. For example, the italicized clause in the following sentence is subordinate: "They all cheered *when I finished the race.*" See the introduction to Chapter 9 (pp. 219–20) for more on subordination. See also *Coordination.*

Summary A condensed form of the essential idea of a passage, article, or entire chapter. A summary is always shorter than the original. See also *Paraphrase, Plagiarism,* and *Direct Quotation.*

Supporting Evidence See *Evidence.*

Syllogism A syllogism is an argument that uses deductive reasoning and consists of a major premise, a minor premise, and a conclusion:

All trees that lose leaves are deciduous. (*Major premise*)
Maple trees lose their leaves. (*Minor premise*)
Therefore, maple trees are deciduous. (*Conclusion*)

See Chapter 21 (p. 545) for more on syllogisms. See also *Deduction.*

Symbol A symbol is a person, place, or thing that represents something beyond itself. For example, the bald eagle is a symbol of the United States, and the maple leaf is a symbol of Canada.

Syntax Syntax refers to the way in which words are arranged to form phrases, clauses, and sentences, as well as to the grammatical relationship among the words themselves.

Synthesis A synthesis is a written discussion that weaves together the ideas of one or more sources with your own. There are two types of synthesis: *informational/explanatory synthesis* and *persuasive/argument synthesis.* See Chapter 10 (pp. 251–53) for more on synthesis.

Technical Language See *Jargon.*

Thesis The thesis, also known as the controlling idea, is the main idea of an essay. It may sometimes be implied rather than stated directly. See the introduction to Chapter 3 (pp. 79–81) for more on the thesis statement.

Title A title is a word or phrase set off at the beginning of an essay to identify the subject, to state the main idea of the essay, or to attract the reader's attention. A title may be explicit or suggestive. A subtitle, when used, explains or restricts the meaning of the main title.

Tone Tone is the manner in which a writer relates to an audience, the "tone of voice" used to address readers. Tone may be friendly, serious, distant, angry, humorous, cheerful, bitter, cynical, enthusiastic, morbid, resentful, warm, playful, and so forth. A particular tone results from a writer's diction, sentence structure, purpose, and attitude toward the subject. See the introduction to Chapter 11 (pp. 289–92) for several examples that display different tones.

Topic Sentence The topic sentence states the central idea of a paragraph and thus limits the content of the paragraph. Although the topic sentence normally appears at the beginning of the paragraph, it may appear at any other point, particularly if the writer is trying to create a special effect. Not all paragraphs contain topic sentences. See also *Paragraph*.

Transition A transition is a word or phrase that links sentences, paragraphs, and larger units of a composition to achieve coherence. Transitions include parallelism, pronoun references, conjunctions, and the repetition of key ideas, as well as many conventional transitional expressions: *moreover, on the other hand, in addition, in contrast, therefore* and so on. See the introduction to Chapter 8 (pp. 192–95) for a detailed discussion of transitions. See also *Coherence*.

Unity Unity is that quality of oneness in an essay that results when all the words, sentences, and paragraphs contribute to the thesis. The elements of a unified essay do not distract the reader. Instead, they harmoniously support a single idea or purpose. See the introduction to Chapter 4 (pp. 98–101) for a detailed discussion of unity.

Verb Verbs can be classified as either strong verbs (*scream, pierce, gush, ravage,* and *amble*) or weak verbs (*be, has, get,* and *do*). Writers prefer to use strong verbs to make their writing more specific, more descriptive, and more action filled.

Voice Verbs can be classified as being in either the active or the passive voice. In the *active voice,* the doer of the action is the grammatical subject. In the *passive voice,* the receiver of the action is the subject:

Active: Glenda questioned all of the children.
Passive: All the children were questioned by Glenda.

Writing Process The writing process is the sequence of activities that most writers usually follow when composing a written work. It consists of four stages:

Prewriting: The stage in the writing process in which you select your subject and topic, gather ideas and information, and determine the thesis and organizational pattern or patterns of a written work.

Drafting: The process of creating the first version of your writing in which you lay out your ideas and information and, through revision, subsequently prepare more focused and polished versions referred to as second and third drafts, and more if necessary.

Revising: The stage in the writing process in which you reconsider and possibly change the large elements of your writing, such as thesis, purpose, content, organization, and paragraph structure.

Editing: The stage in the writing process in which you reconsider and possibly change the small elements of your writing, such as grammar, punctuation, mechanics, and spelling.

Acknowledgments

Diane Ackerman, "Why Leaves Turn Color in the Fall." From *A Natural History of the Senses,* copyright © 1990 by Diane Ackerman. Used by permission of Vintage Publishers, a division of Random House, Inc.

Maya Angelou, "Momma, the Dentist, and Me" from *I Know Why the Caged Bird Sings.* Copyright © 1969 and renewed 1997 by Maya Angelou. Used by permission of Random House, Inc.

Isaac Asimov, "What Is Intelligence Anyway?" Reprinted by permission of Asimov Holdings LLC.

Russell Baker, "Becoming a Writer." Excerpt from Chapter 2 of *Growing Up.* Copyright © 1982 by Russell Baker. Used by permission of Don Congdon Associates, Inc.

Suzanne Britt, "That Lean and Hungry Look." *Newsweek,* October 9, 1978. Reprinted by permission of the author.

Rachel Carson, "Fable for Tomorrow" from *Silent Spring.* Copyright © 1962 by Rachel L. Carson. Used by permission of Houghton Mifflin Harcourt Publishing Company and the Frances Collins Literary Agency. All rights reserved.

Jimmy Carter, "The Home Place" from *An Hour before Daylight: Memoirs of a Rural Boyhood.* Copyright © 2001 by Jimmy Carter. Used by permission of President Jimmy Carter.

Bruce Catton, "Grant and Lee: A Study in Contrasts." Originally published in *The American Story,* ed. Earl Schneck Miers, 1956. Copyright © 1956 U.S. Capitol Historical Society. Used by permission of the U.S. Capitol Historical Society.

Cornell W. Clayton, "Incivility Crisis of Politics Is Just a Symptom of Division." First published in *The Seattle Times,* October 27, 2012. Cornell W. Clayton is a professor of political science at Washington State University.

Judith Ortiz Cofer, "My Rosetta," from *Woman in Front of the Sun: On Becoming a Writer* by Judith Ortiz Cofer. Used by permission of University of Georgia Press.

James Lincoln Collier, "Anxiety: Challenge by Another Name" from *Reader's Digest* (December 1986). Reprinted with the permission of the author.

Barry Commoner, excerpt from *Politics of Energy.* Copyright © 1979 by Barry Commoner. Used by permission of Alfred A. Knopf, an imprint of the Knopf Doubleday Publishing Group, a division of Random House LLC. All rights reserved.

Gabriella Corvese, "Putting 'Action' Back in Activism" from *The Brown Daily Herald,* February 21, 2013. Used by permission of the author.

Michael Dirda, "Readings: Listening to My Father," from *The Washington Post,* June 15, 1997. Copyright © 1997 by The Washington Post Company. All rights reserved. Used by permission and protected by the Copyright Laws of the United States. The printing, copying, redistribution, or retransmission of the Material without express written permission is prohibited.

Lawrence M. Friedman, "What Is Crime?" from *Crime and Punishment in American History.* Copyright © 1993 by Lawrence M. Friedman. Reprinted with the permission of Basic Books, a member of Perseus Books Group, LLC.

Thomas L. Friedman, "My Favorite Teacher" from *The New York Times* (January 9, 2001). Copyright © 2001 by The New York Times Company. All rights reserved. Used by permission and protected by the Copyright Laws of the United States. The printing, copying, redistribution, or retransmission of the Material without express written permission is prohibited.

Martin Gansberg, "Thirty-Eight Who Saw Murder Didn't Call Police," from *The New York Times* (March 17, 1964). Copyright © 1964 by The New York Times Company. All rights reserved. Used by permission and protected by the Copyright Laws of the United States. The printing, copying, redistribution, or retransmission of the Material without express written permission is prohibited.

Henry Louis Gates Jr., "Forty Acres and a Gap in Wealth" from *The New York Times* (November 18, 2007). Copyright © 2007 by The New York Times Company. All rights reserved. Used by permission and protected by the Copyright Laws of the United States. The printing, copying, redistribution, or retransmission of the Material without express written permission is prohibited.

Nancy Gibbs, "The Magic of the Family Meal" from *Time* (June 4, 2006). Copyright © 2006 by Time, Inc. Reprinted with permission of Time, Inc.

Natalie Goldberg, "Be Specific" from *Writing down the Bones: Freeing the Writer Within* by Natalie Goldberg, © Copyright 1986 by Natalie Goldberg. Reprinted by arrangement with Shambhala Publications, Inc. Boston, MA. www.shambhala.com.

Paul Goldberger, from "Disconnected Urbanism." Originally published in *Metropolis*. Copyright © by Paul Goldberger. Used by permission of the author.

Ellen Goodman, "The Company Man" from *Value Judgments*. Copyright © 1993 by Ellen Goodman. Reprinted with the permission of International Creative Management, Inc.

Adam Grant, Ph.D., "Does Trying to Be Happy Make Us Unhappy?" Dr. Adam Grant is a professor at the Wharton School and the bestselling author of *Give and Take*. Used by permission of the author.

Dick Gregory, "Shame." From *Nigger: An Autobiography* by Dick Gregory. Copyright © 1964 by Dick Gregory Enterprises, Inc. Used by permission of Dutton, a division of Penguin Group (USA) LLC and International Creative Management.

Bill Heavey, "The Heart of a Lonely Hunter." As adapted for *The New York Times* from *It's Only Slow Food Until You Try to Eat It*. Used by permission of Grove/Atlantic, Inc. Any third party use of this material, outside of this publication, is prohibited.

Don H. and Sandra Hockenbury, "Encoding Long-Term Memories." Excerpt from *Psychology*, Sixth Edition, copyright © 2013 Worth Publishers, Inc. Used by permission.

Langston Hughes, "Salvation" from *The Big Sea: An Autobiography*. Copyright © 1940 by Langston Hughes. Copyright renewed 1968 by Arna Bontemps and George Houston Bass. Reprinted with the permission of Hill and Wang, a division of Farrar, Straus & Giroux, LLC and Harold Ober Associates.

Barbara Huttmann, "A Crime of Compassion" from *Newsweek* (August 8, 1983). Copyright © 1983 by Barbara Huttmann. Reprinted with the permission of the author.

Jake Jamieson. "The English-Only Movement: Can America Proscribe Language with a Clear Conscience?" Reprinted with the permission of the author.

John I. Jenkins, "Persuasion as the Cure for Incivility" from *The Wall Street Journal*, January 8, 2013. Reprinted by permission. All rights reserved. Used by permission and protected by the Copyright Laws of the United States. The printing, copying, redistribution, or retransmission of the Material without express written permission is prohibited.

Dan M. Kahan, "Shame Is Worth a Try" from *The Boston Globe* (August 5, 2001). Copyright © 2001 by Dan M. Kahan. Reprinted with permission of the author.

Martin Luther King Jr., "The Ways of Meeting Oppression" from *Stride toward Freedom: The Montgomery Story*. Copyright © 1958 by Dr. Martin Luther King Jr. Copyright © 1986 by Coretta Scott King. Reprinted with the permission of the Estate of Martin Luther King Jr., c/o Writer's House as agent for the proprietor.

Stephen King, "Why We Crave Horror Movies." Copyright © Stephen King. Reprinted by permission of Darhansoff & Verrill as agents for the author.

Christina Baker Kline, "Taking My Son to College, Where Technology Has Replaced Serendipity." *blog .NJ.com*, September 1, 2013. Used by permission.

Verlyn Klinkenborg, "Our Vanishing Night." *National Geographic Magazin*e, November 2008. Copyright © 2008 National Geographic Society. Used by permission of the National Geographic Society.

Nicholas D. Kristof, "A Farm Boy Reflects." *The New York Times*, July 13, 2008. Copyright © 2008 by The New York Times, Inc. All rights reserved. Used by permission and protected by the Copyright Laws of the United States. The printing, copying, redistribution, or retransmission of the Material without express written permission is prohibited.

Robert Krulwich, NPR news report entitled "How Do Plants Know Which Way Is Up and Which Way Is Down?" Copyright © 2012 National Public Radio, Inc. Originally published on NPR.org on June 22, 2012, and used with permission of NPR. Any unauthorized duplication is strictly prohibited.

Robert Lake-Thom, aka Medicine Grizzly Bear, "An Indian Father's Plea." Originally published in *Teacher's Magazine*, September 1990. Reprinted with permission of the author.

Anne Lamott, "Polaroids" from *Bird by Bird: Some Instructions on Writing and Life*, by Anne Lamott. Copyright © 1994 by Anne Lamott. Used by permission of Pantheon Books, an imprint of the Knopf Doubleday Publishing Group, a division of Random House, Inc. All rights reserved.

Richard Lederer, "The Case for Short Words" from *The Miracle of Language*. Copyright © 1991 by Richard Lederer. Reprinted with the permission of Pocket Books, a division of Simon & Schuster Adult Publishing Group.

William Lutz, "Doubts about Doublespeak" from *State Government News* (July 1993). Copyright © 1993 by William Lutz. Reprinted with the permission of the author.

Farhad Manjoo, "No, I Do Not Want to Pet Your Dog." *Slate* online, May 9, 2013. All rights reserved.

Myriam Marquez, "Why and When We Speak Spanish in Public" from the *Orlando Sentinel* (June 28, 1999). Copyright © 1999 by the Orlando Sentinel. Reprinted with the permission of the publisher.

Stanley McChrystal, "Lincoln's Call to Service—and Ours." *The Wall Street Journal*, May 29, 2013. Reprinted with permission of the Wall Street Journal. Copyright © 2013 Dow Jones & Company, Inc. All rights reserved. Used by permission and protected by the Copyright Laws of the United States. The printing, copying, redistribution, or retransmission of the Material without express written permission is prohibited.

Cherokee Paul McDonald, "A View from the Bridge" from (Fort Lauderdale, FL) *Sun-Sentinel* (February 12, 1989). Reprinted with permission.

Sean McElwee, "The Case for Censoring Hate Speech." Sean McElwee is a writer based in New York City. Used by permission of the author.

Paul Merrill, "How to Write Poorly (Principles of Poor Writing)" from *The Scientific Monthly,* Vol. 64, No. 1 (Jan 1947). Reprinted with permission from SCIENCE/AAAS.

N. Scott Momaday, "The Flight of the Eagles." Excerpt from pp. 16–17 from *House Made of Dawn* by N. Scott Momaday. Copyright © 1966, 1967, 1968 by N. Scott Momaday. Reprinted by permission of HarperCollins Publishers.

Bharati Mukherjee, "Two Ways to Belong in America." Copyright © 1996 by Bharati Mukherjee. Originally published in *The New York Times*. Reprinted by permission of Janklow & Nesbit Associates on behalf of the author.

Erin Murphy, "White Lies" from *Brevity 33* (first appeared in May 2010 issue). Reprinted with the permission of the author.

Gloria Naylor, "The Meanings of a Word" from *The New York Times* (February 20, 1986). Copyright © 1986 by Gloria Naylor. Reprinted with the permission of SLL/Sterling Lord Literistic, Inc.

Susan Orlean, "The American Man: Age Ten." Reprinted by permission of the author.

Gregory Petsko, "The Blue Marble" from *Genome Biology Online,* April 28, 2011. Reprinted by permission of BioMed Central. Reproduced from the original article *Genome Biology* 2011, **12**:112 doi.10.1186/gb-2011-12-4-112 (http://genomebiology.com/2011/12/4/112) © 2011 BioMed Central Ltd.

Mark D. Pfeifle, "Changing the Face(book) of Social Activism." Copyright by Mark Pfeifle. Reprinted with permission of the author.

Steven Pinker, "In Defense of Dangerous Ideas" from *What Is Your Dangerous Idea?* Jonathan Brockman, ed. Copyright © 2007 by Edge Foundation, Inc. Introduction copyright © 2007 Steven Pinker. Afterword copyright © 2007 by Richard Dawkins. Reprinted by permission of HarperCollins Publishers.

Eduardo Porter, "What Happiness Is" from *The Price of Everything: Solving the Mystery of Why We Pay What We Do* by Eduardo Porter, copyright © 2011 by Eduardo Porter. Used by permission of Portfolio, an imprint of Penguin Group (USA) Inc.

Robert Ramirez, "The Barrio" (original title "The Woolen Serape") from *Pain and Promise: The Chicano Today*, edited by Edward Simmens (New York: New American Library, 1972). Reprinted with the permission of the author.

Carl T. Rowan, "Unforgettable Miss Bessie" from *Reader's Digest*. Copyright © 1985 by The Reader's Digest. Reprinted with permission from Reader's Digest.

Heidi Schlumpf, "'Slacktivism' Makes the World a Better Place from the Couch." *National Catholic Reporter*, August 20, 2012. Used by permission of the National Catholic Reporter.

David Sedaris, "Me Talk Pretty One Day" from *Me Talk Pretty One Day.* Copyright © 2000 by David Sedaris. Reprinted by permission of Little, Brown & Company and Don Congdon Associates, Inc.

Mary Sherry, "In Praise of the F Word" from *Newsweek* (May 6, 1991). Copyright © 1991 by Mary Sherry. Reprinted with the permission of the author.

Laura DeVeau Smith, "The Role of Spirituality and Religion in Mental Health." Reprinted by permission of the author.

Brent Staples, "Black Men and Public Space" from *Harper's*. Copyright © 1987 by Brent Staples. Reprinted by permission of the author.

Cole Stryker, "The Problem with Public Shaming" from *The Nation*, April 24, 2013. Reprinted with permission. For subscription information, call 1-800-333-8536. Portions of each week's *Nation* magazine can be accessed at http://www.thenation.com.

Amy Tan, "Mother Tongue." Copyright © 1989 by Amy Tan. First appeared in *The Threepenny Review*. Reprinted by permission of the author and the Sandra Dijkstra Literary Agency.

June Tangney, "Condemn the Crime, Not the Person" from *The Boston Globe* (August 5, 2001). Copyright © 2001 by June Tangney. Reprinted with the permission of the author.

Eudora Welty, "The Corner Store" from *The Eye of the Story*. Copyright © 1978 by Eudora Welty. Used by permission of Random House, Inc. and Russell & Volkening, Inc.

Diane "Lady Hulk" Williams, "Revolution on Eight Wheels." Reprinted with permission from the July 27, 2011 issue of *The Nation*. For subscription information, call 1-800-333-8536. Portions of each week's *Nation* can be accessed at http://www.thenation.com.

Terry Tempest Williams, "The Clan of the One-Breasted Women" from *Refuge: An Unnatural History of Family and Place*. Copyright ©1991 by Terry Tempest Williams. Used by permission of Pantheon Books, a division of Random House, Inc.

Marion Winik, "Guacamole Is a Cruel Mistress." *Baltimore Fishbowl*, August 15, 2012. Used by permission of the author.

Julie Zhuo, "Where Anonymity Breeds Contempt." From *The New York Times*, November 29, 2010. Used by permission of the New York Times. All rights reserved. Used by permission and protected by the Copyright Laws of the United States. The printing, copying, redistribution, or retransmission of the Material without express written permission is prohibited.

William Zinsser, "Simplicity" from *On Writing Well,* Sixth Edition (New York: HarperCollins Publishers, 1994). Copyright © 1976, 1980, 1985, 1988, 1990, 1994, 1998 by William Zinsser. Reprinted with the permission of the author and Carol Brissie.

Index

Missing something? Instructors may assign the online materials that accompany this text. For access to them, visit **macmillanhighered.com/mfw12e.**

Inside LaunchPad Solo for *Models for Writers*

e-readings

Peace Corps, "What Are Some Ways Peace Corps Volunteers Grow During Service?" [video]
Khalid Latif, "Shattered Silence" [video]
Peter Aguero, "Me & Her & It" [audio]
Sustainable America, "How to Compost in Your Apartment" [infographic]
National Science Foundation, "The Tragedy of the Commons" [animation]
WIRED, "What's Inside Coffee" [video]
CDC, "Screen Time vs. Lean Time" [infographic]
U.S. Department of State, "Help Protect Our Ocean" [video]
Intelligence Squared, "Should College Football Be Banned?" [video]
Lily Myers, "Shrinking Women" [video]
Rader Programs, "Women Are Dying to Be Thin" [infographic]
Kelly Flanagan, "Words From a Father to His Daughter (From the Makeup Aisle)" [audio]
Carrie Arnold, "What's Photoshop Got to Do with It?" [blog]
NEDA, "A Silent Epidemic" [infographic]
Laura DeVeau, "The Role of Spirituality and Religion in Mental Health" [APA-style paper]

LearningCurve

Critical Reading
Topic Sentences and Supporting Details
Topics and Main Ideas
Working with Sources (MLA)
Working with Sources (APA)
Commas
Fragments
Run-ons and Comma Splices
Active and Passive Voice
Appropriate Language
Subject-Verb Agreement

Tutorials

Critical Reading

Active Reading Strategies
Reading Visuals: Audience
Reading Visuals: Purpose

Documentation and Working with Sources

Do I Need to Cite That?
How to Cite Anything

Digital Writing

Photo Editing Basics with GIMP
Audio Editing with Audacity
Presentations
Word Processing
Online Research Tools
Job Search/Personal Branding

Guide to Language, Speaking, and Listening

For Bedford/St. Martin's

Vice President, Editorial, Macmillan Higher Education Humanities: Edwin Hill
Editorial Director for English and Music: Karen S. Henry
High School Publisher: Ann Heath
Executive Editor for Readers: John Sullivan
Senior Sponsoring Editor for High School English: Nathan Odell
Developmental Editor: Caitlin Kaufman
Assistant Production Editor: Lidia MacDonald
Marketing Manager: Jane Helms
Project Management: Matt Rosenquist, Graphic World Inc.
Director of Rights and Permissions: Hilary Newman
Senior Art Director: Anna Palchik
Text Design: Graphic World Inc., Glass Pattern Background image courtesy of istock.

1 2 3 4 5 6 18 17 16 15 14

For information, write: Bedford/St. Martin's, 75 Arlington Street, Boston, MA 02116 (617-399-4000)

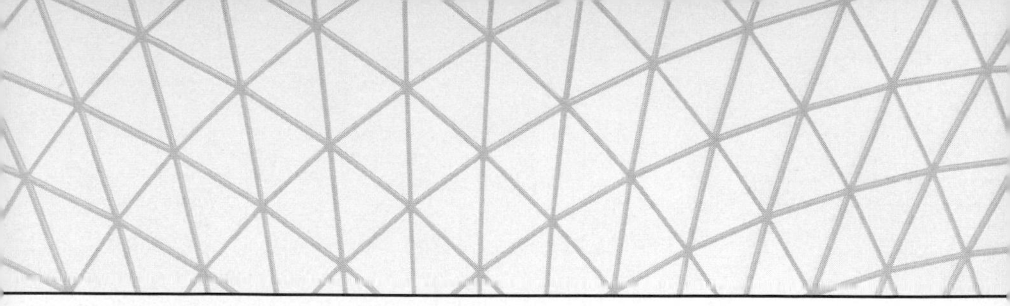

PART ONE
Language

PART TWO
Speaking and Listening

PART ONE

Language

1

Grammatical Sentences

1 ♦ Sentence Fragments

Unlike a complete sentence, a **fragment** is partial or incomplete. It may lack a subject (naming someone or something), a predicate (making an assertion about the subject), or both. A fragment also may otherwise fail to express a complete thought. Unless you add what's missing or reword what's incomplete, a fragment cannot stand alone as a sentence. Even so, we all use fragments in everyday speech, where their context and delivery make them understandable and therefore acceptable.

That bicycle over there.

Good job.

Not if I can help it.

In writing, fragments like these fail to communicate complete, coherent ideas. Notice how much more effective they are as complete sentences.

I'd like to buy that bicycle over there.

You did a good job sanding the floor.

Nobody will steal my seat if I can help it.

Some writers use fragments on purpose. Advertisers are fond of short, emphatic fragments that command attention, like quick jabs to the head.

For seafood lovers. Every Tuesday night. All you can eat.

Those who text-message or tweet compress what they write because time and character space are limited. They rely on the recipient of the message to fill in the gaps.

Thru with lab. CU @ 8. Pizza?

In academic writing, though, it is good practice to express your ideas in complete sentences. Besides, complete sentences usually convey more information than fragments—a big advantage in essay writing.

If you sometimes write fragments without recognizing them, learn to edit your work. Luckily, fragments are fairly easy to correct. Often you can attach a fragment to a neighboring sentence with a comma, a dash, or a colon. Sometimes you can combine two thoughts without adding any punctuation at all.

1a If a fragment is a phrase, link it to a nearby sentence, or make it a complete sentence.

You have two choices for revising a fragment if it is a phrase: (1) link it to an adjoining sentence, using punctuation such as a comma or a colon, or (2) add a missing subject or verb to make it a complete sentence.

Fragment Malcolm has two goals in life. *Wealth and power.*

Sentence Malcom has two goals in life: wealth and power. [The phrase *Wealth and power* has no verb; a colon links it to *goals.*]

Fragment Al ends his stories as he mixes his martinis. *With a twist.*

Sentence Al ends his stories as he mixes his martinis, with a twist. [The prepositional phrase *With a twist* has no subject or verb; a comma links it to the main clause.]

Fragment *To stamp out the union.* That was the bosses' plan.

Sentence To stamp out the union was the bosses' plan. [The infinitive phrase *To stamp out the union* has no main verb or subject; it becomes the sentence subject.]

Fragment The students taking the final exam in the auditorium.

Sentence The students were taking the final exam in the auditorium. [The helping verb *were* completes the verb and makes a sentence.]

1b If a fragment is a subordinate clause, link it to a nearby sentence, or drop the subordinating conjunction.

Some fragments are missing neither subject nor verb. Instead, they are subordinate clauses, unable to express complete thoughts unless linked with main clauses. When you find a subordinating conjunction at the start or in the middle of a word group, that word group may be a subordinate clause. If you have treated it as a complete sentence, you can correct the problem in two ways: (1) combine the fragment with a main clause (a complete sentence) nearby, or (2) make the subordinate clause into a complete sentence by dropping the subordinating conjunction.

Fragment	The new law will help create jobs. *If it passes.*
Sentence	The new law will help create jobs, if it passes.
Fragment	*Because Jay is an avid skier.* He loves winter in the mountains.
Sentence	Because Jay is an avid skier, he loves winter in the mountains.
Sentence	Jay is an avid skier. He loves winter in the mountains.

1c If a fragment has a participle but no other verb, change the participle to a main verb, or link the fragment to a nearby sentence.

A present participle (the *-ing* form of the verb) can serve as the main verb in a sentence only when it is accompanied by a form of *be* ("Sally *is working* harder than usual"). When a writer mistakenly uses a participle alone as a main verb, the result is a fragment.

Fragment Jon was used to the pressure of deadlines. *Having worked the night shift at the daily newspaper.*

One solution is to combine the fragment with an adjoining sentence.

Sentence Jon was used to the pressure of deadlines, having worked the night shift at the daily newspaper.

A second solution is to choose another form of the verb.

Sentence Jon was used to the pressure of deadlines. He *had worked* the night shift at the daily newspaper.

1d If a fragment is part of a compound predicate, link it with the complete sentence containing the subject and the rest of the predicate.

Fragment In spite of a pulled muscle, Jeremy ran the race. *And won.*

A fragment such as *And won* sounds satisfyingly punchy, but it lacks a subject. Create a sentence by linking the two verbs in the compound predicate.

Sentence In spite of a pulled muscle, Jeremy *ran* the race *and won.*

To emphasize the second verb, add punctuation and another subject.

Sentence In spite of a pulled muscle, Jeremy ran the race—and *he* won.

2 ◆ Comma Splices and Fused Sentences

Splice two ropes, or two strips of movie film, and you join them into one. Splice two main clauses by putting only a comma between them, however, and you get a faulty construction called a **comma splice.** Here, for instance, are two perfectly good main clauses, each separate, each able to stand on its own as a sentence:

The detective wriggled on his belly toward the campfire. The drunken smugglers didn't notice him.

Now let's splice those sentences with a comma.

Comma Splice The detective wriggled on his belly toward the campfire, the drunken smugglers didn't notice him.

The resulting comma splice makes for difficult reading.

Even more confusing than a comma splice is a **fused sentence:** two main clauses joined without any punctuation.

Fused Sentence The detective wriggled on his belly toward the campfire the drunken smugglers didn't notice him.

Lacking clues from the writer, a reader cannot tell where to pause. To understand the sentence, he or she must halt and reread.

◆ Sentence Parts at a Glance

The **subject (S)** identifies some person, place, thing, situation, or idea.

The **predicate (P)** includes a verb (expressing action or state of being) and makes an assertion about the subject.

An **object (O)** is the target or recipient of the action described by the verb.

A **complement (C)** renames or describes a subject or object.

S P C S P C

The *campus center is beautiful.* The new *sculpture draws crowds.*

The next two pages show five easy ways to eliminate both comma splices and fused sentences, also called **run-ons.** Your choice depends on the length and complexity of your main clauses and the effect you desire.

2a Write separate complete sentences to correct a comma splice or a fused sentence.

Comma Splice Sigmund Freud has been called an enemy of sexual repression, the truth is that he is not a friend of free love.

Fused Sentence Sigmund Freud has been called an enemy of sexual repression the truth is that he is not a friend of free love.

Neither sentence yields its meaning without a struggle. To point readers in the right direction, separate the clauses.

Sentence Sigmund Freud has been called an enemy of sexual repression. The truth is that he is not a friend of free love.

2b Use a comma and a coordinating conjunction to correct a comma splice or a fused sentence.

If both clauses are of roughly equal weight, you can use a comma to link them–as long as you add a coordinating conjunction after the comma.

Comma Splice Hurricane winds hit ninety miles an hour, they tore the roof from every house on Paradise Drive.

Sentence Hurricane winds hit ninety miles an hour, *and* they tore the roof from every house on Paradise Drive.

2c Use a semicolon or a colon to correct a comma splice or a fused sentence.

A semicolon can connect two closely related thoughts, emphasizing each one.

Comma Splice Hurricane winds hit ninety miles an hour, they tore the roof from every house on Paradise Drive.

Sentence Hurricane winds hit ninety miles an hour; they tore the roof from every house on Paradise Drive.

If the second thought illustrates or explains the first, add it with a colon.

Sentence The hurricane caused extensive damage: it tore the roof from every house on Paradise Drive.

The only punctuation powerful enough to link two main clauses single-handedly is a semicolon, a colon, or a period. A lone comma won't do the job except in the case of joining certain very short, similar main clauses.

Jill runs by day, Tom walks by night.

I came, I saw, I conquered.

Commas are not obligatory with short, similar clauses. If this issue is confusing, you can stick with semicolons to join all main clauses, short or long.

Jill runs by day; Tom walks by night.

I came; I saw; I conquered.

2d Use subordination to correct a comma splice or a fused sentence.

If one main clause is more important than the other or you want to give it more importance, make the less important one subordinate, which throws weight on the main clause. In effect, you show your reader how one idea relates to another: you decide which matters more.

Fused Sentence Hurricane winds hit ninety miles an hour they tore the roof from every house on Paradise Drive.

Sentence *When hurricane winds hit ninety miles an hour,* they tore the roof from every house on Paradise Drive.

Sentence Hurricane winds, *which tore the roof from every house on Paradise Drive,* hit ninety miles an hour.

2e Use a conjunctive adverb with a semicolon and a comma to correct a comma splice or a fused sentence.

If you want to cram more than one clause into a sentence, you may join two clauses with a **conjunctive adverb.** Conjunctive adverbs show relationships such as addition (*also, besides*), comparison (*likewise, similarly*), contrast (*instead, however*), emphasis (*namely, certainly*), cause and effect (*thus, therefore*), or time (*finally, subsequently*). These transitional words and phrases can be a useful way of linking clauses—but only with the right punctuation.

Comma Splice Freud has been called an enemy of sexual repression, however the truth is that he is not a friend of free love.

A writer might consider a comma plus the conjunctive adverb *however* enough to combine the two main clauses, but that glue won't hold. Stronger binding—the semicolon along with a comma—is required.

Sentence Freud has been called an enemy of sexual repression; however, the truth is that he is not a friend of free love.

3 ◆ Verbs

Most verbs are called **action verbs** because they show action (*swim, eat, sleep, win*). Some verbs are called **linking verbs** (*is, become, seem, feel*) because they show a state of being by linking the subject of a sentence with a word that renames or describes it. A few verbs accompany a main verb to give more information about its action; they are called **helping** or **auxiliary verbs** (*have, must, can*).

Verb Forms

3a Use a linking verb to connect the subject of a sentence with a subject complement.

A linking verb (LV) shows what the subject of a sentence *is* or is *like*. The verb creates a sort of equation, either positive or negative, between the subject and its complement (SC)—a noun, a pronoun, or an adjective.

LV SC

Julia will *make* a good *doctor.* [Noun]

LV SC

Jorge *is* not the *one.* [Pronoun]

LV SC

London weather *seems foggy.* [Adjective]

A verb may be a linking verb in some sentences and not in others. If you focus on what the verb means, you can usually tell how it is functioning.

I often *grow* sleepy after lunch.
[Linking verb + subject complement *sleepy*]

I often *grow* tomatoes in my garden.
[Transitive verb + direct object *tomatoes*]

◆ Common Linking Verbs at a Glance

Some linking verbs tell what a noun is, was, or will be.

be, become, remain: I *remain* optimistic.

grow: The sky is *growing* dark.

make: One plus two *makes* three.

prove: His warning *proved* accurate.

turn: The weather *turned* cold.

Some linking verbs tell what a noun might be.

appear, seem, look: The child *looks* cold.

(*continued*)

Most verbs of the senses can operate as linking verbs.

feel, smell, sound, taste: The smoothie *tastes* sweet.

3b Use helping verbs to add information about the main verb.

Adding a **helping** or **auxiliary verb** to a simple verb (*go, shoot, be*) allows you to express a wide variety of tenses and moods (*am going, did shoot, would have been*). (See 3g–3l and 3n–3p.) The parts of this combination, called a **verb phrase,** need not appear together but may be separated by other words.

I probably *am going* to France this summer.

You *should* not *have shot* that pigeon.

This change *may* well *have been contemplated* before the election.

◆ Helping Verbs at a Glance

Of the twenty-three helping verbs, fourteen can also act as main verbs that identify the central action.

be, is, am, are, was, were, being, been

do, does, did

have, has, had

The other nine act only as helping verbs, never as main verbs. As **modals,** they show actions that are possible, doubtful, necessary, required, and so on.

can, could, should, would, may, might, must, shall, will

3c Use the correct principal parts of the verb.

The **principal parts** are the forms the verb can take—alone or with helping verbs—to indicate the full range of times when an action or a state of being does, did, or will occur. Verbs have three principal parts: the base form or infinitive, the past tense, and the past participle.

- The **infinitive** is the simple, base, or dictionary form of the verb (*go, sing, laugh*), often preceded by *to* (*to go, to sing, to laugh*).
- The **past tense** signals completed action (*went, sang, laughed*).
- The **past participle** is combined with helping verbs to indicate action at various past or future times (*have gone, had sung, will have laughed*). With forms of *be*, it makes the passive voice. (See 3m.)

All verbs also have a present participle, the *-ing* form of the verb (*going, singing, laughing*). This form is used to make the progressive tenses. (See 3k and 3l.) It also can modify nouns and pronouns ("the *leaking* bottle") or, as a gerund, function as a noun ("*Sleeping all day* pleases me").

3d Use *-d* or *-ed* to form the past tense and past participle of regular verbs.

Most verbs in English are **regular verbs:** they form the past tense and past participle in a standard, predictable way. Regular verbs that end in *-e* add *-d* to the infinitive; those that do not end in *-e* add *-ed.*

INFINITIVE	PAST TENSE	PAST PARTICIPLE
(to) smile	smiled	smiled
(to) act	acted	acted

3e Use the correct forms for the past tense and past participle of irregular verbs.

At least two hundred **irregular verbs** form the past tense and past participle in some way other than adding *-d* or *-ed*: *go, went, gone.* Most irregular verbs, familiar to native English speakers, pose no problem.

3f Use the correct forms of *lie* and *lay* and *sit* and *set*.

Try taking two easy steps to eliminate confusion between *lie* and *lay.*

- Learn the principal parts and present participles of both.
- Remember that *lie,* in all its forms, is intransitive and never takes a direct object: "The island *lies* due east." *Lay* is transitive, so its forms always require an object to answer "Lay what?": "*Lay* that pistol down."

The same distinction exists between *sit* and *set.* Usually, *sit* is intransitive: "He *sits* on the stairs." *Set,* on the other hand, almost always takes an object: "He *sets* the bottle on the counter." There are, however, a few easily memorized exceptions: The sun *sets.* A hen *sets.* Gelatin *sets.* You *sit* the canter in a horse show.

Tenses

The **simple tenses** indicate whether the verb's action took place in the past, takes place in the present, or will take place in the future. The **perfect tenses** narrow the timing further, specifying that the action was or will be completed by the time of some other action. The **progressive tenses** add precision, indicating that the action did, does, or will continue.

3g Use the simple present tense for actions that take place once, repeatedly, or continuously in the present.

The simple present tense is the infinitive form of a regular verb plus *-s* or *-es* for the third-person singular (used with *a singular noun* or *he, she,* or *it*).

I like, I watch	we like, we watch
you like, you watch	you like, you watch
he/she/it likes, he/she/it watches	they like, they watch

◆ Verb Tenses at a Glance

NOTE: The examples show first person only.

SIMPLE TENSES

Present	***Past***	***Future***
I cook	I cooked	I will cook
I see	I saw	I will see

PERFECT TENSES

Present perfect	***Past perfect***	***Future perfect***
I have cooked	I had cooked	I will have cooked
I have seen	I had seen	I will have seen

PROGRESSIVE TENSES

Present progressive	***Past progressive***	***Future progressive***
I am cooking	I was cooking	I will be cooking
I am seeing	I was seeing	I will be seeing

Present perfect progressive	***Past perfect progressive***	***Future perfect progressive***
I have been cooking	I had been cooking	I will have been cooking
I have been seeing	I had been seeing	I will have been seeing

Some irregular verbs, such as *go,* form their simple present tense following the same rules as regular verbs (*go/goes*). Other irregular verbs, such as *be* and *have,* are special cases for which you should learn the correct forms.

I am, I have	we are, we have
you are, you have	you are, you have
he/she/it is, he/she/it has	they are, they have

You can use the simple present tense for an action happening right now ("I *welcome* this news"), happening repeatedly in the present ("Judy *goes* to church every Sunday"), or ongoing in the present ("Wesley *likes* ice cream"). In some cases, if you want to ask a question, intensify the action, or form a negative, use the helping verb *do* or *does* before the main verb.

I *do think* you should take the job. I *don't think* it will be difficult.

Does Christos *want it? Do* you *want* it? *Doesn't* anyone *want* it?

You can use the simple present for future action: "Football *starts* Wednesday." With *before, after,* or *when,* use it to express a future meaning: "When the team bus *arrives,* the players will board." Use it also for a general or timeless truth, even if the rest of the sentence is in a different tense:

Columbus proved in 1492 that the world *is* round.

Mr. Hammond will argue that people *are* basically good.

3h Use the simple past tense for actions already completed.

Regular verbs form the past tense by adding *-d* or *-ed* to the infinitive; the past tense of irregular verbs must be memorized. Use the past tense for an action at a specific past time, stated or implied.

Jack *enjoyed* the party. [Regular verb]

Akira *went* home early. [Irregular verb]

Though speakers may not pronounce the *-d* or *-ed* ending, standard written English requires that you add it to regular past tense verbs.

Nonstandard I *use* to wear weird clothes when I was a child.

Standard I *used* to wear weird clothes when I was a child.

In the past tense, you can use the helping verb *did* (past tense of *do*) to ask a question or intensify the action. Use *did* (or *didn't*) with the infinitive form of the main verb for both regular and irregular verbs.

I went.	I did go.	Why did I go?
You saw.	You did see.	What did you see?
She ran.	She did run.	Where did she run?

3i Use the simple future tense for actions that are expected to happen but have not happened yet.

Although the present tense can indicate future action ("We *go* on vacation next Monday"), most actions that have not yet taken place are expressed in the simple future tense, including promises and predictions.

George *will arrive* in time for dinner.

Will you please *show* him where to park?

To form the simple future tense, add *will* to the infinitive form of the verb.

I will go	we will go
you will go	you will go
he/she/it will go	they will go

3j Use the perfect tenses for actions completed at the time of another action.

The present perfect, past perfect, and future perfect tenses consist of a form of the helping verb *have* plus the past participle (*-ed* or *-en* form). The tense of *have* indicates the tense of the whole verb phrase.

The action of a **present perfect** verb was completed before the sentence is uttered. Its helping verb is in the present tense: *have* or *has.*

I *have* never *been* to Spain, but I *have been* to Mexico.

Have you *seen* Mr. Grimaldi? Mr. Grimaldi *has gone* home.

You can use the present perfect tense for an action completed before some other action: "I *have washed* my hands of the whole affair, but I am watching from a distance." With *for* or *since,* it shows an action begun in the past and still going on: "Max *has worked* in this office for years."

The action of a **past perfect** verb was completed before some other action in the past. Its helping verb is in the past tense: *had.*

The concert *had ended* by the time we found a parking space.

Until I met her, I *had* not *pictured* Jenna as a redhead.

Had you *wanted* to clean the house before your parents arrived?

In informal writing, the simple past may be used when the relationship between actions is made clear by *when, before, after,* or *until.*

Observers *saw* the plane catch fire before it landed.

The action of a **future perfect** verb will be completed by some point (specified or implied) in the future. Its helping verb is in the future tense: *will have.*

The builders *will have finished* the house by June.

When you get the new dime, *will* you *have collected* every coin you want?

The store *will* not *have closed* by the time we get there.

3k Use the simple progressive tenses for actions in progress.

The present progressive, past progressive, and future progressive tenses consist of a form of the helping verb *be* plus the present participle (the *-ing* form). The tense of *be* determines the tense of the whole verb phrase.

The **present progressive** expresses an action that began in the past and is taking place now. Its helping verb is in the present tense: *am, is,* or *are.*

I *am thinking* of a word that starts with *R.*

Is Stefan *babysitting* while Marie *is visiting* her sister?

You can express future action with the present progressive of *go* plus an infinitive phrase or with other words that make the time clear.

Are you *going to sign up* for the CPR class? Jeff *is taking* it Monday.

Use the present tense, not the present progressive, when verbs express being or emotion (*seem, be, belong, need*) rather than action.

I *guess* that the library is open. I *like* to study there.

The **past progressive** expresses an action that took place continuously at some time in the past, whether or not that action is still going on. Its helping verb is in the past tense: *was* or *were.*

The old men *were sitting* on the porch when we passed.

Lucy *was planning* to take the weekend off.

The **future progressive** expresses an action that will take place continuously at some time in the future. Its helping verb is in the future tense: *will be.* It also can use a form of *be* with *going to be.*

They *will be answering* the phones while she is gone.

She *is going to be flying* to Rome.

Will we *be dining* out every night on our vacation?

3l Use the perfect progressive tenses for continuing actions that began earlier.

Use the present perfect, the past perfect, or the future perfect progressive tense for an action that began earlier and did, does, or will continue.

The **present perfect progressive** indicates an action that started in the past and is continuing in the present. Form it by adding the present perfect of *be* (*has been, have been*) to the present participle (*-ing* form) of the main verb. Often *for* or *since* are used with this tense.

Fred *has been complaining* about his neighbor since the wild parties began.

Have you *been reading* Uma's postcards from England?

The **past perfect progressive** expresses a continuing action that was completed before another past action. Form it by adding the past perfect of *be* (*had been*) to the present participle of the main verb.

By the time Khalid finally arrived, I *had been waiting* for half an hour.

The **future perfect progressive** expresses an action that is expected to continue into the future for a specific time and then end before or continue beyond another future action. Form it by adding *will have been* to the present participle of the main verb.

They *will have been driving* for three days by the time they get to Oregon.

By fall Joanne *will have been attending* school longer than anyone else I know.

Voice

Intelligent students read challenging books.

Challenging books are read by intelligent students.

These two statements convey similar information, but their emphasis is different. In the first sentence, the subject (*students*) performs the verb's action (*read*); in the second sentence, the subject (*books*) receives the verb's action (*are read*). One sentence states its idea directly, the other indirectly. We say that the first sentence is in the **active voice** and the second is in the **passive voice.**

3m Use the active voice rather than the passive voice.

Verbs in the **active voice** consist of principal parts and helping verbs. Verbs in the **passive voice** consist of the past participle (*-ed* or *-en* form) preceded by a form of *be* ("you *are given,*" "I *was given,*" "she *will be given*"). Most writers prefer the active to the passive voice because it is clearer and simpler, requires fewer words, and identifies the actor and the action more explicitly.

Active Voice *Sergeants give* orders. *Privates obey* them.

Normally the subject of a sentence is the focus of readers' attention. If that subject does not perform the verb's action but instead receives the action, readers may wonder: What did the writer mean to emphasize?

Passive Voice *Orders are given* by sergeants. *They are obeyed* by privates.

Other writers misuse the passive voice to try to lend pomp to a humble truth. For example, "Slight technical difficulties are being experienced" may replace "The airplane needs repairs." Some even use the passive voice deliberately to obscure the truth.

You do not need to drop the passive voice entirely from your writing. Sometimes the performer of a verb's action is irrelevant, as in a lab report, which emphasizes the research, not the researcher. Sometimes the performer is understood: "Automobiles are built in Detroit." (It is understood that they are built *by people.*) Other times the performer is unknown and simply omitted: "Many fortunes were lost in the stock market crash of 1929." It's a good idea, though, to substitute the active voice for the passive unless you have a good reason for using the passive.

Mood

Still another characteristic of every verb is its **mood: indicative, imperative, or subjunctive.** The indicative mood is the most common. The imperative and subjunctive moods add valuable versatility.

3n Use the indicative mood to state a fact, to ask a question, or to express an opinion.

Most verbs in English are in the indicative mood.

Fact	Danika *left* home two months ago.
Question	*Will* she *find* happiness as a belly dancer?
Opinion	I *think* not.

3o Use the imperative mood to make a request or to give a command or direction.

The understood but usually unstated subject of a verb in the imperative mood is *you.* The verb's form is the base form or infinitive.

Request	Please *be* there before noon. [*You* please be there. . . .]
Command	*Hurry!* [*You* hurry!]
Direction	*Drive* east on State Street. [*You* drive east. . . .]

3p Use the subjunctive mood to express a wish, requirement, suggestion, or condition contrary to fact.

The subjunctive mood is used in a subordinate clause to suggest uncertainty: the action expressed by the verb may or may not actually take place as specified. In any clause opening with *that* and expressing a requirement, the verb is in the subjunctive mood and takes the base or infinitive form.

Professor Vogt requires that every student *complete* the essay promptly.

She asked that we *be* on time for all meetings.

When you use the subjunctive mood to describe a condition that is contrary to fact, use *were* if the verb is *be*; for other verbs, use the simple past tense. Wishes, whether present or past, follow the same rules.

If I *were* rich, I would be happy.

If I *had* a million dollars, I would be happy.

Elissa wishes that Ted *were* more goal oriented.

Elissa wished that Ted *knew* what he wanted to do.

For a condition that was contrary to fact at some point in the past, use the past perfect tense.

If I *had been* awake, I would have seen the meteor showers.

If Jessie *had known* you were coming, she would have cleaned her room.

Although use of the subjunctive has grown scarcer over the years, it still sounds crude to write "If I *was* you. . . ." If you ever feel that the subjunctive makes a sentence sound stilted, rewrite it with an infinitive phrase.

Professor Vogt requires every student *to complete* the essay promptly.

4 ◆ Subject–Verb Agreement

What does it mean for a subject and a verb to agree? Practically speaking, it means that their forms match: plural subjects take plural verbs, third-person subjects take third-person verbs, and so forth. When your subjects and verbs agree, you prevent a mismatch that could distract readers from your message.

4a A verb agrees with its subject in person and number.

Subject and verb agree in person (first, second, or third):

I write my research papers on my laptop. [Subject and verb in first person]

Eamon writes his papers in the lab. [Subject and verb in third person]

Subject and verb agree in number (singular or plural):

Grace has enjoyed college. [Subject and verb singular]

She and Jim have enjoyed their vacation. [Subject and verb plural]

The present tense of most verbs is the infinitive form, with no added ending except in the third-person singular. (See 3g–3l.)

I enjoy	we enjoy
you enjoy	you enjoy
he/she/it enjoys	they enjoy

Forms of the verb *be* vary.

I am	we are
you are	you are
he/she/it is	they are

4b A verb agrees with its subject, not with any words that intervene.

My *favorite* of O. Henry's short stories *is* "The Gift of the Magi."

Home sales, once driving the local economy, *have fallen* during recent years.

A singular subject linked to another noun or pronoun by a prepositional phrase beginning with wording such as *along with, as well as,* or *in addition to* remains a singular subject and takes a singular verb.

My cousin *James,* as well as his wife and son, *plans* to vote for Levine.

4c Subjects joined by *and* usually take a plural verb.

In most cases, a compound subject takes a plural verb.

"Howl" and "Gerontion" are Barry's favorite poems.

Sugar, salt, and fat adversely *affect* people's health.

However, phrases like *each boy and girl* or *every dog and cat* consider subjects individually, as "each one" or "every one," and use a singular verb.

Each man and woman in the room *has* a different story to tell.

Use a singular verb for two singular subjects that form or are one thing.

Lime juice and soda quenches your thirst.

4d With subjects joined by *or* or *nor*, the verb agrees with the part of the subject nearest to it.

Either they or *Max is* guilty.

Subjects containing *not . . . but* follow this rule also.

Not we but *George knows* the whole story.

You can remedy awkward constructions by rephrasing.

Either they are guilty or Max is.

We do not know the whole story, but George does.

4e Most collective nouns take singular verbs.

When a collective noun refers to a group of people acting as one, use a singular verb.

The *jury finds* the defendant guilty.

When the members of the group act individually, use a plural verb.

The *jury do* not yet *agree* on a verdict.

If you feel that using a plural verb results in an awkward sentence, reword the subject so that it refers to members of the group individually.

The *jurors do* not yet *agree* on a verdict.

4f Most indefinite pronouns take a third-person singular verb.

The indefinite pronouns *each, one, either, neither, anyone, anybody, anything, everyone, everybody, everything, no one, nobody, nothing, someone, somebody,* and *something* are considered singular and take a third-person singular verb.

Someone is bothering me.

Even when one of these subjects is followed by a phrase containing a noun or pronoun of a different person or number, use a singular verb.

Each of you *is* here to stay.

One of the pandas *seems* dangerously ill.

4g The indefinite pronouns *all, any,* and *some* use a singular or plural verb, depending on their meaning.

I have no explanation. *Is any* needed?

Any of the changes considered critical *have* been made already.

All is lost.

All of the bananas *are gone.*

Some of the blame *is* mine.

Some of us *are* Democrats.

None—like *all, any,* and *some*—takes a singular or a plural verb, depending on the sense in which the pronoun is used.

None of you *is* exempt.

None of his wives *were* blond.

4h In a subordinate clause with a relative pronoun as the subject, the verb agrees with the antecedent.

To determine the person and number of the verb in a subordinate clause whose subject is *who, which,* or *that,* look back at the word to which the pronoun refers. This word, known as an **antecedent**, is usually (but not always) the noun closest to the relative pronoun.

I have a sibling *who studies* day and night. [The antecedent of *who* is the third-person singular noun *sibling.* Therefore, the verb in the subordinate clause is third-person singular, *studies.*]

I bought one of the new cars *that have* defective brakes. [The antecedent of *that* is *cars,* so the verb is third-person plural, *have.*]

This is the only one of the mayor's new ideas *that has* any worth. [Here *one,* not *ideas,* is the antecedent of *that.* Thus, the verb in the subordinate clause is third-person singular, *has,* not *have.*]

4i A verb agrees with its subject even when the subject follows the verb.

Introductory expressions such as *there* or *here* change the ordinary order so that the subject follows the verb. Remember that verbs agree with subjects and that *here* and *there* are never subjects.

Here *is* a *riddle* for you.

There *are* twenty *people* in my math class.

Under the bridge *were* a broken-down *boat and* a worn *tire.*

4j A linking verb agrees with its subject, not its subject complement.

When a form of the verb *be* links two or more nouns, the subject is the noun before the linking verb. Nouns that follow the linking verb are subject complements. Make the verb agree with the subject of the sentence, not the subject complement.

Jim is a gentleman and a scholar.

Amy's *parents are* her most enthusiastic audience.

4k When the subject is a title, use a singular verb.

When I was younger, *Harry Potter and the Sorcerer's Stone was* my favorite book.

"People" sung by Barbra Streisand *is* my aunt's favorite song.

4l Singular nouns that end in *-s* take singular verbs.

Some nouns look plural even though they refer to a singular subject: *measles, logistics, mathematics, electronics.* Such nouns take singular verbs.

The *news is* that *economics has become* one of the most popular majors.

5 ◆ Pronoun Reference

The main use of pronouns is to refer in a brief, convenient form to some antecedent that has already been named. A pronoun usually has a noun or another pronoun as its antecedent. Often the antecedent is the subject or object of the same clause in which the pronoun appears.

Josie hit the *ball* after *its* first bounce.

Smashing into *Greg,* the ball knocked off *his* glasses.

The antecedent also can appear in a different clause or even a different sentence from the pronoun.

Josie hit the *ball* when *it* bounced back to *her.*

The *ball* smashed into *Greg. It* knocked off *his* glasses.

A pronoun as well as a noun can be an antecedent.

My *dog* hid in the closet when *she* had *her* puppies. [*Dog* is the antecedent of *she*; *she* is the antecedent of *her*.]

5a Name the pronoun's antecedent: don't just imply it.

When editing, be sure you have identified clearly the antecedent of each pronoun. A writer who leaves a key idea unsaid is likely to confuse readers.

Vague Ted wanted a Norwegian canoe because he'd heard that *they* produce the lightest canoes afloat.

What noun or pronoun does *they* refer to? Not to *Norwegian,* which is an adjective. We may guess that this writer has in mind Norwegian canoe builders, but no such noun has been mentioned. To make the sentence work, the writer must supply an antecedent for *they.*

Clear Ted wanted a Norwegian canoe because he'd heard that Norway produces [*or* Norwegians produce] the lightest canoes afloat.

Watch out for possessive nouns. They won't work as antecedents.

Vague	On William's canoe, *he* painted a skull and bones.
Clear	On his canoe, William painted a skull and bones.
Vague	In Hemingway's story, he describes the powerful sea.
Clear	In the story, Hemingway describes the powerful sea.

5b Adjective Clauses and Relative Pronouns

Be sure to use relative pronouns (*who, whose, which, that*) correctly in sentences with adjective clauses. Use *who,* not *which,* for a person. Select *that* to introduce necessary information that defines or specifies; reserve *which* for additional, but not defining, information.

- Do not omit the relative pronoun when it is the subject within the adjective clause.

Incorrect	The woman *gave us directions to the museum* told us not to miss the Picasso exhibit.
Correct	The woman *who gave us directions to the museum* told us not to miss the Picasso exhibit. [*Who* is the subject of the adjective clause.]

- In speech and informal writing, you can imply (not state) a relative pronoun when it is the object of a verb or preposition within the adjective clause. In formal writing, you should use the relative pronoun.

Formal	Jamal forgot to return the book *that I gave him.* [*That* is the object of *gave.*]
Informal	Jamal forgot to return the book *I gave him.* [The relative pronoun *that* is implied.]
Formal	This is the box *in which we found the jewelry.* [*Which* is the object of the preposition *in.*]
Informal	This is the box *we found the jewelry in.* [The relative pronoun *which* is implied.]

NOTE: When the relative pronoun is omitted, the preposition moves to the end of the sentence but must not be left out.

- *Whose* is the only possessive form of a relative pronoun. It is used with persons, animals, and things.

Incorrect	I bought a chair *that its* legs were wobbly.
Correct	I bought a chair *whose* legs were wobbly.

NOTE: When in doubt about a pronoun, you can rephrase the sentence: I bought a chair *with wobbly legs.*

5c Give the pronoun *it, this, that,* or *which* a clear antecedent.

Vagueness arises, thick as fog, whenever *it, this, that,* or *which* points to something a writer assumes is said but indeed isn't. Often the best way out of the fog is to substitute a specific noun or expression for the pronoun.

Vague I was an only child, and *it* was hard.

Clear I was an only child, and my solitary life was hard.

Vague Judy could not get along with her younger brother. *This* is the reason she wanted to get her own apartment.

Clear Because Judy could not get along with her younger brother, she wanted to get her own apartment.

5d Make the pronoun's antecedent clear.

Confusion strikes if a pronoun points in two or more directions. When more than one antecedent is possible, the reader wonders which the writer means.

Confusing Hanwei shouted to Kenny to take off his burning sweater.

Whose sweater does *his* mean—Kenny's or Hanwei's? Simply changing a pronoun won't clear up the confusion. The writer needs to revise enough to move the two possible antecedents out of each other's way.

Clear "Kenny!" shouted Hanwei. "Your sweater's on fire! Take it off!"

Clear Flames were shooting from Kenny's sweater. Hanwei shouted to Kenny to take it off.

Clear Hanwei realized that his sweater was on fire and shouted to Kenny for help.

5e Place the pronoun close to its antecedent to keep the relationship clear.

Watch out for distractions that slip in between noun and pronoun. If your sentence contains two or more nouns that look like antecedents to a pronoun, your readers may become bewildered.

Confusing Harper steered his dinghy alongside the cabin cruiser that the drug smugglers had left anchored under an overhanging willow in the tiny harbor and eased it to a stop.

What did Harper ease to a stop? By the time readers reach the end of the sentence, they are likely to have forgotten. To avoid confusion, keep the pronoun and its antecedent reasonably close together.

Clear Harper steered his dinghy into the tiny harbor and eased it to a stop alongside the cabin cruiser that the drug smugglers had left anchored under an overhanging willow.

Never force your readers to stop and think, "What does that pronoun stand for?" You, the writer, have to do this thinking for them.

6 ◆ Pronoun–Antecedent Agreement

A pronoun's job is to fill in for a noun, much as an actor's double fills in for the actor. Pronouns are a short, convenient way to avoid repeating the noun.

The sheriff drew a six-shooter; he fired twice.

In this action-packed sentence, first comes a noun (*sheriff*) and then a pronoun (*he*) that refers back to it. *Sheriff* is the antecedent of *he*. Just as verbs need to agree with their subjects, pronouns need to agree with the nouns they stand for without shifting number, person, or gender in midsentence.

6a Pronouns agree with their antecedents in person and number.

A pronoun matches its antecedent in person (first, second, or third) and in number (singular or plural), even when intervening words separate the pronoun and its antecedent.

Faulty All *campers* should bring *your* knapsacks.

Here, noun and pronoun disagree in person: third person *campers*; second person *your*.

Faulty Every *camper* should bring *their* knapsack.

Here, noun and pronoun disagree in number: singular *camper*; plural *their*.

Revised All *campers* should bring *their* knapsacks.

Revised Every *camper* should bring *his or her* knapsack. (See also 6f.)

6b Most antecedents joined by *and* require a plural pronoun.

A **compound subject** is plural; use a plural pronoun to refer to it.

George, who has been here before, *and Jenn,* who hasn't, will need *their* maps.

If the nouns in a compound subject refer to the same person or thing, they make up a singular antecedent. Use a singular pronoun too.

The *owner and founder* of this company carries *his* laptop everywhere.

6c A pronoun agrees with the closest part of an antecedent joined by *or* or *nor*.

If your subject is two or more nouns (or a combination of nouns and pronouns) connected by *or* or *nor,* look closely at the subject's parts. Are they all singular? If so, your pronoun should be singular.

Neither *Joy nor Jean* remembered *her* book last week.

If *Sam, Arthur, or Dieter* shows up, tell *him* I'm looking for *him.*

If the part of the subject closest to the pronoun is plural, the pronoun should be plural.

Neither *Joy nor her sisters* rode *their* bikes today.

If you see *Sam, Arthur, or their friends,* tell *them* I'm looking for *them.*

6d An antecedent that is a singular indefinite pronoun takes a singular pronoun.

Most indefinite pronouns (such as *everyone* and *anybody*) are singular in meaning, so the pronouns that refer to them are also singular.

Either of the boys can do it, as long as *he's* on time.

Warn *anybody* who's still in *her* swimsuit that a shirt is required for dinner.

An indefinite pronoun that is plural (such as *both, many*) takes a plural pronoun.

Tell *both* the guests I will see *them* soon.

6e Most collective nouns used as antecedents require singular pronouns.

When the members of a group (such as a committee, family, jury, or trio) act as a unit, use a singular pronoun to refer to them.

The *cast* for the play will be posted as soon as the director chooses *it.*

When the group members act individually, use a plural pronoun.

The *cast* will go *their* separate ways when summer ends.

6f A pronoun agrees with its antecedent in gender.

If *one of your parents* brings you to camp, invite *him* for lunch.

While technically correct (the singular *he* refers to the singular *one*), this sentence overlooks the fact that some parents are male, some female.

If *one of your parents* brings you to camp, invite *him or her* for lunch.

If your *parents* bring you to camp, invite *them* for lunch.

7 ◆ Adjectives and Adverbs

An adjective's job is to provide information about the person, place, object, or idea named by the noun or pronoun.

Karen bought a *small red* car.

The radios *on sale* are an *excellent* value.

An adverb describes a verb, adjective, or other adverb.

Karen bought her car *quickly*.

The phones arrived *yesterday*; we put them *in the electronics department*.

◆ Adjectives and Adverbs at a Glance

Adjectives:

1. Typically answer the question Which? or What kind?
2. Modify nouns or pronouns

Adverbs:

1. Answer the question How? When? Where? or sometimes Why?
2. Modify verbs, adjectives, and other adverbs

7a Use an adverb, not an adjective, to modify a verb, adjective, or another adverb.

Faulty Karen bought her car *quick*.

Faulty It's *awful* hot today.

Though an informal speaker might get away with these sentences, a writer cannot. *Quick* and *awful* are adjectives, so they can modify only nouns or pronouns. Adverbs are needed to modify the verb *bought* and the adjective *hot*.

Edited Karen bought her car *quickly*.

Edited It's *awfully* hot today.

7b Use an adjective, not an adverb, as a subject complement or an object complement.

If we write, "Her old car looked awful," the adjective *awful* is a **subject complement:** it follows a linking verb and modifies the subject, *car.* An **object complement** completes the description of a direct object and can be an adjective or a noun, but never an adverb.

> Early to bed and early to rise makes a man *healthy, wealthy,* and *wise.* [Adjectives modifying the direct object *man*]

When you are not sure whether you're dealing with an object complement or an adverb, look closely at the word's role in the sentence. If it modifies a noun, it is an object complement and should be an adjective.

> The coach called the referee *stupid* and *blind.* [*Stupid* and *blind* are adjectives modifying the direct object *referee.*]

If it modifies a verb, you want an adverb instead.

> In fact, the ref had called the play *correctly.* [*Correctly* is an adverb modifying the verb *called.*]

7c Use *good* as an adjective and *well* as an adverb.

> This sandwich tastes *good.* [The adjective *good* is a subject complement following the linking verb *tastes* and modifying the noun *sandwich.*]
>
> Al's skin healed *well* after surgery. [The adverb *well* modifies the verb *healed.*]

Only if the verb is a linking verb can you safely follow it with *good.* Other kinds of verbs need adverbs, not subject complements.

Faulty After a bad start, the game ended *good.*

Edited After a bad start, the game ended *well.*

Complications arise when we write or speak about health. It is perfectly correct to say *I feel good,* using the adjective *good* as a subject complement after the linking verb *feel.* However, generations of confusion have nudged the adverb *well* into the adjective category, too. A nurse may speak of "a well baby"; greeting cards urge patients to "get well"—meaning, "become healthy." Just as *healthy* is an adjective here, so is *well.*

When someone asks, "How do you feel?" you can duck the issue with "Fine!" Otherwise, in speech *good* or *well* is acceptable; in writing, use *good.*

7d Form comparatives and superlatives of most adjectives and adverbs with *-er* and *-est* or *more* and *most*.

Comparatives and superlatives are forms that describe one thing in relation to another. Put most adjectives into comparative form (for two things) by adding *-er* and into superlative form (for three or more) by adding *-est.*

The budget deficit is *larger* than the trade deficit.

This year's trade deficit is the *largest* ever.

We usually form the comparative and superlative of potentially cumbersome long adjectives with *more* and *most* rather than with *-er* and *-est*.

The lake is *more beautiful* than I'd imagined.

The shoreline is the *most beautiful* in the region.

For short adverbs that do not end in *-ly*, usually add *-er* and *-est*. With all others, use *more* and *most*. (Also see 7f.)

The trade deficit grows *fastest* and *most uncontrollably* when exports are down.

For negative comparisons, use *less* and *least* for adjectives and adverbs.

Michael's speech was *less dramatic* than Louie's.

Paulette spoke *less dramatically* than Michael.

Use irregular adjectives and adverbs (such as *bad* and *badly*) with care.

Tom's golf game is *bad*, but no *worse* than George's.

Tom plays golf *badly*, but no *worse* than George does.

7e Omit *more* and *most* with an adjective or adverb that is already comparative or superlative.

Some words become comparative or superlative when we tack on *-er* or *-est*. Others, such as *top*, *favorite*, and *unique*, mark whatever they modify as one of a kind. Neither category requires further assistance to make its point. To say "a *more worse* fate" or "my *most favorite* movie" is redundant.

Faulty Lisa is *more uniquely* qualified for the job than any other candidate.

Edited Lisa is *better* qualified for the job than any other candidate.

Edited Lisa is *uniquely* qualified for the job.

7f Use the comparative form of an adjective or adverb to compare two people or things, the superlative form to compare more than two.

No matter how wonderful something is, we can call it the *best* only when we compare it with more than one other thing. Any comparison between two things uses the comparative form (*better*), not the superlative (*best*).

Faulty Chocolate and vanilla are both good, but I like chocolate *best*.

Edited Chocolate and vanilla are both good, but I like chocolate *better*.

8 ◆ Shifts

Just as you can change position to view a scene from different vantage points, in your writing you can change the time or perspective. However, shifting tense or point of view unconsciously or unnecessarily within a passage creates ambiguity and confusion for readers.

8a Maintain consistency in verb tense.

In a passage or an essay, use the same verb tense unless the time changes.

Inconsistent The driver *yelled* at us to get off the bus, so I *ask* him why, and he *tells* me it *is* none of my business.

Consistent present The driver *yells* at us to get off the bus, so I *ask* him why, and he *tells* me it *is* none of my business.

Consistent past The driver *yelled* at us to get off the bus, so I *asked* him why, and he *told* me it *was* none of my business.

8b If the time changes, change the verb tense.

To write about events in the past, use past tense verbs. To write about events in the present, use present tense verbs. If the time shifts, change tense.

> I *do* not *like* the new television programs this year. The comedies *are* too realistic to be amusing, the adventure shows *don't have* much action, and the law enforcement dramas *drag* on and on. Last year the programs *were* different. The sitcoms *were* hilarious, the adventure shows *were* action packed, and the dramas *were* fast paced. I *prefer* last year's reruns to this year's shows.

The time and the verb tense change appropriately from present (*do like, are, don't have, drag*) to past (*were, were, were, were*) back to present (*prefer*), contrasting this year's *present* with last year's *past* programming.

When writing about literature, the accepted practice is to use present tense verbs to summarize what happens in a story, poem, or play. When discussing other aspects of a work, use present tense for present time, past tense for past, and future tense for future.

> Steinbeck *wrote* "The Chrysanthemums" in 1937. [Past tense for past time]

> In "The Chrysanthemums," Steinbeck *describes* the Salinas Valley as "a closed pot" cut off from the world by fog. [Present tense for story summary]

8c Maintain consistency in the voice of verbs.

Shifting unnecessarily from active to passive voice may confuse readers.

Inconsistent My roommates and I *sit* up late many nights talking about our problems. Grades, teachers, jobs, money, and dates *are discussed* at length.

Consistent	My roommates and I *sit* up late many nights talking about our problems. We *discuss* grades, teachers, jobs, money, and dates at length.

8d Maintain consistency in person.

Person indicates your perspective as a writer. First person (*I, we*) establishes a personal, informal relationship with readers as does second person (*you*), which brings readers into the writing. Third person (*he, she, it, they*) is more formal and objective. In a formal scientific report, second person is seldom appropriate, and first, if used, might be reserved for reporting procedures. In a personal essay, using *he, she,* or *one* to refer to yourself would sound stilted. Choose the person appropriate for your purpose, and stick to it.

Inconsistent	College *students* need transportation, but *you* need a job to pay for the insurance and the gasoline.
Consistent	College *students* need transportation, but *they* need jobs to pay for the insurance and the gasoline.
Inconsistent	*Anyone* can go skydiving if *you* have the guts.
Consistent	*Anyone* can go skydiving if *he or she* has the guts.
Consistent	*You* can go skydiving if *you* have the guts.

8e Maintain consistency in the mood of verbs.

Avoid shifts in mood, usually from indicative to imperative.

Inconsistent	Counselors *advised* students to register early. Also *pay* tuition on time. [Shift from indicative to imperative]
Consistent	Counselors *advised* students to register early. They also *advised* them to pay their tuition on time. [Both indicative]

8f Maintain consistency in level of language.

Attempting to impress readers, writers sometimes inflate their language or slip into slang or informal wording. The level of language should be appropriate to your purpose and your audience throughout an essay.

If you are writing a personal essay, use informal language.

Inconsistent	I felt like a typical tourist. I carried an expensive digital camera with lots of icons I didn't quite know how to decode. But I was in a quandary because there was such a plethora of picturesque tableaus to record for posterity.

Instead of suddenly shifting to formal language, the writer could end simply: *But with so much beautiful scenery all around, I couldn't decide where to start.*

If you are writing an academic essay, use formal language.

Inconsistent Puccini's *Turandot* is set in a China of legends, riddles, and fantasy. Brimming with beautiful melodies, this opera is music drama at its most spectacular. It rules!

Cutting the last sentence avoids an unnecessary shift in formality.

9 ◆ Glossary of Grammar Terms

Absolute phrase: An expression, usually a noun followed by a participle, that modifies an entire clause or sentence and can appear anywhere in the sentence: The stallion pawed the ground, *chestnut mane and tail swirling in the wind.*

Antecedent: The word to which a pronoun refers: *Lyn* plays golf, and *she* putts well.

Appositive: A word or group of words that adds information by identifying a subject or object in a different way: my dog *Rover*, Hal's brother *Fred.*

Clause: A group of related words that includes both a subject and a verb: *The sailboats raced* (independent clause) *until the sun set* (subordinate clause).

Collective noun: A singular noun that represents a group of people or items, such as *committee, family, jury, trio.*

Compound predicate: A predicate consisting of two or more verbs linked by a conjunction: My sister *stopped and stared.*

Compound subject: A subject consisting of two or more nouns or pronouns linked by *and: Scott and Liz* drove home.

Conjunction: A linking word that connects words or groups of words through coordination (*and, but*) or subordination (*because, although, unless*).

Conjunctive adverb: A linking word that can connect independent clauses and show a relationship between two ideas: Jen studied hard; *finally*, she passed the exam.

Coordinating conjunction: A one-syllable linking word (*and, but, for, or, nor, so, yet*) that joins elements with equal or near-equal importance: Jack *and* Jill, sink *or* swim.

Correlative conjunction: A pair of linking words (such as *either/or*, *not only/but also*) that appear separately but work together to join elements of a sentence: *Neither* his friends *nor* hers like pizza.

Direct object: The target of a verb that completes the action performed by the subject or asserted about the subject: I met *the sheriff.*

Gerund: A form of a verb, ending in *-ing*, that functions as a noun: Lacey likes *playing* in the steel band.

Indirect object: A person or thing affected by the subject's action, usually the recipient of the direct object, through the action indicated by a verb such as *bring, get, offer, promise, sell, show, tell*, and *write:* Charlene asked *you* a question.

Infinitive: The base form of a verb, often preceded by *to* (*to go, to play*).

Interjection: A word or expression (*oh, alas*) that inserts an outburst of feeling at the beginning, middle, or end of a sentence.

Intransitive verb: A verb that is complete in itself and needs no object: The surgeon *paused.*

Linking verb: A verb (*is, become, seem, feel*) that shows a state of being by linking the sentence subject with a word that renames or describes the subject: The sky *is* blue.

Main clause: A group of words that has both a subject and a verb and can stand alone as a complete sentence: *My friends play softball.*

Modifier: A word (such as an adjective or adverb), phrase, or clause that provides more information about other parts of a sentence: Plays *staged by the drama class* are *always successful.*

Object complement: A noun, an adjective, or a group of words that renames or describes a direct object: The judges rated Hugo *the best skater.*

Object of a preposition: The noun or pronoun that follows the preposition (such as *in, on, at, of, from*) that connects it to the rest of the sentence: She opened the door to the *garage.*

Parenthetical expression: An aside to readers or a transitional expression such as *for example* or *in contrast.*

Personal pronoun: A pronoun (*I, me, you, it, he, we, them*) that stands for a noun that names a person or thing: Mark awoke slowly, but suddenly *he* bolted from the bed.

Phrase: Two or more related words that work together but may lack a subject (*will walk*), a verb (*my uncle*), or both (*to the attic*).

Predicate: The part of a sentence that makes an assertion about the subject involving an action (Birds *fly*), a relationship (Birds *have feathers*), or a state of being (Birds *are warm-blooded*).

Preposition: A transitional word (such as *in, on, at, of, from*) that leads into a phrase such as *in the bar, under a rickety table.*

Prepositional phrase: The preposition and its object (a noun or pronoun), plus any modifiers: *in the bar, under a rickety table.*

Present participle: A form of a verb ending in *-ing* that cannot function alone as a main verb but can act as an adjective: *Leading* the pack, Michael crossed the finish line.

Relative pronoun: A pronoun (*who, which, that, what, whom, whomever, whose*) that opens a subordinate clause, modifying a noun or pronoun in another clause: The gift *that* I received is very practical.

Sentence: A word group that includes both a subject and a predicate and can stand alone.

Subject: The part of a sentence that names something–a person, an object, an idea, a situation–about which the verb in the predicate makes an assertion: The *king* lives.

Subject complement: A noun, an adjective, or a group of words that follows a linking verb and renames or describes the subject: This plum tastes *ripe*.

Subordinate clause: A group of words that contains a subject and a verb but cannot stand alone because it depends on a main clause to help it make sense: *When it snows*, a truck plows our road.

Subordinating conjunction: A word (such as *because, although, if, when*) used to make one clause dependent on, or subordinate to, another: *Unless* you have a key, we are locked out.

Tense: The time when the action of a verb did, does, or will occur.

Transitive verb: An action verb that must have an object to complete its meaning: Alan *hit* the ball.

Verb: A word that shows action (The cow *jumped* over the moon) or a state of being (The cow *is* brown).

2

Effective Sentences

10 • Misplaced and Dangling Modifiers

The purpose of a **modifier,** such as an adjective or adverb, is to give readers more information. To do so, the modifier must be linked clearly to whatever it is meant to modify or describe. If you wrote, "We saw a stone wall around a house on a grassy hill, beautiful and distant," your readers would have to guess what was *beautiful* and *distant:* the wall, the house, or the hill. Edit your modifiers—especially prepositional phrases and subordinate clauses—to make sure each is in the right place.

10a Keep modifiers close to what they modify.

Misplaced modifiers—phrases and clauses that wander away from what they modify—produce results more likely to amuse readers than to inform them. Place your modifiers as close as possible to whatever they modify.

Misplaced She offered toys to all the children in colorful packages. [Does the phrase *in colorful packages* modify *toys* or *children*?]

Clear She offered toys in colorful packages to all the children.

Misplaced We need to remove the dishes from the crates that got chipped. [Does the clause *that got chipped* modify *dishes* or *crates*?]

Clear We need to remove from the crates the dishes that got chipped.

10b Place each modifier so that it clearly modifies only one thing.

A **squinting modifier** is one that looks two ways, leaving the reader uncertain whether it modifies the word before or after it. To avoid ambiguity, place your modifier close to the word it modifies and away from another that might cause confusion.

Squinting	The book that appealed to Amy *tremendously* bored Marcus.
Clear	The book that *tremendously* appealed to Amy bored Marcus.
Clear	The book that appealed to Amy bored Marcus *tremendously*.

10c State something in the sentence for each modifier to modify.

Generally readers assume that a modifying phrase at the start of a sentence refers to the subject of the main clause to follow. If readers encounter a modifying phrase midway through a sentence, they assume that it modifies something just before or (less often) after it.

Feeling tired after the long hike, Jason went to bed.

Alicia, while sympathetic, was not inclined to help.

Sometimes a writer slips up, allowing a modifying phrase to dangle. A **dangling modifier** is one that doesn't modify anything in its sentence.

Dangling	*Noticing a pain behind his eyes,* an aspirin seemed a good idea. [The opening doesn't modify *aspirin* or, in fact, anything.]

To correct a dangling modifier, first figure out what noun, pronoun, or noun phrase the modifier is meant to modify. Then make that word or phrase the subject of the main clause.

Clear	*Noticing a pain behind his eyes, he* decided to take an aspirin.

Another way to correct a dangling modifier is to turn the dangler into a clause that includes the missing noun or pronoun.

Dangling	Her progress, *although talented,* has been slowed by poor work habits.
Clear	*Although she is talented,* her progress has been slowed by poor work habits.

Sometimes rewriting will clarify what the modifier modifies.

Clear *Although talented,* she has been hampered by poor work habits.

11 ◆ Parallel Structure

You use **parallel structure,** or parallelism, when you create a series of words, phrases, clauses, or sentences with the same grammatical form. The pattern created by the series—its parallel structure—emphasizes the similarities or differences among the items, whether things, qualities, actions, or ideas.

My favorite foods are roast beef, apple pie, and linguine with clam sauce.

Louise is charming, witty, intelligent, and talented.

Manuel likes to swim, ride, and run.

Dave likes movies that scare him and books that make him laugh.

Each series is a perfect parallel construction, composed of equivalent words: nouns in the first example, then adjectives, verbs, and adjective clauses.

11a In a series linked by a coordinating conjunction, keep all elements in the same grammatical form.

A coordinating conjunction (*and, but, for, or, nor, so, yet*) cues your readers to expect a parallel structure. Whether your series consists of single words, phrases, or clauses, its parts should balance one another.

Awkward The puppies are *tiny, clumsily bumping* into each other, *and cute.*

Two elements in this series are parallel one-word adjectives (*tiny, cute*), but the third, the verb phrase *clumsily bumping,* is inconsistent.

Parallel The puppies are *tiny, clumsy, and cute.*

Don't mix verb forms, such as gerunds and infinitives, in a series.

Awkward Plan a winter vacation if you like *skiing and to skate.*

Parallel Plan a winter vacation if you like *skiing and skating.*

Parallel Plan a winter vacation if you like *to ski and to skate.*

In a series of phrases or clauses, be sure that all elements in the series are similar in form, even if they are not similar in length.

Awkward The fight in the bar takes place *after the two lovers have their scene together* but *before the car chase.* [The clause starting with *after* is not parallel to the phrase starting with *before.*]

Parallel The fight in the bar takes place *after the love scene* but *before the car chase.*

Awkward You can take the key, or don't forget to leave it under the mat. [The declarative clause starting with *You can* is not parallel to the imperative clause starting with *don't forget.*]

Parallel You can *take the key,* or you can *leave it* under the mat.

11b In a series linked by correlative conjunctions, keep all elements in the same grammatical form.

When you use a correlative conjunction, follow each part with a similarly structured word, phrase, or clause.

Awkward I'm looking forward *to either attending* Saturday's wrestling match *or to seeing* it on closed-circuit TV. [*To* precedes the first part (*to either*) but follows the second part (*or to*).]

Parallel I'm looking forward *either to attending* Saturday's wrestling match *or to seeing* it on closed-circuit TV.

Awkward Take my advice: try *neither to be first nor last* in the lunch line. [*To be* follows the first part but not the second part.]

Parallel Take my advice: try to be *neither first nor last* in the lunch line.

11c Make the elements in a comparison parallel in form.

A comparative word such as *than* or *as* cues the reader to expect a parallel structure. This makes logical sense: to be compared, two things must resemble each other, and parallel structure emphasizes this resemblance.

Awkward Philip likes *fishing* better than *to sail.*

Parallel Philip likes *fishing* better than *sailing.*

Parallel Philip likes *to fish* better than *to sail.*

Awkward *Maintaining* railway lines is as important to the public transportation system as *to buy* new trains.

Parallel *Maintaining* railway lines is as important to the public transportation system as *buying* new trains.

11d Reinforce parallel structure by repeating rather than mixing lead-in words.

Parallel structures are especially useful when a sentence contains a series of clauses or phrases. For example, try to precede potentially confusing clauses with *that, who, when, where,* or some other connective, repeating the same connective every time to help readers follow them with ease.

No one in this country needs a government *that* aids big business at the expense of farmers and workers, *that* ravages the environment in the name of progress, or *that* slashes budgets for health and education.

If the same lead-in word won't work for all elements in a series, try changing the order of the elements to minimize variation.

Awkward	The new school building is large but not very comfortable, and expensive but unattractive.
Parallel	The new school building is large and expensive, but uncomfortable and unattractive.

12 ◆ Sentence Variety

Most writers rely on some patterns more than others to express ideas directly and efficiently, but sometimes they combine sentence elements in unexpected ways to emphasize ideas and to surprise readers.

◆ Types of Sentences at a Glance

A **simple sentence** contains only one main clause, even with modifiers, objects, complements, and phrases in addition to its subject and verb.

MAIN CLAUSE

Even amateur stargazers can easily locate the Big Dipper in the night sky.

It may have a compound subject (*Fred and Sandy*) or a compound verb (*laughed and cried*). Sometimes its subject is unstated but clearly understood: "Run!"

A **compound sentence** consists of two or more main clauses joined by a coordinating conjunction such as *and* or *but*, by a semicolon, or by a semicolon followed by a conjunctive adverb such as *however* or *nevertheless*.

MAIN CLAUSE — MAIN CLAUSE

I would like to accompany you, but I can't.

MAIN CLAUSE — MAIN CLAUSE

My car broke down; therefore, I missed the first day of class.

A **complex sentence** has one main clause and one or more subordinate clauses.

MAIN CLAUSE — SUBORDINATE CLAUSE

I will be at the airport when you arrive.

The relative pronoun linking the clauses may be implied.

MAIN CLAUSE — SUBORDINATE CLAUSE

I know [that] you saw us.

(*continued*)

A **compound-complex sentence** combines a compound sentence (two or more main clauses) and a complex sentence (at least one subordinate clause).

MAIN CLAUSE | SUBORDINATE CLAUSE | SUBORDINATE CLAUSE | MAIN CLAUSE

I'd gladly wait until you're ready; but if I do, I'll miss the boat.

12a Normal Sentences

In a **normal sentence,** a writer puts the subject before the verb at the beginning of the main clause. This pattern is the most common in English because it expresses ideas in the most straightforward manner.

Most high school *students* today *want* interesting classes.

12b Inverted Sentences

In an **inverted sentence,** a writer inverts or reverses the subject–verb order to emphasize an idea in the predicate.

Normal *My peers are uninterested* in reading.

Inverted How *uninterested* in reading *are my peers*!

12c Cumulative Sentences

In a **cumulative sentence,** a writer piles details at the end of a sentence to help readers visualize a scene or understand an idea.

> They came walking out in heavily brocaded yellow and black costumes, the familiar "toreador" suit, heavy with gold embroidery, cape, jacket, shirt and collar, knee breeches, pink stockings, and low pumps.
>
> —Ernest Hemingway, "Bull Fighting a Tragedy"

12d Periodic Sentences

The positions of emphasis in a sentence are the beginning and the end. In a **periodic sentence,** a writer suspends the main clause for a climactic ending, emphasizing an idea by withholding it until the end.

> Leaning back in his chair, shaking his head slowly back and forth, frustrated over his inability to solve the quadratic equation, Franklin scowled.

3

Word Choice

13 ◆ Appropriateness

When you talk to people face-to-face, you can gauge their reactions to what you say. Often their responses guide your tone and your choice of words. When you write, you cannot gauge your readers' reactions as easily because you cannot see them. Instead, you must imagine yourself in their place, focusing especially closely on their responses when you revise.

Besides affecting how well you accomplish your purpose as a writer, your language can also affect how well you are regarded by others. When you accurately assess the tone, formality, and word choice expected in a situation, you use the power of language to enhance your own position. When you misjudge, you may find that others judge you harshly in response. Your prospective employer, your teacher, your supervisor, or others in positions of authority may or may not be aware of their power to set language expectations or of their own responses to your use of language. However, when they see your efforts to write and speak as they feel a situation requires, they will appreciate your effort to become one who can use language powerfully, adjusting it to your audience and situation.

13a Choose a tone appropriate for your topic and audience.

Like a speaker, a writer may come across as friendly or aloof, furious or merely annoyed, playful or grimly serious. This attitude is the writer's **tone** and, like a speaker's tone, it strongly influences the audience's response. A tone that seems right to a reader conveys your concern for the reader's reaction. For instance, taking a humorous approach to a disease such as cancer or AIDS might create an inappropriate tone that ignores a reader's feelings and thus meets with rejection. To convey your tone, use sentence length, level of language, and vocabulary. Choose formal or informal language, coolly objective words, or words loaded with emotional connotations. The key is to be aware of your readers and their expectations.

13b Choose a level of formality appropriate for your tone.

Considering the tone you want to convey to your audience helps you choose words that are neither too formal nor too informal. By **formal** language, we mean the impersonal language of educated persons who consider topics seriously. Usually written, formal language is marked by relatively complex sentences and a large vocabulary. It doesn't use contractions (such as *doesn't*). In contrast, **informal** language more closely resembles ordinary conversation. It uses relatively short sentences and common words. It may include contractions, slang, and references to everyday objects and activities (cheeseburgers, T-shirts, CDs). The writer may use *I* and address the reader as *you*.

The right language for most college essays lies somewhere between formal and informal. If your topic and tone are serious (say, for a research paper on terrorism), then your language may lean toward formality. If your topic is not weighty and your tone is light (say, for a humorous essay about giving your dog a bath), then your language may be informal.

13c Choose common words instead of jargon.

Jargon is the term for the specialized vocabulary used by people in a certain field, such as music, carpentry, law, or sports. Nearly every academic, professional, and recreational field has its own jargon. To a specialist addressing other specialists, jargon is convenient and necessary. Without technical terms, after all, two surgeons could hardly discuss a patient's anatomy. To an outsider, though, such terms may be incomprehensible. To communicate information to readers without making them feel excluded or confused, avoid unnecessary jargon.

Jargon also can include ways of using words. Some politicians and bureaucrats like to make nouns into verbs by tacking on suffixes like *-ize.*

Jargon	The government intends to *privatize* federal land.
Clear	The government intends to *sell* federal land to *private buyers.*

Although *privatize* implies merely "convert to private ownership," usually its real meaning is "sell off"—as might occur were a national park to be auctioned to developers. *Privatize* thus also can be called a *euphemism,* a pleasant term that masks an underlying different meaning (see 13d).

Similarly, technology terms such as *access, format, interface, database,* and *parameters* are useful to explain technical processes. When thoughtlessly applied to nontechnical ideas, they can obscure meaning.

Jargon	A democracy needs the electorate's *input.*
Clear	A democracy needs the electorate *to vote and to express its views to elected officials.*

Avoid needless jargon by favoring a perfectly good old word over a trendy one. Also avoid the jargon of a special discipline—say, psychology or fly-fishing—unless you are writing for readers familiar with the field's details and terms. If you're writing for general readers, define any specialized terms. When you use plain words, you'll rarely go wrong.

13d Use euphemisms sparingly.

Euphemisms are plain truths dressed attractively, sometimes hard facts stated gently. To say that someone *passed away* instead of *died* is a common euphemism—humane, perhaps, in breaking terrible news to an anxious family. In such language, an army that *retreats* makes *a strategic withdrawal,* a person who is *underweight* turns *slim,* and an acne cream treats not *pimples* but *blemishes.* Even if you aren't prone to using euphemisms, note them when you read evidence from partisan sources and spokespersons.

13e Avoid slang in formal writing.

Slang, especially when new, can be colorful ("She's not playing with a full deck"), playful ("He's wicked cute!"), and apt (*ice* for diamonds, a *stiff* for a corpse). Most slang, however, quickly comes to seem as old and wrinkled as the Jazz Age's gleeful *twenty-three skidoo!* Your best bet is to stick to Standard English, seeking words that are usual but exact.

14 ◆ Exact Words

What if you read that a leading citizen is a *pillow of the community*? Good writing depends on knowing what words mean and how to use them precisely.

14a Choose words for their connotations as well as their denotations.

The **denotation** of a word is its basic meaning—its dictionary definition. *Excited, agitated,* and *exhilarated* all denote a similar state of physical and emotional arousal. The **connotations** of a word are the shades of meaning that set it apart from its synonyms. You might be *agitated* by the prospect of final exams next week, but *exhilarated* by your plans for the vacation afterward. When you choose one of several options, you base your choice on connotation.

Imprecise	Advertisers have given light beer a macho image by showing football players *sipping* the product with *enthusiasm.*
Revised	Advertisers have given light beer a macho image by showing football players *guzzling* the product with *gusto.*

◆ *In, On, At*: Prepositions of Location and Time

Location Expressions

Elaine lives *in* Manhattan *at* a swanky address *on* Fifth Avenue.

In means "within" or "inside of" a place, including geographical areas, such as cities, states, countries, and continents.

I packed my books *in* my backpack and left to visit my cousins *in* Canada.

Where ***in*** emphasizes *location* only, ***at*** is often used to refer to a place when a specific *activity* is implied: *at the store* (to shop), *at the office* (to work), *at the theater* (to see a play), and so on.

Angelo left his bicycle *in* the bike rack while he was *at* school.

On means "on the surface of" or "on top of" something and is used with floors of buildings and planets. It is also used to indicate a location *beside* a lake, river, ocean, or other body of water.

The service department is *on* the fourth floor.

We have a cabin *on* Lake Michigan.

In, on, and ***at*** can all be used in addresses. ***In*** is used to identify a general location, such as a city or neighborhood. ***On*** is used to identify a specific street. ***At*** is used to give an exact address.

We live *in* Boston *on* Medway Street.

We live *at* 20 Medway Street.

In and ***at*** can both be used with the verb *arrive*. ***In*** indicates a large place, such as a city, state, country, or continent. ***At*** indicates a smaller place, such as a specific building or address. (*To* is never used with *arrive*.)

Alanya arrived *in* Alaska yesterday; Sanjei will arrive *at* the airport soon.

Time Expressions

In indicates the span of time during which something occurs or a time in the future; it is also used in the expressions *in a minute* (meaning "shortly") and *in* *time* (meaning "soon enough" or "without a moment to spare"). ***In*** is also used with seasons, months, and periods of the day.

He needs to read this book *in* the next three days. [During the next three days]

I'll meet you *in* the morning *in* two weeks. [Two weeks from now]

On is used with the days of the week, with the word *weekend*, and in the expression *on time* (meaning "punctually").

Let's have lunch *on* Friday.

At is used in reference to a specific time on the clock as well as a specific time of the day (*at night, at dawn, at twilight*).

We'll meet again next Monday *at* 2:15 p.m.

◆ *To, For:* Indirect Objects and Prepositions

These sentences mean the same thing:

I sent the president a letter.

I sent a letter to the president.

In the first sentence, *the president* is the **indirect object:** he or she receives the direct object (*a letter*), which was acted on (*sent*) by the subject of the sentence (*I*). In the second sentence, the same idea is expressed using a **prepositional phrase** beginning with *to*.

Some verbs can use either an indirect object or the preposition *to: give, send, lend, offer, owe, pay, sell, show, teach, tell.* Some verbs can use an indirect object or the preposition *for: bake, build, buy, cook, find, get, make.*

I paid *the travel agent* one hundred dollars.

I paid one hundred dollars *to the travel agent.*

Margarita cooked *her family* some chicken.

Margarita cooked some chicken *for her family.*

Some verbs cannot have an indirect object; they must use a preposition. The following verbs must use the preposition *to: describe, demonstrate, explain, introduce,* and *suggest.*

Incorrect Please explain me indirect objects.

Correct Please explain indirect objects *to me.*

The following verbs must use the preposition *for: answer* and *prepare.*

Incorrect He prepared me the punch.

Correct He prepared the punch *for me.*

(*continued*)

Some verbs must have an indirect object; they cannot use a preposition. The following verbs must have an indirect object: *ask* and *cost.*

Incorrect Sasha asked a question to her.

Correct Sasha asked *her* a question.

◆ Two-Word Verbs: Particles, Not Prepositions

Many two-word verbs end with a **particle,** a word that can be used as a preposition on its own but becomes part of a **phrasal verb.** Once the particle is added, the verb takes on a new idiomatic meaning that must be learned.

break up: to separate; to end a romantic relationship; to laugh

decide on: to select or to judge a person or thing

eat at: to worry or disturb a person

feel for [a person]: to sympathize with another's unhappiness

see to: to take care of a person or situation

take in [a person]: to house a person; to trick by gaining a person's trust

14b Avoid clichés.

A **cliché** is a trite expression, once vivid or figurative but now worn out from too much use. When a story begins, "It was a dark and stormy night," then its author is obviously using dull, predictable words. Many a strike is settled after a *marathon bargaining session* that *narrowly averts a walkout.* Fires customarily *race* and *gut.* And when everything is *terrific,* a reader will suspect that it isn't. Clichés abound when writers and speakers try hard to sound lively but don't bother to invent anything vigorous, colorful, and new. When editing your writing, you can often recognize an annoying cliché if you feel a sudden guilty desire to surround it with quotation marks. You might also show your papers to friends, asking them to look for anything trite.

COMMON CLICHÉS

a sneaking suspicion
above and beyond the call of duty
add insult to injury
beyond a shadow of a doubt
come hell or high water
last but not least
little did I dream
make a long story short
piece of cake
stab me in the back

COMMON CLICHÉS

cool as a cucumber
few and far between
greased lightning
hard as a rock
that's the way the ball bounces
through thick and thin
tip of the iceberg
tried and true

14c Use idioms in their correct form.

Every language contains **idioms,** or **idiomatic expressions:** phrases that, through long use, have become standard even though their construction may defy logic or grammar. For example, although *fender bender* may suggest the outcome of a minor collision between two cars, someone unfamiliar with that expression might struggle to connect the literal words with the idiomatic meaning. In addition, many idiomatic expressions require us to choose the right preposition. We work *up* a sweat while working *out* in the gym. We argue *with* someone but *about* something, *for* or *against* it. And someone who decides to *set up* a meeting doesn't expect to be *upset*. Sometimes we must know which article to use before a noun—if any. We can be *in motion,* but we have to be *in the swim.* We're occasionally in *a tight spot* but never in *a trouble.* Idioms also can involve choosing the right verb: we *seize* an opportunity, but we *catch* a plane.

The dictionary can help you choose the appropriate idiom for your sentence. Look up *agree* for instance, and you will probably find examples showing when to use *agree to, agree with,* or *agree that.*

4

Punctuation

15 ◆ End Punctuation

Three marks can signal the end of a sentence: the period, the exclamation point, and the question mark.

15a Use a period to end a declarative sentence, a directive, or an indirect question.

Most sentences are **declarative,** meaning that they make a statement.

Most people on earth are malnourished.

A period, not a question mark, ends an **indirect question,** which states that a question was asked or is being asked.

The counselor asked Marcia why she rarely gets to class on time.

I wonder why Roland didn't show up.

Written as **direct questions,** those sentences require a question mark.

The counselor asked, "Marcia, why do you rarely get to class on time?"

Why, I wonder, didn't Roland show up?

15b Use a period after some abbreviations.

A period within a sentence shows that what precedes it has been shortened.

Dr. Robert A. Hooke's speech will be broadcast at 8:00 p.m.

The names of most organizations (YMCA, PTA), countries (USA, UK), and people (JFK, FDR) are abbreviated using all capitals without periods. Other abbreviations, such as those for designations of time, use periods. When an abbreviation ends a sentence, follow it with one period, not two.

15c Use a question mark to end a direct question.

How many angels can dance on the head of a pin?

The question mark comes at the end of the question even if the question is part of a longer declarative sentence.

"What'll I do now?" Marjorie wailed.

It can indicate doubt about the accuracy of a number or date.

Aristophanes, born in 450(?) BC, became the master comic playwright of Greece's Golden Age.

Often the same purpose can be accomplished more gracefully in words:

Aristophanes, born around 450 BC, became the master comic playwright of Greece's Golden Age.

In formal writing, avoid using a question mark to express irony or sarcasm: *her generous (?) gift.* If your doubts are worth including, state them directly: *her meager but highly publicized gift.*

15d Use an exclamation point to end an interjection or an urgent command.

Rarely used in academic writing, an exclamation point signals strong emotion or emphasis.

We've struck an iceberg! We're sinking! I can't believe it!

It may mark an **interjection** or an urgent directive.

Oh, no! Fire! Hurry up! Help me!

16 ◆ Commas

Like a split-second pause in conversation, a well-placed comma helps your readers to catch your train of thought. It keeps them from stumbling over a solid block of words or drawing an inaccurate conclusion.

Lyman paints fences and bowls.

From this statement, we can deduce that Lyman is a painter who works with both a large and a small brush. But add commas and the portrait changes:

Lyman paints, fences, and bowls.

Now Lyman wields a paintbrush, a sword, and a bowling ball. What we learn about his activities depends on how the writer punctuates the sentence.

16a Use a comma with a coordinating conjunction to join two main clauses.

When you join main clauses with a coordinating conjunction (*and, but, for, or, nor, so, yet*), add a comma after the first clause, right before the conjunction.

The pie whooshed through the air, but the agile Hal ducked.

If your clauses are short and parallel in form, you may omit the comma.

Spring passed and summer came.

They urged but I refused.

Or you may keep the comma to throw emphasis on your second clause.

Spring passed, and summer came.

They urged, but I refused.

Don't use a comma with a coordinating conjunction that links two phrases or that links a phrase and a clause.

Faulty The mustangs galloped, and cavorted across the plain.

Edited The mustangs galloped and cavorted across the plain.

16b Use a comma after an introductory clause, phrase, or word.

Weeping, Lydia stumbled down the stairs.

Before that, Arthur saw her reading an old love letter.

If he knew who the writer was, he didn't tell.

Placed after any such opening word, phrase, or subordinate clause, a comma tells your reader, "Enough preliminaries: now the main clause starts."

However, you need not use a comma after a single introductory word or a short phrase or clause if there is no danger of misreading.

Sooner or later Lydia will tell us the whole story.

16c Use a comma between items in a series.

When you list three or more items, whether they are nouns, verbs, adjectives, adverbs, or entire phrases or clauses, separate them with commas.

> Country ham, sweet corn, and potatoes weighted Grandma's table.
>
> Joel prefers music that shakes, rattles, and rolls.
>
> In one afternoon, we climbed the Matterhorn, voyaged beneath the sea, and flew on a rocket through space.

Notice that no comma *follows* the final item in the series.

Some writers omit the comma *before* the final item in the series. This custom may throw off the rhythm of a sentence and, in some cases, obscure the writer's meaning. Using the comma in such a case is never wrong and is preferred in academic style; omitting it can create confusion.

> I was met at the station by my cousins, brother and sister.

Are these people a brother-and-sister pair who are the writer's cousins? Or are they a group consisting of the writer's cousins, her brother, and her sister? If they are more than two people, a comma would clear up the confusion.

> I was met at the station by my cousins, brother, and sister.

16d Use a comma between coordinate adjectives but not between cumulative adjectives.

Adjectives that function independently of each other, though they modify the same noun, are called **coordinate adjectives.** Set them off with commas.

> Ruth was a clear, vibrant, persuasive speaker.
>
> Life is nasty, brutish, and short.

Don't use a comma after the final adjective before a noun.

Faulty	My professor was a brilliant, caring, teacher.
Edited	My professor was a brilliant, caring teacher.

To check whether adjectives are coordinate, apply two tests. Can you rearrange the adjectives without distorting the meaning of the sentence? (*Ruth was a persuasive, vibrant, clear speaker.*) Can you insert *and* between them? (*Life is nasty and brutish and short.*)

If the answer to both questions is yes, the adjectives are coordinate. Removing any one of them would not greatly affect the others. Use commas between them to show that they are separate and equal.

If you link coordinate adjectives with *and* or another conjunction, omit the commas except in a series (see 16c).

> New York City is huge and dirty and beautiful.

Cumulative adjectives work together to create a single unified picture of the noun they modify. Remove any one of them and you change the picture. No commas separate cumulative adjectives.

Ruth has two small white poodles.

Who's afraid of the big bad wolf?

If you rearrange cumulative adjectives or insert *and* between them, the effect is distorted (*two white small poodles; the big and bad wolf*).

16e Use commas to set off a nonrestrictive phrase or clause.

A **nonrestrictive modifier** adds a fact that, while perhaps interesting and valuable, isn't essential. You could leave it out of the sentence and still make sense. Set off the modifier with commas before and after it.

Potts Alley, *which runs north from Chestnut Street,* is too narrow for cars.

At the end of the alley, *where the fair was held last May,* a getaway car waited.

A **restrictive modifier** is essential. Omit it and you significantly change the meaning of the modified word and the sentence. Such a modifier is called *restrictive* because it limits what it modifies: it specifies this place, person, or action and no other. Because a restrictive modifier is part of the identity of whatever it modifies, no commas set it off from the rest of the sentence.

They picked the alley *that runs north from Chestnut Street* because it is close to the highway.

Anyone *who robs my house* will be disappointed.

Leaving out the modifier in that last sentence changes the meaning from potential robbers to humankind.

Use *that* to introduce (or to recognize) a restrictive phrase or clause. Use *which* to introduce (or to recognize) a nonrestrictive phrase or clause.

The food *that I love best* is chocolate.

Chocolate, *which I love,* is not on my diet.

16f Use commas to set off nonrestrictive appositives.

Like the modifiers discussed in 16e, an **appositive** can be either restrictive or nonrestrictive. If it is nonrestrictive—if the sentence still makes sense when it is omitted or changed—then set it off with commas before and after.

My third ex-husband, *Hugo,* will be glad to meet you.

We are bringing dessert, *a blueberry pie,* to follow dinner.

If the appositive is restrictive—if you can't take it out or change it without changing your meaning—then include it without commas.

Of all the men I've been married to, my ex-husband *Hugo* is the best cook.

16g Use commas to set off conjunctive adverbs.

When you drop a conjunctive adverb into the middle of a clause, set it off with commas before and after it.

Using lead paint in homes has been illegal, *however,* since 1973.

Builders, *indeed,* gave it up some twenty years earlier.

16h Use commas to set off parenthetical expressions.

Use a pair of commas around any parenthetical expression or any aside from you to your readers.

Home inspectors, *for this reason,* sometimes test for lead paint.

Cosmic Construction never used lead paint, *or so their spokesperson says,* even when it was legal.

16i Use commas to set off a phrase or clause expressing contrast.

It was Rudolph, *not Dasher,* who had a red nose.

However, short contrasting phrases beginning with *but* need no commas.

It was not Dasher but Rudolph who had a red nose.

16j Use commas to set off an absolute phrase.

The link between an absolute phrase and the rest of the sentence is a comma or two commas if the phrase falls in midsentence.

Our worst fears drawing us together, we huddled over the letter.

Luke, *his knife being the sharpest,* slit the envelope.

16k Use commas to set off a direct quotation from your own words.

When you briefly quote someone, distinguish the source's words from yours with commas (and, of course, quotation marks). When you insert an explanation into a quotation (such as *he said*), set that off with commas.

Shakespeare wrote, "Some are born great, some achieve greatness, and some have greatness thrust upon them."

"The best thing that can come with success," commented the actress Liv Ullmann, "is the knowledge that it is nothing to long for."

The comma always comes *before* the quotation marks.

However, you should not use a comma with a very short quotation or one introduced by *that.*

Don't tell me "yes" if you mean "maybe."

Jules said that "Nothing ventured, nothing gained" is his motto.

Don't use a comma with any quotation run into your own sentence and read as part of it. Often such quotations are introduced by linking verbs.

Her favorite statement at age three was "I can do it myself."

Shakespeare originated the expression "my salad days, when I was green in judgment."

16l Use commas around *yes* and *no*, mild interjections, tag questions, and the name or title of someone directly addressed.

Yes and No *Yes,* I'd like a Rolls-Royce, but, *no,* I didn't order one.

Interjection *Well,* don't blame it on me.

Tag Question It would be fun to ride in a Silver Cloud, *wouldn't it?*

Direct Address Drive us home, *James.*

16m Use commas to set off dates, states, countries, and addresses.

On June 6, 1990, Ned Shaw was born.

East Rutherford, New Jersey, seemed like Paris, France, to him.

His family moved to 11 Maple Street, Middletown, Ohio.

Do not add a comma between state and zip code: *Bedford, MA 01730.*

16n Do not use a comma to separate a subject from its verb or a verb from its object.

Faulty The athlete driving the purple Jaguar, was Jim Fuld. [Subject separated from verb]

Edited The athlete driving the purple Jaguar was Jim Fuld.

Faulty	The governor should not have given his campaign manager, such a prestigious appointment. [Verb separated from direct object]
Edited	The governor should not have given his campaign manager such a prestigious appointment.

16o Do not use a comma between words or phrases joined by correlative or coordinating conjunctions.

Do not divide a compound subject or predicate unnecessarily with a comma.

Faulty	Neither Peter Pan, nor the fairy Tinkerbell, saw the pirates sneaking toward their hideout. [Compound subject]
Edited	Neither Peter Pan nor the fairy Tinkerbell saw the pirates sneaking toward their hideout.
Faulty	The chickens clucked, and pecked, and flapped their wings. [Compound predicate]
Edited	The chickens clucked and pecked and flapped their wings.

16p Do not use a comma before the first or after the last item in a series.

Faulty	We had to see, my mother's doctor, my father's lawyer, and my dog's veterinarian, in one afternoon.
Edited	We had to see my mother's doctor, my father's lawyer, and my dog's veterinarian in one afternoon.

16q Do not use a comma to set off a restrictive word, phrase, or clause.

A restrictive modifier is essential to the definition or identification of whatever it modifies; a nonrestrictive modifier is not.

Faulty	The fireworks, that I saw on Sunday, were the best I've ever seen.
Edited	The fireworks that I saw on Sunday were the best I've ever seen.

16r Do not use commas to set off indirect quotations.

When *that* introduces a quotation, the quotation is indirect and requires neither a comma nor quotation marks.

Faulty He told us that, we shouldn't have done it.

Edited He told us that we shouldn't have done it.

This sentence also could be recast as a direct quotation.

Edited He told us, "You shouldn't have done it."

17 ◆ Semicolons

A semicolon is a sort of compromise between a comma and a period: it creates a stop without ending a sentence.

17a Use a semicolon to join two main clauses not joined by a coordinating conjunction.

Suppose, having written one statement, you want to add another that is closely related in sense. You decide to keep them both in a single sentence.

Shooting baskets was my brother's favorite sport; he would dunk them for hours at a time.

A semicolon is a good substitute for a period when you don't want to bring your readers to a complete stop.

By the yard life is hard; by the inch it's a cinch.

When you join a subordinate clause to a main one or join two statements with a coordinating conjunction, you can generally use just a comma. Reserve the semicolon to emphasize a close connection or to avoid confusion when long, complex clauses include internal punctuation.

17b Use a semicolon to join two main clauses that are linked by a conjunctive adverb.

You can use a conjunctive adverb to show a relationship between clauses such as addition (*also, besides*), comparison (*likewise, similarly*), contrast (*instead, however*), emphasis (*namely, certainly*), cause and effect (*thus, therefore*), or time (*finally, subsequently*). When a second statement begins with (or includes) a conjunctive adverb, you can join it to the first with a semicolon. No matter where the conjunctive adverb appears, the semicolon is placed between the two clauses.

Bert is a stand-out player; *indeed,* he's the one hope of our team.

We yearned to attend the concert; tickets, *however,* were hard to come by.

17c Use a semicolon to separate items in a series that contain internal punctuation or that are long and complex.

The semicolon is especially useful for setting off one group of items from another. More powerful than a comma, it divides a series of series.

> The auctioneer sold clocks, watches, and cameras; freezers of steaks and tons of bean sprouts; motorcycles, cars, speedboats, canoes, and cabin cruisers; and rare coins, curious stamps, and precious stones.

18 ◆ Colons

A colon introduces a further thought, one added to throw light on a first. In using it, a writer declares: "What follows will clarify what I've just said." Some writers use a capital letter to start any complete sentence that follows a colon; others prefer a lowercase letter. Whichever you choose, be consistent. A phrase that follows a colon always begins with a lowercase letter.

18a Use a colon between two main clauses if the second exemplifies, explains, or summarizes the first.

Like a semicolon, a colon can join two sentences into one. The chief difference is this: a semicolon says merely that two main clauses are related; a colon, like an abbreviation for *that is* or *for example,* says that the second clause gives an example or explanation of the point in the first clause.

> She tried everything: she scoured the Internet, made dozens of phone calls, wrote e-mails, even consulted a lawyer.

18b Use a colon to introduce a list or a series.

A colon can introduce a word, a phrase, a series, or a second main clause, sometimes strengthened by *as follows* or *the following.*

> The dance steps are as follows: forward, back, turn, and glide.

When a colon introduces a series of words or phrases, it often means *such as* or *for instance.* A list of examples after a colon need not include *and* before the last item unless all possible examples have been stated.

> On a Saturday night many kinds of people crowd our downtown area: drifters, bored senior citizens, college students out for a good time.

18c Use a colon to introduce an appositive.

A colon preceded by a main clause can introduce an **appositive.**

> I have discovered the key to the future: robots.

18d Use a colon to introduce a long or comma-filled quotation.

Sometimes you can't conveniently introduce a quoted passage with a comma. Perhaps the quotation is too long or heavily punctuated, or your prefatory remarks demand a longer pause. In either case, use a colon.

> God told Adam and Eve: "Be fruitful, and multiply, and replenish the earth, and subdue it."

18e Use a colon when convention calls for it.

After a Salutation	Dear Mr. James:
Biblical Citations	Genesis 4:7 [The book, chapter, verse]
Titles: Subtitles	*Convergences: Essays on Art and Literature*
Source References	Welty, Eudora. *The Eye of the Story.* New York: Random, 1978.
Time of Day	2:02 p.m.

18f Use a colon only at the end of a main clause.

In a sentence, a colon always follows a complete sentence, never a phrase. Avoid using a colon between a verb and its object, between a preposition and its object, and before a list introduced by *such as.*

Faulty	My mother and father are: Bella and Benjamin.
Revised	My mother and father are Bella and Benjamin.
Faulty	Many great inventors have changed our lives, such as: Edison, Marconi, and Glutz.
Revised	Many great inventors have changed our lives, such as Edison, Marconi, and Glutz.
Revised	Many great inventors have changed our lives: Edison, Marconi, Glutz.

19 ◆ Dashes

A **dash** is a horizontal line used to separate parts of a sentence—a dramatic substitute for a comma, semicolon, or colon. Your software may turn a typed dash, made by hitting your hyphen key twice without adding any spaces, to an unbroken line.

19a Use a dash to indicate a sudden break in thought or shift in tone.

The dash signals that a surprise is in store: a shift in viewpoint, perhaps, or an unfinished statement.

Ivan doesn't care which team wins—he bet on both.

I didn't notice my parents' accented speech—at least not at home.

19b Use a dash to introduce an explanation, an illustration, or a series.

Use a dash to add an informal preparatory pause or to introduce an appositive that needs drama or contains commas.

My advice to you is simple—stop complaining.

Longfellow wrote about three young sisters—grave Alice, laughing Allegra, and Edith with golden hair—in "The Children's Hour."

19c Use dashes to set off an emphatic aside or parenthetical expression from the rest of a sentence.

It was as hot—and I mean *hot*—as the Fourth of July in Death Valley.

19d Avoid overusing dashes.

The dash becomes meaningless if used too often. Use it only when a comma, a colon, or parentheses don't seem strong enough.

Excessive Algy's grandmother—a sweet old lady—asked him to pick up some things at the store—milk, eggs, and cheese.

Edited Algy's grandmother, a sweet old lady, asked him to pick up some things at the store: milk, eggs, and cheese.

20 ◆ Parentheses

Parentheses (singular, *parenthesis*) work in pairs. So do brackets. Both surround bits of information to make a statement perfectly clear. An ellipsis mark is a trio of periods inserted to show that something has been cut.

20a Use parentheses to set off interruptions that are useful but not essential.

FDR (as people called Franklin D. Roosevelt) won four presidential elections.

In fact, he occupied the White House for so many years (1933 to mid-1945) that babies became teenagers without having known any other president.

The material within the parentheses may be helpful, but it isn't essential. Without it, the sentences would still make good sense. Use parentheses to add a qualification, a helpful date, or a brief explanation—words that, in conversation, you might introduce in a changed tone of voice.

20b Use parentheses around letters or numbers indicating items in a series.

> Archimedes asserted that, given (1) a lever long enough, (2) a fulcrum, and (3) a place to stand, he could move the earth.

No parentheses are needed for numbers or letters in an indented list.

5

Mechanics

21 ◆ Capital Letters

Use capital letters only with good reason. If you think a word will work in lowercase letters, you're probably right.

21a Capitalize proper names and adjectives made from proper names.

Proper names designate individuals, places, organizations, institutions, brand names, and certain other distinctive things. Any proper noun can have an adjective form, also capitalized.

Miles Standish	Muir High School	Australian beer
Belgium	a Volkswagen	a Renaissance man
United Nations	a Xerox copier	Shakespearean comedy

21b Capitalize a title or rank before a proper name.

During her second term, Senator Wilimczyk proposed several bills.

In his lecture, Professor Jones analyzed fossil evidence.

Titles that do not come before proper names usually are not capitalized.

Ten senators voted against the research appropriation.

Jones is the department's only full professor.

However, the abbreviation of an academic or professional degree is always capitalized. The informal name of a degree is not capitalized.

Dora E. McLean, MD, also holds a BA in music.

Dora holds a bachelor's degree in music.

21c Capitalize a family relationship only when it is part of a proper name or when it substitutes for a proper name.

Do you know the song about Mother Machree?

I have invited Mother to visit next weekend.

I would like you to meet my aunt, Emily Smith.

21d Capitalize the names of religions, their deities, and their followers.

Christianity	Muslims	Jehovah	Krishna
Islam	Methodists	Allah	the Holy Spirit

21e Capitalize proper names of places, regions, and geographic features.

Los Angeles	the Black Hills	the Atlantic Ocean
Death Valley	Big Sur	the Philippines

Do not capitalize *north, south, east,* or *west* unless it is part of a proper name (*West Virginia, South Orange*) or refers to formal geographic locations.

Drive south to Chicago and then east to Cleveland.

Jim, who has always lived in the South, likes to read about the Northeast.

A common noun such as *street, avenue, boulevard, park, lake,* or *hill* is capitalized when part of a proper name.

Meinecke Avenue	Hamilton Park	Lake Michigan

21f Capitalize days of the week, months, and holidays, but not seasons or academic terms.

During spring term, by the Monday after Passover, I have to choose between the January study plan and junior year abroad.

21g Capitalize historical events, periods, and documents.

Black Monday	the Roaring Twenties
the Civil War [*but* a civil war]	Magna Carta
the Holocaust [*but* a holocaust]	Declaration of Independence
the Bronze Age	Atomic Energy Act

21h Capitalize the names of schools, colleges, departments, and courses.

West End School, Central High School [*but* elementary school, high school]

Reed College, Arizona State University [*but* the college, a university]

Department of History [*but* history department, department office]

Feminist Perspectives in Nineteenth-Century Literature [*but* literature course]

21i Capitalize the first, last, and main words in titles.

When you write the title of a paper, book, article, work of art, television show, poem, or performance, capitalize the first and last words and all main words in between. Do not capitalize articles (*a, an, the*), coordinating conjunctions (*and, but, for, or, nor, so, yet*), or prepositions (such as *in, on, at, of, from*) unless they come first or last in the title or follow a colon.

Essay	"Once More to the Lake"
Novel	*Of Mice and Men*
Volume of Poetry	*Poems after Martial*
Poem	"A Valediction: Of Weeping"

21j Capitalize the first letter of a quoted sentence.

Oscar Wilde wrote, "The only way to get rid of a temptation is to yield to it."

Only the first word of a quoted sentence is capitalized, even when you break the sentence with words of your own.

"The only way to get rid of a temptation," wrote Oscar Wilde, "is to yield to it."

If you quote more than one sentence, start each one with a capital letter.

"Art should never try to be popular," said Wilde. "The public should try to make itself artistic."

Select a quoted passage carefully so that you can present its details accurately as it blends in with your sentence.

22 ◆ Hyphens

The hyphen, the transparent tape of punctuation, is used to join words and to connect parts of words.

22a Use hyphens in compound words that require them.

Compound words in the English language take three forms:

1. Two or more words combined into one (*crossroads, salesperson*)
2. Two or more words that remain separate but function as one (*gas station, high school*)
3. Two or more words linked by hyphens (*sister-in-law, window-shop*)

Compounds fall into these categories more by custom than by rule. When you're not sure which way to write a compound, refer to a current collegiate dictionary. If the compound is not listed, write it as two words.

Use a hyphen in a compound word containing one or more elements beginning with a capital letter.

> Bill says that, as a *neo-Marxist* living in an *A-frame* house, it would be politically incorrect for him to wear a Mickey Mouse *T-shirt*.

Exceptions to this rule include *unchristian*, for one.

22b Use a hyphen in a compound adjective preceding, but not following, a noun.

> Jerome, a devotee of *twentieth-century* music, has no interest in the classic symphonies of the *eighteenth century*.
>
> I'd like living in an *out-of-the-way* place better if it weren't so far *out of the way*.

In a series of hyphenated adjectives with the same second word, you can omit that word (but not the hyphen) in all but the last adjective of the series.

> Julia is a lover of eighteenth-, nineteenth-, and twentieth-century music.

The adverb *well*, when coupled with an adjective, follows the same hyphenation rules as if it were an adjective.

> It is *well known* that Tony has a *well-equipped* kitchen, although his is not as *well equipped* as the hotel's.

Do *not* use a hyphen to link an adverb ending in *-ly* with an adjective.

> The sun hung like a newly minted penny in a freshly washed sky.

22c Use a hyphen after the prefixes *all-*, *ex-*, and *self-* and before the suffix *-elect*.

Lucille's *ex-husband* is studying *self-hypnosis*.

This *all-important* debate pits Senator Browning against the *president elect*.

22d Use a hyphen in most cases if an added prefix or suffix creates a double vowel, a triple consonant, or an ambiguous pronunciation.

It is also acceptable to omit the hyphen in the case of a double *e*: *reeducate*.

The contractor's *pre-estimate* did not cover any *pre-existing* flaws in the house.

The recreation department favors the *re-creation* of a summer program.

22e Use a hyphen in spelled-out fractions and compound whole numbers from twenty-one to ninety-nine.

When her sister gave Leslie's age as six and *three-quarters*, Leslie corrected her: "I'm six and *five-sixths!*"

The fifth graders learned that *forty-four* rounds down to forty while *forty-five* rounds up to fifty.

22f Use a hyphen to indicate inclusive numbers.

The section covering the years 1975-1980 is found on pages 20-27.

22g Use a hyphen to break a word between syllables at the end of a line.

The MLA style guide prefers that you turn off your word processor's automatic hyphenation function. If you are designing a text that requires breaking a word, check your dictionary for its syllable divisions.

23 ◆ Spelling

English spelling so often defies the rules that many writers wonder if, indeed, there *are* rules. How, then, are you to cope? You can proofread carefully and use your spell checker. You can refer to lists of commonly misspelled words and of **homonyms,** words that sound the same, or almost the same, but are spelled differently.

You can also use several tactics to teach yourself to be a better speller.

1. *Use mnemonic devices.* To make unusual spellings stick in your memory, invent associations. Using such mnemonic devices (tricks to aid memory) may help you with whatever troublesome spelling you are determined to remember. *Weird* behaves *weirdly*. Rise ag*ain*, Brit*ain*! One *d* in *dish,* one in *radish.* Why isn't *math*ematics like *ath*letics? You write a *letter* on station*e*ry. Any silly phrase or sentence will do, as long as it brings tricky spellings to mind.
2. *Keep a record of words you misspell.* Buy yourself a little notebook in which to enter words that invariably trip you up. Each time you proofread a paper you have written and each time you receive one back from your instructor, write down any words you have misspelled. Then practice pronouncing, writing, and spelling them out loud until you have mastered them.
3. *Check any questionable spelling by referring to your dictionary,* your good-as-gold best friend. Use it to check words as you come up with them and to double-check them as you proofread and edit. If you are multilingual and originally learned British English, a good dictionary will distinguish American and British spellings (*color, colour; terrorize, terrorise*).
4. *Learn commonly misspelled words.* If you know that you are likely to confuse different words that sound alike, checkmark the words that you consider the trickiest—but don't stop there. Spend a few minutes each day going over them. Spell every troublesome word out loud; write it ten times. Do the same with any common problem words that your spell checker routinely catches, such as *nucular* for *nuclear* or *exercize* for *exercise.* Your spelling will improve rapidly.

24 ◆ Vocabulary

In the past four hundred years, English has continued borrowing from many languages and, as a result, now has one of the world's largest vocabularies. Modern English, then, is a plant growing luxuriously in the soil of multiple language sources.

24a Word roots

As its name suggests, a root is a word from which other words grow, usually through the addition of prefixes or suffixes. From the Latin root *-dic-* or *-dict-* ("speak"), for instance, grows a whole range of words in English: *contradict, dictate, dictator, diction, dictionary, predict,* and others. Here are some other Latin (L) and Greek (G) roots and examples of words derived from them.

ROOT	MEANING	EXAMPLES
-audi- (L)	to hear	audience, audio
-bene- (L)	good, well	benevolent, benefit
-bio- (G)	life	biography, biosphere
-duc(t)- (L)	to lead or to make	ductile, reproduce

ROOT	MEANING	EXAMPLES
-gen- (G)	race, kind	genealogy, gene
-geo- (G)	earth	geography, geometry
-graph- (G)	to write	graphic, photography
-jur-, -jus- (L)	law	justice, jurisdiction
-log(o)- (G)	word, thought	biology, logical
-luc- (L)	light	lucid, translucent
-manu- (L)	hand	manufacture, manual
-mit-, -mis- (L)	to send	permit, transmission
-path- (G)	feel, suffer	empathy, pathetic
-phil- (G)	love	philosopher, bibliophile
-photo- (G)	light	photography, telephoto
-port- (L)	to carry	transport, portable
-psych- (G)	soul	psychology, psychopath
-scrib-, -script- (L)	to write	scribble, manuscript
-sent-, -sens- (L)	to feel	sensation, resent
-tele- (G)	far away	telegraph, telepathy
-tend- (L)	to stretch	extend, tendency
-terr- (L)	earth	inter, territorial
-vac- (L)	empty	vacant, evacuation
-vid-, -vis- (L)	to see	video, envision, visit

PART TWO

Speaking and Listening

6

From A to Z: Overview of a Speech

Persons with little experience in public speaking—and that includes most of us—will benefit from preparing and delivering a first short speech. An audience of as few as two people will be enough to test the waters and help you gain confidence in your ability to "stand up and deliver."

This chapter presents a brief overview of the process of preparing a first speech or presentation (see Figure 6.1). Subsequent chapters expand on these steps.

25 ◆ Steps to Creating a Speech

25a Analyze the audience.

Every audience is unique, with members who have personalities, interests, and opinions all their own, and these factors will influence their responses toward a given topic, speaker, and occasion. Thus, the first task in preparing any speech is to consider the audience. *Audience analysis* is a systematic process of getting to know audience members' attributes and motivations through techniques such as interviews and questionnaires. For a brief first speech, however, gather what information you can about the audience in the time allotted. Consider some *demographic characteristics*: ratio of males to females, age ranges, cultural background, and socioeconomic status. As you mull over topics and the different ways you might present them, think about the potential impact of these variables on audience receptivity.

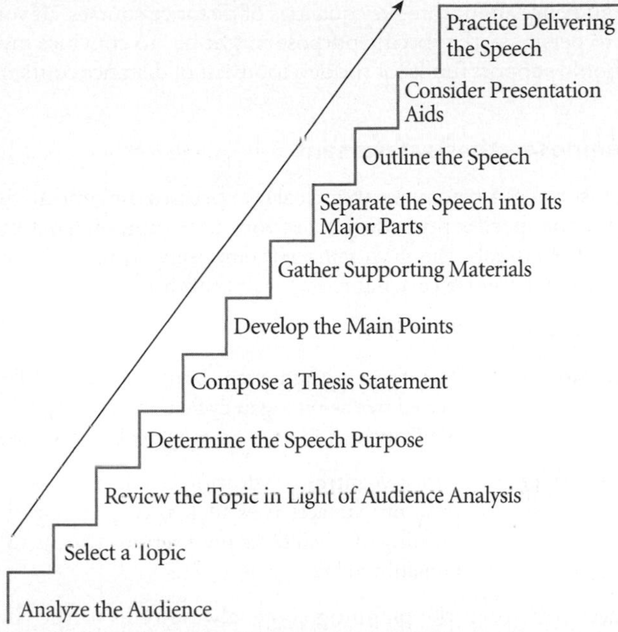

FIGURE 6.1 Steps in the Speechmaking Process

25b Select a topic.

Unless the topic is assigned, use your interests and those of the audience to guide you in selecting something to speak about. What are your areas of interest and expertise? Is there an important current event or outstanding issue affecting the audience that could serve as a topic? Whatever you settle on, you should feel confident that the topic is suitable for both the audience and the speech occasion.

25c Determine the speech purpose.

Decide what you want to accomplish with your speech. For any given topic, you should direct your speech toward one of three *general speech purposes*—to *inform*, to *persuade*, or to *mark a special occasion*. Thus you need to decide whether your goal is to inform your audience about an issue or event, to persuade them to accept one position to the exclusion of other positions, or to mark a special occasion such as a wedding, a funeral, or a dinner event.

Your speech should also have a *specific purpose*. This is a single phrase stating precisely what you want the audience to learn or do as a result of your speech. For example, if your general purpose is to inform, your specific purpose might be "to inform my audience about three key qualities of distance courses." If your general purpose is to persuade, the specific purpose might be "to convince my audience that they should support funds for the development of distance courses."

25d Compose a thesis statement.

Next, compose a thesis statement that clearly expresses the central idea of your speech. While the specific purpose focuses your attention on what *you* want to achieve with the speech, the *thesis statement* concisely communicates to your audience, in a single sentence, what the speech is about:

General Purpose: To inform

Specific Purpose: To inform my audience about the crucial role played by the nitrogen cycle in preserving biodiversity and maintaining healthy ecosystems.

Thesis Statement: Excessive nitrogen additions to the nitrogen cycle from human activities such as crop fertilization and burning of fossil fuels pose serious threats to plant and animal life.

Wherever you are in the planning stage, always refer to the thesis statement to make sure that you are on track to illustrate or prove the central idea of your speech.

25e Develop the main points.

Organize your speech around two or three *main points.* These are the primary pieces of knowledge (in an informative speech) or the key claims (in a persuasive speech). If you create a clear thesis statement for your speech, the main points will be easily identifiable, if not explicit.

25f Gather supporting materials.

Supporting materials illustrate speech points by clarifying, elaborating, and verifying your ideas. They include the entire world of information available to you—from personal experiences to every conceivable kind of external source. Plan to research your topic to provide evidence for your assertions and lend credibility to your message.

25g Separate the speech into its major parts.

Every speech will have an *introduction,* a *body*, and a *conclusion.* Develop each part separately, then bring them together using transition statements. The *introduction* serves to introduce the topic and the speaker, to alert the audience to your thesis, and to catch the audience's attention and interest. Just like the body of a written essay, the speech *body* contains the speech's main points and subpoints, all of which support the speech's thesis. The *conclusion* restates the speech thesis and reiterates how the main points confirm it.

◆ Major Speech Parts

Introduction

- Pique the audience's curiosity with a quotation, a short story, an example, or other kind of attention-getting device.
- Introduce the speech topic and demonstrate its relevance to the audience.
- Preview the thesis and main points.
- Establish your credibility as a speaker to address the topic.

Use a transition to signal the start of the speech body.

Body

- Develop the main points using an organizational pattern that suits the topic, audience, and occasion.

Use a transition to signal the conclusion.

Conclusion

- Restate the thesis and reiterate how the main points confirm it.
- Leave the audience with something to think about, or challenge them to act.

Be prepared to answer questions.

25h Outline the speech.

An outline is the framework upon which to arrange the elements of your speech in support of your thesis. Outlines are based on the principle of *coordination and subordination*—the logical placement of ideas relative to their importance to one another. *Coordinate points* are of equal importance and are indicated by their parallel alignment. *Subordinate points* are given less weight than the main points they support and are placed below and to the right of the points they support.

Coordinate Points

I. Main Point 1
II. Main Point 2
    A. Subpoint 1
    B. Subpoint 2

Subordinate Points

1. Main Point 1
   A. First level of subordination
      1. Second level of subordination
      2. Second level of subordination
         a. Third level of subordination
         b. Third level of subordination

As your speeches become more detailed, you will need to select an appropriate *organizational pattern*. To allow for the full development of your ideas, *working outlines* generally contain points stated in complete sentences. *Speaking outlines* are far briefer and use either short phrases or key words. Speaking outlines are printed out on separate sheets or written on 4″ × 6″ index cards for use during the speech.

25i Consider presentation aids.

As you prepare your speech, consider whether using visual, audio, or a combination of different *presentation aids* will help the audience understand points. A presentation aid can be as simple as writing the definition of a word on a blackboard or as involved as a multimedia slide show.

25j Practice delivering the speech.

Preparation and practice are necessary for the success of even your first speech in class. You will want to feel and appear "natural" to your listeners, an effect achieved by rehearsing both the verbal and nonverbal delivery of your speech. So practice your speech often. It has been suggested that a good speech is practiced at least six times. For a four- to six-minute speech, that's only thirty to forty minutes (figuring in restarts and pauses) of actual practice time.

◆ Practice Your Vocal Delivery

Vocal delivery includes speech volume, pitch, rate, variety, pronunciation, and articulation. As you rehearse, do the following:

- Pay attention to how loudly or softly you are speaking.
- Pay attention to the rate at which you speak. Aim to speak neither too fast nor too slowly.
- Avoid speaking in a monotone.
- Decide how you want to phrase your statements, and then practice saying them.
- Pronounce words correctly and clearly.

◆ Be Aware of Your Nonverbal Delivery

Audiences are highly attuned to a speaker's facial expression, gestures, general body movement, and overall physical appearance. As you rehearse, do the following:

- Practice smiling and otherwise animating your face in ways that feel natural to you. Audiences want to feel that you care about what you are saying, so avoid a deadpan, or blank, expression.
- Practice making eye contact with your listeners. Doing so will make audience members feel that you recognize and respect them.
- Practice gestures that feel natural to you, steering clear of exaggerated movements.

7

Informative Speaking

To *inform* is to communicate knowledge. The goal of **informative speaking** is to impart knowledge in order to raise awareness or deepen understanding of some phenomenon. Informative speeches bring new topics to light, offer new insights on familiar subjects, or provide novel ways of thinking about something. Your speech might be an analysis of an issue, a report of an event; or a physical demonstration of how something works. As long as the audience learns something, the options are nearly limitless.

26 ◆ Gain and Sustain Involvement

Audience members are not simply empty vessels into which you can pour facts and figures for automatic processing. Before your listeners retain information, they must be able to recognize, understand, and relate to it.

26a Use audience analysis.

Use audience analysis to gauge the audience's existing knowledge of your topic and their likely interests and needs with respect to it. Then adjust the amount and complexity of information accordingly. Most people will recall less than half of the information you tell them, so focus on what you most want to convey and trim material that does not strongly support your central idea.

26b Present new and interesting information.

Audiences seek knowledge; they want to learn something new. To satisfy this drive, try to uncover information that is fresh and compelling. Seek out unusual angles, novel interpretations, moving stories, and striking examples. If a speech does not offer audience members anything new, they will feel that their time has been wasted and will rightly be offended.

26c Help listeners follow along.

Audience members cannot put the speaker on "pause" in order to digest information, so help them to stay on track:

- Prepare a well-organized introduction that clearly previews main points.
- Make liberal use of transition words and phrases ("first," "next," "I'll now turn...") to tie speech ideas together and map the logical flow of ideas.
- Use *internal previews* to forecast key points and *internal summaries* to reinforce them.
- Use rhetorical devices such as repetition and parallelism to reinforce information and drive home key ideas.
- Choose an organizational pattern to help listeners mentally organize ideas and see relationships among them.

27 ◆ Subject Matter of Informative Speeches

Broadly speaking, informative speeches may be about *objects* or *phenomena*, *people*, *events*, *processes*, *concepts*, or *issues*. These are not hard-and-fast divisions—a speech can be about both the *process* of dance and the *people* who perform it, for example—nor are they the only way to categorize informative speeches. These categories, however, do indicate the range of potential subject matter suited to an informative purpose, as seen in the following table.

SUBJECT MATTER OF INFORMATIVE SPEECHES	SAMPLE TOPICS
Objects or Phenomena Addresses various aspects of nonhuman subjects (their history and function, for example)	• The health of Lake Michigan • Ribbon use in awareness-raising campaigns • History of graphic novels

(continued)

SUBJECT MATTER OF INFORMATIVE SPEECHES	SAMPLE TOPICS
People Addresses impact of individuals and groups on society (including athletes, authors, inventors, political leaders, refugees, soldiers, and others)	• Rahul Singh, founder, GlobalMedic • Amy Poehler, actress • Ai Weiwei, artist • You, the speaker
Current or Historical Events Addresses noteworthy occurrences, past and present	• 1937 Paris World's Fair • The fall of Libya's dictator • The Battle of Britain
Processes Demonstrates and/or explains how something is done, how it is made, or how it works	• Development of baby penguins • Visualization in sports • Operation of hybrid cars • Interviewing for a job
Concepts Addresses abstract or complex ideas, theories, or beliefs	• Responsible knowledge • Chaos theory • Free speech
Issues Addresses problems or matters of dispute to raise awareness and deepen understanding (rather than to advocate for a position)	• Impact of long-term unemployment • French ban on burkas • Obesity epidemic in the United States

28 ◆ Decide How to Communicate Your Information

Typically, we communicate information by defining, describing, demonstrating, and/or explaining it. Some speeches rely on a single approach (e.g., they focus on *demonstrating* how something works or *explaining* what something means). Oftentimes, speakers combine strategies. As you prepare your speech, ask yourself, "How much emphasis should I give to defining my topic, describing it, demonstrating it, or explaining its meaning?"

DEFINITION When your topic is new to the audience and/or addresses a complex concept (*What is a fractal?*), pay particular attention to providing adequate definitions. To define something is to identify its essential qualities and meaning.

You can approach definition in a number of ways, including the following:

- Defining something by what it does (**operational definition**): *A computer is something that processes information.*

- Defining something by describing what it is not (**definition by negation**): *Courage is not the absence of fear.*
- Defining something by providing several concrete examples (**definition by example**): *Health professionals include doctors, nurses, EMTs, and ambulance drivers.*
- Defining something by comparing it to something synonymous (**definition by synonym**): *A friend is a comrade or a buddy.*
- Defining something by illustrating its root meaning (**definition by word origin**): *Our word* rival *derives from the Latin word* rivalis, *"one living near or using the same stream."*

DESCRIPTION Whether offering your audience a "virtual tour" of the top of Mount Everest, or describing the physical ravages wrought by drug abuse, the point of speeches, or sections of speeches, relying on description is to offer a vivid portrayal of the topic. When you *describe* information, you provide an array of details that paint a mental picture for the audience. Concrete words and vivid imagery will help listeners visualize your depictions.

DEMONSTRATION Sometimes the purpose of an informative speech is to explain how something works or to actually demonstrate it. The many "how to" videos and podcasts on the Web rely on demonstration. A speech may not include an actual physical demonstration (e.g., *how to use social bookmarks*), but the speaker will nevertheless rely on a verbal demonstration of the steps involved.

EXPLANATION Certain informative speech topics are built on *explanation*—providing reasons or causes, demonstrating relationships, and offering interpretation and analysis. The classroom lecture is a classic example of explanation in an informative context. But many kinds of speeches rely on explanation, from those that address difficult or confusing theories and processes (*What is the relationship between the glycemic index and glycemic load?*) to those that present ideas that challenge conventional thinking (*Why do researchers say that sometimes emotion makes us more rather than less logical?*).

29 ◆ Take Steps to Reduce Confusion

New information can be hard to grasp, especially when it addresses a difficult concept (such as *equilibrium* in engineering), a difficult-to-envision process (such as *cash-flow management* in business), or a counterintuitive idea—one that challenges commonsense thinking (such as *drinking a glass of red wine a day can be healthy*).

Useful for almost any speech, the following strategies for communicating information are especially helpful when attempting to clarify complex information.

29a Use analogies to build on prior knowledge.

Audience members will understand a new concept more easily if the speaker uses an analogy to relate it to something that they already know. For example, to explain the unpredictable paths that satellites often take when they fall to earth, you can liken the effect to dropping a penny into water: "Sometimes it goes straight down, and sometimes it turns end over end and changes direction. The same thing happens when an object hits the atmosphere."

29b Demonstrate underlying causes.

Listeners may fail to understand a process because they believe that something "obviously" works a certain way when in fact it does not. To counter faulty assumptions, first acknowledge common misperceptions and then offer an accurate explanation of underlying causes.

30 ◆ Arrange Points in a Pattern

Our understanding of a speech is directly linked to how well it is organized. Informative speeches can be organized using several patterns, including the topical, chronological, spatial, cause-effect, and narrative patterns. (Note that although the problem-solution pattern may be used in informative speeches, it often is a more logical candidate for persuasive speeches.) A speech about the Impressionist movement in painting, for example, could be organized *chronologically,* in which main points are arranged in sequence from the movement's early period to its later falling out of favor. It could be organized *causally* (cause-effect), by demonstrating that Impressionism came about as a reaction to the art movement that preceded it. It could also be organized *topically* (by categories), by focusing on the major figures associated with the movement, famous paintings linked to it, or notable contemporary artists who paint in the style.

8

Persuasive Speaking

To persuade is to advocate, to ask others to accept your views. The goal of **persuasive speaking** is to influence audience members' attitudes, beliefs, values, and actions. Some persuasive speeches attempt to move the audience's attitudes and values closer to the speaker's stance. Others aim for a more explicit response, as when urging listeners to donate money for a cause or to vote for a candidate.

31 • Focus on Motivation

Success in persuasive speaking requires attention to human psychology—to what motivates listeners. Audience analysis is therefore extremely important in persuasive appeals.

Research confirms that you can increase the odds of achieving your persuasive speech goal if you:

- Use information gleaned through audience analysis to make your message personally relevant to listeners.
- Demonstrate how any change you propose will benefit the audience.
- Establish your credibility. Audience members' feelings toward you strongly influence their receptivity toward the message.

- Set modest goals. Expect minor rather than major changes in your listeners' attitudes and behaviors.
- Demonstrate how an attitude or a behavior might keep listeners from feeling satisfied and competent, thereby encouraging receptivity to change.
- Expect to be more successful when addressing an audience whose position differs only moderately from your own.

32 ◆ Balance Reason and Emotion

Persuasion is a complex psychological process of reasoning and emotion, and effective persuasive speeches appeal to not one but both processes in audience members. Emotion gets the audience's attention and stimulates a desire to act; reason provides the justification for the action.

Persuasive speeches use arguments as a framework for making appeals. An **argument** is a stated position, with support, for or against an idea or issue. Appealing to reason and logic—or to what Aristotle termed **logos**—is important in gaining agreement for your argument; it is especially critical when asking listeners to reach a conclusion regarding a complicated issue or to take a specific action. To truly persuade listeners to care about your position, however, you must also appeal to their emotions—to what Aristotle termed **pathos.** Feelings such as pride, love, compassion, anger, shame, and fear underlie many of our actions and motivate us to think and feel as we do.

You can evoke pathos in a speech by using vivid imagery, telling compelling stories (especially ones that touch upon shared values such as patriotism, selflessness, faith, and hope), and using repetition and parallelism.

33 ◆ Stress Your Credibility

Audiences want more than logical and emotional appeals from a speaker; they want what's relevant to them from someone who cares. Aristotle termed this effect of the speaker on the audience **ethos,** or moral character. Modern-day scholars call it **speaker credibility.**

Audience members' feelings about your credibility strongly influence how receptive they will be to your proposals, and studies confirm that attitude change is related directly to the extent to which listeners perceive speakers to be truthful and competent (well prepared).

The following steps will help you establish credibility:

- Emphasize your grasp of the topic; note related expertise.
- Demonstrate trustworthiness by revealing your true speech goals, establishing common ground with audience members, and expressing genuine interest in their welfare.
- Strive for a dynamic delivery.

APPLYING ARISTOTLE'S THREE PERSUASIVE APPEALS	
Appeal to Logos	Targets audience members' reasoning and logic through argument (e.g., claims, evidence, warrants).
Appeal to Pathos	Targets audience members' emotions using techniques of language such as vivid imagery, dramatic storytelling, and repetition.
Appeal to Ethos	Targets audience members' feelings about the speaker's character through demonstrations of trustworthiness, competence, and concern for audience welfare.

34 ◆ Target Listeners' Needs

Audience members are motivated to act on the basis of their needs; thus, one way to persuade listeners is to point to some need they want fulfilled and then give them a way to fulfill it. According to psychologist Abraham Maslow's classic **hierarchy of needs** (see Figure 8.1), each of us has a set of basic needs ranging from essential, life-sustaining ones to less critical, self-improvement ones. Our needs at the lower, essential levels (physiological and safety needs) must be fulfilled before the higher levels (social, self-esteem, and self-actualization needs) become important and motivating. Using Maslow's hierarchy to persuade your listeners to wear seat belts, for example, you would appeal to their need for safety. Critics of this approach suggest that we may be driven as much by *wants* as by needs; nevertheless, the theory points to the fact that successful appeals depend on understanding what motivates the audience. Following are Maslow's five basic needs, along with suggested actions a speaker can take to appeal to them.

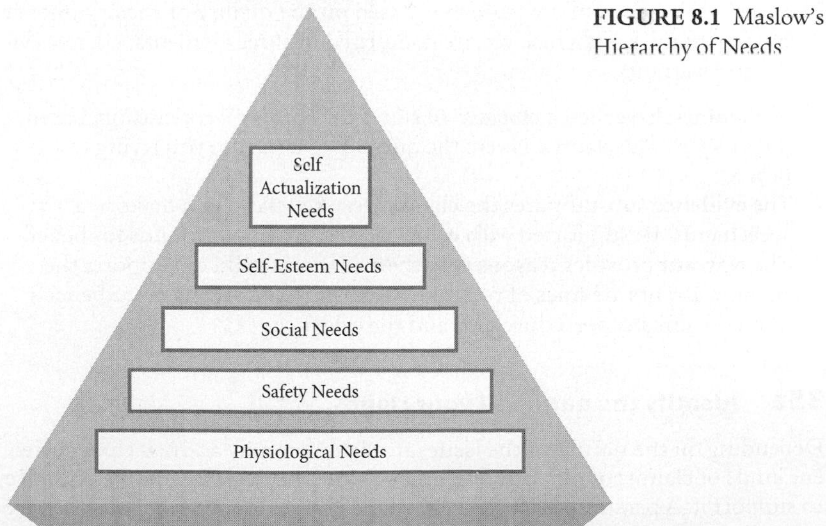

FIGURE 8.1 Maslow's Hierarchy of Needs

NEED	SPEECH ACTION
Physiological needs (to have access to basic sustenance, including food, water, and air)	• Plan for and accommodate the audience's physiological needs–are they likely to be hot, cold, hungry, or thirsty?
Safety needs (to feel protected and secure)	• Appeal to safety benefits–how wearing seat belts or voting for a bill to stop pollution will remove a threat or protect the audience members from harm.
Social needs (to find acceptance; to have lasting, meaningful relationships)	• Appeal to social benefits–if you want teenagers to quit smoking, stress that if they quit they will appear more physically fit and attractive to their peers.
Self-esteem needs (to feel good about ourselves; self-worth)	• Appeal to emotional benefits–stress that the proposed change will make listeners feel better about themselves.
Self-actualization needs (to achieve goals; to reach our highest potential)	• Appeal to your listeners' need to fulfill their potential–stress how adopting your position will help them "be all that they can be."

35 ◆ Construct Sound Arguments

The persuasive power of any speech is based on the quality of the arguments within it. Arguments themselves are comprised of three elements: claims, evidence, and warrants.

1. The **claim** (also called a *proposition*) states the speaker's conclusion, based on evidence. The claim answers the question, "What are you trying to prove?"
2. The **evidence** substantiates the claim. Every key claim you make in a speech must be supported with evidence that provides grounds for belief.
3. The **warrant** provides reasons that the evidence is valid or supports the claim. Warrants are lines of reasoning that substantiate in the audience's mind the link between the claim and the evidence.

35a Identify the nature of your claims.

Depending on the nature of the issue, an argument may address three different kinds of claims: of *fact*, of *value*, and of *policy*. Each type requires evidence to support it. A persuasive speech may contain only one type of claim or, very often, consist of several arguments addressing different kinds of claims. In a persuasive speech, a claim can serve as a main point or it can be the speech thesis (if using only one claim).

- **Claims of fact** focus on whether something is or is not true or whether something will or will not happen. They usually address issues for which two or more competing answers exist, or those for which an answer does not yet exist (called a *speculative claim*). An example of the first is, "Does affirmative action discriminate against non-minority job applicants?" An example of the second is, "Will a woman president be elected in the next U.S. presidential election?"
- **Claims of value** address issues of judgment. Rather than attempting to prove the truth of something, as in claims of fact, speakers arguing claims of value try to show that something is right or wrong, good or bad, worthy or unworthy. For example, "Is assisted suicide ethical?" The evidence in support of a value claim tends to be more subjective than for a fact claim.
- **Claims of policy** recommend that a specific course of action be taken or approved. For example, "Property taxes should be increased to fund classroom expansions in city elementary schools." Notice that in this claim the word "should" appears. A claim of policy speaks to an "ought" condition, proposing that certain better outcomes would be realized if the proposed condition were met.

35b Use convincing evidence.

Every key claim must be supported with convincing *evidence*, supporting material that provides grounds for belief. There are several forms of evidence, including: *examples*, *narratives*, *testimony*, *facts*, and *statistics*. These most common forms of evidence—called "external evidence" because the knowledge does not generate from the speaker's own experience—are most powerful when they impart new information that the audience has not previously used in forming an opinion.

You can also use the *audience's preexisting knowledge and opinions*—what listeners already think and believe—as evidence for your claims. Nothing is more persuasive to listeners than a reaffirmation of their own attitudes, beliefs, and values, especially for claims of value and policy. To use this form of evidence, however, you must first identify what the audience knows and believes about the topic, and then present information that confirms these beliefs.

Finally, when the audience will find your opinions credible and convincing, consider using your own *speaker expertise* as evidence. Be aware, however, that few persuasive speeches can be convincingly built solely on speaker experience and knowledge. Offer your expertise in conjunction with other forms of evidence.

35c Address the other side of the argument.

A persuasive speech message can be either one- or two-sided. A **one-sided message** does not mention opposing claims; a **two-sided message** mentions opposing points of view and sometimes refutes them. Research suggests that two-sided messages generally are more persuasive than one-sided messages, as long as the speaker adequately refutes opposing claims.

All attempts at persuasion are subject to counterargument. Listeners may be persuaded to accept your claims, but once they are exposed to opposing claims they may change their minds. If listeners are aware of opposing claims and you ignore them, you risk a loss of credibility. Yet you need not painstakingly acknowledge and refute all opposing claims. Instead, raise and refute the most important counterclaims and evidence that the audience would know about. Ethically, you can ignore counterclaims that don't significantly weaken your argument.

35d Use effective reasoning.

Reasoning is the process of drawing conclusions from evidence. Arguments can be reasoned inductively, deductively, or causally. Arguments using **deductive reasoning** begin with a general principle or case, followed by a specific example of the case, which then leads to the speaker's conclusion.

In a deductive line of argument, if you accept the general principle and the speaker's specific example of it, you must accept the conclusion:

General Case ("major premise"): All men are mortal.

Specific Case ("minor premise"): Socrates is a man.

Conclusion: Therefore Socrates is mortal.

Reversing direction, an argument using **inductive reasoning** moves from specific cases (minor premises) to a general conclusion supported by those cases. The speaker offers evidence that points to a conclusion that *appears to be*, but *is not necessarily*, true:

Specific Case 1: In one five-year period, the average daily temperature (ADT) on Continent X rose three degrees.

Specific Case 2: In that same period, ADT on Continent Y rose three degrees.

Specific Case 3: In that same period, ADT on Continent Z rose three degrees.

Conclusion: Globally, average daily temperatures appear to be rising by three degrees.

Arguments based on inductive reasoning can be *strong* or *weak*; that is, listeners may decide the claim is probably true, largely untrue, or somewhere in between.

Reasoning by analogy is a common form of inductive reasoning. Here, the speaker compares two similar cases and implies that what is true in one case is true in the other. The assumption is that the characteristics of Case A and Case B are similar, if not the same, and that what is true for B must also be true for A.

Arguments can also follow lines of **causal reasoning,** in which the speaker argues that one event, circumstance, or idea (the cause) is the reason (effect) for another. For example, "Smoking causes lung cancer." Sometimes a speaker can argue that multiple causes lead to a single effect, or that a single cause leads to multiple effects.

35e Avoid fallacies in reasoning.

A **logical fallacy** is either a false or erroneous statement or an invalid or deceptive line of reasoning. In either case, you need to be aware of fallacies in order to avoid making them in your own speeches and to be able to identify them in the speeches of others. Many fallacies of reasoning exist; the following are merely a few.

LOGICAL FALLACY	EXAMPLES
Begging the question An argument that is stated in such a way that it cannot help but be true, even though no evidence has been presented.	• "Intelligent Design is the correct explanation for biological change over time because we can see godly evidence in our complex natural world."
Bandwagoning An argument that uses (unsubstantiated) general opinion as its (false) basis.	• "Nikes are superior to other brands of shoes because everyone wears Nikes."
Either-or fallacy An argument stated in terms of only two alternatives, even though there may be many additional alternatives.	• "If you don't send little Susie to private school this year, she will not gain admission to college."
Ad hominem argument An argument that targets a person instead of the issue at hand in an attempt to incite an audience's dislike for that person.	• "I'm a better candidate than X because, unlike X, I work for a living."

(*continued*)

LOGICAL FALLACY	EXAMPLES
Red herring An argument that relies on irrelevant premises for its conclusion.	• "I fail to see why hunting should be considered cruel when it gives pleasure to many people and employment to even more."
Hasty generalization An argument in which an isolated instance is used to make an unwarranted general conclusion.	• "As shown by the example of a Labrador retriever biting my sister, this type of dog is dangerous and its breeding should be outlawed."
Non sequitur ("does not follow") An argument in which the conclusion is not connected to the reasoning.	• "If we can send a man to the moon, we should be able to cure cancer in five years."
Slippery slope A faulty assumption that one case will lead to a series of events or actions.	• "Helping refugees in the Sudan today will force us to help refugees across Africa and worldwide."
Appeal to tradition An argument suggesting that audience members should agree with a claim because that is the way it has always been done.	• "The president of the United States must be a man because a woman has never been president."

36 ◆ Address Culture

The audience's cultural orientation will significantly affect their responses to persuasion.

CORE VALUES Audience members of the same culture often share core values, such as *self-reliance* and *individual achievement* (in individualist cultures such as the United States); and *interdependence* and *group harmony* (in collectivist cultures such as those of China and India). Usually, appeals that clash with core values are unsuccessful, although globalization may be leading to some cross-pollination of values.

CULTURAL NORMS *Cultural norms* are a group's rules for behavior. Attempts to persuade listeners to think or do things contrary to important cultural norms usually will fail.

CULTURAL PREMISES Listeners sharing a common culture usually hold culturally specific values about identity and relationships, called *cultural premises.* Bear in mind that it is difficult to challenge deeply held cultural premises.

EMOTIONS Culture also influences our responses to emotional appeals. Appeals that touch on *ego-focused* emotions such as pride, anger, happiness, and frustration, for example, tend to find more acceptance among members of individualist cultures; those that use *other-focused* emotions such as empathy, indebtedness, and shame are more apt to encourage identification in collectivist cultures. Usually, it is best to appeal to emotions that lie within the audience's "comfort zone." A good strategy is to avoid undue emphasis on emotions that may make certain audience members feel uncomfortable.

37 ◆ Strengthen Your Case with Organization

Once you've developed your speech claims, the next step is to structure your speech points. Factors to consider when selecting an organizational pattern include the nature of your arguments and evidence; the response you want to elicit from audience members; and your target audience's attitudes toward the topic. Following are organizational patterns especially well-suited to persuasive speeches.

37a Problem–Solution Pattern

Some speech topics or claims clearly suggest a specific design, such as the claim that cigarettes should cost less. Implied is that the current high price of cigarettes represents a problem and that lower prices represent a solution. The **problem–solution pattern of arrangement** is a commonly used design for persuasive speeches, especially those based on *claims of policy*. Here you organize speech points to demonstrate the nature and significance of a problem and then to provide justification for a proposed solution:

I. Problem (define what it is)
II. Solution (offer a way to overcome the problem)

Most problem–solution speeches require more than two points to adequately explain the problem and to substantiate the recommended solution. Thus a three-point **problem–cause–solution pattern** may be in order:

I. The nature of the problem (explain why it's a problem, for whom, etc.)
II. Reasons for the problem (identify its causes, incidence)
III. Proposed solution (explain why it's expected to work, noting any unsatisfactory solutions)

When arguing a claim of policy, it may be important to demonstrate the proposal's feasibility. To do this, use a four-point *problem–cause–solution–feasibility pattern,* with the last point providing evidence of the solution's feasibility.

37b Monroe's Motivated Sequence

The **motivated sequence pattern of arrangement,** developed in the mid-1930s by Alan Monroe, is a five-step sequence that begins with arousing listeners' attention and ends with calling for action. This pattern is particularly effective when you want the audience to do something—buy a product, donate to a cause, and so forth.

STEP 1: ATTENTION The *attention step* addresses listeners' core concerns, making the speech highly relevant to them.

STEP 2: NEED The *need step* isolates the issue to be addressed. If you can show the members of an audience that they have an important need that must be satisfied or a problem that must be solved, they will have a reason to listen to your propositions.

STEP 3: SATISFACTION The *satisfaction step* identifies the solution. This step begins the crux of the speech, offering the audience a proposal to reinforce or change their attitudes, beliefs, and values regarding the need at hand.

STEP 4: VISUALIZATION The *visualization step* provides the audience with a vision of anticipated outcomes associated with the solution. The purpose of this step is to carry audience members beyond accepting the feasibility of your proposal to seeing how it will actually benefit them.

STEP 5: ACTION Finally, in the *action step* the speaker asks audience members to act according to their acceptance of the message. This may involve reconsidering their present way of thinking about something, continuing to believe as they do but with greater commitment, or implementing a new set of behaviors.

37c Comparative Advantage Pattern

Another way to organize speech points is to show how your viewpoint or proposal is superior to one or more alternative viewpoints or proposals. This design, called the **comparative advantage pattern of arrangement,** is most effective when your audience is already aware of the issue or problem and agrees that a need for a solution (or an alternative view) exists. To maintain credibility, make sure to identify alternatives that your audience is familiar with and ones supported by opposing interests.

37d Refutation Pattern

When you feel confident that the opposing argument is vulnerable, consider the **refutation pattern of arrangement,** in which you confront and then refute (disprove) opposing claims to your position. Refutation works best when you can target the audience's chief objections to the opposing argument. If done well, refutation may influence audience members who either disagree with you or are conflicted about where they stand.

Main points arranged in a refutation pattern follow a format similar to this:

Main Point I:	State the opposing position.
Main Point II:	Describe the implications or ramifications of the opposing claim, explaining why it is faulty.
Main Point III:	Offer arguments and evidence for your position.
Main Point IV:	Contrast your position with the opposing claim to drive home the superiority of your position.

38 ◆ Identify the Disposition of the Audience

Where your target audience stands in relation to your topic will significantly affect how they will respond to your persuasive appeals. Are they likely to be receptive to your claims? Critical of them? Persuasion scholar Herbert Simon describes four types of potential audiences and suggests various reasoning strategies and possible organizational patterns for each.

AUDIENCE TYPE	PERSUASIVE STRATEGIES
Hostile audience or those that strongly disagree	• Stress areas of agreement. • Address opposing views. • Don't expect major change in attitudes. • Wait until the end before asking the audience to act, if at all. • Reason inductively: start with evidence, leaving conclusion until last ("tuition should be raised"). • Consider the *refutation* pattern.
Critical and conflicted	• Present strong arguments and evidence. • Address opposing views, perhaps by using the *refutation* pattern.
Sympathetic audience	• Use motivational stories and emotional appeals to reinforce positive attitudes. • Stress your commonality with listeners. • Clearly tell the audience what you want them to think or do. • Consider the *narrative* (storytelling) pattern.
Uninformed, less-educated, or apathetic audience	• Focus on capturing their attention. • Stress personal credibility and "likeability." • Stress the topic's relevance to listeners.

9

Citing Sources in Your Speech

Acknowledging sources is a critical aspect of delivering a speech or presentation. When you credit speech sources, you:

- Demonstrate the quality and range of your research to audience members.
- Demonstrate that reliable sources support your position.
- Avoid plagiarism and gain credibility as an ethical speaker who acknowledges the work of others.
- Enhance your own authority and win more support for your point of view.
- Enable listeners to locate your sources and pursue their own research on the topic.

Ethically, you are bound to attribute any information drawn from other people's ideas, opinions, and theories, as well as any facts and statistics gathered by others, to their original sources. Remember, you need not credit sources for ideas that are *common knowledge*—established information likely to be known by many people and described in multiple places.

39 • Alert Listeners to Key Source Information

An **oral citation** credits the source of speech material that is derived from other people's ideas. For each source, plan on briefly alerting the audience to the following:

1. The *author* or *origin of the source* ("documentary filmmaker *Ken Burns*..."; or "On the *National Science Foundation Web site*...")
2. The *type of source* (magazine, book, personal interview, Web site, blog, online video, etc.)
3. The *title or a description of the source* ("In the book *Endangered Minds*..."; or "In *an article on sharks*...")
4. The *date of the source* ("The article, published in the *October 10th, 2012,* issue..." or "According to a report on cheating on the SAT, posted online September 28, 2012, on the *Daily Beast*...")

Spoken citations need not include a complete bibliographic reference (exact title, full names of all authors, volume, and page numbers); doing so will interrupt the flow of your presentation and unnecessarily divert listeners' attention. However, do keep a running list of source details for a bibliography to appear at the end of your speech draft or outline. In place of bibliographic details, focus on presenting sources in a rhetorically effective manner.

39a Establish the source's trustworthiness.

Too often, inexperienced speakers credit their sources in bare-bones fashion, offering a rote recitation of citation elements. For example, they might cite the publication name and date but leave out key details, such as that the source is a leading authority in his or her field, that could convince the audience to accept the source as reliable and its conclusions as true. But discerning listeners will accept as legitimate the supporting materials you offer for your claims–examples, stories, testimony, facts, and statistics–only if they believe that the sources are reliable and accurate, or credible.

Source reliability refers to our level of trust in a source's credentials and track record for providing accurate information. If you support a scientific claim by crediting it to an unknown student's personal blog, for example, listeners won't find it as reliable as if you credited it to a scientist affiliated with a reputable institution.

While a source that is reliable is usually accurate, this is not always so. Sometimes we have information that contradicts what we are told by a reliable source. For example, a soldier might read a news article in the *Wall Street Journal* about a battle in which he or she participated. The soldier knows the story contains inaccuracies because the soldier was there. In general, however, the soldier finds the *Wall Street Journal* a reliable source. Since even the most reliable source can sometimes be wrong, it is always better to offer a variety of sources, rather than a single source, to support a major point. This is especially the case when your claims are controversial.

To demonstrate a source's trustworthiness, offer a **source qualifier,** or brief description of the source's qualifications to address the topic. Briefly mention relevant affiliations and credentials that will help listeners put the source in perspective and establish credibility (e.g., "columnist for the *Wall Street Journal*").

39b Consider audience perception of sources.

Not every trustworthy source is necessarily appropriate for every audience. For example, a politically conservative audience may reject information from a liberal publication. Thus, audience analysis should factor in your choice of sources. In addition to checking that your sources are reliable, consider whether they will be seen as credible by your particular audience.

39c Avoid a mechanical delivery.

Acknowledging sources need not interrupt the flow of your speech. On the contrary, audience members will welcome information that adds backing to your assertions. The key is to avoid a formulaic, or mechanical, delivery. These strategies can help:

VARY THE WORDING Avoid a rote delivery of sources by varying your wording. For example, if you introduce one source with the phrase, "According to...," switch to another construction, "As reported by...," for the next. Alternating introductory phrases, such as "In the words of..."; "*Baltimore Sun* reporter Jonathan X writes that..."; and so forth contributes to a natural delivery and provides the necessary aural variety.

LEAD WITH THE CLAIM Another means of varying how you cite sources is to discuss a claim first—for example, "Caffeine can cause actual intoxication"—before elaborating on and acknowledging the source of it—for example, "A report in the July 5, 2013, issue of the *New England Journal of Medicine* has found...." Much as transitions help listeners follow along, summarizing and previewing evidence can help listeners process it better.

39d Credit sources in presentation aids.

Just as you acknowledge the ideas of others in the verbal portion of your speech, be sure to credit such material used in any accompanying presentation aids. When reproducing copyrighted material, such as a table or photograph, clearly label it with a copyright symbol (©) and the source information. Even if it is not copyrighted, supporting material listed on a visual aid may require citation. You may cite this material orally, print the citation unobtrusively on the aid, or both.

40 ◆ Overview of Source Types with Sample Oral Citations

Following is an overview of common types of sources cited in a speech, the specific citation elements to mention, and examples of how you might refer to these elements in a presentation. Note that each example includes a source qualifier describing the source's qualifications to address the topic ("Pulitzer

Prize-winning author," "pioneering researcher"). Including a source qualifier can make the difference between winning or losing acceptance for your supporting material.

BOOK

If a book has *two* or *fewer* authors, state first and last names, source qualifier, title, and date of publication. If *three* or *more authors*, state first and last name of first author and "coauthors."

> *Example:* In the book *1948: The First Arab-Israeli War*, published in *2008*, noted *Israeli historian* Benny Morris claims that...

> *Example:* In *The Civic Potential of Video Games,* published in 2009, Joseph Kahne, *noted professor of education and director of the Civic Education Research Group at Mills College,* and his *two coauthors, both educators,* wrote that...

REFERENCE WORK

For a reference work (e.g., atlas, directory, encyclopedia, almanac), note title, date of publication, author or sponsoring organization, and source qualifier.

> *Example:* According to *2012 Literary Marketplace, the foremost guide to the U.S. book publishing industry, Karen Hallard and her coeditors* report that...

PRINT ARTICLE

When citing from a print article, use the same guidelines as you do for a book.

> *Example:* In an article published in the May 2010 edition of *Atlantic Monthly* magazine, Marc Ambider, a *journalist* and *political editor* of the *Atlantic Monthly,* outlines the epidemic of obesity in the United States and describes his own decision to have bariatric surgery....

ONLINE-ONLY MAGAZINE, NEWSPAPER, JOURNAL

Follow the same guidelines as for a book, and identify the publication as "online magazine," "online newspaper," or "online journal."

> *Example: Environmental columnist* Nina Shen Rastogi, writing on the socioeconomic arguments against genetically modified crops in the *May 18, 2010,* edition of the online magazine *Slate*...

ORGANIZATION WEB SITE

Name the Web site, source qualifier, and section of Web site cited (if applicable), and last update.

> *Example:* On its Web site, *last updated September 10, 2012,* the *Society of Interventional Radiology* explains that radio waves are harmless to healthy cells....

If Web site content is undated or not regularly updated, review the site for credibility before use.

BLOG

Name the blogger, source qualifier, affiliated Web site (if applicable), and date of posting.

> *Example:* In a *July 8, 2011,* posting on *Talking Points Memo, a news blog that specializes in original reporting on government and politics, editor* Josh Marshall notes that...

TELEVISION OR RADIO PROGRAM

Name the program, segment, reporter, source qualifier, and date aired.

> *Example:* Judy Woodruff, *PBS Newshour co-anchor*, described in a segment on the auto industry *aired on June 2, 2011*...

ONLINE VIDEO

Name the online video source, program, segment, source qualifier, and date aired (if applicable).

> *Example:* In a session on "What's Next for Mindfulness" delivered at the *University of California, Berkeley's Greater Good Science Center* on *April 20, 2010*, and *broadcast on YouTube,* Jon Kabat-Zinn, *scientist, renowned author, and founding director* of the Stress Reduction Clinic...

TESTIMONY (LAY OR EXPERT)

Name the person, source qualifier, context in which information was offered, and date information was offered.

> *Example:* On *August 3, 2011*, in *congressional testimony* before the *Committee on Foreign Relations Subcommittee on African Affairs*, Nancy E. Lundborg, *USAID Assistant Administrator, Bureau for Democracy, Conflict, and Humanitarian Assistance*, addressed the humanitarian crisis in the Horn of Africa.

INTERVIEW AND OTHER PERSONAL COMMUNICATION

Name the person, source qualifier, and date of the interview/correspondence/e-mail/memorandum.

> *Example:* In an interview I conducted *last week*, Tim Zeutenhorst, *Chairman* of the *Orange City Area Health System Board*, at Orange City Hospital in Iowa, said...

> *Example:* In a June 23 e-mail/letter/memorandum from Ron Jones, a *researcher at the Cleveland Institute*...

10

Speaking with Presentation Aids

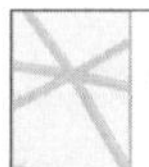

Presentation aids can help listeners process and retain information, convey information in a time-saving fashion, and enhance an image of professionalism. Designed well and used with care, aids can spark interest and even make a speech memorable.

Most people process and retain information best when it is presented both verbally and visually. That is, we learn better from words and pictures than from words alone, a principle dubbed the "multimedia effect." However, no matter how powerful a photograph, chart, or other presentation aid may be, the audience will be less interested in merely gazing at it than in discovering how you will relate it to a specific point. Emphasis should be on using the aids to further the audience's understanding and not on the aids themselves.

41 • Select an Appropriate Aid

Presentation aids include objects, models, pictures, graphs, charts, audio, video, and multimedia. Select the aid, or combination of aids, that will help audience members grasp information most effectively.

41a Props and Models

A **prop** can be any inanimate or even live object—a stone or a snake, for instance—that captures the audience's attention and illustrates or emphasizes key points. A **model** is a three-dimensional, scale-size representation of an object. Presentations in engineering, architecture, medicine, and many other disciplines often make use of models. When using a prop or model:

- In most cases, keep the prop or model hidden until you are ready to use it.

- Make sure it is big enough for everyone to see (and read, if applicable).
- Practice your speech using the prop or model.

41b Pictures

Pictures are two-dimensional representations and include photographs, line drawings, diagrams, maps, and posters. A *diagram* (also called a "schematic drawing") visually explains how something works or is made or operates. *Maps* help listeners visualize geographic areas and understand relationships among them; they also illustrate the proportion of one thing to something else in different areas.

41c Graphs and Charts

A **graph** represents relationships among two or more things. Four types of graphs are line graphs, bar graphs, pie graphs, and pictograms.

A *line graph* uses points connected by lines to demonstrate how something changes or fluctuates in value. Its best use is to represent trends or information that changes over time.

A *bar graph* uses bars of varying lengths to compare quantities or magnitudes; bars may be arranged either vertically or horizontally. Bar graphs are an effective way to compare magnitudes or volume among categories. When creating line and bar graphs:

- Label both axes and start the numerical axis at zero.
- Compare only like variables.
- Put no more than two lines of data on one line graph.

A *pie graph* depicts the division of a whole into slices. Each slice constitutes a percentage of the whole. When creating pie graphs:

- Restrict the number of pie slices to a maximum of seven.
- Identify and accurately represent the values or percentages of each pie slice.

A *pictogram* uses picture symbols (icons) to illustrate relationships and trends; for example, a generic-looking human figure repeated in a row can demonstrate increasing enrollment in college over time. When creating pictograms:

- Clearly indicate what the pictogram symbolizes.
- Make all pictograms the same size.
- Label the axes of the pictogram.

A **chart** visually organizes complex information into compact form. Several different types of charts help listeners grasp key points.

A **flowchart** diagrams the progression of a process, helping viewers visualize a sequence or directional flow.

A **table** (tabular chart) systematically groups data in column form, allowing viewers to examine and make comparisons about information quickly.

41d Audio, Video, and Multimedia

Introducing an *audio clip*—a short recording of sounds, music, or speech—can enliven certain presentations. Similarly, *video*—including movie, television, and other recording instruments—can serve to motivate attention by helping to introduce, transition into, and clarify points. **Multimedia,** which combines stills, sound, video, text, and data into a single production, requires more planning than other forms of presentation aids. Producing multimedia requires familiarity with presentation software programs such as Windows Live Movie Maker and Apple iMovie. When incorporating audio and video into your presentation:

- Use the audio or video clip in a manner consistent with copyright.
- Cue the audio or video clip to the appropriate segment before the presentation.
- Alert audience members to what they will be hearing or viewing before you play it back.
- Reiterate the relevance of the audio or video clip to your key points once it is over.

42 ◆ Decide How to Present the Aid

Many presenters create computer-generated aids shown with digital projectors or LCD displays. On the more traditional side, options for presenting the aids to the audience include overhead transparencies, flip charts, chalkboards, posters, and handouts.

42a Computer-Generated Aids and Displays

With software programs such as Microsoft PowerPoint and Apple Keynote, speakers can create computer-generated slides, which they project using **LCD** (liquid crystal display) **panels** and projectors or the newer **DLP** (digital light processing) **projectors.**

42b Overhead Transparencies

An **overhead transparency** is an image printed on clear acetate that can be viewed by projection. You can create transparencies in advance using PowerPoint, or write on the transparency during the presentation, much like a chalkboard. When using overhead transparencies:

- Check that the projector is in good order before the speech.
- Stand to the *side* of the projector and face the *audience,* not the projected image.
- Use a pointer to indicate specific sections of a transparency—point to the transparency, not to the screen.
- If writing on the transparency, use a water-soluble transparency pen and write clearly.
- Cover the transparencies when finished using them.

42c Flip Charts

A **flip chart** is simply a large (27–34 inch) pad of paper on which a speaker can write or draw. They are often prepared in advance; then, as you progress through the speech, you simply flip through the pad to the next exhibit. You can also write and draw on the pad as you speak.

42d Posters

Speakers use **posters**—large paperboards incorporating text, figures, and images, alone or in combination—to illustrate some aspect of their topic; often the poster rests on an easel.

11

Listeners and Speakers

Most of us understand that giving a speech involves preparation and practice, but few recognize the hard work that listening to a speech requires. Rather than being a passive activity that simply "happens" to us, **listening** is the conscious act of *receiving, comprehending, interpreting, evaluating*, and *responding* to messages.

43 ◆ Effective Listening

43a Recognize that we listen selectively.

In any given situation, no two audience members will process the information in exactly the same way. The reason lies in **selective perception**—people pay attention selectively to certain messages while ignoring others. Several factors influence what we listen to and what we ignore:

- We pay attention to what we hold to be important.
- We pay attention to information that touches our experiences and backgrounds.
- We sort and filter new information on the basis of what we already know (i.e., one way we learn is by analogy).

With these principles in mind, try to:

- Identify what's important to your listeners, including their interests, needs, attitudes, and values.
- Show them early on what they stand to gain from listening to you.
- Touch upon their experiences and backgrounds.
- Build repetition of key ideas into the speech.

- Use analogies to help listeners learn new ideas.
- When appropriate, use presentation aids to visually reinforce your message.

43b Listen responsibly.

As a speaker, you have the power of the podium; but as a listener, you also have considerable power that you can wield constructively or destructively. As listeners, we are ethically bound to refrain from disruptive and intimidating tactics—such as heckling, name-calling, or interrupting—that are meant to silence those with whom we disagree. If we find the arguments of others morally offensive, we are equally bound to speak up appropriately in refutation.

43c Strive for the open exchange of ideas.

In contrast to *monologue*, in which we try merely to impose what we think on another person or group of people, **dialogic communication** is the open sharing of ideas in an atmosphere of respect. For the speaker, this means approaching a speech not as an argument that must be "won," but as an opportunity to achieve understanding with audience members. For listeners, it means maintaining an open mind and listening with empathy.

Speakers and listeners are always responding to one another's signals—whether of interest or disinterest, agreement or disagreement, and so forth. This continual adjustment between speaker and listener is called the **feedback loop.** As a listener, you can encourage dialogic communication and a positive feedback loop by approaching the speaker with an attitude of openness and giving him or her your full attention. This in turn will enable the speaker to deliver the message without impediment.

43d Anticipate the common obstacles to listening.

Active listening—listening that is focused and purposeful—isn't possible under conditions that distract us. As you listen to speeches, try to identify and overcome some common obstacles.

MINIMIZE EXTERNAL AND INTERNAL DISTRACTIONS

A **listening distraction** is anything that competes for the attention we are trying to give to something else. Distractions can originate outside of us, in the environment (external distractions), or within us, in our thoughts and feelings (internal distractions).

To minimize *external listening distractions*, such as the din of jackhammers or competing conversations, try to anticipate and plan for them. If you struggle to see or hear at a distance, arrive early and sit in the front. To reduce *internal listening distractions*, avoid daydreaming, be well rested, monitor yourself for lapses in attention, and consciously focus on listening.

GUARD AGAINST SCRIPTWRITING AND DEFENSIVE LISTENING

When we engage in *scriptwriting*, we focus on what we, rather than the speaker, will say next. Similarly, people who engage in **defensive listening** decide either that they won't like what the speaker is going to say or that they know better. When you find yourself scriptwriting or listening with a defensive posture, remind yourself that effective listening precedes effective rebuttal. Try waiting for the speaker to finish before devising your own arguments.

BEWARE OF LAZINESS AND OVERCONFIDENCE

Laziness and overconfidence can manifest themselves in several ways: We may expect too little from speakers, ignore important information, or display an arrogant attitude. Later, we discover we missed important information. Never assume that you already know exactly what a speaker will say; you'll seldom be right.

WORK TO OVERCOME CULTURAL BARRIERS

Differences in dialects or accents, nonverbal cues, word choice, and even physical appearance can serve as barriers to listening, but they need not if you keep your focus on the message rather than the messenger. Consciously refrain from judging a speaker on the basis of his or her accent, appearance, or demeanor; focus instead on what is actually being said. Whenever possible, reveal your needs to him or her by asking questions.

When speaking, the following will minimize confusion:

- Watch for **idioms,** or colloquial expressions such as "apple of his eye," that non-native speakers might not know. Either eliminate or define them.
- Speak at a rate that is neither too fast nor too slow. Pay particular attention to pronunciation and articulation.
- Be alert to nonverbal cues that suggest that listeners may not comprehend you, and clarify points when indicated.

43e Practice active listening.

Taking the following practical steps can help you listen actively:

- Set listening goals and state them in a way that encourages action: "In my classmate's presentation, I will learn why she believes that a college degree is an important accomplishment."
- Listen for the speaker's main ideas and take note of key points.

- Watch for the speaker's nonverbal cues.
- Try to detect the speaker's organizational pattern.

43f Evaluate evidence and reasoning.

As you listen to speeches, use your critical faculties to do the following:

- *Evaluate the speaker's evidence.* Is it accurate? Are the sources credible?
- *Analyze the speaker's assumptions and biases.* What lies behind the speaker's assertions? Does the evidence support or contradict these assertions?
- *Assess the speaker's reasoning.* Does it betray faulty logic? Does it rely on fallacies in reasoning?
- *Consider multiple perspectives.* Is there another way to view the argument? How do other perspectives compare with the speaker's?
- *Summarize and assess the relevant facts and evidence.*

43g Offer constructive and compassionate feedback.

Follow these guidelines when evaluating the speeches of others:

- *Be honest and fair in your evaluation.*
- *Adjust to the speaker's style.* Don't judge the content of a speaker's message by his or her style.
- *Be compassionate in your criticism.* Always start by saying something positive, and focus on the speech, not the speaker.
- *Be selective in your criticism.* Make specific rather than global statements. Rather than statements such as, "I just couldn't get into your topic," give the speaker something he or she can learn from: "I wanted more on why the housing market is falling. . . ."

12

Communicating in Groups

Most of us will spend a substantial portion of our educational and professional lives participating in **small groups** or teams (usually between three and twenty people); and many of the experiences we have as speakers—in the classroom, workforce, and in virtual groups online—occur in a group setting. Groups often report on the results they've achieved, and some groups form solely for the purpose of coordinating oral presentations. Thus, understanding how to work cooperatively within a group setting is a critical skill.

44 • Effective Group Communication

44a Focus on goals.

How well or poorly you meet the objectives of the group is largely a function of how closely you keep sight of the group's goals and avoid behaviors that detract from these goals. Setting an **agenda** can help participants stay on track by identifying items to be accomplished during a meeting; often it will specify time limits for each item.

44b Plan on assuming dual roles.

In a group, you will generally assume dual roles: a task role and a maintenance role. **Task roles** are the hands-on roles that directly relate to the group's accomplishment of its objectives. Examples include "recording secretary" (takes notes) and "moderator" (facilitates discussion). Members also adopt various **maintenance roles** that help facilitate effective group interaction, such as "the harmonizer" (smoothes out tension) and "the gatekeeper" (keeps the discussion moving and gets everyone's input). Online maintenance roles include the "moderator" or "master" (coordinates and sometimes screens members' comments) and the "elder" (long-standing and respected group member).

Sometimes, group members focus on individual needs irrelevant to the task at hand. **Anti-group roles** such as "floor hogger" (not allowing others to speak), "blocker" (being overly negative about group ideas; raising issues that have been settled), and "recognition seeker" (calling attention to oneself rather than to group tasks) do not further the group's goals and should be avoided.

44c Center disagreements around issues.

Whenever people come together to consider an important issue, conflict is inevitable. But conflict doesn't have to be destructive. In fact, the best decisions are usually those that emerge from productive conflict. In *productive conflict,* group members clarify questions, challenge ideas, present counterexamples, consider worst-case scenarios, and reformulate proposals. Productive conflict centers disagreements around issues rather than personalities. In *person-based conflict,* members argue with one another instead of about the issues, wasting time and impairing motivation; *issues-based conflict* allows members to test and debate ideas and potential solutions. It requires each member to ask tough questions, press for clarification, and present alternative views.

44d Resist groupthink.

For groups to be truly effective, members need to form a *collective mind*, that is, engage in communication that is critical, careful, consistent, and conscientious. At the same time, they must avoid **groupthink,** the tendency to accept information and ideas without subjecting them to critical analysis. Groups prone to groupthink typically exhibit these behaviors:

- Participants reach a consensus and avoid conflict in order not to hurt others' feelings, but without genuinely agreeing.
- Members who do not agree with the majority feel pressured to conform.
- Disagreement, tough questions, and counterproposals are discouraged.
- More effort is spent justifying the decision than testing it.

44e Optimize decision making in groups.

Research suggests that groups can reach the best decisions by adopting two methods of argument: **devil's advocacy** (arguing for the sake of raising issues

Missing something? Instructors may assign the online materials that accompany this text. To access them, visit **macmillanhighered.com/mfw12e.**

Inside LaunchPad Solo for *Models for Writers*

e-readings

Peace Corps, "What Are Some Ways Peace Corps Volunteers Grow During Service?" [video]
Khalid Latif, "Shattered Silence" [video]
Peter Aguero, "Me & Her & It" [audio]
Sustainable America, "How to Compost in Your Apartment" [infographic]
National Science Foundation, "The Tragedy of the Commons" [animation]
WIRED, "What's Inside Coffee" [video]
CDC, "Screen Time vs. Lean Time" [infographic]
U.S. Department of State, "Help Protect Our Ocean" [video]
Intelligence Squared, "Should College Football Be Banned?" [video]
Lily Myers, "Shrinking Women" [video]
Rader Programs, "Women Are Dying to Be Thin" [infographic]
Kelly Flanagan, "Words From a Father to His Daughter (From the Makeup Aisle)" [audio]
Carrie Arnold, "What's Photoshop Got to Do with It?" [blog]
NEDA, "A Silent Epidemic" [infographic]
Laura DeVeau, "The Role of Spirituality and Religion in Mental Health" [APA-style paper]

LearningCurve

Critical Reading
Topic Sentences and Supporting Details
Topics and Main Ideas
Avoiding Plagiarism (MLA)
Avoiding Plagiarism (APA)
Commas
Fragments
Run-ons and Comma Splices
Active and Passive Voice
Appropriate Language
Subject-Verb Agreement

Tutorials

Critical Reading

Active Reading Strategies
Reading Visuals: Audience
Reading Visuals: Purpose

Documentation and Working with Sources

Do I Need to Cite That?
How to Cite Anything

Digital Writing

Photo Editing Basics with GIMP
Audio Editing with Audacity
Presentations
Word Processing
Online Research Tools
Job Search/Personal Branding

or concerns about the idea under discussion) and **dialectical inquiry** (devil's advocacy that goes a step further by proposing a countersolution to the idea). Both approaches help expose underlying assumptions that may be preventing participants from making the best decision. As you lead a group, consider how you can encourage both methods of argument.